What's New and Important in this 3rd Printing – Updated Forms

"Lowest interest rates of our lifetime. Buy now!"

In the last couple of years, mortgage interest rates have been driven to all-time lows. This has allowed homeowners and investors with good credit to secure loans with low monthly payments. It is a great time to purchase all types of real estate assets with low fixed payments for 30-year or 40-year loans. The Federal Reserve Board's (FED) primary job is to keep interest rates low in order to control inflation without triggering a recession.

Financial Crisis Started in 2007

The financial crisis that started in 2007 continues to cause widespread changes in the financial regulatory system. The following are just two of the major pieces of legislation that will significantly impact the real estate industry, but have not been fully written or implemented.

Dodd-Frank

The **Dodd-Frank Wall Street Reform and Consumer Protection Act** (H.R. 4173) is a federal statute that was signed into law in 2010. The Act changes the existing regulatory structure of the US financial system by creating numerous new agencies, as well as merging and removing agencies in an effort to streamline the regulatory process. The Federal Reserve Act was amended by Dodd-Frank to increase the oversight of specific institutions. It has and will dramatically influence our economy, and institutions that are regarded as "too big to fail." The Dodd-Frank Act is meant to protect our economy from another near-catastrophic meltdown like that in recent years.

HARP

Due to the deep recession that we're currently slowly recovering from, millions of homeowners found themselves "under water" meaning they owed more money on their homes than they were worth. As a result the Federal Housing Agency created the **Home Affordable Refinance Program (HARP)** which allows some homeowners to refinance on better terms. Currently, only homeowners whose loans were sold to Fannie Mae or Freddie Mac prior to May 31, 2009 are eligible for the HARP programs.

The latest version (HARP 3.0) is winding its way through Congress and will purportedly remove the requirement that the original loan was purchased by Fannie Mae or Freddie Mac.

HARP is scheduled to sunset (expire) on December 31, 2013.

SAFE Act (Licensing)

The **Secure and Fair Enforcement for Mortgage Licensing Act of 2008 (SAFE Act)** is designed to enhance consumer protection and reduce fraud by the setting of minimum standards for the licensing and registration of state-licensed mortgage loan originators.

Pre-Licensure Education (PE): The SAFE Act requires all **Mortgage License Originator (MLO)** license applicants to complete at least 20 hours of pre-license education through a **Nationwide Mortgage Licensing System (NMLS)** approved provider, including the following specific areas:

a. 3 hours of federal law and regulations.
b. 3 hours of ethics, including fraud, consumer protection, and fair lending issues.
c. 2 hours of training related to lending standards for the nontraditional mortgage product marketplace.

Certification: is the process by which state agencies certify that licensed mortgage loan originators have successfully completed state education and/or state testing requirements.

Continuing Education (CE): SAFE requires 8 hours of continuing education to be completed **each year** prior to renewal.

SAFE MLO TEST: Licensees must pass both the National and State Components of the SAFE MLO Test. Once passed, the National Component satisfies all state requirements. The State Component must be passed for each state in which you seek licensing.

Criminal Background Check: All MLOs must submit fingerprints for a criminal background check.

Credit Report: A credit report will be pulled through NMLS.

All states have now fully implemented the requirements of the Safe Act (licensing). Any Mortgage Loan Originators are required to comply with the licensing and educational requirements of the NMLS.

Every state has a different agency to contact regarding NMLS requirements:

- California is the Department of Real Estate (DRE) (**dre.ca.gov**)
- Texas is the Texas Dept. of Savings and Mortgage Lending (**sml.state.tx.us**)
- Arizona is the Dept. of Financial Institutions (**azd.fi.gov**)
- New York is the State of New York Banking Dept. (**banking.state.ny.us**)

Contact the NMLS at **www.mortgage.nationwidelicensingsystem.org**.

REAL ESTATE FINANCE

SEVENTH EDITION

3rd Printing – Updated Forms

WALT HUBER, MS FINANCE
GLENDALE COLLEGE

LEVIN P. MESSICK, IFAC
MT. SAN ANTONIO COLLEGE
PRESIDENT, AC APPRAISALS, INC.

EDUCATIONAL TEXTBOOK COMPANY, INC.
P. O. Box 3597
Covina, California 91722
(626) 339-7733
FAX (626) 332-4744
etctextbooks.com

Call Glendale College Bookstore to order all ETC books:

1-818-240-1000 ext. 3024
1-818-242-1561 (Direct)

Library of Congress Cataloging-in-Publication Data
Real Estate Finance/Huber, Walt, MS; Messick, Levin P. , IFAC - 7th ed.
Includes index

1. Real property—United States—Finance. 2. Mortgage loans—United States.
3. Housing—United States—Finance.

ISBN: 0-916772-48-9 (10-digit Number)
ISBN: 978-0-916772-48-2 (13-digit Number)

Printed in the United States of America

3rd Printing – Updated Forms

Preface

We, the authors, have designed *Real Estate Finance* to be a flexible tool for both novice and professional alike. We've highlighted essential finance concepts for particular emphasis, bolded definitions within the material for memory enhancement, and included concise summaries for easy review. Our unique approach clarifies the process of qualifying standards, disclosure requirements, and loan documents, making this the most user-friendly finance book on the market.

The text is divided into three-chapter increments for a total of six parts. Each section covers a specific area of interest and eliminates the need to wade through all the material to find the desired subject matter. In addition, we've condensed the subjects into fifteen nationally oriented chapters, including the basics, such as primary and secondary lenders, information on credit scoring, and loan applications. Part six (the last three chapters) covers loan information specific to individual states, as well as escrow procedures. Our unique formatting is just one of the methods we employ to create a textbook that is applicable to everyone, making it both an educational tool and a valuable reference source.

The authors would like to extend a warm thank you to the following individuals and companies for their help, encouragement, and constructive criticism during the writing of this text: Larry Bivins, Michael Layne, Sanford T. Jones, and Lawrence P. Woodard of AC Appraisals, Inc., who took time to read and comment on the manuscript draft. Don Kinnsch, Mike Woods, and Pam Woods of Factory Built Financial and Ron Perrot of All Lenders Mortgage provided information and examples of many of the documents used in the loan process. Steve Costello of Collateral DNA very kindly provided information on comparable property data collection. Tim Cullen, IFAC, California Commercial Appraisers, for providing commercial appraisal information. Darlene Messick provided invaluable assistance in helping to format the rough text, and Tom and Jenny Messick assisted with the ads and forms. We also received helpful advice and suggestions from the California Department of Real Estate (**www.dre.ca.gov**), and the California Association of REALTORS® (www.**car.org**).

A special debt of gratitude is owed for the invaluable assistance we received from the designers and editors of this book, including: Colleen Taber, executive editor; Rick Lee, layout and pre-press editor; Philip Dockter, art director; and Melinda Winters, cover design. Further acknowledgement is gratefully given to: Linda Serra, Business Division Chairperson from Glendale College, appraiser Edward S. Stahl; Donna Grogan, CPM from El Camino College; William Nunally from Sacramento City College; Kim Tyler, real estate law specialist from Shasta College; Jim Michaelsen, from Santa Rosa Junior College; Nick Zoumbos, accounting specialist, from Crafton Hills College, and Joe Newton, fellow author from Bakersfield College. And as always, thanks to William Pivar, a trusted friend, excellent author, and a heck of a fisherman. Finally, a special thanks to Mary Ann Zamel and Arlette Lyons from Mount San Antonio College, and financial analyst Walt Zozula from Glendale College and mortgage broker at Banker Group in Woodland Hills, CA.

Acknowledgments

Joseph DiRuscio
Allan Hancock College

Matthew Roberts
Allan Hancock College

Chris M. Hamilton
Antelope Valley College

Dorothy Ables
Coastline Community College

Richard Helgeson
Collin County College

Ivan G. Eagleson
De Anza College

Doug Housley
College of the Canyons

Jeff Eddy
College of the Sequoias

Rick Chehab
De Anza College

Ken Combs
Del Mar College

Olivia Anderson
East Los Angeles College

Elliot Dixon
East Los Angeles College

Dr. Robert Bowers
Fullerton College

Sonia Banks
Gavilan College

Walt Zozula
Glendale College

Alfred E. Fabian
Ivy Tech State College

Jim Cunningham
Long Beach City College

Ron Maricich
Los Angeles Harbor College

Sal Mesa
Los Angeles Southwest College

Patricia Moore
Los Medanos College

Ignacio Gonzalez
Mendocino College

Ed Culbertson
MiraCosta College

Larry Cowart
Morehead State University

Edwin Estes, Jr.
Mt. San Antonio College

J. Stango
Mt. San Jacinto College

David Kemp
Palomar College

Bonnie Frazier
Palomar College

Fred Henning
Riverside City College

Patrick Hogarty
Sacramento City College

Nick Zoumbos
San Bernardino Valley College

Dr. Nick Sacorafas
San Diego Mesa College

Nick Faklis
San Joaquin Delta College

Gary Goldberg
Santa Barbara City College

Steve Herndon
Santa Rosa Junior College

Joel Carlson
Santiago Canyon College

Sandra Johnson
Shoals School of Business

Gail Stockin
Southwestern College

Mike Anderson
Ventura College

Chris Grover
Victor Valley College

Dana J. Gordon
Victor Valley College

Jerome L. Fox
West Los Angeles College

Dean Piller
West Los Angeles College

Ruben Ramos
Yuba College

360 Training.com
Austin, Texas

CELI
Canton, Texas

CETC
Garland, Texas

Key Realty School
Las Vegas, Nevada

Rod Rodriguez, JD
Texas Attorney

Preview of Internet Sites

The History of Credit
www.didyouknow.cd/creditcards.htm

Board of Governors: Federal Reserve
www.federalreserve.gov

Employee Mall
www.employeemall.com

One West Bank (Formerly IndyMac Federal Bank)
www.onewestbank.com

U.S. Census Bureau
www.census.gov

Fannie Mae
www.fanniemae.com

Ginnie Mae
www.ginniemae.gov

Freddie Mac
www.freddiemac.com

FIRREA (18 U.S.C.)
www.fear.org/fedstat2.html

History of the '80s – Lessons for the Future
www.fdic.gov/bank/historical/history/vol1.html

Credit Unions Online
www.creditunionsonline.com

Real Estate Investment Trust
www.reit.com

Farm Service Agency
www.fsa.usda.gov/FSA

Farmer Mac
www.farmermac.com/plane/frames.htm

Bankrate.com
www.bankrate.com/brm/ratehm.asp

HUD
www.hud.gov/offices/hsg/sfh/buying/buyhm.cfm

Single Family Insurance Programs
www.hud.gov/offices/hsg/sfh/insured.cfm

FHA Mortgage Limits
https://entp.hud.gov/idapp/html/hicostlook.cfm

203(k) Rehab Mortgage Insurance
www.hud.gov/offices/hsg/sfh/203k/203k--df.cfm

VA Home Loan Guaranty Services
www.homeloans.va.gov

Marshall & Swift: The Building Cost People
www. marshallswift.com/comp-39 -residential-cost-handbook.aspx

California Housing Finance Agency
www.calhfa.ca.gov

Online Mortgage Calculator
www.quickenloans.com/mortgage-calculator

State Housing Agencies
www.trackproservices.com/links/statelnk.html

State and Local Government Information
www.statelocalgov.net

Alaska Home Loan Program
www.ahfc.state.ak.us/Department_Files/Mortgage/loans-main-page.htm

Delaware State Housing Authority (DSHA)
www.destatehousing.com

Florida Housing Finance Corporation (FHFC)
www.floridahousing.org/home

Maryland Mortgage Program
www.dhcd.state.md.us/website/home/index.aspx

Nationwide Mortgage Licensing System (NMLS)
www.mortgage.nationwidelicensingsystem.org

New Jersey Mortgage Opportunity Program (MOP)
www.state.nj.us/dca/hmfa

State of New York Mortgage Agency (SONYMA)
www.nyhomes.org/home/index.aspx

Oregon Housing and Community Services (OHCS)
www.oregon.gov/OHCS/SFF_OregonBondHome.shtml

Texas Veterans' Housing Assistance Program (VHAP)
www. glo.state.tx.us/vlb/vhap/index.html

Wisconsin Department of Veterans Affairs (WDVA)
http://dva.state.wi.us

In this era of bank failures, government bailouts, real estate crashes, and stock market volatility, it's more important than ever to re-establish consumer confidence and return to the fundamentals of finance, particularly in the real estate and lending businesses. Economic stability can only be achieved by proper knowledge and practice of the principles of finance.

Table of Contents

Part I – Introduction to Real Estate Finance

– Part I –

Chapters 1, 2, and 3
Introduction To Real Estate Finance

Chapter 1 – A Short History of Finance and the Fed

The roots of our modern financial system extend back to the Roman Empire. These roots are evident in the language of finance today. The United States bases its system of laws, banking, finance, and real estate ownership on British models.

The **Federal Reserve System (the "Fed")** regulates the U.S. banking system by:

1. issuing of currency from the Treasury and controlling the reserve requirements.
2. control of interest rates.
3. buying and selling U.S. bonds and securities.

Chapter 2 – The Real Estate Cycle and the Secondary Market

The real estate cycle has four phases, beginning with an expansion of real estate activity that leads to a peak, and then a decline to a bottom or trough. The establishment of a national secondary market to buy and sell mortgages has worked to diminish drastic swings in the real estate cycle by insuring that mortgage money is available at all stages within the cycle.

Chapter 3 – Sources of Funds: The Primary Market

The ***PRIMARY MARKET*** *is mostly made up of local banks, savings banks, and mortgage bankers and brokers*. Deregulation of banking laws had an adverse effect on the S&Ls and permitted other lenders to take over part of their market share. This same deregulation has allowed other institutions such as credit unions, insurance companies, and pension plans to enter the primary market.

SAFE Act

The **Secure and Fair Enforcement for Mortgage Licensing Act of 2008 (SAFE Act)** is designed to enhance consumer protection and reduce fraud by the setting of minimum standards for the licensing and registration of state-licensed mortgage loan originators (MLOs). In addition to pre-licensing (PE) and annual continuing education (CE) requirements, MLOs must pass both state and federal exams, be fingerprinted, have a background and credit check performed and pay a fee.

Chapter 1
A Short History of Finance and the Fed

I. Lending in Ancient Times

A. THE ROMAN INFLUENCE

The American financial system has roots that extend back to the ancient Roman Empire. The Roman system of finance is reflected in the language that we use today. The term ***FIDUCIARY**, meaning a relationship of financial trust*, is from the Latin word *fides*, which means faith or trust. The Latin word *moneta* is the origin for the word money. ***MONEY** is any paper currency or metallic coin authorized by a government to represent value and accepted as a medium of exchange.*

Roman law and customs would not disappear with the empire but would continue on in various forms throughout western civilization.

B. MEDIEVAL INFLUENCES

The medieval period of western civilization saw the rise of feudalism throughout Europe.

In this system, the king owned all the land (**real property**) and would parcel it out to faithful retainers for their loyal services. These retainers, in turn, would further parcel

CHAPTER OUTLINE

out their holdings to others loyal to them. All such holdings were considered a life estate only, and would revert to the king upon the death of the holder. A ***LIFE ESTATE*** *is an interest in real estate or real property that is limited to the lifetime of the owner.*

In the middle of society were tradesmen and craftsmen. Most were required to be members of a guild and undergo a lengthy apprenticeship before being able to practice their trades. The lowest classes of citizens, if they could be called that, were serfs. Serfs were considered chattel and were bound to the land, meaning they were transferred with it to each new owner and lord. ***CHATTEL*** *is personal property.* Today, chattel may or may not be transferred with the real estate.

Serfdom was a form of slavery.

Our understanding of the system is based greatly on the study of the *Domesday Book.* This was a survey and tax roll commissioned by William the Conqueror in 1085 to ensure that the king knew the value and extent of all his new holdings.

As might be imagined, there was little room for upward mobility within society. Further, loans on real estate were virtually nonexistent. Such lending, as existed, was for an amount given against a ***PLEDGE*** *(pawn)* of personal property or real estate if the loan was defaulted. Any such loan generally did not bear interest, as medieval religious authorities interpreted any payment of interest as usury. Today, ***USURY*** *is defined as an interest payment in excess of the legally permitted rate.*

C. THE END OF FEUDALISM IN ENGLAND

This political, economic, and social life arrangement would be wrenched apart in England by the events of the 14th century. First the English would engage in a costly century-long war in France. Then, in 1348, England was struck by a bubonic plague epidemic called the "Black Death." The death toll was so severe that the entire social, political, and economic life of the country was disrupted. Serfdom, in England, ceased to exist as peasants flocked to the cities to take jobs formerly open only to guild members. There were too few lords alive to force them to return to the land. The advances in navigation that would soon bring about the discovery of new colonial lands to the west would also accelerate the opportunities for trade and the need for a stable financial system as well.

II. Banking in the Renaissance

In the rest of Europe, both the forces of the Renaissance and the Reformation would gradually allow the formation of modern banking practices.

The History of Credit

Credit was first used in Assyria, Babylon, and Egypt 3000 years ago. The **bill of exchange**—the forerunner of banknotes—was established in the 14th century. Debts were settled by one-third cash and two-thirds bill of exchange. Paper money followed only in the 17th century.

The first advertisement for credit was placed in 1730 by Christopher Thornton, who offered furniture for sale that could be paid off weekly.

From the 18th century until the early part of the 20th century, "tallymen" sold clothes in return for small weekly payments. They were called tallymen because they kept a record, or tally, of what people had bought on a wooden stick. One side of the stick was marked with notches to represent the amount of debt and the other side was a record of payments. In the 1920s, a shopper's plate—a "buy now, pay later" system—was introduced in the USA. They could only be used in the shops that issued them.

In 1950, **Diners Club** and **American Express** launched their charge cards in the USA, the first "plastic money." In 1951, Diners Club issued the first credit card to 200 customers who could use it at 27 restaurants in New York. But it wasn't until the establishment of standards for the magnetic strip in 1970 that the credit card became part of the information age.

From "Did You Know?"
www.didyouknow.cd/creditcards.htm

The wars of religion and nationalism were expensive for monarchs. They were often forced to borrow from the new wealthy merchant class to finance their wars. Two wealthy merchant families in particular would rise to prominence in this period as lenders. These were the Medici family in Italy and the Fugger family in Germany. These merchant princes would also underwrite commercial expeditions for a share in the merchant's profits. An ***UNDERWRITER*** *makes loans based on assessment of risk.*

A. BRITISH INFLUENCES

By the 17th Century, England was an established trading nation with the beginnings of a colonial empire abroad.

The English Civil War, early in the century, had further restricted the power of English kings. The monarch operated in a constitutional role and his power was regulated by a parliament. Individual property rights were considered to be in fee simple estate. A ***FEE SIMPLE ESTATE*** *is the highest legal form of property ownership with rights that are assumed to continue forever.*

The country did indeed seem to be a "nation of shopkeepers," as Napoleon would call it a century later. These shopkeepers were becoming increasingly wealthy in cash assets with no safe place to keep their extra cash.

1. Goldsmith Accounts: The Birth of English Banking

While the British treasury might be a perfectly secure place to store money, the suspicion remained that the king and his ministers might conveniently forget whose money it really was. Thus, most merchants preferred to place their extra cash with the London goldsmiths. In return for the cash, the goldsmiths provided receipts that were redeemable on demand. The goldsmiths soon discovered that their clients often left the money in their keeping for very long periods of time and often continued to deposit additional sums of money with them. Many customers, rather than withdrawing their gold to pay a debt, would simply sign over their receipt to whomever they owed the debt. As a convenience to their customers, the goldsmiths created notes that were payable to the owner or to "the bearer on demand." A ***BEARER NOTE*** *is payable to whomever presents it.*

Goldsmiths' bearer notes marked the beginning of the first circulating paper currency.

The fact that the customers did not often withdraw all their money also allowed the goldsmiths to make loans of this additional cash. As an inducement to the depositors to keep their money in the goldsmiths' strongboxes, the goldsmiths shared the profits of the loans with the depositors in the form of an interest payment. For many goldsmiths the lending of money was becoming more profitable than making jewelry.

2. Stocks and Bonds

During this same time period, England was launching great private trading ventures. Among these were the Muscovy Company, the Hudson's Bay Company, and the East India Company. The great size and cost of these enterprises brought about the idea of "stock subscription" to fund their endeavors. ***STOCK*** *is an ownership interest in an institution or company.*

This allowed the cost of funding to be borne by many rather than a few. Additionally, the government also invested in these enterprises. However, the size and scope of these companies often exhausted these sources of initial funding and they were forced to borrow money. They managed this by the issue of "bonds." ***BONDS** are debt instruments that bear a stated "face value" or principal amount payable to the bearer in a specified time.* They are generally sold at a discount from this amount and the difference between the stated amount and the discount is the rate of interest return. As might be imagined, the London goldsmiths/ bankers saw opportunities to make additional money in the bond market.

3. The Bank of England

In 1694, a consortium of bankers, led by William Patterson, established the Bank of England.

The bank made a loan of its entire capital to the British government. From that point forward, the British treasury deposited all its monetary reserves in the bank. In return, the bank received the sole right to issue notes and engage in commercial lending. In effect, it became the banker's banker. With the right of issue, it controlled the circulating currency. It also acted as a lender of last resort to other banks. It was then, and is now, what we call a central bank. ***CENTRAL BANKS** control the economy of a nation.* The Federal Reserve System (Fed) is the U.S. central bank.

III. The American Colonies

The American Colonies were a mixture of proprietary land grants and direct royal holdings.

In most cases, these large holdings were sold in fee simple estate to individual colonists. A great problem throughout the colonial period was the lack of sufficient currency to support the needs of colonial trade. This was solved, in part, by the establishment of land office banks by the various colonies. The land office banks would make loans to colonists against a mortgage on their land. The mortgage monies were paid out in the form of bearer notes issued in the name of the colony (see **Figure 1-1**).

This provided a greatly needed form of circulating currency in the colonial period. The British outlawed this practice in 1741. However, like many British laws of the period, it was conveniently ignored by the colonists.

A. A NEW NATION

The issue of fiat paper money by the colonies and the Continental Congress financed the American Revolution. So much worthless paper money was issued that the phrase "not worth a Continental" was added to the American vocabulary. ***FIAT MONEY** is*

Figure 1-1

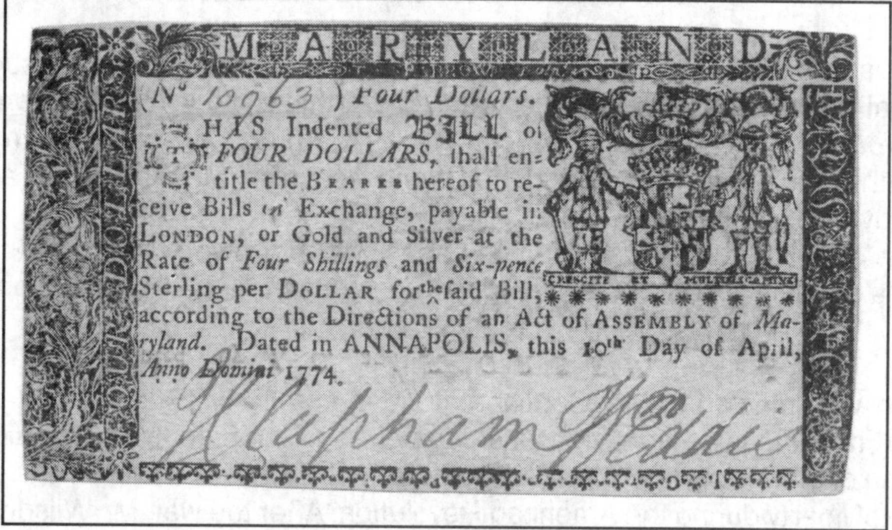

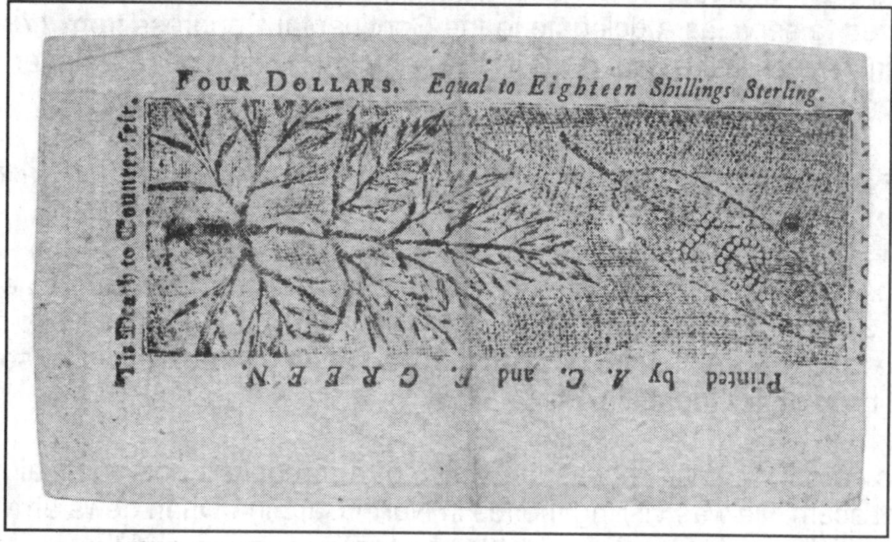

issued by decree of the state, often in times of war. It is issued with no regard for economic stability. It is almost always paper money and always inflationary.

This new distrust of paper money would later be enshrined in the U.S. Constitution by the requirement that the states could make nothing but gold and silver legal tender. ***LEGAL TENDER*** *is money that is legally required to be accepted by the public in payment of any debt*. This well-intentioned requirement on the part of our founding fathers would later be circumvented by court interpretations that everyone except state governments could issue paper currency!

Historical Note: James Wilson

James Wilson was one of the men who signed those banknotes issued by the Continental Congress that would become so worthless they were the origin of the phrase *"Not worth a Continental."* Wilson (1742-1798) was a Scottish immigrant who arrived in this country in 1765 during the Stamp Act crisis. Mr. Wilson was an attorney and an advocate of freedom. He is of interest to us in that he was an investor in real estate and often leveraged his purchases with borrowed funds. He very rapidly amassed a small fortune from his investments. In a sense, he was the Donald Trump of his day.

Mr. Wilson was elected to the Continental Congress in 1775 and 1776, along with Benjamin Franklin, as a Pennsylvania delegate. As a delegate, he was a signer of the Declaration of Independence. Mr. Wilson would spend most of his fortune in supporting the cause of liberty during the American Revolution. After the war, Mr. Wilson continued his winning ways with real estate and gradually began to rebuild his fortune. He was also selected to serve as a delegate to the Continental Congress from 1785 to 1787. Once again, he was in the right place at the right time and became a signer of the U.S. Constitution.

James Wilson was one of only five men to have signed both the Declaration and the Constitution

Mr. Wilson was appointed as an Associate Justice of the U.S. Supreme Court by President George Washington. While Mr. Wilson had hoped to be appointed Chief Justice, he readily accepted the position that had been offered. He would serve on the court until his untimely death in 1798.

Late in his career, Mr. Wilson was the victim of a fraudulent and criminal real estate investment scam. He was visiting friends in North Carolina when news arrived that he had lost every penny of his money in this speculative venture and that there was also a criminal warrant for his arrest, because the authorities believed he was an active participant in the scam. On receiving the news, Mr. Wilson collapsed from a stroke. He remained in a coma and died within three days. The moral of this tale is that Mr. Wilson would certainly have benefited from proper underwriting and appraisal of the properties he invested in. Unfortunately, these modern investment protections were not available in his time.

James Wilson appears among the signers on the reverse of the most recent $2 bill.

B. THE BANK OF THE UNITED STATES

The first Treasurer of the United States was Alexander Hamilton.

Hamilton was a fiscal conservative who was well aware of the stability provided to the British economy by the Bank of England. He persuaded congress to establish a central bank, based on the British model, to ensure that the new nation would commence on a sound financial footing. Congress went along with the plan, but was only willing to allow the new experiment in national finance a twenty-year charter. The charter lapsed in 1811. The result of this bad timing was that the government was forced to issue treasury bills to pay for the War of 1812 at high interest and state chartered banks with dubious capital assets multiplied.

In 1817, Congress rechartered the bank as the **Second Bank of the United States**. Once again, it had only a twenty-year charter. Both banks provided the young nation with financial stability and safety while allowing moderate growth. The first experiment with central banking was curtailed by President Andrew Jackson, a westerner who was distrustful of a central monetary authority of any kind. He also had a great distrust of the eastern establishment, who he thought was choking off western financial expansion. Jackson felt that federal monies would be safer spread around in state banks. He proceeded to veto the recharter of the Bank of the United States and withdrew all federal funds from the bank. The end result of this action was a massive loss of federal funds and a severe depression. However, this occurred after Jackson left the presidency and the blame for it was attached to his successor, Martin Van Buren.

C. STATE-CHARTERED BANKING

The era that ensued after the demise of the Bank of the United States in 1837 was a period of great territorial and business expansion in the United States. Initially, the nation went through a great depression from 1837-1840. However, in 1841, the establishment of a subtreasury system for federal funds provided security and safety, at least, for the governments monies. After 1841, the nation would experience inflationary conditions until another depression in 1857.

1. The Wildcat Era

With no central bank and a lack of federal or, in most cases, state regulation, banks proliferated like rabbits. While many of these institutions were honest and sound, many more were fraudulent. The term "wildcat banking" was coined to describe institutions that shared quarters out with the wildcats. In other words, they were located where it was impossible to find them if someone desired to redeem one of the many beautifully engraved notes that they issued (see **Figure 1-2**).

Figure 1-2

In the period from 1837-1863, over 16,000 banks existed, of which at least 5,000 were totally fraudulent.

These banks issued over 36,000 different designs of currency. The average citizen who accepted a bad note could only console himself with the thought that he at least held a nice example of contemporary art.

However, there were positive developments during this period. The first building and loan societies started up during the 1830s. These were the precursors of the modern savings and loans. Mutual savings banks appeared in the 1840s. They provided a safe haven for workers' deposits and functioned in a similar way to today's credit unions. Many states created lending and usury laws in an attempt to regulate predatory banking and real estate lending practices by individuals and institutions.

D.THE NATIONAL BANKING ACT OF 1863

The Civil War (1861-1865) was the most costly war in the nation's history up to that time.

Gold and silver were hoarded by the population, forcing the government to ask the banks for large loans of currency. The banking system was quite happy to loan the government their notes and deluged the Treasury with them. The problem was that these notes were of all different designs, values, and sizes. Those that circulated outside their local areas did so at a heavy discount. Secretary of the Treasury Salmon P. Chase, in an effort to introduce some sort of order into the chaos that ensued, issued U.S. notes (greenbacks) that had no backing other than the government's promise to pay. Further, he persuaded the administration to submit a bill to Congress to create a uniform note issue for the entire nation.

The result was the ***NATIONAL BANKING ACT OF 1863****, which set minimum capitalization and reserves for any bank that applied for a National Bank Charter*. The banks could then buy government bonds with their capital. Upon deposit of their bonds with the U.S. Treasury, the banks could then make loans of up to 90% of the value of the bonds they had deposited. The loans would be made using a standardized national banknote provided by the government. This system provided the government with low interest loans. Further, it provided the banks with interest on the bonds and interest again on the loans that they made. Lastly, it provided the nation with a uniform circulating currency that was backed by government securities and not subject to discount. This system worked so well that in 1865 congress drove out all privately issued bank notes by placing a 10% federal tax on them that had to be paid each time they were exchanged.

While the nation had a secure uniform circulating currency, several problems remained to be addressed. The rapid industrialization and westward farm and ranch expansion of the nation after the Civil War created dramatic swings in the business cycle. The nation went through severe depressions in 1873, 1893, and 1907. Because the banking system was still local in nature, it was unable to respond to these crises and often the response of the local banks worsened the problems. Perhaps the most troubling aspect was that national banks were not allowed to engage in mortgage lending. ***MORTGAGE LENDING*** *is the practice of loaning money that is secured by real estate and real property. The loan document is called a* ***MORTGAGE LIEN***.

Mortgage lending during this period was still largely carried out by private individuals or by the building and loans (now more frequently called savings banks). Most mortgages were short term and often had a balloon payment at the end. A ***BALLOON PAYMENT*** *is a large lump-sum payment of principle at the end of a series of smaller periodic mortgage payments, typically much higher than the previous payments.* A consequence is that the loan generally has to be refinanced. At the end of the 19th

century, it was becoming apparent that the U.S. economy was functioning sluggishly as a result of a lack of cohesiveness and direction in the lending system.

IV. The Federal Reserve Act of 1913

The passage of the Federal Reserve Act of 1913 attempted to solve the existent problems of the banking system.

The original purpose of the system was to discount ***COMMERCIAL PAPER*** *(unsecured promissory notes sold by large banks to meet short-term debt obligations)* and provide additional bank regulation. A positive aspect of this law was that it allowed the member national banks of the system to engage in mortgage lending. For the first time since the demise of the Bank of the United States in 1837, the nation had a central banking system. The system would slowly begin to assume a centralized control over the economic life of the nation. It would really commence its modern functions during the Great Depression.

The primary responsibility of the central bank is to influence the flow of money and credit in the nation's economy.

A. THE ROLE OF THE FEDERAL RESERVE SYSTEM (Fed)

The ***FEDERAL RESERVE SYSTEM*** *serves as the central bank for the United States*. For its member banks, it is the "lender of last resort" or "the banker's banker." The Federal Reserve is made up of thousands of member banks (see **Figures 1-3** and **1-4**). It has regulatory control over the entire U.S. banking system.

Figure 1-3 **The Federal Reserve System**

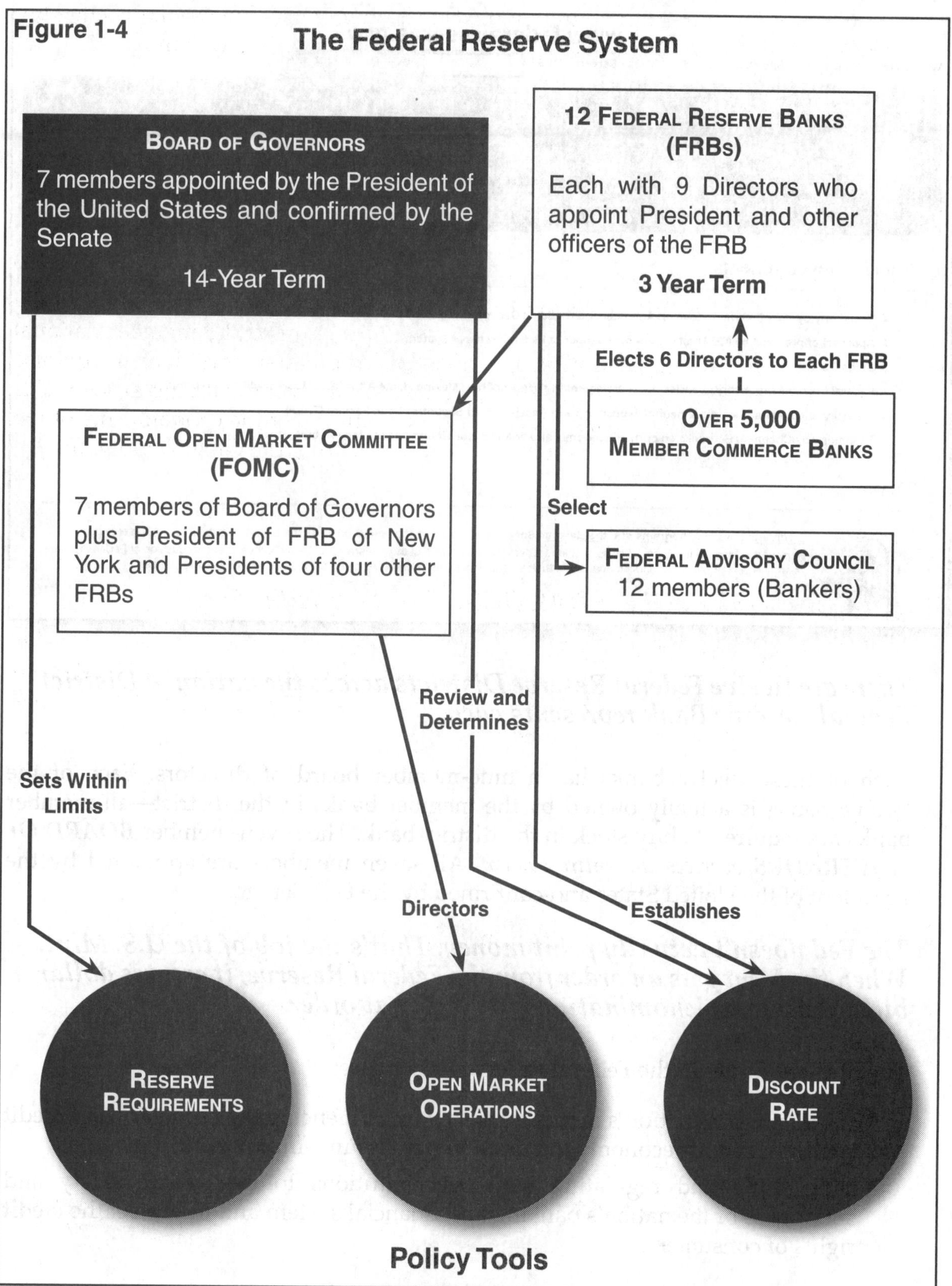
Figure 1-4
The Federal Reserve System
BOARD OF GOVERNORS
7 members appointed by the President of the United States and confirmed by the Senate
14-Year Term
12 FEDERAL RESERVE BANKS (FRBs)
Each with 9 Directors who appoint President and other officers of the FRB
3 Year Term
Elects 6 Directors to Each FRB
OVER 5,000 MEMBER COMMERCE BANKS
FEDERAL OPEN MARKET COMMITTEE (FOMC)
7 members of Board of Governors plus President of FRB of New York and Presidents of four other FRBs
Select
FEDERAL ADVISORY COUNCIL
12 members (Bankers)
Review and Determines
Sets Within Limits
Directors
Establishes
RESERVE REQUIREMENTS
OPEN MARKET OPERATIONS
DISCOUNT RATE
Policy Tools

www.federalreserve.gov

What's New · What's Next · Site Map · A-Z Index · FAQs · Careers · RSS   Search   Advanced Search

Board of Governors of the Federal Reserve System

The Federal Reserve, the central bank of the United States, provides the nation with a safe, flexible, and stable monetary and financial system.

About the Fed | News & Events | Monetary Policy | Banking Information & Regulation | Payment Systems | Economic Research & Data | Consumer Information | Community Development | Reporting Forms | Publications

Recent Developments

- Testimony by Vice Chairman Kohn on American International Group
- Approval of proposal by ICE Trust to become member of Federal Reserve System
- Beige Book
- Federal financial regulatory agencies issue statement in support of the "Making Home Affordable" loan modification program
- Treasury and Federal Reserve announce launch of Term Asset-Backed Securities Loan Facility (TALF)
- Testimony by Chairman Bernanke on current economic and financial conditions and the federal budget

Features

Credit and Liquidity Programs and the Balance Sheet Expands information provided about the policy tools the Federal Reserve has employed to address the financial crisis. Includes a detailed explanation of the Federal Reserve's balance sheet, discussion of Federal Reserve risk-management practices, and information on the types and amounts of collateral being pledged at various lending facilities.

There are twelve Federal Reserve Districts across the nation. A District Federal Reserve Bank represents each.

Each of these twelve banks has a nine-member board of directors. Each of the twelve banks is actually owned by the member banks in the district—all member banks are required to buy stock in the district bank. The seven-member ***BOARD OF GOVERNORS*** *oversees the entire system.* All seven members are appointed by the President of the United States and confirmed by the U.S. Senate.

The Fed doesn't actually print money. That's the job of the U.S. Mint. When the Mint gets an order from the Federal Reserve, it creates dollar bills of various denominations to meet that order.

The primary duties of the Federal Reserve System are:

1. conducting the nation's monetary policy by influencing the monetary and credit conditions in the economy in pursuit of maximum employment, and
2. supervising and regulating banking institutions to ensure the safety and soundness of the nation's banking and financial system and to protect the credit rights of consumers.

The Federal Reserve Banks distribute currency (paper money) and coin to depository institutions to meet the public's need for cash.

The Federal Reserve controls the **monetary policy** of the United States in a number of ways.

1. The Power of Currency Issue

The Federal Reserve is now the only entity to have the power to issue currency.

The ***POWER OF CURRENCY ISSUE*** *is the legal authority to print money.* During the 1930s, the Federal Reserve would begin the withdrawal of National Bank notes from circulation. Government gold and silver certificates, as well as U.S. notes, would also be withdrawn. In their place, a new uniform federal reserve currency was issued. This process is still ongoing.

The banks are required by law to hold a percentage of the customers' deposits in ready cash or the equivalent of cash.

The "Fed," as the Federal Reserve is known, also controls the ***RESERVE REQUIREMENTS*** *of the member banks. Ostensibly, this permits the Fed to require its member banks to retain enough reserves to ensure that sufficient funds are on hand to satisfy customer withdrawal needs.* Actually, this power is also used as a tool to manage the banking system's ability to make loans.

By raising the "reserve requirement" of banks, the Fed limits the amount of money available for loans. By lowering the reserve requirement, more money becomes available for loans.

2. Control of Interest Rates

The Fed also controls interest rates throughout the nation. This is accomplished by the discount rate. The ***DISCOUNT RATE*** *is the interest rate that the Federal Reserve charges to member banks to loan them money.*

A bank can borrow money from the Fed by pledging its **commercial paper (short-term promissory notes)** for the loan. The rate of interest to the bank is known as the prime rate. The ***PRIME RATE*** *is a bank's lowest rate, generally given only to its best customers.*

The Fed controls the "margin rate," which is the percentage of the amount an investor can borrow when purchasing stock. It is currently about 50%. For example, an investor buying $40,000 worth of stock can only borrow $20,000 from the securities company.

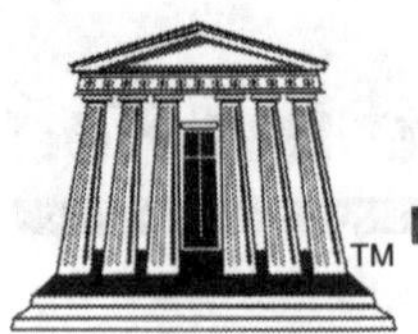

Upward or downward changes in this rate will create upward or downward changes in the rate charged by the bank to its customers. The rate to a bank's customers will generally be higher than the prime rate. The ***FEDERAL FUNDS RATE*** *is the interest rate at which depository institutions lend balances at the Federal Reserve to other depository institutions overnight.*

While the Federal Reserve rate is for short-term loans only, it is often used as a benchmark for the rates that banks set to their customers for other loans.

3. Open Market Operations (Buying and Selling of U.S. Bonds)

The Fed also carries out open market operations that have an effect on the nation's economy. ***OPEN MARKET OPERATIONS*** *consist of the buying and selling of United States Treasury bonds, as well as the securities of federal agencies such as the Federal Home Loan Bank System, Federal Housing Administration (FHA), and Ginnie Mae.* Sales of these securities have the effect of tightening the money supply.

Buying bonds from investors increases the money supply in the U.S. and selling bonds to investors reduces the money supply in the U.S. This is perhaps the most important tool in the Federal Reserve's arsenal.

The ***FEDERAL OPEN MARKET COMMITTEE*** *carries out open market operations.* The importance of this committee may be gauged by the fact that seven of the twelve members of the committee are the Board of Governors themselves. The other five members consist of one member from the Federal Reserve Bank of New York and four other members who serve in rotation from the other eleven district banks.

4. Truth in Lending Law (Regulation Z)

The Fed is also responsible for supervising the Truth in Lending Law. The ***TRUTH IN LENDING LAW*** *requires lenders to inform borrowers of the total costs of obtaining a loan.* This law (including interest rates and terms) is also known as **Regulation Z**. Since the Fed regulates the economy, and by extension the lenders, it was made responsible for enforcing the act.

V. The Role of the Federal Government and Government Agencies

The actions of the federal government have a great impact on the economic life of the nation. Increases in government spending beyond the income taken in by the government in the form of taxes require the U.S. Treasury to borrow funds on the open market. This has the effect of making money less available for private borrowers. It also creates higher interest rates for private borrowers who are competing with the government for available funds.

Since the 1930s, the federal government has taken an active role in trying to assure home ownership for all Americans. A number of government agencies have been created to provide loan insurance and to create a market for mortgage securities. The actions of these agencies have an effect on the real estate market and on the national economy as well. We will discuss these agencies and their operations in the chapters that follow.

Collapse of the Secondary Market – 2008

- Bear Stearns was acquired by J.P. Morgan Chase in March 2008 for $1.2 billion. The sale was conditional on the Fed's lending Bear Sterns $29 billion on a nonrecourse basis.
- IndyMac Bank, America's leading Alt-A originator in 2006 was placed into conservatorship by the FDIC on July 11, 2008, citing liquidity concerns. A bridge bank, IndyMac Federal Bank, FSB, was established under the control of the FDIC. It was sold to a group of investors and is still in business.
- Fannie Mae and Freddie Mac were both placed under the conservatorship of the Federal Housing Finance Agency (FHFA) in September 2008. The two GOVERNMENT SECURED ENTERPRISES (GSEs) guarantee or hold mortgage backed securities(MBS), mortgages and other debt with a value of more than $5 trillion.
- Merrill Lynch was acquired by Bank of America in September 2008 for $50 billion.
- Lehman Brothers declared bankruptcy on September 15, 2008, after the Secretary of the Treasury Henry Paulson, citing moral hazard, refused to bail it out.
- AIG received an $85 billion emergency loan in September 2008 from the Federal Reserve, which AIG is expected to repay by gradually selling off its assets. In exchange, the Federal government acquired a 79.9% equity stake in AIG.
- Washington Mutual (WaMu) was seized in September 2008 by the USA Office of Thrift Supervision (OTS). Most of WaMu's untroubled assets were to be sold to J.P. Morgan Chase.
- In November 2008, the U.S. government announced it was purchasing $27 billion of preferred stock in Citigroup, a USA bank with over $2 trillion in assets, and warrants on 4.5% of its common stock. The preferred stock carries an 8% dividend. This purchase follows an earlier purchase of $25 billion of the same preferred stock using TARP funds.

The ***TROUBLED ASSET RELIEF PROGRAM (TARP)*** *is a U.S. government program to purchase* assets and equity from financial institutions in order to strengthen the financial sector. Instigated in 2008, it was one of the measures taken by the government to address the subprime mortgage crisis (discussed in the following chapter). A government ***BAILOUT*** *is the act of loaning or giving capital to a failing business in order to save it from bankruptcy, insolvency, or total liquidation and ruin.*

VI. The Future of Money

Our forefathers could never have anticipated that gold, silver, and finally paper money would one day be replaced by credit and debit cards with magnetic strip coding, let alone wireless banking and computer chip technology. Nor can we, in the 21st century, possibly imagine the changes and advances that will be made in our future. Perhaps we will one day become a truly "cashless society." With technology growing in leaps and bounds, it doesn't seem so farfetched as it would have just a few years ago.

In order to understand some of the advances the future may hold, it is necessary to look at how the banking industry has changed recently. Some of the advances seen just in the past few decades include the advent of credit cards, automated teller machines (ATMs), debit cards, and online banking, bill paying, and check writing.

A. AUTOMATED TELLER MACHINES (ATMs)

Automated teller machines (ATMs) save banks money by reducing the need for tellers. Initially, they were only installed inside or immediately outside their banks' branch offices.

To encourage customers to embrace the (then) new technology and overcome their fears about putting checks into an ATM rather than a teller's hands, banks did not initially charge customers any fees for ATM use. Banks that embraced the ATM prospered, growing far faster than those who did not. Soon banks began imposing fees. First, they began charging their own customer's "off-use" fees when they used another bank's machine. As is often the case, this "nickel-and-dime 'em" strategy irritated consumers, but didn't enrage them. Also, the banks had the political wisdom to spend millions of dollars on campaign contributions and top lobbyists—and to not impose fees on ATMs located in or near government offices.

A number of large banks elected to charge a second fee for the exact same operation, but with a different justification; banks should be allowed to charge noncustomers for using their machines. In other words, banks should be compensated for installing ATMs and for their wear and tear. Legislation was introduced in the U. S. Senate to ban the surcharge. Also, at least two dozen states later attempted to ban surcharges legislatively. All these efforts failed. However, in the wake of the ordinances banning the ATM surcharge in Santa Monica and San Francisco, California, surcharge legislation is not a dead issue. What will happen to ATM fees is not clear, but it is clear that ATMs are larger profit machines than their promoters could have ever imagined 25 years ago.

B. DEBIT CARDS

Debit cards, also known as "check cards," look like credit cards or ATM cards, but operate like cash or a personal check. Debit cards differ from credit cards in that credit cards are a way to "pay later," whereas debit cards are a way to "pay now." When you use a debit card, your money is quickly deducted from your checking or savings account.

C. ELECTRONIC BANKING

Consumers can now have their paychecks directly deposited electronically to their checking or savings accounts. In addition, computers have made it possible to have the bank pay their bills online. Or they can pay the bills themselves by debiting their account. The banks also provide electronic copies of all transactions to their consumers. This saves both the bank and the consumer time and paperwork. Other banking services such as personal and mortgage loan applications can be carried out online. There have been concerns by consumer groups that consumers may suffer greater exposure to the possibility of identity theft by computer hackers. This has actually occurred, in several instances, where large segments of information were stolen from bank data sources thought to be secure. However, many cases of stolen identity have also occurred when consumers entered websites that masqueraded as the bank sites or by answering financial questions to an e-mail or PDF from a fraudulent site. Banking, regulatory, and consumer protection groups have been working together to educate the public to practice safe online banking practices, as well as how to recognize consumer online scams. At present, it appears that the speed and convenience of the electronic medium outweighs any perceived problems by consumers about the security of the online services.

D. ONLINE REAL ESTATE SALES AND MORTGAGE LENDING SERVICES

For some time now, consumers have been able to shop for properties online through online brokerage services. In addition, many lenders have set up proprietary online loan programs. The newest wrinkle in this fast moving electronic world is the concept of using **Aggregation** of services to target **Affinity Groups**.

AGGREGATION means the bundling of different services into one consumer-friendly package. An *AFFINITY GROUP consists of individuals involved in a group undertaking or industry to increase profit.*

One of the pioneering companies in this area is EmployeeMall, Inc. This company works with major corporations and government agencies to help them provide additional employment benefits to both hourly and management employees at

www.employeemall.com
Employee Mall
Our Services
Members Login
About Us
Contact
EmployeeMall is the leading provider of Employee Discount Programs
An employee discount shopping program is the one employee benefit that an employee can use every day of the year. EmployeeMall will save your staff significant amounts of money on the goods and services they use most.
Best-in-Class Partners
EmployeeMall carefully selects its partners in order to provide only the very best goods and services with the deepest discounts possible.
Best-in-Class Clients
Our clients range from the Fortune 500 to small businesses. All have one thing in common: The desire to provide the best benefits for their employees.

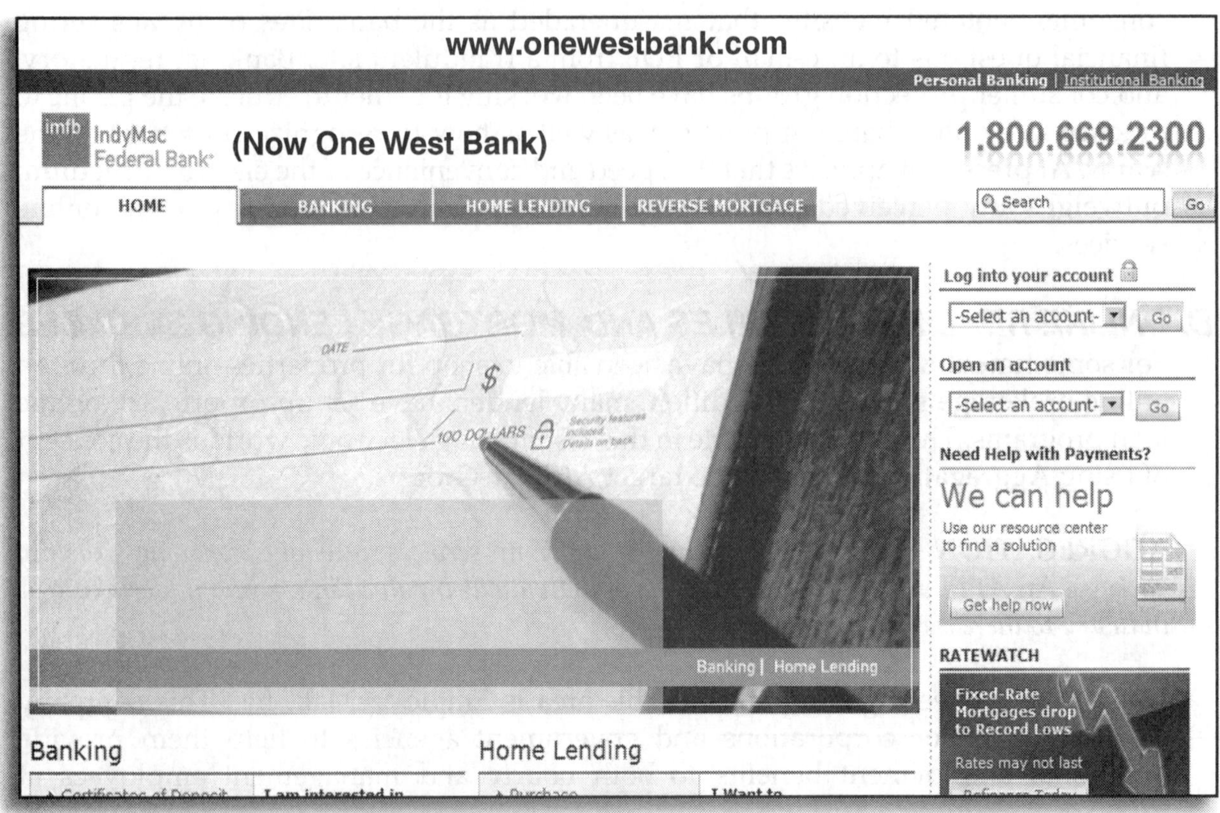
www.onewestbank.com
Personal Banking | Institutional Banking
imfb IndyMac Federal Bank
(Now One West Bank)
1.800.669.2300
HOME
BANKING
HOME LENDING
REVERSE MORTGAGE
Search
Go
Log into your account
-Select an account-
Go
Open an account
-Select an account-
Go
Need Help with Payments?
We can help
Use our resource center to find a solution
Get help now
RATEWATCH
Fixed-Rate Mortgages drop to Record Lows
Rates may not last
Banking | Home Lending
Banking
Home Lending

minimal additional cost to the companies involved. The company sets up employee websites with each of its clients. The employees can then navigate the site to get substantial discounts from major retail firms. The newest venture for EmployeeMall (**employeemall.com**)has been to join together major real estate and lending firms with the employees of government and business entities. The client firm's employees now not only have access to retail discounts but real estate and loan discounts as well.

Participating real estate and mortgage firms typically offer discounts on commissions, points, and fees. In return, they get access to a national market of buyers and borrowers who have excellent job prospects, impeccable credit, and discretionary income. All participants save money by having one site that is centrally managed and accessible to all the users.

VII. CHAPTER SUMMARY

The roots of our modern financial system extend back to the Roman Empire. These roots may be seen in the language of finance today. The United States based its system of laws, banking, finance, and real estate ownership on British models. After the failure of the first central bank, neither the federal government nor the states did much to regulate financial activity before the Civil War, and chaos was often the result. In the aftermath of the Civil War, and throughout the 20th century, the federal government assumed an increasing role in the national economy.

With the establishment of the Federal Reserve System (the Fed) as the nation's powerful central banking system, and the creation of federal agencies to foster home ownership, the nation finally had a financial system that was capable of moderating severe swings in the business cycle. This system, while not foolproof, is a role model for the world.

The Federal Reserve System (the "Fed") regulates the U.S. banking system by:

1. issuing of currency from the Treasury and controlling the reserve requirements.
2. control of interest rates.
3. buying and selling U.S. bonds and securities.

VIII. TERMINOLOGY

Affinity Groups	Life Estate
Bailout	Margin Rates
Balloon Payment	Money
Bearer Note	Mortgage Lending
Bonds	Mortgage Lien
Central Bank	Open Market Operations (OMO)
Chattel	Pledge
Commercial Paper	Primary Market
Discount Rate	Prime Rate
Federal Funds Rate	Power of Currency Issue
Federal Open Market Committee	Regulation Z
Federal Reserve System (Fed)	Reserve Requirements
Fee Simple Estate	Stock
Fiat Money	TARP
Fiduciary	Truth in Lending Law
Government Sponsored Enterprise (GSE)	Underwriter
Legal Tender	Usury

IX. CHAPTER QUIZ

1. Personal property that is often included with real estate is called:
   a. fee estate.
   b. chattel.
   c. serfs.
   d. pawn.

2. A fiduciary is:
   a. a person who is a lawyer.
   b. a person who lends money.
   c. a person who has a relationship of financial trust.
   d. a person who invests in real estate.

3. The highest form of property ownership is a:
   a. life estate.
   b. fee simple estate.
   c. fiduciary estate.
   d. mortgaged estate.

4. The first central bank in the world was:
   a. the Bank of the United States.
   b. the Federal Reserve System.
   c. the Bank of England.
   d. the National Banking System.

5. A central bank:
   a. has the power of issue.
   b. is a depository for a nation's treasury.
   c. regulates the economy of a nation.
   d. is all the above.

6. The Federal Reserve System controls interest rates with all of the following, except:
   a. the discount rate.
   b. the federal funds rate.
   c. open market operations.
   d. Regulation Z.

7. Usury is defined as:
   a. a legal tender.
   b. an excessive interest rate.
   c. a mortgage lien.
   d. none of the above.

8. The London goldsmiths:
   a. developed deposit banking.
   b. developed bearer notes.
   c. made loans from their clients' money.
   d. all the above.

9. The first federal legislation concerning banking was:
   a. the National Banking Act of 1863.
   b. the establishment of the Federal Reserve System.
   c. the establishment of the Sub-Treasury System.
   d. the establishment of the Bank of the United States.

10. Open Market Operations are:
    a. carried out by the U.S. Treasury Department.
    b. sales and purchases of U.S. Treasury Bonds by the Federal Reserve.
    c. government loans to homeowners carried out by the GNMA and the FHA.
    d. sales of mortgages to the Federal Reserve.

ANSWERS: 1. b; 2. c; 3. b; 4. c; 5. d; 6. d; 7. b; 8. d; 9. d; 10. b

FOR SALE
Gulf Coast
Realty Group inc.
434-3699
FIAT-ALLIS

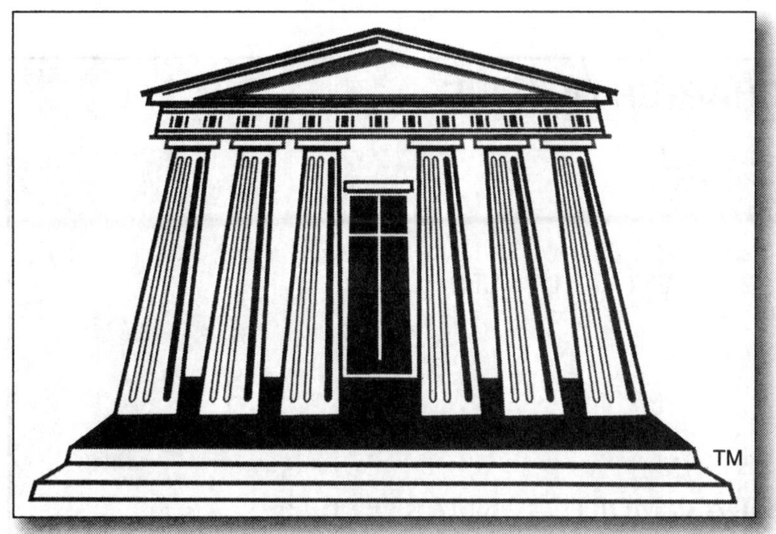

Chapter 2
The Real Estate Cycle and the Secondary Market

I. The Real Estate Cycle

Activity in the real estate market fluctuates according to the real estate cycle.

The ***REAL ESTATE CYCLE****, like the business cycle, refers to the activity of the real estate market as it reacts to the forces of supply and demand.* A cycle is characterized by a general expansion of real estate activity that peaks and then begins to contract, leading to a bottoming out of activity. At this point activity again turns up, leading to a new peak of activity. This cycle has four phases, which are shown in **Figure 2-1**. A widely accepted rule of economics is that all business activity, including the real estate market, reacts to the forces of supply and demand. It is also an accepted principle that supply and demand will always seek to balance each other.

The four phases of the business cycle are:

1. *Peak (top)*
2. *Recession (contraction or slump)*
3. *Bottom (trough)*
4. *Recovery (expansion or boom)*

Chapter 2

CHAPTER OUTLINE

2007 Credit Crisis

The ***SUBPRIME MORTGAGE CRISIS was a financial crisis triggered by a dramatic rise in mortgage delinquencies and foreclosures in America, negatively affecting banks and financial markets around the world***. The seeds of the crisis began germinating in the year 2000 with the Community Redevelopment Act and came to fruition in 2007, exposing widely spread weaknesses in financial industry regulation and the U.S./global financial system.

Many U.S. mortgages issued in recent years were made to ***SUBPRIME BORROWERS, defined as those with lesser ability to repay the loan based on various criteria like credit score and credit history***. When housing prices began to decline in the spring of 2008, mortgage delinquencies soared, particularly in the subprime market, and securities backed with subprime mortgages, widely held by financial firms, lost most of their value. The result was a large decline in the capital of many banks and US government sponsored enterprises, tightening credit around the world.

The financial crisis actually began with the revelation of questionable accounting practices by Fannie Mae and Freddie Mac in 2006.

Figure 2-1

Real Estate and Business Cycles

Four Phases of All Business-Type Cycles

The real estate cycle described here is a generalization of the business cycles we actually experience. No two cycles are quite the same, yet they all have much in common. In real life, actual business cycles will vary, but the characteristic patterns described here (peaks, recession, bottom, and recovery) can always be observed. You should learn to identify the distinctive aspects of each phase of peaks, recession, bottom, and recovery. Each phase is characterized by different economic conditions.

PEAK (TOP)

The ***PEAK** is the highest point in a new business cycle, and is usually higher than the peak of the previous cycle*. It is the upper or top part of the business cycle. Goods sell briskly and inventory selection is good. Good jobs are available and unemployment is low.

RECESSION (CONTRACTION OR SLUMP)

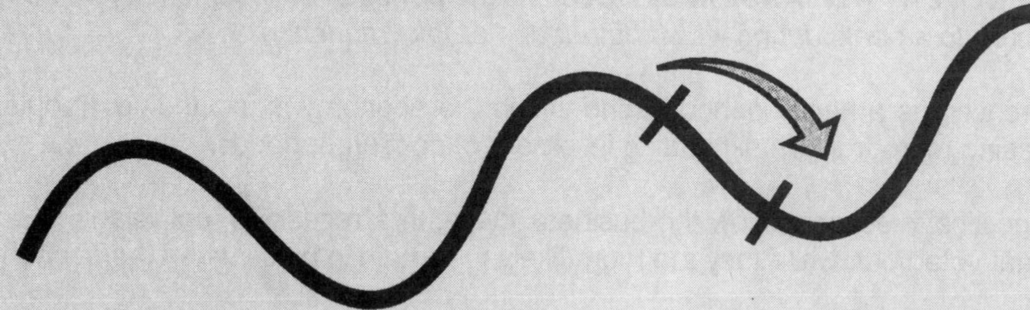

A ***CONTRACTION*** *or* ***SLUMP*** *is the period in the business cycle from the peak down to a trough, during which output and employment fall.*

Recession follows the peak with a slow downturn in business activity. Interest rates may be increasing. People are experiencing job losses as inventories are reduced and production is cut back to reduce operating costs.

As unemployment increases, the demand for goods and services also decreases, which can result in even further cutbacks in business.

BOTTOM (TROUGH)

The ***BOTTOM (TROUGH)*** *is evidenced by a fall in output and employment, followed by an increase in business activity.* At the end of the bottom, interest rates usually have been lowered by the Fed and remain low in order to stimulate a recovery.

RECOVERY (EXPANSION OR BOOM)

The ***RECOVERY (EXPANSION or BOOM)*** *is the period in the business cycle from the bottom up to a peak, during which output and employment rise.*

The recovery is a happy period during which the economy is expanding. People are purchasing more from an expanding inventory of consumer goods.

Even political elections follow the business cycle. In a recession, politicians in power often get voted out, while they are more likely to remain in office when the economy is strong.

SEASONAL VARIATIONS AND TRENDS

One must realize that seasonal patterns and long-term trends will disturb the business cycle. Retail sales go up every Christmas and beach area hotels are crowded every summer. Long-term trends, such as the automobile industry trends, are on the rise and must be taken into consideration when evaluating the business cycle. Business conditions never remain static. Prosperity is eventually followed by an economic recession, although in good times, people tend to expect prosperity to continue unabated.

A. SUPPLY AND DEMAND

When demand for a product (such as housing) exceeds the supply, the price for the product tends to increase. In real estate this period is often called a ***SELLER'S MARKET****.* Higher prices encourage the suppliers, in this case home builders, to increase production. As production increases, more of the demand is satisfied until a point is reached where production outstrips demand. *At that point, prices begin to fall and production will taper off until demand catches up with supply, and the cycle begins again. This period is called a* ***BUYER'S MARKET****.*

B. BALANCE

Economic theory holds that in a healthy economy, supply and demand should be in balance.

BALANCE *is the economic principle that value is created and maintained when opposing economic market forces are in a state of equilibrium.* In the real world however, this is an idealized situation. The forces that affect supply and demand are constantly changing and thereby constantly shifting supply and demand out of balance. However, as long as supply and demand are reasonably close to balanced, the economy will function quite well. The economy will suffer when either supply or demand greatly exceeds one or the other (see **Figure 2-2**).

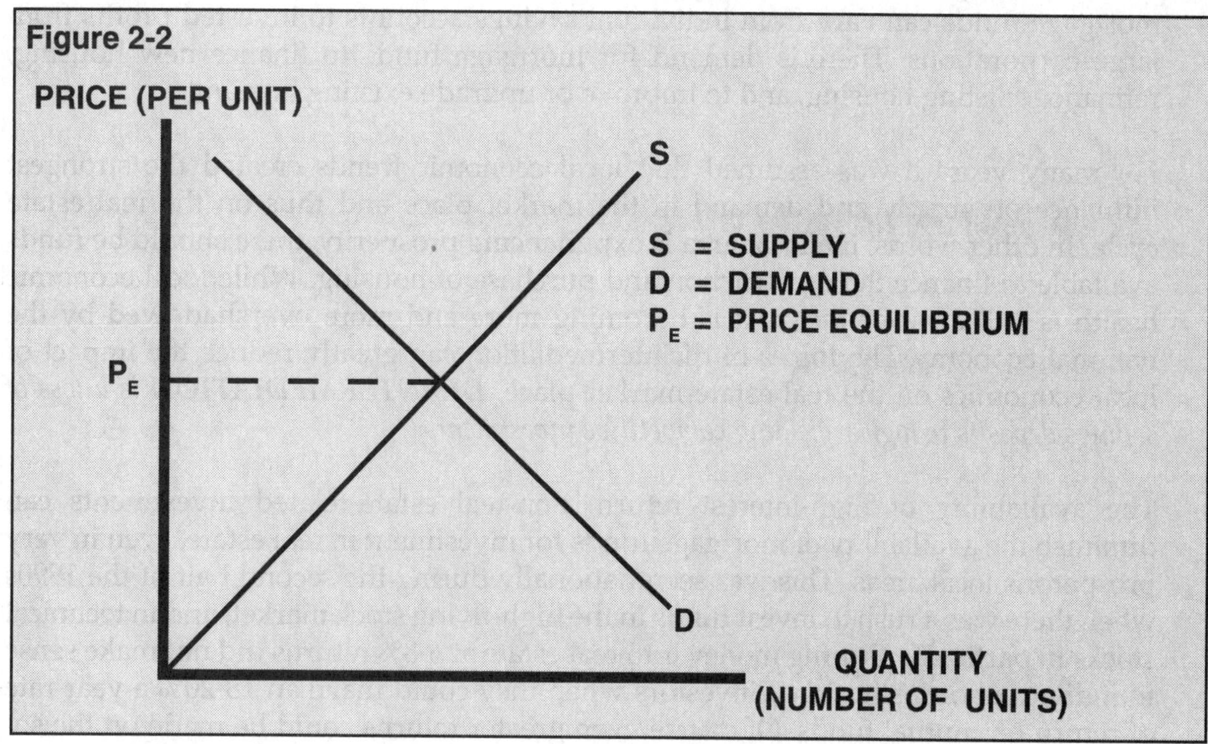

II. Factors Influencing Real Estate Cycles

Imbalances in supply and demand may be either short term or long term, depending on their causes.

It is not always possible to know whether a particular cycle is short term or long term, because a number of different factors interact to create the cycles. Among the causes that influence the cycle are the availability of mortgage funds, demographic changes within the population, the state of local and national economies, the cost of labor and materials, and finally political and social attitudes.

A. MORTGAGE FUNDS

The availability of mortgage funding affects both supply and demand for housing.

While there are buyers and sellers at all points along the real estate cycle, they are all affected by the availability of mortgage funds. A house is generally the largest purchase a consumer will make in his or her lifetime. In most cases the buyer does not have sufficient assets to purchase a house outright. Quite simply, most housing is either built or purchased with borrowed money. The availability and cost of this money directly affects both the supply and demand for housing. The source of these mortgage funds can vary from individual savings accounts to invested profits from large corporations. There is demand for mortgage funds to finance new housing, refinance existing housing, and to improve or upgrade existing housing.

For many years it was assumed that local economic trends created the strongest influence on supply and demand in the market place and thus on the real estate cycle. In other words, if a local area is experiencing prosperity, there should be funds available to finance the construction and purchase of housing. While local economic health is still a major factor, it is becoming more and more overshadowed by the national economy. The forces of disintermediation can greatly reduce the impact of local economics on the real estate market place. ***DISINTERMEDIATION*** *is a loss of savings deposits to higher yielding competitive investments.*

The availability of high-interest return, non-real estate-related investments can diminish the availability of mortgage funds for investment in real estate, even in very prosperous local areas. This was seen nationally during the second half of the 1990s when there was a rush to invest funds in the high-flying stock market, and in technical stocks in particular. Putting money into real estate at 6-8% returns did not make sense to individual or institutional investors when they could make an 18-20% a year rate of return on mutual funds. Of course even greater returns could be made on the so-called "dot com" stock.

The collapse of the "dot com" market of the late 90s, along with a downturn in market prices, made money available at lower rates for real estate loans.

However, after the events of September 11, 2001, the economy had weakened, creating problems for new homebuyers. Many became jobless and unable to afford the cost of a down payment on a house. Fortunately, Americans weather disaster well, and this situation had sharply changed within two years. The housing market saw an increase in both sales and prices, while rates continued to remain low between 2003 and 2006. However, the Federal Reserve raised interest rates several times in 2006. This had the effect of slowing the real estate market and a slight "cooling off" of prices for homes.

As previously mentioned, housing is the highest cost purchase made by most consumers. The high interest rates provided nationally by other forms of investment tend to limit the amount of money available to the housing market. The housing market is itself very sensitive to minor changes in the interest rate. A very small upward change in either the interest rate or the price of housing can cause home ownership to become unaffordable for many.

> **Example:** Let us assume that a house has a sale price of $100,000. The buyer puts down 20% of the sale price as a down payment. The monthly payment for an $80,000 thirty-year mortgage on the house at 7.5% interest is $559.37. Now let's assume that the price of the house increases to $150,000 and the rate remains the same. The down payment is still $20,000. The monthly payment for a thirty-year mortgage on $130,000 at 7.5% will be $908.98. A one-percent increase to an 8.5% rate would make the payment $999.59.

The example above does not exaggerate what has happened in many areas of the country. Typically, lenders expect the borrower to pay a down payment of 10-20% of the sales price on the purchase of a house. In addition, most lending guidelines note that the monthly payments should not exceed 25% of the buyer's monthly income. Thus, for the example above at $559.37, the buyer should have a monthly income of approximately $2,400 per month. At $908.98, that qualifying income would increase to $3,900 per month. The one percent increase in rate would require an additional $400 per month in qualifying income.

Many prosperous local markets have seen a rapid growth in employment, along with a huge demand for housing.

As expected, this has caused existing housing prices to rise rapidly in those areas, in many cases far exceeding the ability of buyers to afford them. In the past, this acted as a magnet to builders who would start up new construction of both single-family homes and apartment rental units to meet the increased demand and thus "cool off"

home prices and help assure affordability. These, in turn, would create demand for more commercial support facilities and provide more jobs and more demand for housing. Yet, in some areas this has not occurred and, as a result, has threatened these prosperous local economies. To fully understand these phenomena we need to examine some of the other factors that influence the real estate cycle.

B. POPULATION

Population demographics are an important factor in the success of a local real estate market.

DEMOGRAPHICS *refer to the study and description of the population of an area.* Demographics include such factors as age, education, gross income, disposable income, number of family members, and savings and spending patterns. Also studied are patterns of migration and establishment of employment centers. Demographic data at the national level may be obtained from the Bureau of the Census. Many local communities and chambers of commerce also are sources of demographic data.

www.census.gov
U.S. Census Bureau

The nation has undergone enormous changes within the past two decades. We have changed from a "smokestack" industrial nation to a technical and service-oriented nation. This has created tremendous dislocation within communities that were factory oriented due to plant closings and job layoffs. In addition, many smaller rural farming communities have experienced a loss in population as a result of the growth of agribusiness and the closing down of family farms. At the same time, those communities that were successful in attracting the new technical and service-oriented businesses often found that their infrastructures were overwhelmed by the sudden influx of population that these new businesses attracted. While many industrial towns and farming areas had more housing stock than they needed, the new technical communities were often totally lacking in housing stock altogether.

Another demographic factor that is affecting housing needs is a population that is gradually growing older.

Demographic data is important to community planners, developers, politicians, and real estate professionals in order to recognize and plan for changing trends in their areas and communities.

C. SOCIAL ATTITUDES

A major factor that has impacted both the availability of housing and mortgage funding has been the changing social behavior patterns of the population. A modern example is the increase in the portion of the population that is in its prime homebuying years. Both baby boomers and their children are now seeking housing, which has been a major factor in the overwhelming demand for housing that has pushed up prices so drastically in the past decade. High divorce rates and a trend toward later marriages have also stimulated demand because there are fewer people per household. These trends, along with a gradually aging population of baby boomers, have been a significant factor in creating the modern phenomenon of condominiums.

While demand has been stimulated dramatically, the ability of builders to satisfy this demand has often been hampered by environmental, political, and social forces.

D. POLITICAL ACTIVITY

The supply and demand for housing and credit depends on notoriously unpredictable political forces (taxation and spending).

Because the national government is the largest borrower in the country, its activities have a huge influence on the economy. ***DEFICIT SPENDING*** *by Congress forces the government to borrow money, making less money available for construction and home loans.* On the other hand, action by the Federal Reserve to loosen credit will rapidly increase available loan money supplies. If the Federal Reserve lowers interest rates too much, it may create inflationary pressure that will only serve to increase the price of housing.

E. REGULATION

Regulation by local, state, and federal governments is pervasive in almost every activity engaged in by our citizenry. The real estate and financial markets are no exception.

This regulation takes the form of federal, state, and local tax laws, environmental regulations, lending laws, and local zoning and building codes. The vast majority of these laws and regulations have been enacted to protect the environment, promote public safety, or to protect consumers from predatory loan practices. ***PREDATORY LOAN PRACTICES*** *include usury, deception, and fraud and refer to a variety of abusive lending practices, such as excessive or hidden fees, refinancing of loans at no benefit to the borrower, offering a loan knowing the borrower lacks the means to repay it, and using high-pressure sales tactics to sell a loan.*

Individual home ownership is encouraged at the federal and state levels by the provision for the home mortgage interest deduction in the income tax codes. However, at the local level, homes are subject to property taxes. These taxes are necessary to provide local services such as streets, lighting, schools, and fire and police protection. In some areas, these local property taxes have become oppressive. Some communities have implemented so-called "impact fees" in addition to the regular property taxes

collected. ***IMPACT FEES** are charged to all new housing that is developed within the community and are levied to pay for community infrastructure.* Often, these fees are really a part of "no-growth" attitudes on the part of a segment of the population that is already living in the community. The fees are often so high that any new construction is totally discouraged.

Environmental regulations have often worked to remove large segments of land that would have been available for development. Additionally, builders are often forced to commission studies or environmental impact reports (EIRs) before development of a housing tract can begin. Builders must also undergo review of their plans by local building and planning commissions. The bottom line, even in a community that does not discourage development, is that the process is often expensive and lengthy for the builder. Projects are often cancelled because the process has taken so long that the economic conditions that supported development have changed for the worse. Compliance with real estate and lending consumer protection laws adds hidden costs to the price of housing and to the mortgage loan as well. Builders, real estate professionals, and lenders are required to generate additional paperwork and carry out due diligence procedures to insure that they do not run afoul of the various laws and regulations. This requires additional overhead expense on their part. All of the costs of compliance with political factors are passed along to the consumer.

In some areas of the country it is estimated that the cost of compliance with political, environmental, and regulatory rules adds from $30,000 to $50,000 to the final price of a new home.

III. The Role of the Secondary Mortgage Market

The supply of funds available for investment in real estate mortgages is channeled into either the primary or secondary market. The ***PRIMARY MARKET** is made up of lenders, such as savings banks, commercial banks, and mortgage companies, who make mortgage loans directly to borrowers.* These lenders sometimes sell their mortgages into the secondary market, such as FNMA and GNMA.

For example, if a borrower wishes to borrow money to finance the purchase of a home, he or she will seek a loan from a local bank, savings bank, or mortgage company. The source of funds for the loan will largely be made up of the savings from individuals and businesses from the local area. These funds would soon dry up if the lending institution was not able to sell some of the mortgage loans it has already made to other investors. The ability to sell off these mortgage loans frees up additional money for lending, which allows the institution to continue providing continuous services to the community by being able to provide additional real estate financing.

Primary lenders sell their mortgages into the secondary market. The ***SECONDARY MARKET** consists of private, quasi-public, and government agencies that buy and sell existing* *mortgages or mortgage-backed securities from primary lenders and in so doing provide greater availability of funds for additional mortgage lending by primary lenders.* Presently, private investors do not have the same influence on the real estate market that the agencies created by the government have. Therefore, we will focus our discussion on them.

A real estate loan is an investment, just like stocks or bonds.

The lender (be it a bank, savings bank, or private party) commits its funds to an enterprise (in this case the purchase or construction of a home) in the expectation that the money will generate a return in the form of interest payments. Real estate loans can be bought and sold just like other investments. The present value (cash today) of the lender's right to receive future payments over the life of the loan can be calculated by comparing the rate of return on the loan to the rate of return on other investments with the same degree of risk.

Example: A bank makes a home loan of $135,000 at 11% interest, secured by a deed of trust. One year later, approximately $134,500 of principal remains to be paid on the loan. If market interest rates have gone up to 12.5% for similar quality investments, then the present value of the loan is less than $134,500. The **present value** is the total amount of cash today it would take to generate the same amount of income at a 12.5% rate of return. An 11% return on $134,500 would be $14,795 per year. This same return could be achieved by investing $118,360 at 12.5% interest, so the present value of the loan (all other factors being equal) is $118,360, rather than its face value of $134,500.

It should be noted that many other factors can influence the value of a loan. A primary influence is the degree of risk associated with the loan. The ***DEGREE OF RISK*** *refers to the likelihood of default by the borrower and also to the ability of the lender to recover the loan proceeds by selling (foreclosing) the security property.*

The degree of risk in real estate loans is controlled mainly by qualifying the borrower and the property before the loan is made. Stricter guidelines have made qualifying for a loan more difficult than ever.

To ***QUALIFY A BORROWER*** *is to insure that he or she has a large enough and stable enough income to minimize the risk of default.* To ***QUALIFY A PROPERTY*** *is to make sure the property is worth enough to satisfy the loan in the event of default and foreclosure.*

Why buy and sell loans? The secondary market serves two vital functions: it promotes investments in real estate by making funds available for real estate loans, and it provides a measure of stability in the primary (local) market by moderating the adverse effects of real estate cycles. Consider the following examples.

Example: A-1 Savings Bank has a long list of prospective borrowers who need funds for the purchase of homes. A-1's problem is that all of its deposits are already tied up in real estate loans. But, by selling its existing mortgage loans to a secondary market investor, A-1 can get the funds it needs to make the new loans and thereby satisfy its credit-hungry customers. The effects of a tight money market in A-1's local community are moderated because A-1 can get funds in the national market.

Example: If A-1 Savings Bank had a surplus of deposits instead of a shortfall, it might encounter difficulty finding enough local investments to absorb its funds. In this case, A-1 could buy real estate loans on the secondary market, in essence investing in real estate located all over the country. Because of the uniform standards applied to secondary market loans, A-1 can feel fairly secure in its investments, even though it may never see the actual borrowers and properties it is helping to finance.

The availability of funds in the primary market depends on the existence of the secondary market.

This can be seen by taking a brief look at the flow of mortgage funds: first, mortgage funds are given to the homebuyer by a lending institution in the primary market; the mortgage is then sold to a secondary market agency, which may in turn sell it to other investors in the form of mortgage-backed securities. As mortgage-backed securities are sold by the agency, more funds (cash) become available to the secondary market for the purchase of new mortgages from the primary market. As more mortgages are purchased from the primary market, more funds become available for lenders to pass on to borrowers.

The secondary market provides cash liquidity to primary lenders through the purchase of mortgages. These mortgages are then used as collateral for the sale of mortgage-backed bonds to investors by the secondary market institutions.

IV. Agencies of the Secondary Market

For the purposes of our discussion, the secondary market may be said to include three agencies:

1. Federal National Mortgage Association (FNMA) – Fannie Mae
2. Government National Mortgage Association (Ginnie Mae)
3. The Federal Home Loan Mortgage Corporation (FHLMC or "Freddie Mac")

The secondary market is able to function as it does because of the standardized underwriting criteria applied by these agencies. ***UNDERWRITING CRITERIA*** *are used to qualify the borrower and the property and include such items as loan-to-value ratios and income-to-expense ratios.* Every mortgage issued by each individual lender must conform to the secondary market. These standards assure a uniform quality control, which inspires confidence in the purchasers of the mortgage-backed securities. The purchasers know that the mortgages that back the securities must be of a minimum quality. This lessens their risk in investing in properties they cannot view or assess for themselves. Without the assurance of the underlying underwriting standards, someone in California would be unlikely to invest in sight-unseen property in New Jersey.

Because the secondary market performs such an important function in providing liquidity of mortgage funds, the standards set by the secondary market have a large influence on lending activities in the primary market.

As an example, once secondary agencies began accepting adjustable rate mortgages (ARMs), 15-year fixed-rate mortgages, and convertible ARMs, these types of financing became more readily available in the primary market. Lenders were more willing to make these kinds of loans when they knew the loans could be sold to the secondary market.

A relatively recent development in the activities of the secondary market is the current streamlined online underwriting programs (loans) developed by "Fannie Mae" and "Freddie Mac," thus further expanding the availability of funds available for mortgage lending purposes.

A. FEDERAL NATIONAL MORTGAGE ASSOCIATION (FNMA) "Fannie Mae"

The Federal National Mortgage Association (FNMA), also known as "Fannie Mae," dominates the secondary mortgage market. Originally it bought and sold only FHA and VA loans. In 1968 it became a private corporation and now sells securities over the stock exchange to get money so that it can buy and sell conventional loans in addition to government-backed notes. It is not a demand source for funds.

Fannie Mae is the nation's largest investor in residential mortgages.

The Federal National Mortgage Association (FNMA) was created in 1938 as the first government-sponsored secondary market institution. It was originally formed as a wholly owned government corporation. While the specific purpose of FNMA was to provide a secondary market for FHA-insured mortgages, FNMA did not start buying FHA mortgages on a large scale until 1948. At that same time, FNMA was also authorized to purchase VA-guaranteed loans.

The role of FNMA was further expanded in 1970 (after it became a private corporation) with the passage of the Emergency Home Finance Act, which permitted FNMA to purchase conventional mortgages as well as FHA and VA mortgages.

FNMA underwent several reorganizations and became a privately owned and managed corporation that was supervised by HUD. In 2008 it was placed under conservatorship by the newly formed Federal Housing Finance Agency (FHFA).

In 2008, the federal government took control of Fannie Mae and Freddie Mac in an effort to keep the two mortgage giants from failing, disasters that would have made home loans still harder to get.

The government agreed to pump billions of dollars into Fannie Mae and Freddie Mac and assume responsibility for trillions of dollars of their debt, while handing control of the companies to federal regulation by the Federal Housing Finance Agency (FHFA).

"Fannie Mae" funds its operation by selling securities that are backed by its pool of mortgages to the public. It buys the mortgages from lenders. Lenders who wish to sell loans to FNMA are required to own a certain amount of stock in , the required amount being based on the principal balance of mortgage loans. FNMA posts the prices daily that it is willing to pay for the standard loan programs approved for purchase. The required yield and process may also be obtained from a hotline operated by FNMA and from various financial services and publications. Loans sold to FNMA may be serviced by FNMA or by the originating lender. FNMA pays a service fee to the lender if it continues to service the loan.

In 1981, FNMA started a participation program with lenders. A master participation agreement is entered into between a lender and FNMA. The lender then assembles a pool (collection) of loans and a participation interest in that pool (50-95%) is then sold to FNMA. In this way, both the lender and FNMA own an interest in the loans instead of the lender selling them outright. In that same year, FNMA also announced the sale of conventional mortgage-backed securities that are guaranteed by FNMA as to full and timely payments of both principal and interest. A service fee is charged by FNMA for issuing securities backed by the mortgage pool, as well as a monthly fee for the guarantee provision.

The most recent development by FNMA is the ***DESKTOP UNDERWRITER®****, an automated online underwriting system that is intended to reduce the time, cost, and subjectivity associated with the traditional process.* The system permits brokers to go online and submit a borrower's application and loan request. The system will then analyze the borrower's credit history and ability to pay, as well as whether the loan meets FNMA's eligibility requirements. The system will then provide either an immediate loan approval, referral to a traditional underwriter, or will reject the loan as out of the scope of FNMA's lending criteria.

In those cases requiring traditional underwriting and assessment of the loan collateral, the process has been shortened as well. In assessing the collateral, the system will determine if a full appraisal is warranted or if the new streamlined **Limited Appraisal Form (Form 2055)** can be used. Often the appraisal is also submitted online to the lender by the appraiser. Lastly, Desktop Underwriter® provides access to the proprietary automated underwriting systems of Countrywide Home Loans and GMAC Residential

Funding Corporation to underwrite case files for jumbo and other nonconforming loans that do not meet FNMA's eligibility requirements. FNMA provides both online registration and training for lending institutions and brokers, as well as regional classes and in-office training.

www.fanniemae.com
Fannie Mae

B. GOVERNMENT NATIONAL MORTGAGE ASSOCIATION (GNMA)

The ***GOVERNMENT NATIONAL MORTGAGE ASSOCIATION**, or **"Ginnie Mae,"** was created with the passage of the **Housing and Urban Development Act (1968)**.* It is a wholly owned government corporation, which in effect, replaced FNMA when FNMA became privately owned.

GNMA operates under the Department of Housing and Urban Development (HUD).

At the time of its creation, GNMA was given the responsibility for managing and eventually liquidating the remaining FNMA mortgages. Another function of GNMA is that of "special assistance": GNMA assists the financing of urban renewal and housing projects by providing below-market rates to low-income families.

A primary function of GNMA is to promote investment by guaranteeing the payment of principal and interest on FHA and VA mortgages. GNMA carries out this function through its mortgage-backed securities program. GNMA's activities in the "special assistance" area have lessened in importance as activities in its mortgage-backed securities program have increased. This program, supported by the federal government's borrowing power, guarantees timely interest and principal mortgage payments to the mortgage holders. The added security of the guarantee enables the mortgage holders to pledge a pool of their loans as collateral for securities. The repayment of the mortgages is the source of the funds used to pay off the securities when they become due. The mortgage-backed securities offer safety to investors, they can be easily traded, and they can be purchased in smaller denominations than many comparable investment instruments.

In order to issue GNMA mortgage-backed securities, the issuer must be an FHA or VA-approved mortgagee, be an acceptable GNMA servicer-seller, and have a specified net worth. A fee is paid for the GNMA commitment to guarantee the mortgage pool. The issuer (lender) continues to service the mortgage.

Mortgage-backed securities fall into two general types: bond-type securities and pass-through securities. ***BOND-TYPE SECURITIES** are long term, pay interest semiannually, and provide for repayment at a specified redemption date. **PASS-THROUGH SECURITIES** pay interest and principal on a monthly basis.*

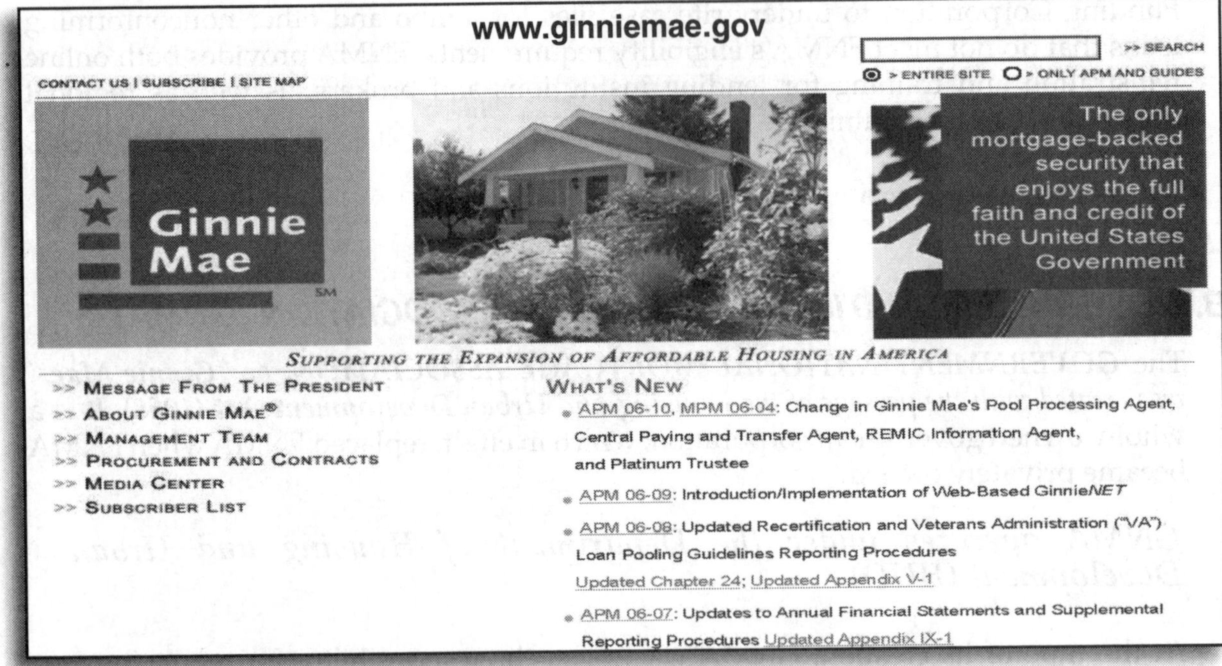

Pass-through securities are the more prevalent.

***FULLY MODIFIED PASS-THROUGH SECURITIES** pay interest and principal monthly, regardless of whether the payments have been collected from the mortgagors.* Any proceeds from foreclosure or prepayment are also passed on to the security holder as soon as received. If the issuer of the security (the lender) fails to make the payments, GNMA takes over the mortgage pool and makes the payments. Straight pass-through securities pay monthly interest and principal only when they are collected from the mortgagor.

C. FEDERAL HOME LOAN MORTGAGE CORPORATION (FHLMC)

The ***FEDERAL HOME LOAN MORTGAGE CORPORATION (FHLMC)**, which is also known as **"Freddie Mac,"** was created through the **Emergency Home Finance Act (1970)**.* Initially, FHLMC was a nonprofit, federally chartered institution, which was controlled by the Federal Home Loan Bank System. The primary function of FHLMC was to aid savings and loan associations who were hit particularly hard by the recession of 1969-1970. FHLMC helped S&Ls acquire additional funds for lending in the mortgage market by purchasing the mortgages they already held. FHLMC was authorized to deal in FHA, VA, and conventional mortgages. In 1989, FHLMC became a private corporation and basically operates in a manner that is similar to FNMA.

In 2008 FHLMC (Freddie Mac) was placed under conservatorship by the Federal Housing Finance Agency. Conservatorship is not ownership, but overseeing; although they may purchase up to 79% of dividend paying stock.

FHLMC emphasizes the purchase of conventional mortgage loans, and also actively sells the mortgage loans from its portfolio, thus acting as a conduit for mortgage investments. The funds that are generated by the sale of the mortgages are then used to purchase more mortgages.

"Freddie Mac" has been actively involved in developing underwriting standards for conventional mortgage loans, furthering assistance to savings banks who deal chiefly in conventional mortgages. All members of the Federal Home Loan Bank System, now under the Office of Thrift Supervision, are eligible to sell mortgages to FHLMC. Commercial banks, credit unions, and other nonmembers may be approved by FHLMC as eligible sellers. Nonmember sellers are charged an additional fee for the mortgage purchase.

FHLMC issues its own mortgage-backed securities, which are backed by the conventional mortgages it purchases. FHLMC purchases mortgages through its immediate delivery program or its forward commitment purchase program. In the ***IMMEDIATE DELIVERY PROGRAM****, sellers have up to 60 days in which to deliver the mortgages FHLMC has agreed to purchase.* Failure to deliver can mean that the seller will be banned from making sales to FHLMC for two years. The immediate loan delivery program can involve either whole loan purchases or participation purchases. Under the ***FORWARD COMMITMENT PURCHASE PROGRAM****, commitments are made for six- and eight-month periods.* Delivery of the mortgages is at the option of the seller. There is a nonrefundable commitment fee payable to FHLMC.

FHLMC also has an automated underwriting process. This system, established in 1996, is similar to that of FNMA.

www.freddiemac.com
Freddie Mac

V. Quality Control

The secondary market has an enormous influence on the primary market, not only because of the increased availability of funds that it provides, but also because of the standards of quality it imposes on lenders. Because lenders wish to be able to sell their loans to the secondary agencies, they must follow the underwriting guidelines of those agencies. In the 1980s and early 1990s, the rate of mortgage delinquencies and foreclosures rose sharply. In response to this higher loss rate, both FNMA and FHLMC implemented changes in their underwriting guidelines. The secondary market is trying to improve the quality of the loans it purchases and ensure the reputation of residential mortgages as a safe investment.

In their efforts to increase the quality of the loans they purchase, the agencies necessarily force the lenders to upgrade the quality of the loans they make. Not only can the agencies refuse to purchase loans that do not follow their underwriting guidelines, they can also request lenders to repurchase loans already sold if it is later discovered the lender violated an underwriting guideline.

The secondary market encourages lenders to implement their own quality control programs.

The secondary market considers it the lender's responsibility to submit investment quality loans for purchase. According to FHLMC, an ***INVESTMENT QUALITY LOAN*** *is "a loan from a borrower whose timely repayment of the debt can be expected, that is secured by a property of sufficient value to recover the lender's investment if a mortgage default occurs."* By encouraging lenders to carefully review property appraisals, legal documentation (e.g., the mortgage instrument), origination documentation (e.g., the loan application, credit report, and employment verification), and the ultimate underwriting decision, the secondary market exerts its influence to increase the overall quality of loans made and to decrease the rate of delinquency and foreclosure.

Both Fannie Mae and Freddie Mac are GSEs – Government Sponsored Enterprises.

VI. CHAPTER SUMMARY

The real estate cycle has four phases, beginning with an expansion of real estate activity that leads to a peak, and then a decline to a bottom or trough. Expansion then begins again, leading to another peak and the completion of the cycle. The cycle is driven by supply and demand. Supply and demand for both real estate and mortgage money is affected by economic, social, and political factors. Political regulation of housing and lending, while intended to protect consumer health, safety, and quality of life, has often tended to increase the price of housing for consumers. Supply and demand are seldom in balance, however, balance is critical to maintaining the value of real estate. The establishment of a national secondary market to buy and sell mortgages has worked to soften drastic swings in the real estate cycle by insuring that mortgage money is available at all stages within the cycle. The major players in the secondary market are FNMA, GNMA, and FHLMC. These institutions have recently utilized the Internet to streamline the mortgage lending process and lower both the costs and time required to obtain a loan.

VII. TERMINOLOGY

Balance
Bond-Type Securities
Buyer's Market
Conservatorship
Deficit Spending
Desktop Underwriters
Demand
Demographics
Disintermediation
Emergency Home Finance Act (1970)
Federal Housing Finance Agency (FHFA)
FHLMC ("Freddie Mac")
FNMA ("Fannie Mae")
Forward Commitment Purchase Program
GNMA ("Ginnie Mae")
Government Sponsored Enterprise(GSE)
Housing and Urban Development Act (1968)
Immediate Delivery Program
Impact Fees
Limited Appraisal (Form 2055)
Pass-Through Securities
Predatory Loan Practices
Primary Market
Qualifying a Borrower
Qualifying a Property
Real Estate Cycle
Secondary Market
Seller's Market
Subprime Mortgages
Supply
Underwriting Criteria

VIII. CHAPTER QUIZ

1. Predatory loan practices include:
   a. usury.
   b. deception.
   c. fraud.
   d. all the above.

2. When the demand for housing increases:
   a. it is a buyer's market.
   b. prices decrease.
   c. prices increase.
   d. prices remain in balance.

3. Value is created and maintained by:
   a. buyers.
   b. political regulation.
   c. the secondary market.
   d. balance.

4. The study and description of the population of an area is called:
   a. disintermediation.
   b. demographics.
   c. demand analysis.
   d. population analysis.

5. FHLMC and FNMA are:
   a. government agencies.
   b. primary lenders.
   c. part of the secondary market.
   d. regulatory bodies.

6. Pass-through securities pay interest:
   a. annually.
   b. quarterly.
   c. semiannually.
   d. monthly.

7. Disintermediation is:
   a. a loss of savings deposits to higher-paying investments.
   b. a gain of savings deposits by local lenders.
   c. mortgage securities sales to investors by the secondary market.
   d. the sale of mortgages to the secondary market by primary lenders.

8. The primary market is made up of:
   a. local lending institutions.
   b. first time homebuyers.
   c. federal agencies.
   d. all the above.

9. Which of the following is a false statement regarding political regulation of the housing market?
   a. Regulation serves to protect consumers from deceptive practices.
   b. Regulation helps keep housing prices low.
   c. Regulation increases housing prices.
   d. Regulation protects health and safety.

10. Which of the following is a government agency?
   a. FHLMC
   b. FNMA
   c. GNMC
   d. GNMA

ANSWERS: 1. *d;* 2. *c;* 3. *d;* 4. *b;* 5. *c;* 6. *d;* 7. *a;* 8. *a;* 9. *b;* 10. *d*

MUTUAL
SAVINGS
BANK
tyme
NO FEE ATM
DO NOT
ENTER

Chapter 3
Sources of Funds: The Primary Market

The "primary market" for real estate loan funds is from individuals and institutions that make loans directly to borrowers.

As noted in the previous chapter, many of these lenders are local in nature and obtain their funds from the deposits of local savers and businesses. However, some mortgage firms have established a national presence in the marketplace.

I. Traditional Direct Lenders

The market for real estate loans dates back to the establishment of the original building and loan societies in the 1830s. The modern market did not begin until the great depression a hundred years later. It was during this time that the beginnings of a viable secondary market were established. This encouraged the traditional banks and savings and loans to expand their real estate activities. This period was marked by a generally well regulated, stable, and predictable market. The 1980s saw many changes in both the attitudes and practices of the real estate lending institutions.

These changes were brought about by several factors. The first of these was that economic conditions were constantly fluctuating. The forces of disintermediation created by these conditions made it difficult for traditional lending institutions to maintain the stable interest rates that had formerly prevailed. They lobbied for deregulation so that they

Chapter 3

CHAPTER OUTLINE

could compete with other forces in the marketplace. They were successful, for the most part, in obtaining much of the regulatory relief that they sought. By the end of the decade, many of the traditional institutions were victims of the old axiom "be careful what you wish for, you just might get it!" Unfortunately, the financial/credit/real estate crisis of 2008-2009 once again proved this to be true.

A. SAVINGS AND LOANS

The savings and loan associations (S&Ls) were the oldest and largest source of funds for financing residential property.

Over the years, ***SAVINGS AND LOANS*** *carried out their historic function of investing on average 75% of their funds in the single-family residential market*. They were able to dominate local mortgage markets despite the fact that commercial banks had more assets. The deposits placed with the savings and loans were in the form of savings accounts that were less susceptible to immediate withdrawal than the demand (checking) deposits held by commercial banks.

Between 1945 and the late 1970s, the S&Ls expanded their mortgage loan operations aggressively. While other lenders were afraid of the inherent risk associated with long-term conventional loans, the S&Ls believed that they could succeed based on their intimate knowledge of local market conditions and their ability to attract long-term deposits. Because they were able to offer higher interest rates than the commercial banks, they had no trouble attracting deposits during the period of prosperity from World War II until the 1970s. However, the surge in interest rates in the late 1970s and early 1980s turned the tables on this strategy. Because the savings and loans were restricted by law with respect to how much interest they could pay to their depositors, they found themselves in the unfamiliar and uncomfortable position of being unable to offer attractive enough rates of return to their depositors. The result was that they lost a large portion of their deposits to competing investments, such as money market funds and government bonds that offered much higher rates of return. ***MONEY MARKET FUNDS*** *are private, noninsured investment accounts.*

To make matters worse, the S&Ls found themselves holding long-term, nonliquid mortgages at low rates of interest (by 1980s standards). These loans could not be liquidated into the secondary market and had to be held in portfolio. A ***PORTFOLIO LOAN*** *is a loan held by a lender rather than sold into the secondary market*. The reason for this was that historically the savings and loans had set their own property and borrower standards based on what they considered to be their superior knowledge of the local market. In many cases, those standards were not of a level that was acceptable to the national secondary market.

The S&Ls attacked the problem on two fronts. The first was to ask for deregulation so that they could compete with the money market funds by being able to invest in other

areas. The second was the gradual adoption of the secondary market procedures for new real estate loans to enable them to sell into the secondary market.

With banking deregulation, S&Ls were free to compete with alternative investments.

For many S&Ls, this was a green light to pour money into the most risky investments.

In the heady rush to increase returns, S&Ls forgot the first rule of interest returns: the higher the rate of return, the greater the risk.

Often the investments were made in areas that neither the S&Ls nor their regulators had any ability to evaluate. The industry was led by a group of managers with a "good old boy mentality" who were, at best, incompetent and, at worst, fraudulent. The result was a rapid increase in the rate of failure of savings and loans. By late 1986 and early 1987, the problem had reached such epic proportions that it attracted the attention of the U.S. Congress, who held hearings to determine how to rescue the nation's financial system. The result of these hearings was The Financial Institutions Reform, Recovery, and Enforcement Act (FIRREA).

1. Financial Institutions Reform, Recovery, and Enforcement Act (FIRREA)

The Financial Institutions Reform, Recovery, and Enforcement Act (FIRREA) governs all federally related transactions.

FIRREA would do more than just address the savings and loans problems. It affects every institution and every person who deals in a federally related transaction. A ***FEDERALLY RELATED TRANSACTION*** *is any transaction in which the federal government is involved*. Any real estate transaction, or any loan in which there is federal involvement of any kind, is affected.

FIRREA protects the federal deposit insurance funds. The FDIC increased its deposit insurance ceiling from $100,000 to $250,000 in 2008.

www.fear.org/fedstat2.html
FIRREA (18 U.S.C.)

Another result of the bill was that minimum standards for lending, underwriting, and appraisal were set in place for all lending institutions that are either regulated by the federal government or have access to federal funds.

Under FIRREA, the ***OFFICE OF THRIFT SUPERVISION (OTS)*** *was formed to regulate the S&Ls*. This had been handled by the Federal Home Loan Bank Board (FHLBB), which was eliminated by FIRREA. The Federal Deposit Insurance Corporation (FDIC) was granted initial responsibility for the ***RESOLUTION TRUST CORPORATION (RTC)****, which was formed to liquidate the assets of fraudulent and failed S&Ls*. By the time this was complete, hundreds of S&Ls had ceased to exist. FIRREA also eliminated the old Federal Savings and Loan Insurance Corporation (FSLIC), granting the FDIC permanent responsibility for managing the ***SAVINGS ASSOCIATION INSURANCE FUND (SAIF)****, which replaced the old FSLIC in insuring savings banks (the new name for S&Ls)*.

www.fdic.gov/bank/historical/history/vol1.html
History of the '80s – Lessons for the Future

FIRREA's purpose was to restore the public's confidence in the savings and loan industry. It gave the FDIC the responsibility of insuring the deposits of thrift institutions in its place.

It also set procedures for lending in federal transactions. As a result, depositors were reassured and many again began to invest in the savings and loans. As a result of the massive failures and the reorganizations, the number of savings and loans decreased drastically. Financially secure organizations survived (now known as savings banks), and continue to play an important role in real estate finance.

B. COMMERCIAL BANKS

Commercial banks remain the largest source of investment funds in the country today.

As their name implies, ***COMMERCIAL BANKS*** *are oriented towards commercial lending activities, supplying capital for business ventures and construction activities on a comparatively short-term basis*. Until relatively recently, residential mortgages were not a major part of their business, primarily because of government limitations on the amount of long-term investments they could make. Those limitations were imposed because the vast majority of deposits held by commercial banks are **demand deposits** or **checking accounts**, which are payable on demand whenever a depositor elects.

Demand deposits are considered less reliable for reinvestment in long-term real estate loans than the more stable savings deposits.

Nevertheless, commercial banks then increased their participation in home mortgage lending. The S&L crisis allowed them to gain an increased market share of new depositors at the expense of the S&Ls. At the same time, the banks wanted to be able to offer their customers mortgage loans rather then send them off to competing lenders.

Frequently, the bank is able to sell the loan into the secondary market while retaining the servicing of the loan. ***SERVICING A MORTGAGE LOAN*** *means that the bank collects the mortgage payments for the loan even though it has been sold into the secondary market.* The bank receives a fee for doing this and the borrower remains happy in the belief that his or her loan is still held by the bank.

By offering mortgage loans, the bank is able to attract new customers for its other services such as checking accounts, credit cards, and equity lines of credit.

Banks saw growth in consumer loans, while business loans have remained stable at best. Because of the tax deductibility of mortgage loan interest, banks expected mortgage loans to make up a larger portion of their consumer loan business.

Changes in government banking regulations also spurred commercial banks to engage in more mortgage lending activity.

Government regulations require that banks hold different percentages of funds on reserve for different types of loans, based on the perceived risk of the loans. First-lien home mortgages are in the lowest risk category. That means that banks have to maintain less money on reserve for home mortgage loans than for other types of loans. This leaves more funds available for additional loans or for other investments. All commercial banks are part of the Federal Reserve System and have the ability to borrow funds from that system. This gives them more flexibility in changing markets than other types of lenders.

C. CREDIT UNIONS

Credit unions are one of the relatively new kids on the block in the field of mortgage lending.

CREDIT UNIONS *were set up in 1970 as membership associations made up of employees and others who worked for individual institutions with a common association of interest, such as teachers and defense and aircraft workers.* These members invested savings and could then borrow against the membership funds to finance personal purchases of goods and services. Generally, loans were only for personal property. Interest rates were low and served to pay expenses, with any remaining profit credited quarterly to each individual member's account.

The deregulation of the banking industry provided a growth opportunity for credit unions, but was also impacted by the financial crisis.

Credit unions originated in rural Germany over 150 years ago as a way for older farmers to help support younger farmers and not pay income taxes as an association.

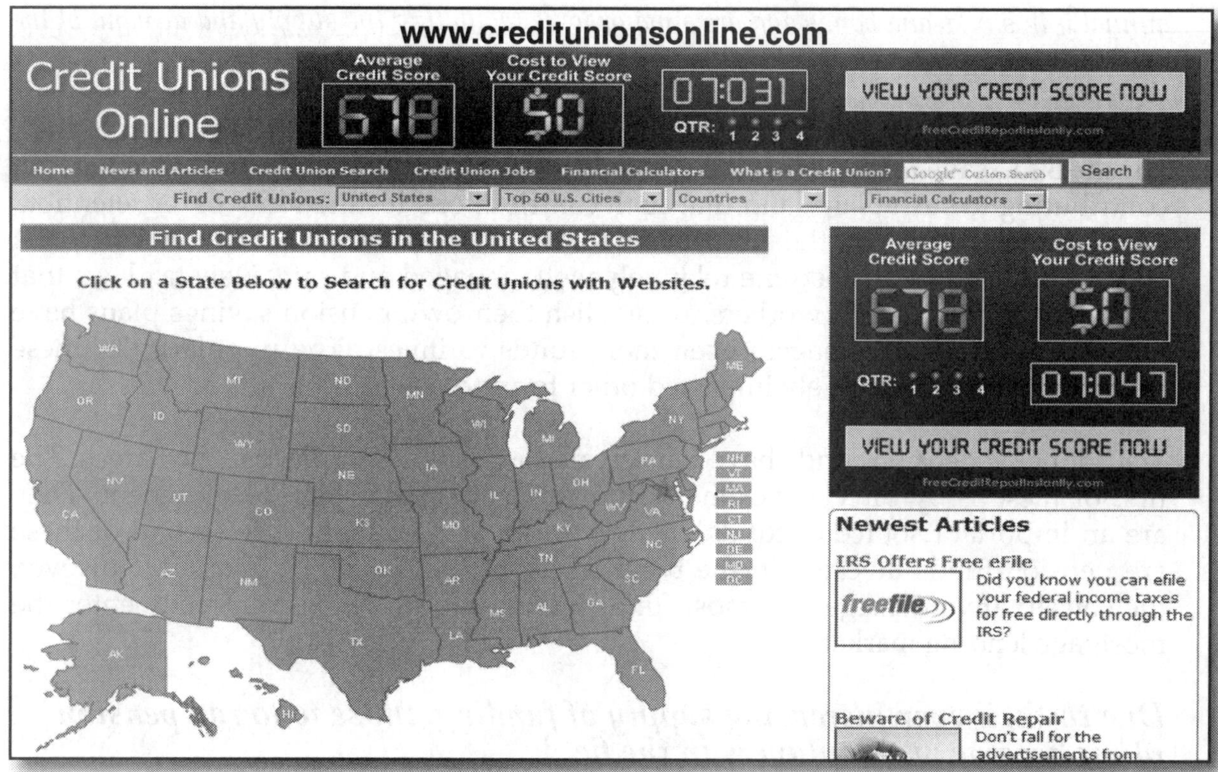

They have their own insurance fund and their own national regulator (similar to the FDIC), the **National Credit Union Administration**. The two major wholesale credit unions were seized in 2009: U.S. Central in Lenexa, Kansas, and Western Corporate, or "WestCor," in San Dimas, California. With a combined total of $57 billion in assets, these unions had a significant chunk of the $80.8 billion industry. Most credit unions have portfolios of loans made for mortgages, vehicles, and other assets.

Credit unions, along with small and midsized banks, do much of the nation's small-business lending that drives job creation.

While credit unions have entered the field of mortgage lending, at this time their overall share of the mortgage lending market remains small.

II. Indirect Lenders

A. PENSION FUNDS

About 50% of American workers have personal or union pension plans.

A **PENSION FUND** *is a fund set up by a corporation, labor union, government entity, or other organization to pay the pension benefits of retired workers. These funds invest billions*

annually in stocks and bonds and are a major force regulating the supply and demand of the markets.

American workers insisted on plans that allowed them to set aside a portion of their paychecks to save for retirement. Large corporations discovered the tax advantages of contributing to such plans, and that such contributions resulted in worker retention. With the enactment of the **Employee Retirement Income Security Act of 1974 (ERISA)**, all such plans became relatively well managed and safe. New tax laws that permitted self-employed workers to establish their own pension savings plans have given pension fund managers even more funds to invest. The popularity of these funds has actually adversely impacted other forms of savings.

Traditionally, pension funds have participated in the market place in two areas. The first of these is by direct investment in commercial real estate development. They are an important source of funds for developers and builders. The second of these are pension funds invested in the bond issues of the secondary market. However, the conservative managers of most funds have been unwilling to directly enter the mortgage lending market.

Due to their ever-increasing supply of funding, those who ran pension plans became major players in the field.

B. INSURANCE COMPANIES

INSURANCE COMPANIES *control vast amounts of capital in the form of insurance premiums, which are held for relatively long terms.* Money invested in insurance policies is generally not subject to early or sudden withdrawal (as are the deposits in banks or savings banks) and does not earn the high-interest returns that are now common in other investment forms. For these reasons, insurance companies are able to safely invest large sums of money in long-term real estate loans.

In the past, insurance companies preferred direct investments in large scale commercial projects, as opposed to investment in residential lending. Often, the insurance companies would also engage in participation loans with commercial developers to increase their rate of return. A ***PARTICIPATION LOAN*** *is one in which the lender assumes a percentage of ownership in addition to the loan proceeds.* This gives them an ongoing permanent share of the profits of the business to which they have loaned the money.

Insurance companies have a lower cost of funds than their competitors in the mortgage lending business.

In addition to whole life policies, which pay minimal dividends or interest, they have even greater sums of money to invest from term policies, on which they pay no interest at all. This has given them a formidable advantage in the investment marketplace.

For many years, insurance companies have been major players in the secondary market through the purchase of bonds issued against mortgages issued by FHLMC, FNMA, and others. Recently, some insurance companies have entered the primary market by establishing subsidiary multitiered mortgage companies that allow them to compete directly in the primary market.

III. The Role of the Correspondent

In some states, such as California, real estate brokers can act as mortgage brokers.

A. MORTGAGE BROKERS

Mortgage brokers fill a role in the marketing of loans to consumers. ***MORTGAGE BROKERS*** *are financial "go-betweens" or coordinators.* They arrange financing for borrowers, and work as intermediaries between the lender and the borrower. The mortgage broker does not loan his or her own funds. He/she is a knowledgeable real estate and loan professional who handles the origination of a loan with the consumer. The broker then "shops" the loan with a variety of primary mortgage lenders who have programs for which the borrower will qualify. The broker then matches the borrower with the lender that will provide the best program at the best price to the borrower. The broker handles all the paperwork involved, helps the lender and the borrower set up escrow, orders the appraisal for the lender, and takes care of the closing paperwork for the lender and the borrower after the loan is funded. The mortgage broker provides an important service to both borrowers and lenders. By acting as a go-between, the broker frees up valuable time for the primary lender, reduces their need for personnel, and is able to advise and guide the borrower through an often lengthy and complex process.

A mortgage broker finds you the loan, the mortgage banker or financial institution lends you the money.

B. MORTGAGE BANKER/MORTGAGE COMPANIES

Mortgager bankers, or mortgage companies, also act in the role of intermediaries in the lending of capital. ***MORTGAGE BANKERS/MORTGAGE COMPANIES*** *originate, service, and sell loans to investors.* They are often local in nature, and receive lending funds from large national investors, such as insurance companies and pension plans. The major national investors often are not aware of local market conditions and depend on the mortgage bankers to make stable loans for them in the local markets. While the mortgage bankers originate loans themselves, they also work with mortgage brokers. The mortgage bankers do not keep portfolio loans. They will sell their loans into the secondary market as soon as they have "seasoned." A ***SEASONED LOAN*** *is one that* *has been held for a sufficient time to establish that the borrower is making his/her payments in a timely manner, often 6-12 months.* Often, the mortgage banker will retain or sell the servicing of the loan separately from the loan itself.

Because mortgage bankers/mortgage companies invest little of their own money, their activities are largely controlled by the availability of capital in the secondary market.

As might be expected, their loan qualification criteria must reflect the standards of the national market in order to resell their loans into the secondary market.

IV. The Role of the Private Investor

A. REAL ESTATE INVESTMENT TRUST (REITs)

A *REAL ESTATE INVESTMENT TRUST (REIT) is an unincorporated association of real estate investors managed by a trustee.* In 1960, by means of the **Real Estate Investment Trust Act**, Congress made it possible for investors to enjoy the flow-through tax advantages of a partnership. The Act allows investors who prefer real estate as an investment to receive tax benefits similar to those granted to mutual funds and other regulated investment companies. **Unlike ordinary corporations, whose earnings are subject to double taxation (first at the corporate level and again as personal income when distributed to stockholders), the real estate investment trust earnings are taxed only once, after they have been distributed to their investors.** There are several requirements for a REIT:

1. It cannot hold property primarily for sale to customers.
2. It must have at least 100 beneficial owners.
3. No five persons or less can hold over 50% of the beneficial interest.
4. It must issue shares or certificates of interest.
5. Each share must have a proportionate vote in trust policy decisions.
6. 95% of its gross income must be from investments.
7. 75% of its income must be from real estate investments.

The reason people invest in REITs is because they are tax free if they distribute 95% of their income to their investors.

B. PRIVATE INDIVIDUALS

Private individuals have always been a force in the world of real estate finance.

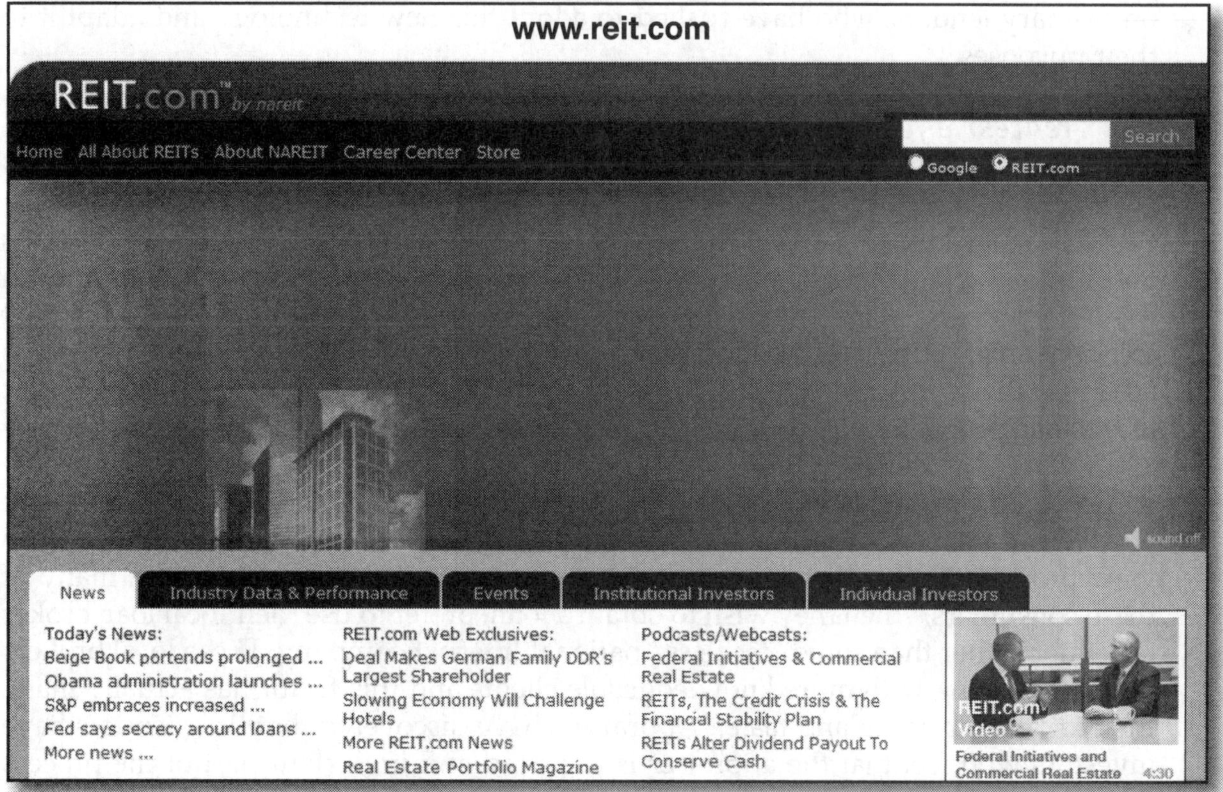

The majority of these individuals are sellers who extend credit to their purchasers. This is referred to as "taking back" or "carrying back" a part of the sales price, often in the form of a second mortgage. A ***SECOND MORTGAGE*** *is often a source of funds when a lender will not loan the full amount of the purchase price of a residence. It may also be a source of funds for home repairs for a homeowner who does not wish to renegotiate the terms of his original mortgage.*

"Seconds" are generally for shorter periods of time and at higher rates than "firsts."

When interest rates are high or money is in short supply, a buyer may be inclined to ask a property owner to sell his or her property on installment terms.

Private financing becomes much more prevalent when funds from traditional lenders are scarce, too expensive, or both.

C. THE INTERNET

The authors would be remiss if the effect of the Internet on lending was not discussed. Over the past ten years, the use of both home computers and of the Internet has become available to virtually every American household. This fact has not been lost on primary lenders, who have rushed to adopt this new technology and adapt it to their purposes.

The greatest effect of the Internet has been on how fast transactions can take place.

Some primary lenders viewed the Internet as a means to both speed up transactions and remove what some of them viewed as bottlenecks (brokers and appraisers) in the loan process. Many brokers, appraisers, and others saw this attempt at direct electronic marketing as a threat to their livelihoods and worked to use the Internet to advertise their services to clients, reduce their overhead costs, and speed up their part of the loan process.

It is still too early to assess the full impact of the computer/Internet revolution, but after ten years, several trends have become clear. Consumers do use the Internet to view properties and shop for loan rates and other information. However, many of these consumers, when they wish to obtain a loan, prefer to use their local loan broker or lender rather than some "faceless" national Internet company. These local brokers now are dealing with more knowledgeable clients and this factor has actually made the broker's job easier and faster. Appraisers have discovered that their lenders have investors who feel that the appraiser is a trusted and important part of the process that they do not wish to go away.

The adoption of computerization and the Internet has both lowered consumer costs and increased productivity throughout the industry.

1. Online Loan Applications – A Good Start

Like many aspects of the loan industry, the application process can be started online. An applicant accesses a website and fills out a simple form to begin the process. In theory, the applicant will receive a number of offers. It has been the author's experience that most loans cannot be fully completed through the Internet. It usually takes at least one face-to-face meeting, as well as other correspondence, to complete the process.

Don't assume that loans generated online will be at the lowest net cost to the consumer. The Internet is a good starting point for the shopping-around process, but other avenues should be explored to find the best deal. It would be ill-advised to automatically rule out your local savings bank or credit union and real estate agents. With their experience and expertise, they can be excellent resources and a place to start the shopping process.

www.lendingtree.com
www.bloomberg.com
www.indymacmortgage.com
http://quickenloans.quicken.com

V. CHAPTER SUMMARY

The primary market is mostly made up of local banks, savings banks, and mortgage companies. Funds for the primary market come from savings by local businesses, local deposits, and individual investors. For many years residential lending was dominated by the savings and loans. Banking deregulation had an adverse effect on the S&Ls and permitted other lenders to take over part of their market share. This same deregulation has allowed other institutions, such as credit unions, insurance companies, and pension plans to enter the primary market. Real Estate Investment Trusts allow ordinary individual investors to invest in real estate loans and provide a tax advantage for their investments. Loans by private individuals have always been a part of the primary mortgage loan market. These loans are primarily in the form of second trust mortgages. The Internet has helped to shorten the length of the loan process, reduce consumer expense, and increase industry productivity.

VI. TERMINOLOGY

Commercial Banks
Credit Unions
Employment Retirement Income Security Act of 1974 (ERISA)
FDIC
Federally Related Transaction
FIRREA
Insurance Companies
Money Market Funds
Mortgage Banker/Mortgage Companies
Mortgage Brokers
Office of Thrift Supervision (OTS)
Participation Loan
Pension Funds
Portfolio Loan
Primary Market
Real Estate Investment Trust (REIT)
Real Estate Investment Trust Act
Resolution Trust Corporation (RTC)
Savings and Loans
Savings Association Insurance Fund (SAIF)
Seasoned Loan
Second Mortgage
Servicing a Mortgage Loan

VII. CHAPTER QUIZ

1. What percentage of its net income must a REIT derive from real estate investments?
   a. 95%
   b. 75%
   c. 50%
   d. 100%

2. The collection of principal and interest payments by one lender on behalf of another is called:
   a. loan seasoning.
   b. loan participation.
   c. loan portfolio.
   d. loan servicing.

3. A federally related transaction is:
   a. any transaction that involves the federal government.
   b. any loan by a bank or savings bank.
   c. any loan by a credit union.
   d. all the above.

4. A mortgage broker:
   a. acts as a loan coordinator.
   b. loans his/her own money.
   c. services loans.
   d. all of the above.

5. The practice of holding a loan for a specified period before it may be sold into the secondary market is called:
   a. loan seasoning.
   b. loan participation.
   c. loan portfolio.
   d. loan servicing.

6. The deposit insurance fund for both banks and savings banks is managed by:
   a. FSLIC.
   b. FNMA.
   c. FDIC.
   d. None of the above.

7. Requiring a percentage of a developer's profit, as well as principal and interest, is known as:

   a. loan seasoning.
   b. loan participation.
   c. loan portfolio.
   d. loan servicing.

8. Money market funds are:

   a. privately insured.
   b. federally insured.
   c. not insured.
   d. none of the above.

9. Loans that are not sold into the secondary market are called:

   a. seasoned loans.
   b. participation loans.
   c. portfolio loans.
   d. serviced loans.

10. The usage of computers and the Internet:

   a. increases productivity.
   b. saves time.
   c. lowers consumer cost.
   d. all the above.

ANSWERS: 1. *b*; 2. *d*; 3. *a*; 4. *a*; 5. *a*; 6. *c*; 7. *b*; 8. *c*; 9. *c*; 10. *d*

on the Internet

www.freddiemac.com

Home

Home

More Loans

Less Work

Home

– Part II –
Chapters 4, 5, and 6
Lending Rules

Chapter 4 – The Secondary Market and Federal Credit Agencies

While loans are made directly to borrowers at the local level by savings banks, banks, credit unions, and mortgage bankers from local deposits by individuals and businesses, these sources of funds are often not enough to maintain continued lending, especially during periods of high demand. The establishment of the secondary market has provided these lenders with a stable market in which to sell their mortgages.

Chapter 5 – Federal Regulation and Consumer Protection

The federal government has long taken an active role in assuring that all citizens will be able to enjoy the benefits of property ownership. In addition to support of the capital markets that make real estate loans possible, particular care has been taken to assure that no citizen will be discriminated against on the basis of race, religion, sex, disability, or ethnicity.

Chapter 6 – State Regulation of Lending

The 10th Amendment to the U.S. Constitution reserves all powers to the states that are not specifically given to the federal government in the Constitution. As a result, the states have regulated, by law, the form and manner of property ownership as well as the documentation required for ownership.

Chapter 4
The Secondary Market and Federal Credit Agencies

In Chapter 2, we discussed the history of some of the major agencies that make up the secondary market and their interaction with the primary market. In this chapter we will discuss the interaction of the secondary market with the investment community. As we have seen, mortgages that originate in the primary market are sold into the secondary market, and the funds received from them by the primary lenders are the source of new mortgage loans to borrowers.

I. The Secondary Mortgage Market

The participants who make up the secondary mortgage market (Fannie Mae, Freddie Mac, and Ginnie Mae) must raise the necessary funds to purchase the mortgages from the primary lenders by selling bonds to the general public.

***SECURITIES** are any form of ownership that can be easily traded on a secondary market, such as stocks and bonds. The mortgages that have been purchased by the participants in the secondary market act as collateral for the bonds they issue. These bonds are referred to as **MORTGAGE-RELATED SECURITIES**.* These bonds, or securities, have found a ready market for several reasons. The first is that the mortgage pools that underlie the bonds are broad based. The mortgages that make up a pool are national in scope rather than regional.

Chapter 4

CHAPTER OUTLINE

Thus, even though one region of the country might be experiencing the sort of economic difficulties that could lead to default, the rest of mortgages in the pool are from regions that are stable. ***DEFAULT** is the nonpayment of the mortgage by the borrower*. The effects of defaults are diluted by the number and mix of mortgages in the pool.

The second reason that the bonds are attractive to investors is the establishment of underwriting guidelines by the agencies that participate in the market. This provides assurance to the investors that the mortgages rest on credit-worthy borrowers and sound collateral from the underlying real estate. The third reason that these bonds are popular is that in most cases, they are not double taxed. Also, each offering of bonds is rated for overall credit quality by such agencies as Standard & Poor's and Moody's. Lastly, there is the perception (which may or may not be true) that some of these bonds, such as those offered by FNMA and the FHLMC, are protected by the government.

A. PASS-THROUGH SECURITIES

The first popular mortgage-backed security was the pass-through security. These were securities offered by the Government National Mortgage Association, or GNMA. GNMA ("Ginnie Mae") is a government agency within the Department of Housing and Urban Development (HUD). ***PASS-THROUGH SECURITIES** provide the investor with an "undivided interest" in the mortgage pool. In essence, the investor is an owner and will receive the principal and interest on their share of the mortgages plus any prepayments of the mortgage*. These payments are guaranteed by GNMA. Pass-through securities have a relatively high yield when compared to other investments that are considered safe, such as treasury bonds, which are liquid, and as they are guaranteed by a government agency, risk-free. A ***LIQUID INVESTMENT** may be instantly sold into an established marketplace*. Stocks and bonds are examples of liquid investments. All of these factors contribute to popularity with investors.

However, there is also a downside to pass-through securities. Cash flows are often not predictable due to the propensity of borrowers to prepay their mortgages. This tends to happen when interest rates decline and borrowers refinance to obtain the lower rates. This means that investors must reinvest the funds obtained from the prepayments at lower rates as well.

In addition to the GNMA pass-through securities, there are also similar programs that are offered by private entities. These programs meet the expectations of investors for safety in two ways. First, the collateral properties are evaluated by a rating service, such as Standard & Poor's or Moody's. Secondly, the issuing entity also receives a rating based on its ability to pay the principal and interest on any defaulted loans. This rating is based on property type and loan-to-value (LTV) ratio as well as whether or not the properties involved are covered by government insurance or private mortgage insurance. **Private mortgage insurance (PMI)** is required on loans that exceed 80 percent of the value of the property.

Very often the issuing entity will "over-collateralize" the securities package. For example, the private secondary lender may issue a securities pool with a principal balance of $100 million. However, the pool will contain $110 million worth of mortgages. *The $100 million principal balance would be called a **SENIOR PASS-THROUGH**. The additional $10 million in mortgages would be called a **SUBORDINATE PASS-THROUGH***. Thus, payments on $110 million in mortgages are used to pay off the $100 million in the securities issue. This provides safety from defaults or early payoffs for the investor.

B. MORTGAGE-BACKED SECURITIES

***MORTGAGE-BACKED SECURITIES** are instruments issued by various agencies, such as GNMA, to raise investment funds.* These securities are similar to the familiar corporate bond. They pay interest at intervals until maturity, at which time the face value of the bond is paid to the holder. They differ from the pass-through in that the investor does not have any ownership interest in the mortgages themselves. Generally, the interest amount will be below the interest rates of the underlying mortgages that back the bonds. These bonds also rely on over-collateralization of the mortgages, which back them to provide safety to the investors. The mortgages are held by a trustee who will track the interest rates in the market as well as the interest rates paid on the bonds. When market rates decline to a point where the investment safety of the pool might be endangered, the trustee will require that the issuing entity purchase more mortgages to place into the pool. This process is called marking to market. ***MARKING TO MARKET** is the process of tracking and comparing mortgage interest rates held in a pool to current market interest rates (yield).*

These bonds are also rated by the ratings agencies. Ratings are based on the quality, quantity, and diversification of the mortgages held in the individual investment pool.

The packaging and selling of risky subprime mortgage-backed securities contributed greatly to the financial crisis of 2008-2009.

C. COLLATERALIZED MORTGAGE OBLIGATIONS (CMOs)

The ***COLLATERALIZED MORTGAGE OBLIGATION** allows the creation of multi-class mortgage securities.* These mortgage securities rearrange the cash flows into a series of securities with different maturity dates. *The different classes of securities are called **TRANCHES**.* An investor can select either a long-term tranch or a short-term tranch with or without pass-through privileges. There are also interest-only and principal-only securities. One class of investors receives payment from principle on the mortgages only and the other class receives payments from the interest on the mortgages only. These complex securities initially ran into the problem of double taxation by the Internal Revenue Service (once at the corporate level and again at the individual investor level). In 1986, Congress addressed this problem and created the Real Estate Mortgage Investment Conduit. A ***REAL ESTATE MORTGAGE INVESTMENT CONDUIT (REMIC)*** *is an entity that can issue CMO securities without double income taxation.*

A partnership, corporation, or trust may issue collateralized mortgage obligations if it establishes itself as a REMIC.

At this point, it will not be subject to the double taxation rules for CMO-related activity. A REMIC is prohibited from receiving any income from any activity that is not a qualified mortgage in the securities pool. It is not allowed to receive fees or other compensation, other than servicing income from its mortgage portfolio, nor is it allowed to buy or sell mortgages outside of the established pool. Proceeds from sales of securities within the pool must be disbursed to investors within 90 days.

II. FNMA and FHLMC

We have noted that FNMA and the Federal Home Loan Mortgage Corporation (FHLMC) were originally set up by the federal government to establish a strong secondary market. They are not, however, agencies of the federal government. **While they are chartered by Congress, they are private corporations**. The government does not guarantee their obligations in any manner. However, the public, both borrowers and investors, have the perception that somehow they are federal agencies. This perception has been bolstered by the fact that Congress has expressed the intention of federal support in the case of a default on the part of either of the agencies. To back up this statement of intent, Congress passed the ***FEDERAL HOUSING ENTERPRISE FINANCIAL SAFETY AND SOUNDNESS ACT*** *in 1992. This act set capital guidelines for both FNMA and FHLMC.* The act also established the ***OFFICE OF SECONDARY MARKET EXAMINATION AND OVERSIGHT (OSMEO)*** *as an agency within the Department of Housing and Urban Development to monitor the capital requirements of both FNMA and FHLMC.*

As a result of the 2008 financial meltdown, Congress changed the framework for regulation of Fannie Mae and Freddie Mac by placing them in conservatorship with a new federal agency called the **Federal Housing Finance Agency (FHFA)**. This agency replaced HUD as regulator of FNMA, FHLMC, and FHFB.

Conservatorship is not ownership, but overseeing; although they may purchase up to 79% of dividend paying preferred stock.

III. Federal Credit Agencies

There are a number of federal agencies that provide both primary and secondary market support. Many of these agencies were formed particularly to support mortgage loans in

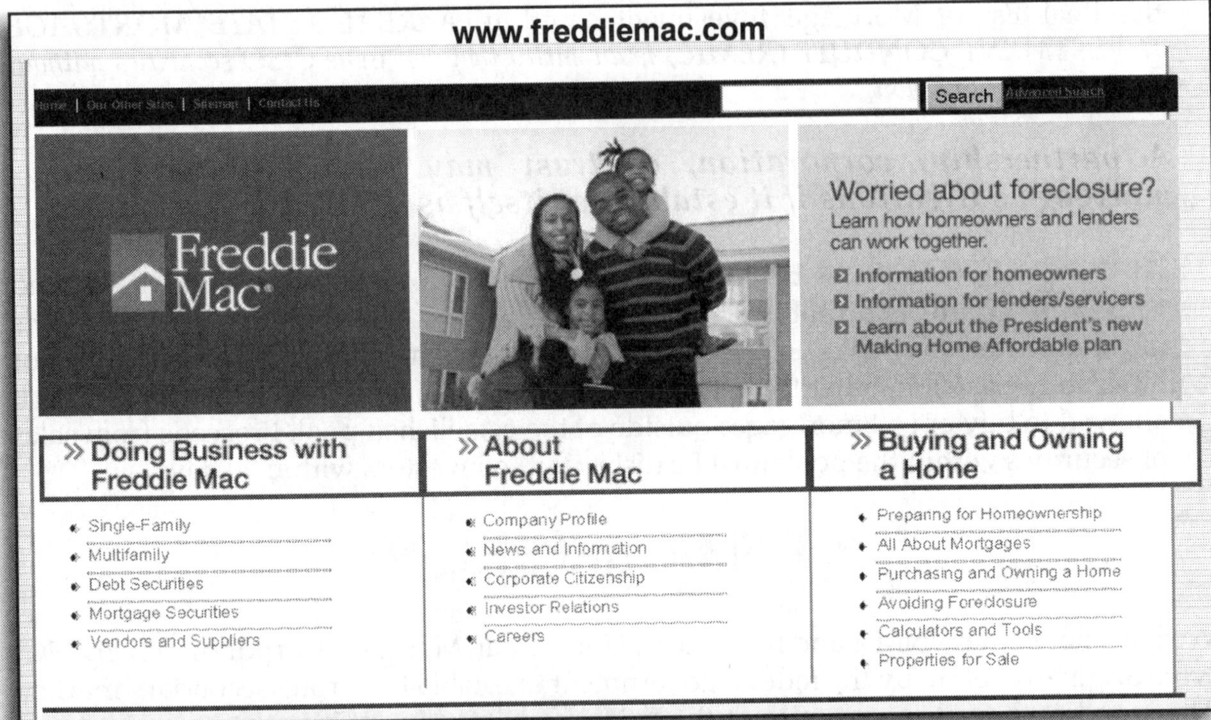

the agricultural sector of the economy. Typically, conventional lenders are reluctant to loan on farms, as income from agriculture is highly dependent on a number of variables. Among these are weather, crop yields, and national and world market prices at time of harvest (food is highly perishable and must be immediately processed). All of those inherently uncertain factors contribute to the lender's concern regarding the borrower's ability to repay the loan.

A. FARM SERVICE AGENCY (FSA)

The mission of the U.S. Department of Agriculture's ***FARM SERVICE AGENCY (FSA)*** *is to stabilize farm income, help farmers conserve land and water resources, provide credit to new or disadvantaged farmers and ranchers, and help farm operations recover from the effects of disaster.*

FSA was set up when the Department was reorganized in 1994, incorporating programs from several agencies including the Agricultural Stabilization and Conservation Service, the Federal Crop Insurance Corporation (now a separate Risk Management Agency), and the Farmers Home Administration. Though FSA's name has changed over the years, the agency's relationship with farmers goes back to the 1930s.

In the 1930s, Congress set up a unique system under which federal farm programs are administered locally. Farmers who are eligible to participate in these programs elect a three-to-five-person county committee that reviews county office operations and makes decisions on how to apply the programs. This grassroots approach gives

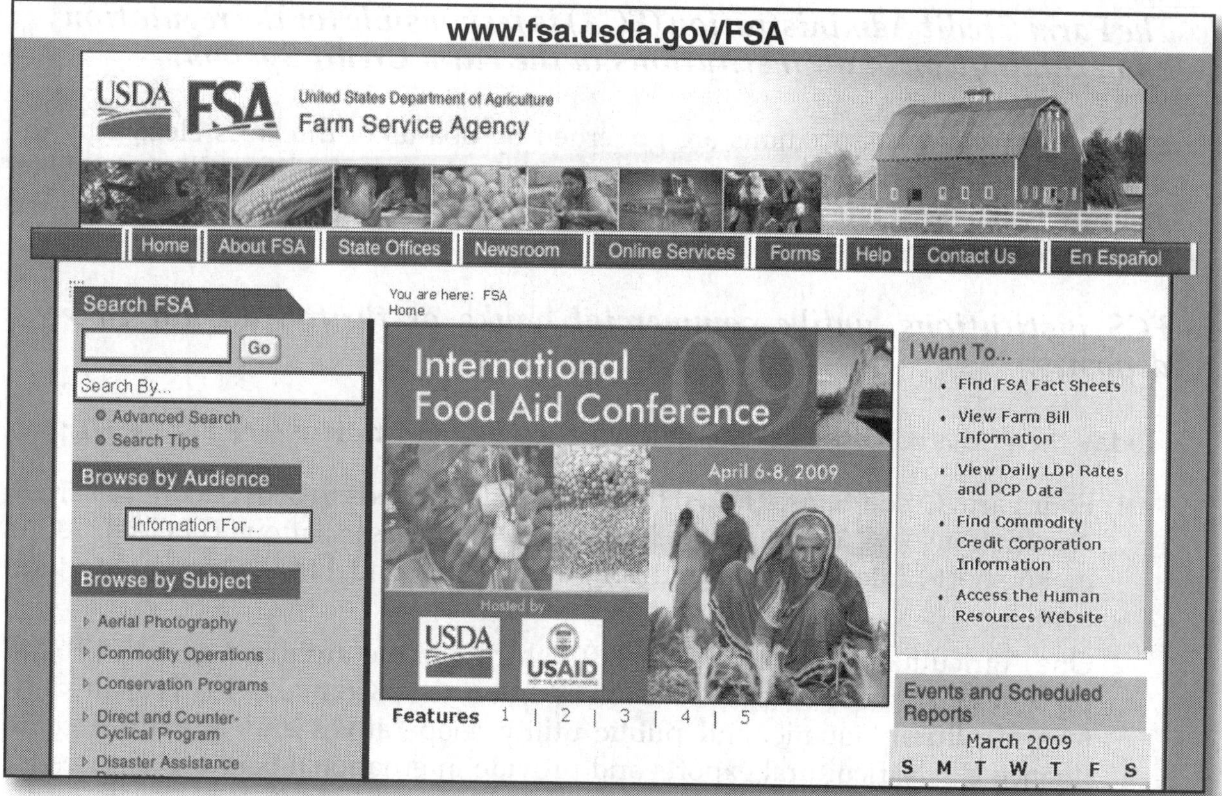

farmers a much-needed say in how federal actions affect their communities and their individual operations. After more than 60 years, it remains a cornerstone of FSA's efforts to preserve and promote American agriculture.

The Farm Service Agency was set up to provide relief and emergency farm financing. The agency requires that a borrower be unable to obtain funds from more traditional lending sources before they will finance or insure a loan. Direct loans may be made at lower-than-market rates to those who qualify.

In general, the agency serves low-income family farmers and the elderly, or veterans who are farmers.

B. FARM CREDIT SYSTEM (FCS)

The ***FARM CREDIT SYSTEM (FCS)*** *specializes in providing credit and related services to farmers, ranchers, and producers or harvesters of aquatic products.* FCS is a network of borrower-owned lending institutions and related service organizations serving all 50 states and the Commonwealth of Puerto Rico. Loans may also be made to finance the processing and marketing activities of these borrowers. In addition, loans may be made to rural homeowners, certain farm-related businesses, and agricultural, aquatic, and public utility cooperatives.

The Farm Credit Administration (FCA) is responsible for the regulation and examination of all institutions in the Farm Credit System.

All FCS banks and associations are governed by boards of directors elected by the stockholders who are farmer/borrowers of each institution. Additionally, federal law requires that at least one member of the board be elected from outside the FCS by the other directors.

FCS institutions, unlike commercial banks or thrifts, do not take deposits.

Today the FCS is composed of the following lending institutions (see **Figure 4-1**):

1. Four Farm Credit Banks (FCBs) that provide loan funds to 81 Agricultural Credit Associations (ACAs), and 9 Federal Land Credit Associations (FLCAs). ACAs make short-, intermediate-, and long-term loans and FLCAs make long-term loans.
2. One Agricultural Credit Bank (ACB), which has the authority of an FCB and provides loan funds to four ACAs. In addition, the ACB makes loans of all kinds to agricultural, aquatic, and public utility cooperatives and is authorized to finance U.S. agricultural exports and provide international banking services for farmer-owned cooperatives.

Figure 4-1 **Farm Credit System District Territories**

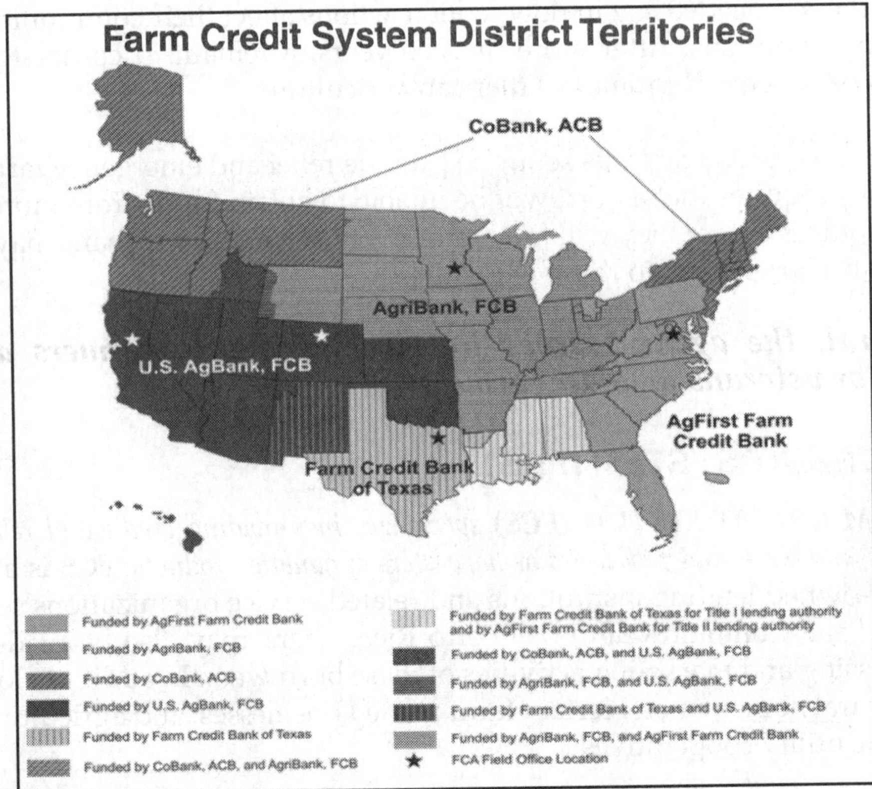

1. Federal Credit System Financial Assistance Corporation

The **FEDERAL CREDIT SYSTEM FINANCIAL ASSISTANCE CORPORATION** *was created by the Agricultural Credit Act to provide capital to farm credit banks that were in financial difficulty.* Approximately $1.26 billion in funds was provided by the Assistance Corporation before its authority to raise additional funds expired on December 31, 1992. It will continue to operate until all funds used to provide the assistance are repaid.

2. Federal Agricultural Mortgage Corporation (FAMC)

The FAMC is better known as "Farmer Mac."

The **FEDERAL AGRICULTURAL MORTGAGE CORPORATION (FAMC)** *was also created as a chartered corporation by the Agricultural Credit Act. It is similar in concept to the Government National Mortgage Corporation in operation, but exists solely to provide a secondary market for farm mortgages.* The agency is part of the Farm Credit System. It examines mortgage pools and provides a guarantee on repayment of principle and interest by the borrowers. The mortgages in the pools are then used as the basis for pass-through securities to be sold to investors. However, there is a basic difference between the guaranties issued by FAMC and GNMA. Farmer Mac will only guarantee up to 90 percent of the principle and interest. However, that guarantee is backed by a direct line of credit with the U.S. Treasury, which has, as yet, never been needed.

C. FINANCING CORPORATION (FICO)

The **FINANCING CORPORATION (FICO)** *was chartered by the Federal Home Loan Bank Board in 1987 to help resolve the crisis created by the widespread collapse of the savings and loans.* The purpose of the agency was to stabilize and recapitalize the FSLIC (later replaced by SAIF), which had virtually exhausted its funds and was at the point of bankruptcy. FICO was authorized to issue bonds. The proceeds of the bonds were to be used by the FSLIC to resolve the S&L insolvencies. The bonds had no federal guarantee.

The abbreviation FICO, for the Financing Corporation, has nothing to do with a person's FICO score.

D. FEDERAL FINANCING BANK (FFB)

The **FEDERAL FINANCING BANK (FFB)** *came about as a result of the passage of the Federal Financing Act of 1973. The purpose of this agency was to consolidate the financing activities of a number of different federal agencies in one place.* The bank issues securities for many different agencies. Among them are NASA and the U.S. Postal Service. While

most mortgage-related activities are excluded, FFB does purchase HUD Section 108 guaranteed loans.

E. FHA AND VA

While it is commonplace for brokers, borrowers, lenders, and investors to refer to "FHA loans" or "VA loans" neither of these government agencies buys or sells mortgage loans.

The FHA and VA are issuers of government mortgage insurance. The activities of both of these agencies will be more fully discussed in Chapter 11.

IV. CHAPTER SUMMARY

Loans are made directly to borrowers by savings banks, banks, credit unions, and mortgage bankers from local deposits by individuals and businesses. However, these sources of funds are often not enough to maintain continued lending, especially during periods of high demand. The establishment of the secondary market has provided these lenders with a stable market in which to sell their mortgages. This secondary market has to raise the necessary funds to provide this essential service to the primary market. This has been accomplished by the establishment of both private firms and government agencies for this purpose.

The firms and agencies have been successful for a number of reasons. The most important of these has been the creation of national mortgage loan underwriting guidelines that assure investors of the quality of the mortgage loans that back the investment pools. The members of the secondary market issue mortgage-related securities and bonds that are attractive to investors because the underlying mortgages are broad based, have sound collateral, and are often free from double taxation, unlike other investments such as stocks and bonds. Securities issued by private firms in this market are often covered by private mortgage insurance and are over-collateralized to enhance their safety as investments. The securities of the secondary market are also rated by third-party investment rating services.

FNMA, FHLMC, and GNMA are the major issuers of residential mortgage-related securities. The three major types of securities that are issued are: pass-through securities, mortgage-backed bonds, and collateralized mortgage obligations. The federal government has been an active supporter of this market, either through direct federal agency support or beneficial regulation. In addition, a number of federal agencies have been established to provide mortgage lending for farm and rural areas. The best known of these are the Farm Service Agency (FSA) and the Federal Agricultural Mortgage Corporation (FAMC), or "Farmer Mac." The secondary market has made home ownership a realization for millions of Americans, rather than just a dream.

V. TERMINOLOGY

Agricultural Credit Act
Collateralized Mortgage Obligation
Default
Farm Credit Agency (FCA)
Farm Credit System (FCS)
Farm Service Agency (FSA)
Federal Agricultural Mortgage Corporation (FAMC)
Federal Financing Bank (FFB)
Financing Corporation (FICO)
Liquidity
Marking to Market
Mortgage-Backed Securities
Mortgage-Related Securities
Pass-Through Securities
Private Mortgage Insurance (PMI)
Real Estate Mortgage Invvestment Conduit (REMIC)
Senior Pass-Through
Subordinate Pass-Through
Tranches

VI. CHAPTER QUIZ

1. An investment is said to be liquid when:
   a. it is guaranteed by the government.
   b. it can be readily sold.
   c. it is worthless.
   d. it is difficult to sell.

2. Mortgage-related securities are:
   a. easily bought and sold.
   b. issued by participants in the secondary market.
   c. have real estate mortgages as their collateral.
   d. all the above.

3. When a borrower prematurely stops making loan payments, the loan is said to be:
   a. paid off.
   b. in arrears.
   c. in suspense.
   d. in default.

4. Standard and Poor's and Moody's are:
   a. primary lenders.
   b. private secondary lenders.
   c. rating services.
   d. mortgage insurance companies.

5. FNMA and FHLMC are:
   a. government agencies.
   b. government-chartered private corporations.
   c. primary lenders.
   d. funded by the U.S. Treasury.

6. If $100 million worth of mortgages are used to collateralize $90 million of securities, the additional $10 million is known as a(n):
   a. subordinate pass-through.
   b. senior pass-through.
   c. overcapitalized pass-through.
   d. junior pass-through.

7. Private Mortgage Insurance (PMI) is required on loans that exceed what percentage of the value of the property?
   a. 60%
   b. 70%
   c. 80%
   d. 90%

8. The process of tracking mortgages in a pool and comparing their rates to current market rates is called:
   a. an investment rating.
   b. pool analysis.
   c. market analysis.
   d. marking to market.

9. A tranch is a(n):
   a. rating.
   b. investment pool.
   c. portion of a multiclass security.
   d. REMIC

10. The Agricultural Credit Act:
   a. provides direct farm loans.
   b. superceded and consolidated previous farm credit legislation.
   c. forbids the sale of farm-based mortgage securities.
   d. was passed to rescue the failing Department of Agriculture.

ANSWERS: 1. b; 2. d; 3. d; 4. c; 5. b; 6. a; 7. c; 8. d; 9. c; 10. b

AFTER HOUR
DIEBOLD
DEPOSITORY

Chapter 5
Federal Regulation and Consumer Protection

The federal government has a long history of legislation that protects property ownership and prohibits discrimination. The U.S. Constitution severely limits the government's ability to take the private property of citizens, except for public use. In addition, the Bill of Rights assures the citizens of the United States extraordinary personal freedom. These freedoms were expanded by the adoption of the 13th, 14th, and 15th Amendments to the Constitution immediately after the Civil War. These amendments not only did away with slavery, but addressed the concept of anti-discrimination as well.

Additionally, during this period, Congress also passed specific anti-discriminatory legislation that addressed ownership of real estate. Since that time, Congress has strengthened that original legislation with additional laws that cover real estate sales, ownership, rental, lending, and appraisal. In addition to laws prohibiting discrimination, there are laws that prohibit abusive sales and loan practices, as well as legislation that addresses disclosure. ***DISCLOSURE*** *requires that all pertinent information about a property or a loan be provided to enable a consumer to make informed choices in the lending process.* It is important that professional real estate and finance practitioners should be aware of, understand, and comply with all these federal laws.

Chapter 5

CHAPTER OUTLINE

I. Anti-Discrimination Legislation

A. CIVIL RIGHTS ACT OF 1866

The Civil Rights Act of 1866 was the first piece of legislation passed by Congress after the Civil War that dealt with real estate in particular.

The ***CIVIL RIGHTS ACT OF 1866*** *provides that "all citizens of the United States shall have the same right, in every state and territory, as is enjoyed by white citizens thereof to inherit, purchase, lease, sell, hold, and convey real and personal property." The act specifically prohibits any discrimination based on race or ancestry.* The law was not really enforced after the latter part of the 19th century, and it was not challenged in court until 1968. In the historic *Jones v. Mayer* case, the U.S. Supreme Court ruled that the 1866 federal law "prohibits all racial discrimination, private or public, in the sale or rental of property." The court upheld the constitutionality of the law based on the 13th Amendment to the U.S. Constitution, which prohibits slavery.

B. FEDERAL FAIR HOUSING ACT

The Federal Fair Housing Act is contained in Title VIII of the Civil Rights Act of 1968.

With this law, congress broadened the protections of the Civil Rights Act of 1866. The ***FEDERAL FAIR HOUSING ACT*** *makes it illegal to discriminate on the basis of race, color, religion, sex, national origin, or handicap, or against families with children, in the sale or lease of residential property or in the sale or lease of vacant land for the construction of residential buildings.*

Some residential sales and leases are exempt from the provisions of the Fair Housing Act. The sale of a single-family home is exempt if three conditions are met:

1. the owner does not own more than three such homes at one time;
2. there is no real estate broker or agent involved in the transaction, and
3. there is no discriminatory advertising.

This exemption is limited to one transaction in any 24-month period, unless the owner was the most recent occupant of the home.

Religious discrimination is permitted, with respect to rentals, in dwellings owned by religious organizations. Lodging in private clubs is also exempt from the anti-discrimination law if the club is truly private and noncommercial. Discrimination against families with children is permitted by apartment complexes, condominiums, and other developments that qualify as "housing for older persons" under the act. These exemptions were permitted in order to allow the constitutional guarantee of "freedom of association."

Violations of the act include: refusing to sell, rent, or negotiate the terms of a sale or lease for residential property; changing the terms of a sale or lease for different people; discriminating in advertising; making false representations regarding the availability of property; blockbusting; steering, and limiting participation in a multiple listing service (MLS).

***BLOCKBUSTING** is the illegal practice of inducing property owners in a neighborhood to sell by predicting the entrance of minorities into the neighborhood.* The person making the prediction buys the property and then resells it for a profit. ***STEERING** is the channeling of various applicants to specific areas in order to maintain or change the character of those neighborhoods.*

The Fair Housing Act also makes it unlawful to discriminate in lending practices based on a borrower's race, color religion, sex, national origin, or handicap. In addition, it specifically prohibits redlining. ***REDLINING** is the illegal practice of refusing to make loans on properties in a particular area based on racially discriminatory reasons.*

C. EQUAL CREDIT OPPORTUNITY ACT (ECOA)

The ***EQUAL CREDIT OPPORTUNITY ACT** is a federal law prohibiting those who lend money from discriminating against borrowers based on their race, sex, color, religion, handicap, national origin, age, or marital status.*

Enacted in 1974, this Act was a result of hearings by the National Commission on Consumer Finance that focused on the denial of credit to women. Married women were often denied credit in their own name, even when they were the principal breadwinner in the family. If they should divorce their husbands, all credit was in the husbands' names and thus the women had no credit history and, by extension, no creditworthiness. The information gathered in this series of hearings was utilized by both Houses of Congress to develop a bill to protect the rights of women, both married and unmarried, in the lending process. Congress revisited the bill and expanded it to include additional protections based on age, race, color, religion, and those on welfare.

The Equal Credit Opportunity Act (ECOA) ensures that all consumers are given an equal chance to obtain credit.

The law has several provisions that attempt to remove discrimination from the process and provide regulatory oversight of lenders efforts to be nondiscriminatory in the lending process. Lenders are required to notify loan applicants within thirty days of their decision as to whether or not to extend credit. If credit is denied, the lender must state the reasons for the denial in writing to the borrower. Questions regarding sex, marital status, religion, national origin, and welfare status on an application are forbidden. For loan purposes, married women have the right to maintain a separate credit history and have it considered separately from her husband's credit, regardless of his creditworthiness.

While the attempt to provide inclusiveness to minority and underrepresented groups in the lending process is laudable, it sometimes flies in the face of simple economics. Minorities are indeed underrepresented in the ability to acquire credit. However, many lenders argue that this is because they do not meet the credit guidelines that have been established to properly qualify borrowers for a loan, and not from some hidden agenda to deny them credit because they are a member of a minority group. The lenders argue, quite reasonably, that the same federal government that requires minority inclusiveness sets many of the lending guidelines that protect both the federal insurance programs and the investors in the marketplace. They further argue that they are in the business of making money. Good loans to creditworthy borrowers, regardless of their minority status, help them to make money. Loans to borrowers who are not creditworthy are risky and prone to foreclosure, thereby driving the price of credit up for everyone. These arguments are certainly valid and have been considered in the oversight of the law by the Federal Reserve Board.

The Federal Reserve Board oversees compliance with the Equal Credit Opportunity Act.

The Federal Reserve Board issued Regulation B to provide guidelines for lenders in this sensitive area. ***REGULATION B*** *notes that it is illegal to discriminate by "intent," by "practice," or by "effect."* It is often virtually impossible to prove discrimination by intent without clear written or taped evidence. However, the board's guidelines focus on practices through the implementation of regulations that force the lenders to treat each application in a uniform manner. The board also addresses effects through periodic reviews of a lender's records in an attempt to uncover evidence of loan redlining.

D. HOME MORTGAGE DISCLOSURE ACT

The ***HOME MORTGAGE DISCLOSURE ACT (1975)*** *was specifically passed by Congress to deal with the problem of redlining.* As previously noted, redlining is the practice by lenders of refusing to make loans in certain neighborhoods based on neighborhood decline that is attributed to racial composition or a perception of higher crime rates. The lenders often justified "redline areas" by incorrectly analyzing both census data and the contents of appraisal reports in their possession. This improper application of data was then used to deny loans to borrowers who lived in those areas.

The new law would use the very same data collection by the Bureau of the Census and the information that it contains to correct lending inequity. The law requires any lender with assets of $10 million or more to make a report of all of its loans both within and outside of the Standard Metropolitan Statistical Area in which it has either a main office or a branch office. A ***STANDARD METROPOLITAN STATISTICAL AREA (SMSA)*** *is a city and its suburbs having a population of 50,000 persons or more.* The distribution of loans must be indicated by the census tracts in which they were made. A ***CENSUS TRACT*** *is the smallest demographic area used by the Bureau of the Census. It consists of areas of approximately 4,000 persons in neighborhoods of similar economic conditions*. The law requires use of current census data. This means that the SMSAs and census tracts must be drawn from the 2000 census. State-chartered lenders are exempt only if their state has similar requirements. In other words, they are not really exempt.

It is easy for the regulators to determine if a lender is not making loans in any nearby census tract area and to initiate inquiries to determine why they are not.

E. COMMUNITY REINVESTMENT ACT

The ***COMMUNITY REINVESTMENT ACT (1978)*** *was passed to make all federally regulated institutions responsive to the needs of their communities by requiring them to publicize how well they were serving their local communities*. To properly comply with the act, the institutions must define the area from which it accepts deposits and to which it makes loans. It must provide the public with information about all the types of loans and accounts available. The institution must post a notice in all its places of business that notifies the public who it is regulated by and that the public is invited to comment on its practices at any appropriate hearing. Finally, it must make periodic reports to its regulators about its efforts to make credit available to the community that it serves. This report is called a community support statement. A ***COMMUNITY SUPPORT STATEMENT*** *is a report to the institution's regulators that details exactly how well the federally regulated institution serves its community*. Based on the community support statement, as well as input from the community itself, the regulators may or may not permit the further expansion of a particular lending institution.

F. FINANCIAL INSTITUTIONS REFORM, RECOVERY, AND ENFORCEMENT ACT (FIRREA)

The ***FINANCIAL INSTITUTIONS REFORM, RECOVERY, AND ENFORCEMENT ACT (FIRREA)*** *of 1989 was a response to the failure of the savings and loan industry in the 1980s. It revised the regulation of thrift organizations and created several new agencies, such as the Office of Thrift Supervision (OTS) and the Resoluton Trust Corporation (RTC).* It would make sweeping changes in the operations of all individuals and institutions involved in federally related lending transactions.

FIRREA defines a federally related transaction as any transaction that involves the use of federal monies or access to federal monies.

The Act includes all mortgage lenders, including the primary and secondary market, that are not affiliated with depository institutions, as well as mortgage brokers and appraisers. FIRREA requires mortgage and home improvement lenders to report the sex, race, and income levels of loan applicants. In particular, the law requires that all data on rejected applications submitted by mortgage loan brokers be filed with the regulators.

FIRREA regulations insure that redlining and other discriminatory acts do not occur at any level in the lending process.

Under the Act, lenders are evaluated publicly on how well they meet a community's lending needs. The evaluations consist of "outstanding," "satisfactory," "in need of improvement," or "in noncompliance." Any rating of "less-than-satisfactory" will require immediate remedy on the part of the lender to maintain access to the federal credit market. The Act also requires that regulators keep secret the names of any persons who lodge complaints of possible discrimination with an institution's regulators.

FIRREA requires the licensing of appraisers by all fifty states and sets up the ***APPRAISAL SUBCOMMITTEE*** *as a federal agency to monitor the actions of lenders, state regulators, the Appraisal Foundation, and other federal regulatory agencies.* The agency has representatives from all federal financial regulatory agencies on its board. The agency is concerned with safe-guarding the financial security of financial institutions, uniformity of regulations among its member regulatory agencies, and anti-discriminatory practices and competency in the appraisal process.

FIRREA applies to everyone associated with a federally related transaction.

The Federal Reserve Board is charged with implementing regulations as needed for lenders. FIRREA carries both civil and criminal penalties for violations of the Act.

G. REAL ESTATE SETTLEMENT PROCEDURES ACT (RESPA)

The ***REAL ESTATE SETTLEMENT PROCEDURES ACT (RESPA)*** *of 1974 requires lenders, mortgage brokers, or servicers of home loans to provide borrowers with pertinent and timely disclosures of the nature and costs of the real estate settlement process. The act also protects borrowers against certain abusive practices, such as kickbacks, and places limitations upon the use of escrow accounts.*

Consumers had long complained about the various fees and commissions paid in the loan process. A home purchase can be an unsettling experience. For many consumers, it is one of the most confusing transactions that they will undertake in a lifetime. The settlement charges on a loan seem endless. Among the charges are: fees for a credit report, appraisal, termite inspection, title search and insurance, escrow, recording and transfer fees, taxes, prepaid interest, and various lender fees (also known as "garbage fees"). How is a consumer to know if the fees are valid and customary or if he or she is being overcharged? How can a consumer shop intelligently for the best deal?

Congress has asked the same questions. In addition, Congress was concerned that the potential existed for lenders to provide kickbacks to real estate agents who steered clients towards them. The potential for this sort of activity existed throughout the process. For example, lenders might receive kickbacks from appraisers, escrow companies, and title companies for using their services. The kickbacks could then be concealed as charges for services in the settlement statements provided by the lenders to the borrowers.

RESPA dealt with these problems by requiring all lenders to provide three disclosure statements to the borrower:

1. A HUD booklet that explains the loan settlement process and outlines standard procedures.
2. A **Good Faith Estimate** of all settlement charges.
3. A **Uniform Settlement Statement** prior to close of escrow.

The HUD booklet not only explains the loan process and the standard procedures and documentation required, but also provides the borrower with information about the various remedies that he or she may seek if RESPA has been violated. A ***GOOD FAITH ESTIMATE*** *is provided to the borrower at the beginning of the loan process. This document lists estimates of the charges that the borrower will have to pay and whether or not any special relationship exists between any of the parties to the transaction* (see **Figure 5-1**). Charges listed must be for actual services provided and must be based on actual current market costs. The ***UNIFORM SETTLEMENT STATEMENT*** *must be provided to the borrower before the settlement. This document provides a complete statement of all charges and may contain no estimates.* The lender must keep a copy on file for at least two years after the settlement. The lender is not allowed to charge any fee for completing the forms (see **Figure 5-2**).

RESPA forbids kickbacks or the use of required title companies, and limits the amount of funds required to be deposited to escrow accounts.

No more than 1/12 of annual taxes or insurance may be required to be deposited in escrow. Additionally, the lender is required to tell the borrower if the lender intends to sell the mortgage, what percentage of its loans were sold in the preceding year, and how many it plans to sell in the next year. RESPA provides for both civil and criminal penalties for violations of the Act. A borrower may obtain up to three times the actual damages incurred, as well as attorney and court costs.

Figure 5-1

GOOD FAITH ESTIMATE

Applicants:
Property Addr:
Prepared By: FACTORY BUILT FINANCIAL Ph. 951-693-1086
28780 OLD TOWN FRONT ST. STE C-8, Temecula, CA 92590

Application No:
Date Prepared:
Loan Program:

The information provided below reflects estimates of the charges which you are likely to incur at the settlement of your loan. The fees listed are estimates-actual charges may be more or less. Your transaction may not involve a fee for every item listed. The numbers listed beside the estimates generally correspond to the numbered lines contained in the HUD-1 settlement statement which you will be receiving at settlement. The HUD-1 settlement statement will show you the actual cost for items paid at settlement.

Total Loan Amount $ Interest Rate: % Term: mths

800	**ITEMS PAYABLE IN CONNECTION WITH LOAN:**		
801	Loan Origination Fee		$
802	Loan Discount		
803	Appraisal Fee		
804	Credit Report		
805	Lender's Inspection Fee		
808	Mortgage Broker Fee		
809	Tax Related Service Fee		
810	Processing Fee		
811	Underwriting Fee		
812	Wire Transfer Fee		
1100	**TITLE CHARGES:**		
1101	Closing or Escrow Fee:		$
1105	Document Preparation Fee		
1106	Notary Fees		
1107	Attorney Fees		
1108	Title Insurance:		
1200	**GOVERNMENT RECORDING & TRANSFER CHARGES:**		
1201	Recording Fees:		$
1202	City/County Tax/Stamps:		
1203	State Tax/Stamps:		
1300	**ADDITIONAL SETTLEMENT CHARGES:**		
1302	Pest Inspection		$
		Estimated Closing Costs	
900	**ITEMS REQUIRED BY LENDER TO BE PAID IN ADVANCE:**		
901	Interest for days @ $	per day	$
902	Mortgage Insurance Premium		
903	Hazard Insurance Premium		
904			
905	VA Funding Fee		
1000	**RESERVES DEPOSITED WITH LENDER:**		
1001	Hazard Insurance Premiums months @ $	per month	$
1002	Mortgage Ins. Premium Reserves months @ $	per month	
1003	School Tax months @ $	per month	
1004	Taxes and Assessment Reserves months @ $	per month	
1005	Flood Insurance Reserves months @ $	per month	
	months @ $	per month	
	months @ $	per month	
		Estimated Prepaid Items/Reserves	
TOTAL ESTIMATED SETTLEMENT CHARGES			

TOTAL ESTIMATED FUNDS NEEDED TO CLOSE:	TOTAL ESTIMATED MONTHLY PAYMENT:
	Principal & Interest
	Other Financing (P & I)
	Hazard Insurance
	Real Estate Taxes
	Mortgage Insurance
	Homeowner Assn. Dues
	Other
	Total Monthly Payment

These estimates are provided pursuant to the Real Estate Settlement Procedures Act of 1974, as amended (RESPA). Additional information can be found in the HUD Special Information Booklet, which is to be provided to you by your mortgage broker or lender, if your application is to purchase residential real property and the lender will take a first lien on the property. The undersigned acknowledges receipt of the booklet "Settlement Costs," and if applicable the Consumer Handbook on ARM Mortgages.

Applicant Date Applicant Date

Figure 5-2

A. U.S. DEPARTMENT OF HOUSING AND URBAN DEVELOPMENT SETTLEMENT STATEMENT	B. TYPE OF LOAN 1. [ ] FHA 2. [ ] FmHA 3. [X] Conv. unis 4. [ ] VA 5. [ ] Conv. ins 6. ESCROW NUMBER: 1-10533 7. LOAN NUMBER: 8. MORTGAGE INSURANCE NUMBER:

THIS NOTE IS FURNISHED TO GIVE YOU A STATEMENT OF THE ACTUAL SETTLEMENT COSTS. AMOUNTS PAID TO AND BY THE SETTLEMENT AGENT ARE SHOWN. ITEMS MARKED "(P.O.C.)" WERE PAID OUTSIDE OF THE CLOSING; THEY ARE SHOWN HERE FOR INFORMATIONAL PURPOSES AND ARE NOT INCLUDED IN THE TOTALS.

D. NAME OF BORROWER:	E. NAME OF SELLER:	F. NAME OF LENDER:
JOHN BUYER JANE BUYER 123 Purchase Lane Glendale, CA	JOHN SELLER JANE SELLER	GET SMART SAVINGS AND LOAN 123 Lending Lane Beverly Hills, CA 91020

G. PROPERTY LOCATION:	H. SETTLEMENT AGENT: COLONIAL ESCROW, INC.	I. SETTLEMENT DATE:
123 PURCHASE LANE GLENDALE, CA	PLACE OF SETTLEMENT: 601 EAST GLENOAKS BLVD. SUITE 210 GLENDALE, CA 91207 P.O. BOX 433 GLENDALE, CA 91209-0433	06/01/20

J. SUMMARY OF BORROWER'S TRANSACTIONS		K. SUMMARY OF SELLER'S TRANSACTIONS	
100. GROSS AMOUNT DUE FROM BORROWER		**400. GROSS AMOUNT DUE TO SELLER**	
101. CONTRACT SALES PRICE	800,000.00	401. CONTRACT SALES PRICE	800,000.00
102. PERSONAL PROPERTY		402. PERSONAL PROPERTY	
103. SETTL. CHRGS. TO BORROWER (LINE 1400)	10,122.01	403. DEPOSITS	
104.		404.	
105.		405.	
Adjustments: items paid by seller in advance		Adjustments: items paid by seller in advance	
106. CITY/TOWN TAXES		406. CITY/TOWN TAXES	
107. COUNTY TAXES		407. COUNTY TAXES	
108. ASSESSMENTS		408. ASSESSMENTS	
109. TAXES : 06/01/20 TO 07/01/20	666.67	409. TAXES : 06/01/20 TO 07/01/20	666.67
110.		410.	
111.		411.	
112.		412.	
120. GROSS AMOUNT DUE FROM BORROWER	810,788.68	420. GROSS AMOUNT DUE TO SELLER	800,666.67
200. AMOUNTS PAID BY OR IN BEHALF OF BORROWER		**500. REDUCTIONS IN AMOUNT DUE TO SELLER**	
201. DEPOSITS	91,000.00	501. EXCESS DEPOSIT	
202. PRINCIPAL AMOUNT OF NEW LOAN(S)	640,000.00	502. SETTL. CHRGS. TO SELLER (LINE 1400)	54,845.00
203. EXISTING LOAN(S) TAKEN SUBJECT TO		503. EXISTING LOAN(S) TAKEN SUBJECT TO	
204. NEW 2ND TRUST DEED	80,000.00	504. PAYOFF TO MOST SUPERIOR SAVINGS AND L	490,000.00
205.		505. INTEREST FROM 05/01/20 TO 06/01/20	4,161.64
206.		506. FORWARDING FEE	50.00
207.		507. RECONVEYANCE FEE	60.00
208.		508. NEW 2ND TRUST DEED	80,000.00
209.		509.	
Adjustments: Items unpaid by seller		Adjustments: Items unpaid by seller	
210. CITY/TOWN TAXES		510. CITY/TOWN TAXES	
211. COUNTY TAXES		511. COUNTY TAXES	
212. ASSESSMENTS		512. ASSESSMENTS	
213.		513.	
214.		514.	
215.		515.	
216.		516.	
217.		517.	
218.		518.	
219.		519.	
220. TOTAL PAID BY/FOR BORROWER	811,000.00	520. TOTAL REDUCTION AMOUNT DUE SELLER	629,116.64
300. CASH AT SETTLEMENT FROM/TO BORROWER		**600. CASH AT SETTLEMENT TO/FROM SELLER**	
301. Gross amounts due from borrower (line 120)	810,788.68	601. Gross amount due to seller (line 420)	800,666.67
302. Less amounts paid by/for borrower (line 220)	811,000.00	602. Less reductions in amount due seller (line 520)	629,116.64
303. CASH FROM[ ] TO[X] BORROWER	211.32	603. CASH FROM[ ] TO[X] SELLER	171,550.03

- 2 -

L. SETTLEMENT STATEMENT

700. TOTAL SALES/BROKER'S COMMISSION	PAID FROM BORROWER'S FUNDS AT SETTLEMENT	PAID FROM SELLER'S FUNDS AT SETTLEMENT
BASED ON PRICE $ 800,000.00 @ 6.00%		
701. BROKER: J. Q. SMART 48,000.00		
702.		
703.		
704. COMMISSIONS PAID AT SETTLEMENT		48,000.00
800. ITEMS PAYABLE IN CONNECTION WITH LOAN		
801. LOAN FEE	6,400.00	
802. LOAN DISCOUNT		
803. APPRAISAL	350.00	
804. CREDIT REPORT	45.00	
805. LENDER'S INSPECTION FEE		
806. MORTGAGE INSURANCE APPLICATION FEE		
807. ASSUMPTION FEE		
808. TAX SERVICE	89.00	
809. DOCUMENT FEE	250.00	
810.		
811.		
900. ITEMS REQUIRED BY LENDER TO BE PAID IN ADVANCE		
901. INTEREST AT 7.5000% FROM 05/31/20 TO 06/01/20	131.51	
902. MORTGAGE INSURANCE		
903. PROPERTY INSURANCE, INC. FOR FIRE INSURANCE	1,000.00	
904.		
905.		
1000. RESERVES DEPOSITED WITH LENDER		
1001. HAZARD INSURANCE		
1002. MORTGAGE INSURANCE		
1003. CITY PROPERTY TAXES		
1004. COUNTY PROPERTY TAXES		
1005. ANNUAL ASSESSMENTS		
1006.		
1007.		
1008.		
1100. ESCROW AND TITLE CHARGES		
1101. ESCROW FEE TO COLONIAL ESCROW, INC.	900.00	900.00
1102. ABSTRACT OR TITLE SEARCH		
1103. TITLE EXAMINATION		
1104. TITLE INSURANCE BINDER		
1105. DOCUMENT PREPARATION TO COLONIAL ESCROW, INC.		
1106. MESSENGER FEE TO COLONIAL ESCROW, INC.	50.00	
1107. ATTORNEY'S FEES		
1108. TITLE POLICY TO AMERICAN COAST TITLE	628.50	2,165.00
1109. LENDERS COVERAGE $ 640,000.00		
1110. OWNERS COVERAGE $ 800,000.00		
1111. PROCESSING DEMANDS TO COLONIAL ESCROW, INC.		35.00
1112. DOCUMENT FEE TO COLONIAL ESCROW, INC.		85.00
1113. LOAN TIE IN FEE TO COLONIAL ESCROW, INC.	125.00	
1200. GOVERNMENT RECORDING AND TRANSFER CHARGES		
1201. RECORDING FEES: DEED $8.00; MORTGAGE $20.00; RELEASES $5.00	28.00	5.00
1202. DOCUMENTARY TRANSFER TAX		880.00
1203. STATE TAX/STAMPS		
1204.		
1205.		
1300. ADDITIONAL SETTLEMENT CHARGES		
1301. SURVEY		
1302. PEST CONTROL, INC. FOR TERMITE REPORT/WORK		1,000.00
1303. SUB ESCROW FEE TO AMERICAN COAST TITLE	75.00	75.00
1304. TITLE ENDORSEMENT FEE(S) TO AMERICAN COAST TITLE	50.00	
1305. STREET ASSESSMENT BOND TO AMERICAN COAST TITLE		1,300.00
1306. HOME WARRANTY, INC. FOR HOME PROTECTION POLICY		400.00
1307.		
1400. TOTAL SETTLEMENT CHARGES (ENTER ON LINES 103 SECTION J AND 502, SECTION K)	10,122.01	54,845.00

The advent of the Internet has actually been a boon to consumers as major primary lenders have rushed to advertise their rates and charges almost on an hourly basis.

This permits consumers to shop rates and fees between the various lenders. It also serves to make borrowers more familiar with the entire process. Many traditional loan brokers at first believed Internet advertising might have a detrimental effect on their business. Research has shown, however, that there is enough business to go around and that consumers like a familiar person that they can interact with to handle their loans. Informed consumers have lightened the workload of many brokers by familiarizing themselves with the process, fees, and necessary required documentation that they must provide before they arrive at their local loan broker's office to begin the process.

RESPA protects consumers from predatory lending practices.

H. TRUTH IN LENDING ACT (Consumer Credit Protection Act)

The Truth in Lending Act standardized the method of calculating the cost of credit by disclosing the annual percentage rate (APR).

It contains several important provisions that are administered by the Federal Reserve. The Federal Reserve Board of Governors issued Regulation Z to implement the Act. ***REGULATION Z*** *requires that the lender provide the consumer with the total of all finance charges and the Annual Percentage Rate (APR) of the loan* (see **Figure 5-3**). This disclosure must be in writing and be more prominent than other items in the disclosure. This disclosure must be made to the borrower, in writing, within three business days from the time the lender receives the application.

FINANCE CHARGES *include interest charges, discount points, appraisal fees, inspection fees, origination fees, and any credit life or mortgage insurance fees.* The ***ANNUAL PERCENTAGE RATE (APR)*** *is the effective yield on the loan.* It will be higher than the quoted loan rate if upfront charges, such as origination fees and discount points, are included.

To find the best loan, compare APRs and choose the lowest.

Another important borrower right provided by Regulation Z is the ***RIGHT OF RESCISSION (RIGHT TO CANCEL)***, *which means that a borrower may cancel any agreement entered into within three business days after the close of the transaction* (see **Figure 5-4**). A lender is required to inform the consumer of the right to rescind by providing a notice of rescission. This must be in writing and separate from any other sale or credit document. The rescission document must describe the acquisition of the security interest, how the right of rescission is to be exercised, the effects of the rescission, and the date the right of rescission expires. This allows a borrower to back out of any

Figure 5-3

TRUTH-IN-LENDING DISCLOSURE STATEMENT

(THIS IS NEITHER A CONTRACT NOR A COMMITMENT TO LEND)

Applicants: Prepared By:

Property Address:

Application No: Date Prepared:

ANNUAL PERCENTAGE RATE	FINANCE CHARGE	AMOUNT FINANCED	TOTAL OF PAYMENTS
The cost of your credit as a yearly rate	The dollar amount the credit will cost you	The amount of credit provided to you or on your behalf	The amount you will have paid after making all payments as scheduled
%	$	$	$

☐ REQUIRED DEPOSIT: The annual percentage rate does not take into account your required deposit

PAYMENTS: Your payment schedule will be:

Number of Payments	Amount of Payments **	When Payments Are Due	Number of Payments	Amount of Payments **	When Payments Are Due	Number of Payments	Amount of Payments **	When Payments Are Due
		Monthly Beginning:			Monthly Beginning:			Monthly Beginning:

☐ DEMAND FEATURE: This obligation has a demand feature.

☐ VARIABLE RATE FEATURE: This loan contains a variable rate feature. A variable rate disclosure has been provided earlier.

CREDIT LIFE/CREDIT DISABILITY: Credit life insurance and credit disability insurance are not required to obtain credit, and will not be provided unless you sign and agree to pay the additional cost.

Type	Premium	Signature	
Credit Life		I want credit life insurance.	Signature:
Credit Disability		I want credit disability insurance.	Signature:
Credit Life and Disability		I want credit life and disability insurance.	Signature:

INSURANCE: The following insurance is required to obtain credit:

☐ Credit life insurance ☐ Credit disability ☐ Property insurance ☐ Flood insurance

You may obtain the insurance from anyone you want that is acceptable to creditor

☐ If you purchase ☐ property ☐ flood insurance from creditor you will pay $ for a one year term.

SECURITY: You are giving a security interest in:

☐ The goods or property being purchased ☐ Real property you already own.

FILING FEES: $

LATE CHARGE: If a payment is more than days late, you will be charged % of the payment

PREPAYMENT: If you pay off early, you

☐ may ☐ will not have to pay a penalty.

☐ may ☐ will not be entitled to a refund of part of the finance charge.

ASSUMPTION: Someone buying your property

☐ may ☐ may, subject to conditions ☐ may not assume the remainder of your loan on the original terms.

See your contract documents for any additional information about nonpayment, default, any required repayment in full before the scheduled date and prepayment refunds and penalties

☐ * means an estimate ☐ all dates and numerical disclosures except the late payment disclosures are estimates.

* * NOTE: The Payments shown above include reserve deposits for Mortgage Insurance (if applicable), but exclude Property Taxes and Insurance.

THE UNDERSIGNED ACKNOWLEDGES RECEIVING A COMPLETED COPY OF THIS DISCLOSURE.

(Applicant) (Date) (Applicant) (Date)

(Applicant) (Date) (Applicant) (Date)

(Lender) (Date)

Figure 5-4

Notice of Right to Cancel

Name(s) of Customer(s) ______________________________

Type of Loan ______________________________

Amount of Loan ______________________________ $ ______________

You have entered into a transaction which will result in a deed of trust or mortgage on your home. You have a legal right under federal law to cancel this transaction, without cost, within three business days from whichever of the following occurs last:

1. the date of the transaction, which is ______________________________ : or
2. the date you received your Truth in Lending disclosures: or
3. the date you received this notice of your right to cancel.

If you cancel the transaction, the deed of trust or mortgage is also cancelled. Within 20 calendar days after we receive your notice, we must take the steps necessary to reflect the fact that the deed of trust or mortgage on your home has been cancelled, and we must return to you any money or property you have given to us or to anyone else in connection with this transaction.

You may keep any money or property we have given you until we have done the things mentioned above, but you must then offer to return the money or property. If it is impractical or unfair for you to return the property, you must offer its reasonable value. You may offer to return the property at your home or at the location of the property. Money must be returned to the address below. If we do not take possession of the money or property within 20 calendar days of your offer, you may keep it without further obligation.

ACKNOWLEDGEMENT OF RECEIPT

I hereby acknowledge receipt of TWO copies of the foregoing Notice of Right to Cancel.

______________________, 20 ______ (Date)

______________________________ (Customer's Signature)

______________________________ (All joint owners must sign)

HOW TO CANCEL

If you decide to cancel this transaction, you may do so by notifying us in writing, at the following address:

____
(Creditor's Name)

____
(Address)

____
(City, State. Zip Code)

You may use any written statement that is signed and dated by you and states your intention to cancel, or you may use this notice by dating and signing below. Keep one copy of this notice because it contains important information about your rights.

If you cancel by mail or telegram, you must send the notice no later than midnight of ______________________ (date)

(or midnight of the third business day following the latest of the three events listed above). If you send your written notice to cancel some other way, it must be delivered to the above address no later than that time.

______________________,20 ______ (Date)

______________________________ (Customer's Signature)

transaction into which they have either been pressured or have "buyer's remorse" over. The borrower may not waive his or her right of rescission. The right of rescission does not apply to the purchase of any property other than their principal residence.

Business or corporate entities do not qualify for the right of rescission.

Regulation Z also contains provisions that apply to advertising. Prior to passage of the Act, an advertiser might have disclosed only the most attractive credit terms, thus distorting the true costs of the financing.

Regulation Z requires that advertisers disclose all the terms of the financing if the ad contains any information about a single financing term.

These terms include, but are not limited to, the cash price, interest rate, or payment amounts. These are known as ***TRIGGERS***. If any trigger is used, the advertiser must disclose all the terms of the financing. Such information is not allowed to be contained in a "fine print" section of the advertisement (See **Figures 5-5** and **5-6**).

Anyone who places an advertisement for consumer credit must comply with the provisions of the Act; this includes lenders, real estate agents, and builders.

Figure 5-5

(WRONG)

Now
Get A Home
Equity Loan With
No Application Fee,
No Appraisal Fee
And No Points.

(triggering terms)

BUT ONLY UNTIL

If you own a house, a condo, or a co-op, can save you a lot of money on a Home Equity Loan.

There's no application fee. Saving you up to $200.

There's no appraisal cost. Saving you up to $250.

And there are no points at closing for an additional savings.

Also, your Home Equity Loan or Home Equity Line of Credit can be used for almost any purpose and your interest payments may be 100% tax-deductible. (Consult your tax advisor.)

To apply for a loan or to find out how much you can borrow, visit any of our branches. Or call at But do it soon. Offer ends

(required disclosures needed)

All loans are secured by a mortgage on your home and are subject to credit approval
Available through Applications must be received by

Figure 5-6

(CORRECT)

Great Value at Golden Hawk Ridge

The Oakwood is an extraordinary value for a 3-Bedroom 2-bath Executive Home.

Close to major shopping malls, schools, and commuter transportation this development is only minutes away from downtown on I-40. Homes range from 1600 to 2400 square feet and start at $250,000.00.

(proper disclosure) → Typical financing: The Oakwood (at Golden Hawk Ridge) – cash price $250,000, $50,000 down payment (20%) at 6% interest (6.09 annual percentage rate). Mortgage $200,000 to be paid in 360 equal and consecutive monthly payments of $1,218 plus taxes and insurance. We pay all closing costs except prepaid items and loan origination fees.

(triggering term) → Conventional Financing

(proper disclosure of rate of finance charge) → 6% Interest (6.09% Annual Percentage Rate)

II. CHAPTER SUMMARY

The federal government has long taken an active role in assuring that all citizens will be able to enjoy the benefits of property ownership. In addition to support of the capital markets that make real estate loans possible, particular care has been taken to assure that no citizen will be discriminated against on the basis of race, religion, sex, disability, or ethnicity. In addition, the government has sought to curb both abusive and predatory sales and lending practices. The government has required full disclosure throughout the lending process, both to protect consumers and to allow them to be well informed. This legislation has also benefited lenders, as it has rooted out anti-competitive lending practices.

III. TERMINOLOGY

Annual Percentage Rate (APR)
Appraisal Subcommittee
Blockbusting
Census Tract
Civil Rights Act of 1866
Civil Rights Act of 1968
Consumer Credit Protection Act
Community Reinvestment Act
Community Support Statement
Disclosure
Equal Credit Opportunity Act
Federal Fair Housing Act
Financial Institutions Reform, Recovery, and Enforcement Act (FIRREA)
Finance Charges
Good Faith Estimate
Home Mortgage Disclosure Act
Real Estate Settlement Procedures Act (RESPA)
Redlining
Regulation Z
RESPA
Right of Rescission (Right to Cancel)
Standard Metropolitan Statistical Area (SMSA)
Steering
Triggers
Uniform Settlement Statement

IV. CHAPTER QUIZ

1. RESPA is the:
    a. Real Estate Security and Procedures Act.
    b. Real Estate Safety and Practices Act.
    c. Real Estate Settlement and Practices Act.
    d. Real Estate Settlement Procedures Act.

2. The Civil Rights Act of 1866:
    a. requires disclosure.
    b. prevents discrimination in real property ownership.
    c. requires lenders to publish information on loans to minority borrowers.
    d. does not apply to modern lending.

3. Redlining is:
    a. refusal to loan in certain neighborhoods.
    b. marking boundaries of census tracts.
    c. not lending to bad credit consumers.
    d. not lending on insufficient collateral.

4. The Federal Fair Housing Act prohibits acts based on:
    a. blockbusting.
    b. steering.
    c. redlining.
    d. all the above.

5. The Consumer Protection Act:
    a. contains the truth in lending laws.
    b. defines abusive practices.
    c. requires a good-faith estimate.
    d. none of the above.

6. FIRREA applies to:
    a. appraisers only.
    b. lenders only.
    c. everyone involved in a federally related transaction.
    d. regulators only.

7. A Community Support Statement is provided by:
   a. lenders to their local news media.
   b. lenders to the borrower.
   c. lenders to their regulators.
   d. community leaders to the lender.

8. A good faith estimate is:
   a. provided at the end of the loan process.
   b. provided at the beginning of the loan process.
   c. an estimate of the annual percentage rate only.
   d. an estimate of the time it will take to complete the loan.

9. It is illegal to discriminate:
   a. by intent.
   b. by effect.
   c. by practice.
   d. all the above.

10. Regulation Z:
    a. prohibits redlining.
    b. prohibits racial discrimination.
    c. allows a married woman to maintain separate credit.
    d. is overseen by the Federal Reserve Board.

ANSWERS: 1. d; 2. b; 3. a; 4. d; 5. a; 6. c; 7. c; 8. b; 9. d; 10. d

Federal Regulation and Consumer Protection

Chapter 6
State Regulation of Lending

This chapter will examine the role played by state governments in the lending process.

The 10th Amendment to the U.S. Constitution reserved all powers not specifically enumerated (listed) in the Constitution to the states. A read of the Constitution would make apparent to the reader that the states seemed to retain more powers than they gave up.

The U.S. Constitution and the first ten amendments do not specifically address the issues of banking, finance, real estate law, or consumer legislation. In the beginning, Congress was content with the power to coin money and provide a uniform money system through the establishment of the Bank of the United States. As we saw in the last chapter, federal interest in discrimination, consumer rights, and lending did not really begin until after the Civil War. Even then the amount of federal involvement was minor until the era of the great depression and later. It was left up to the states to develop laws that would protect consumers from usury, develop mortgage and real estate laws, and charter local banking institutions.

Chapter 6

CHAPTER OUTLINE

I. Real Estate Laws

The United States was initially made up of a group of former English colonies that had become states within the constitutional union. It is therefore not surprising that they would, for the most part, adopt the British common law systems of legal Real Property and Real Estate ownership. ***REAL ESTATE*** *is the ownership of the physical land itself.* ***REAL PROPERTY*** *consists of those rights that come with the ownership of the real estate.* Very often, real property rights are more valuable than the physical property itself. Real property rights are often stated as:

1. The right to possess.
2. The right to use.
3. The right to borrow money against.
4. The right to rent to others.
5. The right to dispose of (by, sale, will, or transfer).
6. The right to quiet enjoyment.
7. The right to exclude others.
8. The right to do nothing at all.

These real property rights are often referred to as the ***BUNDLE OF RIGHTS****. An individual in control of all those rights is said to own the property in* ***FEE SIMPLE****.* These rights are limited by the power of eminent domain under the Constitution and by zoning laws in most jurisdictions. As our pioneering ancestors spread outward into the territories, they brought this imminently sensible system of ownership with them. This is the system of land and real property ownership throughout the United States, with only minor variations from state to state.

A. ESTATES

An ***ESTATE*** *is a possessory interest in real estate or real property.*

"Fee simple" is the highest form of possessory interest.

There are several estates that have less than the full possessory rights. The most important of these is the ***LEASED FEE ESTATE****, which is the interest held by a landlord.* In essence, a landlord has given up his right of possession to the property to a tenant for a specified period. Both the right to the rents and the right to the ***REVERSION*** *(return of the property)* at the end of the lease may be sold or lent upon. Additionally, *the tenant's possessory interest, called the* ***LEASEHOLD ESTATE****,* may also have loan or sale value, particularly if the tenant's rents are below market. This could easily happen in the case of a long-term lease. While the various states and territories of the United States recognize a number of other forms of ownership estates, they are, for the most part, beyond the scope of this book.

B. DEEDS

***TITLE** is a term that signifies the proof of ownership*. The title to a property is based on the legal chain of documents that show ownership interests and transfers from owner to owner. *Title to real estate and real property is transferred from one person to another by use of a legal document called a* **DEED**. *The owner who is making the transfer is called the* **GRANTOR**. *The person receiving title is called the* **GRANTEE**. A deed must be in writing in all jurisdictions and must meet all requirements of the state in which the property is located.

Originally, title was researched and individual deeds were drawn up by attorneys. Over time, and with the advent of title insurance, this practice has been reduced somewhat. ***TITLE INSURANCE** is insurance written by a title company to protect the property owner against loss if the title is imperfect*. Individual deeds, however, are still widely used today in the east and the south. The acceptance of preprinted legal form deeds by many states has also served to reduce the need for the services of attorneys.

The advantage of title insurance is that it also protects against hidden or unknown claims against title.

The use of title insurance is required for any loan that is sold into the secondary market. Title companies are supervised by agencies of the states in which they operate.

1. General Warranty Deeds

In most states, general warranty deeds are the most commonly used deeds in real estate transactions.

A ***GENERAL WARRANTY DEED** offers the most complete warranty regarding the quality of the title. The grantor warrants that the title he or she is conveying is free and clear of all claims except those specifically listed in the deed*. Specifically, the deed will guarantee free and clear legal title to the property, that the grantor has the right to convey the property, and that the grantor will compensate the grantee for loss of property or eviction if it is discovered that someone else has any claim to the property.

A general warranty deed covers all transfers of the property from the original source of title to the present.

2. Special Warranty Deeds

A ***SPECIAL WARRANTY DEED** makes the same warranties as a general warranty deed except it limits the application of defects to the title to those discovered while under ownership of the grantor*. It does not apply to title problems caused by owners previous to the current grantor.

3. Grant Deeds

The grant deed is very popular in the western states.

A ***GRANT DEED*** *transfers absolute legal title to a property.* It is sometimes called a "naked title deed" (see **Figure 6-1**). A grant deed carries only two implied warranties: 1) that the grantor has not transferred title to anyone else at the same time, and 2) that the grantor is transferring the estate free of any encumbrances made by the grantor other than those disclosed to the grantee. The interesting thing about this form of transfer is that the deed does not state that the grantor is the owner of the property or that the property is not encumbered by debt or liens not made by the grantor. It merely implies that the grantor has not made a deed to others and that the grantor has not encumbered the property with debt or liens. As a result, it is absolutely necessary to obtain a policy of title insurance at the time of any transfer. However, the beneficial result is that the title insurance company carries the full legal liability for any title claims against the property rather than the grantor, grantee, or previous owners.

4. Quitclaim Deed

The ***QUITCLAIM DEED*** *is most often used to remove items from the public record, such as easements or recorded restrictions. It merely says that the grantor is relinquishing any interest that he or she has in the property* (see **Figure 6-2**).

A quitclaim deed contains no warranties, written or implied.

5. Gift Deed

A ***GIFT DEED*** *is often used to transfer real estate to children or other loved ones.* Generally, no monetary legal consideration is required to transfer the property.

A gift deed can be invalidated if it is discovered that it was used to defraud creditors.

6. Sheriff's Deed/Commissioner's Deed

A ***SHERIFF'S DEED*** *is used to transfer property that has been ordered to be sold by a court of law.* This can happen as a result of a monetary judgment against the owner. The property is then sold by the court to satisfy the judgment. In some states this is known as a commissioner's sale and a commissioner's deed.

A sheriff's deed or commissioner's deed carries no warranties.

Figure 6-1

RECORDING REQUESTED BY

AND WHEN RECORDED MAIL DOCUMENT AND TAX STATEMENT TO:

NAME

STREET ADDRESS

CITY, STATE & ZIP CODE

TITLE ORDER NO. ____________

ESCROW NO. ____________

S	R	U	PAGE	SIZE	DA	MISC	LONG	RFD	COPY
M	A	L	465	426	PCOR	NCOR	SMF	NCHG	EXAM
					T:		CTY	UNI	

SPACE ABOVE THIS LINE FOR RECORDER'S USE ONLY

GRANT DEED

TRA: ____________

APN: ____________

The undersigned grantor(s) declare(s)
DOCUMENTARY TRANSFER TAX $ ____________
☐ computed on full value of property conveyed, or
☐ computed on full value less liens and encumbrances remaining at time of sale.
☐ Unincorporated Area City of ____________

FOR VALUABLE CONSIDERATION, receipt of which is hereby acknowledged, I (We) ____________

(NAME OF GRANTOR(S))

hereby remise, release and grant to ____________

(NAME OF GRANTEE(S))

the following described real property in the City of ____________, County of ____________,

State of ____________.

(Insert Legal Description)

DATED: ____________

STATE OF CALIFORNIA }
COUNTY OF ____________ }

On ____________ before me, ____________ personally appeared
(here insert name and title of the officer)

____________,
who proved to me on the basis of satisfactory evidence to be the person(s) whose name(s) is/are subscribed to the within instrument and acknowledged to me that he/she/they executed the same in his/her/their authorized capacity(ies), and that by his/her/their signature(s) on the instrument the person(s), or the entity upon behalf of which the person(s) acted, executed the instrument.

I certify under PENALTY OF PERJURY under the laws of the State of California that the foregoing paragraph is true and correct.

WITNESS my hand and official seal.

Signature ____________ (SEAL)

MAIL TAX STATEMENT AS DIRECTED ABOVE

Figure 6-2

RECORDING REQUESTED BY

AND WHEN RECORDED MAIL DOCUMENT AND TAX STATEMENT TO:

NAME

STREET ADDRESS

CITY, STATE & ZIP CODE

TITLE ORDER NO. ____________

ESCROW NO. ____________

S	R	U	PAGE	SIZE	DA	MISC	LONG	RFD	COPY
M	A	L	465	426	PCOR	NCOR	SMF	NCHG	EXAM
						T:	CTY	UNI	

SPACE ABOVE THIS LINE FOR RECORDER'S USE ONLY

QUITCLAIM DEED

TRA: ____________

APN: ____________

The undersigned grantor(s) declare(s)
DOCUMENTARY TRANSFER TAX $ ____________
☐ computed on full value of property conveyed, or
☐ computed on full value less liens and encumbrances remaining at time of sale.
☐ Unincorporated Area City of ____________

FOR VALUABLE CONSIDERATION, receipt of which is hereby acknowledged, I (We) ____________

____
(NAME OF GRANTOR(S))

hereby remise, release and quitclaim to ____________

____
(NAME OF GRANTEE(S))

the following described real property in the City of ____________, County of ____________, State of ____________.

(Insert Legal Description)

DATED: ____________ ____________

____

STATE OF CALIFORNIA
COUNTY OF ____________

On ____________ before me, ____________, personally appeared
(here insert name and title of the officer)

____________,
who proved to me on the basis of satisfactory evidence to be the person(s) whose name(s) is/are subscribed to the within instrument and acknowledged to me that he/she/they executed the same in his/her/their authorized capacity(ies), and that by his/her/their signature(s) on the instrument the person(s), or the entity upon behalf of which the person(s) acted, executed the instrument.

I certify under PENALTY OF PERJURY under the laws of the State of California that the foregoing paragraph is true and correct.

WITNESS my hand and official seal.

Signature ____________ (SEAL)

MAIL TAX STATEMENT AS DIRECTED ABOVE

7. Tax Deed

A ***TAX DEED*** *is issued by a tax collector after the sale of property that has been seized by the state, county, or local municipality for nonpayment of taxes due.* Again, no warranty of the deed is expressed or implied.

8. Deed of Trust/Deed of Reconveyance

These deeds are types of financing instruments and will be discussed in Chapter 7.

All states have laws that require legal delivery of a deed from the grantor to the grantee.

In general, all states have laws that will invalidate a deed if the grantor is incompetent at the time the deed is made, if the deed is never delivered, or if the deed is a forgery or fraudulently altered. Case law in each state prescribes how the validity of a deed is determined and what other provisions may apply to property transfers.

C. MORTGAGES

A ***MORTGAGE*** *is a legal document that pledges the property of the borrower to a lender as security for a loan (lien).* This, again, was an area that was originally the exclusive domain of attorneys. While attorneys are still engaged in drawing up some mortgages, the advent of preprinted legal forms for residential transactions has served to lessen the involvement of attorneys in this area. Mortgage law has traditionally been within the jurisdiction of state law. To be valid, a mortgage must meet the requirements of the state in which it is drawn up. The federal government, as we have seen, has become more involved in the field of mortgage lending in the past century and has acted to preempt certain state laws. The federal government has overturned state laws restricting the "due on sale" clause, some usury laws, established conditions that allow prepayment of mortgages, and set ceilings on prepayment penalties.

D. RECORDING

All the states have enacted laws known as recording acts. These vary by individual state.

The general intent of recording is to create a publicly available record that establishes the chain of ownership of any individual property.

These laws were enacted to protect the claims of owners and to protect prospective purchasers. Virtually all states require recording to protect an ownership claim. The places and methods of recordation vary from state to state.

E. STATE-CHARTED BANKS

As we saw in Chapter 1, banking in general was unregulated in the early nation, with the exception of the establishment of the Bank of the United States. The states established banking laws and regulations at a very early period to protect the public. While state laws still govern state-chartered institutions, the effect of their regulation has been tempered by the fact that most real estate lending is now governed by federal laws and regulations.

F. USURY LAWS

Beginning in the 1830s, many states, in an effort to limit predatory lending practices, passed laws to limit the interest charges that individual lenders and banks operating within their states could charge a borrower, called **USURY LAWS**. The implementation and enforcement of these laws would become very popular nearly a century later during the Great Depression. The laws were designed to protect consumers from grossly unfair interest rates charged by lenders. Lenders argued that in many cases such state-regulated rates were set at levels that made lending impossible during times of high interest rates. The lenders found a sympathetic ear in the federal government, at least in the case of real estate loans.

To insure that the system works smoothly and provides reasonable rates to all, the federal courts overturned many state usury laws, or at least those sections dealing with federally related real estate transactions. Most states still have usury laws that deal with other types of consumer credit.

II. The Rise of Federalism

Over the last century, the federal government has gradually extended its control of lending within the United States.

Federal authorities have virtually taken over the entire banking system. Many real estate loans are now subject to federal loan guarantees. This makes the loans subject to federal regulation. The federal government has also entered the domain of consumer law. This has been carried out by utilizing laws that were designed to prohibit discrimination and were themselves based on the 13th, 14th, and 15th Amendments to the U.S. Constitution. The beneficial effect has been that the process of the law in the nation has become more uniform and the lending system has been protected.

The adverse effect of federal regulation has been that federal incursion has come at the expense of the states and property owners.

The demise of usury laws has created a system in which the federal government sets interest rates. The passage of the **Garn-St. Germain Act** in 1982 set the stage for the

enforcement of the due-on-sale clause. A ***DUE-ON-SALE CLAUSE*** *in a mortgage allows the lender to demand payment in full if the property is sold*. It also means that many real estate loans are not assumable. An ***ASSUMABLE LOAN*** *allows the owner to take a down payment for his equity and permits the purchaser to assume the current loan on the property*. Lenders are perfectly willing in times of low rates to allow a new borrower to assume a loan, particularly if the rate on the loan is the same or higher than the current market rates. However, if the rate is below current market, they want the power to force the buyer to have to make a new loan at a new higher rate. The problem with this is that often the buyer will not qualify for the new rate and the sale is lost. When sales are lost, the market declines and so do home prices. As home prices decline, more loan defaults take place and the lenders lose money. Before 1982, many states had prohibitions on the due-on-sale clause.

The effect of the Garn-St. Germaine Bill was to transfer a part of a property owner's rights to the lenders.

III. The Modern Role of the States

The modern role of the state remains that of a protector of the interests of its citizens.

States still control deeds and recording laws. In addition, they regulate appraisers, real estate agents, and loan brokers. In the areas of anti-discrimination, consumer law, and anti-redlining, many state laws are actually more severe than federal law. Also, many states have **state lending agencies**.

The state lending agencies provide state financial assistance at two levels. The first level consists of loans to communities to attract new business to an area and the second level consists of loans to improve housing in local communities. Some states and local communities also have special low-interest loan programs for veterans, teachers, and other professionals that allow the state or community to attract and retain people in designated fields. Further information about some of these programs may be found in Chapters 17 and 18.

IV. CHAPTER SUMMARY

The 10th Amendment to the U.S. Constitution reserves all powers to the states that are not specifically given to the federal government. As a result, the states have regulated by law the form and manner of property ownership, as well as the documentation required for ownership. This law was, for the most part, based on English Common Law and was adopted in each new territory throughout the United States during the past two centuries. The highest and most common form of property ownership is fee simple, which has with it a bundle of rights. This bundle of rights consists of real property rights.

Title to real estate is generally transferred by a deed. The most common form of deed used in the United States is the general warranty deed. This form of deed is the most comprehensive and assures a grantee (buyer) that the title to the property is free and clear and that the warranty extends back through the entire chain of ownership. In the western states, the grant deed is popular. This deed, when used in conjunction with title insurance, shifts any title liability to the title insurance company.

States have also carried out the very important function of publicly recording all documents relating to real estate, such as deeds and mortgages. While federal lending laws have, in some cases, adversely impacted a state's ability to regulate real estate lending, the states have retained their role as regulators of agents, brokers, and appraisers.

V. TERMINOLOGY

Assumable Loan
Bundle of Rights
Deed
Due-on-Sale Clause
Estate
Fee Simple
Garn-St. Germaine Act
General Warranty Deed
Gift Deed
Grant Deed
Grantee
Grantor
Leased Fee Estate
Leasehold Estate
Mortgage
Real Estate
Real Property
Recording Acts
Reversion
Special Warranty Deed
Title
Usury Laws

VI. CHAPTER QUIZ

1. A grantor is:
    a. one who sells or transfers property.
    b. one who receives property by deed.
    c. an agency that guarantees title.
    d. none of the above.

2. A Special Warranty Deed:
    a. warranties the title for the entire chain of ownership.
    b. does not carry any warranty of title by the grantor.
    c. warranties the title only for actions of the grantor.
    d. warranties actions of the grantee.

3. A landlord holds title in:
    a. fee simple estate.
    b. leasehold estate.
    c. leased fee estate.
    d. life estate.

4. The return of property to the landlord at the end of a lease is called a:
    a. reversion.
    b. release.
    c. transfer.
    d. none of the above.

5. A grant deed is also called:
    a. a special warranty deed.
    b. a title deed.
    c. a nonwarranted deed.
    d. a naked title deed.

6. Real property is:
    a. the physical land only.
    b. the rights of property ownership.
    c. tangible.
    d. none of the above.

7. The constitutional amendment that reserves all powers not granted to the federal government to the states is the:

   a. 10th amendment.
   b. 11th amendment.
   c. 12th amendment.
   d. 13th amendment.

8. An estate is a:

   a. form of ownership interest.
   b. type of deed.
   c. type of mortgage.
   d. type of sales contract.

9. The most common form of deed in the U.S. is the:

   a. General Warranty deed.
   b. Special Warranty Deed.
   c. Grant Deed.
   d. Quitclaim Deed.

10. A lender's right to limit or deny a buyer's ability to assume a loan is called:

   a. the Garn-St. Germaine Bill.
   b. the due-on-sale clause.
   c. a trust deed.
   d. a special warranty deed.

ANSWERS: *1. a; 2. c; 3. c; 4. a; 5. d; 6. b; 7. a; 8. a; 9. a; 10. b*

SEARS SAVINGS BANK

GLENDALE PLAZA BRANCH

HOURS
MONDAY-THURSDAY
9:00 TO 4:00
FRIDAY
9:00 TO 6:00

NO SOLICITING

MEMBER
FSLIC

A MEMBER OF THE
SEARS FINANCIAL NETWORK

– Part III –

Chapters 7, 8, and 9
How the Loan Process Works

Chapter 7 – Finance Instruments

Instruments of real estate finance are documents that provide evidence of debt and give the lender the right to proceed against the collateral property if the borrower defaults on the loan. The promissory note is the basic instrument of debt. Mortgages, deeds of trust, and real estate contracts give the lender or seller the right to foreclose against or repossess the property if the buyer defaults. The deed of trust provides a speedier method of foreclosure than does a mortgage.

Chapter 8 – Overview of the Loan Process

The loan process consists of four general steps. By supplying all the necessary data the lender needs, the borrower can ensure a much smoother loan process for all concerned.

Chapter 9 – Conventional Financing

The majority of conventional loans are fixed-rate, fully amortized 30-year loans. However, 15-year loans have been gaining in popularity because of the significant savings in interest payments. Also, loans may be fully amortized, partially amortized, or interest only with a balloon payment.

Chapter 7
Finance Instruments

This chapter on real estate finance instruments is an introduction to the contents and operation of these instruments. It is not intended as a substitute for competent professional advice and it should not be used as the basis for personal action, or to advise clients or customers regarding the operation of particular documents. The laws governing creditor-debtor relations are subject to change by judicial or legislative action. Therefore, it is advisable to consult an attorney for current, local advice concerning the effect of these instruments in any particular transaction.

The "instruments" that will be discussed in this chapter are written documents.

Written agreements are an integral part of most real estate financing transactions.

This chapter will discuss promissory notes, mortgages, deeds of trust (or trust deeds), real estate contracts, and some of the more common and, for the real estate practitioner, more significant clauses found in these documents.

Chapter 7

CHAPTER OUTLINE

I. Promissory Notes

Before a lender will finance the purchase of a house, the borrower must promise to repay the funds. That promise is put in writing in the form of a promissory note (see **Figure 7-1**). A ***PROMISSORY NOTE*** *is a written promise to pay money. The one promising to pay the money is called the **MAKER** of the note.* Usually, the maker is the homebuyer. *The one promised payment is called the **PAYEE**.* Usually, the payee is either a lender (if the purchaser has borrowed money from a bank or other lender to buy the property) or a seller (if the seller is financing the transaction in whole or in part by taking back a promissory note and mortgage or deed of trust).

The promissory note is the basic evidence of debt: it shows who owes how much money to whom.

Promissory notes are usually brief and simple documents. They normally are less than a page long and state:

1. the names of the parties,
2. the amount of the debt,
3. how and when the money is to be paid,
4. whether there is an acceleration clause (discussed below),
5. the payee's remedies if the money is not properly repaid, and
6. the signature of the maker.

Other provisions of the financing agreement between the debtor (maker or buyer) and the creditor (payee or lender/seller) are found in the mortgage or deed of trust.

A. NEGOTIABLE INSTRUMENTS

Virtually all promissory notes used in real estate financing are negotiable instruments.

NEGOTIABLE INSTRUMENTS *are promissory notes that are freely transferable.* ***FREELY TRANSFERABLE*** *means a bank or other creditor can sell the note and obtain immediate cash.* The sale is usually made at a discount, meaning the note is sold for a cash amount that is less than the face value of the note. The **Uniform Commercial Code (UCC)**, which governs negotiable instruments, defines a **negotiable instrument** as a written, unconditional promise or order to pay a certain sum of money, either on a certain date or on demand, payable either to order or to bearer, and signed by the maker.

The promissory note is almost always accompanied by a security instrument. A ***SECURITY INSTRUMENT*** *gives the creditor the right to have the security property sold to satisfy the debt if the debtor fails to pay the debt according to the terms of the agreement.* The

Figure 7-1

NOTE

...., 19.........   ...., ...
[City]   [State]

....
[Property Address]

1. BORROWER'S PROMISE TO PAY

In return for a loan that I have received, I promise to pay U.S. $.................... (this amount is called "principal"), plus interest, to the order of the Lender. The Lender is................................' Savings and Loan Association I understand that the Lender may transfer this Note. The Lender or anyone who takes this Note by transfer and who is entitled to receive payments under this Note is called the "Note Holder".

2. INTEREST

Interest will be charged on unpaid principal until the full amount of principal has been paid. I will pay interest at a yearly rate of..........................%.

The interest rate required by this Section 2 is the rate I will pay both before and after any default described in Section 6(B) of this Note.

3. PAYMENTS

(A) Time and Place of Payments

I will pay principal and interest by making payments every month.

I will make my monthly payments on the 1st day of each month beginning on .... 20........ I will make these payments every month until I have paid all of the principal and interest and any other charges described below that I may owe under this Note. My monthly payments will be applied to interest before principal. If, on .... I still owe amounts under this Note, I will pay those amounts in full on that date, which is called the "maturity date".

I will make my monthly payments at .... or at a different place if required by the Note Holder.

(B) Amount of Monthly Payments

My monthly payment will be in the amount of U.S. $..

4. BORROWER'S RIGHT TO PREPAY

I have the right to make payments of principal at any time before they are due. A payment of principal only is known as a "prepayment." When I make a prepayment, I will tell the Note Holder in writing that I am doing so.

I may make a full prepayment or partial prepayments without paying any prepayment charge. The Note Holder will use all of my prepayments to reduce the amount of principal that I owe under this Note. If I make a partial prepayment, there will be no changes in the due date or in the amount of my monthly payment unless the Note Holder agrees in writing to those changes.

5. LOAN CHARGES

If a law, which applies to this loan and which sets maximum loan charges, is finally interpreted so that the interest or other loan charges collected or to be collected in connection with this loan exceed the permitted limits, then: (i) any such loan charge shall be reduced by the amount necessary to reduce the charge to the permitted limit; and (ii) any sums already collected from me which exceeded permitted limits will be refunded to me. The Note Holder may choose to make this refund by reducing the principal I owe under this Note or by making a direct payment to me. If a refund reduces principal, the reduction will be treated as a partial prepayment.

6. BORROWER'S FAILURE TO PAY AS REQUIRED

(A) Late Charge for Overdue Payments

If the Note Holder has not received full amount of any monthly payment by the end of the 16th calendar day after the date it is due, I will pay a late charge to the Note Holder. The amount of the charge will be 5% of my overdue payment of principal and interest. I will pay this late charge promptly but only once on each late payment.

(B) Default

If I do not pay the full amount of each monthly payment on the date it is due, I will be in default.

(C) Notice of Default

If I am in default, the Note Holder may send me a written notice telling me that if I do not pay the overdue amount by a certain date, the Note Holder may require me to pay immediately the full amount of principal which has not been paid and all the interest that I owe on that amount. That date must be at least 30 days after the date on which the notice is delivered or mailed to me.

(D) No Waiver By Note Holder

Even if, at a time when I am in default, the Note Holder does not require me to pay immediately in full as described above, the Note Holder will still have the right to do so if I am in default at a later time.

(E) Payment of Note Holder's Costs and Expenses

If the Note Holder has required me to pay immediately in full as described above, the Note Holder will have the right to be paid back by me for all of its costs and expenses in enforcing this Note to the extent not prohibited by applicable law. Those expenses include, for example, reasonable attorneys' fees.

7. GIVING OF NOTICES

Unless applicable law requires a different method, any notice that must be given to me under this Note will be given by delivering it or by mailing it by first class mail to me at the Property Address above or at a different address if I give the Note Holder a notice of my different address.

Any notice that must be given to the Note Holder under this Note will be given by mailing it by first class mail to the Note Holder at the address stated in Section 3(A) above or at a different address if I am given a notice of that different address.

MULTISTATE FIXED RATE NOTE—Single Family—**FNMA/FHLMC UNIFORM INSTRUMENT**

8. OBLIGATIONS OF PERSONS UNDER THIS NOTE

If more than one person signs this Note, each person is fully and personally obligated to keep all of the promises made in this Note, including the promise to pay the full amount owed. Any person who is a guarantor, surety or endorser of this Note is also obligated to do these things. Any person who takes over these obligations, including the obligations of a guarantor, surety or endorser of this Note, is also obligated to keep all of the promises made in this Note. The Note Holder may enforce its rights under this Note against each person individually or against all of us together. This means that any one of us may be required to pay all of the amounts owed under this Note.

9. WAIVERS

I and any other person who has obligations under this Note waive the rights of presentment and notice of dishonor. "Presentment" means the right to require the Note Holder to demand payment of amounts due. "Notice of dishonor" means the right to require the Note Holder to give notice to other persons that amounts due have not been paid.

10. UNIFORM SECURED NOTE

This Note is a uniform instrument with limited variations in some jurisdictions. In addition to the protections given to the Note Holder under this Note, a Mortgage, Deed of Trust or Security Deed (the "Security Instrument"), dated the same date as this Note, protects the Note Holder from possible losses which might result if I do not keep the promises which I make in this Note. That Security Instrument describes how and under what conditions I may be required to make immediate payment in full of all amounts I owe under this Note. Some of those conditions are described as follows:

> **Transfer of the Property or a Beneficial Interest in Borrower.** If all or any part of the Property or any interest in it is sold or transferred (or if a beneficial interest in Borrower is sold or transferred and Borrower is not a natural person) without Lender's prior written consent, Lender may, at its option, require immediate payment in full of all sums secured by this Security Instrument. However, this option shall not be exercised by Lender if exercise is prohibited by federal law as of the date of this Security Instrument.
>
> If Lender exercises this option, Lender shall give Borrower notice of acceleration. The notice shall provide a period of not less than 30 days from the date the notice is delivered or mailed within which Borrower must pay all sums secured by this Security Instrument. If Borrower fails to pay these sums prior to the expiration of this period, Lender may invoke any remedies permitted by this Security Instrument without further notice or demand on Borrower.

WITNESS THE HAND(S) AND SEAL(S) OF THE UNDERSIGNED.

....(Seal)
-Borrower

....(Seal)
-Borrower

....(Seal)
-Borrower

[Sign Original Only]

security instrument may be either a deed of trust or a mortgage. The relative rights of the creditor and debtor under these security instruments vary according to whether it is a deed of trust or a mortgage. The next two sections of this chapter will cover deeds of trust and mortgages, the rights of the parties, the methods of foreclosure, and the advantages and disadvantages of the two documents.

II. The Deed of Trust (Trust Deed)

The *DEED OF TRUST (or TRUST DEED) is a commonly used security device in the western United States to finance real estate. It is a three-party device. The borrower is called the **GRANTOR** or **TRUSTOR**; the lender is called the **BENEFICIARY**, and there is an independent third party, the **TRUSTEE**.* The trust deed was originally designed to convey naked title (legal title with no rights to possession) to the trustee throughout the period of indebtedness. *In some states, called **TITLE THEORY STATES**, the trust deed still conveys title. In most states, called **LIEN THEORY STATES**, the deed of trust creates a lien against the property in favor of the beneficiary.*

The deed of trust (lien) gives the creditor the right to force the sale of the property if the debtor defaults on the obligations under the promissory note or the trust deed.

A. REQUIREMENTS FOR A VALID TRUST DEED

To be valid, a deed of trust must contain certain provisions. These include:

1. A statement pledging the property as collateral for a debt (a granting clause).
2. A complete and unambiguous property description.
3. The amount of the debt.
4. The maturity date of the debt.
5. A defeasance clause (stating that the trust deed will be cancelled when the debt is paid).
6. A power-of-sale clause.

When the debt is paid in full, the beneficiary directs the trustee to reconvey the title to the trustor (maker). The trustee releases the lien of the trust deed by signing and recording a deed of reconveyance. A *DEED OF RECONVEYANCE returns full title to the maker (trustor) of the debt.*

When a beneficiary fails to release a trustor in a timely manner, the beneficiary is liable in an action for damages and subject to statutory penalties.

The first page of a standard deed of trust is shown in **Figure 7-2**. Most lenders use this standard FNMA/FHLMC trust deed form so the loan will be easily salable to these agencies. If FNMA or FHLMC had to carefully inspect the provisions of each individual deed of trust they purchase, it would be an impractical, time-consuming process. When all lenders use a standard form, secondary investors can be assured of receiving a deed of trust with acceptable provisions.

B. FORECLOSURE

A deed of trust allows the beneficiary to foreclose the lien without the burden of bringing a legal action. This is called a ***NONJUDICIAL FORECLOSURE**, which is foreclosure without having to go to court.*

C. POWER OF SALE

The deed of trust contains a power-of-sale clause that authorizes the trustee to sell the property without court supervision if the debtor defaults. A typical power-of-sale clause might read as follows:

If the default is not cured on or before the date specified in the notice, lender, at its option, may require immediate payment in full of all sums secured by this security instrument without further demand and may invoke the power of sale. If lender invokes the power of sale, lender shall execute or cause trustee to execute a written notice of the occurrence of an event of default and of lenders election to cause the property to be sold.

D. TRUSTEE'S SALE

*At the direction of the beneficiary, the trustee conducts an out-of-court sale, or auction, called a **TRUSTEE'S SALE**.* The proceeds from the sale are used to pay off the trustor's debt.

However, before the trustee can sell the property, certain legal requirements must be met. First, the beneficiary (lender) prepares a document called the **Declaration of Default**, requesting the trustee to begin the foreclosure proceedings. The trustee then prepares a **Notice of Default and Election to Sell**, which is sent to the borrower. The trustee also notifies anyone who has subsequently recorded a request for notice of default and sale. The trustee is required to provide notice to all lien holders.

The borrower can prevent the sale of the property by reinstating the loan. A loan is reinstated by paying all past due installments, plus late charges, interest, and other costs.

A borrower may reinstate the loan at any time from the notice of default until five business days before the sale date.

Figure 7-2

_____________ [Space Above This Line For Recording Data] _____________

DEED OF TRUST

THIS DEED OF TRUST ("Security Instrument") is made on ...., 20.......... The trustor is .... ("Borrower"). The trustee is .... ("Trustee"). The beneficiary is ...., which is organized and existing under the laws of ...., and whose address is .... ("Lender"). Borrower owes Lender the principal sum of .... Dollars (U.S. $..................................). This debt is evidenced by Borrower's note dated the same date as this Security Instrument ("Note"), which provides for monthly payments, with the full debt, if not paid earlier, due and payable on .... This Security Instrument secures to Lender: (a) the repayment of the debt evidenced by the Note, with interest, and all renewals, extensions and modifications; (b) the payment of all other sums, with interest, advanced under paragraph 7 to protect the security of this Security Instrument; and (c) the performance of Borrower's covenants and agreements under this Security Instrument and the Note. For this purpose, Borrower irrevocably grants and conveys to Trustee, in trust, with power of sale, the following described property located in .... County, California:

which has the address of ...., ...
[Street] [City]

California .... ("Property Address");
[Zip Code]

TOGETHER WITH all the improvements now or hereafter erected on the property, and all easements, rights, appurtenances, rents, royalties, mineral, oil and gas rights and profits, water rights and stock and all fixtures now or hereafter a part of the property. All replacements and additions shall also be covered by this Security Instrument. All of the foregoing is referred to in this Security Instrument as the "Property."

BORROWER COVENANTS that Borrower is lawfully seised of the estate hereby conveyed and has the right to grant and convey the Property and that the Property is unencumbered, except for encumbrances of record. Borrower warrants and will defend generally the title to the Property against all claims and demands, subject to any encumbrances of record.

THIS SECURITY INSTRUMENT combines uniform covenants for national use and non-uniform covenants with limited variations by jurisdiction to constitute a uniform security instrument covering real property.

CALIFORNIA—Single Family—FNMA/FHLMC UNIFORM INSTRUMENT Form 3005 12/83

To see the full document, go to www.efannie.com and search for form 3005.

If the loan is not reinstated within three months of the notice of default, the trustee publishes a Notice of Sale of the property in a newspaper of general circulation. A ***NOTICE OF SALE*** *warns not only the borrower, but also other lien holders that the property is being sold to recover the monies owed against it.* The notice must appear weekly and the sale cannot take place until at least 20 days have elapsed from the first date of publication. Additionally, a notice of sale must be sent to the borrower and posted on the property.

At the sale (usually a public auction), any person, including the debtor or creditor, may bid. The trustee can reject any or all inadequate bids and can postpone the sale if there are no acceptable bids. Otherwise, the sale is made to the highest bidder. The purchaser receives a ***TRUSTEE'S DEED****, which eliminates all liens junior to the trust deed being foreclosed, and any interest the debtor had in the property.* The trustee applies the sale proceeds in the following order:

1. To pay the trustee's costs and sale expenses.
2. To satisfy the beneficiary's debt.
3. To junior lien holders in order of priority.
4. To the debtor, if any surplus.

The entire process of selling property through the power of sale clause in a deed of trust may be accomplished in well under a year, without the expenses involved in court proceedings. There are, of course, expenses connected with a trustee's sale, but these are usually substantially less than those connected with a court-ordered sheriff's sale.

The relative speed and economy of the trustee's sale has caused trust deeds to all but replace mortgages in many states.

Because no court is involved in the trust deed foreclosure process, it is impossible to obtain a deficiency judgment in a trustee's sale.

A deficiency judgment may only be granted by a court of law. The courts are not involved in the trustee's sale process.

If the sale of the property fails to cover the debt, the beneficiary cannot then sue the debtor for the remainder. He or she must be satisfied with the proceeds of the trustee's sale. However, it is possible to foreclose a deed of trust like a mortgage, whereby all the procedures and rights relating to mortgages are applicable.

E. ADVANTAGES AND DISADVANTAGES OF THE TRUST DEED

For the creditor, the primary advantage of the deed of trust is the quick and inexpensive nonjudicial sale process, with no post-sale right of redemption for the borrower. The primary disadvantage is that a deficiency judgment is unobtainable after a nonjudicial foreclosure.

From the borrower's point of view, the protection against deficiency judgements is probably the main advantage of the trust deed. The speed of the process, the lack of judicial supervision, and the lack of redemption rights following the trustee's sale are all disadvantages for the borrower.

III. Mortgages

A ***MORTGAGE*** *is a two-party instrument in which the borrower (called the* ***MORTGAGOR****) mortgages his or her property to the lender (called the* ***MORTGAGEE****) as security for the repayment of the loan.*

For the most part, lenders prefer the deed of trust to the mortgage.

A. FORECLOSURE

A foreclosure under a mortgage requires a court-ordered sale conducted by the sheriff or other court-appointed official. This type of foreclosure process is called ***JUDICIAL FORECLOSURE***. In the event of default, the mortgagee accelerates the due date of the debt to the present and notifies the defaulting debtor to pay off the entire outstanding balance at once. *If the debtor fails to do so, the mortgagee initiates a lawsuit, called a* ***FORECLOSURE ACTION****, in the county where the land is located*. The purpose of this legal proceeding is to get a judge to order the county sheriff to seize and sell the property. *The judge's order is called an* ***ORDER OF EXECUTION***. Acting under the order of execution, the sheriff notifies the public of the place and date of the sale. This requires posting notices at the property and the courthouse and running an advertisement of the sale in a newspaper circulated in the county. This process takes several weeks.

1. Redemption

At any time up until the sheriff's sale, the debtor may save the property by paying the mortgagee what is due. *This right to save or redeem the property before the sale is called the* ***EQUITABLE RIGHT OF REDEMPTION***. The debtor may also be obligated to pay delinquent interest, court costs, attorney's fees, and sheriff's fees in order to redeem the property.

2. Sheriff's Sale

The ***SHERIFF'S SALE*** *is a public auction, normally held at the courthouse door, and anyone can bid on the property*. The property is sold to the highest bidder and the proceeds are used to pay for the costs of the sale and to pay off the mortgage. As with the trust deed, any surplus goes to the debtor.

If the property does not bring enough money at the sale to pay off the mortgage, the debtor may be able to obtain a deficiency judgment against the debtor for the remaining debt. To obtain a deficiency judgment, the creditor must apply to the court within three months of the judicial sale.

In some states, such as California, deficiency judgments are prohibited if the mortgage secured a loan to purchase a one-to-four-unit personal residence occupied by the owner.

3. Post-Sale Redemption

After the sale, the debtor has another opportunity to save or redeem the property. The debtor can do this by paying the purchaser the amount paid for the property plus accrued interest from the time of the sale. *This right to redeem the property following the sheriff's sale is called the* **STATUTORY RIGHT OF REDEMPTION**.

Depending on the court congestion and the availability of the sheriff for foreclosures, a judicial mortgage foreclosure may take anywhere from several months to several years from the time of default until a sheriff's deed is delivered to the purchaser, which finally divests the debtor of title.

The period of post-sale redemption lasts one year in some states, if the proceeds are less than the amount needed to satisfy the indebtedness, or three months if the proceeds satisfy the indebtedness. This period varies in other states.

B. ADVANTAGES AND DISADVANTAGES OF THE MORTGAGE

For the creditor (mortgagee), the main advantage of a mortgage is the right to obtain a personal judgment against the debtor (mortgagor) for any deficiency if the property does not bring enough at the sheriff's sale to satisfy the debt.

The main disadvantages to the creditor concern the time and expense involved in executing a judicial foreclosure. Legal fees and court costs may easily amount to several thousand dollars, which must be paid out of the creditor's pocket, and may or may not be recovered at the sale. The entire process, as has already been mentioned, can take a long time to complete.

The advantages and disadvantages of a mortgage for the debtor (mortgagor) generally correspond to those for the creditor, but in reverse. Because court proceedings are slow, a mortgagor usually has a longer time to get the money together to prevent the foreclosure than a trust deed borrower. And even after the foreclosure sale, the mortgagor still has a chance to redeem the property. On the other hand, the mortgagor faces the possibility of a deficiency judgment (even after the foreclosure has taken place and the property is lost for good), and a portion of the debt may have to be repaid.

IV. Real Estate Contracts

Real estate contracts are also called contracts for deed, installment sales contracts, conditional sales contracts, and land contracts.

Real estate contracts differ significantly from mortgages and deeds of trust. Under both mortgage and trust deed security arrangements, the debtor acquires title to the property. Under a ***REAL ESTATE CONTRACT**, the seller (**VENDOR**) retains legal title until the buyer (**VENDEE**) pays off the entire contract* (see **Figure 7-3**). During the period the purchaser is paying on the contract, which may be many years, the purchaser has the right to possess and enjoy the property, but is not the legal owner.

In some states, real estate contracts often provide that if the buyer defaults on the contract obligation, all the buyer's rights in the property are forfeited; any payments made may be retained by the seller as liquidated damages, and the seller has a right to retake possession of the property immediately. In other states, such as California, such provisions are no longer enforceable. In these states, the seller is required to reimburse the buyer when repossessing the property, although the reimbursement may be reduced by any damages the seller incurred. The buyer has the right to reinstate the contract after default, and once a substantial portion of the contract price has been paid, the buyer gains a right of redemption.

A. ADVANTAGES AND DISADVANTAGES OF REAL ESTATE CONTRACTS

For the seller (vendor), one advantage of contract sales is the personal satisfaction or security that the seller may feel by remaining the title owner—by not giving the buyer (vendee) a deed until the entire purchase price has been paid. However, since it may be necessary to file a quiet title action to regain the property, this feeling of security may be largely illusory. A ***QUIET TITLE** is a title granted by a court that clears away all liens and other claims against a title.*

The main disadvantage for the vendor under a real estate contract is similar to the main disadvantage for the creditor under a mortgage: the expense and time required for terminating the contract and retaking possession of the property.

A serious disadvantage for the vendee under the contract is the fact that the vendor remains the legal owner, unlike mortgages or deeds of trust.

This often makes it difficult, if not impossible, for the vendee to obtain bank financing for construction or improvements. Banks are usually reluctant to lend to persons who do not have legal title because the vendor remains the legal owner.

Figure 7-3

RECORDING REQUESTED BY

AND WHEN RECORDED MAIL TO

SPACE ABOVE THIS LINE FOR RECORDER'S USE

LONG FORM SECURITY (INSTALLMENT) LAND CONTRACT WITH POWER OF SALE
AND REQUEST FOR NOTICE OF DEFAULT
(PRIOR LOAN PAYMENTS *NOT* INCLUDED)

THIS AGREEMENT, made and entered into this day of between
herein called VENDOR, and

herein called VENDEE, and

STEWART TITLE OF CALIFORNIA, INC., a California corporation, herein called TRUSTEE.

The signature of Vendor and Vendee of this contract shall also constitute their signature of the

REQUEST FOR NOTICE OF DEFAULT

In accordance with California Civil Code section 2924(b), request is hereby made by the undersigned Vendor and Vendee that: (1) a copy of any Notice of Default and a copy of any Notice of Sale under Deed of Trust recorded ____________________, in Book ________ Page ______________, Document No. ______________ Official Records of ______________ County, California, as affecting the herein described property, executed by ______________

as Trustor, in which ____________________
is named as Beneficiary, and ____________________ as Trustee, be mailed to Vendor and Vendee at address immediately below; and (2) a copy of any Notice of Default and a copy of any Notice of Sale under Deed of Trust recorded ______________ in Book ______, Page ________, Document No. ______________, Official Records of ______________ County, California, as affecting the herein described property, executed by ______________ as Trustor, in which ____________________ is named as Beneficiary, and ____________________Trustee, be mailed to Vendor and Vendee at address below.

Vendee

Address

Vendor

Address

LANDContract.doc

V. Typical Clauses in Security Instruments

We will now take a brief look at some clauses commonly used in real estate finance instruments. These clauses are generally used to safeguard the interests of the lender in the event of a default by the borrower. They are also often used to insure that the lender receives additional monies in the event of a prepayment of the mortgage debt.

A. ACCELERATION CLAUSE

Almost all promissory notes, mortgages, deeds of trust, and many real estate contracts contain an acceleration clause. An ***ACCELERATION CLAUSE*** *allows the creditor or seller to accelerate the debt, that is, to declare the entire outstanding balance immediately due and payable in the event of default.* This means that a debtor who misses one payment may discover the following month that he or she does not owe just two payments, but rather the entire remaining balance. Most lenders will wait until payments are at least 90 days delinquent before they enforce an acceleration clause. The following is a typical acceleration clause:

In case the mortgagor (or trustor) shall fail to pay any installment of principal or interest secured hereby when due to keep or perform any covenant or agreement aforesaid, then the whole indebtedness hereby secured shall forthwith become due and payable, at the election of the mortgagee (or beneficiary).

Under California law, if the loan is secured by owner-occupied residential property (one-to-four-units), the borrower must be allowed to prepay up to 20% of the original loan amount in one year without penalty. (Exception for seller financing: a seller can prohibit prepayment in the year of sale.) Any penalty imposed may not be more than six months' interest on the amount of prepayment over 20%. Once the loan has been in place for five years, no further prepayment penalties can be charged. Other states have slightly differing requirements.

B. PREPAYMENT CLAUSE

Many conventional loans have prepayment provisions. (They are prohibited on FHA and VA loans.) While the time periods and the amount of payment vary considerably, the basic effect of a prepayment provision is to charge the debtor for paying off the loan too early and depriving the lender of receiving the anticipated interest. An example might be a provision that charges the debtor 3% of the original loan amount if more than 20% of the principal is repaid in any one of the first five years of the loan. An example of the wording of a typical prepayment penalty clause is as follows:

If, within five years from the date of this note, borrower makes any prepayments of principal in excess of twenty percent of the original principal amount in any 12-month period beginning with the date of this note or anniversary dates thereof ("loan year"), borrower shall pay the note holder three percent of the original principal amount.

C. ALIENATION CLAUSE

Alienation refers to transfer of ownership.

***ALIENATION CLAUSES** in loan documents limit the debtor's right to transfer the property without the creditor's permission.* Depending on the clause, it may be triggered by a transfer of title or the transfer of any interest in the property (such as a land contract, a long-term lease, or even a lease with an option to purchase). *The alienation clause may give the lender the right to declare the entire loan balance due immediately, in which case it is called a* **DUE-ON-SALE CLAUSE**, to raise the interest rate if current rates are higher than the loan's rate, or to do either at its option.

Although alienation clauses are common in fixed-rate loans, adjustable-rate mortgage (ARM) loans seldom include them.

An ARM's rate adjustment feature allows the lender to keep the interest rate at or near market rates, even if ownership does change hands. The following is a typical due-on-sale clause:

If all or any part of the property, or an interest therein, is sold or transferred by borrower without lender's prior written consent, lender may, at lender's option, declare all the sums secured by this instrument to be immediately due and payable.

Before 1982, the enforceability of such clauses varied widely from state to state. Some states regarded such provisions as enforceable according to their terms. Other states refused to enforce them unless the lender could show that its security was impaired by the transfer. Still other states distinguished between the various types of clauses, regarding some as enforceable and others as unenforceable.

In 1982, two actions on the federal level had the effect of limiting the power of the states with respect to the enforceability of due on sale clauses. The first action resulted from a lawsuit involving the enforceability of alienation clauses by a savings and loan association in California (*Fidelity Savings and Loan Association v. De La Cuesta, et al.*). In that case, the U.S. Supreme Court upheld a Federal Home Loan Bank Board regulation which preempted state law and permitted federally chartered savings and loans to enforce due-on-sale clauses, regardless of whether such clauses were enforceable under state law.

This decision affected only the enforceability of alienation clauses by federal savings and loans; it was not directly applicable to actions by other lenders. However, passage of the Deposit Insurance Flexibility Act (**Garn-St. Germain Act**) in the same year gave

all lenders the right to enforce due-on-sale clauses in their security instruments. The act provided for a three-year transition period from October 15, 1982, to October 15, 1985, to phase in enforceability of alienation clauses in states where they had previously been unenforceable. In those states, the enforceability of due-on-sale clauses in loans, which had been made during the period beginning when state law declared alienation clauses unenforceable and ending with passage of the Garn-St. Germain Act, was delayed until October 15, 1985. The states where the window period applied were given the right to extend the window period by action of their state legislature.

In California, the window period ran between August 1978 (the date of California Supreme Court decision ruling alienation clauses unenforceable) and October 1982.

NOTE: If the seller decides to sell the property without assuming the existing mortgage (e.g., the buyer takes out a new mortgage, the proceeds of which are used to pay off the seller's mortgage), any prepayment penalty provision may then apply. This "due-on-sale catch-22" is something the seller should be aware of.

In California, a lender may not enforce the alienation clause and also the prepayment penalty on one-to-four-unit dwellings. On other properties, the lender may enforce both clauses only if the borrower has separately agreed to pay a prepayment penalty on acceleration.

D. SUBORDINATION CLAUSE

Generally, the priority among mortgages, trust deeds, and real estate contracts is determined by the date of recording, the first recorded instrument being the first in priority. In some situations, however, the parties may desire that a later recorded instrument have priority over an earlier recorded instrument. This is particularly common in construction financing. Due to the high-risk nature of construction loans, construction lenders frequently refuse to lend any money unless they can be assured of first lien priority. Because the developer, in many circumstances, has purchased the land on some sort of deferred payment plan, there is often a security instrument (mortgage, trust deed, or contract) that has already been recorded. In order for the later construction loan mortgage or trust deed to take priority over the earlier instrument, the earlier instrument must contain a subordination clause, or the earlier lender must sign a separate subordination agreement.

A ***SUBORDINATION CLAUSE*** *states that the instrument in which it is contained will be subordinate (junior) to a construction loan lien (mortgage or deed of trust) to be recorded later.* A subordination agreement accomplishes the same thing, but may be executed at any time (for example, when the later loan is made). The following is a typical subordination clause:

Lender agrees that this instrument shall be subordinate to a lien given by borrower to secure funds for the construction of improvements on the property, provided said lien is duly recorded and also provided that the amount secured by said lien does not exceed $95,000.00.

E. PARTIAL RELEASE, SATISFACTION, OR RECONVEYANCE CLAUSE

A ***PARTIAL RELEASE, SATISFACTION, OR RECONVEYANCE CLAUSE*** *obligates the creditor to release part of the property from the lien when part of the debt has been paid.*

Example: A real estate contract for the purchase of five acres of land may contain a clause stating that when the vendee has paid 20% of the purchase price, the vendor will execute a deed to the vendee for one acre of the land. This would allow the vendee to acquire clear title to one acre, which may then be used to build upon.

The fact that the vendee has title will make it much easier to obtain construction financing. Such clauses are also frequently found in blanket mortgages or trust deeds covering subdivisions in the process of being developed and sold.

The partial release (for real estate contracts), partial satisfaction (for mortgages), or partial reconveyance (for trust deeds) clause permits the developer to acquire, and therefore convey, clear title to one lot for which he or she has a purchaser, without having to pay off the entire lien against the development.

The following is a typical partial release clause:

Upon payment of all sums due with respect to any lot subject to this lien, lender shall release said lot from the lien at no cost to the borrower.

VI. CHAPTER SUMMARY

Instruments of real estate finance are documents that provide evidence of debt and give the lender the right to proceed against the collateral property if the borrower defaults on the loan. The promissory note is the basic instrument of debt, signed by the borrower and showing the amount of the loan, interest rate, method and manner of repayment, and the borrower's promise to repay the debt. Mortgages, deeds of trust, and real estate contracts give the lender or seller the right to foreclose against or repossess the property if the buyer defaults. The deed of trust provides a speedier method of foreclosure than does a mortgage.

Some particular clauses found in many mortgages, trust deeds, and installment contracts include acceleration clauses, prepayment provisions, and alienation (due-on-sale) clauses. Subordination agreements and partial release or satisfaction clauses are less common in residential loans, but are frequently found in construction or development loans.

VII. TERMINOLOGY

Acceleration Clause
Alienation Clause
Beneficiary
Declaration of Default
Deed of Reconveyance
Deed of Trust
Deficiency Judgment
Due-on-Sale Clause
Equitable Right of Redemption
Foreclosure Action
Freely Transferable
Garn-St. Germain Act
Grantor
Judicial Foreclosure
Lien Theory States
Maker
Mortgage
Mortgagee
Mortgagor
Negotiable Instruments
Nonjudicial Foreclosure
Notice of Default and Election to Sell
Notice of Sale
Order of Execution
Partial Release, Satisfaction, or Reconveyance Clause
Payee
Promissory Note
Quiet Title
Real Estate Contract
Security Instrument
Sheriff's Sale
Statutory Right of Redemption
Subordination Clause
Title Theory States
Trust Deed
Trustee
Trustee's Deed
Trustor
Uniform Commercial Code (UCC)
Vendee
Vendor

VIII. CHAPTER QUIZ

1. In a promissory note, the borrower is called the:
   a. payee.
   b. maker.
   c. trustee.
   d. beneficiary.

2. A deed of reconveyance is provided by the:
   a. trustee.
   b. trustor.
   c. beneficiary.
   d. payee.

3. A deficiency judgment:
   a. is part of a deed of reconveyance.
   b. is exercised by the vendee.
   c. may only be granted by a court of law.
   d. none of the above.

4. The seller of a real estate contract is known as the:
   a. payee.
   b. vendee.
   c. payer.
   d. vendor.

5. The right of a borrower to redeem property after a sheriff's sale is called:
   a. the equitable right of redemption.
   b. the statutory right of redemption.
   c. a deficiency judgment.
   d. a quiet title action.

6. A lender's right to declare a balance immediately due and payable in the event of default is called:
   a. prepayment.
   b. acceleration.
   c. alienation.
   d. due on sale.

7. A mortgage that is junior to another is called:
   a. a priority lien.
   b. a nonpriority lien.
   c. subordinate.
   d. none of the above.

8. A foreclosure that does not have to be taken to court is called:
   a. nonjudicial.
   b. judicial.
   c. a reconveyance deed.
   d. a nonrecurring foreclosure.

9. A declaration of default is prepared by a:
   a. judge.
   b. trustee.
   c. lender.
   d. borrower.

10. A notice of sale:
   a. requires a 30-day notice.
   b. must be approved by a judge.
   c. is sent by the county sheriff.
   d. is published in a newspaper.

ANSWERS: 1. *b*; 2. *a*; 3. *c*; 4. *d*; 5. *b*; 6. *b*; 7. *c*; 8. *a*; 9. *c*; 10. *d*

Finance Instruments

HERE

Countrywide®
HOME LOANS

JOB
POSTINGS

Chapter 8
Overview of the Loan Process

While the principles behind real estate finance are fairly straightforward, they will be easier to understand after taking a brief look at the financing process. The procedures for financing real estate can be conveniently broken down into four steps:

1. Filling out the loan application;
2. Analyzing the borrower and property;
3. Processing the loan application, and
4. Closing the loan.

A fifth step could be added: servicing and sale to the secondary market. However, because this step takes place after the loan has been placed, it is primarily a matter of administration rather than analysis and judgment.

I. The Loan Process

This chapter will provide an overview of the steps in the process. A more detailed analysis of the process will be provided in chapters 13 and 14. These chapters deal with the qualification of the borrower and the qualification of the property.

CHAPTER OUTLINE

A. THE LOAN APPLICATION

The first step in obtaining a real estate loan is to fill out the loan application. The loan application is not designed for those merely inquiring about real estate loans, but for those who will follow through and actually borrow the funds (provided the loan is approved). The home buyer (or the real estate agent on behalf of the buyer) sets up an appointment with the lender. The buyer will attend this appointment armed with a good deal of personal and financial data, which will be the basis of the lender's decision whether or not to make the loan. The types of information the buyer should take to this interview will be discussed shortly. It should be noted that if the buyer does not have all the necessary data at the interview, it will be necessary to provide the missing information at a later date, which will cause a delay in the loan application process.

A borrower must provide personal and financial information when applying for a loan.

During the initial interview, the buyer will learn about the various types of financing programs offered by the lender. These will probably include 30-year, fixed rate mortgages, 15-year, fixed rate mortgages, and adjustable-rate mortgages (ARMs). Based on the information given by the lender and the buyer's own personal circumstances, the buyer will decide which program best suits his or her needs.

The lender will also require a deposit to cover the expenses that must be paid up front. These include the costs of the credit report, property appraisal, and preliminary title report. This deposit will assure the lender that these fees will be paid for, even if the loan does not close.

A borrower pays for a credit report, property appraisal, and preliminary title report up front.

The **purchase agreement** will be examined at this interview as well (see **Figure 8-1**). This is so the lender can be sure that the terms of the agreement are in keeping with the terms of the loan the lender can offer (e.g., interest rate and length of the term of the loan). Of particular concern is the agreed-upon closing date. Often, the purchase agreement will provide for a closing date that is far too early to be realistic. If it is impossible for the lender to meet the closing date, a more feasible one can be agreed on and later frustration avoided.

A purchase agreement is given to a home purchaser by the seller; it contains the sale terms and the date that the parties expect the transaction to close.

Figure 8-1

CALIFORNIA RESIDENTIAL PURCHASE AGREEMENT AND JOINT ESCROW INSTRUCTIONS

For Use With Single Family Residential Property — Attached or Detached
(C.A.R. Form RPA-CA, Revised 4/10)

Date *June 14, 20xx*

1. OFFER:
   A. THIS IS AN OFFER FROM *Walter Buyer, Debbie Buyer* ("Buyer").
   B. THE REAL PROPERTY TO BE ACQUIRED is described as *264 Beach Lane, Costa Mesa CA 92627* , Assessor's Parcel No. ______, situated in *Costa Mesa* , County of *Orange* , California, ("Property").
   C. THE PURCHASE PRICE offered is *Eight Hundred Thousand* (Dollars $ *800,000.00*).
   D. CLOSE OF ESCROW shall occur on ______ (date) (or ☒ *90* Days After Acceptance).
2. AGENCY:
   A. DISCLOSURE: Buyer and Seller each acknowledge prior receipt of a "Disclosure Regarding Real Estate Agency Relationships" (C.A.R. Form AD).
   B. POTENTIALLY COMPETING BUYERS AND SELLERS: Buyer and Seller each acknowledge receipt of a disclosure of the possibility of multiple representation by the Broker representing that principal. This disclosure may be part of a listing agreement, buyer representation agreement or separate document (C.A.R. Form DA). Buyer understands that Broker representing Buyer may also represent other potential buyers, who may consider, make offers on or ultimately acquire the Property. Seller understands that Broker representing Seller may also represent other sellers with competing properties of interest to this Buyer.
   C. CONFIRMATION: The following agency relationships are hereby confirmed for this transaction:
   Listing Agent *Sail Realty* (Print Firm Name) is the agent of (check one): ☒ the Seller exclusively; or ☐ both the Buyer and Seller.
   Selling Agent *Ramos Realty* (Print Firm Name) (if not the same as the Listing Agent) is the agent of (check one): ☒ the Buyer exclusively; or ☐ the Seller exclusively; or ☐ both the Buyer and Seller. Real Estate Brokers are not parties to the Agreement between Buyer and Seller.
3. FINANCE TERMS: Buyer represents that funds will be good when deposited with Escrow Holder.
   A. INITIAL DEPOSIT: Deposit shall be in the amount of .... $ *10,000.00*
   (1) Buyer shall deliver deposit directly to Escrow Holder by personal check, ☐ electronic funds transfer, ☐ Other ______ within 3 business days after acceptance (or ☐ Other ______);
   OR (2) (If checked) ☒ Buyer has given the deposit by personal check (or ☐ ______) to the agent submitting the offer (or to ☒ ______), made payable to *ABC Escrow* . The deposit shall be held uncashed until Acceptance and then deposited with Escrow Holder (or ☐ into Broker's trust account) within 3 business days after Acceptance (or ☐ Other ______).
   B. INCREASED DEPOSIT: Buyer shall deposit with Escrow Holder an increased deposit in the amount of .... $ ______
   within ______ Days After Acceptance, or ☐ ______.
   If a liquidated damages clause is incorporated into this Agreement, Buyer and Seller shall sign a separate liquidated damages clause (C.A.R. Form RID) for any increased deposit at the time it is deposited.
   C. LOAN(S):
   (1) FIRST LOAN: in the amount of .... $ *640,000.00*
   This loan will be conventional financing or, if checked, ☐ FHA, ☐ VA, ☐ Seller (C.A.R. Form SFA), ☐ assumed financing (C.A.R. Form PAA), ☐ Other ______. This loan shall be at a fixed rate not to exceed *8.000* % or, ☐ an adjustable rate loan with initial rate not to exceed ______ %. Regardless of the type of loan, Buyer shall pay points not to exceed *2.00* % of the loan amount.
   (2) ☐ SECOND LOAN: in the amount of .... $ ______
   This loan will be conventional financing or, if checked, ☐ Seller (C.A.R. Form SFA), ☐ assumed financing (C.A.R. Form PAA), ☐ Other ______. This loan shall be at a fixed rate not to exceed ______ % or, ☐ an adjustable rate loan with initial rate not to exceed ______ %. Regardless of the type of loan, Buyer shall pay points not to exceed ______ % of the loan amount.
   (3) FHA/VA: For any FHA or VA loan specified above, Buyer has 17 (or ☐ ______) Days After Acceptance to Deliver to Seller written notice (C.A.R. Form FVA) of any lender-required repairs or costs that Buyer requests Seller to pay for or repair. Seller has no obligation to pay for repairs or satisfy lender requirements unless otherwise agreed in writing.
   D. ADDITIONAL FINANCING TERMS: ______
   E. BALANCE OF PURCHASE PRICE OR DOWN PAYMENT: in the amount of .... $ *150,000.00*
   to be deposited with Escrow Holder within sufficient time to close escrow.
   F. PURCHASE PRICE (TOTAL): .... $ *800,000.00*

Buyer's Initials (______)(______) Seller's Initials (______)(______)

EQUAL HOUSING OPPORTUNITY

RPA-CA REVISED 4/10 (PAGE 1 OF 8)

Reviewed by ______ Date ______

CALIFORNIA RESIDENTIAL PURCHASE AGREEMENT (RPA-CA PAGE 1 OF 8)

Agent: WALT HUBER Phone: Fax: Prepared using zipForm® software
Broker: WALT HUBER REALTOR

Property Address: 264 Beach Lane Costa Mesa, CA 92627 Date: June 14, 20xx

G. VERIFICATION OF DOWN PAYMENT AND CLOSING COSTS: Buyer (or Buyer's lender or loan broker pursuant to 3H(1)) shall, within 7 (or ☐ ________) Days After Acceptance, Deliver to Seller written verification of Buyer's down payment and closing costs. (If checked, ☐ verification attached.)

H. LOAN TERMS:

(1) LOAN APPLICATIONS: Within 7 (or ☐ ________) Days After Acceptance, Buyer shall Deliver to Seller a letter from lender or loan broker stating that, based on a review of Buyer's written application and credit report, Buyer is prequalified or preapproved for any NEW loan specified in 3C above. (If checked, ☐ letter attached.)

(2) LOAN CONTINGENCY: Buyer shall act diligently and in good faith to obtain the designated loan(s). Obtaining the loan(s) specified above is a contingency of this Agreement unless otherwise agreed in writing. Buyer's contractual obligations to obtain and provide deposit, balance of down payment and closing costs are not contingencies of this Agreement.

(3) LOAN CONTINGENCY REMOVAL:

(i) Within 17 (or ☐ ________) Days After Acceptance, Buyer shall, as specified in paragraph 14, in writing remove the loan contingency or cancel this Agreement;

OR (ii) (if checked) ☐ the loan contingency shall remain in effect until the designated loans are funded.

(4) ☐ NO LOAN CONTINGENCY (If checked): Obtaining any loan specified above is NOT a contingency of this Agreement. If Buyer does not obtain the loan and as a result Buyer does not purchase the Property, Seller may be entitled to Buyer's deposit or other legal remedies.

I. APPRAISAL CONTINGENCY AND REMOVAL: This Agreement is (or, if checked, ☐ is NOT) contingent upon a written appraisal of the Property by a licensed or certified appraiser at no less than the specified purchase price. If there is a loan contingency, Buyer's removal of the loan contingency shall be deemed removal of this appraisal contingency (or, ☐ if checked, Buyer shall, as specified in paragraph 14B(3), in writing remove the appraisal contingency or cancel this Agreement within 17 (or ________) Days After Acceptance). If there is no loan contingency, Buyer shall, as specified in paragraph 14B(3), in writing remove the appraisal contingency or cancel this Agreement within 17 (or ________) Days After Acceptance.

J. ☐ ALL CASH OFFER (If checked): Buyer shall, within 7 (or ☐ ________) Days After Acceptance, Deliver to Seller written verification of sufficient funds to close this transaction. (If checked, ☐ verification attached.)

K. BUYER STATED FINANCING: Seller has relied on Buyer's representation of the type of financing specified (including but not limited to, as applicable, amount of down payment, contingent or non contingent loan, or all cash). If Buyer seeks alternate financing, (i) Seller has no obligation to cooperate with Buyer's efforts to obtain such financing, and (ii) Buyer shall also pursue the financing method specified in this Agreement. Buyer's failure to secure alternate financing does not excuse Buyer from the obligation to purchase the Property and close escrow as specified in this Agreement.

4. ALLOCATION OF COSTS (If checked): Unless otherwise specified in writing, this paragraph only determines who is to pay for the inspection, test or service ("Report") mentioned; it does not determine who is to pay for any work recommended or identified in the Report.

A. INSPECTIONS AND REPORTS:

(1) ☐ Buyer ☒ Seller shall pay for an inspection and report for wood destroying pests and organisms ("Wood Pest Report") prepared by Bug B Gone a registered structural pest control company.

(2) ☐ Buyer ☐ Seller shall pay to have septic or private sewage disposal systems pumped and inspected ________.

(3) ☐ Buyer ☐ Seller shall pay to have domestic wells tested for water potability and productivity ________.

(4) ☐ Buyer ☐ Seller shall pay for a natural hazard zone disclosure report prepared by ________.

(5) ☐ Buyer ☐ Seller shall pay for the following inspection or report ________.

(6) ☐ Buyer ☐ Seller shall pay for the following inspection or report ________.

B. GOVERNMENT REQUIREMENTS AND RETROFIT:

(1) ☐ Buyer ☒ Seller shall pay for smoke detector installation and/or water heater bracing, if required by Law. Prior to Close Of Escrow, Seller shall provide Buyer written statement(s) of compliance in accordance with state and local Law, unless exempt.

(2) ☐ Buyer ☐ Seller shall pay the cost of compliance with any other minimum mandatory government retrofit standards, inspections and reports if required as a condition of closing escrow under any Law. ________.

C. ESCROW AND TITLE:

(1) ☒ Buyer ☒ Seller shall pay escrow fee 50%/50%.

Escrow Holder shall be ABC Escrow.

(2) ☒ Buyer ☐ Seller shall pay for owner's title insurance policy specified in paragraph 12E ________.

Owner's title policy to be issued by ________.

(Buyer shall pay for any title insurance policy insuring Buyer's lender, unless otherwise agreed in writing.)

D. OTHER COSTS:

(1) ☐ Buyer ☐ Seller shall pay County transfer tax or fee ________.

(2) ☐ Buyer ☐ Seller shall pay City transfer tax or fee ________.

(3) ☐ Buyer ☐ Seller shall pay Homeowner's Association ("HOA") transfer fee ________.

(4) ☐ Buyer ☐ Seller shall pay HOA document preparation fees ________.

(5) ☐ Buyer ☐ Seller shall pay for any private transfer fee ________.

(6) ☐ Buyer ☐ Seller shall pay the cost, not to exceed $ ________, of a one-year home warranty plan, issued by ________, with the following optional coverages:

☐ Air Conditioner ☐ Pool/Spa ☐ Code and Permit upgrade ☐ Other: ________.

Buyer is informed that home warranty plans have many optional coverages in addition to those listed above. Buyer is advised to investigate these coverages to determine those that may be suitable for Buyer.

(7) ☐ Buyer ☐ Seller shall pay for ________.

(8) ☐ Buyer ☐ Seller shall pay for ________.

Buyer's Initials (________) (________) Seller's Initials (________) (________)

RPA-CA REVISED 4/10 (PAGE 2 OF 8) Reviewed by ________ Date ________

EQUAL HOUSING OPPORTUNITY

CALIFORNIA RESIDENTIAL PURCHASE AGREEMENT (RPA-CA PAGE 2 OF 8)

Cal Principles -

Property Address: 264 Beach Lane Costa Mesa, CA 92627 Date: June 14, 20xx

5. **CLOSING AND POSSESSION:**
   A. Buyer intends (or ☐ does not intend) to occupy the Property as Buyer's primary residence.
   B. **Seller-occupied or vacant property:** Possession shall be delivered to Buyer at 5 PM or (☒ 11 ☒ AM ☐ PM), on the date of Close Of Escrow; ☐ on ______ ; or ☐ no later than ______ **Days** After Close Of Escrow. If transfer of title and possession do not occur at the same time, Buyer and Seller are advised to: **(i)** enter into a written occupancy agreement (C.A.R. Form PAA, paragraph 2); and **(ii)** consult with their insurance and legal advisors.
   C. **Tenant-occupied property:**
      (i) Property shall be vacant at least **5** (or ☐ ______) **Days** Prior to Close Of Escrow, unless otherwise agreed in writing. **Note to Seller: If you are unable to deliver Property vacant in accordance with rent control and other applicable Law, you may be in breach of this Agreement.**
      OR **(ii)** (if checked) ☐ **Tenant to remain in possession.** (C.A.R. Form PAA, paragraph 3)
   D. At Close Of Escrow, **(i)** Seller assigns to Buyer any assignable warranty rights for items included in the sale, and **(ii)** Seller shall Deliver to Buyer available Copies of warranties. Brokers cannot and will not determine the assignability of any warranties.
   E. At Close Of Escrow, unless otherwise agreed in writing, Seller shall provide keys and/or means to operate all locks, mailboxes, security systems, alarms and garage door openers. If Property is a condominium or located in a common interest subdivision, Buyer may be required to pay a deposit to the Homeowners' Association ("HOA") to obtain keys to accessible HOA facilities.
6. **STATUTORY DISCLOSURES (INCLUDING LEAD-BASED PAINT HAZARD DISCLOSURES) AND CANCELLATION RIGHTS:**
   A. **(1)** Seller shall, within the time specified in paragraph 14A, Deliver to Buyer, if required by Law: **(i)** Federal Lead-Based Paint Disclosures (C.A.R. Form FLD) and pamphlet ("Lead Disclosures"); and **(ii)** disclosures or notices required by sections 1102 et. seq. and 1103 et. seq. of the Civil Code ("Statutory Disclosures"). Statutory Disclosures include, but are not limited to, **a Real Estate Transfer Disclosure Statement ("TDS")**, Natural Hazard Disclosure Statement ("NHD"), notice or actual knowledge of release of illegal controlled substance, notice of special tax and/or assessments (or, if allowed, substantially equivalent notice regarding the Mello-Roos Community Facilities Act and Improvement Bond Act of 1915) and, if Seller has actual knowledge, of industrial use and military ordinance location (C.A.R. Form SPQ or SSD).
      (2) Buyer shall, within the time specified in paragraph 14B(1), return Signed Copies of the Statutory and Lead Disclosures to Seller.
      (3) In the event Seller, prior to Close Of Escrow, becomes aware of adverse conditions materially affecting the Property, or any material inaccuracy in disclosures, information or representations previously provided to Buyer, Seller shall promptly provide a subsequent or amended disclosure or notice, in writing, covering those items. **However, a subsequent or amended disclosure shall not be required for conditions and material inaccuracies** of which Buyer is otherwise aware, or which are **disclosed in reports provided to or obtained by Buyer or ordered and paid for by Buyer**.
      (4) If any disclosure or notice specified in 6A(1), or subsequent or amended disclosure or notice is Delivered to Buyer after the offer is Signed, Buyer shall have the right to cancel this Agreement within **3 Days** After Delivery in person, or **5 Days** After Delivery by deposit in the mail, by giving written notice of cancellation to Seller or Seller's agent.
      (5) Note to Buyer and Seller: Waiver of Statutory and Lead Disclosures is prohibited by Law.
   B. **NATURAL AND ENVIRONMENTAL HAZARDS:** Within the time specified in paragraph 14A, Seller shall, if required by Law: **(i)** Deliver to Buyer earthquake guides (and questionnaire) and environmental hazards booklet; **(ii)** even if exempt from the obligation to provide a NHD, disclose if the Property is located in a Special Flood Hazard Area; Potential Flooding (Inundation) Area; Very High Fire Hazard Zone; State Fire Responsibility Area; Earthquake Fault Zone; Seismic Hazard Zone; and **(iii)** disclose any other zone as required by Law and provide any other information required for those zones.
   C. **WITHHOLDING TAXES:** Within the time specified in paragraph 14A, to avoid required withholding, Seller shall Deliver to Buyer or qualified substitute, an affidavit sufficient to comply with federal (FIRPTA) and California withholding Law, (C.A.R. Form AS or QS).
   D. **MEGAN'S LAW DATABASE DISCLOSURE:** Notice: Pursuant to Section 290.46 of the Penal Code, information about specified registered sex offenders is made available to the public via an Internet Web site maintained by the Department of Justice at www.meganslaw.ca.gov. Depending on an offender's criminal history, this information will include either the address at which the offender resides or the community of residence and ZIP Code in which he or she resides. (Neither Seller nor Brokers are required to check this website. If Buyer wants further information, Broker recommends that Buyer obtain information from this website during Buyer's inspection contingency period. Brokers do not have expertise in this area.)
7. **CONDOMINIUM/PLANNED DEVELOPMENT DISCLOSURES:**
   A. **SELLER HAS: 7 (or ☐ ______) Days** After Acceptance to disclose to Buyer whether the Property is a condominium, or is located in a planned development or other common interest subdivision (C.A.R. Form SPQ or SSD).
   B. If the Property is a condominium or is located in a planned development or other common interest subdivision, Seller has **3 (or ☐ ______) Days** After Acceptance to request from the HOA (C.A.R. Form HOA): **(i)** Copies of any documents required by Law; **(ii)** disclosure of any pending or anticipated claim or litigation by or against the HOA; **(iii)** a statement containing the location and number of designated parking and storage spaces; **(iv)** Copies of the most recent 12 months of HOA minutes for regular and special meetings; and **(v)** the names and contact information of all HOAs governing the Property (collectively, "CI Disclosures"). Seller shall itemize and Deliver to Buyer all CI Disclosures received from the HOA and any CI Disclosures in Seller's possession. Buyer's approval of CI Disclosures is a contingency of this Agreement as specified in paragraph 14B(3).
8. **ITEMS INCLUDED IN AND EXCLUDED FROM PURCHASE PRICE:**
   A. **NOTE TO BUYER AND SELLER:** Items listed as included or excluded in the MLS, flyers or marketing materials are **not** included in the purchase price or excluded from the sale unless specified in 8B or C.
   B. **ITEMS INCLUDED IN SALE:**
      (1) All EXISTING fixtures and fittings that are attached to the Property;
      (2) EXISTING electrical, mechanical, lighting, plumbing and heating fixtures, ceiling fans, fireplace inserts, gas logs and grates, solar systems, built-in appliances, window and door screens, awnings, shutters, window coverings, attached floor coverings, television antennas, satellite dishes, private integrated telephone systems, air coolers/conditioners, pool/spa equipment, garage door openers/remote controls, mailbox, in-ground landscaping, trees/shrubs, water softeners, water purifiers, security systems/alarms; (If checked ☐ stove(s), ☐ refrigerator(s); and
      (3) The following additional items: ______
      (4) Seller represents that all items included in the purchase price, unless otherwise specified, are owned by Seller.
      (5) All items included shall be transferred free of liens and without Seller warranty.
   C. **ITEMS EXCLUDED FROM SALE:** Unless otherwise specified, audio and video components (such as flat screen TVs and speakers) are excluded if any such item is not itself attached to the Property, even if a bracket or other mechanism attached to the component is attached to the Property; and ______

Buyer's Initials (______) (______) Seller's Initials (______) (______)

RPA-CA REVISED 4/10 (PAGE 3 OF 8)

Reviewed by ______ Date ______

EQUAL HOUSING OPPORTUNITY

CALIFORNIA RESIDENTIAL PURCHASE AGREEMENT (RPA-CA PAGE 3 OF 8)

Cal Principles -

264 Beach Lane
Property Address: Costa Mesa, CA 92627 Date: June 14, 20xx

9. **CONDITION OF PROPERTY:** Unless otherwise agreed: **(i) the Property is sold (a) in its PRESENT physical ("as-is") condition as of the date of Acceptance and (b) subject to Buyer's Investigation rights; (ii)** the Property, including pool, spa, landscaping and grounds, is to be maintained in substantially the same condition as on the date of Acceptance; and **(iii)** all debris and personal property not included in the sale shall be removed by Seller by Close Of Escrow.
   A. Seller shall, within the time specified in paragraph 14A, DISCLOSE KNOWN MATERIAL FACTS AND DEFECTS affecting the Property, including known insurance claims within the past five years, and make any and all other disclosures required by law.
   B. Buyer has the right to inspect the Property and, as specified in paragraph 14B, based upon information discovered in those inspections: (i) cancel this Agreement; or (ii) request that Seller make Repairs or take other action.
   C. **Buyer is strongly advised to conduct investigations of the entire Property in order to determine its present condition. Seller may not be aware of all defects affecting the Property or other factors that Buyer considers important. Property improvements may not be built according to code, in compliance with current Law, or have had permits issued.**
10. **BUYER'S INVESTIGATION OF PROPERTY AND MATTERS AFFECTING PROPERTY:**
   A. Buyer's acceptance of the condition of, and any other matter affecting the Property, is a contingency of this Agreement as specified in this paragraph and paragraph 14B. Within the time specified in paragraph 14B(1), Buyer shall have the right, at Buyer's expense unless otherwise agreed, to conduct inspections, investigations, tests, surveys and other studies ("Buyer Investigations"), including, but not limited to, the right to: **(i)** inspect for lead-based paint and other lead-based paint hazards; **(ii)** inspect for wood destroying pests and organisms; **(iii)** review the registered sex offender database; **(iv)** confirm the insurability of Buyer and the Property; and **(v)** satisfy Buyer as to any matter specified in the attached Buyer's Inspection Advisory (C.A.R. Form BIA). Without Seller's prior written consent, Buyer shall neither make nor cause to be made: **(i)** invasive or destructive Buyer Investigations; or **(ii)** inspections by any governmental building or zoning inspector or government employee, unless required by Law.
   B. Seller shall make the Property available for all Buyer Investigations. Buyer shall **(i)** as specified in paragraph 14B, complete Buyer Investigations and, either remove the contingency or cancel this Agreement, and **(ii)** give Seller, at no cost, complete Copies of all Investigation reports obtained by Buyer, which obligation shall survive the termination of this Agreement.
   C. Seller shall have water, gas, electricity and all operable pilot lights on for Buyer's Investigations and through the date possession is made available to Buyer.
   D. **Buyer indemnity and Seller protection for entry upon property:** Buyer shall: **(i)** keep the Property free and clear of liens; **(ii)** repair all damage arising from Buyer Investigations; and **(iii)** indemnify and hold Seller harmless from all resulting liability, claims, demands, damages and costs of Buyer's investigations. Buyer shall carry, or Buyer shall require anyone acting on Buyer's behalf to carry, policies of liability, workers' compensation and other applicable insurance, defending and protecting Seller from liability for any injuries to persons or property occurring during any Buyer Investigations or work done on the Property at Buyer's direction prior to Close Of Escrow. Seller is advised that certain protections may be afforded Seller by recording a "Notice of Non-responsibility" (C.A.R. Form NNR) for Buyer Investigations and work done on the Property at Buyer's direction. Buyer's obligations under this paragraph shall survive the termination or cancellation of this Agreement and Close of Escrow.
11. **SELLER DISCLOSURES; ADDENDA; ADVISORIES; OTHER TERMS:**
   A. **Seller Disclosures (if checked):** Seller shall, within the time specified in paragraph 14A, complete and provide Buyer with a:
   ☒ Seller Property Questionnaire (C.A.R. Form SPQ) **OR** ☐ Supplemental Contractual and Statutory Disclosure (C.A.R. Form SSD)
   B. **Addenda (if checked):** ☐ Addendum # (C.A.R. Form ADM)
   ☐ Wood Destroying Pest Inspection and Allocation of Cost Addendum (C.A.R. Form WPA)
   ☒ Purchase Agreement Addendum (C.A.R Form PAA) ☐ Septic, Well and Property Monument Addendum (C.A.R. Form SWPI)
   ☐ Short Sale Addendum (C.A.R. Form SSA) ☐ Other
   C. **Advisories (if checked):** ☑ Buyer's Inspection Advisory (C.A.R. Form BIA)
   ☐ Probate Advisory (C.A.R. Form PAK) ☒ Statewide Buyer and Seller Advisory (C.A.R. Form SBSA)
   ☐ Trust Advisory (C.A.R. Form TA) ☐ REO Advisory (C.A.R. Form REO)
   D. **Other Terms:**
12. **TITLE AND VESTING:**
   A. Within the time specified in paragraph 14, Buyer shall be provided a current preliminary title report, which shall include a search of the General Index. Seller shall within 7 Days After Acceptance give Escrow Holder a completed Statement of Information. The preliminary report is only an offer by the title insurer to issue a policy of title insurance and may not contain every item affecting title. Buyer's review of the preliminary report and any other matters which may affect title are a contingency of this Agreement as specified in paragraph 14B.
   B. Title is taken in its present condition subject to all encumbrances, easements, covenants, conditions, restrictions, rights and other matters, whether of record or not, as of the date of Acceptance except: **(i)** monetary liens of record unless Buyer is assuming those obligations or taking the Property subject to those obligations; and **(ii)** those matters which Seller has agreed to remove in writing.
   C. Within the time specified in paragraph 14A, Seller has a duty to disclose to Buyer all matters known to Seller affecting title, whether of record or not.
   D. At Close Of Escrow, Buyer shall receive a grant deed conveying title (or, for stock cooperative or long-term lease, an assignment of stock certificate or of Seller's leasehold interest), including oil, mineral and water rights if currently owned by Seller. Title shall vest as designated in Buyer's supplemental escrow instructions. THE MANNER OF TAKING TITLE MAY HAVE SIGNIFICANT LEGAL AND TAX CONSEQUENCES. CONSULT AN APPROPRIATE PROFESSIONAL.
   E. Buyer shall receive a CLTA/ALTA Homeowner's Policy of Title Insurance. A title company, at Buyer's request, can provide information about the availability, desirability, coverage, survey requirements, and cost of various title insurance coverages and endorsements. If Buyer desires title coverage other than that required by this paragraph, Buyer shall instruct Escrow Holder in writing and pay any increase in cost.
13. **SALE OF BUYER'S PROPERTY:**
   A. This Agreement is NOT contingent upon the sale of any property owned by Buyer.
   OR B. ☐ (If checked): The attached addendum (C.A.R. Form COP) regarding the contingency for the sale of property owned by Buyer is incorporated into this Agreement.

Buyer's Initials (________) (________) Seller's Initials (________) (________)

RPA-CA REVISED 4/10 (PAGE 4 OF 8) Reviewed by ________ Date ________ EQUAL HOUSING OPPORTUNITY

CALIFORNIA RESIDENTIAL PURCHASE AGREEMENT (RPA-CA PAGE 4 OF 8) Cal Principles -

Property Address: *264 Beach Lane Costa Mesa, CA 92627* Date: *June 14, 20xx*

14. **TIME PERIODS; REMOVAL OF CONTINGENCIES; CANCELLATION RIGHTS: The following time periods may only be extended, altered, modified or changed by mutual written agreement. Any removal of contingencies or cancellation under this paragraph by either Buyer or Seller must be exercised in good faith and in writing (C.A.R. Form CR or CC).**

A. **SELLER HAS: 7 (or ☐ __________) Days** After Acceptance to Deliver to Buyer all Reports, disclosures and information for which Seller is responsible under paragraphs 4, 6A, B and C, 7A, 9A, 11A and B, and 12. Buyer may give Seller a Notice to Seller to Perform (C.A.R. Form NSP) if Seller has not Delivered the items within the time specified.

B. (1) **BUYER HAS: 17 (or ☐ __________) Days** After Acceptance, unless otherwise agreed in writing, to:

(i) complete all Buyer Investigations; approve all disclosures, reports and other applicable information, which Buyer receives from Seller; and approve all other matters affecting the Property; and

(ii) Deliver to Seller Signed Copies of Statutory and Lead Disclosures Delivered by Seller in accordance with paragraph 6A.

(2) Within the time specified in 14B(1), Buyer may request that Seller make repairs or take any other action regarding the Property (C.A.R. Form RR). Seller has no obligation to agree to or respond to Buyer's requests.

(3) Within the time specified in 14B(1) (or as otherwise specified in this Agreement), Buyer shall Deliver to Seller either (i) a removal of the applicable contingency (C.A.R. Form CR), or (ii) a cancellation (C.A.R. Form CC) of this Agreement based upon a contingency or Seller's failure to Deliver the specified items. However, if any report, disclosure or information for which Seller is responsible is not Delivered within the time specified in 14A, then Buyer has **5 (or ☐ __________) Days** After Delivery of any such items, or the time specified in 14B(1), whichever is later, to Deliver to Seller a removal of the applicable contingency or cancellation of this Agreement.

(4) **Continuation of Contingency:** Even after the end of the time specified in 14B(1) and before Seller cancels this Agreement, if at all, pursuant to 14C, Buyer retains the right to either (i) in writing remove remaining contingencies, or (ii) cancel this Agreement based upon a remaining contingency or Seller's failure to Deliver the specified terms. Once Buyer's written removal of all contingencies is Delivered to Seller, Seller may not cancel this Agreement pursuant to 14C(1).

C. SELLER RIGHT TO CANCEL:

(1) **Seller right to Cancel; Buyer Contingencies:** If, within time specified in this Agreement, Buyer does not, in writing, Deliver to Seller a removal of the applicable contingency or cancellation of this Agreement then Seller, after first Delivering to Buyer a Notice to Buyer to Perform (C.A.R. Form NBP) may cancel this Agreement. In such event, Seller shall authorize return of Buyer's deposit.

(2) **Seller right to Cancel; Buyer Contract Obligations:** Seller, after first Delivering to Buyer a NBP may cancel this Agreement for any of the following reasons: **(i)** if Buyer fails to deposit funds as required by 3A or 3B; **(ii)** if the funds deposited pursuant to 3A or 3B are not good when deposited; **(iii)** if Buyer fails to Deliver a notice of FHA or VA costs or terms as required by 3C(3) (C.A.R. Form FVA); **(iv)** if Buyer fails to Deliver a letter as required by 3H; **(v)** if Buyer fails to Deliver verification as required by 3G or 3J; **(vi)** if Seller reasonably disapproves of the verification provided by 3G or 3J; **(vii)** if Buyer fails to return Statutory and Lead Disclosures as required by paragraph 6A(2); or **(viii)** if Buyer fails to sign or initial a separate liquidated damage form for an increased deposit as required by paragraphs 3B and 25. In such event, Seller shall authorize return of Buyer's deposit.

(3) **Notice To Buyer To Perform:** The NBP shall: **(i)** be in writing; **(ii)** be signed by Seller; and **(iii)** give Buyer at least **2 (or ☐ ________) Days** After Delivery (or until the time specified in the applicable paragraph, whichever occurs last) to take the applicable action. A NBP may not be Delivered any earlier than **2 Days** Prior to the expiration of the applicable time for Buyer to remove a contingency or cancel this Agreement or meet an obligation specified in 14C(2).

D. **EFFECT OF BUYER'S REMOVAL OF CONTINGENCIES:** If Buyer removes, in writing, any contingency or cancellation rights, unless otherwise specified in a separate written agreement between Buyer and Seller, Buyer shall with regard to that contingency or cancellation right conclusively be deemed to have: **(i)** completed all Buyer Investigations, and review of reports and other applicable information and disclosures; **(ii)** elected to proceed with the transaction; and **(iii)** assumed all liability, responsibility and expense for Repairs or corrections or for inability to obtain financing.

E. **CLOSE OF ESCROW:** Before Seller or Buyer may cancel this Agreement for failure of the other party to close escrow pursuant to this Agreement, Seller or Buyer must first give the other a demand to close escrow (C.A.R. Form DCE).

F. **EFFECT OF CANCELLATION ON DEPOSITS:** If Buyer or Seller gives written notice of cancellation pursuant to rights duly exercised under the terms of this Agreement, Buyer and Seller agree to Sign mutual instructions to cancel the sale and escrow and release deposits, if any, to the party entitled to the funds, less fees and costs incurred by that party. Fees and costs may be payable to service providers and vendors for services and products provided during escrow. **Release of funds will require mutual Signed release instructions from Buyer and Seller, judicial decision or arbitration award. A Buyer or Seller may be subject to a civil penalty of up to $1,000 for refusal to sign such instructions if no good faith dispute exists as to who is entitled to the deposited funds (Civil Code §1057.3).**

15. **REPAIRS:** Repairs shall be completed prior to final verification of condition unless otherwise agreed in writing. Repairs to be performed at Seller's expense may be performed by Seller or through others, provided that the work complies with applicable Law, including governmental permit, inspection and approval requirements. Repairs shall be performed in a good, skillful manner with materials of quality and appearance comparable to existing materials. It is understood that exact restoration of appearance or cosmetic items following all Repairs may not be possible. Seller shall: **(i)** obtain receipts for Repairs performed by others; **(ii)** prepare a written statement indicating the Repairs performed by Seller and the date of such Repairs; and **(iii)** provide Copies of receipts and statements to Buyer prior to final verification of condition.

16. **FINAL VERIFICATION OF CONDITION:** Buyer shall have the right to make a final inspection of the Property within **5 (or __________) Days** Prior to Close Of Escrow, NOT AS A CONTINGENCY OF THE SALE, but solely to confirm: **(i)** the Property is maintained pursuant to paragraph 9; **(ii)** Repairs have been completed as agreed; and **(iii)** Seller has complied with Seller's other obligations under this Agreement (C.A.R. Form VP).

17. **PRORATIONS OF PROPERTY TAXES AND OTHER ITEMS:** Unless otherwise agreed in writing, the following items shall be PAID CURRENT and prorated between Buyer and Seller as of Close Of Escrow: real property taxes and assessments, interest, rents, HOA regular, special, and emergency dues and assessments imposed prior to Close Of Escrow, premiums on insurance assumed by Buyer, payments on bonds and assessments assumed by Buyer, and payments on Mello-Roos and other Special Assessment District bonds and assessments that are a current lien. The following items shall be assumed by Buyer WITHOUT CREDIT toward the purchase price: prorated payments on Mello-Roos and other Special Assessment District bonds and assessments and HOA special assessments that are a current lien but not yet due. Property will be reassessed upon change of ownership. Any supplemental tax bills shall be paid as follows: **(i)** for periods after Close Of Escrow, by Buyer; and **(ii)** for periods prior to Close Of Escrow, by Seller (see C.A.R. Form SPT or SBSA for further information). TAX BILLS ISSUED AFTER CLOSE OF ESCROW SHALL BE HANDLED DIRECTLY BETWEEN BUYER AND SELLER. Prorations shall be made based on a 30-day month.

Buyer's Initials (________) (________) Seller's Initials (________) (________)

RPA-CA REVISED 4/10 (PAGE 5 OF 8)

Reviewed by ________ Date ________

EQUAL HOUSING OPPORTUNITY

CALIFORNIA RESIDENTIAL PURCHASE AGREEMENT (RPA-CA PAGE 5 OF 8)

Cal Principles -

Property Address: 264 Beach Lane Costa Mesa, CA 92627 Date: June 14, 20xx

18. **SELECTION OF SERVICE PROVIDERS:** Brokers do not guarantee the performance of any vendors, service or product providers ("Providers"), whether referred by Broker or selected by Buyer, Seller or other person. Buyer and Seller may select ANY Providers of their own choosing.
19. **MULTIPLE LISTING SERVICE ("MLS"):** Brokers are authorized to report to the MLS a pending sale and, upon Close Of Escrow, the sales price and other terms of this transaction shall be provided to the MLS to be published and disseminated to persons and entities authorized to use the information on terms approved by the MLS.
20. **EQUAL HOUSING OPPORTUNITY:** The Property is sold in compliance with federal, state and local anti-discrimination Laws.
21. **ATTORNEY FEES:** In any action, proceeding, or arbitration between Buyer and Seller arising out of this Agreement, the prevailing Buyer or Seller shall be entitled to reasonable attorney fees and costs from the non-prevailing Buyer or Seller, except as provided in paragraph 26A.
22. **DEFINITIONS:** As used in this Agreement:
    - A. **"Acceptance"** means the time the offer or final counter offer is accepted in writing by a party and is delivered to and personally received by the other party or that party's authorized agent in accordance with the terms of this offer or a final counter offer.
    - B. **"C.A.R. Form"** means the specific form referenced or another comparable form agreed to by the parties.
    - C. **"Close Of Escrow"** means the date the grant deed, or other evidence of transfer of title, is recorded.
    - D. **"Copy"** means copy by any means including photocopy, NCR, facsimile and electronic.
    - E. **"Days"** means calendar days. However, After Acceptance, the last **Day** for performance of any act required by this Agreement (including Close Of Escrow) shall not include any Saturday, Sunday, or legal holiday and shall instead be the next Day.
    - F. **"Days After"** means the specified number of calendar days after the occurrence of the event specified, not counting the calendar date on which the specified event occurs, and ending at 11:59PM on the final day.
    - G. **"Days Prior"** means the specified number of calendar days before the occurrence of the event specified, not counting the calendar date on which the specified event is scheduled to occur.
    - H. **"Deliver", "Delivered" or "Delivery"**, regardless of the method used (i.e. messenger, mail, email, fax, other), means and shall be effective upon (i) personal receipt by Buyer or Seller or the individual Real Estate Licensee for that principal as specified in paragraph D of the section titled Real Estate Brokers on page 8; OR (ii) if checked, ☐ per the attached addendum (C.A.R. Form RDN).
    - I. **"Electronic Copy" or "Electronic Signature"** means, as applicable, an electronic copy or signature complying with California Law. Buyer and Seller agree that electronic means will not be used by either party to modify or alter the content or integrity of this Agreement without the knowledge and consent of the other party.
    - J. **"Law"** means any law, code, statute, ordinance, regulation, rule or order, which is adopted by a controlling city, county, state or federal legislative, judicial or executive body or agency.
    - K. **"Repairs"** means any repairs (including pest control), alterations, replacements, modifications or retrofitting of the Property provided for under this Agreement.
    - L. **"Signed"** means either a handwritten or electronic signature on an original document, Copy or any counterpart.
23. **BROKER COMPENSATION:** Seller or Buyer, or both, as applicable, agrees to pay compensation to Broker as specified in a separate written agreement between Broker and that Seller or Buyer. Compensation is payable upon Close Of Escrow, or if escrow does not close, as otherwise specified in the agreement between Broker and that Seller or Buyer.
24. **JOINT ESCROW INSTRUCTIONS TO ESCROW HOLDER:**
    - A. **The following paragraphs, or applicable portions thereof, of this Agreement constitute the joint escrow instructions of Buyer and Seller to Escrow Holder,** which Escrow Holder is to use along with any related counter offers and addenda, and any additional mutual instructions to close the escrow: 1, 3, 4, 6C, 11B and D, 12, 13B, 14F, 17, 22, 23, 24, 28, 30, and paragraph D of the section titled Real Estate Brokers on page 8. If a Copy of the separate compensation agreement(s) provided for in paragraph 23, or paragraph D of the section titled Real Estate Brokers on page 8 is deposited with Escrow Holder by Broker, Escrow Holder shall accept such agreement(s) and pay out of Buyer's or Seller's funds, or both, as applicable, the respective Broker's compensation provided for in such agreement(s). The terms and conditions of this Agreement not specifically referenced above, in the specified paragraphs are additional matters for the information of Escrow Holder, but about which Escrow Holder need not be concerned. Buyer and Seller will receive Escrow Holder's general provisions directly from Escrow Holder and will execute such provisions upon Escrow Holder's request. To the extent the general provisions are inconsistent or conflict with this Agreement, the general provisions will control as to the duties and obligations of Escrow Holder only. Buyer and Seller will execute additional instructions, documents and forms provided by Escrow Holder that are reasonably necessary to close the escrow.
    - B. A Copy of this Agreement shall be delivered to Escrow Holder within 3 business days after Acceptance (or ☐ ____________________). Escrow Holder shall provide Seller's Statement of Information to Title company when received from Seller. Buyer and Seller authorize Escrow Holder to accept and rely on Copies and Signatures as defined in this Agreement as originals, to open escrow and for other purposes of escrow. The validity of this Agreement as between Buyer and Seller is not affected by whether or when Escrow Holder Signs this Agreement.
    - C. Brokers are a party to the escrow for the sole purpose of compensation pursuant to paragraphs 23 and paragraph D of the section titled Real Estate Brokers on page 8. Buyer and Seller irrevocably assign to Brokers compensation specified in paragraphs 23, respectively, and irrevocably instruct Escrow Holder to disburse those funds to Brokers at Close Of Escrow or pursuant to any other mutually executed cancellation agreement. Compensation instructions can be amended or revoked only with the written consent of Brokers. Buyer and Seller shall release and hold harmless Escrow Holder from any liability resulting from Escrow Holder's payment to Broker(s) of compensation pursuant to this Agreement. Escrow Holder shall immediately notify Brokers: **(i)** if Buyer's initial or any additional deposit is not made pursuant to this Agreement, or is not good at time of deposit with Escrow Holder; or **(ii)** if either Buyer or Seller instruct Escrow Holder to cancel escrow.
    - D. A Copy of any amendment that affects any paragraph of this Agreement for which Escrow Holder is responsible shall be delivered to Escrow Holder within 2 business days after mutual execution of the amendment.

Buyer's Initials (________) (________) Seller's Initials (________) (________)

RPA-CA REVISED 4/10 (PAGE 6 OF 8) Print Date | Reviewed by ________ Date ________ | EQUAL HOUSING OPPORTUNITY

CALIFORNIA RESIDENTIAL PURCHASE AGREEMENT (RPA-CA PAGE 6 OF 8) Cal Principles -

Property Address: *264 Beach Lane Costa Mesa, CA 92627* Date: *June 14, 20xx*

25. **LIQUIDATED DAMAGES: If Buyer fails to complete this purchase because of Buyer's default, Seller shall retain, as liquidated damages, the deposit actually paid. If the Property is a dwelling with no more than four units, one of which Buyer intends to occupy, then the amount retained shall be no more than 3% of the purchase price. Any excess shall be returned to Buyer. Release of funds will require mutual, Signed release instructions from both Buyer and Seller, judicial decision or arbitration award. AT TIME OF THE INCREASED DEPOSIT BUYER AND SELLER SHALL SIGN A SEPARATE LIQUIDATED DAMAGES PROVISION FOR ANY INCREASED DEPOSIT. (C.A.R. FORM RID).**

Buyer's Initials _______ / _______ Seller's Initials _______ / _______

26. DISPUTE RESOLUTION:

A. **MEDIATION:** Buyer and Seller agree to mediate any dispute or claim arising between them out of this Agreement, or any resulting transaction, before resorting to arbitration or court action. **Buyer and Seller also agree to mediate any disputes or claims with Broker(s), who, in writing, agree to such mediation prior to, or within a reasonable time after, the dispute or claim is presented to the Broker.** Mediation fees, if any, shall be divided equally among the parties involved. If, for any dispute or claim to which this paragraph applies, any party (i) commences an action without first attempting to resolve the matter through mediation, or (ii) before commencement of an action, refuses to mediate after a request has been made, then that party shall not be entitled to recover attorney fees, even if they would otherwise be available to that party in any such action. THIS MEDIATION PROVISION APPLIES WHETHER OR NOT THE ARBITRATION PROVISION IS INITIALED. **Exclusions from this mediation agreement are specified in paragraph 26C.**

B. **ARBITRATION OF DISPUTES:**
Buyer and Seller agree that any dispute or claim in Law or equity arising between them out of this Agreement or any resulting transaction, which is not settled through mediation, shall be decided by neutral, binding arbitration. Buyer and Seller also agree to arbitrate any disputes or claims with Broker(s), who, in writing, agree to such arbitration prior to, or within a reasonable time after, the dispute or claim is presented to the Broker. The arbitrator shall be a retired judge or justice, or an attorney with at least 5 years of residential real estate Law experience, unless the parties mutually agree to a different arbitrator. The parties shall have the right to discovery in accordance with Code of Civil Procedure §1283.05. In all other respects, the arbitration shall be conducted in accordance with Title 9 of Part 3 of the Code of Civil Procedure. Judgment upon the award of the arbitrator(s) may be entered into any court having jurisdiction. Enforcement of this agreement to arbitrate shall be governed by the Federal Arbitration Act. Exclusions from this arbitration agreement are specified in paragraph 26C.

"NOTICE: BY INITIALING IN THE SPACE BELOW YOU ARE AGREEING TO HAVE ANY DISPUTE ARISING OUT OF THE MATTERS INCLUDED IN THE 'ARBITRATION OF DISPUTES' PROVISION DECIDED BY NEUTRAL ARBITRATION AS PROVIDED BY CALIFORNIA LAW AND YOU ARE GIVING UP ANY RIGHTS YOU MIGHT POSSESS TO HAVE THE DISPUTE LITIGATED IN A COURT OR JURY TRIAL. BY INITIALING IN THE SPACE BELOW YOU ARE GIVING UP YOUR JUDICIAL RIGHTS TO DISCOVERY AND APPEAL, UNLESS THOSE RIGHTS ARE SPECIFICALLY INCLUDED IN THE 'ARBITRATION OF DISPUTES' PROVISION. IF YOU REFUSE TO SUBMIT TO ARBITRATION AFTER AGREEING TO THIS PROVISION, YOU MAY BE COMPELLED TO ARBITRATE UNDER THE AUTHORITY OF THE CALIFORNIA CODE OF CIVIL PROCEDURE. YOUR AGREEMENT TO THIS ARBITRATION PROVISION IS VOLUNTARY."

"WE HAVE READ AND UNDERSTAND THE FOREGOING AND AGREE TO SUBMIT DISPUTES ARISING OUT OF THE MATTERS INCLUDED IN THE 'ARBITRATION OF DISPUTES' PROVISION TO NEUTRAL ARBITRATION."

Buyer's Initials _______ / _______ Seller's Initials _______ / _______

C. ADDITIONAL MEDIATION AND ARBITRATION TERMS:

(1) **EXCLUSIONS: The following matters shall be excluded from mediation and arbitration: (i) a judicial or non-judicial foreclosure or other action or proceeding to enforce a deed of trust, mortgage or installment land sale contract as defined in Civil Code §2985; (ii) an unlawful detainer action; (iii) the filing or enforcement of a mechanic's lien; and (iv) any matter that is within the jurisdiction of a probate, small claims or bankruptcy court. The filing of a court action to enable the recording of a notice of pending action, for order of attachment, receivership, injunction, or other provisional remedies, shall not constitute a waiver or violation of the mediation and arbitration provisions.**

(2) **BROKERS: Brokers shall not be obligated or compelled to mediate or arbitrate unless they agree to do so in writing. Any Broker(s) participating in mediation or arbitration shall not be deemed a party to the Agreement.**

27. TERMS AND CONDITIONS OF OFFER:
This is an offer to purchase the Property on the above terms and conditions. The liquidated damages paragraph or the arbitration of disputes paragraph is incorporated in this Agreement if initialed by all parties or if incorporated by mutual agreement in a counter offer or addendum. If at least one but not all parties initial such paragraph(s), a counter offer is required until agreement is reached. Seller has the right to continue to offer the Property for sale and to accept any other offer at any time prior to notification of Acceptance. If this offer is accepted and Buyer subsequently defaults, Buyer may be responsible for payment of Brokers' compensation. This Agreement and any supplement, addendum or modification, including any Copy, may be Signed in two or more counterparts, all of which shall constitute one and the same writing.

28. TIME OF ESSENCE; ENTIRE CONTRACT; CHANGES: Time is of the essence. All understandings between the parties are incorporated in this Agreement. Its terms are intended by the parties as a final, complete and exclusive expression of their Agreement with respect to its subject matter, and may not be contradicted by evidence of any prior agreement or contemporaneous oral agreement. If any provision of this Agreement is held to be ineffective or invalid, the remaining provisions will nevertheless be given full force and effect. Except as otherwise specified, this Agreement shall be interpreted and disputes shall be resolved in accordance with the laws of the State of California. **Neither this Agreement nor any provision in it may be extended, amended, modified, altered or changed, except in writing Signed by Buyer and Seller.**

Buyer's Initials (_______) (_______) Seller's Initials (_______) (_______)

RPA-CA REVISED 4/10 (PAGE 7 OF 8)

Reviewed by _______ Date _______

EQUAL HOUSING OPPORTUNITY

CALIFORNIA RESIDENTIAL PURCHASE AGREEMENT (RPA-CA PAGE 7 OF 8)

Cal Principles -

Property Address: *264 Beach Lane Costa Mesa, CA 92627* Date: *June 14, 20xx*

29. **EXPIRATION OF OFFER:** This offer shall be deemed revoked and the deposit shall be returned unless the offer is Signed by Seller and a Copy of the Signed offer is personally received by Buyer, or by ______________________, who is authorized to receive it, by 5:00 PM on the third Day after this offer is signed by Buyer (or, if checked, ☐ by ______________ ☐ AM ☐ PM, on ______________ (date)).

Buyer has read and acknowledges receipt of a Copy of the offer and agrees to the above confirmation of agency relationships.

Date *June 14, 20xx* Date *June 14, 20xx*

BUYER ______________ BUYER ______________

Walter Buyer *Debbie Buyer*
(Print name) **(Print name)**

100 Boat Avenue, Marina del Rey CA 90292
(Address)

☐ Additional Signature Addendum attached (C.A.R. Form ASA).

30. **ACCEPTANCE OF OFFER:** Seller warrants that Seller is the owner of the Property, or has the authority to execute this Agreement. Seller accepts the above offer, agrees to sell the Property on the above terms and conditions, and agrees to the above confirmation of agency relationships. Seller has read and acknowledges receipt of a Copy of this Agreement, and authorizes Broker to Deliver a Signed Copy to Buyer.

☐ (If checked) **SUBJECT TO ATTACHED COUNTER OFFER (C.A.R. Form CO) DATED:** ______________.

Date *June 15, 20xx* Date *June 15, 20xx*

SELLER ______________ SELLER ______________

Tony Seller *Ramona J. Seller*
(Print name) **(Print name)**

264 Beach Lane, Costa Mesa, CA 92627
(Address)

☐ Additional Signature Addendum attached (C.A.R. Form ASA).

(_____ / _____) (Initials) **CONFIRMATION OF ACCEPTANCE:** A Copy of Signed Acceptance was personally received by Buyer or Buyer's authorized agent on (date) *June 15, 20xx* at *11* ☒ AM ☐ PM. **A binding Agreement is created when a Copy of Signed Acceptance is personally received by Buyer or Buyer's authorized agent whether or not confirmed in this document. Completion of this confirmation is not legally required in order to create a binding Agreement. It is solely intended to evidence the date that Confirmation of Acceptance has occurred.**

REAL ESTATE BROKERS:

A. **Real Estate Brokers are not parties to the Agreement between Buyer and Seller.**
B. **Agency relationships are confirmed as stated in paragraph 2.**
C. If specified in paragraph 3A(2), Agent who submitted the offer for Buyer acknowledges receipt of deposit.
D. **COOPERATING BROKER COMPENSATION:** Listing Broker agrees to pay Cooperating Broker **(Selling Firm)** and Cooperating Broker agrees to accept, out of Listing Broker's proceeds in escrow: **(i)** the amount specified in the MLS, provided Cooperating Broker is a Participant of the MLS in which the Property is offered for sale or a reciprocal MLS; or **(ii)** ☐ (if checked) the amount specified in a separate written agreement (C.A.R. Form CBC) between Listing Broker and Cooperating Broker. Declaration of License and Tax (C.A.R. Form DLT) may be used to document that tax reporting will be required or that an exemption exits.

Real Estate Broker (Selling Firm) *Ramos Realty* DRE Lic. # *00 000 000*
By *Joseph Ramos* DRE Lic. # *00 000 000* Date *06/14/20xx*
Address *777 Newport Blvd.* City *Newport Beach* State *CA* Zip *92663*
Telephone *(714) 647-0000* Fax *(714) 647-0001* E-mail *jr@ramosrealty.com*

Real Estate Broker (Listing Firm) *Sail Realty* DRE Lic. # *00 000 000*
By *Carmen Caro* DRE Lic. # *00 000 000* Date *06/15/20xx*
Address *227 Harbor Blvd.* City *Costa Mesa* State *CA* Zip *92627*
Telephone *(714) 626-2828* Fax *(714) 626-2829* E-mail *carmen@sailrealty.com*

ESCROW HOLDER ACKNOWLEDGMENT:

Escrow Holder acknowledges receipt of a Copy of this Agreement, (if checked, ☐ a deposit in the amount of $______________), counter offer numbered ______________, ☐ Seller's Statement of Information and ☐ Other ______________, and agrees to act as Escrow Holder subject to paragraph 24 of this Agreement, any supplemental escrow instructions and the terms of Escrow Holder's general provisions if any.

Escrow Holder is advised that the date of Confirmation of Acceptance of the Agreement as between Buyer and Seller is ______________.

Escrow Holder ______________ Escrow # ______________
By ______________ Date ______________
Address ______________
Phone/Fax/E-mail ______________
Escrow Holder is licensed by the California Department of ☐ Corporations, ☐ Insurance, ☐ Real Estate. License # ______________

PRESENTATION OF OFFER: (__________) Listing Broker presented this offer to Seller on ______________ (date).
Broker or Designee Initials

REJECTION OF OFFER: (______) (______) No counter offer is being made. This offer was rejected by Seller on ______________ (date).
Seller's Initials

Published and Distributed by:
REAL ESTATE BUSINESS SERVICES, INC.
a subsidiary of the California Association of REALTORS®
525 South Virgil Avenue, Los Angeles, California 90020

Reviewed by
Broker or Designee ______________ Date ______________

EQUAL HOUSING OPPORTUNITY

REVISION DATE 4/10

CALIFORNIA RESIDENTIAL PURCHASE AGREEMENT (RPA-CA PAGE 8 OF 8)

Cal Principles -

1. Credit Scoring

***CREDIT SCORING** gives lenders a fast, objective measurement of your ability to repay a loan or make timely credit payments.* It is based solely on information in consumer credit reports maintained at one of the credit reporting agencies. Factors comprising a credit score include:

1. **Payment History** – What is your track record?
2. **Amounts Owed** – How much is too much?
3. **Length of Credit History** – How established is yours?
4. **New Credit** – Are you taking on more debt?
5. **Types of Credit Use** – Is it a "healthy" mix?

*The most widely used credit bureau scores are developed by Fair, Isaac and Company. These are known as **FICO SCORES**.* See **Figure 8-2** for a fuller description of credit scoring, which is often difficult to explain.

B. ANALYSIS OF THE BORROWER AND THE PROPERTY

Once the application has been properly filled out, the lender can begin gathering other pertinent information on the buyer. Verification forms will be sent out to the buyer's employer, banks, or other financial institutions, and any previous mortgage lender. The lender will order a credit report and have a preliminary title report prepared. A *CREDIT REPORT verifies the borrower's good credit standing.* An approved appraiser will also be contacted to have an appraisal done on the property. An *APPRAISAL provides a professional third-party opinion of the value of the property.*

After examining the application, the lender may also ask the buyer to submit further information, including:

1. a copy of any divorce decree (to verify any child support or alimony obligations and any settlement agreement that may be the source of the down payment);
2. an investment account record;
3. pension plan documentation;
4. tax returns (if the buyer is self-employed or retired and living on investment income), and
5. any other documentation that may have an effect on the buyer's income or credit status. (See **Figures 8-3** through **8-5**).

The lender will be very concerned with the source of the buyer's down payment. Personal savings, the previous sale of a home, or gifts are all acceptable sources of the down payment.

Figure 8-2

Credit Scoring

The higher your credit score, the better your interest rates and terms of the loan.

WHAT IS CREDIT SCORING?

Credit scores are assigned numbers used by lenders to determine whether a consumer will get a loan and at what interest rate. Individual lenders often contract with a credit reporting agency such as TransUnion (**transunion.com**), Experian (**experian.com**), or Equifax (**equifax.com**) who compile consumer credit information. These companies then contract with different credit scoring companies, such as Fair, Isaac and Company (www.fairisaac.com), who own the mathematical model used to create the 3-digit FICO score. They provide the lender with a list of "reason codes" that the lender can choose from when receiving scores for consumers applying for mortgages. The reason codes can include things like, "too few bank card accounts," "too many subprime accounts," etc. The credit scoring company uses information from a consumer's credit report, together with these reason codes and the mathematical formula to create an individual's credit score.

In an effort to better predict the likelihood of default, Fair Isaac recently introduced **FICO 08**. Changes in the existing method of credit scoring include those involving:

Authorized Users – An authorized user is a person that is permitted by another account holder to use their account. The new scoring model eliminates "piggybacking" which allowed individuals with bad credit to leverage the payment histories of "stronger" credit card holders by becoming an authorized user on their accounts.

Delinquencies – The second change in the scoring model has to do with payment patterns - especially those that are greater than 90 days late in making a payment.

The FICO 08 model will be more forgiving to consumers that are in arrears in one area, but have a number of other accounts that are in good standing.

The law:

1. requires lenders to provide consumers with their specific credit score, what credit information went into making up the score, and an explanation of how credit scores work in the loan approval process;
2. compels credit reporting agencies to correct inaccurate information in a timely manner, and
3. requires credit reporting agencies to correct inaccurate information more quickly and provide consumers with additional legal recourse if an agency continues to report inaccurate information once they become aware that a mistake has been made.

FICO scores generally range from 300 to 850, with the lower score indicating likely borrower default and the higher score indicating just a slight chance of borrower default. Lenders will receive three different credit scores, from FICO (Experian), Beacon (Equifax), and Empirica (TransUnion), and usually pick the middle score.

Figure 8-3

GIFT LETTER

Applicant(s): Loan Number:

I, ______________________ (Donor), do hereby certify the following:

(1) I have made a gift of $ ________ (Amount) to ______________ (Recipient)

Whose relationship is: ______________ (Relationship)

(2) This gift is to be applied toward the purchase of the property located at:

______________________ (Property Address)

(3) No repayment of the gift is expected or implied in the form of cash or by future services of the recipient.

(4) The funds given to the homebuyer were not made available to the donor from any person or entity with an interest in the sale of the property including the seller, real estate agent or broker, builder, loan officer, or any entity associated with them.

(5) The source of this gift is: ______________ (Source)

Donor Signature Date	Borrower Signature
Donor Name (Print or Type)	Borrower Signature
Donor Address	
( ) Donor Phone Number	

WARNING: Our signatures above indicate that we fully understand that it is a Federal Crime punishable by fine, imprisonment, or both to knowingly make any false statement concerning any of the above facts as applicable under the provision of Title 18, United States Code, Section 1012 and 1014.

Attachments:

1. **Evidence of Donor's Ability to Provide Funds.**
2. **Evidence of Receipt of Transfer of Funds.**

Figure 8-4

Form **4506**
(Rev. January 2012)
Department of the Treasury
Internal Revenue Service

Request for Copy of Tax Return

OMB No. 1545-0429

▶ **Request may be rejected if the form is incomplete or illegible.**

Tip. You may be able to get your tax return or return information from other sources. If you had your tax return completed by a paid preparer, they should be able to provide you a copy of the return. The IRS can provide a **Tax Return Transcript** for many returns free of charge. The transcript provides most of the line entries from the original tax return and usually contains the information that a third party (such as a mortgage company) requires. See **Form 4506-T, Request for Transcript of Tax Return,** or you can quickly request transcripts by using our automated self-help service tools. Please visit us at IRS.gov and click on "Order a Transcript" or call 1-800-908-9946.

1a Name shown on tax return. If a joint return, enter the name shown first.	**1b First social security number on tax return, individual taxpayer identification number, or employer identification number (see instructions)**
2a If a joint return, enter spouse's name shown on tax return.	**2b Second social security number or individual taxpayer identification number if joint tax return**

3 Current name, address (including apt., room, or suite no.), city, state, and ZIP code (see instructions)

4 Previous address shown on the last return filed if different from line 3 (see instructions)

5 If the tax return is to be mailed to a third party (such as a mortgage company), enter the third party's name, address, and telephone number.

Caution. *If the tax return is being mailed to a third party, ensure that you have filled in lines 6 and 7 before signing. Sign and date the form once you have filled in these lines. Completing these steps helps to protect your privacy. Once the IRS discloses your IRS return to the third party listed on line 5, the IRS has no control over what the third party does with the information. If you would like to limit the third party's authority to disclose your return information, you can specify this limitation in your written agreement with the third party.*

6 **Tax return requested.** Form 1040, 1120, 941, etc. and all attachments as originally submitted to the IRS, including Form(s) W-2, schedules, or amended returns. Copies of Forms 1040, 1040A, and 1040EZ are generally available for 7 years from filing before they are destroyed by law. Other returns may be available for a longer period of time. Enter only one return number. If you need more than one type of return, you must complete another Form 4506. ▶ ____________

Note. *If the copies must be certified for court or administrative proceedings, check here* . . . . ☐

7 **Year or period requested.** Enter the ending date of the year or period, using the mm/dd/yyyy format. If you are requesting more than eight years or periods, you must attach another Form 4506.

________ ________ ________ ________

________ ________ ________ ________

8 **Fee.** There is a $57 fee for each return requested. **Full payment must be included with your request or it will be rejected. Make your check or money order payable to "United States Treasury." Enter your SSN or EIN and "Form 4506 request" on your check or money order.**

a	Cost for each return	$ **$57.00**
b	Number of returns requested on line 7	
c	Total cost. Multiply line 8a by line 8b	$

9 If we cannot find the tax return, we will refund the fee. If the refund should go to the third party listed on line 5, check here . . . . . . ☐

Caution. Do not sign this form unless all applicable lines have been completed.

Signature of taxpayer(s). I declare that I am either the taxpayer whose name is shown on line 1a or 2a, or a person authorized to obtain the tax return requested. If the request applies to a joint return, **either** husband or wife must sign. If signed by a corporate officer, partner, guardian, tax matters partner, executor, receiver, administrator, trustee, or party other than the taxpayer, I certify that I have the authority to execute Form 4506 on behalf of the taxpayer. **Note.** *For tax returns being sent to a third party, this form must be received within 120 days of the signature date.*

Phone number of taxpayer on line 1a or 2a

Sign Here

▶ **Signature** (see instructions) — Date

▶ **Title** (if line 1a above is a corporation, partnership, estate, or trust)

▶ **Spouse's signature** — Date

For Privacy Act and Paperwork Reduction Act Notice, see page 2. Cat. No. 41721E Form **4506** (Rev. 1-2012)

Figure 8-5

Form **4506-T** (Rev. January 2012) Department of the Treasury Internal Revenue Service

Request for Transcript of Tax Return

▶ **Request may be rejected if the form is incomplete or illegible.**

OMB No. 1545-1872

Tip. Use Form 4506-T to order a transcript or other return information free of charge. See the product list below. You can quickly request transcripts by using our automated self-help service tools. Please visit us at IRS.gov and click on "Order a Transcript" or call 1-800-908-9946. If you need a copy of your return, use **Form 4506, Request for Copy of Tax Return.** There is a fee to get a copy of your return.

1a Name shown on tax return. If a joint return, enter the name shown first.	**1b First social security number on tax return, individual taxpayer identification number, or employer identification number (see instructions)**
2a If a joint return, enter spouse's name shown on tax return.	**2b Second social security number or individual taxpayer identification number if joint tax return**

3 Current name, address (including apt., room, or suite no.), city, state, and ZIP code (see instructions)

4 Previous address shown on the last return filed if different from line 3 (see instructions)

5 If the transcript or tax information is to be mailed to a third party (such as a mortgage company), enter the third party's name, address, and telephone number.

Caution. *If the tax transcript is being mailed to a third party, ensure that you have filled in lines 6 through 9 before signing. Sign and date the form once you have filled in these lines. Completing these steps helps to protect your privacy. Once the IRS discloses your IRS transcript to the third party listed on line 5, the IRS has no control over what the third party does with the information. If you would like to limit the third party's authority to disclose your transcript information, you can specify this limitation in your written agreement with the third party.*

6 **Transcript requested.** Enter the tax form number here (1040, 1065, 1120, etc.) and check the appropriate box below. Enter only one tax form number per request. ▶ ______

a **Return Transcript,** which includes most of the line items of a tax return as filed with the IRS. A tax return transcript does not reflect changes made to the account after the return is processed. Transcripts are only available for the following returns: Form 1040 series, Form 1065, Form 1120, Form 1120A, Form 1120H, Form 1120L, and Form 1120S. Return transcripts are available for the current year and returns processed during the prior 3 processing years. Most requests will be processed within 10 business days ☐

b **Account Transcript,** which contains information on the financial status of the account, such as payments made on the account, penalty assessments, and adjustments made by you or the IRS after the return was filed. Return information is limited to items such as tax liability and estimated tax payments. Account transcripts are available for most returns. Most requests will be processed within 30 calendar days ☐

c **Record of Account,** which provides the most detailed information as it is a combination of the Return Transcript and the Account Transcript. Available for current year and 3 prior tax years. Most requests will be processed within 30 calendar days ☐

7 **Verification of Nonfiling,** which is proof from the IRS that you **did not** file a return for the year. Current year requests are only available after June 15th. There are no availability restrictions on prior year requests. Most requests will be processed within 10 business days ☐

8 **Form W-2, Form 1099 series, Form 1098 series, or Form 5498 series transcript.** The IRS can provide a transcript that includes data from these information returns. State or local information is not included with the Form W-2 information. The IRS may be able to provide this transcript information for up to 10 years. Information for the current year is generally not available until the year after it is filed with the IRS. For example, W-2 information for 2010, filed in 2011, will not be available from the IRS until 2012. If you need W-2 information for retirement purposes, you should contact the Social Security Administration at 1-800-772-1213. Most requests will be processed within 45 days ☐

Caution. *If you need a copy of Form W-2 or Form 1099, you should first contact the payer. To get a copy of the Form W-2 or Form 1099 filed with your return, you must use Form 4506 and request a copy of your return, which includes all attachments.*

9 **Year or period requested.** Enter the ending date of the year or period, using the mm/dd/yyyy format. If you are requesting more than four years or periods, you must attach another Form 4506-T. For requests relating to quarterly tax returns, such as Form 941, you must enter each quarter or tax period separately. ______ ______ ______ ______

Check this box if you have notified the IRS or the IRS has notified you that one of the years for which you are requesting a transcript involved **identity theft** on your federal tax return ☐

Caution. Do not sign this form unless all applicable lines have been completed.

Signature of taxpayer(s). I declare that I am either the taxpayer whose name is shown on line 1a or 2a, or a person authorized to obtain the tax information requested. If the request applies to a joint return, **either** husband or wife must sign. If signed by a corporate officer, partner, guardian, tax matters partner, executor, receiver, administrator, trustee, or party other than the taxpayer, I certify that I have the authority to execute Form 4506-T on behalf of the taxpayer. **Note.** *For transcripts being sent to a third party, this form must be received within 120 days of the signature date.*

Phone number of taxpayer on line 1a or 2a

Sign Here

▶ **Signature** (see instructions) Date

▶ **Title** (if line 1a above is a corporation, partnership, estate, or trust)

▶ **Spouse's signature** Date

For Privacy Act and Paperwork Reduction Act Notice, see page 2. Cat. No. 37667N Form **4506-T** (Rev. 1-2012)

Using borrowed funds for the down payment is usually not permitted.

1. Equal Credit Opportunity Act (ECOA)

The federal ***EQUAL CREDIT OPPORTUNITY ACT*** *prohibits discrimination based on age, sex, race, marital status, color, religion, or national origin*. Senior citizens, young adults, and single persons must be considered on the basis of income adequacy, satisfactory net worth, job stability, and satisfactory credit rating. Lenders must apply their credit guidelines to each potential borrower in the same manner.

The ECOA ensures that all consumers are given an equal chance to obtain credit.

C. PROCESSING THE LOAN APPLICATION

When the credit report, verification forms, preliminary title report, and appraisal have all been received by the lender, a loan package is put together and submitted to the underwriting department. The loan underwriter thoroughly examines the loan package and then makes the decision to approve it, reject it, or approve it under certain conditions. A conditional approval usually requires the submission of additional information, such as:

1. the closing statement from the sale of the buyer's previous home;
2. pay stubs to verify employment;
3. a final inspection report, and
4. a commitment for private mortgage insurance (PMI) if the down payment is less than 20% of the purchase price.

D. CLOSING THE LOAN

After the conditions are met, all the necessary documents are prepared for closing. The closing process ordinarily takes about one week if everything goes smoothly.

The mechanics of closing are normally the responsibility of the escrow agent.

This escrow holder may be an "in-house" escrow department of the lender, an independent escrow company, or a title insurance company (depending on the region). The escrow agent simultaneously follows the instructions of both the buyer and the seller, and is responsible for providing the lender with a certified copy of the **escrow instructions**. The escrow agent gathers together all the necessary documents (e.g., the promissory note and deed of trust) and makes sure that all the documents are properly signed by the parties. The escrow agent calculates the various prorations, adjustments, and charges to be assessed against each party, makes sure that all required funds and documents are deposited, and furnishes each party with a settlement (for closing) statement.

If there are no unforeseen problems during closing (e.g., the seller does not have title to the property), the loan papers are signed and sent to the funding department. This department makes one final check to be sure that everything is in order and that it has the necessary instructions for the release of the funds. The loan funds are then disbursed to the proper parties.

II. Filling Out The Loan Application

As mentioned earlier, the buyer fills out a loan application at the initial interview with the lender. A copy of such a loan application is shown in **Figure 8-6**. This standard loan application is used throughout the United States for a conventional (nongovernment-insured) loan.

Lenders expect the loans they make to be repaid without collection, loan servicing, or foreclosure problems. They are obviously careful to make loans only to those borrowers who can be expected to repay the loan in a timely manner. Therefore, employment stability, income potential, history of debt management, and net worth are important considerations to the lender. These are the types of information the loan application is designed to elicit.

A. (Section I) TYPE OF MORTGAGE AND TERMS OF LOAN

The lender notes the type of loan provided, i.e., Conventional, FHA, VA, as well as the loan amount, and the interest rate.

B. (Section II) PROPERTY INFORMATION

The application begins with a section on the property. Questions as to the type of loan sought, the terms of the loan, location and legal description of the property, the property's value, and the manner of taking title must be completed. This information is used to determine how much security for the loan will be provided.

Because lenders must live with their lending decisions for long periods of time, they are interested in the trend of the collateral's value as well as its current value.

Figure 8-6

Uniform Residential Loan Application

This application is designed to be completed by the applicant(s) with the Lender's assistance. Applicants should complete this form as "Borrower" or "Co-Borrower," as applicable. Co-Borrower information must also be provided (and the appropriate box checked) when ☐ the income or assets of a person other than the Borrower (including the Borrower's spouse) will be used as a basis for loan qualification or ☐ the income or assets of the Borrower's spouse or other person who has community property rights pursuant to state law will not be used as a basis for loan qualification, but his or her liabilities must be considered because the spouse or other person has community property rights pursuant to applicable law and Borrower resides in a community property state, the security property is located in a community property state, or the Borrower is relying on other property located in a community property state as a basis for repayment of the loan.

If this is an application for joint credit, Borrower and Co-Borrower each agree that we intend to apply for joint credit (sign below):

Borrower ____________________ Co-Borrower ____________________

I. TYPE OF MORTGAGE AND TERMS OF LOAN

Mortgage Applied for:	☐ VA ☐ FHA	☐ Conventional ☐ USDA/Rural Housing Service	☐ Other (explain):	Agency Case Number	Lender Case Number

Amount $	Interest Rate %	No. of Months	**Amortization Type:**	☐ Fixed Rate ☐ GPM	☐ Other (explain): ☐ ARM (type):

II. PROPERTY INFORMATION AND PURPOSE OF LOAN

Subject Property Address (street, city, state & ZIP)	No. of Units
Legal Description of Subject Property (attach description if necessary)	Year Built

Purpose of Loan	☐ Purchase ☐ Refinance	☐ Construction ☐ Construction-Permanent	☐ Other (explain):	Property will be: ☐ Primary Residence ☐ Secondary Residence ☐ Investment

Complete this line if construction or construction-permanent loan.

Year Lot Acquired	Original Cost	Amount Existing Liens	(a) Present Value of Lot	(b) Cost of Improvements	Total (a + b)
	$	$	$	$	$

Complete this line if this is a refinance loan.

Year Acquired	Original Cost	Amount Existing Liens	Purpose of Refinance	Describe Improvements ☐ made ☐ to be made
	$	$		Cost: $

Title will be held in what Name(s)	Manner in which Title will be held	Estate will be held in: ☐ Fee Simple ☐ Leasehold (show expiration date)
Source of Down Payment, Settlement Charges, and/or Subordinate Financing (explain)		

III. BORROWER INFORMATION

Borrower				Co-Borrower			
Borrower's Name (include Jr. or Sr. if applicable)				Co-Borrower's Name (include Jr. or Sr. if applicable)			
Social Security Number	Home Phone (incl. area code)	DOB (mm/dd/yyyy)	Yrs. School	Social Security Number	Home Phone (incl. area code)	DOB (mm/dd/yyyy)	Yrs. School
☐ Married ☐ Unmarried (include single, divorced, widowed) ☐ Separated		Dependents (not listed by Co-Borrower) no. ages		☐ Married ☐ Unmarried (include single, divorced, widowed) ☐ Separated		Dependents (not listed by Borrower) no. ages	
Present Address (street, city, state, ZIP) ☐ Own ☐ Rent ____No. Yrs.				Present Address (street, city, state, ZIP) ☐ Own ☐ Rent ____No. Yrs.			
Mailing Address, if different from Present Address				Mailing Address, if different from Present Address			

If residing at present address for less than two years, complete the following:

Former Address (street, city, state, ZIP) ☐ Own ☐ Rent ____No. Yrs.	Former Address (street, city, state, ZIP) ☐ Own ☐ Rent ____No. Yrs.

IV. EMPLOYMENT INFORMATION

Borrower			Co-Borrower		
Name & Address of Employer	☐ Self Employed	Yrs. on this job Yrs. employed in this line of work/profession	Name & Address of Employer	☐ Self Employed	Yrs. on this job Yrs. employed in this line of work/profession
Position/Title/Type of Business	Business Phone (incl. area code)		Position/Title/Type of Business	Business Phone (incl. area code)	

If employed in current position for less than two years or if currently employed in more than one position, complete the following:

Uniform Residential Loan Application
Freddie Mac Form 65 7/05 (rev.6/09) **Page 1 of 5** **Fannie Mae Form 1003 7/05 (rev.6/09)**

IV. EMPLOYMENT INFORMATION (cont'd)

Borrower			Co-Borrower		
Name & Address of Employer	☐ Self Employed	Dates (from – to)	Name & Address of Employer	☐ Self Employed	Dates (from – to)
		Monthly Income $			Monthly Income $
Position/Title/Type of Business	Business Phone (incl. area code)		Position/Title/Type of Business	Business Phone (incl. area code)	
Name & Address of Employer	☐ Self Employed	Dates (from – to)	Name & Address of Employer	☐ Self Employed	Dates (from – to)
		Monthly Income $			Monthly Income $
Position/Title/Type of Business	Business Phone (incl. area code)		Position/Title/Type of Business	Business Phone (incl. area code)	

V. MONTHLY INCOME AND COMBINED HOUSING EXPENSE INFORMATION

Gross Monthly Income	Borrower	Co-Borrower	Total	Combined Monthly Housing Expense	Present	Proposed
Base Empl. Income*	$	$	$	Rent	$	
Overtime				First Mortgage (P&I)		$
Bonuses				Other Financing (P&I)		
Commissions				Hazard Insurance		
Dividends/Interest				Real Estate Taxes		
Net Rental Income				Mortgage Insurance		
Other (before completing, see the notice in "describe other income," below)				Homeowner Assn. Dues		
				Other:		
Total	$	$	$	Total	$	$

* **Self Employed Borrower(s) may be required to provide additional documentation such as tax returns and financial statements.**

Describe Other Income

Notice: **Alimony, child support, or separate maintenance income need not be revealed if the Borrower (B) or Co-Borrower (C) does not choose to have it considered for repaying this loan.**

B/C		Monthly Amount
		$

VI. ASSETS AND LIABILITIES

This Statement and any applicable supporting schedules may be completed jointly by both married and unmarried Co-Borrowers if their assets and liabilities are sufficiently joined so that the Statement can be meaningfully and fairly presented on a combined basis; otherwise, separate Statements and Schedules are required. If the Co-Borrower section was completed about a non-applicant spouse or other person, this Statement and supporting schedules must be completed about that spouse or other person also.

Completed ☐ Jointly ☐ Not Jointly

ASSETS Description	Cash or Market Value	**Liabilities and Pledged Assets.** List the creditor's name, address, and account number for all outstanding debts, including automobile loans, revolving charge accounts, real estate loans, alimony, child support, stock pledges, etc. Use continuation sheet, if necessary. Indicate by (*) those liabilities, which will be satisfied upon sale of real estate owned or upon refinancing of the subject property.		
Cash deposit toward purchase held by:	$			
List checking and savings accounts below		**LIABILITIES**	**Monthly Payment & Months Left to Pay**	**Unpaid Balance**
Name and address of Bank, S&L, or Credit Union		Name and address of Company	$ Payment/Months	$
Acct. no.	$	Acct. no.		
Name and address of Bank, S&L, or Credit Union		Name and address of Company	$ Payment/Months	$
Acct. no.	$	Acct. no.		
Name and address of Bank, S&L, or Credit Union		Name and address of Company	$ Payment/Months	$
Acct. no.	$	Acct. no.		

Uniform Residential Loan Application
Freddie Mac Form 65 7/05 (rev. 6/09)

Page 2 of 5

Fannie Mae Form 1003 7/05 (rev.6/09)

VI. ASSETS AND LIABILITIES (cont'd)

Assets		Liabilities		
Name and address of Bank, S&L, or Credit Union		Name and address of Company	$ Payment/Months	$
Acct. no.	$	Acct. no.		
Stocks & Bonds (Company name/ number & description)	$	Name and address of Company	$ Payment/Months	$
		Acct. no.		
Life insurance net cash value Face amount: $	$	Name and address of Company	$ Payment/Months	$
Subtotal Liquid Assets	$			
Real estate owned (enter market value from schedule of real estate owned)	$			
Vested interest in retirement fund	$			
Net worth of business(es) owned (attach financial statement)	$	Acct. no.		
Automobiles owned (make and year)	$	Alimony/Child Support/Separate Maintenance Payments Owed to:	$	
Other Assets (itemize)	$	Job-Related Expense (child care, union dues, etc.)	$	
		Total Monthly Payments	$	
Total Assets a.	$	Net Worth (a minus b) ▶ $	**Total Liabilities b.**	$

Schedule of Real Estate Owned (If additional properties are owned, use continuation sheet.)

Property Address (enter S if sold, PS if pending sale or R if rental being held for income) ▼		Type of Property	Present Market Value	Amount of Mortgages & Liens	Gross Rental Income	Mortgage Payments	Insurance, Maintenance, Taxes & Misc.	Net Rental Income
			$	$	$	$	$	$
		Totals	$	$	$	$	$	$

List any additional names under which credit has previously been received and indicate appropriate creditor name(s) and account number(s):

Alternate Name	Creditor Name	Account Number

VII. DETAILS OF TRANSACTION		
a.	Purchase price	$
b.	Alterations, improvements, repairs	
c.	Land (if acquired separately)	
d.	Refinance (incl. debts to be paid off)	
e.	Estimated prepaid items	
f.	Estimated closing costs	
g.	PMI, MIP, Funding Fee	
h.	Discount (if Borrower will pay)	
i.	Total costs (add items a through h)	

VIII. DECLARATIONS

If you answer "Yes" to any questions a through i, please use continuation sheet for explanation.	Borrower Yes	Borrower No	Co-Borrower Yes	Co-Borrower No
a. Are there any outstanding judgments against you?	☐	☐	☐	☐
b. Have you been declared bankrupt within the past 7 years?	☐	☐	☐	☐
c. Have you had property foreclosed upon or given title or deed in lieu thereof in the last 7 years?	☐	☐	☐	☐
d. Are you a party to a lawsuit?	☐	☐	☐	☐
e. Have you directly or indirectly been obligated on any loan which resulted in foreclosure, transfer of title in lieu of foreclosure, or judgment? (This would include such loans as home mortgage loans, SBA loans, home improvement loans, educational loans, manufactured (mobile) home loans, any mortgage, financial obligation, bond, or loan guarantee. If "Yes," provide details, including date, name, and address of Lender, FHA or VA case number, if any, and reasons for the action.)	☐	☐	☐	☐

Uniform Residential Loan Application
Freddie Mac Form 65 7/05 (rev.6/09) **Page 3 of 5** **Fannie Mae Form 1003 7/05 (rev.6/09)**

VII. DETAILS OF TRANSACTION	
j. Subordinate financing	
k. Borrower's closing costs paid by Seller	
l. Other Credits (explain)	
m. Loan amount (exclude PMI, MIP, Funding Fee financed)	
n. PMI, MIP, Funding Fee financed	
o. Loan amount (add m & n)	
p. Cash from/to Borrower (subtract j, k, l & o from i)	

VIII. DECLARATIONS	Borrower		Co-Borrower	
If you answer "Yes" to any questions a through i, please use continuation sheet for explanation.	Yes	No	Yes	No
f. Are you presently delinquent or in default on any Federal debt or any other loan, mortgage, financial obligation, bond, or loan guarantee?	☐	☐	☐	☐
g. Are you obligated to pay alimony, child support, or separate maintenance?	☐	☐	☐	☐
h. Is any part of the down payment borrowed?	☐	☐	☐	☐
i. Are you a co-maker or endorser on a note?	☐	☐	☐	☐
j. Are you a U.S. citizen?	☐	☐	☐	☐
k. Are you a permanent resident alien?	☐	☐	☐	☐
l. Do you intend to occupy the property as your primary residence? If Yes," complete question m below.	☐	☐	☐	☐
m. Have you had an ownership interest in a property in the last three years?	☐	☐	☐	☐
(1) What type of property did you own—principal residence (PR), second home (SH), or investment property (IP)?	______		______	
(2) How did you hold title to the home— by yourself (S), jointly with your spouse (SP), or jointly with another person (O)?	______		______	

IX. ACKNOWLEDGEMENT AND AGREEMENT

Each of the undersigned specifically represents to Lender and to Lender's actual or potential agents, brokers, processors, attorneys, insurers, servicers, successors and assigns and agrees and acknowledges that: (1) the information provided in this application is true and correct as of the date set forth opposite my signature and that any intentional or negligent misrepresentation of this information contained in this application may result in civil liability, including monetary damages, to any person who may suffer any loss due to reliance upon any misrepresentation that I have made on this application, and/or in criminal penalties including, but not limited to, fine or imprisonment or both under the provisions of Title 18, United States Code, Sec. 1001, et seq.; (2) the loan requested pursuant to this application (the "Loan") will be secured by a mortgage or deed of trust on the property described in this application; (3) the property will not be used for any illegal or prohibited purpose or use; (4) all statements made in this application are made for the purpose of obtaining a residential mortgage loan; (5) the property will be occupied as indicated in this application; (6) the Lender, its servicers, successors or assigns may retain the original and/or an electronic record of this application, whether or not the Loan is approved; (7) the Lender and its agents, brokers, insurers, servicers, successors, and assigns may continuously rely on the information contained in the application, and I am obligated to amend and/or supplement the information provided in this application if any of the material facts that I have represented herein should change prior to closing of the Loan; (8) in the event that my payments on the Loan become delinquent, the Lender, its servicers, successors or assigns may, in addition to any other rights and remedies that it may have relating to such delinquency, report my name and account information to one or more consumer reporting agencies; (9) ownership of the Loan and/or administration of the Loan account may be transferred with such notice as may be required by law; (10) neither Lender nor its agents, brokers, insurers, servicers, successors or assigns has made any representation or warranty, express or implied, to me regarding the property or the condition or value of the property; and (11) my transmission of this application as an "electronic record" containing my "electronic signature," as those terms are defined in applicable federal and/or state laws (excluding audio and video recordings), or my facsimile transmission of this application containing a facsimile of my signature, shall be as effective, enforceable and valid as if a paper version of this application were delivered containing my original written signature.

Acknowledgement. Each of the undersigned hereby acknowledges that any owner of the Loan, its servicers, successors and assigns, may verify or reverify any information contained in this application or obtain any information or data relating to the Loan, for any legitimate business purpose through any source, including a source named in this application or a consumer reporting agency.

Borrower's Signature X	Date	Co-Borrower's Signature X	Date

X. INFORMATION FOR GOVERNMENT MONITORING PURPOSES

The following information is requested by the Federal Government for certain types of loans related to a dwelling in order to monitor the lender's compliance with equal credit opportunity, fair housing and home mortgage disclosure laws. You are not required to furnish this information, but are encouraged to do so. The law provides that a lender may not discriminate either on the basis of this information, or on whether you choose to furnish it. If you furnish the information, please provide both ethnicity and race. For race, you may check more than one designation. If you do not furnish ethnicity, race, or sex, under Federal regulations, this lender is required to note the information on the basis of visual observation and surname if you have made this application in person. If you do not wish to furnish the information, please check the box below. (Lender must review the above material to assure that the disclosures satisfy all requirements to which the lender is subject under applicable state law for the particular type of loan applied for.)

BORROWER ☐ I do not wish to furnish this information	CO-BORROWER ☐ I do not wish to furnish this information
Ethnicity: ☐ Hispanic or Latino ☐ Not Hispanic or Latino	Ethnicity: ☐ Hispanic or Latino ☐ Not Hispanic or Latino
Race: ☐ American Indian or Alaska Native ☐ Asian ☐ Black or African American ☐ Native Hawaiian or Other Pacific Islander ☐ White	Race: ☐ American Indian or Alaska Native ☐ Asian ☐ Black or African American ☐ Native Hawaiian or Other Pacific Islander ☐ White
Sex: ☐ Female ☐ Male	Sex: ☐ Female ☐ Male

To be Completed by Loan Originator:
This information was provided:
- ☐ In a face-to-face interview
- ☐ In a telephone interview
- ☐ By the applicant and submitted by fax or mail
- ☐ By the applicant and submitted via e-mail or the Internet

Loan Originator's Signature X		Date
Loan Originator's Name (print or type)	Loan Originator Identifier	Loan Originator's Phone Number (including area code)
Loan Origination Company's Name	Loan Origination Company Identifier	Loan Origination Company's Address

Uniform Residential Loan Application
Freddie Mac Form 65 7/05 (rev.6/09) **Page 4 of 5** **Fannie Mae Form 1003 7/05 (rev.6/09)**

CONTINUATION SHEET/RESIDENTIAL LOAN APPLICATION

Use this continuation sheet if you need more space to complete the Residential Loan Application. Mark B f or Borrower or C for Co-Borrower.	Borrower:	Agency Case Number:
	Co-Borrower:	Lender Case Number:

I/We fully understand that it is a Federal crime punishable by fine or imprisonment, or both, to knowingly make any false statements concerning any of the above facts as applicable under the provisions of Title 18, United States Code, Section 1001, et seq.

Borrower's Signature X	Date	Co-Borrower's Signature X	Date

C. (Section III) BORROWER INFORMATION/INCLUDING DEPENDENTS

The next section of the application requests the borrower's name, address, telephone number, social security number, marital status, and employer. There is a parallel section for the same information on any co-borrower (e.g., spouse). This information helps the lender determine both the borrower's ability and willingness to repay the loan.

The lender will want to know how many dependents the borrower must support. Although children help stabilize a borrower, they also add considerably to the financial obligations of the borrower.

D. (Section IV) EMPLOYMENT INFORMATION

The next section of the form asks for the borrower's employment information and how to contact the borrower's employer to confirm the information given. If the borrower has been employed less than two years, previous employers must be listed as well.

E. (Section V) MONTHLY INCOME AND COMBINED HOUSING EXPENSE INFORMATION

The section regarding income provides spaces for primary employment income, overtime, bonuses, commissions, dividends and interest, net rental income, and information regarding income from any other sources.

The monthly housing expense is made up of such items as rent, principal and interest payments, any secondary financing payments, hazard insurance premiums, real estate taxes, mortgage insurance premiums, and homeowners' association dues.

F. (Section VI) ASSETS AND LIABILITIES

In this section of the form, the borrower is required to list all assets and liabilities. Assets include cash deposits, checking and savings accounts, stocks and bonds, life insurance policies, owned real estate, retirement funds, automobiles, and other personal property. Liabilities include any installment debts, automobile loans, real estate loans, alimony, and/or child support payments.

G. (Section VII) DETAILS OF TRANSACTON

The next section asks for information on the real estate transaction itself. The buyer is to fill in the purchase price, closing costs, prepaid escrow expenses, mortgage amount, any secondary financing amounts, other equity, amount of cash deposit, closing costs to be paid by the seller, and an estimate of the cash amount that the borrower will be required to pay at the close of the transaction.

H. (Section VIII) DECLARATIONS

In this section, the buyers are required to note if there have been any legal judgments against them; if they have had a foreclosure within the past seven years; if they have declared bankruptcy within the past seven years, and if they are a party to any lawsuit. The answers to these questions will be of extreme interest to the lender. Obviously, an affirmative answer to any one of them could possibly adversely affect the ability of a borrower to obtain a loan.

I. (Section IX) ACKNOWLEDGEMENT AND AGREEMENT

The borrower agrees that any false statements contained in the application that have been made by the borrower may be criminally prosecuted under U.S. law. The borrower signs and dates the application here.

J. (Section X) INFORMATION FOR GOVERNMENT MONITORING PURPOSES

This section asks for the race, national origin, and sex of the borrower. This information is entirely voluntary on the part of the borrower and is collected to carry out the federal government's anti-discrimination laws.

III. Loan Application Checklist

In order to properly fill out the loan application, the borrower will need to know a variety of information that may not be easily recalled from memory. To ensure that all necessary data is at the borrower's fingertips, it would be wise for him or her to take the following information to the initial interview:

1. The purchase agreement.
2. A residence history.
   a. Where the buyer has lived for the past two years.
   b. If the buyer is currently renting, the landlord or rental agency's name, address, and phone number.
   c. If the buyer owns his or her present home, the name, address, and phone number of the lender and the type of loan (e.g., FHA or conventional).
3. Employment history.
   a. Names, addresses, and zip codes of where the buyer has been employed for the last two years; the position held; whether the employment was full-time, part-time or temporary, and the income being earned at the time of departure.

b. If self-employed or fully commissioned, the tax returns for the past two calendar years, plus a year-to-date income and expense statement.

c. If a major stockholder in a corporation (owns 25% or more of the stock), three years of corporate tax returns.

4. Income.

   a. The amount and sources, including regular salary and secondary sources, such as:

      1. military retirement,
      2. company pensions,
      3. social security benefits,
      4. disability benefits, and
      5. child support or alimony will require a copy of the divorce decree.

5. A list of assets.

   a. Names, addresses, and account numbers for all bank accounts.

   b. The value of household goods and personal property.

   c. The make, model, year, and market value of automobiles.

   d. The cash and face value of insurance policies.

   e. The address, description, and value of any other real estate owned (income properties should have a spreadsheet showing relevant data, similar to the one shown in **Figure 8-7**).

Figure 8-7

SCHEDULE OF REAL ESTATE								
ADDRESS	MARKET VALUE	MORTGAGE BALANCE	EQUITY	GROSS RENT	MORTGAGE PAYMENT	INCOME	MORTGAGEE NAME, LOAN NUMBER, & MAILING ADDRESS	SUBDIVISION NAME & COMMENTS

6. A copy of a gift letter.
   a. If a gift is the source of the down payment or closing costs.
   b. The letter must be signed by the donor (a close relative) and state that the funds are not to be repaid.

7. A list of liabilities.
   a. The name, address, and phone number for each creditor and the balance, monthly payment, and account number.
   b. A copy of the divorce decree if there is any child support or alimony obligation.

8. A Certificate of Eligibility for VA loans.

9. If there is to be the sale of a present home.
   a. The net dollar amount from the sale after deducting the sales commission and any expenses.
   b. If the buyer is being relocated by an employer who is paying all or part of the closing costs, a letter from the employer stating exactly what costs will be paid by the company.

IV. CHAPTER SUMMARY

The loan process consists of four general steps:

1. Filling out the loan application;
2. Analyzing the borrower and property;
3. Processing the loan application, and
4. Closing the loan.

Each of these steps can be simplified if the borrower (and real estate agent) knows what is required of him or her. By supplying all the necessary data the lender needs, the borrower can ensure a much smoother loan process for all concerned. Some of the information the lender will require include the following:

1. The purchase agreement
2. A residence history
3. An employment history
4. Income information
5. A list of assets
6. A copy of any gift letter
7. A list of liabilities

Lenders use 3-digit FICO scores to determine a borrower's creditworthiness. A high FICO score can ensure lower interest rates and terms.

V. TERMINOLOGY

Appraisal
Credit Report
Credit Scoring
Equal Credit Opportunity Act
Escrow Agent
Escrow Instructions
FICO Score
Loan Application
Purchase Agreement

VI. CHAPTER QUIZ

1. An escrow agent:
   a. fills out the loan application.
   b. acts on the instructions of the parties to the loan.
   c. determines the value of the property.
   d. none of the above.

2. An appraiser:
   a. provides an opinion of the value of the loan.
   b. provides an opinion of the value of the borrower's credit.
   c. provides an opinion of the value of the property.
   d. none of the above.

3. A purchase agreement is:
   a. provided by the lender at the close of the loan.
   b. provided by the borrower at the close of the loan.
   c. not required.
   d. a document that shows the terms of sale and expected closing date.

4. A credit report is:
   a. not necessary.
   b. paid for at the time of application.
   c. provided by the borrower.
   d. ordered by the escrow agent.

5. A bankruptcy would be noted on what section of the application?
   a. Assets and liabilities
   b. Borrower information
   c. Declarations
   d. Income

6. Real estate loans would be noted on what part of the form?
   a. Assets and liabilities
   b. Declarations
   c. Details of purchase
   d. Monthly housing expense

7. Information provided for government monitoring purposes is:
   a. required.
   b. voluntary.
   c. highly intrusive.
   d. used to redline borrowers based on their race.

8. A borrower must provide employment status for the past:
   a. one year.
   b. two years.
   c. three years.
   d. five years.

9. Discrimination in the loan process is prohibited by:
   a. the Fair Housing Act.
   b. the Credit Bureau Act.
   c. the Equal Credit Opportunity Act.
   d. none of the above.

10. Bankruptcies and foreclosures must be reported if they have occurred in the past:
    a. five years.
    b. three years.
    c. seven years.
    d. ten years.

ANSWERS: 1. *b*; 2. *c*; 3. *d*; 4. *b*; 5. *c*; 6. *a*; 7. *b*; 8. *b*; 9. *c*; 10. *c*

Overview of the Loan Process

www.QuickenMortgag
Shop
Compare

Chapter 9
Conventional Financing

For the sake of simplicity and organization, we have divided the subject of financing programs into three general categories:

1. Conventional loan programs
2. Creative financing methods
3. Government insured or guaranteed loan programs

Since the Federal Housing Administration (FHA) was formed in 1934, conventional loans, government-sponsored loans, and certain forms of creative financing have provided the solutions to virtually all real estate financing problems.

Until the late 1970s, most real estate loans (conventional, creative, or government-sponsored) involved long-term, fixed-rate repayment plans. A ***LONG-TERM, FIXED-RATE REAL ESTATE LOAN*** *is one that is repaid over 15-30 years at an unchanging rate of interest.*

The fixed-rate mortgage has been the cornerstone financing instrument since the Great Depression.

Chapter 9

CHAPTER OUTLINE

However, in times of high or volatile interest rates, the fixed-rate mortgage is not favored by real estate lenders, due primarily to its slow payback of principal and its inability to keep pace with inflation and rising interest rates. A fixed-rate mortgage bearing 7% interest will provide a 7% return throughout its term (up to 30 years), regardless of what happens to the cost of money during that time.

A fixed-rate mortgage remains at the same rate of interest for the life of the loan.

If real estate is to attract investment money, it will be on the promise of return yields that are competitive with other investment alternatives. This means homebuyers today, and in the future, will have to pay interest rates that provide a similar return to that of the stock and bond markets. Furthermore, because interest levels are subject to significant change over relatively short periods, it's reasonable to expect lenders to protect themselves by committing their funds for shorter terms (15 years and less), or by offering variable rate loans, like adjustable-rate mortgages (ARMs).

I. Conventional Loans

A ***CONVENTIONAL LOAN*** *is any loan not insured or guaranteed by a government agency.* The best way to explain contemporary nongovernment financing is to start with a look at conventional loans as they've been structured in the past, and then follow with a recital of the changes that resulted in today's conventional financing programs.

A. AMORTIZED LOANS

Conventional loans made over the past several decades have generally been long-term, fixed-rate, fully amortizing loans. An ***AMORTIZED LOAN*** *is one that provides for repayment within an agreed period (term) by means of regular level payments (usually monthly), which include a portion for principal and a portion for interest.* As each payment is received, the appropriate amount of principal is deducted from the debt and the remainder of the payment, which represents the interest, is retained by the lender as earnings or profit. With each payment, the amount of the debt is reduced. Every month the interest portion of the payment is reduced and the principal portion is increased (see **Figure 9-1**).

The long-term, fully amortized or level payment loan has obvious advantages for the borrower.

1. Its repayment is spread out over 15-30 years, which keeps the monthly payment at a manageable level.
2. It is self-liquidating as the loan balance steadily declines to zero (the borrower is not faced with balloon payments of any kind).

Figure 9-1

Example: $90,000 loan @ 10¼%, 30-year term (figures approximate)					
PYMT. NO.	**PRINCIPAL BALANCE**	**TOTAL PYMT.**	**INTEREST PORTION**	**PRNCPL. PORTION**	**ENDING BALANCE**
1	$90,000.00	$806.49	$768.75	$37.74	$89,962.26
2	89,962.26	806.49	768.43	38.06	89,924.20
3	89,924.20	806.49	768.10	38.39	89,885.81
4	89,885.81	806.49	767.77	38.72	89,847.09
5	89,847.09	806.49	767.44	39.05	89,808.04

3. The principal and interest payment remains constant for the entire term of the debt.

The long-term, fully amortized, fixed-rate real estate loan is the loan type that borrowers are most familiar with and, in most cases, the type they would like to obtain when financing a home.

B. 15-YEAR, FIXED-RATE MORTGAGE

The 15-year, fixed-rate mortgage has gained increasing popularity over the last three decades. Before the advent of the Federal Housing Administration in 1934, a home loan normally was made for a period of five, seven, or 15 years. However, most of those loans involved partial or no amortization with balloon payments at the conclusion of their terms.

In the 80s and 90s lenders began to report that as many as 30% of their mortgages were 15-year fixed-rate. The secondary agencies also reported an increase in volume of 15-year mortgages. This growth rate has slowed within the past several years.

1. Advantages of 15-Year Mortgages

A 15-year mortgage saves money.

There are several advantages to the 15-year mortgage. One is that lenders will frequently offer lower fixed interest rates on a 15-year than a 30-year mortgage because the shorter term means less risk for the lender. A 15-year mortgage also offers free and clear home ownership in half the time. The major benefit is the thousands of dollars that borrowers can save because of lower total payments over the life of the loan. A borrower who can do simple arithmetic will understand that for the relatively small additional monthly payment, the 15-year mortgage offers significant savings over its 30-year counterpart. In **Figure 9-2**, a comparison is made between a $70,000, $100,000, and $125,000 mortgage at 10% for 15-year terms and 10.5% for 30-year terms.

Figure 9-2

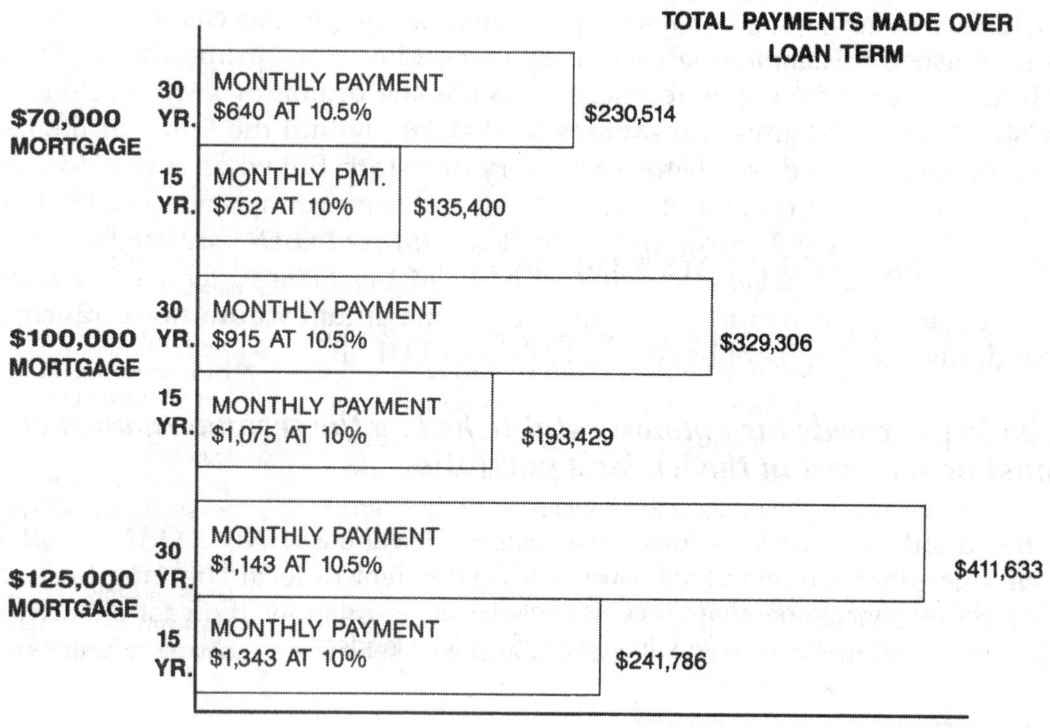

2. Disadvantages of 15-Year Mortgages

The growth in the use of 15-year mortgages has slowed somewhat in the past decade due to several disadvantages. A 15-year mortgage requires higher monthly payments. Larger down payments are often required to reduce the monthly payments. This combination of larger down payment and higher monthly payments has made it difficult for many young first-time buyers to utilize the 15-year mortgage. In addition, the homeowner loses the tax deduction on the interest payments sooner because homeownership is attained sooner. Lastly, because borrowers usually have the option of making extra payments on a 30-year mortgage, they can choose to retire the debt early, without being legally obligated to make the higher payments.

C. CONFORMING VS. NONCONFORMING LOANS

Nonconforming loans are those that do not fit Fannie Mae (FNMA) or Freddie Mac (FHLMC) limits either because they are subprime or jumbo loans.

The particulars of the conventional loan programs detailed in this chapter reflect the criteria established by the national secondary market investors, primarily the FNMA and FHLMC. Every conventional lender who has the option of keeping its loans in portfolio (primarily banks and savings banks) can, within the limits of the law, deviate from the standards set by the secondary investors. But when a loan does not meet secondary market criteria, it's considered nonconforming and is not salable on the secondary market. For example, so-called ***JUMBO LOANS*** *are nonconforming loans that exceed the maximum loan limits set by FNMA or FHLMC for a single-family residence.* A loan larger than the FNMA/FHLMC maximum would not conform to their standards and could not be sold to FNMA or FHLMC.

A jumbo loan exceeds the amount established by the secondary market and must be retained in the lender's portfolio.

Today the trend is almost exclusively towards ***CONFORMING LOANS***, *that is, loans that meet secondary market standards.* While lenders in local communities may occasionally set policies that differ from those explained below, the vast majority of their loans will conform to the policies and standards set by the secondary market.

D. 80% CONVENTIONAL LOAN

For many years now, the standard conventional loan-to-value ratio (LTV) has been 80% of the appraised value or the sales price, whichever is less.

With this type of loan the buyer makes a 20% down payment and obtains a 30-year, fixed-rate conventional loan for the balance of the purchase price.

If a buyer does not have enough money for a 20% down payment but still wants a conventional loan, he or she has a number of options, including:

1. A 90% conventional loan with a 10% down payment.
2. A 95% conventional loan with a 5% down payment.
3. A down payment of 10% with a conventional loan for up to 75% and the seller carrying a second mortgage for the remaining portion of the purchase.

Example: $120,000 sales price

$90,000	75% first mortgage
$18,000	15% second mortgage (seller's)
$12,000	10% down payment
$120,000	

Asking the seller to carry a portion of the purchase price on installment has been a popular way to finance conventional transactions ever since the long-term, fully amortized loan came into existence in the 1930s.

Its popularity increases when interest rates are high and money from institutional sources (banks and savings banks) is scarce.

E. LOAN ORIGINATION FEE

To cover the administrative costs of making a real estate loan, the lender will always charge a ***LOAN ORIGINATION FEE****, also called a "loan fee" or "loan service fee." The loan fee is a percentage of the loan amount, not the sales price. On conventional loans it will range from 1-3% or more.*

Example:

$120,000	sales price
x .80	80% loan-to-value ratio
$96,000	loan amount
x .02	2% loan fee
$1,920	loan fee

The fee is customarily paid by the buyer. The lender generally charges lower loan fees on loans with 80% or lower ratios, and higher fees on the riskier 90% and 95% loans.

F. SECONDARY FINANCING

When a purchaser borrows money from any source to pay a portion of the required down payment or settlement costs, it is called ***SECONDARY FINANCING***. In the preceding example, a 25% down payment would have been $30,000 ($120,000 purchase price less $90,000 loan equals $30,000 down payment). However, the borrower arranged for the seller to "carry" a portion of the purchase price over a period of time. In effect, the borrower has been extended credit by the seller and it's viewed as secondary financing, just as if the money had been borrowed from a lender. Conventional lenders allow secondary financing, provided the following requirements are met.

The borrower must make a 10% down payment. For owner-occupied property, the total of the first and second mortgage must not exceed 90% of the appraised value or

the sales price, whichever is less. The borrower must pay the remaining 10% of the purchase price out of his or her own funds. The first mortgage may not exceed 75% loan to value.

Term not to exceed 30 years or to be less than five years. The "term" of a loan, in this context, refers to secondary financing, which cannot extend beyond 30 years. The rationale for the 30-year limit is that it should not take longer to pay off a second mortgage than it will take to pay off a first mortgage, and traditionally the repayment period for a long-term, fully amortized first mortgage has been 30 years.

No prepayment penalty permitted. The second mortgage must be payable in part or in full at any time without a prepayment penalty.

Scheduled payments must be due on a regular basis. Payments on the second may be monthly, quarterly, semiannual, or on any other regular basis. The scheduled payments can be designed to fully amortize the debt during its term or to pay interest only with a balloon payment at the conclusion of the term.

No negative amortization. The payment on the second mortgage must at least equal the interest on the loan. No negative amortization is allowed. ***NEGATIVE AMORTIZATION*** *occurs when the monthly payment is insufficient to pay the monthly interest and principle.* Thus, the unpaid interest is added back into the loan and the balance owed increases rather than decreases.

The buyer must be able to afford the payments on both the first and second mortgages. In other words, the first mortgage lender takes the payments on the secondary mortgage into account when applying the qualifying ratios to the borrower's income.

1. Fully Amortized Second Mortgage

A five-year, $9,000 fully amortized second mortgage bearing 9.25% interest will cost the borrower approximately $190.12 per month. When underwriting the loan, the lender will include this amount in the borrower's monthly housing expense.

Example:

$632.00	payment on 10%, 30-year, and $60,000 first mortgage (includes principle, interest, real estate taxes, and insurance)
+$190.12	payment on 9.75%, five-year, $9,000 second mortgage (fully amortized)
$822.12	total housing expense

2. Partially Amortized Second Mortgage with Balloon Payment

If a second mortgage is fully amortized (so that the loan is completely paid off by the end of the loan term), the monthly payments will be larger than if it is only partially amortized over the same period (so that the regular payments pay off only part of the loan by the end of the term, and a balloon payment is necessary). The thinking behind the partially amortized mortgage is that the smaller monthly payments make the total housing expense less burdensome for the borrower, and thus easier to qualify for the loan.

Example:

$632.00	payment on 10%, 30-year, $60,000 first mortgage (includes taxes and insurance)
+$77.32	payment on 9.75%, five-year, $9,000 second (partially amortized, based on 30-year repayment schedule)
$709.32	

When compared to the example for the fully amortized second mortgage, it's clear the partially amortized second mortgage eases the qualifying burden somewhat. It may be a preferred financing arrangement when a borrower's income is insufficient to qualify for the higher monthly payments.

3. Setting Up a Partial Amortization Schedule

The above example states that the payments for the partially amortized mortgage are based on a 30-year repayment (amortization) plan. This means the payments were scheduled as though the debt would be paid in full over a 30-year period, even though the entire balance would be due and payable after five years. When the repayment term is 30 years, as opposed to five years, the payments are lower and the debt is retired very gradually. In fact, after five years, payments based on 30-year amortization will have reduced the original loan balance by a relatively small amount, and if the second mortgage is to be paid at that time, there will be a substantial balloon payment. The following chart (**Figure 9-3**) illustrates how the $9,000 second mortgage balance would steadily decline over 30 years if allowed to do so. A 30-year, $9,000 loan at 9.75% will have an $8,677 (approximate) balance at the end of five years. This would be the amount of the balloon payment.

4. Interest-Only Second Mortgage

The second mortgage can call for "interest only," which will reduce the amount of the monthly payments still more. Of course, if no principal is paid during the term of the loan, the balloon payment will be the original amount (in the case of our prior example, $9,000). Monthly interest-only payments are computed by

Figure 9-3

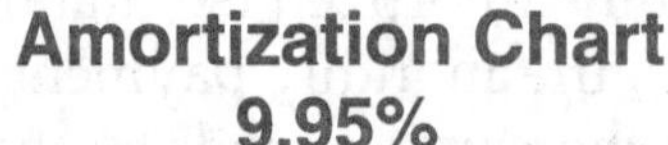

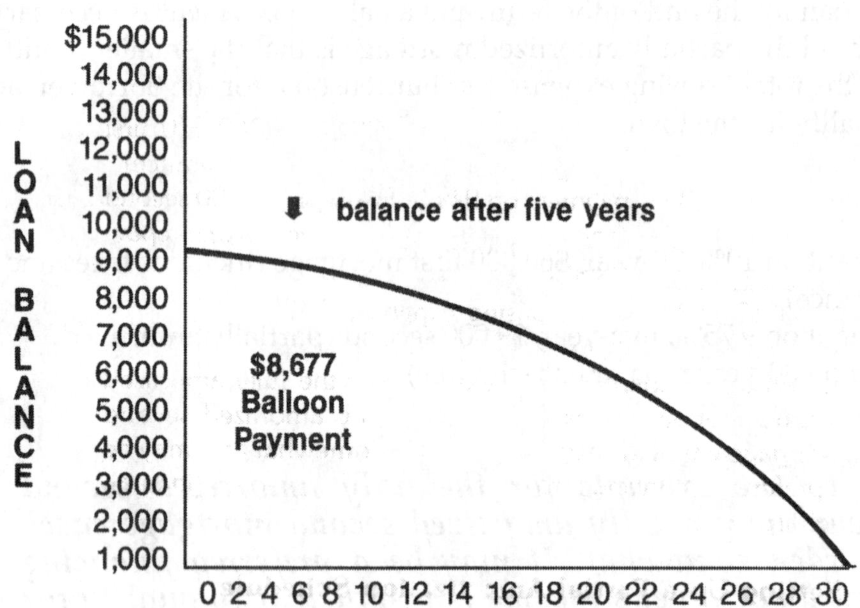

multiplying the mortgage debt by the stipulated interest and dividing that figure by 12 (months).

Example:

$9,000 x .0975 = $877.50
$877.50 ÷ 12 = $73.13 monthly interest payment

5. Lender First and Lender Second Mortgage

The seller does not necessarily have to carry the second mortgage when secondary financing is included. The lender, for example, can make a normal 80% loan and a 10% second loan. The buyer makes a 10% down payment. A typical lender second under these circumstances might have payments based on 30-year amortization with a five-year ***CALL PROVISION*** *(balloon payment in five years)*, or it might be a fully amortized ten-year loan. The repayment plan is a matter of agreement between borrower and lender. Keep in mind: the lender will normally charge a loan fee for both the first and second loans.

G. PRIVATE MORTGAGE INSURANCE (PMI)

Eighty-percent conventional loans have traditionally been considered "safe" by the mortgage industry because the substantial equity the borrower has in the property (20% of the purchase price) is a strong incentive to keep mortgage payments current.

Even if there is a default, a foreclosure sale of the property is more than likely to produce enough funds to cover 80% of the original sales price (or appraised value). However, once borrowers begin making down payments of less than 20% of the sales price, lenders regard the loan as more risky. Under these circumstances, the lender will require the borrower to pay for private mortgage insurance as protection against loss.

The presence of mortgage insurance reduces the lender's risk of loss in the event of a borrower default.

Both FNMA and FHLMC require third-party insurance on home loans with less than 20% down payments. Needless to say, the smaller down payment requirement of the 90% loan made it very popular with buyers, sellers, and real estate agents. Mortgage insurance is sometimes available for loans with up to 95% LTV.

1. How Mortgage Insurance Works

When insuring a loan, the mortgage insurance company shares the lender's risk, but actually assumes only the primary element of risk. This is to say the insurer does not insure the entire loan amount, but rather the upper portion of the loan. The amount of coverage can vary, but typically it's 20% to 25% of the loan amount.

Example: 20% coverage

$200,000	sales price
x.90	LTV
$180,000	90% loan
x.20	amount of coverage
$36,000	amount of policy

In the event of default and foreclosure, the lender, at the insurer's option, will either sell the property and make a claim for reimbursement of actual losses (if any) up to the face amount of the policy, or relinquish the property to the insurer and make a claim for actual losses up to the policy amount. Losses incurred by the lender take the form of unpaid interest, property taxes and hazard insurance, attorney's fees, and costs of preserving the property during the period of foreclosure and resale, as well as the expense of selling the property itself. The following example is an illustration of how a claim is determined:

1. $10,950 unpaid interest
2,061 unpaid taxes and insurance
1,750 attorney's fees
6,075 resale costs
+ 310 miscellaneous expenses
$21,146 total cost of foreclosure and resale

2. $195,000 resale price
-187,000 loan balance
$8,000 gross profit on resale

3. $8,000 gross profit on resale
-21,146 foreclosure and resale costs
<$13,146> net loss – amount of claim

In return for insuring the loan, the mortgage insurance company charges an initial premium at the time the loan is made, and a recurring fee, called a ***RENEWAL PREMIUM****, that is added to the borrower's mortgage payment. Real estate agents and lenders refer to the charges as the* ***PMI (PRIVATE MORTGAGE INSURANCE)*** *or the* ***MIP (MORTGAGE INSURANCE PREMIUM)****.*

The initial premium charged at loan closing for a 90% fixed-rate mortgage is generally less than 1% of the loan amount, depending upon the amount of coverage requested. Typical coverage would call for an initial premium of .5% of the loan amount for 20% coverage.

Example:

$155,000 sales price
$139,500 90% loan
$139,500 loan amount
x .0050 initial premium
$698 PMI at closing

The renewal premium for a standard fixed-rate, 90% loan averages about .34% of the loan amount annually. The annual fee is divided by 12 and added to the buyer's monthly payment.

Example:

$139,500 loan amount
x .0034 (.34%)
$474.30 annual premium
$474.30 ÷ 12 = $39.53 monthly premium

Figure 9-4 is a mortgage insurance rate chart for primary residences published by a national mortgage insurance company. Although the focus of this discussion has been on insuring fixed-rate mortgages, private mortgage insurance companies also insure adjustable-rate mortgages (ARMs). Today, rates vary somewhat between companies for different types and amounts of coverage. **The chart is intended to serve only as a general example and not as a current price guide.**

2. One-Time PMI Premium

Some private mortgage insurance companies offer one-time premium programs as an alternative to the traditional program of an initial premium plus renewal premiums. Under this alternative, the initial premium and renewal premiums are combined into a single, one-time premium. The one-time premium is financed over the loan term rather than paid as a lump sum; the premium amount is simply added to the mortgage amount before calculating the monthly payment. The one-time premium has two advantages for borrowers: there is no cash requirement at closing, and the monthly payments, including a share of the amortized one-time premium, are usually smaller than the monthly payments, including a share of the renewal premium required under the traditional program.

3. Cancellation

Lenders require mortgage insurance on high loan-to-value, low down-payment loans as protection against borrower default.

Once the increased risk of borrower default is eliminated, usually when the loan balance has been reduced to 80% or less of the home's present value, the mortgage insurance has fulfilled its purpose. Originally, a lender was not required to cancel the insurance policy, even once the risk was reduced.

The mortgage insurance policy is a contract between the insurer and the lender—not the borrower—so only the lender can cancel it.

In many cases, the lender either did not cancel the policy, or cancelled it without passing the savings on to the borrower.

Example: Sometimes insurance premiums are written into the interest rate charged on the loan. If the lender's interest rate is 7% and the cost of the mortgage insurance is .5%, the total interest rate on the mortgage will be 7.5%. In the past, when the lender cancelled the insurance policy, it might have kept the interest rate at 7.5% instead of lowering it back to 7%. This practice is called **loaded couponing**.

FHLMC revised its mortgage insurance cancellation rule in 1985 to prevent this and other practices. Under FHLMC's rule, when the insurance is cancelled the

Figure 9-4

FIXED PAYMENT MORTGAGES (1) (7)

MGIC Coverage	LTV	SINGLE Term to 80% (8) No Refund	 Refund (9)	ANNUAL 1st-Year Premiums	RENEWAL PREMIUMS Declining(3)	 Constant (4) Yrs. 2-10	 Yrs. 11-Term
25%	90.01 - 95%	3.60%	4.40%	1.10%	.50%	.49%	.25%
	85.01 - 90%	2.50	3.10	.65	.35	.34	.25
	85% & under	2.15	2.45	.50	.35	.34	.25
22%	90.01 - 95%	3.25	4.30	1.00	.50	.49	.25
	85.01 - 90%	2.35	3.00	.55	.35	.34	.25
	85% & under	2.05	2.40	.45	.35	.34	.25
20%	90.01 - 95%	3.05	4.15	.90	.50	.49	.25
	85.01 - 90%	2.20	2.95	.50	.35	.34	.25
	85% & under	1.95	2.35	.40	.35	.34	.25
17%	85.01 - 90%	2.00	2.85	.40	.35	.34	.25
	85% & under	1.75	2.30	.35	.35	.34	.25
12%	85.01 - 90%	1.70	2.80	.35	.35	.34	.25
	85% & under (5)	1.50	2.00	.30	.30	.29	.25

NONFIXED PAYMENT MORTGAGES (2) (7)

MGIC Coverage	LTV	SINGLE Term to 80% (8) No Refund	 Refund (9)	ANNUAL 1st-Year Premiums	RENEWAL PREMIUMS Declining(3)	 Constant (4) (6) Yrs. 2-10	 Yrs. 11-Term
25%	90.01 - 95%	4.20%	5.20%	1.35%	.55%	.54%	.25%
	85.01 - 90%	3.15	3.90	.75	.45	.44	.25
	85% & under	2.50	3.15	.60	.45	.44	.25
22%	90.01 - 95%	3.85	5.05	1.20	.55	.54	.25
	85.01 - 90%	2.90	3.80	.65	.45	.44	.25
	85% & under	2.35	3.10	.55	.45	.44	.25
20%	90.01 - 95%	3.60	4.90	1.10	.55	.54	.25
	85.01 - 90%	2.75	3.75	.60	.45	.44	.25
	85% & under	2.20	3.05	.50	.45	.44	.25
17%	85.01 - 90% (5)	2.50	3.65	.50	.45	.44	.25
	85% & under	2.00	2.65	.40	.40	.39	.25
12%	85.01 - 90%	2.05	3.20	.40	.40	.39	.25
	85% & under (5)	1.65	2.30	.35	.35	.34	.25

(*An ARM will only be insured by many mortgage insurance companies if the only negative amortization that occurs is a result of payment caps; scheduled negative amortization is not allowed.)

lender must modify the mortgage interest rate to reflect the cancellation. However, cancellation is not automatic; the borrower must request the cancellation and often must pay the costs of a new appraisal.

"Loaded Couponing" is the practice of retaining a higher interest rate that includes the premiums for PMI after the insurance has been cancelled.

FHLMC now requires lenders to drop coverage, at the request of borrowers, under certain conditions.

1. The insurance must be cancelled if the loan is at least seven years old and has been paid down to 80% or less of the home's current value.
2. If the mortgage is less than seven years old, lenders must cancel the policy only if the loan has been paid down to 80% of the home's value and the borrower meets established payment history criteria.
3. If the borrower has a fixed payment mortgage, payments must not have been more than 30 days past due in the immediately preceding 12 months.
4. If the loan is an adjustable-rate mortgage, there must have been no payment over 30 days past due for the preceding 24 months.

FNMA also requires lenders to cancel PMI under certain conditions. In 1987, FNMA implemented a rule that requires all lenders who sell their mortgages to FNMA to cancel PMI if a new appraisal shows that the loan has been paid down to 80% of the property's current value (no matter how old the loan is). See **Figure 9-5**.

The borrower must pay for a lender-approved appraisal, and if the appraisal shows the loan balance to be 80% or less of current value, the borrower then makes a formal request to terminate the PMI. The lender must cancel the policy and reduce the monthly mortgage payment by the amount of the PMI premium.

Cancelling mortgage insurance, but failing to pass on the savings to the borrower, is a violation of the Real Estate Settlement Procedures Act (RESPA), according to the Department of Housing and Urban Development (HUD).

The practice of collecting premiums on cancelled insurance, referred to as ***SELF-INSURANCE,*** is thought to be common, although no accurate figures are available. The RESPA ruling is similar to the HUD policy on FHA loans, which considers self-insurance a fraudulent practice.

Figure 9-5

FHLMC Mortgage Insurance Cancellation Rules

IF:	REQUIREMENT:
1. Insurance is cancelled	Lender must reduce interest to reflect cancellation.
2. Loan is at least seven years old and has been paid down to 80%	Insurance must be cancelled and rate reduced.
3. **Fixed rate** loan is less than seven years old but paid down to 80% of home's current value*	Insurance must be cancelled and rate reduced, provided no mortgage payments have been more than 30 days past due during the preceding **12 months**.
4. **Adjustable-rate** loan is less than seven years old but paid down to 80% of home's current value*	Same as above, except no mortgage payments have been more than 30 days past due during the preceding **24 months.**

*** Buyer must obtain appraisal at own expense.**

4. Rising Mortgage Delinquency

In the early 1980s and again in the early 1990s (and yet AGAIN in recent years), the amount of past-due mortgages and foreclosures began to rise dramatically. Indeed, in the early 1990s the rate reached historic levels not seen since the Great Depression. These increases in loan delinquencies and foreclosures prompted the mortgage insurance industry to raise its premiums and to institute new underwriting guidelines. Having learned nothing from these past failures, delinquencies are on the rise again. It remains to be seen what additional safeguards private mortgage insurance companies will apply to new mortgages in the future.

Most loan defaults occur between the third and fifth year of the life of the loan.

The losses experienced in 1984-1985 and 1991-1993 (and yet again in 2008-2009) were largely due to loans originated in 1980-1982, 1987-1990, and 2006-2007. The defaults occurred at a time of high unemployment and high interest rates, which depressed home values and the housing market. Those who lost their jobs lost their homes as well, because they could not sell at a price equal to or greater than the mortgage balance.

The lesson that needs to be learned is that homebuyers and lenders can no longer expect inflation alone to bail them out of problem loans, as was the case in the past.

Previous high inflation rates in the 1975 to 1985 period almost always ensured that the selling price of the home would exceed the original mortgage balance, so that a hard-pressed homeowner could sell the home for a profit, or at least enough to pay off the mortgage. When inflation levels lowered and the economy became depressed, the values of the homes declined drastically and homeowners were unable, in many cases, to sell their homes for enough money to cover the amount that had been loaned on them.

This same scenario, taken to nightmarish proportions, repeated itself again in 2007-2008.

As a result of this experience, mortgage insurance companies began to exert considerable effort to increase the quality of the loans they insure in an attempt to avoid future losses. These efforts resulted in both new policies, procedures, and new products.

A major change in the private mortgage insurance process is the active role that mortgage insurance companies are taking with their own underwriting procedures.

No longer are these companies simply reviewing loans made by lenders and then accepting them with few questions. Mortgage insurance companies now have their own comprehensive set of underwriting guidelines. For example, one national insurance company has its own list of documentation requirements, including lender loan application, credit report, verification of employment and income, verification of deposit, sales agreement, appraisal, and borrower payment history. The mortgage insurance company also requires a comprehensive borrower analysis, involving his or her personal history, employment history, an income ratio analysis, a review of assets, credit ratings, and credit reports. There are certain acceptable sources of equity (cash, gift letters, lot equity, sweat equity, etc.) and a set policy for property appraisals.

In another effort to improve quality control in underwriting, one national mortgage insurance company provides in its master policy that the insurance will not cover losses suffered from misrepresentation, negligence, or fraud. Representations made by lender, borrower, or any other party are considered to be the lender's own representation. It's hoped that these provisions encourage more care in the underwriting process because lenders will bear the burden of any misrepresentation or fraud that escapes their attention. The effect of these types of policy provisions may be somewhat modified by state law. Many states have passed laws providing that fraudulent statements in applications and attached documents for mortgage insurance will block a claim to recover. In some of these laws, if the application contains incorrect information that's not fraudulent, the legislation provides that the misrepresentation shall not prevent a recovery unless it was material to the acceptance of the risk, or the insurer in good faith would not have issued the policy if the true facts had been known. At least 30 states have passed similar legislation.

Another step taken by mortgage insurers, in an effort to control losses, includes employing spot-check appraisers to reevaluate the value of loan properties. Both lenders and insurers are becoming increasingly careful of those with whom they do business. Lenders are examining the financial health of the mortgage insurance company to ensure that they are able to pay all claims. Mortgage insurance companies are rechecking the underwriting standards of the lender to make sure that the loans being made are sound and less likely to default. Many insurance companies have refused to do business with those lenders who have made a large number of defaulted loans. Usually, a very small number of lenders are responsible for most of the loans that default.

One mortgage insurance company concluded that 90% of its defaults had come from only 10% of its lenders.

H. 90% CONVENTIONAL LOAN

Ninety-percent loans became increasingly popular with the advent of private mortgage insurance.

The qualifying standards for such loans tend to be more stringent and lenders adhere to those standards more strictly (even though the loan is insured). Marginal buyers and properties are more likely to be rejected if the loan amount requested exceeds 80% of the value or purchase price, whichever is less.

When seeking a 90% loan, the buyer must make at least a 5% down payment out of his or her own cash reserves. The rest of the down payment may be a gift from a family member, equity in other property traded to the seller, or credit for rent already paid under a lease/purchase.

Ninety-percent loans usually call for larger loan origination fees and higher interest rates than do 80% loans. This is a generalization and there are certainly exceptions. When thinking in terms of 90% financing, it's a good idea to expect a more expensive loan.

I. 95% CONVENTIONAL LOAN

The success of the 90% loan in the 1960s, 1970s, and early 2000s encouraged lenders and private mortgage insurers to experiment with even higher loan-to-value ratios. With the 95% loan, made primarily by savings banks and mortgage companies, it's possible to obtain conventional financing with as little as 5% cash down.

Applying the generalization "the smaller the down payment, the greater the risk of default" (which represents the view of most lenders), it's easy to understand why in most cases the 95% conventional loan is more costly than 80% and 90% loans. Both interest rates and loan fees are generally increased for 95% loans. In fact, private mortgage insurance companies may charge up to a 1.10% premium at closing for 95% loans, as opposed to the .65% for 90% loans (at 25% coverage). Also, the borrower's renewal premium on 95% loans is usually higher than on 90% loans. Depending on the type of coverage requested, the renewal premium will be around .49%.

Figure 9-6 shows a comparison of the mortgage insurance rates for loans with different loan-to-value ratios.

Figure 9-6

PMI Comparison Chart
(for $95,000 loan at 20% coverage)

LTV	1st Year	Annual Renewal Premium
80%	(Mortgage Insurance not required)	
90%	$475.00 (.50%)	$323.00 (.34%)
95%	$855.00 (.90%)	$465.50 (.49%)

No secondary financing is allowed for 95% conventional loans. The buyer must make the down payment on his or her own, without resorting to secondary financing or gifts.

Ninety-five percent conventional loans are extremely difficult to obtain.

Underwriting guidelines are extremely strict for 95% loans, more so than they have been in the past, due to the high foreclosure rate of high loan-to-value loans. A marginal buyer will rarely qualify for a 95% loan. Underwriters "ride the credit line" when evaluating risk with just 5% down. If a borrower's application is weak in certain areas, it's probably advisable that some alternate form of financing be considered, such as government-insured or seller financing.

Owner occupancy is required for a 95% loan.

1. FNMA Guidelines for 95% Loans

As an example of stricter underwriting requirements for 95% loans, FNMA guidelines state that the borrower should fall into one of the following three sets of circumstances:

1. The borrower has a good mortgage payment history, good credit, sufficient financial assets, and a credit history indicating the borrower is willing and able to devote a substantial portion of his or her income to a mortgage payment.
2. The borrower has no mortgage payment history (first-time buyer), good credit, sufficient financial assets, and the borrower's total monthly debt service-to-income ratio is 30% or less.
3. The borrower has no mortgage payment history, but has good credit, sufficient financial assets and financial reserves to carry the mortgage payment. The borrower must normally have on deposit sufficient cash, or other very liquid assets, to cover **two months' mortgage payments** (principal, interest, taxes, insurance, and mortgage insurance) after the down payment and closing costs.

Private mortgage insurers usually require three months' mortgage payments in reserve, an even stricter standard than FNMA.

J. 100% OR MORE CONVENTIONAL LOAN

In the late 1990s, some lenders were advertising loans from 100-125%. These loans were made on two assumptions. The first was that borrowers who had a good credit history were unlikely to default. The second assumption was that rapidly increasing property values would soon make up the gap between the property's actual value at the time of the loan and the overall loan amount. As we've seen from past experience, these are very dangerous assumptions to make. Such a loan creates a situation in which a borrower is more likely to default in a severe economic downturn when property values decrease. Indeed, it might be very advantageous for the borrower to default rather than remain "buried" under such a loan.

K. EASY DOCUMENTATION LOANS

In accordance with the general rule that lower down-payment loans are more expensive and subject to stricter underwriting scrutiny, higher down-payment loans are generally less expensive for the borrower and underwriting standards have been less stringently applied. For example, many lenders have been willing to waive verification of employment or documentation of income if the borrower is willing to make a larger than normal down payment, usually at least 25-30%, and has good credit. These loans are often referred to as "easy qualifier," "time saver," "low documentation," or "no documentation" loans. They are particularly attractive for high-income borrowers whose income is from self-employment or from a variety of sources, and for whom documentation may be more burdensome than for borrowers whose income is solely from wages or salary.

In addition to the simplified, faster qualifying procedure, these low loan-to-value ratio loans are often less expensive because the lender may impose lower loan fees or slightly lower interest rates. Also, because the down payment is well over 20%, mortgage insurance is not required.

In times of rising delinquency rates, lenders become skeptical about low documentation loans and often refuse to do them.

As may be imagined, in 2008, as a result of the economic crisis, "easy doc" and "no doc" loans disappeared.

L. ASSUMING CONVENTIONAL LOANS

Agents should not take chances when writing sales that call for assumption of existing conventional loans. Don't give buyers and sellers advice on whether a loan is assumable, unless it is a certainty.

When there is some question about what will happen if an assumption is attempted, consult the lender, an attorney, or other individual who is particularly qualified to advise you. When a buyer attempts to assume a loan, one of three things will happen:

1. The lender will accept the assumption and the loan terms will be left intact.
2. The lender will accept the assumption but will insist on an assumption fee and/or will increase the loan's interest rate, possibly to present market levels. This frequently defeats the purpose of the assumption, which was to take advantage of the loan's lower-than-market interest rate. Assumption fees vary from lender to lender, some are inconsequential, others are prohibitive (up to 3% of the loan balance or more). The charges are usually spelled out in the mortgage instrument.
3. The lender will refuse to allow the assumption and will call the note, which means demanding full payment of the loan at once. The right to do this must be spelled out in the promissory note or mortgage. If the buyer is an investor, the lender will usually require that the loan be paid down to a 75% loan-to-value ratio.

Don't discover after the sale what the lender plans or is entitled to do. Find out before creating the sales contract, even if it means not making the sale at all.

M. CONVENTIONAL PREPAYMENT PENALTIES

Historically, most conventional lenders have penalized borrowers who paid off their loans sooner than agreed. Some still do. But because of the volatility of interest rates today, lenders are inclined to make short-term loans. They like the idea of being able to invest their money in real estate at today's rates, to recover it after a relatively short period (3-15 years for real estate loans), and to reinvest the funds at whatever rates prevail at the time.

Prepayment penalties discourage early payment of a loan, and this runs counter to most lenders' objectives in today's real estate market. FNMA and FHLMC don't have prepayment penalties in their standard promissory notes and mortgages or trust deeds. In many states, lenders are prohibited from charging prepayment penalties beyond the first five years of the life of the loan for loans on owner-occupied, one-to-four-unit dwellings.

II. CHAPTER SUMMARY

The majority of conventional loans are fixed-rate, fully amortized 30-year loans. However, 15-year loans have been gaining in popularity because of the significant savings in interest payments. Also, loans may be fully amortized, partially amortized, or interest-only with a balloon payment. Today, virtually all conventional loans are conforming loans, meaning they conform to FNMA/FHLMC standards.

1. Different standards apply to loans of different loan-to-value ratios: loans of not more than 80% LTV, loans of more than 80% LTV, and loans of more than 90% LTV. Generally speaking, the smaller the down payment, the stricter the underwriting standards applied. The loan fees also tend to be higher for loans with higher loan-to-value ratios.
2. Secondary financing is allowed on many conventional loans, but there are specific restrictions that must be followed. For example, a borrower may borrow part of the down payment from another source but must pay at least 10% out of his/her own resources. Also, no prepayment penalties are allowed on the second loan.
3. For loans over 80% LTV, private mortgage insurance is required to insure the lender for part of the loan amount. The borrower pays an initial fee and then an annual renewal premium for the mortgage insurance. Requirements of private mortgage insurers impose another set of standards in addition to the FNMA/FHLMC guidelines for underwriting loans.
4. Before trying to assume a conventional loan, study the original loan papers carefully. Lenders often have the option of charging an assumption fee, raising the interest rate, or refusing the assumption altogether. Conventional loans may or may not include prepayment charges and/or alienation clauses.

III. TERMINOLOGY

Amortization
Amortized Loans
Call Provision
Conforming Loans
Conventional Loan
Fixed-Rate Mortgage
Jumbo Loan
Loaded Couponing
Loan Origination Fee
Low Documentation Loans
LTV (Loan-to-Value)
MIP (Mortgage Insurance Payment)
Negative Amortizaton
No Documentation Loans
PMI (Private Mortgage Insurance)
Renewal Premium
Self Insurance
Secondary Financing

IV. CHAPTER QUIZ

1. A mortgage that remains at the same rate for the life of the loan is called a:
   a. single-rate mortgage.
   b. fixed-rate mortgage.
   c. closed-rate mortgage.
   d. nonassumable mortgage.

2. A loan that exceeds the maximum amount that FNMA or FHLMC will lend is called a:
   a. variable-rate mortgage.
   b. maximum loan.
   c. jumbo loan.
   d. none of the above.

3. Conforming Loans meet what standards?
   a. Primary market
   b. Secondary market
   c. Banks only
   d. Credit unions only

4. Jumbo loans:
   a. may be sold into the secondary market.
   b. are no longer offered by lenders.
   c. must be held in the lender's portfolio.
   d. none of the above.

5. A loan origination fee:
   a. is the commission paid to salespersons.
   b. is paid to the borrower by the lender for the privilege of processing the loan.
   c. is a fee to cover administrative costs.
   d. is prohibited by FNMA and FHLMC.

6. The standard loan-to-value (LTV) ratio has historically been:
   a. 95%.
   b. 90%.
   c. 80%.
   d. 75%.

7. In a loan with negative amortization, the balance owed:
   a. decreases over time.
   b. remains the same.
   c. increases over time.
   d. none of the above.

8. The practice of continuing to charge interest for PMI that was included within the interest charges on a loan after the insurance has been cancelled is called:
   a. default.
   b. a mortgage insurance premium.
   c. a noncancellation policy.
   d. loaded couponing.

9. The practice of collecting mortgage insurance premiums on a policy that has been cancelled by the lender:
   a. is called self-insurance.
   b. a violation of RESPA.
   c. is a fradulent practice.
   d. all of the above.

10. The greatest risk of default is caused by:
   a. large down payments.
   b. small or no down payments.
   c. overpriced housing.
   d. high interest rates.

ANSWERS: 1. *b*; 2. *c*; 3. *b*; 4. *c*; 5. *c*; 6. *c*; 7. *c*; 8. *d*; 9. *d*; 10. *b*

E-LOAN
www.eloan.com

– Part IV –

Chapters 10, 11, and 12
Other Types of Financing

Chapter 10 – Alternative Financing

Alternate financing programs were originally developed in the 1980s to meet the dual challenges of higher home prices and higher interest rates. In order to make it easier for borrowers, many of these alternate financial plans involve the payment of discount points, temporary buydowns, or permanent buydowns to reduce the borrower's interest or lower the payments.

Chapter 11 – Government Programs: FHA and VA Loans

The FHA and VA loan programs are huge federal insurance programs that are backed by the full faith and credit of the U.S. government. Both programs have found ready acceptance by lenders and borrowers alike. The FHA has been a boon to the lending, construction, and real estate markets since its beginning. The VA programs are designed to provide veterans returning to civilian life an opportunity to enjoy the benefits of home ownership.

Chapter 12 – Seller Financing

Seller financing provides an almost limitless variety of creative alternatives to institutional financing and is particularly attractive in tight money markets when loans from institutional lenders often have prohibitive interest rates.

Chapter 10
Alternative Financing

The last two decades have presented the real estate and lending industries with a unique assortment of challenges. The paramount challenge has been to reconcile the investor's need for a high rate of return with the borrower's need for an affordable loan. The search for a solution to this problem spawned many innovative plans, such as buydowns, adjustable-rate mortgages (ARMs), graduated payment mortgages (GPMs), and growth equity mortgages (GEMs).

As interest rates declined from the high point reached in the early 1980s, interest in most alternative financing plans quickly evaporated. The return of affordable fixed-rate conventional financing relegated many of the alternate financing plans to the dustbin (with the sole exception of ARMs). However, today's lower interest rates are not guaranteed to continue, and rising rates can easily rekindle interest in alternative financing programs.

In this chapter, we will examine some of the most popular and successful of the alternative financing methods: buydowns, ARMs, and GEMs.

Alternative financing plans are popular in times of high interest rates.

Chapter 10

CHAPTER OUTLINE

I. Discount Points

Before discussing specific alternative financing programs, it is important to explain **discount points**, often referred to simply as "points." The term "point" is short for "percentage point." A ***POINT*** *is one percentage point (one percent) of the loan amount*. For example, with a $100,000 loan, one point would be $1000; six points would be $6,000.

Lenders charge two different types of points in real estate loan transactions. One type, called a loan origination fee, loan fee, service fee, or administrative charge, is designed to pay the administrative costs the lender incurs in processing the loan. For example, a borrower might be required to pay a loan origination fee of 2% of the loan amount (two points).

The other type of point is a discount point. ***DISCOUNT POINTS*** *are used to increase the lender's yield from the loan without raising the interest rate*. If the loan is discounted (that is, if discount points are paid), the lender can charge the borrower a lower interest rate than it would otherwise have to charge in order to meet its minimum yield requirements. *The interest rate stated in the promissory note, called the* **NOMINAL RATE** *or the* **COUPON RATE**, *is less than the* **EFFECTIVE RATE**, *which is the lender's effective yield from the loan.*

Discount points were traditionally associated with FHA and VA financing, but they have become increasingly common in conventional loans.

Points may be paid by either the buyer or the seller, but they are most often paid by the seller in a sales transaction. Keep in mind that discounts are computed based on the loan amount, not the sales price. The borrower would, of course, pay the discount points in a refinance transaction.

Example:

$222,000	sales price
$177,600	loan amount
6%	discount
$177,600	
x.06	
$10,656	discount amount

Discount points are paid at closing by deducting the amount of the points from the amount of the loan to be advanced.

For instance, if the loan were for $145,000 and the lender required four discount points, 4% of the loan ($5,800) would be deducted from the amount actually advanced to the

borrower (the loan would be discounted 4%) and the remainder, $139,200, would be delivered to the borrower to finance the purchase. The borrower would sign a promissory note and mortgage agreeing to repay the entire $145,000 at the stipulated rate of interest. The lender would advance only $139,200, but would be repaid $145,000. The buyer would transfer the loan proceeds ($139,200) to the seller without making up the difference. In effect, the seller would have paid the lender $5,800 to induce the lender to make the loan with a lower-than-market interest rate. The $5,800 would have compensated the lender for the lower yielding loan.

A. POINTS IN VA TRANSACTIONS

Payment of discount points has long been a part of most VA loans.

The interest rates on VA loans are usually somewhat lower than prevailing market rates. This means that a lender making a VA loan does not charge the borrower as much interest as it would for a conventional loan. Lenders have traditionally required the seller to pay enough points to increase the lender's yield on VA loans to a rate that is competitive with conventional loans.

Under VA regulations, the buyer is prohibited from paying any discount points. Any points required by the lender must be paid by the seller or a third party, such as a builder.

B. POINTS IN CONVENTIONAL LOANS

The purpose of points in conventional loan transactions is usually to increase the lender's yield from the rate the borrower is willing or able to pay to the rate the lender requires as a yield on its loans. While the buyer is not prohibited from paying discount points on conventional or FHA loans, in most instances the seller is the one who pays the points as a way of reducing the interest rate to be paid by the buyer. In effect, this makes the property more marketable. *When the seller (or a third party) pays points to reduce the buyer's interest rate, it is called a* ***BUYDOWN***. It is far easier to sell property if the buyer's interest rate is relatively low and affordable.

C. HOW MANY POINTS?

The question of how many points must be paid can only be answered with up-to-the-minute information concerning yields required by lenders, which are affected to a large degree by existing market conditions.

The number of points required to increase the lender's yield by 1% is affected by many factors, including prevailing interest rates, the average time that loans are outstanding before being paid off, and to some degree, the terms of the loan documents themselves.

The number of points to be paid is often computed on the assumption that it takes six points to increase the lender's yield on a 30-year loan by 1%. This is a "rule of thumb" approach to computing yields and should be confirmed with the lender before a final quote is made.

Example:

$90,000 proposed 30-year loan
11% required yield
10% interest rate preferred by borrower

$90,000
x.06
$5,400 discount (usually paid by seller)

$90,000
- 5,400
$84,600 advanced by lender after discount

$90,000 note
x.10 nominal rate paid by borrower
$9,000 interest paid by borrower

$9,000 ÷ $84,600 = .11 yield to lender

II. Buydown Plans

One of the easiest and most agreeable ways to make expensive loans less expensive is the "buydown."

A buydown is a way to lower a purchaser's initial monthly mortgage payments as an aid to qualifying for a loan. The seller, builder, or any other person, including the buyer, makes a lump sum payment to the lender at the time the loan is made. The money that has been paid to the lender is used to reduce the borrower's monthly payments either early in or throughout the life of the loan. The following examples will utilize high interest rates, as these are precisely the sort of market conditions under which buydowns become popular.

Example:

$65,000 30-year, 15% loan
$3,900 buydown (6 points)

$822 quoted 15% loan payment
- 770 buyer's payment at 14%
$52 savings resulting from buydown

In the above example, the quoted rate is 15%, but the borrower's interest rate has been bought down by 1%, reducing the interest rate to 14%, for a savings of $52 per month.

Buydown sellers pay upfront payments to reduce buyers' mortgage rates.

A. TWO ADVANTAGES TO A BUYDOWN

There are two fairly obvious advantages to a buydown plan:

1. The buyer's monthly payment is lower than normal.
2. The lender evaluates the buyer on the basis of the reduced payment, thereby making it easier to qualify for the loan.

B. PERMANENT BUYDOWNS

A buydown can be permanent or temporary. If a portion of a buyer's interest rate is permanently bought down (e.g., for 30 years), the lender's nominal rate (the rate stated in the promissory note) will be reduced by that amount.

Example: Lender quotes 15% for a 30-year loan of $65,000. Builder agrees to buydown the note rate to 14%. Lender agrees to make the loan at this rate if Builder makes a lump sum payment to Lender of $3,900 to buy down the interest rate by 1%.

1. How to Compute Permanent Buydowns

There are two ways to be completely accurate when determining a permanent interest rate buydown. One way is to obtain a discount/yield table booklet from a lender or title company and learn to use it. The other way is to call your lender for a quote. If you just want a rough estimate of the buydown amount, the six points per 1% interest formula referred to earlier is reasonably accurate.

C. TEMPORARY BUYDOWNS

When interest rates are high, temporary buydowns are very popular as a means of reducing a buyer's payments—sometimes substantially—in the early months or years of the loan.

Many buyers feel they can grow into a larger payment but need time to get established. Temporary buydown plans take two forms: level payment and graduated payment.

1. Level Payment Buydown Plan

A ***LEVEL PAYMENT BUYDOWN PLAN*** *calls for an interest reduction that is constant throughout the buydown period.*

Example: Lender makes a 30-year loan for $65,000 at 15% interest. The seller agrees to buydown the purchaser's interest rate to 13% for three years (See **Figure 10-1**).

Figure 10-1

Year	Note Interest Rate	Buydown %	Effective Interest Rate	Monthly Payment at 15%	Actual Monthly Payment	Monthly Subsidy	Annual Subsidy
1.	15%	2%	13%	$822	$719	$103	$1,236
2.	15%	2%	13%	$822	$719	$103	$1,236
3.	15%	2%	13%	$822	$719	$103	$1,236
4.	15%	-0-	15%	$822	$822	-0-	-0-
						TOTAL BUYDOWN	$3,708

2. Graduated Payment Buydown Plan

A ***GRADUATED PAYMENT BUYDOWN PLAN*** *calls for the largest subsidies in the first year or two of the loan, with progressively smaller subsidies in each of the remaining years of the buydown period.*

Example: Lender makes a 30-year loan for $70,000 at 14.75% interest. Builder agrees to buydown purchaser's interest rate by 3% the first year, 2% the second year, and 1% the third year (See **Figure 10-2**).

Figure 10-2

Year	Note Interest Rate	Buydown %	Effective Interest Rate	Monthly Payment at 14.75%	Actual Monthly Payment	Monthly Subsidy	Annual Subsidy
1.	14.75%	3%	11.75%	$871	$707	$164	$1,968
2.	14.75%	2%	12.75%	$871	$761	$110	$1,320
3.	14.75%	1%	13.75%	$871	$816	$55	$660
4.	14.75%	-0-	14.75%	$871	$871	-0-	-0-
						TOTAL BUYDOWN	$3,948

An example of a typical temporary buydown is the "3-2-1" plan, in which the buyers' mortgage rates are lowered by 3 percentage points during the first year, 2 percent the second year, and one point the third year. After that, the buyers make the full payment themselves.

3. How to Compute Temporary Buydowns

To be 100% accurate, use the yield/discount tables previously mentioned or obtain a quote from your lender. As an alternative, temporary buydowns can be computed with considerable accuracy with the use of the interest rate factors in Chapter 15 of this book, or a hand calculator programmed to calculate amortized loan payments. The subsidy computation by this method is simple:

1. Compute the buyer's monthly principal and interest payment without the subsidy.
2. Determine the buyer's monthly payment with the subsidy.
3. Subtract the subsidized payment from the actual payment and multiply by twelve for the annual subsidy.
4. Multiply the annual subsidy by the number of years in the buydown plan.

Example: Level Payment Buydown

$76,000	loan amount
16.25%	coupon (note) rate
14.25%	subsidized rate (five years)

1. Determine monthly principal and interest without subsidy.

$76,000	
x .0136494	16.25%, 30-year interest factor
$1,037.35	monthly payment without subsidy

2. Determine payment with subsidy.

$76,000	
x .0120469	14.25%, 30-year interest factor
$915.56	monthly payment with subsidy

3. Subtract subsidy payment from actual payment and multiply by 12 (months).

$1,037.35	actual payment
- 915.56	subsidized payment
$121.79	monthly subsidy
x 12	
$1,461.48	annual subsidy

4. With a level payment plan, the annual subsidy is constant for the entire buydown period (in the case of this example, five years). So the final step is to multiply the annual subsidy by the number of years in the buydown plan.

$1,461.48	annual subsidy
x 5	years in buydown plan
$7,307.40	total buydown (subsidy)

III. FNMA/FHLMC Limits on Buydowns

FNMA and FHLMC guidelines impose loan limits on discounts, buydowns, and other forms of contributions by sellers or other interested parties for the purpose of paying for financing costs, including prepaid interest and impounds for property taxes, hazard insurance, and mortgage insurance. Contributions are limited to a percentage of the sales price or appraised value, whichever is less.

If the contributions exceed FNMA and FHLMC guidelines, the contribution amount must be deducted from the value or sales price before determining the maximum loan amount (with the exception of contributions by an employer or immediate family member, which are not subject to these limits) (see **Figure 10-3**).

Figure 10-3

Maximum Contribution	LTV Ratio
2%	Investment property
3%	Principal residence and greater than 90% LTV
6%	Principal residence and 76%-90% LTV
9%	Principal residence or second home and 75% LTV or less

Example:

$100,000	sales price (principal residence)
105,000	appraised value
90,000	90% loan
6,000	maximum contribution

Any contribution in excess of $6,000 would be deducted from the sales price (or appraised value, if it were less), with a corresponding reduction in the loan amount.

IV. Adjustable-Rate Mortgages (ARMs)

Perhaps the most popular and widely accepted form of alternate financing is the adjustable-rate mortgage, universally referred to as an ARM.

Because the ARM shifts the risk of interest rate fluctuations to the borrower, lenders normally charge a lower rate for an ARM than for a fixed-rate loan. Although the majority of borrowers prefer the security of a fixed-rate (provided the rate is not too high), ARMs have maintained a place in the market despite comparatively low mortgage rates.

Generally, as interest rates rise and fall, so does the popularity of adjustable-rate mortgages.

A. WHAT IS AN ADJUSTABLE-RATE MORTGAGE?

An ***ADJUSTABLE-RATE MORTGAGE (ARM)*** *is a mortgage that permits the lender to periodically adjust the interest rate so it will accurately reflect fluctuations in the cost of money.* ARMs are made primarily by banks and mortgage companies.

The ARM passes the risk of fluctuating interest levels on to borrowers, where many lenders feel it belongs.

With an ARM, it is the borrower who is affected by interest movements. If rates climb, the borrower's payments go up; if they decline, the payments go down.

B. HOW DOES AN ARM WORK?

The borrower's interest rate is determined initially by the cost of money at the time the loan is made. Once the rate has been set, it is tied to one of several widely recognized and published indexes, and future interest adjustments are based on the upward and downward movements of the index. An ***INDEX*** *is a statistical report that is a generally reliable indicator of the approximate change in the cost of money.* There are several acceptable indexes published periodically that are easily available to lenders and borrowers alike. Examples include:

1. the indexes for the monthly average yield on three-year Treasury securities;
2. the monthly average of the weekly auction rate on Treasury bills;
3. the national average mortgage contract rate for major lenders on purchases of previously occupied homes, and
4. the cost of funds (based on the lenders' cost of funds).

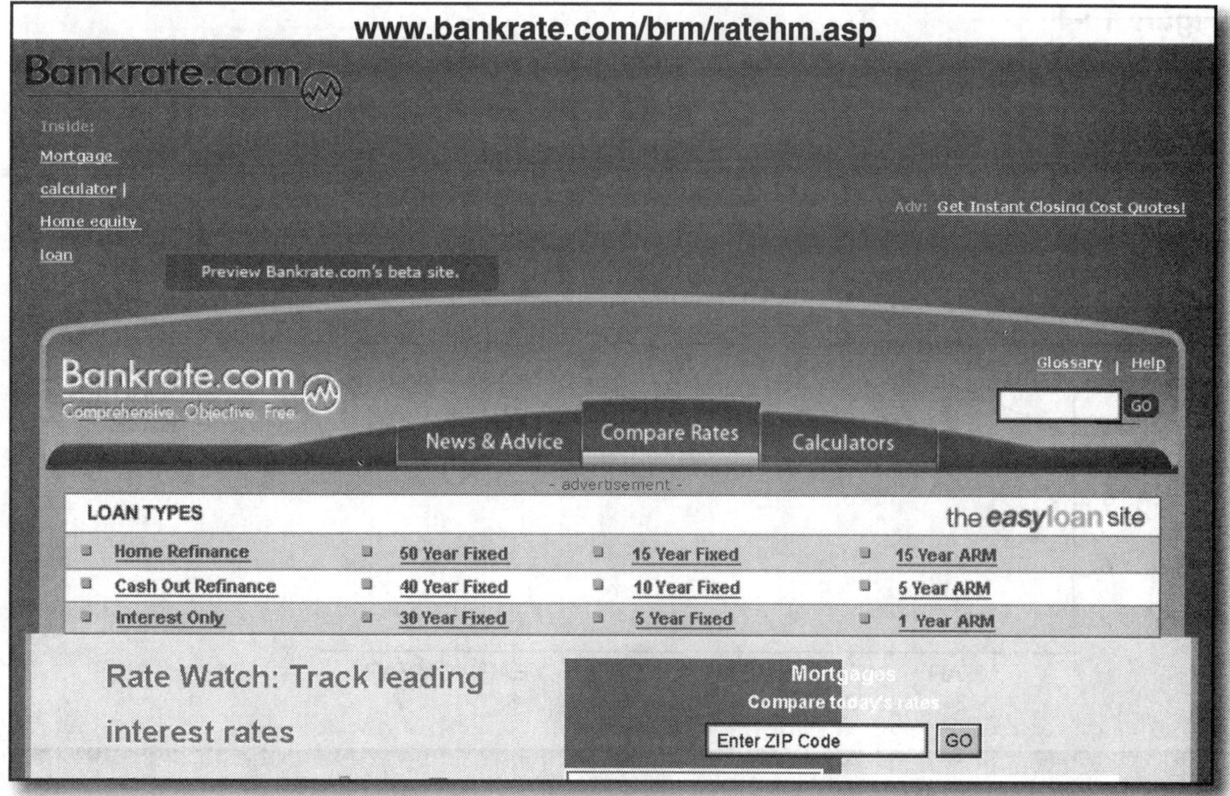

At the time a loan is made, the index preferred by the lender is selected, and thereafter the loan interest rate will rise and fall with the rates reported by the index. Since the index is a reflection of the lender's cost of money, it is necessary to add a "margin" to the index to ensure sufficient income for administrative expenses and profit. In fact, between lenders who use the same index, it is the size of the margin that makes the difference in interest charges. Margins will usually vary from 2% to 3%. The index plus the margin equals the adjustable interest rate.

It is the index rate that fluctuates during the term of the loan and causes the borrower's interest rate to increase and decrease; the lender's margin remains constant.

It should be noted that the lender has the option of increasing or leaving unchanged the borrower's interest rate when the selected index rises. But if the index falls, a reduction in the borrower's rate is mandatory.

Example: The lender has selected the one-year Treasury securities index. The lender's margin is 2%. When the index rate is raised, the ARM's interest rate is raised, and when the index rate falls, the ARM's rate falls. The margin stays the same (see **Figure 10-4**).

Figure 10-4

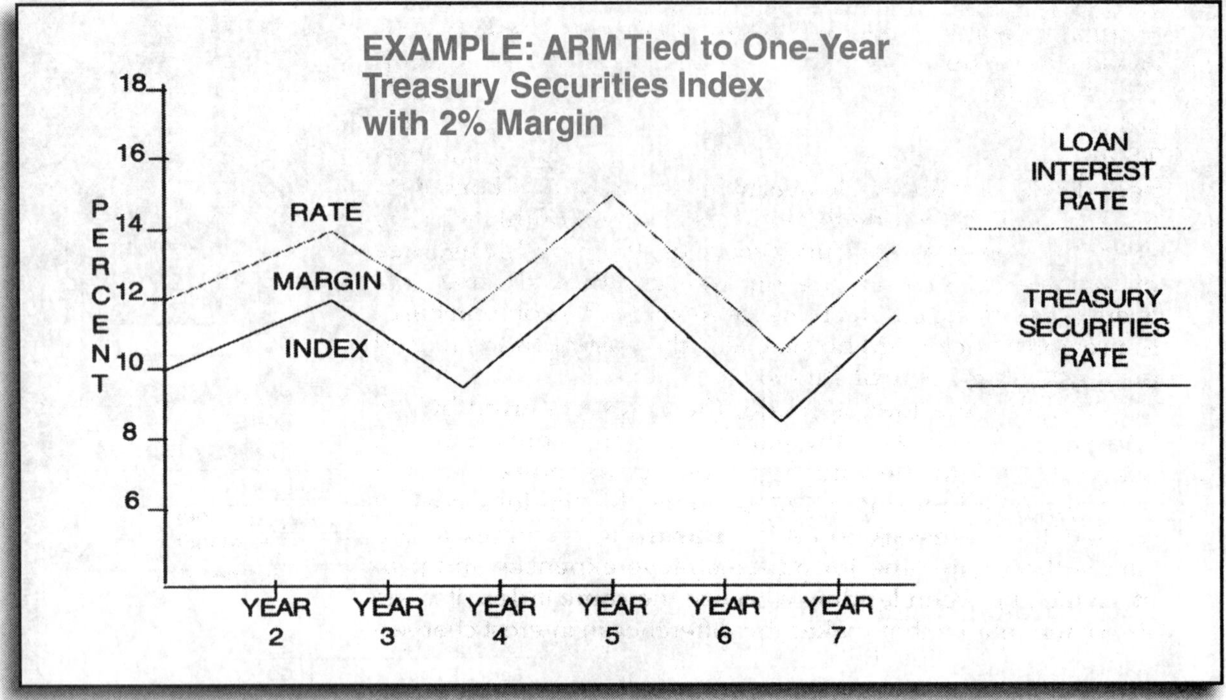

Terms, rate changes, and other aspects of ARMs are regulated by the government agencies that oversee lending institutions (principally the Office of Thrift Supervision and the Federal Reserve). Any applicable guidelines or requirements of FNMA, FHLMC, FHA, and/or private mortgage insurers must be followed as well.

C. ELEMENTS OF AN ARM LOAN

There are several elements that give form to an adjustable-rate mortgage. They include:

1. the index;
2. the margin;
3. the rate adjustment period;
4. the interest rate cap (if any);
5. the mortgage payment adjustment period;
6. the mortgage payment cap (if any);
7. the negative amortization cap (if any), and
8. a conversion option (if any).

1. The Index

Most lenders try to use an index that is very responsive to economic fluctuations. Thus, most ARMs have either a Treasury rate (usually one year) or the cost of funds as an index. The ***COST OF FUNDS INDEX (COFI)*** *is an average of the interest rates savings and loan associations pay for deposits and other borrowings with a certain range of maturities.*

The cost of funds index is more stable than the Treasury index rate.

The cost of funds index doesn't rise as much as the Treasury index over the long term, but neither does it fall as much. The Treasury index is more volatile, going both lower and higher than the cost of funds index.

2. Margin

The ***MARGIN*** *is the difference between the index value and the interest charged to the borrower.* It remains constant throughout the loan term.

Example:

9.25%	current index value
2.00%	margin
11.25%	mortgage interest rate (note rate)

3. Rate Adjustment Period

The ***RATE ADJUSTMENT PERIOD*** *refers to the intervals at which a borrower's interest rate is adjusted,* e.g., six months, one year, or three years. After referring to the rate movement in the selected index, the lender will notify the borrower in writing of any rate increase or decrease. Annual rate adjustments are most common.

4. Interest Rate Cap

Lenders use two different mechanisms to limit the magnitude of payment changes that occur with interest rate adjustments: interest rate caps and payment caps. *If a limit is placed on the number of percentage points an interest rate can be increased during the term of a loan, it is said to be* ***CAPPED***. Today, most ARMs have caps of some kind.

Lenders, consumers, and congressional leaders alike are concerned with a phenomenon called payment shock. ***PAYMENT SHOCK*** *results from increases in a borrower's monthly payments which, depending upon the amount and frequency of payment increases, as well as the borrower's income, may eliminate the borrower's ability to continue making mortgage payments.*

5. Teaser Rates

When lenders discovered the residential adjustable-rate mortgage instrument in late 1979, they recognized an opportunity to increase earnings and to insulate themselves from the staggering losses caused by too many fixed-rate mortgages that were yielding less than the prevailing cost of money. As public acceptance of ARMs grew, so did the prevailing cost of money. As public acceptance of ARMs grew, so did the competition for adjustable-rate mortgage loans.

To compete, lenders lowered the first-year interest rates on the loans they offered and introduced borrowers to discounts and buydowns. *The low initial rates have subsequently been dubbed* ***TEASER RATES***. Many lenders offered attractive teaser rates merely to enlarge their portfolio of ARMs. But since most ARMs were without interest rate caps prior to 1984, there were many instances where initial interest rates were increased by five to six percent. Clearly a crisis was developing. Consumers were losing confidence in the ARM and lenders were afraid they might experience unprecedented defaults, a phenomenon appropriately referred to as portfolio shock.

Industry leaders (especially the secondary market investors) began demanding more uniform ARM lending practices and a period of self-regulation began. To protect borrowers from payment shock and themselves from portfolio shock, lenders began imposing caps on their ARMS.

6. FNMA and FHLMC Caps

Both FNMA and FHLMC have guidelines relating to ARM interest rate caps. There are many different ARM plans, but as a general guideline, most ARMs purchased by FNMA are limited to rate increases of no more than 2% per year and 5% over the life of the loan. FHLMC rate adjustment guidelines limit rate increases to 2% per year and 5% over the life of the loan.

While FNMA and FHLMC guidelines do not take the form of government regulations, most lenders include these or stricter caps in their loans.

The Federal Home Loan Mortgage Corporation (FHLMC) has developed a set of ARM guidelines that, in its opinion, sets parameters acceptable for "investment quality" ARM loans. Guidelines for periodic interest rate caps are illustrated on the next page. The column titled "Illustrative Maximum Payment Increase" shows how a monthly payment would increase on a 30-year, $50,000 loan at a 12% interest rate with initial payments of $514.31 (see **Figure 10-5**).

Figure 10-5

Federal Home Loan Mortgage Corporation
Guidelines for Periodic Interest Rate Caps

	Per Rate Adjustment Period	
Rate Adjustment Period	Maximum Rate Adjustment	Illustrative Maximum Payment Increase*
Less than six months	0.167%	$6.43
Six months or more, but less than one year	1.0%	$38.79
One year or more, but less than two years	2.0%	$78.13
Two years or more, but less than three years	3.0%	$117.91
Three years or more	5.0%	$198.53

* $50,000 loan, 30 years at 12% interest

7. Mortgage Payment Adjustment Period

The ***MORTGAGE PAYMENT ADJUSTMENT PERIOD*** *defines the intervals at which a borrower's actual principal and interest payments are changed.* It is possible they will not coincide with the interest rate adjustments. There are two ways the rate and payment adjustments can be handled:

1. The lender can adjust the rate periodically as called for in the loan agreement and then adjust the mortgage payment to reflect the rate change.
2. The lender can adjust the rate more frequently than the mortgage payment is adjusted. For example, the loan agreement may call for interest rate adjustments every six months but changes in mortgage payments every three years.

If a borrower's principal and interest payment remains constant over a three-year period but the loan's interest rate has steadily increased or decreased during that time, then too little or too much interest will have been paid in the interim. When this happens, the difference is subtracted from or added to the loan balance. *When the minimum monthly payments are not large enough to pay all the interest due on the*

loan and this unpaid interest is added to the remaining balance of the loan, it is called ***NEGATIVE AMORTIZATION***. The danger of negative amortization is that the borrower may end up owing more than the original amount of the loan.

In an earlier illustration, it was shown how a borrower's ARM payments would parallel a chosen index, but this is not always the case. If the loan agreement calls for regular rate changes, but only occasional payment adjustments, the payments will not parallel the index at all, as indicated by **Figure 10-6**.

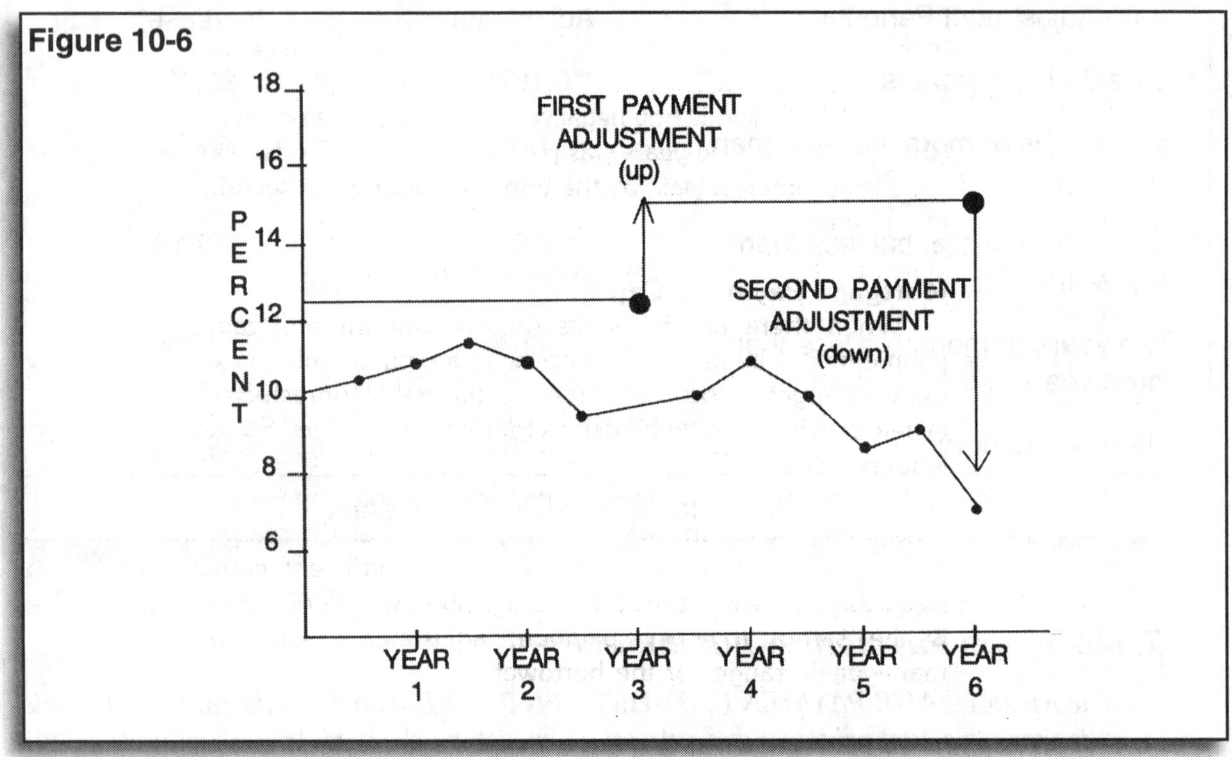

Example: A borrower's interest payment is set at 12.5%, which includes a 2.5% margin and a beginning index value of 10%. The lender will use the six-month Treasury bill index for biannual rate adjustments, and the borrower's mortgage payment will be adjusted every three years.

You will notice that throughout the loan's first level payment period (years 1-3), rates were increased four times and decreased twice. Though it is impossible to say by looking at the graph, it would appear that the rate increases during this period were more sustained and, in at least one instance, sharper than the rate declines. There is a good likelihood that during this period there was more interest due than paid, resulting in negative amortization. In the second three years, with only two moderate and relatively brief exceptions, the index value declined. Any negative amortization that occurred during the first three years was probably more than offset by the surplus interest paid by the borrower during the second three years.

8. Mortgage Payment Cap

When there are no limits on the amount mortgage payments can be increased, borrowers are vulnerable to extreme changes in the cost of money. Inevitably, unrestricted increases would create hardships for many borrowers. Some lenders incorporate payment caps into their ARMs, usually in the area of 7.5% annually. Other lenders only impose annual interest rate caps that work to limit payment increases. Still other lenders impose both rate and payment caps. Regardless of which policy a lender embraces, the objective is the same: to keep payment adjustments within a manageable range for the borrower.

9. Negative Amortization

There has been a dramatic movement away from plans that can result in negative amortization. This is probably because mortgage plans that provide for, or at least have a possibility of, negative amortization are not as attractive to borrowers as plans that do not permit negative amortization. In general, today's borrowers are better informed with respect to adjustable-rate loans.

Many lenders see annual interest and payment hikes, with acceptable limitations, as a means of avoiding interest shortfalls and the need for negative amortization. Interest rate fluctuations in recent times have been minor compared to the fluctuations between 1981 and 1982. By establishing rate and payment caps (during 1984), lenders began sharing more of the risk of increased interest rates than they did in the preceding three years. But if interest rates reach the high pre-1983 levels, the rate and payment caps in use today might prove too expensive for lenders, and that could signal the return of negative amortization as a means of keeping borrower's payments at manageable levels.

10. Negative Amortization Cap

Negative amortization has to be watched carefully or it could become an unmanageable problem for both the homeowner and the lender.

Various lenders handle the problem in different ways. Negative amortization becomes more critical at higher initial loan-to-value ratios. The current industry practice is to set a limit between 110%-125% of the initial loan balance. Another approach is to set the limit at 100% of the initial appraised value. This allows households that make larger down payments to have lower payments for a longer period of time. If negative amortization reaches the ceiling, the loan must be recast and further negative amortization is prohibited.

Bear in mind that negative amortization ceilings can be reached only if the interest rate increases several percentage points a year, for a number of years, without

relief. The payment caps previously mentioned allow payment increases that are substantial enough to prevent negative amortization in most cases. Negative amortization is most likely to occur when there are frequent rate changes (e.g., every six months) and infrequent payment adjustments (e.g., every three years).

11. Periodic Reamortization

As mentioned just above, many ARM loans with a possibility of negative amortization have a maximum cap for the amount of negative amortization. If the cap is reached, the loan payments are reamortized to a level sufficient to pay off the loan over the remaining term, without regard to any payment cap that might otherwise apply. Some ARMs provide for periodic reamortization of the loan, instead of or in addition to setting maximum caps for negative amortization. For example, the loan agreement might provide that every fifth year the monthly payments will be adjusted, with no payment cap, so that the new payments fully amortize the loan balance over its remaining term. These reamortizations are in addition to the normal reamortization and new payment levels made in connection with the regularly scheduled rate and/or payment adjustments.

Example: Original loan of $65,000 at 12.75% (10% index value + 2.75% margin). During the first five years, overall rate increases have exceeded payment adjustments, resulting in negative amortization of $2,250. The loan balance is $67,250. Index value at the fifth year is 12.25%; the margin remains constant at 2.75% for an adjusted rate of 15%.

$67,250	adjusted loan balance
15%	adjusted interest rate
25 years	remaining term on original 30-year loan

To determine the reamortized payment, refer to the principal and interest factors in Chapter 15.

$67,250	adjusted loan balance
x .0128084	factor for 15%, 25-year loan
$861.36	reamortized payment

This periodic reamortization reduces the possibility of a large buildup in the homeowner's debt, which would otherwise have to be paid in the form of a balloon payment when the house is sold or the loan becomes due.

D. CONVERTIBLE ARMs

One of the most popular innovations in ARM loans is the conversion option. A convertible ARM is one in which the borrower has the right to convert from an adjustable-rate loan to a fixed-rate loan. ARMs with a conversion option normally include the following:

1. Higher interest rate (often both the initial rate and the converted rate are higher);
2. Limited time to convert (e.g., between the first and fifth year), and
3. Conversion fee (typically about 1%).

For example, in one convertible ARM program, the loan may be converted between the 13th and 60th month for a $250 conversion fee paid to the lender. The initial rate on the ARM loan is the same as for other ARMs, but if converted, the fixed rate is 1/8% higher than the standard fixed rate at the time of conversion.

E. ARM LOAN-TO-VALUE (LTV) RATIOS

ARMs with loan-to-value ratios of 80%, 90%, and 95% are available. However, higher LTV loans are often subject to some restrictions. For example, many lenders refuse to make 90% or 95% ARM loans if there is a possibility of negative amortization. In most cases, borrowers seeking 90% or 95% ARMs will be required to occupy the property being purchased. FNMA and FHLMC require owner occupancy for all ARMs. Owner-occupants are considered better risks than nonoccupant borrowers.

F. FHLMC AND FNMA LTV GUIDELINES FOR ARMs

FNMA and FHLMC have stricter guidelines for adjustable-rate mortgages than the guidelines established for fixed-rate mortgages.

Loan-to-value ratios may not exceed 90% for ARMs. The lower loan-to-value requirements are due to the potential risk involved from payment increases when the interest rate is adjusted.

G. DISCOUNTS AND SUBSIDY BUYDOWNS ON ARMs

Some ARMs have initial interest rate discounts or subsidy buydowns. A discounted rate in this context means the borrower pays less than the ***NOTE RATE*** *(index rate plus margin)* prior to the first interest rate adjustment. The discounted rate is frequently referred to as a **teaser rate**. Loans with a subsidy buydown reduce the borrower's initial rate by payment of funds in advance. The subsidy buydown is usually paid by the seller. The probability that payment shock will occur is increased, because a payment increase after the first adjustment period is almost inevitable, even if there has been no increase in the value of the index in the interim. Of course, an increase in the index during this same period would make the payment shock even greater.

Moreover, initial rate discounts and subsidy buydowns have been used to make ARMs more attractive to borrowers who have trouble qualifying for financing at higher rates.

Thus, these loans are inherently more risky than most other types of loans, and lenders now underwrite them conservatively.

For ARMs with a 2% annual interest rate adjustment cap and an LTV over 80%, FHLMC requires the borrower to be qualified on the basis of payments made on the mortgage at the initial rate plus 2% (the maximum second-year mortgage rate increase). For example, a borrower seeking an ARM loan with an initial interest rate of 9% would have to qualify at an 11% interest rate (initial rate plus 2%).

Similarly, when an ARM involves a buydown, FNMA requires the borrower to be qualified on the basis of the original interest rate without the buydown. FNMA limits seller contributions to 2% if the loan-to-value ratio is over 90%, and to 9% if the loan-to-value ratio is 90% or less.

H. HOUSING EXPENSE-TO-INCOME RATIOS ON ARMs

Certain ARMs contain features that increase the likelihood that housing expense-to-income ratios will increase to dangerous levels after the first rate adjustment. (Expense-to-income ratios are covered in *Qualifying the Buyer*, Chapter 13.) ARMs with no rate or payment caps have the potential for large increases in the ratios. Likewise, loans with rate discounts or subsidy buydowns that exceed 2% add to the chances of significant payment shock. When ARMs are made with these features, secondary market investors, and many private mortgage insurance companies, are insisting that the traditional housing expense-to-gross income and total monthly debt payment-to-income ratios of 28% and 36% be disregarded in favor of lower, more conservative ratios.

The FHLMC recommends a 25% housing expense-to-income ratio, and a 33% total monthly debt service-to-income ratio, for ARM loans with any of the following features:

1. rate or payment cap outside FHLMC guidelines, or no caps;
2. discount or subsidy buydown exceeds 2%;
3. rate cap over 1% or payment cap over 7.5%, or
4. difference between rate and payment adjustment periods exceeds three years, and the payment cap does not meet FHLMC guidelines.

I. APPRAISALS ON PROPERTIES SECURED BY ARMs

Because ARMs introduce additional elements of risk to mortgage lending, many lenders adhere more strictly to their underwriting guidelines when evaluating an application for an ARM. A lender is particularly likely to review the appraisal for an ARM with special care.

Today, lenders insist that appraisal reports accurately reflect property values influenced by buydowns or other financing concessions. If a comparable property was sold with special financing arrangements, the buyers may have paid more for it than they would have without those arrangements. The appraiser must take the effect of the financing arrangements into account when using the comparable's selling price as an indication of the subject property's value.

When underwriting an ARM, the underwriter will review the appraisal report very closely to determine if the appraiser has performed this analysis satisfactorily. If not, the appraisal will be considered deficient.

J. ARM STANDARDIZATION

The widespread acceptance of ARMs represents a major evolutionary phase in the housing industry.

Initially, the estimated 200-plus adjustable-rate plans fueled sharp criticism. Customers were understandably confused by the proliferation of ARM programs. The threat of government regulation, increased dangers of foreclosure, and the refusal of the secondary market to buy ARMs caused lenders to standardize many of their ARM programs.

Uniform ARM underwriting standards have since been adopted and the secondary market agencies purchase ARMs. Originally, lenders were underwriting ARMs on the basis of their own standards and were largely keeping them in portfolio.

With standardization, lenders follow secondary market guidelines and resell ARMs just as they do fixed-rate loans.

K. ARM DISCLOSURE

Lenders offering adjustable-rate mortgages must comply with the Federal Reserve's guidelines under Regulation Z of the Truth in Lending Act requiring certain disclosures to be made to ARM borrowers.

These rules require a **general brochure** to be given to borrowers and **certain specific disclosures** to be made if relevant to the particular ARM program. They also establish guidelines for calculating and disclosing the annual percentage rate (APR). Disclosures must be provided to the borrower when the loan application is made or before payment of any nonrefundable fee, whichever occurs first.

A lender may comply with the requirement to provide a general informational brochure on adjustable-rate loans by giving the loan applicant the *Consumer Handbook on Adjustable-Rate Mortgages*, which has been prepared by the Federal Reserve and the Federal Home Loan Bank Board. The following disclosures must be made, if appropriate, to the individual loan program applied for:

1. The index used to determine the interest rate.
2. Where the borrower may find the index.
3. An explanation of how the interest rate and payment will be determined.
4. A suggestion that the borrower ask the lender about the current margin and interest rate.
5. If the initial rate is discounted, a disclosure of that fact and a suggestion that the borrower inquire as to the amount of the discount.
6. The interest and payment adjustment periods.
7. Any rules regarding changes in the index, interest rate, payment amount, or loan balance (including an explanation of any caps, a conversion option, or the possibility of negative amortization).
8. An explanation of how to calculate the payments for the loan.
9. A statement that the loan has a demand feature (that is, a "call" provision or acceleration clause).
10. A description of the information that will be included in the adjustment notices and when those notices will be provided.
11. A statement that disclosure forms are available for the lender's other ARM programs.

The lender must also give the borrower a historical example illustrating how the payments on a $10,000 loan would have been affected by rate changes over the past 15 years, and an example of how the maximum interest rate and payment would be calculated for a $10,000 loan.

The lender must give the borrower advance notice of any change in the payment, interest rate, index, or loan balance. These disclosures must be provided at least 25 days, but no more than 120 days, before a new payment level goes into effect, and at least once in each year in which the interest rate changes without a corresponding payment adjustment.

When calculating the annual percentage rate for an adjustable-rate mortgage, a lender is allowed to base the APR on the loan's initial interest rate.

At closing, this is usually the only interest rate for the loan that the lender can be sure of. The rates that will apply later on are uncertain because they depend on changes in the index to which the loan is tied. However, the lender is required to state that the APR may increase (e.g., "10.41% APR, subject to increase after closing").

If the loan has a teaser rate (a special low initial interest rate) and the interest rate is scheduled to rise by a specific amount, the APR must be a composite figure taking into account every interest rate that the lender knows at closing will apply to the loan. The APR can't be based on the teaser rate alone.

The guidelines are an effort to ensure that when mortgage rates are adjusted, borrowers, whose disclosure forms are based only on a discounted initial rate, are not faced with unexpectedly large increases in their payments.

L. WHAT YOU NEED TO KNOW ABOUT ARMs

As an agent, you must always be prepared to answer buyers' and sellers' questions. You are expected to be knowledgeable. When it comes to ARM financing, it would be reasonable to expect the following questions:

1. What Will My Interest Rate Be?

It is usually not necessary to break the rate down into index and margin. The buyer is concerned only with the total. Monitor local rates; they change regularly.

2. How Often Will My Interest Rate Change?

The rate adjustments will be spelled out in the loan agreement. Depending on lender preference (index used), they will occur every six months, annually, every three years, or every five years. The six-month and one-year intervals are most common. In order to be specific, you have to know your lenders and their policies.

3. How Often Will My Payment Change?

Again, in order to give an accurate answer, you have to be familiar with the policies of the local lenders. The majority of lenders have shown a preference for simultaneous rate and payment changes, but there are many exceptions.

4. Is There Any Limit To How Much My Interest Rate Can Be Increased?

Most ARMs have payment caps. The most common life-of-the-loan caps are 5% and 6% caps imposed by FHLMC and FNMA. Annual interest rate caps are usually between 1% and 2%.

5. Is There Any Limit To How Much My Payment Can Be Increased At Any One time?

Some ARMs have payment caps while others keep payment hikes under control with interest rate caps. Where payment caps exist, they are usually limited to 7.5%-15% of the payment amount or the equivalent of a 1%-2% interest rate change.

6. What Is The Probability Of Runaway Negative Amortization?

The answer is: remote to nonexistent. Interest rate caps, negative amortization caps, and re-amortization requirements protect borrower and lender in this regard. The best protection is undoubtedly the changing nature of the money market itself. Interest rates rise and fall; they always have. A borrower's rate will be increased at one interval and reduced at another. If, at one point, there is negative amortization because the interest due exceeded interest paid, there is an excellent chance that not long afterwards index declines will result in the opposite: accelerated amortization. This up-and-down pattern, though always unpredictable, continues throughout the life of the loan.

7. Can My ARM Be Converted To A Fixed-Rate Loan?

Many ARMs now contain a conversion option that permits the borrower to convert to a fixed-rate loan for a fee at certain periods or points in the loan term. ARMs with a conversion option often have higher interest rates than those without.

V. The Growth Equity Mortgage (GEM)

Sometimes called a **building equity mortgage (BEM)** or **rapidly amortizing mortgage (RAM)**, the growth equity mortgage (GEM) solves many of the problems that have limited the appeal of ARMs. Still, today it enjoys only limited public acceptance.

Though there are numerous variations of the growth equity mortgage, all of them share the following characteristics:

1. The interest rate is fixed over the life of the loan.
2. First-year payments of principal and interest are based on a 30-year term.
3. The borrower's payments are increased at specified intervals (usually annually) for all, or a portion of, the life of the loan.
4. Because the interest rate is fixed, 100% of the annual payment increases are used to reduce the principal balance.

A. DETERMINING ANNUAL PAYMENT ADJUSTMENTS

There are any number of annual payment adjustment plans, but by far the most popular method is to increase the payments by a fixed percentage—typically 3% or 5%.

Example: $86,000 loan at 10.25% (fixed rate) based on a 30-year term. Payments to be increased 3% annually.

$86,000	
x .0089610	10.25%, 30-year factor
$770.65	initial monthly payment

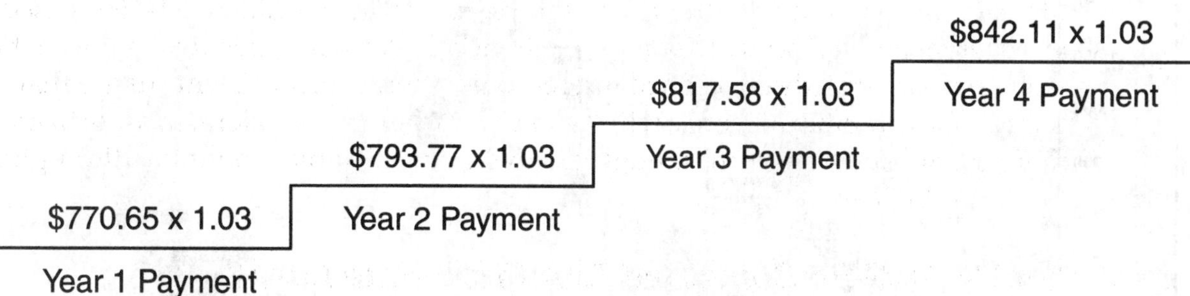

In the example above, the borrower's payments are increased by 3% each year, and the entire increase is always applied to the loan balance.

B. EQUITY BUILDS UP QUICKLY

Because payment increases are used to reduce the mortgage debt, a borrower will pay off a GEM much sooner than a 30-year fixed-rate mortgage. If payments are increased 3% per year on a 15% loan, the entire debt will be retired in 13 years and 7 months; with 5% annual increases, the same loan will pay off in just 11 years and 4 months. A GEM's repayment term is dependent on the interest rate and the magnitude of the annual payment increases. Most GEMs pay off in 11 to 17 years. **Figure 10-7** demonstrates the difference between the repayment patterns of a GEM and a 30-year fixed-rate mortgage.

It is clearly illustrated by the Comparison of Repayment Pattern graph that GEM payments become substantially higher than the level fixed-rate payments. In the past, this annual rate of increase was well below the inflationary trends and GEM payment increases did not rise as fast as borrowers' incomes. Borrowers had few difficulties adjusting to payment hikes, and furthermore, to many borrowers the payment increase drawback was insignificant when weighed against the remarkable advantage of accelerated equity accumulation. A 30-year, fixed-rate mortgage shows a balance of $65,620.93 after 13 years and 4½ months. At the end of the same period, the GEM loan is paid in full. At current low rates of inflation, the GEM payment increases do not look so attractive. The primary advantages of GEMs, fast amortization and predictable

Figure 10-7

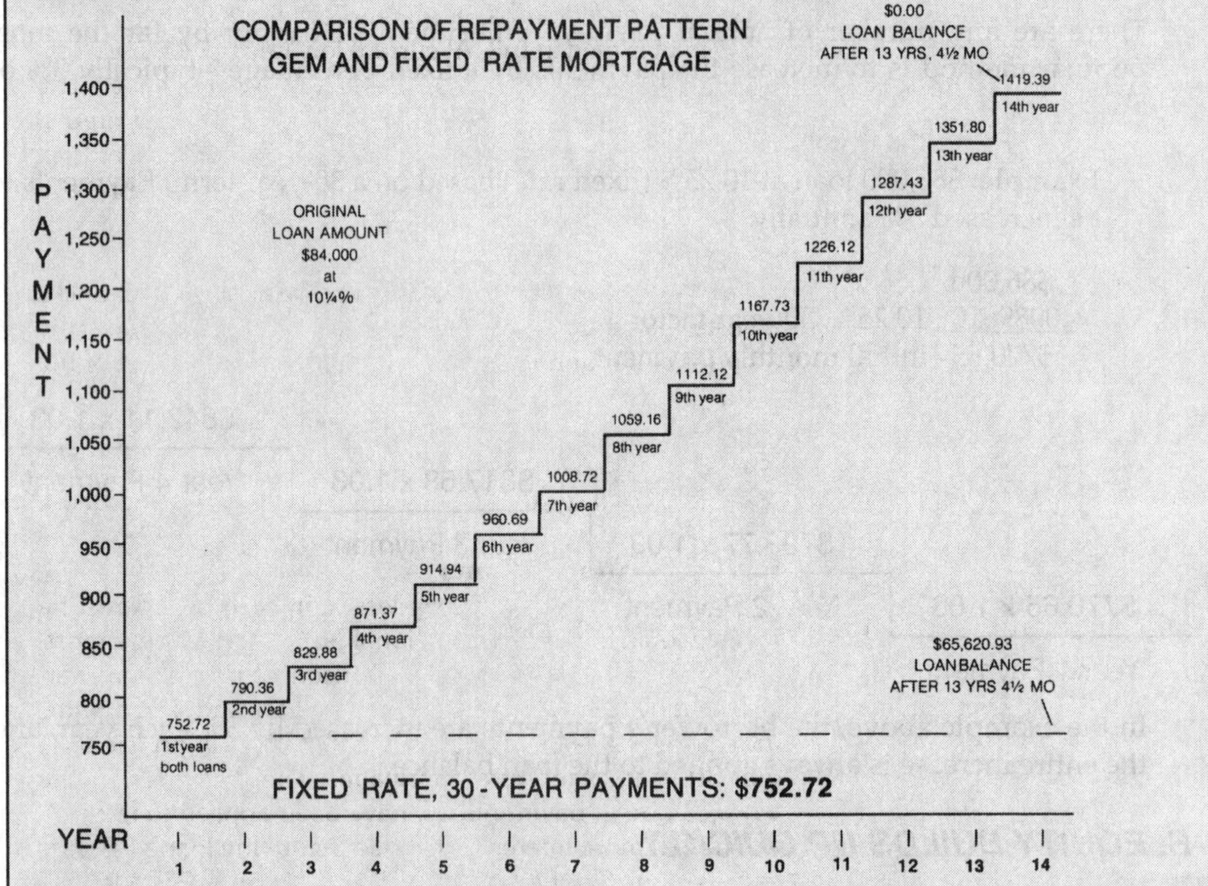

payments, are also available with the more popular level payment 15-year, fixed-rate loans discussed in the previous chapter.

C. PAYMENTS ARE PREDICTABLE

The borrower's payments will increase annually, but unlike adjustable-rate mortgages that are tied to an index, the amount of the annual increase is known at the outset of the loan.

D. NO NEGATIVE AMORTIZATION

To the contrary, with a GEM, there is accelerated positive amortization.

E. REDUCED INTEREST COSTS

A GEM borrower will pay less than half the interest he or she would pay with a traditional 30-year, fixed-rate mortgage.

By referring back to the "Comparison of Repayment Pattern" chart (Figure 10-7), you can see that after 13 years and 4½ months the borrower will have paid only $18,379.07 in principal on the 30-year, fixed-rate mortgage. The balance of the $120,811.56 in payments will have been applied to interest, with much more interest to be paid before the loan's 30-year term is over. On the other hand, interest on a GEM loan is much less, and the interest portion of each succeeding payment will decline as rapidly as the loan balance itself.

F. SIMPLICITY OF LOAN

In contrast to ARMs, the GEM is easy to understand and explain. There is little doubt buyers are reluctant to commit to a major debt, like a home loan, if they do not understand how it works.

G. LOWER-THAN-MARKET INTEREST RATE

Very often lenders are willing to make GEM loans at lower-than-market rates because they will recapture the principal so quickly. Recaptured principal can be reinvested at competitive market rates. The lower-than-market rate makes it easier to qualify for the loan.

VI. Reduction Option Mortgage

A ***REDUCTION OPTION MORTGAGE*** *is a fixed-rate loan that gives the borrower a limited opportunity to reduce the interest rate without paying refinancing costs.* For example, on a 30-year reduction option mortgage, the borrower might be given the option of reducing the interest rate once at any time during the second through fifth years of the loan term. There might be some additional limitations. For example, the borrower might not be allowed to exercise the option unless market interest rates had declined at least 2%.

If the borrower chose to exercise the option, the lender would charge a processing fee, usually in the neighborhood of a few hundred dollars. This is substantially less than the fees typically charged for refinancing, which are ordinarily between 1% and 2% of the loan amount. Other costs of refinancing, such as an appraisal fee, are also avoided with a reduction option mortgage. Interest rates for reduction option mortgages tend to be slightly higher than for fixed-rate loans without the reduction option.

VII. Biweekly Loans

A ***BIWEEKLY LOAN*** *is a fixed-rate mortgage set up in a fashion similar to a standard 30-year conventional loan. Both interest rate and payments are fixed.* However, payments are made every two weeks instead of every month. Each payment is equal to half of what

the monthly payment would be for a fully amortized 30-year, fixed-rate loan of the same amount at the same interest rate.

Biweekly loans offer significant savings over the life of a loan. For example, if a $70,000 loan at an interest rate of 10.5% is paid on a biweekly schedule instead of a monthly payment plan, the borrower would save approximately $60,000 in interest. Because payments are made every two weeks (not twice a month), 26 payments are made each year (i.e., the equivalent of an extra monthly payment is made each year). As interest is calculated on the remaining balance, this provides a rather large interest savings. Biweekly loans are generally paid off in approximately 20 to 21 years, instead of 30 years.

Example: A $70,000 loan with a 10.5% fixed rate and a 30-year amortization schedule would have the following results:

Schedule of Payments	Payment	# of payments	Total Amount Paid
Monthly	$640.32	360	$230,515.20
Biweekly	$320.21	532	$170,352.39

The biweekly loan would pay off in about 20½ years, with total interest payments of approximately $60,189.81 less than the monthly payment schedule.

NOTE: In this example, biweekly payments are slightly more than one-half the monthly payment in order to avoid a partial final payment.

Although biweekly loans have been available for some time, especially in the Northeast and Midwest, they have not been widely promoted by lenders because of the increased servicing costs associated with handling 26 payments instead of 12 payments per year. However, FNMA began purchasing biweekly loans in February 1988. With FNMA available as a purchaser for the loans, lenders are relieved of the burden of packaging biweekly mortgages for private investors, which may lead to some growth in their popularity. Loans with a payment schedule that coincides with the way many people are paid would seem to have some natural appeal.

VIII. Home Equity Conversion Mortgages (Reverse Mortgages)

A ***REVERSE MORTGAGE****, also known as a* ***reverse annuity mortgage (RAM)****, enables older homeowners (62+) to convert their home equity into tax-free income without having to sell their home, give up title, or take on a mortgage payment. The loan is repaid when the borrower dies or permanently moves away.*

A reverse mortgage borrower generally must be over age 62 and own a home with little or no outstanding mortgage balance.

Typically, the homeowner mortgages his or her home to a bank or savings bank and, in return, receives a monthly check from the lender. The amount of the monthly payment depends on the appraised value of the home, the age of the homeowner, the length of the loan, when the loan must be repaid, and the amount of interest charged.

The most basic reverse mortgage is the ***TERM LOAN****, which provides monthly advances for a fixed period of time (generally three to 12 years)*. At the end of the period, all principal advances, plus interest, are due.

Term loans have had limited success because borrowers fear having to sell their home at the end of the term.

The ***SPLIT-TERM LOAN*** *is similar to the basic term loan, except that it does not have to be repaid until the borrower moves, dies, or sells the house*. This type of reverse mortgage provides more peace of mind for the borrower.

Under a ***TENURE LOAN****, the lender makes monthly payments only as long as the borrower occupies the house as a principal residence*. Tenure payments are generally lower than other types of reverse mortgages because of the uncertainty as to when the mortgage will be repaid.

The ***LINE OF CREDIT LOAN*** *is slightly different from the other reverse mortgages in that payments are not made on a regular basis*. The borrower withdraws funds whenever necessary, up to a maximum number of times. Repayment is deferred until the borrower dies, sells, or moves. In the past decade, the equity line of credit has also become popular. This loan is based on the owner's equity in the home and may be withdrawn in a similar manner as the line of credit. However, repayments begin with the first withdrawal.

IX. Shared Appreciation Mortgages

The Shared Appreciation Mortgage (SAM) was originally introduced in the 1980s.

With a SAM, the lender shares the appreciation of equity in your home with you.

Typically, the lender is willing to reduce the interest rate of the mortgage for a share of the equity buildup in your home. The rate reduction in the past has been as much as 2%. For this reduction the lender wants anywhere from 25-50% of the equity in your home. These loans often have prepayment penalties that do not allow the borrower to get out from under an adverse turn in the market. This loan could be a good deal for a borrower

if interest rates are increasing and the home is held through a period of declining home values. This type of mortgage could have been a very bad choice for a borrower in the past few years in California.

For example:

> A borrower who had financed the $350,000 purchase of his home with a SAM at 5% interest, approximately 2% less than the going rate in 2000, would have seen interest rates decline to 3% during the succeeding five-year period, while home prices went up 100-150%. The borrower who could resell in 2005-06 for $700,000 would have had to pay the lender $175,000 at a 50% shared rate of the appreciated value at the time of closing. During the life of the loan, under this scenario, the borrower would have been repaying the loan at an above-market rate as well.

A SAM could be costly to a borrower who paid off the mortgage under one of these plans and planned to remain in the residence. They would have to come up with the lender's share of the equity appreciation (as measured by an appraisal) in cash. In the case of the example above this could be a staggering amount.

Scenarios such as those given above are the reason that this type of mortgage has not enjoyed the popularity of other mortgage types such as the ARM.

X. CHAPTER SUMMARY

Alternative financing programs were originally developed in the 1980s to meet the dual challenges of higher home prices and higher interest rates. The combination of these two factors made it extremely difficult for buyers to qualify for a home loan. In order to make it easier for borrowers, many of these alternate financial plans involve the payment of discount points, temporary buydowns, or permanent buydowns to reduce the borrower's interest or lower the payments.

Out of the many programs introduced, only a few have achieved continued acceptance and popularity with consumers. These consist primarily of the various ARM programs offered by lenders. Borrowers contemplating applying for an ARM should be made aware of the following important elements: the lender's index for adjusting the interest rate, the lender's margin above the index rate, rate and payment adjustment periods, the possibility of negative amortization, whether there is an option to convert to a fixed-rate loan, and whether there are any periodic or lifetime caps on the interest rate.

XI. TERMINOLOGY

Adjusted-Rate Loan
Adjustable-Rate Mortgage (ARM)
AML
APR
Biweekly Loan
Buydown
Capped
Certain Specific Disclosures
Cost of Funds Index (COF)
Coupon Rate
Discount Points
Effective Rate
General Brochure
Growth Equity Mortgage (GEM)
Graduated Payment Mortgage (GPM)
Index
Line of Credit
Loan
Margin
Mortgage Payment Adjustment Period
Negative Amortization
Note Rate
Payment Shock
Point
Reduction Option Mortgage
Reverse Annuity Mortgage (RAM)
Reverse Mortgage
Shared Appreciation Mortgage (SAM)
Split-Term Loan
Teaser Rate
Tenure Loan
Term Loan

XII. CHAPTER QUIZ

1. A loan balance that grows rather than decreases due to unpaid interest being added back into the loan is said to have:

   a. a split term.
   b. a margin.
   c. negative amortization.
   d. positive amortization.

2. Alternate financing plans are popular:

   a. during times of low interest rates.
   b. during times of high interest rates.
   c. with older borrowers.
   d. with younger borrowers.

3. The payment of points to reduce the amount of interest on a loan is called:

   a. meeting margin.
   b. an index loan.
   c. a cap.
   d. a buydown.

4. An amount added to cover administrative costs and profit is called:

   a. an index.
   b. cost of funds.
   c. margin.
   d. a cap.

5. Mortgage payment caps are generally limited by lenders to an annual increase of:

   a. 1%.
   b. 2%.
   c. 5%.
   d. 7.5%.

6. A borrower who has a 90% loan at 6.5% interest with a 2% annual interest rate must qualify at:

   a. 7%.
   b. 7.5%.
   c. 8%.
   d. 8.5%.

7. Lenders offering adjustable-rate mortgages must:
   a. comply with Regulation Z.
   b. provide the borrower with a general brochure.
   c. make certain specific disclosures.
   d. all the above.

8. In a Growth Equity Mortgage (GEM):
   a. payments increase annually.
   b. payments decrease annually.
   c. interest increases annually.
   d. interest decreases annually.

9. "One Point" is:
   a. $1,000.
   b. 1% of the sales price.
   c. 1% of the loan amount.
   d. none of the above.

10. What age must a reverse mortgage borrower be?
   a. Under 60
   b. Over 62
   c. Over 64
   d. Over 65

ANSWERS: 1. *c;* 2. *b;* 3. *d;* 4. *c;* 5. *d;* 6. *d;* 7. *d;* 8. *a;* 9. *c;* 10. *b*

Real Estate Español.com
Real Estate for Hispanic-Americans
Sell
Refina
Purch

Chapter 11
Government Programs: FHA and VA Loans

Congress is continually reforming the FHA and VA loan programs.

This chapter will examine the function of two government agency programs misleadingly labeled "loan" programs: Federal Housing Administration (FHA) and Department of Veterans Affairs (VA) loans.

Neither FHA nor VA makes loans directly to the public. FHA insures, but VA guarantees.

The FHA and VA are also not part of the secondary market—they do not buy loans or sell loan-backed securities. Instead, they act as giant federal insurance agencies and insure approved lenders against losses caused by borrower default. Each agency has a number of separate programs that have made homeownership possible for millions of Americans who otherwise might not have been eligible for conventional loans.

Lenders are extremely comfortable with the insurance programs of each agency as they are backed by the full faith and credit of the United States government.

CHAPTER OUTLINE

www.makinghomeaffordable.gov

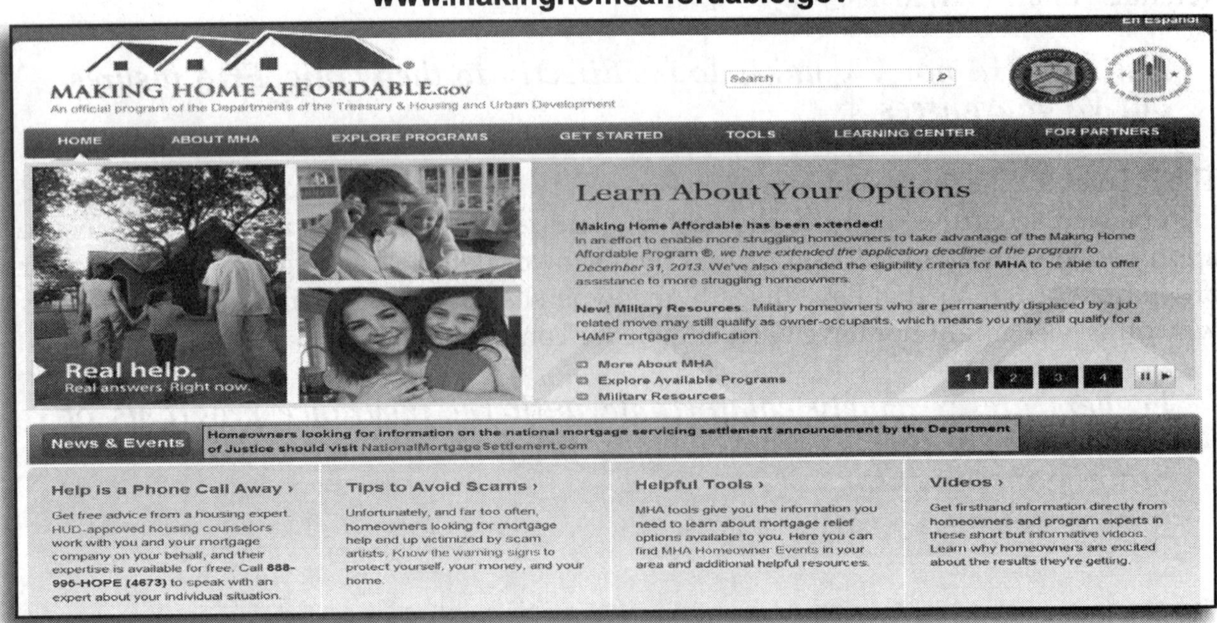

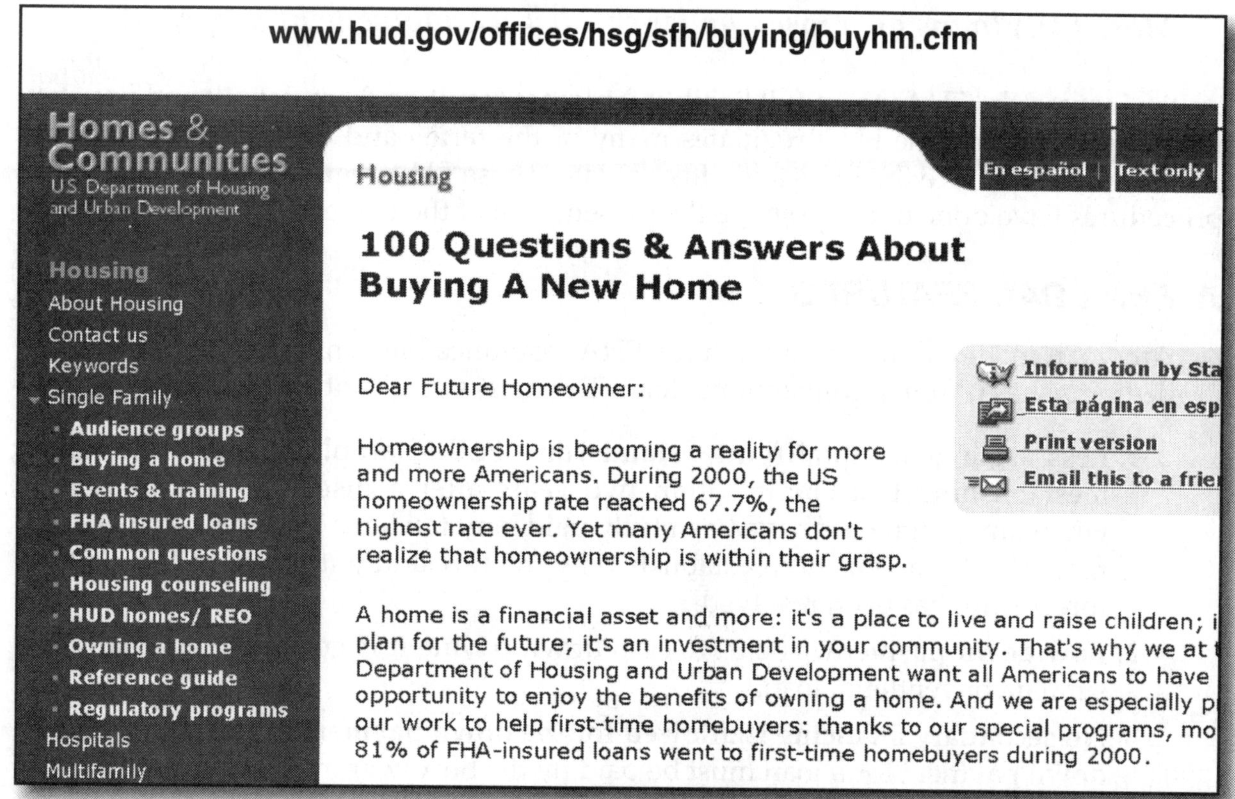
www.hud.gov/offices/hsg/sfh/buying/buyhm.cfm

Homes & Communities
U.S. Department of Housing and Urban Development

Housing
About Housing
Contact us
Keywords
Single Family
Audience groups
Buying a home
Events & training
FHA insured loans
Common questions
Housing counseling
HUD homes/ REO
Owning a home
Reference guide
Regulatory programs
Hospitals
Multifamily

En español | Text only

Housing

100 Questions & Answers About Buying A New Home

Information by Sta
Esta página en esp
Print version
Email this to a frie

Dear Future Homeowner:

Homeownership is becoming a reality for more and more Americans. During 2000, the US homeownership rate reached 67.7%, the highest rate ever. Yet many Americans don't realize that homeownership is within their grasp.

A home is a financial asset and more: it's a place to live and raise children; i plan for the future; it's an investment in your community. That's why we at Department of Housing and Urban Development want all Americans to have opportunity to enjoy the benefits of owning a home. And we are especially p our work to help first-time homebuyers: thanks to our special programs, mo 81% of FHA-insured loans went to first-time homebuyers during 2000.

I. Federal Housing Administration (FHA)

The Federal Housing Administration (FHA) was created by Congress in 1934 as part of the *NATIONAL HOUSING ACT. The purpose of the act and of the FHA was to generate new jobs through increased construction activity, to exert a stabilizing influence on the mortgage market, and to promote the financing, repair, and sale of real estate nationwide.* Today, the FHA is part of the Department of Housing and Urban Development (HUD).

> ***The FHA's primary function is to insure loans. FHA approved lenders are insured against losses caused by borrower default.***

The FHA insurance program is called the **Mortgage Insurance Premium (MIP)**. Under the plan, lenders who have been approved by the FHA to make insured loans either submit applications from prospective borrowers to the local FHA office for approval, or, if authorized by the FHA to do so, perform the underwriting functions themselves (review of appraisal, mortgage credit examinations, etc.). *Lenders who are authorized by the FHA to fully underwrite their own FHA loan applications are called* ***DIRECT ENDORSEMENT LENDERS (DE LENDERS).*** A direct endorsement lender is responsible for the entire mortgage process, from application through closing. When a DE lender has approved and closed a loan, the application for mortgage insurance is submitted to the FHA.

Most FHA loans are closed under the direct endorsement program.

As the insurer, the FHA incurs full liability for losses resulting from default and property foreclosure. In turn, the FHA regulates many of the terms and conditions of the loan. FHA regulations have the force and effect of law. These FHA regulations, practices, and procedures have done much to shape the present face of the real estate lending industry.

A. FHA LOAN FEATURES

Any loan intended for submission for FHA insurance has a number of features that distinguishes it from a conventional loan. The most significant of these features are:

1. **Less stringent qualifying standards**. For example: FHA will allow reestablishment of credit within two years after a discharge of bankruptcy; when any judgments have been fully paid, any tax liens have been repaid, or a repayment plan has been established by the IRS, and within three years after a foreclosure has been resolved.
2. **Low down payment**. The 3.5% cash down payment is generally less than for a similar conventional loan.
3. **No secondary financing is allowed for the down payment**. The FHA minimum down payment for a loan must be paid by the borrower in cash. The borrower is not allowed to resort to secondary financing from the seller or from any lender to make up any part of the down payment. The FHA permits the use of either a nonrepayable gift of money, credit from a portion of rents from a rent/purchase contract between a buyer and seller, or some home repairs made by the purchaser ("sweat equity") to be used to satisfy the statutory 3.5% down payment costs. This is ordinarily not permitted with conventional loans.
4. **Some closing costs may cover down payment**. While a borrower may not finance any of the closing costs along with the sales price, FHA permits the use of some closing costs to satisfy the 3.5% statutory down payment requirement.
5. **FHA mortgage insurance is required for the loan regardless of the amount of the down payment.** In contrast, conventional loans usually do not require mortgage insurance unless the loan-to-value ratio exceeds 80%.
6. **No prepayment penalties are allowed.** Some conventional loans have substantial prepayment penalties for the first few years of the mortgage term. An FHA loan may be paid off in full at any time with no additional charges. A lender is allowed to require that any such payment be made on a regular installment due date. Loans that were made before August 1985 require a 30-day notice of the intention to prepay the loan.
7. **The property must be owner occupied.** The FHA used to insure investor properties but they have virtually eliminated all such programs. Two-to-four-unit properties qualify if they are owner occupied.

B. OTHER CHARACTERISTICS OF FHA LOANS

The typical FHA loan has a thirty-year term. However, FHA offers loan terms as short as fifteen years. They also offer adjustable loans and home repair loans, which will be discussed in the section on FHA programs.

The FHA requires their loans to have a first lien position.

The FHA used to set the maximum interest rates, but now the rate is freely negotiable between the borrower and the lender. They still tend to be lower than conventional rates because the lender's risk is lessened by the FHA mortgage insurance.

A lender may only charge a 1% origination fee on an FHA loan, but is allowed to charge discount points. Typically, discount points allow a lender to recover any interest loss up front. These points may be paid by either the buyer or another party.

Although discount points may be paid by the buyer in an FHA transaction, they are almost always paid by the seller.

The lender is required to obtain an appraisal of the property from an FHA-approved appraiser. The appraiser will note any major health and safety deficiencies on the Uniform Residential Appraisal Report (URAR). FHA no longer uses the Valuation Conditions Form or the Homebuyer Summary Form. FHA now states, in a letter to mortgagees and appraisers, that it has shifted its historical emphasis on the repair of minor deficiencies and now only requires repair for those property conditions that rise above the level of cosmetic defects, or normal wear and tear. Some cosmetic defects listed are such items as worn-out carpet, trip hazards, cracked or broken window glass, crawl spaces filled with trash and debris, and missing stair rails. In addition, well water tests and septic system tests are no longer required unless the appraiser has evidence of contamination or they are required by a local authority.

Major problems to be addressed by the appraiser include standing water against a foundation, damp basements, and hazardous materials in the improvements or on the site. This causes the question to arise as to whether trash, such as flammable material in the crawl space, is hazardous. Faulty or defective mechanical systems, including plumbing and heating devices, are included in the list. Last, but not least, bulging foundation walls are to be reported.

Unlike many conventional loans, FHA loans are fully assumable without any increase in interest rates. A lender is also prohibited from exercising any "due on sale" clause on an FHA transfer. As of 1989, sellers are released from all liability under an assumption; however, buyers must qualify under the standard FHA 203b income rules.

https://entp.hud.gov/idapp/html/hicostlook.cfm

Homes & Communities

hud home page | search | privacy statement

U.S. DEPARTMENT OF HOUSING AND URBAN DEVELOPMENT

fha mortgage limits

Welcome to the FHA Mortgage Limits page. This page allows you to look up the FHA mortgage limits for your area or several areas, and then list them by state, county, or Metropolitan Statistical Area. Detailed **help** is available, or send questions to the Single Family Administrator.

Sorted By: State

State: All States

County:

County Code:

MSA Name:

MSA Code:

Last Revised: / /

Send Reset

FHA loans are not assumable by investors.

C. INCOME QUALIFICATIONS AND MAXIMUM LOAN AMOUNTS

There is no minimum income requirement for an FHA loan. Borrowers must show two years of steady employment and demonstrate that they have consistently paid their bills on time. The FHA has a ratio of 31% and 43%. This means that the payments for a home loan may not exceed 31% of the borrower's gross monthly income and all installment debt, including the home loan payment, may not exceed 43%. These figures are more liberal than the conventional limits underwritten by FNMA and FHLMC.

The FHA sets maximum mortgage loan amounts. These amounts, which vary by state as well as location within a state, are adjusted yearly. The maximum amount for low-cost areas, such as Wyoming, was $271,050. The maximum for a high-cost area, such as Los Angeles, California, was $729,750. Section 214 of the National Housing Act provides that Alaska, Hawaii, Guam, and the Virgin Islands may have a maximum of $1,094,625.

D. MORTGAGE INSURANCE PREMIUM (MIP)

All FHA loans require a mortgage insurance premium.

The mortgage insurance is referred to as **MORTGAGE INSURANCE PREMIUM (MIP).** FHA charges an up-front premium of 1.75% - 2.25% of the loan amount. In addition, FHA charges a monthly premium equal to .05% of the loan amount annually. If the property is sold within the first 84 months of the loan term, any unused portion of the up-front MIP will be returned to the borrower. When the loan balance drops below 78% of the original purchase price, the monthly payment may be cancelled, provided the borrower has made monthly payments for five years on a thirty-year mortgage.

II. FHA Programs

A. FHA 203b FIXED-RATE PROGRAM

With a ***203b FIXED-RATE PROGRAM****, a down payment of 3.5% of the sales price is required* (see **Figure 11-1**). Gifts from family members are allowed, as are payments from government or nonprofit agencies that are designed to help first-time or low-income buyers. FHA does not require the borrower to have cash reserves. As noted earlier, only two years of employment prior to application is required. Lenders may only charge closing fees that are found on an FHA-approved list. Fees for document preparation, processing fees, underwriting fees, and lender's tax services are not allowed. All owner-occupied one-to-four-unit family residences are eligible. Homes located in planned unit developments (PUDs) must be HUD-approved projects.

B. FHA 251 ADJUSTABLE PROGRAM

The ***FHA 251 ADJUSTABLE PROGRAM*** *is a thirty-year adjustable rate mortgage*. It is indexed to the one-year Treasury Bill rate and is adjusted annually. The adjusted rate may not move higher or lower than 1% per year. The rate adjustment is capped at 5%. This means that the rate may not go higher than 5% over the life of the loan. To qualify for the 251 Adjustable Program, a borrower must qualify at 1% above the initial rate. Eligible property types, mortgage insurance premiums, closing costs rules, down payment requirements, and qualifying ratios are the same as for the 203b program.

C. FHA 203k PURCHASE AND REHABILITATION PROGRAM

The ***FHA 203k PURCHASE AND REHABILITATION PROGRAM*** *was developed to help revitalize communities and neighborhoods*. It was developed by HUD and is administered by the FHA. Many areas have older housing stock that is basically sound, but in need of extensive repairs. Normally, in conventional practice, a homebuyer must first purchase the home and then obtain construction financing to rehabilitate the home. This often creates multiple short-term mortgages at high interest rates. In most cases, conventional lenders will not make a mortgage loan until all repairs are completed. As a result, many basically sound properties in need of repair were left vacant, and at risk of further deterioration and vandalism, simply because prospective homebuyers were unable to afford the purchase price without a loan.

It may be possible to combine Section 203(k) with other financial resources, such as HUD's HOME, HOPE, and Community Development Block Grant Programs, to assist borrowers.

FHA.com
another American dream comes true

What is HOPE for Homeowners?

When the subprime mortgage crisis reached its peak in the fall of 2008, the federal government took steps to help stabilize the American housing market. The Emergency Economic Stabilization Act of 2008 was signed into law on October 3, 2008. Part of that new law includes a requirement to help qualified homeowners avoid foreclosure through federal loan guarantees and credit enhancements.

The HOPE for Homeowners act is designed to prevent qualified home owners from defaulting on their loans, and avert foreclosure. This is done through refinancing into affordable, fixed-rate mortgages.

If you are in danger of defaulting on your home loan, it's very important to contact your lender immediately and request an evaluation of your situation. If you are able to qualify, your loan officer can help you begin the paperwork to prevent foreclosure. If you are already in discussions with the bank, your loan officer may suggest HOPE for Homeowners as a way to proceed.

AM I ELIGIBLE?

Homeowners may be eligible for HOPE for Homeowners program if they meet the following criteria as specified in the HOPE for Homeowners act 2008:

- The original mortgage is dated on or before January 1, 2008
- The homeowner did not default on the original loan intentionally
- The homeowner is not invested in multiple home loans
- All information on the original mortgage is true (including income sources and job details)
- The homeowner has not been convicted of fraud

HOPE for Homeowners is not a simple refinancing program. While it does allow qualified borrowers who are stuck in variable-rate mortgages to refinance into affordable, fixed-rate mortgages, there is a trade-off known as equity sharing.

WHAT IS EQUITY SHARING?

Those who apply and are accepted for the HOPE program must agree to an equity sharing program. Equity is the difference between the amount of your original loan and the actual value of the home; if you sell or refinance your home after entering the HOPE program, under the terms of HOPE you are required to share any equity with the FHA. How much the government receives depends on how long you wait to sell or refinance. If you sell in the first year of your participation in HOPE, the government receives 100% of the equity. There is a sliding scale after the first year:

- Year two – homeowners can keep 10% of the equity, FHA gets 90%
- Year three – homeowners keep 20%, FHA gets 80%
- Year four – homeowners keep 30%, FHA gets 70%
- Year five—homeowners keep 40%, FHA gets 60%

After year five, homeowners split the equity from sale or refinancing 50/50 with the Federal Housing Administration. If there is no equity or negative equity at the time of sale or refinancing, the FHA receives nothing.

WHAT ARE THE BENEFITS OF HOPE?

The benefits of participating in HOPE for Homeowners include;

- Keeping your home
- Getting a 30-year fixed-rate mortgage (extendable to 40 years in some cases)
- Lower monthly mortgage payments which do not change

The 30-year loan is extendable in some situations. Extending the terms to 40 years is helpful in cases where the homeowner has a large amount of debt; the 40-year term reduces mortgage payments further. There are requirements and restrictions on these extended loans. Check with your lender to see if you qualify for the 40-year loan terms under the HOPE program.

The HOPE for Homeowners program runs until September 20, 2011.

Figure 11-1

203(k) Rehab Mortgage Insurance

Summary:

Section 203(k) insurance enables homebuyers and homeowners to finance both the purchase (or refinancing) of a house and the cost of its rehabilitation through a single mortgage or to finance the rehabilitation of their existing home.

Purpose:

Section 203(k) fills a unique and important need for homebuyers. When buying a house that needs repair or modernization, homebuyers usually have to follow a complicated and costly process. The interim acquisition and improvement loans often have relatively high interest rates, short repayment terms and a balloon payment. However, Section 203(k) offers a solution that helps both borrowers and lenders, insuring a single, long term, fixed or adjustable rate loan that covers both the acquisition and rehabilitation of a property. Section 203(k) insured loans save borrowers time and money. They also protect the lender by allowing them to have the loan insured even before the condition and value of the property may offer adequate security.

For less extensive repairs/improvements, see **Streamlined 203(k)**. For housing rehabilitation activities that do not also require buying or refinancing the property, borrowers may also consider HUD's **Title I Home Improvement Loan program**.

Type of Assistance:

Section 203(k) insures mortgages covering the purchase or refinancing and rehabilitation of a home that is at least a year old. A portion of the loan proceeds is used to pay the seller, or, if a refinance, to pay off the existing mortgage, and the remaining funds are placed in an escrow account and released as rehabilitation is completed. The cost of the rehabilitation must be at least $5,000, but the total value of the property must still fall within the FHA mortgage limit for the area. The value of the property is determined by either (1) the value of the property before rehabilitation plus the cost of rehabilitation, or (2) 110 percent of the appraised value of the property after rehabilitation, whichever is less.

Many of the rules and restrictions that make FHA's basic single family mortgage insurance product (**Section 203(b)**) relatively convenient for lower income borrowers apply here. But lenders may charge some additional fees, such as a supplemental origination fee, fees to cover the preparation of architectural documents and review of the rehabilitation plan, and a higher appraisal fee.

Eligible Customers:

All persons who can make the monthly mortgage payments are eligible to apply. Cooperative units are not eligible; individual condominium units may be insured if they are in projects that have been approved by FHA or the Department of Veterans Affairs, or meet certain Fannie Mae guidelines.

Eligible Activities:

The extent of the rehabilitation covered by Section 203(k) insurance may range from relatively minor (though exceeding $5000 in cost) to virtual reconstruction: a home that has been demolished or will be razed as part of rehabilitation is eligible, for example, provided that the existing foundation system remains in place. Section 203(k) insured loans can finance the rehabilitation of the residential portion of a property that also has non-residential uses; they can also cover the conversion of a property of any size to a one-to-four unit structure. The types of improvements that borrowers may make using Section 203(k) financing include:

- structural alterations and reconstruction
- modernization and improvements to the home's function
- elimination of health and safety hazards
- changes that improve appearance and eliminate obsolescence

- reconditioning or replacing plumbing; installing a well and/or septic system
- adding or replacing roofing, gutters, and downspouts
- adding or replacing floors and/or floor treatments
- major landscape work and site improvements
- enhancing accessibility for a disabled person
- making energy conservation improvements

HUD requires that properties financed under this program meet certain basic energy efficiency and structural standards.

Application:

Applications must be submitted through an FHA approved lender.

Technical Guidance:

Insurance for rehabilitation is authorized under Section 203(k) of the National Housing Act (12 U.S.C. 1709(4k)). Program regulations are at 24 CFR 203.50. For more information contact the **FHA Resource Center.**

For More Information:

A brochure, *Rehab a Home with HUD's 203(k)*, is available online. A set of **questions and answers about 203(k) loans** is also available.

www.hud.gov/offices/hsg/sfh/203k/203k--df.cfm
203(k) Rehab Mortgage Insurance

The 203k program permits a borrower to obtain a property in need of rehabilitation with just one loan. Available loans may be either at a fixed rate or adjustable rate. The maximum amount of the loan, including acquisition and rehabilitation, is eligible for FHA insurance when the mortgage proceeds are disbursed and a rehabilitation account is established. Thus, the lender can have a fully insured FHA loan, acceptable to the secondary market.

A 203k loan combines acquisition cost and rehabilitation cost in one mortgage loan.

The program allows loans on one-to-four-unit family dwellings that are at least one-year old. Loans may also be made on properties that have been demolished, as long as the foundation remains. The program allows conversion of single-family dwellings into two-to-four-unit dwellings and conversion of larger than four-unit dwellings into one-to-four-unit dwellings. It also permits a dwelling to be transported from one site to another. The 203k program also allows loans on mixed-use properties. A ***MIXED-USE PROPERTY*** *combines a single-family residence with a commercial building*. The loans are limited to no more than 25% commercial use on a one-story property, 49% on a two-story property, and 33% on a three-story property.

Condominium units are also eligible for 203k mortgages, as long as they are owner-occupied and the borrower is not an investor. The rehabilitation of the unit is restricted to the interior of the building only. In addition, the rules dictate that after rehabilitation, individual buildings within the project may not contain more than four units.

A 203k loan has a minimum requirement of $5,000 in needed repairs. Eligible repairs are those that cover the health and safety of the occupants. These would include, but are not limited to, repair of structural damage, elimination of lead-based paint, room additions, replacement of roofing, flooring, energy-efficient improvements, electrical systems, plumbing systems, and heating and air conditioning systems. Improvements that provide handicapped accessibility are fully covered. Repairs that are not eligible for loans include such luxury items as new swimming pools, gazebos, and tennis courts. The maximum mortgage amount is either the "as-is" value of the property plus the cost of repairs, or 110% of the expected market value of the property after the completion of all repairs.

1. Steps in the 203k Program

The steps in the process are slightly different than in a regular purchase. First, after locating a prospective property, the buyer and his or her real estate agent make a preliminary analysis of the extent of repairs necessary and a rough estimate of the cost of the work to be carried out. Then a sales contract is executed, including provisions that the borrower has applied for 203k financing and that the contract is contingent upon approval of this financing. The buyer then contacts an approved FHA lender. The lender will, at this stage, recommend an FHA-approved 203k consultant (generally a contractor) to help the buyer draw up the necessary work writeups and cost estimates. Upon receipt of these documents, the lender will ask the FHA to issue a case number and assign an FHA-approved plan reviewer, appraiser, and inspector. The plan reviewer will meet with the buyer and the consultant (contractor) at the property to insure that the repairs are acceptable. The appraiser will then carry out an appraisal of the property. The lender will review the application and issue a conditional commitment and statement of appraised value. After the buyer has completed the necessary documentation for an FHA loan, the lender will issue a firm commitment. This document will detail the maximum amount that can be loaned. The mortgage will then close and the lender will submit the closing documents to FHA. FHA then issues a mortgage insurance certificate to the lender. Repair work may begin at the time of closing and must be completed within six months. The repair funds are disbursed as each stage of rehabilitation is completed. Upon overall completion, a final inspection is carried out by the FHA-approved inspector.

D. FHA TITLE I PROGRAM

The ***FHA TITLE I PROGRAM*** *is designed to allow homeowners to finance light repairs or permanent improvements to their homes*. Loans of up to $25,000.00 will be insured for a maximum of twenty years. Interest rates are set at market by the lender. The borrower also pays a mortgage insurance premium for a Title I loan. Title I loans are only available through FHA-approved Title I lenders.

III. VA Loan Guaranties

In 1944, a grateful U.S. Congress passed the Serviceman's Readjustment Act to provide returning World War II veterans with education, medical, and home loan benefits to help them readjust to civilian life. *This law is often referred to as the* ***G.I. BILL***. The original act has been amended many times over the years. These amendments have served to broaden and extend the earned benefits for veterans of conflicts that our nation has been involved in, as well as the original WWII veterans. *Veterans' benefits are managed by the* ***DEPARTMENT OF VETERANS AFFAIRS (VA)***. One very important benefit is the VA home loan guaranty. This guaranty is extended to eligible veterans to assist them in the purchase of owner-occupied residential property of up to four units. No investor loans of any type are guaranteed by the VA.

The G.I. Bill is the legislation that provides for VA loan guaranties.

A. VA LOAN GUARANTY CHARACTERISTICS

The VA program has a number of features that are attractive to borrowers who qualify:

1. A VA loan may not have prepayment penalties.
2. A VA loan may be assumed by anyone; the new buyer does not have to be a veteran.
3. No mortgage insurance is required.
4. Funding fees may be financed.
5. Builder warranty is required on new homes.
6. Closing costs may be paid by seller.

While no mortgage insurance is required, the VA charges a funding fee that is currently set at 2.15% on non-down payment loans. For second-time users with eligibility, the fee is 3.3%. With a down payment of 5%, the fee for both first- and second-time users is 1.5%. For a 10% down payment, the fee drops to 1.25%. The fee may be financed in the loan.

Closing costs are not permitted to be financed in the loan. However, the VA sets maximum fees for these items. These fees are changed from time to time by the VA. Current closing cost items include:

1. A maximum 1% origination fee.

2. Appraisal fees are set by Regional VA offices. The fee may not be more than is reasonable and customary for the area.
3. Credit report fees may not exceed the cost charged to the lender. Credit research fees of $50.00 charged by Loan Prospector® are allowed.
4. The veteran may pay for hazard and flood insurance, if required.
5. The veteran may pay for title insurance.
6. The veteran must pay the VA funding fee.
7. The veteran may pay for recording fees.
8. The veteran is responsible for prorated interest and property taxes.

Aside from the veteran borrower, the seller or any other party may pay closing cost fees.

1. Sale by Assumption

Veterans who obtain loans guaranteed by the VA are legally obligated to indemnify (pay back) the United States government for any claim paid out by the VA under the loan guaranty.

This is the case for the life of the loan, regardless of whether the property has been sold, foreclosed, or transferred to another. It is important that the veteran who sells or transfers a home, where the VA loan will not be paid off in full, be made aware of this fact. A veteran may be released from liability on that loan only if the following three conditions are met:

1. The loan must be current.
2. The purchaser must be an acceptable credit risk.
3. The purchaser must assume the obligations and liabilities of the veteran on the loan, including the indemnity obligation. The ***INDEMNITY OBLIGATION*** *means that the veteran must reimburse the U.S. Government for any loss on the loan.* The assumption of the obligations must be evidenced by a written agreement as specified by the VA.

To facilitate a veteran's release from liability on a loan a new buyer intends to assume, it is best to include in the sales contract a provision to that effect. The sales agreement should provide that the buyer will assume all the seller's loan obligations, including the liability for indemnity on the VA loan, and that the sale will not be closed unless and until the VA approves the credit and income of the purchaser. The seller must apply to the VA for a formal release of liability.

Unfortunately, this procedure is often neglected and sales are consummated without submitting the application for release of liability to the VA, and in many cases, without the new buyer formally agreeing to assume payment of the loan. If the sale closes without first obtaining the release from the VA, the veteran will find that he or she is fully liable in the case of a default.

2. Restoration of Entitlement

A veteran who has paid off his or her loan and has sold the house on which the loan was secured, may have all his or her entitlement restored. ***ENTITLEMENT** is the maximum insurance amount that the VA will provide for the veteran's home loan.* By act of Congress, the veteran is entitled to the amount by virtue of his or her service in the armed forces. Entitlement may also be restored if the property is sold to another veteran who substitutes his or her entitlement for the seller's. To restore entitlement, the veteran must apply to the VA and fill out the necessary forms.

3. Eligibility

Eligibility requirements for a VA loan vary depending on when and where a veteran served and the length of the service. In general, the periods for active wartime service are:

WWII	09/16/40 - 07/25/47
Korean Conflict	06/27/50 - 01/31/55
Vietnam Era	08/05/64 - 05/07/75

The veteran must have had a minimum of **90 days** of active service and have been discharged under conditions other than dishonorable.

Persian Gulf War 08/02/90-TBD

Gulf War veterans must have completed 24 months of active duty or the full period (at least 90 days) for which they were called up to active war duty. A veteran who was discharged for a service-connected disability, for hardship, or at the convenience of the government, is also eligible.

Peacetime veterans are also eligible for the periods:

07/26/47 to 06/26/50
02/01/55 to 08/04/64
05/08/75 to 09/07/80 (enlisted) 10/16/81 (officer)

Veterans must have had at least **181 days of continuous active duty** and a discharge under other than dishonorable conditions. Peacetime veterans after 09/07/80 to 08/01/90 must have had 24 months of active duty service and similar discharge requirements. Current active duty personnel are eligible after 90 days of continuous service. Selected reserves and National Guard are eligible after six years of service and having attended weekend drills and two-week active duty for training, or if they have been honorably discharged, retired, or transferred to Standby Reserve or Ready Reserve. They may be eligible before six years for a service-connected disability. Eligibility for Selected Reservists expired on 09/30/2007. Members of the military who have served in Iraq and Afghanistan or are currently serving are eligible for all benefits.

The spouse of a serviceperson who died while in service from a service-connected disability, became missing in action, or became a prisoner of war may also be eligible for VA home loan benefits. In addition, certain U.S. citizens who served in the armed forces of the allied nations during WWII are also eligible. Lastly, public health service officers, cadets at the service academies, some merchant seamen of WWII, and officers of the National Oceanic and Atmospheric Administration may be eligible as well.

4. VA Loan Guaranty Amounts

The VA does not guarantee the entire amount of a loan. What is guaranteed is the top portion of the loan; where the lender is most at risk in the event of default. A veteran may use the maximum entitlement in effect at the time of the purchase, which is $36,000. This may be adjusted upwards on certain loans.

On October 10, 2008 the President signed the **Veterans Benefits Improvement Act of 2008**. The following are the highlights of the changes to the program:

1. Authority to guarantee adjustable rate mortgages (ARMs) and hybrid ARMs has been extended through 9-30-2012.
2. Refinance loans are available for up to 100% of the appraised value of a home rather than the previous 89%.
3. Guaranty amounts for loans of $417,000 or less are unaffected.
4. On loans for more than $417,000, the VA will guarantee 25% of the original loan amount up to maximum guaranty. Maximum guaranty amount varies depending on location of the property.

At the time of this printing, the high-end figure for the Contiguous U.S. was $729,750 and, for Alaska, Guam, Hawaii, and the U.S. Virgin Islands, the figure was as high as $1,094,625. These figures are always changing (adjusted annually), so please consult **fhaoutreach.com** to calculate the maximum guaranty for a particular property.

5. Partial Entitlement

A veteran who used his entitlement to purchase a home in the past may use that portion of his remaining entitlement to purchase a second home.

Example: A veteran used the maximum entitlement of $25,000 that was available in 1978 to purchase a home. Today he wishes to purchase a second vacation home. The home is priced at $100,000. The veteran has $11,000 remaining in entitlement ($36,000 - $25,000 = $11,000).

B. THE VA LOAN PROCESS

The first step in the process is to determine if the veteran has a Certificate of Eligibility. A ***CERTIFICATE OF ELIGIBILITY*** *notifies the lender that the veteran is eligible for a VA loan and what his or her entitlement will be.* Presently, veterans receive this form as part of their discharge papers. If the veteran does not have this form, he or she will have to apply to the VA for a Certificate of Eligibility. This is done by submitting a **Request for a Certificate of Eligibility (VA Form 26-1880 - Figure 11-2)** along with a copy of his or her DD-214 (discharge paper). This form needs to be submitted before any other part of the loan goes forward because only the VA may determine the veteran's eligibility for a loan, and it is likely that this process will take some time.

The VA allows the use of uniform loan application forms and encourages the use of electronic loan underwriting utilizing FHLMC's Loan Prospector® and FNMA's Desktop Underwriter®. All lenders are responsible for conforming in full to VA requirements. This includes the use of VA-approved appraisers and underwriters. All VA loans require the following additional documents from the lender:

1. VA Form 26-0286 Loan Summary Sheet
2. VA Form 26-8320 Certificate of Eligibility
3. VA Form 26-8998 Acknowledgement of Receipt of Funding Fee
4. VA Form 26-1843 Certificate of Reasonable Value (provided with appraisal)
5. VA Form 26-1820 Report and Certification of Loan Disbursement.
6. A HUD-1 Settlement Statement
7. Name and mailing address to be used in requesting file for audit
8. E-mail address to be used in lieu of mailings

Figure 11-2

OMB Control No. 2900-0086
Respondent Burden: 15 minutes

Department of Veterans Affairs

REQUEST FOR A CERTIFICATE OF ELIGIBILITY

FOR VA USE ONLY
COE REF. NO.

MAIL COMPLETED APPLICATION TO:
Atlanta Regional Loan Center
Attn: COE (262)
P. O. Box 100034
Decatur, GA 30031

NOTE: Please read information on reverse before completing this form. If additional space is required, attach a separate sheet.

1. NAME OF VETERAN *(First, Middle, Last)*
2. DATE OF BIRTH
3. SOCIAL SECURITY NUMBER

4A. DID YOU SERVE UNDER ANOTHER NAME?
☐ YES ☐ NO *(If "Yes," complete Item 4B)*

4B. NAME(S) USED DURING MILITARY SERVICE *(If different from name in Item 1)*

5. DAYTIME TELEPHONE NUMBER
6. E-MAIL ADDRESS *(If applicable)*

7A. ADDRESS *(Number and street or rural route, city or P.O., State and ZIP Code)*

7B. MAIL CERTIFICATE OF ELIGIBILITY TO: *(Complete ONLY if the Certificate is to be mailed to an address different from the one listed in Item 7A.)*

8A. WERE YOU DISCHARGED, RETIRED, OR SEPARATED FROM SERVICE BECAUSE OF DISABILITY?
☐ YES ☐ NO

8B. VA CLAIM NUMBER *(If known)*

MILITARY SERVICE (SEE INSTRUCTIONS FOR PROOF OF SERVICE ON THE NEXT PAGE)

9A. ARE YOU CURRENTLY ON ACTIVE DUTY? *(If you currently serving on active duty, leave the "Date Separated" field blank.)*
☐ YES ☐ NO

IMPORTANT: Please provide your dates of service. In many cases eligibility can be established based on data in VA systems. However, it is recommended that proof of service be provided, if readily available. Proof of service is required for persons who entered service after September 7, 1980 and were discharged after serving less than 2 years.	BRANCH OF SERVICE	DATE ENTERED	DATE SEPARATED	OFFICER OR ENLISTED	SERVICE NUMBER *(If different from Social Security Number)*
9B. ACTIVE SERVICE - ***Do not*** *include any periods of Active Duty for Training or Active Guard Reserve service.* ***Do*** *include any activation for duty under Title 10 U.S.C. (e.g. Reserve or Guard unit mobilized.)*					
9C. RESERVE OR NATIONAL GUARD SERVICE *Include any periods of Active Duty for Training (ADT) or Active Guard Reserve service.* ***Do not*** *include any activation for duty under Title 10 U.S.C. (e.g. Reserve or Guard unit mobilized.)*					

PREVIOUS VA LOANS (SEE INSTRUCTIONS ON THE NEXT PAGE - Attach a separate sheet if information for all homes will not fit in Item 10)

10A. DO YOU NOW OWN ANY HOME(S) PURCHASED OR REFINANCED WITH A VA-GUARANTEED LOAN?
☐ YES *(If "Yes," complete Items 10B through 10D)*
☐ NO *(If "No," skip to Item 14)*
☐ NOT APPLICABLE (NA) - I HAVE NEVER OBTAINED A VA-GUARANTEED HOME LOAN *(If "NA," skip to Item 14)*

10B. DATE OF LOAN *(Month and Year)* | 10C. STREET ADDRESS | 10D. CITY AND STATE

11A. ARE YOU APPLYING FOR THE **ONE-TIME ONLY RESTORATION** OF ENTITLEMENT TO PURCHASE ANOTHER HOME?
☐ YES ☐ NO *(If "Yes," complete Items 11B through 11D)*

11B. DATE OF LOAN *(Month and Year)* | 11C. STREET ADDRESS | 11D. CITY AND STATE

12A. ARE YOU APPLYING FOR A RESTORATION OF ENTITLEMENT TO OBTAIN A **REGULAR (CASH-OUT) REFINANCE** ON YOUR CURRENT HOME?
☐ YES ☐ NO *(If "Yes," complete Items 12B through 12D)*

12B. DATE OF LOAN *(Month and Year)* | 12C. STREET ADDRESS | 12D. CITY AND STATE

13A. ARE YOU REFINANCING AN EXISTING VA LOAN TO OBTAIN A LOWER INTEREST RATE **WITHOUT RECEIVING** ANY CASH PROCEEDS (IRRRL)?
☐ YES ☐ NO *(If "Yes," complete Items 13B through 13D)*

13B. DATE OF LOAN *(Month and Year)* | 13C. STREET ADDRESS | 13D. CITY AND STATE

I CERTIFY THAT the statements in this document are true and complete to the best of my knowledge.

14A. SIGNATURE OF VETERAN *(Do NOT print)*
14B. DATE SIGNED

FEDERAL STATUTES PROVIDE SEVERE PENALTIES FOR FRAUD, INTENTIONAL MISREPRESENTATION, CRIMINAL CONNIVANCE OR CONSPIRACY PURPOSED TO INFLUENCE THE ISSUANCE OF ANY GUARANTY OR INSURANCE BY THE SECRETARY OF VETERANS AFFAIRS

FOR VA USE ONLY *(Please do not write below this line)*
DATE RETURNED

REASON(S) FOR RETURN

VA FORM SEP 2011 **26-1880**
SUPERSEDES VA FORM 26-1880, MAR 2011, WHICH WILL NOT BE USED.

INSTRUCTIONS FOR VA FORM 26-1880

PRIVACY ACT NOTICE - VA will not disclose information collected on this form to any source other than what has been authorized under the Privacy Act of 1974 or Title 38, Code of Federal Regulations 1.576 for routine uses (for example: the authorized release of information to Congress when requested for statistical purposes) identified in the VA system of records, 55VA26, Loan Guaranty Home, Condominium and Manufactured Home Loan Applicant Records, Specially Adapted Housing Applicant Records, and Vendee Loan Applicant Records - VA, and published in the Federal Register. Your obligation to respond is required in order to determine the qualifications for a loan.

RESPONDENT BURDEN - This information is needed to help determine a veteran's qualifications for a VA guaranteed home loan. Title 38, U.S.C., section 3702, authorizes collection of this information. We estimate that you will need an average of 15 minutes to review the instructions, find the information, and complete this form. VA cannot conduct or sponsor a collection of information unless a valid OMB control number is displayed. You are not required to respond to a collection of information if this number is not displayed. Valid OMB control numbers can be located on the OMB Internet Page at www.reginfo.gov/public/do/PRAMain. If desired, you can call 1-800-827-1000 to get information on where to send comments or suggestions about this form.

A. YOUR IDENTIFYING INFORMATION

Item 1 - Tell us your complete name, *as you would like it to appear on your Certificate of Eligibility (COE).*
Item 4B - If you served under another name, provide the name as it appears on your discharge certificate (DD Form 214).
Item 7 - You can have your Certificate of Eligibility sent to you at your current mailing address, or directly to your lender, or to any mailing address you provide in Item 7B.
Item 8B - In most cases, your VA claim number is the same as your Social Security Number. If you are not sure of your VA claim number, leave this field blank.

B. MILITARY SERVICE

Item 9 - **NOTE** - Cases involving other than honorable discharges will usually require further development by VA. This is necessary to determine if the service was under other than dishonorable conditions.

Item 9A - If you are currently serving on regular active duty, eligibility can usually be established based on data in VA systems. However, in some situations you may be asked to provide a statement of service signed by, or by direction of, the adjutant, personnel officer, or commander of your unit or higher headquarters. The statement may be in any format; usually a standard or bulleted memo is sufficient. It should identify you by name and social security number, and provide: (1) your date of entry on your current active duty period and (2) the duration of any time lost (or a statement noting there has been no lost time). Generally this should be on military lettherhead.

Item 9B - **Active Service** *(not including Active Duty Training or Active Guard Reserve service)* - the best evidence to show your service is your discharge certificate (DD Form 214) showing active duty dates and type of discharge. If you were separated after October 1, 1979, the DD214 was issued in several parts (copies). We are required to have a copy showing the character of service (Item 24) and the narrative reason for separation (Item 28). We prefer the MEMBER-4 copy, however, we can accept any copy that contains these items. The copy number is shown on the bottom right of the form. We don't need the original; a photocopy is acceptable. Any Veterans Services Representative in the nearest Department of Veterans Affairs office or center will assist you in securing necessary proof of military service.

NOTE - A reservist or member of the National Guard can be called to active duty under either of two legal authorities. Title 10 U.S. Code covers those who are ordered to regular active duty under federal call up. Reservists may also be called to active service under the authority of Title 32 U.S. Code. Service covered under Title 32 U. S. Code includes basic training (Initial Active Duty for Training or IADT) annual training, as well as certain types of full-time duty may be called Active Guard Reserve, Active Duty for Special Work. Full-time National Guard Duty or Active Duty Support. Service under Title 10 U.S. Code is qualifying active duty for the VA Home Loan Benefit. Active service under Title 32 U.S. Code, however, does NOT qualify under the active duty requirements. Service under Title 32 U.S. Code can be used to meet the 6-year requirement to qualify as a member of the Selected Reserve or National Guard.

Item 9C - **National Guard Service:** You may submit NGB Form 22, Report of Separation and Record of Service, or NGB Form 23, Retirement Points Accounting, or their equivalent. We are required to have a copy showing character of service.

Selected Reserve Service (Including Active Duty Training and Active Guard Reserve) - You may submit (Including Active Duty Training and Active Guard Reserve) a copy of your latest annual retirement points statement and evidence of honorable service. There is no single form used by the Reserves similar to the DD Form 214 or NGB Form 22. The following forms are commonly used, but others may be acceptable:

Army Reserve	DARP FM 249-2E
Naval Reserve	NRPC 1070-124
Air Force Reserve	AF 526
Marine Corps Reserve	NA VMC 798
Coast Guard Reserve	CG 4174 or 4175

If you are still serving in the Selected Reserves or the National Guard, you must include an original statement of service signed by, or by the direction of, the adjutant, personnel officer, or commander of your unit or higher headquarters showing your date of entry and the length of time that you have been a member of the Selected Reserves. At least 6 years of honorable service must be documented.

C. PREVIOUS VA LOANS

Items 10 through 14. Your eligibility is reusable depending on the circumstances. Normally, if you have paid off your prior VA loan and no longer own the home, you can have your used eligibility restored for additional use. Also, on a one-time only basis, you may have your eligibility restored if your prior VA loan has been paid in full but you still own the home. Normally VA receives notification that a loan has been paid. In some instances, it may be necessary to include evidence that a previous VA loan has been paid in full. Evidence can be in the form of a paid-in-full statement from the former lender, a satisfaction of mortgage from the clerk of court in the county where the home is located, or a copy of the HUD-1 settlement statement completed in connection with a sale of the home or refinance of the prior loan. Many counties post public documents (like the satisfaction of mortgage) online.

Item 11A. **One-Time Restoration.** If you have paid off your VA loan, but still own the home purchased with that loan, you may apply for a one-time only restoration of your entitlement in order to purchase another home that will be your primary residence. Once you have used your one-time restoration, you must sell all homes before any other entitlement can be restored.

Item 12A. **Regular (cash-out) Refinance.** You may refinance your current VA or non-VA loan in order to pay off the mortgage and/or other liens of record on the home. This type of refinance requires an appraisal and credit qualifying.

Item 13A. **Interest Rate Reduction Refinancing Loan (IRRRL).** You may refinance the balance of your current VA loan in order to obtain a lower interest rate, or convert a VA adjustable rate mortgage to a fixed rate. The new loan may not exceed the sum of the outstanding balance on the existing VA loan, plus allowable fees and closing costs, including VA funding fee and up to 2 discount points. You may also add up to $6,000 of energy efficiency improvements into the loan. **A certificate of eligibility is not required for IRRRL.** Instead, a Prior Loan Validation, obtained through our online system WebLGY can be used in lieu of a COE. Presently, this application is only available to lenders. In WebLGY, a lender can select Eligibility from the toolbar and then Prior Loan Validation. Enter the veteran's Social Security Number and Last Name. The system will then, in most cases, pull up the veteran's active loan information. Print the prior Loan Validation screen and use it in lieu of the COE.

VA FORM 26-1880, SEP 2011

IV. CHAPTER SUMMARY

The FHA and VA loan programs are huge federal insurance programs that are backed by the full faith and credit of the U.S. government. Both programs have found ready acceptance by lenders and borrowers alike. The FHA has been a boon to the lending, construction, and real estate markets since its beginning. The insurance provided by the FHA is called the Mortgage Insurance Premium (MIP). An FHA insured mortgage has less stringent down payment and qualifying requirements and is readily assumable. The FHA has several programs; the most notable of these are the 203b fixed-rate program, which is the most frequently used, and the 203k program, which allows a sale and major rehabilitation construction costs to be combined into one loan. The FHA also has a Title I home repair loan program which allows homeowners to carry out minor repairs to their homes without having to resort to refinancing their original loan.

The VA programs are designed to provide veterans returning to civilian life an opportunity to enjoy the benefits of home ownership. This program, which was instituted following WWII, has been periodically updated by the U.S. Congress to keep pace with the rise in the price of housing over the past five decades. A VA loan may have no prepayment penalties and may be assumed by anyone. No mortgage insurance is required. However, the veteran is directly liable to the U.S. government until the loan is either paid off in full or has been assumed by someone else who also assumes this "indemnity" obligation to the government. In the case of a property loan assumption, it is important that both real estate and lending professionals inform their clients about the indemnity obligation and the adverse consequences that will occur in the event of a default. A veteran may have his or her entitlement restored once his or her loan is paid in full and the house is sold. A veteran may also use any partial entitlement remaining from the purchase of his or her first home to use in the purchase of a second home. Both wartime and peacetime veterans are eligible for VA loans.

The Veterans Benefits Act of 2008 raised the VA Loan Guaranty Program maximum amount and extended the ARM program through 9-30-2012.

V. TERMINOLOGY

Certificate of Eligibility	Mixed-Use Property
Certificate of Reasonable Value (CRV)	Mortgage Insurance Premium (MIP)
Department of Veterans Affairs (VA)	National Housing Act
Direct Endorsement Lender	Request For Certificate of Eligibility (VA Form 26-1880)
Discount Points	203b Fixed-Rate Program
Entitlement	203k Purchase and Rehabilitation Program
FHA 251 Adjustable Program	Request for a Certificate of Eligibility (VA Form 26-1880)
FHA Title I Program	Valuations Condition Form
G.I. Bill	
Homebuyer's Summary	
HOPE Program	
Indemnity Obligation	

VI. CHAPTER QUIZ

1. The statutory FHA down payment is:

   a. 2%.
   b. 3.5%.
   c. 4%.
   d. 5%.

2. The FHA maximum debt ratios are:

   a. 31% and 43%.
   b. 25% and 29%.
   c. 43% and 52%.
   d. None of the above.

3. The current basic maximum entitlement for a VA loan guaranty is:

   a. $240,000.
   b. $144,000.
   c. $36,000.
   d. $261,000.

4. What FHA loan program is designed to allow homeowners to finance light repairs or permanent improvements to their homes?

   a. Title I
   b. Title II
   c. Title III
   d. Title IV

5. After an appraisal inspection, an FHA lender must give the borrower a:
   a. Certificate of Eligibility.
   b. Valuation Conditions Form.
   c. Certificate of Reasonable Value.
   d. none of the above.

6. The program that permits rehabilitation costs to be included with acquisition costs is:
   a. Title I.
   b. FHA 203b.
   c. FHA 203k.
   d. FHA 251.

7. On a "mixed use" property, the commercial usage for a single-story building must not be more than:
   a. 33%.
   b. 25%.
   c. 49%.
   d. 23%.

8. What amount in needed property repairs qualifies for a 203K loan?
   a. $20,000
   b. $5,000
   c. $10,000
   d. None of the above

9. The maximum origination fee for both FHA and VA loans is:
   a. 1%.
   b. 1.5%.
   c. 2%.
   d. None of the above.

10. The Mortgage Insurance Premium (MIP) may be cancelled when the loan balance:
   a. drops to 78% of the original purchase price and loan payments for 5 years.
   b. drops to 80% of the original purchase price and loan payments for 5 years.
   c. payments have been made for ten years.
   d. is fully paid off.

ANSWERS: 1. b; 2. a; 3. c; 4. a; 5. d; 6. c; 7. b; 8. b; 9. a; 10. a

Chapter 12
Seller Financing

In tight money markets, it's not uncommon for a seller to make a deal to finance part of the purchase price. Mortgage money from traditional lenders may be too costly in terms of interest rates, or simply unavailable. Buyers may be unable to come up with the necessary cash for the down payment required by a conventional mortgage, or simply wish to take advantage of the low interest rate on the seller's existing mortgage. In any case, sellers can often enhance the salability of their properties by offering financing in the form of purchase money mortgages or land contracts.

I. Purchase Money Mortgage/Trust Deed

A ***PURCHASE MONEY MORTGAGE*** *is given by a buyer to a seller to finance the purchase. The seller is the* ***MORTGAGEE*** *or* ***BENEFICIARY***. Institutions such as banks and savings banks are not the only ones who make loans secured by mortgages or deeds of trust. An individual seller can just as easily be a mortgagee or beneficiary. The advantage of this arrangement is that sellers are not bound by institutional policies regarding loan ratios, interest rates, or qualifying standards. To make the sale, a seller may finance the entire purchase price for the buyer (relying on a mortgage as security), charge below market interest, and/or offer financing to a buyer who is considered a credit risk by institutional lenders.

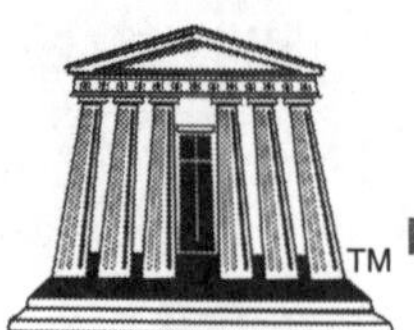

CHAPTER OUTLINE

The seller is taking a risk with a purchase money mortgage, but it may be justified if it allows the sale to proceed or enables the seller to get a higher price for his or her home.

As with any other form of seller financing, purchase money financing can be advantageous if the seller does not need immediate cash from the sale. Because the profit from the sale is spread over several years, the seller may benefit from a lower rate of income taxation.

Taking the full profit at the time of sale could push the seller into a higher tax bracket. But when the profit is paid on an installment basis, only the amount actually received in a given year is considered taxable income for that year.

A. UNENCUMBERED PROPERTY

The simplest form of purchase money financing is where the seller has clear title to the property, free of any mortgages or other liens. The buyer and seller simply negotiate the amount and terms of their financing arrangement and draw up the appropriate documents. Purchase money financing may take any of the many forms discussed in earlier chapters, such as variable interest rates, graduated payments, or partial amortization with balloon payment. Virtually the only limit is the imagination of the parties.

Example: Grandma Perkins decides to move to her sister's farm in the country and wants to sell her townhouse. The mortgage on the townhouse has long since been paid. Mr. and Mrs. Jenkins want to buy the townhouse, but cannot qualify for conventional financing. However, Grandma believes they are honest and reliable people who can be trusted to pay off a loan, so she offers them the following deal: sales price of $90,000, with $8,000 down and the balance in the form of a purchase money loan, secured by deed of trust with Grandma as the beneficiary. Interest will accrue at the rate of 6% for the first year, and increase ½ of 1% per year until it reaches 7.5%, where it will stay for the balance of the 30-year loan term. Payments are to be interest only for the first six years, and the principal then fully amortized over the balance of the term.

B. ENCUMBERED PROPERTY

Because many residential properties are encumbered by existing mortgages or deeds of trust, seller financing often involves assumption or refinancing of existing debt. There are several ways to deal with an existing mortgage. Perhaps the most simple method is to allow the buyer to assume liability for the existing note.

1. Assumption

If the seller's existing mortgage does not contain an alienation clause (due-on-sale clause), it is assumable.

The buyer can simply agree to take over payment of the seller's debt with the terms of the note unchanged. The property still serves as the basic security for the loan, but the buyer becomes primarily liable for repayment of the debt. If there is a foreclosure and the proceeds are insufficient to satisfy the debt, the lender may sue the buyer for the deficiency.

2. Assumption and Release

An assumption can take two forms. In the first case, it is an agreement strictly between the buyer and seller. The buyer assumes liability for the loan, but the seller is not completely released from responsibility; he or she remains **secondarily liable**. If the lender cannot recover the loan amount from the buyer or through foreclosure, it may still sue the seller for the deficiency. In order for the seller to be relieved of this responsibility, he or she must obtain a **release** from the lender. In this instance, the lender agrees to accept the buyer as the new mortgagor and to release the seller from all obligations on the mortgage. The lender will normally charge a loan assumption fee on assumable loans, renegotiate the loan assumption fee on assumable loans, or renegotiate the interest rate if the mortgage contains an alienation clause. A lender and/or an attorney who is familiar with real estate finance should always be consulted to determine if a loan is assumable.

A seller must obtain a release of liability from a lender or he/she may still be liable for the loan if the buyer defaults.

Example: Ned Taylor sells a rental house to Sam Jones, who assumes Ned's existing $90,000 mortgage. Ned does not get a release from the lender. A year later, with $88,000 still owing on the mortgage, Sam encounters financial difficulties and decides to bail out. He leaves his obligations behind, but does not leave a forwarding address. The mortgage payments are not made, so the lender forecloses, obtaining only $70,000 at the foreclosure sale, due to the dilapidated condition in which Sam's tenants left the property. By the time of the sale, the total amount owed, including delinquent interest and the costs of foreclosure and sale, reaches $93,500, leaving a deficiency of $23,500 ($93,500 debt - $70,000 sale proceeds = $23,500 deficiency). The lender cannot locate Sam to collect the deficiency, so it sues Ned. Ned may be held responsible for the deficiency because he was never released from liability on the mortgage when it was assumed by Sam.

3. Alienation Clause

The seller's existing mortgage may contain an *ALIENATION CLAUSE, which is designed to restrict the seller's right to transfer the property*. The clause may be triggered by the transfer of title or by the transfer of significant interest in the property (e.g., a long-term lease). The alienation clause may give the lender the right to declare the entire loan balance immediately due and payable, the right to raise the interest rate on the loan, or the right to do either at its option.

C. PURCHASE MONEY SECOND MORTGAGE

Even in cases where there is an assumable loan, or where the buyer can obtain financing from an institutional lender, it may be beneficial for the seller to provide additional financing in the form of a second mortgage or second deed of trust. If the buyer does not have sufficient cash to cover the difference between the sales price and the institutional financing, a purchase money second mortgage can be the key to closing the sale.

Example: George Hatfield owns property with an existing $45,000 mortgage. The mortgage is assumable, and has 120 payments of $582.30 remaining. Ray McCarthy is interested in buying the property, but does not have the $55,000 cash needed to meet the sales price of $100,000. Ray offers to buy the house with a $20,000 down payment if George will take back a second deed of trust for the remaining $35,000. George agrees and the sale is finalized.

Seller-sponsored second mortgages are subject to the same lien priority rules as institutional mortgages.

In the event of default and foreclosure, the first mortgage is paid in full from the proceeds of sale before any proceeds are allocated to the second mortgage. Sellers who take back second mortgages should keep this in mind when negotiating the amount of seller financing. This is especially true if there is a possibility of declining property values, or if the financing is set up to result in negative amortization over the early years of the loan.

D. SELLER-SPONSORED WRAPAROUND FINANCING

A *WRAPAROUND MORTGAGE is a loan transaction in which the lender assumes responsibility for an existing mortgage*. The wraparound mortgage or all-inclusive trust deed is a device sometimes used in place of an assumption. By using a wraparound installment mortgage sales contract, the seller can pass on the benefit of an existing loan at lower-than-market interest rates, even if the buyer is unwilling to directly assume the loan. The "wrap" is sometimes used to get around the provisions of an alienation clause (which limits the ability to assume a loan). If the lender becomes aware of the subterfuge, the transaction can be foreclosed under the terms of the alienation clause.

> **Example:** Mary Cudahy wants to sell her house for $91,000. There is an existing $32,000, 8% deed of trust on the property. Jeff Cochran offers to buy with $20,000 down and a seller-financed second deed of trust for the balance of $71,000. Under the terms of the agreement, a portion of Jeff's monthly payments will be used to make the payment on Mary's loan, which remains a lien on the property.

The attractiveness of the wraparound is that it enables the buyer to obtain financing at below-market interest rates while still providing a market rate of return for the seller. An example will illustrate this apparent contradiction.

> **Example:** Seller Johnson has a $51,000, 10% trust deed against his property. He sells to Abernathy for $69,000, with $8,000 down and the $61,000 balance secured by a wraparound deed of trust at 12% interest based on 30-year amortization with a balloon payment for the entire balance in 15 years. Seller Johnson will receive 12% interest on the $61,000 wraparound, but has actually extended only $10,000 in credit.

$69,000	sales price
- 8,000	down payment
- 51,000	underlying trust deed
$10,000	credit extended – net owed to seller

To determine the seller's yield in the first year:

1. Calculate the interest the seller will receive in the first year on the wraparound trust deed.

   $61,000
   x .12
   $7,320

2. Calculate the interest the seller will pay the same year on the underlying trust deed.

   $51,000
   x .10
   $5,100

3. Determine the net interest to the seller.

   $7,320
   -5,100
   $2,220

4. Divide the net interest to the seller by the amount of credit actually extended.

   2,220 ÷ 10,000 = 22%

Stated more simply, the seller is paying out $5,100 a year in interest on the original deed of trust and is receiving $7,320 in interest on the wrap from the buyer. This leaves the seller with a net gain of $2,220. The amount of credit actually extended by the seller under the wrap is $10,000, so the seller is receiving $2,220 in interest payments on $10,000 of credit. The yield on the credit extended is thus 22%. If the market interest rates are at 12.5%, the seller is receiving 9.5% over the market rate while the buyer is paying .5% below the market rate. Even if the rate charged by the seller on the wrap is not below the market rate, the arrangement may still be attractive to the buyer because of the greater flexibility of seller financing. The example shows the excellent return that is available to the seller when the amount of credit actually extended by the seller is relatively small.

The more credit extended by the seller, the lower the return.

E. WRAPAROUND VS. ASSUMPTION PLUS SELLER SECOND

In an assumption, the buyer receives the benefit of an existing low interest rate loan. If the transaction is structured with a wraparound loan at market rates, the seller receives the benefit of the existing low interest rate loan and is able to receive a very attractive rate of return on the portion of the financing that is actually extended by the seller.

> **Example:** A sale is made for a price of $100,000, with the buyer making a $20,000 down payment. The seller's existing loan with a balance of $60,000 carries an interest rate of 9%. Prevailing market interest rates at the time of sale are approximately 12% (see **Figure 12-1**).

As you can see from Figure 12-1, if a wraparound loan is made at market rates, the seller enjoys a high yield on the portion of credit extended by the seller. If the transaction is structured with an assumption and a second mortgage to the seller at market rates, the buyer enjoys financing at a very low overall rate.

A wraparound transaction can also be structured so that the seller receives above-market rates on the credit actually extended and, at the same time, the buyer pays below-market rates on the total amount financed. It can appear as if both of them are getting a good deal. If in the example given in Figure 12-1 the wraparound loan was made at an interest rate of 10.5%, the buyer would be paying an overall rate 1.5% less than the prevailing market rates of 12%. At the same time, the seller would be receiving a rate of approximately 15% on the $20,000 of credit extended by the seller.

Figure 12-1

	Wraparound	Assume + 2nd
Sales price	$100,00	$100,000
Down payment	$20,000	$20,000
Balance financed	$80,000@12% wrap	$60,000@9% assumed $20,000@12% 2nd
Credit extended by seller	$20,000	$20,000
Approximate yield to seller on credit extended	21%	12%
Approximate overall interest to buyer on $80,000 financed	12%	9.75%

F. RESALE OF PURCHASE MONEY SECURITIES

If a seller wants the option of cashing out at some time in the future, he or she can do so without giving up the ability to offer purchase money financing. Since 1980, FNMA has been willing to buy purchase money securities on the secondary market. The catch is that the securities must conform to FNMA underwriting standards, which defeats some of the advantages of seller financing, such as freedom from loan-to-value ratios, and other institutional limitations. If the seller desires to resell his or her loan immediately or in the future, the seller should use standard FNMA forms for writing the financing agreement with the buyer. This will ensure that the loan meets FNMA standards. The only other requirement is that the loan be serviced by a FNMA approved lender. The seller then has the option, at any time, of ordering the lender to pass the loan through to FNMA, thereby cashing out the seller. By choosing the proper time to resell (when market interest rates are low), the seller can pass the loan through with a minimum discount.

II. Land Contract

In some areas, a popular form of purchase money financing is the land contract. This type of financing has many of the same advantages as purchase money mortgages and trust deeds, such as freedom from institutional loan qualifying standards, deferral of income taxation, and flexibility of terms. Its main disadvantage, when compared to purchase money mortgages, is that land contracts cannot be resold to FNMA, although a few private secondary market investors may be willing to buy contracts.

The distinguishing feature of a land contract is that the seller retains legal title to the property until the buyer has made all of the payments on the contract.

In its simplest form, the land contract is made by a seller who owns the property free and clear. Such a seller need only negotiate the term and interest rate of the contract, along with the amount of down payment, if any.

Example: Assume a ten-year, fully amortized contract at 12%.

Real Estate Contract

Buyer agrees to pay $15,000 as down payment, including deposit. The balance shall be paid as follows: $85,000 in the form of a real estate contract, payable at $1,219.50 or more per month, including principal and interest, at the rate of 12% per year for 120 months until the balance is paid in full.

Example: Assume a five-year, partially amortized contract at 14%.

Real Estate Contract

Buyer agrees to pay $15,000 as down payment, including deposit. The balance shall be paid as follows: $85,000 in the form of a real estate contract, payable at $1,007.14 or more per month, including principal and interest, at the rate of 14% per year, computed on the basis of a 30-year amortization, for 60 months, at which time the balance shall be due and payable in full.

In a partially amortized contract, a portion of the principal balance remains unpaid at the conclusion of the contract term. The buyer will have to pay this balance ("balloon" payment) in cash at that time, or else refinance the property.

A. CONTRACT SUBJECT TO EXISTING MORTGAGE

It is rare to find a seller whose property is not encumbered by some form of mortgage lien. When this is the case, the existing mortgage(s) must be taken into account. The simplest way to do this is to make the contract subject to the existing mortgage. The contract is written for the full purchase price, but the buyer's property rights under the contract are subject to the rights of the seller's mortgagee. The seller remains liable to make the payments on the loan and the property may be foreclosed if the seller defaults.

The obvious problem with this arrangement, from the buyer's point of view, is how to make sure the seller does not default on the loan payments. If this should occur, the buyer may lose everything; the seller will no longer have title to convey after a foreclosure **(remember that the buyer doesn't get a deed until the contract is paid**

in full) and the buyer will be forced to resort to a lawsuit to try to recover his or her payments on the contract. The solution is to include in the contract a provision requiring the seller to make timely payments on his or her loan and allowing the buyer to make such payments directly to the lender if the seller fails to do so.

Example: Seller shall maintain the existing mortgage in good standing. In the event that seller fails to make any payment when due, or in any other way causes or allows the loan to go into default, buyer shall be entitled to cure such default, and deduct all costs from the amounts due next to seller on this contract.

In order for a provision like the one above to be effective in preventing foreclosure, there must be some way for the buyer to receive notice when the seller falls into arrears. This may be the true crux of the problem, as the only sure way to obtain such notice is to request it from the seller's lender. This is a routine procedure, unless the seller's mortgage contains an enforceable **alienation (due-on-sale) clause**. There is always the possibility that when the lender learns of the proposed sale, it will elect to enforce the alienation provision in the existing mortgage, thus frustrating the sale.

1. Contract Escrow

One approach that is sometimes used to ensure the seller makes the payments on the existing mortgage is to set up an escrow account or servicing agreement for the contract payments. This is fairly simple to do, especially since a deed is usually placed in escrow pending completion of the contract anyway. In a ***CONTRACT ESCROW**, the buyer makes payments into the escrow account, and the escrow agent pays the seller's loan payments out of the account*. The balance in the account (after the loan payments are made) is disbursed to the seller. In this fashion, the buyer is protected from the consequences of a default by the seller.

Sample Escrow Instructions

1. Seller shall place a deed to the property in escrow, to be conveyed to buyer upon full payment of the contract debt.
2. Buyer shall make all payments into an escrow account to be maintained by the escrow agent.
3. Upon receipt of each monthly payment, the escrow agent shall immediately make all payments due on seller's mortgage.
4. The escrow agent shall maintain a balance in the account equal to two monthly mortgage payments; all funds in excess of this minimum balance shall be disbursed to seller after compliance with provision three of these instructions.

2. Estoppel Letter

It is always good practice, in any transaction where an existing mortgage is to be left in place, to obtain the lender's written consent to the proposed transaction.

This is not essential where there is no alienation clause in the seller's promissory note or mortgage. Where alienation clauses do exist, most lenders will insist on renegotiation of the loan to reflect current interest rates, or demand that the loan be paid off entirely. But occasionally a lender will consent to a sale without any change in the existing mortgage. *The lender's consent is given in the form of a letter, called an* ***ESTOPPEL LETTER***, acknowledging the transfer and waiving the lender's right to accelerate the loan on account of the transfer. By writing the letter, the lender is ***ESTOPPED*** *(legally prevented)* from later trying to accelerate the loan on the basis of the sale.

An estoppel letter is often requested even in transactions where the underlying financing does not contain an alienation clause. The holder of the underlying mortgage or contract is asked to state in the estoppel letter the amount of the outstanding principal balance and to acknowledge that the loan is not in default. The buyer then has written confirmation from the lien holder as to the amount of the obligation the buyer is planning to assume, or take subject to, and is also assured that the seller is current on the payments and other obligations.

B. CONTRACT WITH ASSUMPTION OF EXISTING MORTGAGE

In the previous section, we saw how a seller could enter into a land contract while still maintaining his or her existing mortgage. If the seller does not wish to remain liable for the mortgage payments, but the buyer cannot (or will not) refinance the debt, the buyer may be able to assume (take over) the seller's mortgage and pay the balance of the purchase price under a contract. In this arrangement, the buyer becomes personally liable for payment of the mortgage debt; the buyer makes one payment to the mortgagee and another payment to the seller.

Example: Jim Dalton wishes to sell his home for $70,000. The property is encumbered by an assumable 9.5% mortgage with a balance of $34,000 and monthly payments of $336.35 (204 payments remain to be made). Andy Smith agrees to buy the property at the proposed price, with $10,000 down, assumption of the mortgage, and the balance to be paid over ten years on a contract at 12.75%.

$70,000	purchase price
- 10,000	down payment
- 34,000	assumed loan
$26,000	balance due on contract

$26,000	contract balance
x .0147840	10-year 12.75% amortization factor
$384.38	monthly contract payment

Thus, Andy will pay:

1. $10,000 down payment to seller
2. $336.35/mo. for 204 months to seller's mortgagee
3. $384.38/mo. for 120 months to seller

The advantage of an assumption for the buyer is the ability to get financing at lower-than-market interest rates. Of course, if the seller's loan bore a higher interest rate than the buyer could obtain elsewhere, there would be no point in assuming the loan. The advantage for the seller is that his or her property is more attractive when it can be financed at the lower rate, and he or she is also relieved of responsibility for making the monthly payments to the lender.

C. CONTRACT PLUS ASSUMPTION PLUS INSTITUTIONAL SECOND

In some transactions, the seller will be willing to let the buyer assume the existing mortgage and also be willing to finance part of the price on a land contract, but he or she will desire at least a partial cash-out of his or her equity, perhaps to use as a down payment on another purchase. This is no problem if the buyer can provide a sufficient down payment to cover the seller's cash requirements. But even if the buyer cannot come up with the cash from his or her own assets, there is still an alternative: an institutional second mortgage.

Example: Arthur Dodge has listed his property with a sales price of $160,000. He has an assumable first mortgage in the amount of $95,000, and is willing to finance a portion of the balance on a land contract, but he needs at least $50,000 in cash from the sale. Olga Turner would like to buy Art's property, but has only $20,000 towards a down payment. Olga asks Art whether he would agree to a second mortgage from an institutional lender, which would take priority over the land contract. Art says yes, and the deal is closed on the following terms:

$20,000	cash from Olga
+ $30,000	cash from 2nd mortgage
$50,000	cash to seller

$50,000	cash to seller
+ $95,000	assumed 1st mortgage
+ $15,000	land contract
$160,000	total purchase price

Olga applies to Sam's Mortgage Company, which loans her $30,000 secured by a second mortgage on the property. The original (assumed) mortgage remains first in priority, and both mortgages have priority over the land contract.

Note that the buyer may have difficulty obtaining an institutional second because most lenders would hesitate to loan money on property where the title remains with the seller (as with a land contract).

1. Lien Priority

The significance of lien priority becomes apparent only when the borrower defaults. If the property must be sold through foreclosure to satisfy a debt, then each lender is paid from the proceeds of the sale according to its priority. If there is only enough money to pay the first lender, then the other (secondary) lenders are out of luck because their security has been exhausted.

> **Example:** Using the facts from the previous example, assume that Olga defaults and the property is sold under foreclosure, the proceeds of the sale (after taxes, costs, etc.) amounting to $120,000. The first mortgage is paid first, in the amount of $95,000, leaving $25,000 in proceeds. The remaining $25,000 is paid to the second mortgagee, which takes a $5,000 loss because its loan was for $30,000. Art gets nothing at all, because he is last in priority and there are no more proceeds.

2. Deeds and Security

In the preceding example, Olga did not receive a deed to the property because part of the purchase price was secured by a land contract; Art still holds the deed as security for the repayment of the contract debt. If Olga did not have legal title to the property, how could she get a second mortgage? There are two possible answers. The most likely is that Art, the legal title holder, consented to the mortgage. Art could agree to let the property stand as security for the loan without assuming personal responsibility for its repayment, meaning that the second mortgagee could recover the property if Olga defaulted, but could not sue Art for any deficiency.

The other alternative would have been for Olga to mortgage her equitable interest in the property; that is, her right to acquire title by making timely payments on the land contract. Such an equitable interest may be used as security, but most lenders do not prefer it. In foreclosure of such an interest, the lender would merely acquire Olga's contract rights, not the property itself. In order to obtain title, the lender would still have to pay off the contract. Under this second arrangement, the so-called "second" mortgage is really third in priority because it can never result in a sale of the property until after the contract has been paid off.

Example: Using the same circumstances as in the foregoing example, assume that Art did not consent to a second mortgage, but that Olga was still able to borrow $30,000 with her equitable interest (contract rights) as security. If Olga defaults on the loan, Sam's Mortgage Company can take over her rights under the contract. Sam's can acquire title by paying off the contract, and then attempt to sell the property in order to recover its loan. Note that the property is still encumbered by the original $95,000 mortgage.

III. Other Forms of Creative Financing

As mentioned at the beginning of this chapter, imagination is the only limit to the types of seller financing that are possible. In the final section of this chapter, we will review some of the less conventional arrangements that are being used today.

A. LEASE/OPTION

The lease/option plan is comprised of two elements: a lease, and an option to purchase the leased property within a specific time period (usually within the term of the lease).

Obviously the lease/option is not the equivalent of a sale, but there is at least a strong possibility that a sale will eventually take place under the terms of the lease/option.

An ***OPTION*** *is an agreement to keep open, for a predetermined period of time, the right to purchase or sell property. The prospective purchaser is referred to as the* ***OPTIONEE****; the property owner is the* ***OPTIONOR***. For the most part, the option contract is designed to assure the optionee the right to purchase the property at an agreed upon price and within a specified period of time. Usually, the optionee is keenly interested in the property, but will not exercise the right to complete the purchase unless certain problems are resolved or questions answered beforehand. Some of the instances in which an option might be used are:

1. **Speculation.** The prospective purchaser believes that the property will increase in value. For example, it is soon to be rezoned. However, the purchaser wants to wait until the change in zoning actually occurs before purchasing the property.
2. **Investment.** The prospective purchaser thinks the property will be a good investment but wants to wait until he or she can find other investors willing to contribute capital and share the risk before actually purchasing the property.
3. **Comparison.** The prospective purchaser thinks the property is a good buy but wants to investigate other properties before coming to a final decision.
4. **Profit.** The purchaser plans on selling the option (if the option is assignable) for a profit.

5. **Time to acquire cash to close.** The prospective purchaser needs additional time to save for the down payment, to sell other property, to obtain the down payment, or otherwise obtain the cash needed to close the transaction.
6. **Qualifying.** The buyer is unable to qualify for a loan at present, but has reason to believe that circumstances will change shortly and that he or she will be able to qualify for a loan within the next year. For example, perhaps the buyer is expecting a raise and will soon pay off another debt, thereby reducing his or her monthly obligations. Or, the buyer may be able to save or otherwise obtain a larger down payment, or perhaps simply hopes that the property will increase in value enough over the next year so that he or she can obtain a larger loan than is now possible and be able to pay the seller the purchase price.
7. **Rent credit.** The buyer and seller may agree to credit part or all of the lease payments to the down payment, loan amount, or sales price (which would reduce both the down payment and the necessary loan amount), making it easier for the buyer to make the purchase in another six months or year.

When property values are in decline and buyers are wary of purchasing a home that might be worth less than the price they paid for it in the foreseeable future, a lease/option can benefit both a buyer and seller.

8. **Avoiding foreclosure.** A seller, rather than sell a property for less than what he or she owes on a loan or succumb to foreclosure may benefit from leasing the property to a potential buyer willing to pay more than the market rate for rent in order to eventually purchase the property.

9. **Declining value.** A buyer who is hesitant to purchase a home when property values are declining, may benefit from a lease/option so that he or she has the option to back out of a purchase deal if the property decreases in value over time.

1. Consideration for an Option

To be enforceable, an option must be supported by consideration. The ***CONSIDERATION*** *is something of value given by the optionee to the optionor in return for a commitment to sell the property to the optionee at some time in the future. The consideration is usually a sum of money, but it can be anything of value. It is sometimes called the* ***OPTION MONEY***.

In most cases, the consideration must pass to the optionor for the option contract to be binding. In other words, if the purchaser simply promised to pay the property owner $5,000 in return for the owner's promise to sell him the property, but had not actually delivered the option money to the owner, the option contract would not be enforceable.

Once paid, the option money is not refundable, regardless of whether the optionee proceeds with the purchase.

In many instances, purchasers and sellers agree that the option money will be credited to the purchase price, much like a good faith deposit in an ordinary purchase and sale agreement.

Example:

$73,000 purchase price
- 5,000 option money
$68,000 balance due if sale is consummated

This is not always the case, however, so such an arrangement should be clearly spelled out in the option contract. If the buyer and seller have not clearly agreed in the written option contract to credit the option money against the purchase price, the presumption is that the balance due would be the entire price recited in the option.

Example:

$73,000 purchase price
$5,000 option money
$73,000 balance due if sale is consummated

2. Other Option Essentials

An option is required to include all of the terms of the underlying contract of sale.

This means that a binding contract is formed at the moment the optionee exercises his or her option to purchase. Required information includes, but is not necessarily limited to, the following:

1. names and addresses of the optionor and the optionee;
2. date of the option;
3. nature and amount of consideration;
4. words indicating that an option is being given;
5. date option expires, and
6. purchase price and essential terms.

3. How Does a Lease/Option Work?

The seller/landlord leases the property to the buyer/tenant for a specific term (six months, one year, etc.), with the provision that part of the rental payments may be applied to the purchase price if the tenant decides to buy before the lease expires.

> **Example:** Mavis Rutland is selling her house for $75,000. Huey Anderson is interested in the property, but will not be able to qualify for a loan until he receives a raise, which he expects in two months. Huey and Mavis agree that Huey will rent the property for six months at $500.00/month, with half the rental payments being applicable to the sales price if Huey buys within six months. Huey also gets an option, which means that Mavis agrees not to sell to anyone else within the six-month lease period. If Huey decides to buy after six months, he will pay $73,500, the amount still due after deducting half the rental payments. However, failure to exercise the option will not entitle Huey to a refund of the portion that would have been applied to the purchase price had the property been purchased.

The essential terms of a lease/option, in addition to the option requirements recited previously, include:

1. rental amount;
2. rent credit, if any;
3. reference to security deposit, if any;
4. a statement that a default by the optionee/lessee in connection with the lease agreement will result in a forfeiture of option rights, and
5. type of acceptable financing.

4. Advantages and Disadvantages of the Lease/Option

The main advantage of the lease/option is keeping a sale alive until the parties are in a position to close.

Although this could be done with a simple option agreement, the lease/option also allows the "buyer" to reduce the selling price over a period of time, making it easier to come up with a down payment or to qualify for a loan when the option is exercised. Also, the "seller" is receiving some income from the property, which can be used to make payments on a new house until the old house is sold, or to cover payments on existing financing on the old house.

The primary disadvantage of the lease/option is that the "seller" cannot sell the property to anyone other than the tenant during the term of the option.

Thus the lease/option is used only when it seems unlikely that other offers will be forthcoming in the near future. In addition, the "seller" cannot occupy the property during the term of the lease, so this plan normally involves sellers who have already purchased a new home or who have been holding the subject property for income production rather than as a personal residence.

5. Ways to Structure a Lease/Option

The crediting of rental payments may be done in a variety of ways, depending on the needs of the buyer. Rental payments may be credited towards the amount needed for a down payment if the buyer is short on cash, or they may be used to reduce the amount of financing required if the buyer cannot qualify for an appropriate loan. If desired, part of the credit may be applied to the purchase price, reducing both the down payment and the loan balance.

B. LEASE CONTRACT SEPARATE FROM OPTION CONTRACT

A problem with the lease/option agreement is that too often the optionee/tenant does not exercise the right to purchase. The result is wasted effort, with no sale and no commission.

Why the lease/option has such a high mortality rate is arguable, but there are at least two characteristics inherent in every lease/option agreement that promise trouble:

1. The prospective buyer's minimal cash investment—sometimes as little as a first and last lease payment.
2. The prospective buyer's extended occupancy of the property before a commitment is made.

Every property, especially a resale property, is flawed to some extent, and frequently optionees who have not yet committed themselves to a purchase will point to every minor imperfection when the time for a decision arrives. They will either refuse to exercise their right to buy or they will try to use the problems with the property, however inconsequential they might be, to negotiate further concessions on the part of the owner. A more forceful, and consistently more successful, method of structuring lease/option arrangements is to treat the lease and the option as two separate contracts. Generally, the transaction would be formed as follows:

1. The lease agreement would be written as a ***TRIPLE-NET LEASE*** *(in addition to rent, buyer is responsible for payment of property taxes, insurance, and utilities)*. If possible, rental payments would be set at above-market rates. The above-normal rental commits the buyer to the property and acts as an incentive to exercise the option to buy at the earliest possible date.
2. Secure the option with substantial cash consideration. Because it is not refundable, the consideration immediately passes to the seller. Because of the substantial nature of the option money, it is usually applied to the purchase price when the option to buy is exercised.

The agent's commission can be paid from the option money immediately, thereby emphasizing to the prospective buyer that a lease/option is a viable form of seller financing.

Experience shows that once a purchaser is financially committed to a property, he or she is not likely to walk away from it. Minor imperfections seem less important to someone who has already made a substantial investment in a property.

Of course, the amount of consideration to be paid by the optionee is negotiable.

The general rule is simple: the more option money paid, the more secure the transaction.

To make the effort worthwhile for an agent, the option money should, at a minimum, equal the amount of the commission.

C. LEASE/PURCHASE OR LEASE/SALE

A lease/purchase or lease/sale is quite similar to a lease/option. The primary difference is that, along with a lease, the buyer and seller sign a purchase and sale agreement instead of an option. The purchase contract is normally written with a substantial nonrefundable deposit and with a closing date set six months or a year in the future.

Most agents believe that a lease/purchase arrangement is more likely to result in a successful sale than a lease/option.

The fact that the buyer is willing to sign a purchase agreement is an indication that he or she has already decided to buy the property and will do so, instead of delaying that decision for another six months or year, as would be the case with an option.

Although the buyer's willingness to sign a written contract to buy the property may certainly be an indication of the buyer's intent, the differences between a lease/purchase and a lease/option may be more psychological than financial. The practical consequences of a lease/purchase are pretty much the same as a lease/option. Lease/purchase agreements are usually written so that the seller is entitled to the deposit if the buyer does not close the transaction as agreed in the purchase and sale agreement. This means that the buyer forfeits the deposit if he or she fails to go through with the purchase, which is little different from paying the option money.

As with a lease/option, the most reliable indicator of a successful lease/purchase is usually the amount of money put up by the buyer.

However, even though the economic realities of lease/purchase and lease/option transactions may be essentially the same, many sellers prefer a lease/purchase (lease/sale). Therefore, structuring a transaction as a "sale" with a closing one year later, instead of as a one-year option, may be acceptable to some sellers who would be reluctant to agree to an option.

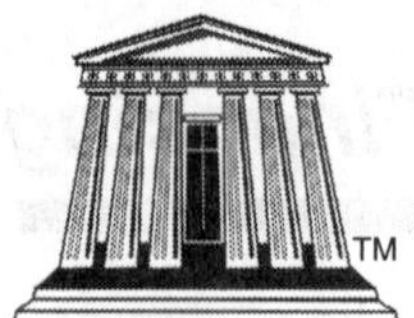

D. EQUITY EXCHANGES

When a buyer cannot come up with sufficient cash for a sale, the difference can be made up with other assets, such as land, another house, cars, boats, or any other property in which the buyer has an equity interest and that the seller would be willing to accept as part of the down payment. If the transaction involves an exchange of real estate that is used in a trade or business, or is held for the production of income or investment, some or all of the capital gain can be deferred in a "tax-free" exchange.

The tax-free exchange is not available for the parties' residences or for property held for sale by a dealer.

If the transaction does qualify for tax-free exchange treatment, any gain that is purely a result of the exchange is deferred. However, any property or money that does not qualify (i.e., is not "like-kind" property held for income business or investment) is treated as "boot" and is taxable.

> **Example:** Ben Hummel owns a rental house that he would like to sell. He lists the house for $174,000, including an assumable mortgage of $127,000. Cathy Collier is interested in the property, but has only $15,000 cash for a down payment. Bill Broker suggests an exchange of Cathy's triplex, valued at $115,000 with an assumable mortgage of $80,000, for Ben's house, with Cathy to assume Ben's loan. Ben will receive $35,000 in the form of Cathy's equity in the triplex, and $12,000 cash. He will assume Cathy's loan, which will result in "mortgage relief" of $47,000. He owed $127,000 on the loan that is to be assumed by Cathy and will owe only $80,000 on the loan that he is to assume (a difference of $47,000).

In the above example, Cathy will pay no income tax on the sale of her triplex. She will receive only qualifying property in return for her property. Ben will owe taxes on the $12,000 in cash received and also on the $47,000 of mortgage relief. Both are treated as taxable boot.

E. PARTICIPATION LOAN (Shared Equity Loan)

In a ***PARTICIPATION LOAN*** *or* ***shared equity loan****, the buyer enters into a form of partnership with an investor who provides cash for the sale.* The investor may be the seller, a bank, or any private investor. Instead of charging interest, the investor in a participation plan receives a percentage of the equity (the difference between the property's value and the indebtedness secured by the property). Different investors will have varying requirements as to the percentage of equity to be shared, and as to the method of repayment of the investment. These issues are a matter of institutional policy or negotiation between buyer and investor. The important points to consider when arranging a participation loan are listed below.

1. **How will the loan be applied?** An investor may simply put up cash for the down payment, or the primary lender may reduce the interest rate in exchange for a share of the equity. In the first case, the participation loan is essentially a form of secondary financing, with "interest" paid in the form of a share of the equity instead of a percentage of the loan amount.

   Example:

$100,000	sales price
- 20,000	participation loan
80,000	conventional loan

   In the second instance, the participation loan is a variation of the permanent buydown, except that the buyer must repay the buydown when the equity is divided.

   Example:

   $100,000 sales price; the lender quotes 15% interest rate for the $80,000, 30-year conventional loan. The lender agrees to 13% interest rate in exchange for a share of the equity. The buyer makes a $20,000 down payment.

2. **How will the equity be calculated?** *EQUITY is the difference between the value of the property and the outstanding indebtedness secured by the property.* For the purposes of a participation loan, the buyer and investor must agree at the outset as to how the property is to be valued. Any method acceptable to both parties may be used. The value of the property at the time of purchase may be periodically adjusted according to an agreed-upon index, or the parties many choose a particular appraiser whose opinion of value they will accept.

   The parties should also determine whether the participation loan is to be considered part of the indebtedness on the property. A critical factor here is whether the participation loan is secured by a lien against the property. If it is, then it reduces the equity.

   Example:

$110,000	value of property
- 72,000	balance on participation loan
$38,000	equity to be shared

3. **What percentage of the equity will the investor receive?** This amount is negotiable, but should be large enough to provide at least a market rate of return to the investor. Factors of influence in this regard are:

1. the amount of the participation loan in proportion to the value of the property;
2. the projected rate of increase in the value of the property;
3. the rate at which any conventional financing will be paid off (that is, the rate of equity growth if the value of the property remains constant), and
4. the term of the participation.

4. **When will the investor be repaid?** The investor may cash out his or her share of equity at a pre-agreed time (e.g., after five years), or else at the time the property is sold. Notice that if the investor is cashed out before the property is sold, the buyer will most likely have to refinance at that time. If the investor is to be repaid when the property is sold, provision should be made for establishing an acceptable resale price for the property.

5. **How will improvements be handled?** The agreement should specify whether the investor will share in any changes in equity resulting from improvements made on the property. If the buyer invests $5,000 of her own funds in an addition that adds $7,000 to the value of the property, does the investor get a share of the $2,000 equity created by the addition? Conversely, if a $5,000 remodeling project only adds $3,000 to the overall value of the property, does the investor share in the $2,000 reduction of equity? Questions such as these should be addressed in the original loan agreement.

6. **Who will be responsible for payment of taxes and insurance?** Usually the buyer will pay the property taxes and homeowner's insurance premiums, but this point may be negotiable in the case of some private investors.

You will note from the foregoing discussion that participation plans can be fairly complex in comparison to other creative financing methods. Agreements such as these should be clearly spelled out, with provisions for all possible contingencies.

The services of an experienced real estate attorney should always be obtained when preparing participation plan financing.

IV. Broker's Responsibilities

Several creative financing arrangements have been explained in this chapter, but this is by no means an exhaustive survey of the possibilities for imaginative buyers and sellers. The old saying "where there's a will, there's a way" is particularly true of creative finance. The advantages of open-minded negotiation among buyer, seller, lender, and agent cannot be overemphasized. However, when using an arrangement that has not been tried and proven by others in the past, the greatest care should be taken to protect the rights of all parties through detailed specification of all terms of the agreement, preferably with the advice and assistance of legal counsel.

As you have seen, the variety of creative financing plans is almost without limit. The variety of plans and the associated wide variety of rights and obligations of all parties—the buyer, the seller, the lender (if any), and the real estate agent—require that professional real estate agents involved in negotiating creative transactions be especially well informed and take particular care to properly represent their clients and to make proper disclosures. In many cases, it will be advisable to seek the counsel of real estate attorneys and/or certified public accountants.

The area of law that governs such creative financing transactions is as yet unsettled, but one California case should serve as notice to real estate agents and brokers working in this field. In *Peirce v. Hom*, the real estate broker arranged two mortgage loans for the purchaser, who was an elderly widow. When she ultimately was unable to make the payments and lost the property through foreclosure, she sued the broker. The California Court of Appeal held that real estate agents, holding themselves out as having professional knowledge in the area of real estate finance, have an obligation to give expert advice to their clients regarding the economic consequences of a transaction. In this particular case, the widow, after making both mortgage payments, had scarcely enough money to pay for the necessities of life. The court held that the broker should have inquired into the buyer's ability to repay the loans and possibly advised her of a more prudent way to obtain the money.

V. CHAPTER SUMMARY

Seller financing provides an almost limitless variety of creative alternatives to institutional financing and is particularly attractive in tight money markets when loans from institutional lenders often have prohibitive interest rates. Seller financing is also attractive to borrowers who cannot qualify for an institutional loan. However, for seller financing to be a feasible alternative, the seller must not have an immediate need for cash from the sale.

The same financial instruments are used for seller financing that are used by institutional lenders, such as promissory notes and mortgages. The simplest form of seller financing is when the seller owns the property free and clear. However, most seller-financed sales are of properties that are encumbered by previous financing. In this case, the buyer must take the property subject to the prior financing. There are various ways to structure such a transaction, and they include:

1. Assumption
2. Wraparound Financing
3. Land Contract Subject to Existing Financing
4. Contract With Assumption of Existing Mortgage
5. Contract Plus Assumption Plus Institutional Second Mortgage
6. Lease Option
7. Lease Contract Separate from Option Contract
8. Lease/Purchase
9. Equity Exchange
10. Participation Plan

Finally, professional brokers and agents who are involved in creative financing need to exercise caution, enlisting the services of a qualified real estate attorney. The agent/broker has a professional obligation to determine the best financial course for the buyer to adopt, and the ability of the participants in the transaction to understand the transaction before proceeding.

VI. TERMINOLOGY

Alienation Clause
Beneficiary
Consideration
Contract Escrow
Equity
Estopped
Estoppel Letter
Mortgagee
Option
Optionee
Option Money
Optionor
Purchase Money Mortgage
Release
Secondarily Liable
Triple Net Loans
Wraparound Mortgage

VII. CHAPTER QUIZ

1. An estoppel letter is used to:

   a. prevent a lender from participating in a mortgage.
   b. protect an agent entering into a creative financing transaction.
   c. prevent a lender from exercising the due-on-sale clause.
   d. prevent the state from forbidding a seller-financed transaction.

2. The simplest form of purchase money financing is:

   a. when the property is encumbered.
   b. when the property is unencumbered.
   c. when the property is estopped.
   d. when the property is in foreclosure.

3. An alienation clause:

   a. allows the lender to estoppel the property.
   b. allows the lender to exercise foreclosure rights.
   c. allows the lender to encumber the property.
   d. allows the lender to make its loan due and payable at time of sale.

4. A purchaser of an option is called the:

   a. optionor.
   b. optionee.
   c. lessee.
   d. lessor.

5. To prevent secondary liability, a seller must obtain a(n):
   a. release from the lender.
   b. estoppel letter.
   c. option.
   d. none of the above.

6. A wraparound mortgage can:
   a. provide a market rate of return to the seller.
   b. allow the buyer to have a below-market interest rate.
   c. be used in place of an assumption.
   d. all the above.

7. A form of purchase money financing where the seller retains legal title to the property until the buyer has made all the payments on the contract is called a(n):
   a. assumption.
   b. wraparound mortgage.
   c. land contract.
   d. none of the above.

8. The order in which lenders are paid in the event of a default is called:
   a. equitable foreclosure.
   b. option exercise.
   c. default priority.
   d. lien priority.

9. A lease/option is used to:
   a. keep a sale alive.
   b. reduce the selling price over time.
   c. provide income to the seller while awaiting the close of the sale.
   d. all the above.

10. Those who participate in creative financing should:
   a. consult a real estate attorney.
   b. exercise caution.
   c. both a and b.
   d. none of the above.

ANSWERS: 1. *c*; 2. *b*; 3. *d*; 4. *b*; 5. *a*; 6. *d*; 7. *c*; 8. *d*; 9. *d*; 10. *c*

Seller Financing

– Part V –
Chapters 13, 14, and 15
Qualifying By The Numbers

Chapter 13 – Qualifying the Borrower

The loan underwriting process evaluates both the property and the borrower's willingness and ability to pay off the loan. This analysis will be made by applying the guidelines of the agency that will be involved in the loan.

Chapter 14 – Qualifying the Property

Lenders demand professional appraisals because they want an entirely objective opinion of the true market values of the properties upon which they loan. The appraisers utilized by lenders are Licensed or Certified. The appraiser's client is the lender, not anyone else associated with the transaction.

Chapter 15 – Real Estate Finance Mathematics

Agents, brokers, and loan officers need to be able to solve basic real estate math problems in order to provide professional service to their clients. It is of particular importance to be able to answer a client's questions regarding interest rates, appreciation in value, and proration of closing costs.

Chapter 13
Qualifying the Borrower

Before agreeing to make a real estate loan, a lender will evaluate both the borrower's ability and willingness to repay the loan, and whether or not the property is of sufficient value to serve as collateral for the loan. This evaluation process is called **LOAN UNDERWRITING**. *The individual who conducts this process is called an* **UNDERWRITER**.

The primary concern of the underwriter is to minimize the amount of the lender's risk.

The degree of risk in any individual loan is determined by answering two fundamental questions:

1. Does the borrower's overall financial situation, which is comprised of income, assets, and credit history, indicate that he or she can reasonably be expected to make the proposed monthly loan payments in a timely manner?
2. Is there sufficient value in the property pledged as collateral to assure recovery of the loan amount in the event of a default?

The Federal Home Loan Mortgage Corporation (FHLMC – "Freddie Mac") deals with loans which have met these questions in an affirmative manner as **INVESTMENT QUALITY LOANS**.

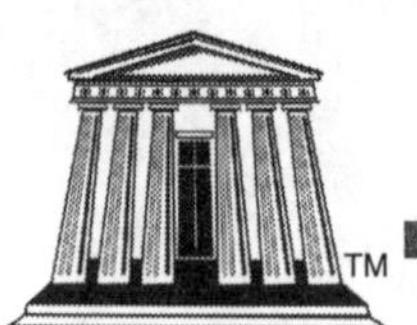

CHAPTER OUTLINE

Until the 1980s, it was not uncommon for lenders to have their own individual underwriting guidelines. Loans were quite often made from funds obtained from local deposits. The lending guidelines of many local institutions were often liberal. The lenders made their own rules because it was their money. Any loan that did not meet the requirements of the secondary market was simply kept in the lender's portfolio. However, in the 1980s, lenders experienced a massive loss of deposits by depositors who were attracted to other higher paying investments. This situation is called **disintermediation.** To continue to make loans, the lenders who did not fail during this period were required to sell their loans into the secondary market. This meant that they had to play by the rules of the secondary market.

Because most lenders now underwrite to the FNMA and the FHLMC conventional underwriting standards, which for all practical purposes are nearly the same, it is important that real estate agents and loan brokers be familiar with those standards in order to expertly prequalify their clients. FHA and VA have some slight differences that will also be addressed. Property collateral issues will be addressed in the following chapter.

I. FHLMC/FNMA Underwriting Standards

According to the Federal Home Loan Mortgage Corporation (FHLMC), *"underwriting mortgage loans is an art, not a science. It cannot be reduced to mathematical formulas, but requires sensitive weighing of the many aspects of the loan."* There are many factors related to the borrower's loan application that an underwriter will consider; they will all relate to income, net worth, and credit history (see **Figures 13-1 and 13-2**).

A. INCOME

Conventional lenders consider a borrower's income adequate for a loan if the proposed payment of principal, interest, taxes, and insurance does not exceed 28% of his or her stable monthly income.

STABLE MONTHLY INCOME *is the borrower's gross monthly income from primary base employment and any secondary income that is considered reliable and likely to endure.* We will take a closer look at acceptable income sources shortly.

Example:

$2,900 stable monthly income
$700 proposed mortgage payment*

700 ÷ 2,900 = .24

*Includes principal, interest, taxes, insurance (PITI), and private mortgage insurance (PMI), if applicable.

Figure 13-1

Uniform Underwriting and Transmittal Summary

I. Borrower and Property Information

Borrower Name ____ SSN ____
Co-Borrower Name ____ SSN ____
Property Address ____

Property Type
- 1 unit
- 2- to 4-units
- Condominium
- PUD
- Co-op
- Manufactured Housing
  - Single Wide
  - Multiwide

Project Classification

Freddie Mac
- Streamlined Review
- Established Project
- New Project
- Detached Project
- 2- to 4-unit Project
- Reciprocal Review

Fannie Mae
- P Limited Review New Detached
- Q Limited Review Established
- R Expedited Review New
- S Expedited Review Established
- T Fannie Mae Review
- U FHA-approved
- V Refi Plus™
- E PUD
- F PUD
- T PUD
- 1 Co-op
- 2 Co-op
- T Co-op

Occupancy Status
- Primary Residence
- Second Home
- Investment Property

Additional Property Information
Number of Units ____
Sales Price $ ____
Appraised Value $ ____

Property Rights
- Fee Simple
- Leasehold

Project Name ____ CPM Project ID# (if any) ____

II. Mortgage Information

Loan Type
- Conventional
- FHA
- VA
- USDA/RHS

Amortization Type
- Fixed-Rate—Monthly Payments
- Fixed-Rate—Biweekly Payments
- Balloon
- ARM (type) ____
- Other (specify) ____

Loan Purpose
- Purchase
- Cash-Out Refinance
- Limited Cash-Out Refinance (Fannie)
- No Cash-Out Refinance (Freddie)
- Home Improvement
- Construction to Permanent

Lien Position
- First Mortgage

Amount of Subordinate Financing
$ ____
(If HELOC, include balance and credit limit)
- Second Mortgage

Note Information
Original Loan Amount $ ____
Initial P&I Payment $ ____
Initial Note Rate ____ %
Loan Term (in months) ____

Mortgage Originator
- Seller
- Broker
- Correspondent

Broker/Correspondent Name and Company Name: ____

Buydown
- Yes
- No

Terms ____

If Second Mortgage
Owner of First Mortgage
- Fannie Mae
- Freddie Mac
- Seller/Other

Original Loan Amount of First Mortgage
$ ____

III. Underwriting Information

Underwriter's Name ____ Appraiser's Name/License# ____ Appraisal Company Name ____

Stable Monthly Income

	Borrower	Co-Borrower	Total
Base Income	$	$	$ 0.00
Other Income	$	$	$ 0.00
Positive Cash Flow (subject property)	$	$	$ 0.00
Total Income	$ 0.00	$ 0.00	$ 0.00

Present Housing Payment: $ ____

Proposed Monthly Payments
Borrower's Primary Residence
First Mortgage P&I $ ____
Second Mortgage P&I $ ____
Hazard Insurance $ ____
Taxes $ ____
Mortgage Insurance ____
HOA Fees $ ____
Lease/Ground Rent $ ____
Other $ ____
Total Primary Housing Expense $ 0.00

Other Obligations
Negative Cash Flow (subject property) $ ____
All Other Monthly Payments $ ____
Total All Monthly Payments $ 0.00

Qualifying Ratios
Primary Housing Expense/Income ____ %
Total Obligations/Income ____ %
Debt-to-Housing Gap Ratio (Freddie) ____ %

Loan-to-Value Ratios
LTV ____ %
CLTV/TLTV ____ %
HCLTV/HTLTV ____ %

Qualifying Rate
- Note Rate ____ %
- ____ % Above Note Rate ____ %
- ____ % Below Note Rate ____ %
- Bought-Down Rate ____ %
- Other ____ %

Level of Property Review
- Exterior/Interior
- Exterior Only
- No Appraisal

Form Number: ____

Borrower Funds to Close
Required $ ____
Verified Assets $ ____

Risk Assessment
- Manual Underwriting
- AUS
  - DU
  - LP
  - Other

AUS Recommendation ____
DU Case ID/LP AUS Key# ____
LP Doc Class (Freddie) ____

Escrow (T&I)
- Yes
- No

Source of Funds ____
No. of Months Reserves ____
Interested Party Contributions ____ %

Community Lending/Affordable Housing Initiative Yes No
Home Buyers/Homeownership Education Certificate in file Yes No

Representative Credit/Indicator Score ____

Underwriter Comments

____

IV. Seller, Contract, and Contact Information

Seller Name ____
Seller Address ____
Seller No. ____ Investor Loan No. ____
Seller Loan No. ____

Contact Name ____
Contact Title ____
Contact Phone Number ____ ext. ____
Contact Signature ____

Freddie Mac Form 1077 06/09 Page 1 of 1 Fannie Mae Form 1008 06/09

Figure 13-2

Page 1 of 2

STATE OF CALIFORNIA
DEPARTMENT OF REAL ESTATE
Providing Service, Protecting You

MORTGAGE LOAN DISCLOSURE STATEMENT

RE 883 (Rev. 10/10)

❖ For any federally related mortgage loan, HUD/RESPA laws require that a Good Faith Estimate (GFE) be provided in addition to this disclosure form.

❖ This disclosure statement meets the requirement described in Business and Professions Code (B&P) Section 10240 for loan products offered to the consumer that DO NOT allow the borrower to defer payment of principal and interest (P&I). Each payment will include the full amount of P&I due.

❖ For a non-traditional mortgage loan for a 1-4 Unit Residential Property - THIS IS THE WRONG FORM. See RE 885.

This Mortgage Loan Disclosure Statement does not constitute a loan commitment.

BORROWER'S NAME(S)

REAL PROPERTY COLLATERAL: THE INTENDED SECURITY FOR THIS PROPOSED LOAN WILL BE A DEED OF TRUST OR MORTGAGE ON (STREET ADDRESS OR LEGAL DESCRIPTION)

THIS MORTGAGE LOAN DISCLOSURE STATEMENT IS BEING PROVIDED BY THE FOLLOWING CALIFORNIA REAL ESTATE BROKER ACTING AS A MORTGAGE BROKER

INTENDED LENDER TO WHOM YOUR LOAN APPLICATION WILL BE DELIVERED (IF KNOWN) ☐ Unknown

❖ B&P Section 10241 requires the disclosure of all costs and expenses incurred with origination of real estate mortgage loans. The required fee disclosures must include, but are not limited to, the following fees and expenses:

BROKER COMMISSION	ORIGINATION FEE	DISCOUNT POINTS	APPRAISAL FEE	CREDIT REPORTING FEE	TAX SERVICE FEE
PROCESSING FEE	UNDERWRITING FEE	WIRE TRANSFER FEE	FIRE INSURANCE PREMIUM	ESCROW FEE	TITLE INSURANCE FEE
NOTARY FEE	RECORDING FEE	ASSUMPTION FEE	FORWARDING FEE	TRANSFER FEES	TOTAL
BENEFICIARY STATEMENT FEE	FLOOD INSURANCE	OTHER	OTHER	OTHER	

ADDITIONAL REQUIRED CALIFORNIA DISCLOSURES

Proposed Loan Amount $________

Total Fees, Costs, and Expenses from Above $________

Down Payment or Payoffs Liens/Creditors (list) $________

________ $________

________ $________

________ $________

________ $________

Subtotal $________ $________

Estimated Cash at Closing ☐ To You ☐ That You Must Pay $________

GENERAL INFORMATION ABOUT LOAN

PROPOSED INTEREST RATE: ________ %

☐ FIXED RATE ☐ INITIAL VARIABLE RATE

Proposed Monthly Loan Payments: $________ Principal & Interest (P&I)
If the loan is a variable interest rate loan, the payment will vary. See loan documents for details.

Total Number of Installments: ________
Loan Term: ______ Years ______ Months

PREPAYMENT PENALTY

IS THERE A PREPAYMENT PENALTY? ☐ Yes ☐ No

TERMS OF PREPAYMENT

Compensation to Broker

Yield Spread Premium, Service Release Premium or Other Rebate Received from Lender $________

Yield Spread Premium, Service Release Premium or Other Rebate Credited to Borrower $________

Total Amount of Compensation Retained by Broker $________

✱ Note: The purchase of Credit Life and/or Disability Insurance is NOT required as a condition of making this proposed loan.

RE 883 — Page 2 of 2

OTHER LIENS

LIENS CURRENTLY ON THIS PROPERTY FOR WHICH THE BORROWER IS OBLIGATED

Lienholder's Name	*Amount Owing*	*Priority*

LIST LIENS THAT WILL REMAIN OR ARE ANTICIPATED TO REMAIN ON THIS PROPERTY AFTER THE PROPOSED LOAN FOR WHICH YOU ARE APPLYING IS MADE OR ARRANGED (INCLUDING THE PROPOSED LOAN FOR WHICH YOU ARE APPLYING):

Lienholder's Name	*Amount Owing*	*Priority*

Notice to Borrower: Be sure that you state the amount of all liens as accurately as possible. If you contract with the broker to arrange this loan, but the loan cannot be arranged because you did not state these liens correctly, you may be liable to pay commissions, costs, fees, and expenses even though you do not obtain the loan.

BALLOON PAYMENT INFORMATION

IS THIS LOAN SUBJECT TO A BALLOON PAYMENT?	DUE DATE OF FINAL BALLOON PAYMENT (ESTIMATED MONTH/DAY/YEAR)	BALANCE DUE AT MATURITY
☐ Yes ☐ No		$

IF YES, THE FOLLOWING PARAGRAPH APPLIES:

NOTICE TO BORROWER: IF YOU DO NOT HAVE THE FUNDS TO PAY THE BALLOON PAYMENT WHEN IT COMES DUE, YOU MAY HAVE TO OBTAIN A NEW LOAN AGAINST YOUR PROPERTY TO MAKE THE BALLOON PAYMENT. IN THAT CASE, YOU MAY AGAIN HAVE TO PAY COMMISSIONS, FEES, AND EXPENSES FOR THE ARRANGING OF THE NEW LOAN. IN ADDITION, IF YOU ARE UNABLE TO MAKE THE MONTHLY PAYMENTS OR THE BALLOON PAYMENT, YOU MAY LOSE THE PROPERTY AND ALL OF YOUR EQUITY THROUGH FORECLOSURE. KEEP THIS IN MIND IN DECIDING UPON THE AMOUNT AND TERMS OF THIS LOAN.

ARTICLE 7 COMPLIANCE

If this proposed loan is secured by a first deed of trust in a principal amount of less than $30,000 or secured by a junior lien in a principal amount of less than $20,000, the undersigned broker certifies that the loan will be made in compliance with Article 7 of Chapter 3 of the Real Estate Law.

WILL THIS LOAN BE MADE WHOLLY OR IN PART FROM BROKER CONTROLLED FUNDS AS DEFINED IN SECTION 10241(J) OF THE BUSINESS AND PROFESSIONS CODE?

☐ May ☐ Will ☐ Will Not

Note: If the broker indicates in the above statement that the loan "may" be made out of broker-controlled funds, the broker must inform the borrower prior to the close of escrow if the funds to be received by the borrower are in fact broker-controlled funds.

NOTICE TO BORROWER: THIS IS NOT A LOAN COMMITMENT

Do not sign this statement until you have read and understood all of the information in it. All parts of this form must be completed before you sign it. Borrower hereby acknowledges the receipt of a copy of this statement.

NAME OF BROKER	LICENSE ID NUMBER / NMLS ID NUMBER	BROKER'S REPRESENTATIVE	LICENSE ID NUMBER / NMLS ID NUMBER
BROKER'S ADDRESS			
BROKER'S SIGNATURE	DATE	OR SIGNATURE OF REPRESENTATIVE	DATE
BORROWER'S SIGNATURE	DATE	BORROWER'S SIGNATURE	DATE

Department of Real Estate license information telephone number: 877-373-4542, or check license status at www.dre.ca.gov

National Mortgage Licensing System: http://mortgage.nationwidelicensingsystem.org/about/pages/nmlsconsumeraccess.aspx

The Real Estate Broker negotiating the loan shall retain on file for a period of three years a true and correct copy of this disclosure signed and dated by the borrower(s).

A second but equally important concern is that the total of the borrower's housing expenses, plus any installment debts with more than ten (10) remaining payments, as well as alimony, child support, or maintenance payments, if any, not exceed 36% of his or her stable monthly income.

Example:

$2,900 stable monthly income

$700 proposed mortgage payment
$225 auto payment (18 installments remain)
+ 100 child support
$1,025

1,025 ÷2,900 = .35 total expense-to-income ratio

The total expense-to-income ratio, called a total ***DEBT SERVICE RATIO****,* frequently is a more realistic measure of the borrower's ability to support the loan payments because it takes into account the borrower's other recurring financial obligations.

Using these ratios, it is a simple matter to determine the maximum mortgage payment for which a borrower will qualify. First, take the borrower's stable monthly income and multiply that by the maximum housing expense-to-income ratio (0.28). The answer is the maximum mortgage payment allowable under the first ratio. Then, take the stable monthly income and multiply that by the maximum total debt service ratio (0.36). The answer is the amount of total monthly long-term debts the borrower is permitted to have. Take this total amount and subtract the monthly long-term obligations (not including mortgage payments), and the resulting figure is the largest mortgage payment allowed under the total debt service ratio. The mortgage payment determined through calculating the total debt service ratio is more than likely to be smaller than the housing expense-to-income figure. This is because other monthly debts are taken into consideration. Because the borrower must qualify under both ratios, the smaller of the two is the maximum allowable mortgage payment.

Example: Mary Smith has a stable monthly income of $3,200. She has three long-term monthly debt obligations: a $220 car payment, a $75 personal loan payment, and a $50 revolving charge card payment. What is the maximum monthly mortgage payment for which she can qualify?

Housing expense-to-income ratio: 28%

$3,200.00	monthly income
x .28	expense to income ratio
$896.00	maximum mortgage payment under housing expense-to-income ratio

Total debt service ratio: 36%

$3,200.00	monthly income
x .36	income ratio
$1,152.00	maximum total debt service

$1,152.00	maximum total debt service
- 220.00	car payment
- 75.00	personal loan
- 50.00	revolving charge card payment
$807.00	maximum mortgage payment under total debt service ratio

The maximum monthly mortgage payment Mary would qualify for would be $807. Remember, Mary must qualify under both ratios, so the lower figure is the most Mary can get. Of course, if she could pay off some of her debts and reduce her total long-term monthly obligations, she would be able to qualify for a larger mortgage payment.

Loans with a loan-to-value ratio of 90-95% now have a total expense-to-monthly income ratio of 28%. The housing expense ratio may not exceed 36%.

FNMA/FHLMC Ratios		
Loan-to-Value	**Housing Expense**	**Total Debt Service/ Fixed Payments**
90% or less (down payment 10% or more)	28%	36%
FNMA more than 90% (down payment 5%)	28%	36%

1. Stable Monthly Income

As mentioned earlier, stable monthly income is the base income of the borrower (both husband and wife), plus earnings from acceptable secondary sources. ***SECONDARY EARNINGS*** *take the form of, but are not limited to, bonuses, commissions (over and above base salary), part-time employment, social security payments, military disability and retirement payments, interest on savings or other investments, and the like.*

Analyzing a borrower's income is a three-dimensional procedure. Before concluding there is a sufficient quantity of income, the underwriter must decide what portion of the total verified earnings are acceptable as a part of his or her stable monthly income. This is accomplished by studying the quality (dependability) of the income source(s) and the durability (probability of continuance) of the income.

a. Quality

A ***QUALITY SECONDARY SOURCE*** *is one that is reasonably reliable, such as an established employer, government agency, interest-yielding investment account, etc.*

b. Durability

DURABLE INCOME *is that income which can be expected to continue for a sustained period.* Permanent disability, retirement earnings, and interest on established investments clearly are enduring types of income.

c. Bonuses, Commissions, and Part-Time Earnings

These sources are considered durable if they can be shown to have been a consistent part of the borrower's overall earnings pattern for at least one, but preferably two, years. Proof of such consistency can be obtained by submitting copies of the borrower's W-2 forms or federal income tax statements from the previous year, or a verification of employment and earnings from the employer.

d. Overtime

Overtime earnings are technically eligible for inclusion in a borrower's stable monthly income, but underwriters are most reluctant to rely on such earnings because their durability is so uncertain.

It is recommended that you not count on overtime earnings when qualifying your buyers, unless they are clearly a consistent part of his or her earnings pattern.

e. Unemployment and Welfare

These earnings are almost never treated as stable monthly income because they are viewed as temporary.

f. Alimony, Child Support, or Maintenance

These sources of income can be considered part of the borrower's stable monthly income if it is determined they are likely to be consistently made. Such a determination is dependent on whether the payments are required by written agreement or court decree, the length of time the payments have been received, the age of the child (child support payments generally stop at age 18), the overall financial and credit status of the payer, and the ability of the borrower to compel payment if necessary.

A copy of the divorce decree is generally sufficient to establish the amount and the enforceability of the required payments. In some instances, where the underwriter is not satisfied that the full payments are received regularly, the borrower may be asked to submit proof of receipt.

The closer a child gets to age 18, the less durable child support income paid for he or she appears. There is no official cut-off date used by underwriters, but it is safe to say that once the child is between 16 and 17 years of age, most underwriters will see the support payments as terminal and will not include them in the stable monthly income.

g. Income From Other Family Members

Generally, only the earnings of the head(s) of household will be considered when calculating the stable monthly income. Support income from teenage children or other family members could stop without notice; income of this sort lacks both quality and durability.

h. Self-Employment Income

Self-employed borrower's should be prepared to provide, if possible, audited profit and loss statements and balance sheets for the two years prior to the loan application. Additionally, the underwriter will require copies of the borrower's federal income tax statements for the same two years (see **Figure 13-3**).

If a borrower has been self-employed for less than two years, it will be difficult to qualify him or her for a loan; more difficult still if the borrower has been in business for less than one year.

Underwriters are wary of new businesses and are generally unswerving in their insistence that the self-employed borrower must have operated the business profitably for at least two years.

The requirement for documentation of income may be waived in some cases. Some lenders offer "easy qualifier" or "no documentation" loans for borrowers meeting certain requirements. A borrower with sufficient assets, good credit, and who is able to make a large down payment (usually at least 30%) may be able to obtain a loan without providing documentation of income and income tax returns for the preceding two years. Recently, these types of loans have suffered a high default rate and are currently in disfavor.

i. Comortgagor

Frequently, a comortgagor is used to aid a primary borrower in qualifying for a loan. Today, parents often lend their established earnings pattern and financial status to their children who otherwise would be unable to purchase a home. A ***COMORTGAGOR*** *is simply a co-borrower; an individual who, along with the primary borrower, accepts responsibility for repayment of the loan by signing the promissory note and mortgage.* Like the primary borrower, the comortgagor must have earnings, assets, and a credit history that are acceptable to the underwriter.

Keep in mind that if a comortgagor is used, he or she must be able to support both his or her own housing expense and a proportionate share, if not all, of the proposed housing expense. Marginal comortgagors should not be relied on very heavily; they may do more harm than good to a loan application.

j. Rental Income

Income from rental properties can be counted as stable monthly income if a stable pattern of rental income can be verified. Authenticated copies of the

Figure 13-3

Self-Employed Income Analysis

Borrower Name ______________________

Property Address ______________________

General Instructions: This form is to be used as a guide in Underwriting the Self-employed borrower. The underwriter has a choice in analysing the individual Tax return by either the Schedule Analysis Method or the Adjusted Gross Income (AGI) Method.

The AGI Method begins with adjusted gross income from the individual tax returns and either increases or decreases that figure after analysing specific lines and schedules of the return. This method derives total income (both business and non-business).
If the borrower has passive activity unallowed losses or loss carryovers, use the Schedule Analysis Method of analysing income.

Adjusted Gross Income (AGI) Method

A. Individual Tax Return (1040)	____	____	____
1. Adjusted Gross Income			
Income Section:			
2. Wages, salary considered elsewhere	(-)		
3. Taxable Interest Income	(-)		
4. Tax-exempt Interest Income	(+)		
5. Dividend Income	(-)		
6. Taxable Refunds	(-)		
7. Alimony	(-)		
8. Business Income or Loss - Schedule C			
a. Depletion	(+)		
b. Depreciation	(+)		
c. 50% Meals and Entertainment Exclusion	(-)		
9. (-) Capital Gain or (+) Capital Loss - Schedule D			
10. IRA Distributions (non-taxable)	(+)		
11. Pensions and Annuities (non-taxable)	(+)		
12. Schedule E - Depreciation	(+)		
13. Schedule F - Depreciation	(+)		
14. Unemployment Compensation	(-)		
15. Social Security Benefits (non-taxable)	(+)		
16. Other			
______________________			
______________________			
Adjustment Section:			
17. IRA Deduction	(+)		
18. One-Half of Self-Employed Tax	(+)		
19. Self-Employed Health Insurance	(+)		
20. Keogh Retirement Plan	(+)		
21. Penalty for Early Withdrawal	(+)		
22. Alimony Paid	(+)		
Additional Schedules:			
23. Form 2106 Unreimbursed Expenses(not fully deductible)	(-)		
24. Form 4562 Amortization	(+)		
25. Total			

Complete sections B, C, and D, only if the borrower needs more income to qualify for the loan than is shown in section A and the borrower has the legal right to draw additional income from the business to qualify for the loan.

B. Corporate Tax Return Form (1120) - Corporate Income to qualify the borrower will be considered only if the borrower can provide evidence of access to the funds.

1. Taxable Income (Tax and Payments Section)	(+)		
2. Total Tax (Tax and Payments Section)	(-)		
3. Depreciation (Deductions Section)	(+)		
4. Depletion (Deductions Section)	(+)		
5. Mortgages, notes bonds payable in less than one year (Balance Sheets Section)	(-)		
6. Subtotal			
7. Times individual percentage of ownership	x %	x %	x %
8. Subtotal			
9. Dividend Income reflected on the borrower's individual income tax returns	(-)		
10. Total Income available to borrower			

C. S Corporation Tax Returns (Form 1120s) or Partnership Tax Returns (Form 1065) - Partnership or S Corporation income to qualify the borrower will be considered only if the borrower can provide evidence of access to the funds.

1. Depreciation (Deductions Section)	(+)		
2. Depletion (Deductions Section)	(+)		
3. Mortgages, notes bonds payable in less than one year (Balance Sheets Section)	(-)		
4. Subtotal			
5. Times individual percentage of ownership	x %	x %	x %
6. Total income available to borrower			
Total Income Available (add A, B, C)	I	II	III

D. Year-to-Date Profit and Loss

Year-to-Date income to qualify the borrower will be considered only if that income is in the line with the previous year's earnings or if audited financial statements are provided.

1. Salary/Draws to Individual $ ______
2. Total Allowable add back ______ x ______ % of individual ownership = $ ______
3. Total net profit ______ x ______ % of individual ownership = $ ______
4. Total $ ______

Combined Total I, II, III, YTD = $ ______ divided by ______ months = $ ______ Monthly Average

owner's books showing gross earnings and operating expenses for the previous two years should be submitted along with the borrower's application for loan approval.

k. Verifying Income

Until early 1987, lenders were required to verify income by sending an income verification form directly to the applicant's employer. The employer filled out the form and then sent it directly back to the lender. The borrower was not allowed to have any contact with the verification forms. However, FNMA and FHLMC have changed income verification procedures and income may now be verified by the borrower. The borrower can substantiate his or her own employment and income by providing W-2 forms for the previous two years and payroll stubs or vouchers for the previous 30-day period. The pay stubs must identify the borrower, employer, and the borrower's gross earnings for both the current pay period and year-to-date. Lenders then confirm the employment and earnings by a phone call to the employer.

2. Computing Monthly Earnings

When converting hourly wages to monthly earnings, multiply the hourly wage by 40 (hours in a work week), then multiply by 52 (weeks in a year) and divide by 12 (months in a year).

Example:

Hourly Wage: $20.00
Weekly Income: $20.00 x 40 = $800
Annual Income: $800 x 52 = $41,600
Monthly Income: $41,600 ÷ 12 = $3,466.67

3. Employment History

When evaluating the elements of a borrower's income (quantity, quality, and durability), the underwriter will analyze the individual's employment stability using the **Request for Verification of Employment** (see **Figure 13-4**). A borrower with a history of steady, full employment will be given more favorable consideration than one who has changed employers frequently, unless the changes are properly explained.

As a general rule, a borrower should have continuous employment for at least two years in the same field.

However, every borrower is unique and if there is not an established two-year work history, there may be explainable circumstances that would warrant loan

Figure 13-4

Request for Verification of Employment

Privacy Act Notice: This information is to be used by the agency collecting it or its assignees in determining whether you qualify as a prospective mortgagor under its program. It will not be disclosed outside the agency except as required and permitted by law. You do not have to provide this information, but if you do not your application for approval as a prospective mortgagor or borrower may be delayed or rejected. The information requested in this form is authorized by Title 38, USC, Chapter 37 (if VA); by 12 USC, Section 1701 et. seq. (if HUD/FHA); by 42 USC, Section 1452b (if HUD/CPD); and Title 42 USC, 1471 et. seq., or 7 USC, 1921 et. seq. (if USDA/FmHA).

Instructions: Lender - Complete items 1 through 7. Have applicant complete item 8. Forward directly to employer, named in item 1.
Employer - Please complete either Part II or Part III as applicable. Complete Part IV and return directly to lender named in item 2.
The form is to be transmitted directly to the lender and is not to be transmitted through the applicant or any other party.

Part I - Request

1. To (Name and address of employer)	2. From (Name and address of lender) **FACTORY BUILT FINANCIAL** **28780 OLD TOWN FRONT ST. STE C-8** **Temecula, CA 92590**

I certify that this verification has been sent directly to the employer and has not passed through the hands of the applicant or any other interested party.

3. Signature of Lender	4. Title	5. Date	6. Lender's No. (Optional)

I have applied for a mortgage loan and stated that I am now or was formerly employed by you. My signature below authorizes verification of this information.

7. Name and Address of Applicant (include employee or badge number)	8. Signature of Applicant

Part II - Verification of Present Employment

9. Applicant's Date of Employment	10. Present Position	11. Probability of Continued Employment

12A. Current **Gross** Base Pay (Enter Amount and Check Period)

☐ Annual ☐ Hourly
☐ Monthly ☐ Other (Specify)
$ ☐ Weekly ☐

12B. Gross Earnings

Type	Year To Date Thru ____	Past Year ____	Past Year ____
Base Pay	$	$	$
Overtime	$	$	$
Commissions	$	$	$
Bonus	$	$	$
Total	$	$	$

13. For Military Personnel Only

Pay Grade	
Type	Monthly Amount
Base Pay	$
Rations	$
Flight or Hazard	$
Clothing	$
Quarters	$
Pro Pay	$
Overseas or Combat	$
Variable Housing Allowance	$

14. If Overtime or Bonus is Applicable, Is Its Continuance Likely?

Overtime Yes ☐ No ☐
Bonus Yes ☐ No ☐

15. If paid hourly-average hours per week

16. Date of applicant's next pay increase

17. Projected amount of next pay increase

18. Date of applicant's last pay increase

19. Amount of last pay increase

20. Remarks (if employee was off work for any length of time, please indicate time period and reason)

Part III - Verification of Previous Employments

21. Date Hired	23. Salary/Wage at Termination Per (Year)(Month)(Week)			
22. Date Terminated	Base	Overtime	Commissions	Bonus

24. Reason for Leaving	25. Position Held

Part IV - Authorized Signature

Federal statutes provide severe penalties for any fraud, intentional misrepresentation, or criminal connivance or conspiracy purposed to influence the issuance of any guaranty or insurance by the VA Secretary, the U.S.D.A., FmHA/FHA Commissioner, or the HUD/CPD Assistant Secretary.

26. Signature of Employer	27. Title (Please print or type)	28. Date
29. Print or type name signed in Item 26	30. Phone No.	

approval, such as having recently finished college or been discharged from the service.

4. Advancement

If the borrower has changed employers for the sake of advancement within the same line of work, the underwriter will likely view the change favorably. On the other hand, persistent job hopping without advancement usually signifies a problem of some kind and an underwriter will tend to regard the individual's earnings as unstable.

5. Education and Training

Special education or training that prepares an individual for a specific kind of work can strengthen a loan application. Such education or training can offset minor weaknesses with respect to earnings or job tenure if the underwriter is convinced there is a continuing demand for individuals in this line of work. The type of work should promote job stability and opportunities for advancement.

B. NET WORTH

According to FNMA, *"accumulation of net worth is a strong indication of credit worthiness."* A borrower who has built up a significant net worth from earnings, savings, and other investment activities clearly has the ability to manage financial affairs and accumulate wealth. An individual's ***NET WORTH*** *is determined by subtracting personal liabilities from total assets.*

If a borrower has a marginal debt service-to-income ratio, an above normal net worth can offset the deficiency. Underwriters know that net worth in liquid form can be used to pay unexpected bills or to support a borrower when there has been a temporary interruption in income.

1. Required Reserves After Closing

As a safeguard against unexpected bills or temporary loss of income, and as a general indicator of financial ability, FNMA requires the borrower to have sufficient cash on deposit, or in the form of highly liquid assets, to cover two months' payments (principal, interest, taxes, insurance, and if applicable, mortgage insurance) after making the down payment and paying all closing costs. FHLMC guidelines require a minimum of two months' payments for all owner-occupant loans, without regard to loan-to-value ratio, and three to six months for non-owner-occupant loans.

2. Verification of Assets

Included in every loan application is a section devoted to assets. The underwriter will take whatever steps are necessary to verify the nature and value of assets held by the borrower. The purpose of the asset verification process is twofold:

1. It must be determined that the borrower has sufficient liquid assets to make the cash down payment and pay the closing costs and other expenses incidental to the purchase of the property. ***LIQUID ASSETS** include cash and any other assets that can be quickly converted to cash.*
2. The underwriter wants to know that the borrower has sufficient reserves to handle typical household emergencies, whatever they might be and whenever they might arise.

3. Verification of Deposit

The underwriter will use the **Request for Verification of Deposit** form (**Figure 13-5**) to prove the borrower has the necessary funds in his or her bank account(s). This form is sent directly to the bank and returned to the underwriter without passing through the borrower's hands. When the underwriter receives the completed verification of deposit, there are four things he or she will look for:

1. Does the verified information conform to the statements in the loan application?
2. Does the borrower have enough money in the bank to meet the expenses of purchase?
3. Has the bank account been opened only recently (within the last couple of months)?
4. Is the present balance notably higher than the average balance?

Recently opened accounts or higher than normal balances must be explained, as these are strong indications that the buyer has resorted to borrowed funds to pay the down payment and closing costs.

4. Alternative Verification Method

When FNMA changed its rules regarding verification of income (early 1987), it also changed its rules on verification of deposits. Lenders may now use an alternative method of verifying deposits: the borrower may submit the original bank statements for the previous three months to verify sufficient cash for closing.

5. Financial Statement (Income Statement and Balance Sheet)

If a borrower's assets are substantial and diverse, an audited financial statement may be the best way to explain the borrower's creditworthiness to the underwriter.

Figure 13-5

Request for Verification of Deposit

Privacy Act Notice: This information is to be used by the agency collecting it or its assignees in determining whether you qualify as a prospective mortgagor under its program. It will not be disclosed outside the agency except as required and permitted by law. You do not have to provide this information, but if you do not your application for approval as a prospective mortgagor or borrower may be delayed or rejected. The information requested in this form is authorized by Title 38, USC, Chapter 37 (if VA); by 12 USC, Section 1701 et. seq. (if HUD/FHA); by 42 USC, Section 1452b (if HUD/CPD); and Title 42 USC, 1471 et. seq., or 7 USC, 1921 et. seq. (if USDA/FmHA).

Instructions: Lender - Complete items 1 through 8. Have applicant complete item 9. Forward directly to depository named in item 1.
Depository - Please complete items 10 through 18 and return directly to lender named in item 2.
The form is to be transmitted directly to the lender and is not to be transmitted through the applicant(s) or any other party.

Lender's Phone No. **951-693-1086**

Part I - Request

1. To (Name and address of depository)	2. From (Name and address of lender)
	FACTORY BUILT FINANCIAL **28780 OLD TOWN FRONT ST. STE C-8** **Temecula, CA 92590**

I certify that this verification has been sent directly to the bank or depository and has not passed through the hands of the applicant or any other interested party.

3. Signature of Lender	4. Title	5. Date	6. Lender's No. (Optional)

7. Information To Be Verified

Type of Account	Account in Name of	Account Number	Balance
			$
			$
			$
			$

To Depository: I/We have applied for a mortgage loan and stated in my/our financial statement that the balance on deposit with you is as shown above. You are authorized to verify this information and to supply the lender identified above with the information requested in items 10 through 13. Your response is solely a matter of courtesy for which no responsibility is attached to your institution or any of your officers.

8. Name and Address of Applicant(s)	9. Signature of Applicant(s)
	X
	X

To Be Completed by Depository

Part II - Verification of Depository

10. Deposit Accounts of Applicant(s)

Type of Account	Account Number	Current Balance	Average Balance For Previous Two Months	Date Opened
		$	$	
		$	$	
		$	$	
		$	$	

11. Loans Outstanding To Applicant(s)

Loan Number	Date of Loan	Original Amount	Current Balance	Installments (Monthly/Quarterly)	Secured By	No. of Late Payments
		$	$	$ per		
		$	$	$ per		
		$	$	$ per		

12. Please include any additional information which may be of assistance in determination of credit worthiness (Please include information on loans paid-in full in item 11 above.)

13. If the name(s) on the account(s) differ from those listed in item 7, please supply the name(s) on the account(s) as reflected by your records.

Part III - Authorized Signature

Federal statutes provide severe penalties for any fraud, intentional misrepresentation, or criminal connivance or conspiracy purposed to influence the issuance of any guaranty or insurance by the VA Secretary, the U.S.D.A., FmHA/FHA Commisioner, or the HUD/CPD Assistant Secretary.

14. Signature of Depository Representative	15. Title (Please print or type)	16. Date

17. Please print or type name signed in item 14	18. Phone No.

A *FINANCIAL STATEMENT (balance sheet) is a summary of facts showing the individual's financial condition; it contains an itemized list of assets and liabilities which serves to disclose net worth* (see **Figure 13-6**).

6. Real Estate for Sale

If a borrower is selling a property to raise cash to buy the subject property, the equity may be counted as a legitimate asset. ***EQUITY*** *is the difference between the market value of the property and the sum of the selling expenses, mortgages, and other liens against the property.* Equity is what the buyer should receive from the sale of the property. In cases where the equity is the primary or exclusive source of money for the purchase of the subject property, the underwriter might require, before making the new loan, evidence that the former property has been sold and the proceeds from that sale have been received by the borrower.

If the purpose of the loan is to finance the construction of a home on a lot owned by the borrower, the underwriter will treat the borrower's equity in that lot as cash or its equivalent.

Example:

$75,000	estimated construction costs
+ 10,000	lot value
$85,000	total property value
$85,000	total property value
x .80	loan-to-value ratio (80%)
$68,000	maximum loan amount
$85,000	total property value
- 68,000	maximum loan amount
$17,000	required down payment
$10,000	lot value
- 4,000	liens against lot (mortgage)
$6,000	borrower's equity

The borrower shows $6,000 equity in the lot, which is included in the list of assets necessary to satisfy the down payment and settlement cost requirements.

7. Other Assets

Any assets held by the borrower will help the loan application. Assets, other than cash and real estate, typically listed in a loan application include automobiles, furniture, jewelry, stocks and bonds, and cash value in a life insurance policy.

Figure 13-6

Personal Financial and Credit Statement

U.S. Department of Housing and Urban Development
Office of Housing
Federal Housing Commissioner

OMB No. 2502-0001 (Exp. 09/30/2012)

Public reporting burden for this collection of information is estimated to average 8 hours per response, including the time for reviewing instructions searching existing data sources, gathering and maintaining the data needed, and completing and reviewing the collection of information. This information is required to obtain benefits. HUD may not collect this information, and you are not required to complete this form, unless it displays a currently valid OMB control number.
Section 207(b)(1) and (2) of the National Housing Act authorizes the Secretary of the Department of Housing and Urban Development to insure mortgages on property held by Federal or State instrumentalities, municipal corporate instrumentalities of one or more States, or housing corporations restricted by Federal or State laws or regulations of State banking or insurance departments as to rents, charges, capital structure, rate of return, or methods or operations; or to ensure the property any mortgagor approved by the Secretary. Assurances of confidentiality are pledged to respondents as stated in the Privacy Act. HUD may disclose this data on y in response to a Freedom of Information request.

Privacy Act Statement: HUD is authorized to collect this information by P. L. 479.48, Stat.1246, 12 USC 1701 et. seq.; and the Housing and Community Development Act of 1987, 42 USC 3543, to collect the Social Security Number (SSN). This report is authorized by law (24 CFR 207.1). It will be used as a minimum, to make a determination of the financial and credit status of the respondent. HUD may disclose this information to Federal, State and local agencies when relevant civil, criminal, or regulatory investigations and prosecutions. It will not be otherwise disclosed or released outside of HUD, except as required and permitted by law. Providing the SSN is mandatory. Failure to provide any of the information may result in your disapproval of participation in this HUD program and/or delay action on your proposal.

Project Name:	Project Number:	
Project Location:	Name & Address of Person(s) making this Statement:	
	Date Prepared :	Date of Statement:

Assets		
Cash on hand in banks Name of depository	Balance	Total
Depository and Account No. - Restricted		$
Depository and Account No. - Unrestricted		$
Accounts Receivable	$	
Less: Doubtful Accounts		$
Notes Receivable	$	
Less: Doubtful Notes		$
Stocks and Bonds - Market Value (Schedule A - reverse side)		$
Other Current Assets: (describe)		
		$
Total Current Assets		$
Real Property — at net * (Schedule B — reverse side)		$
Machinery Equipment and Fixtures — at net		$
Life Insurance (Cash value less loans)		$
Other Assets (describe)		
		$
Total Assets		$

Liabilities and Net Worth		
Accounts Payable		$
Notes Payable		$
Debts payable in less than one year (secured by mortgages on land and buildings)		$
Debts payable in less than one year (secured by chattel mortgages or other liens on assets)		$
Other current liabilities: (describe)		
		$
Total Current Liabilities:		$
Debts payable in more than one year (secured by mortgages on land and buildings)		$
Debts payable in more than one year (secured by chattel mortgages or other liens on assets)		$
Other liabilities (describe)		
		$
Total Liabilities		$
Net Worth		$
Total Liabilities and Net Worth		$

* Cost, including improvements, less depreciation.

Page 1 of 4

form **HUD-92417** (05/2003)
ref. Handbook 4470.1

Accounts and Notes Receivable Partner (P) Employee (E) Relative (R) or other (O)*			
Name (Indicate also P,E,R or O)*	Address	Maturity Date	Amount
Name (Indicate also P,E,R or O)*	Address	Maturity Date	Amount
Name (Indicate also P,E,R or O)*	Address	Maturity Date	Amount
Name (Indicate also P,E,R or O)*	Address	Maturity Date	Amount
Name (Indicate also P,E,R or O)*	Address	Maturity Date	Amount

Life Insurance	Face Value	Beneficiary

Delinquencies (starting with Federal Indebtedness)		
Type Liability	Amount	Circumstances
Type Liability	Amount	Circumstances
Type Liability	Amount	Circumstances
Type Liability	Amount	Circumstances
Type Liability	Amount	Circumstances

Accounts and Notes Payable Partner (P) Employee (E) Relative (R) or other (O)*			
Name (Indicate also P,E,R or O)*	Address	Amount	Maturity Date
Name (Indicate also P,E,R or O)*	Address	Amount	Maturity Date
Name (Indicate also P,E,R or O)*	Address	Amount	Maturity Date
Name (Indicate also P,E,R or O)*	Address	Amount	Maturity Date
Name (Indicate also P,E,R or O)*	Address	Amount	Maturity Date

Pledged Assets		
Type Pledged	Amount	Offsetting Liability
Type Pledged	Amount	Offsetting Liability
Type Pledged	Amount	Offsetting Liability
Type Pledged	Amount	Offsetting Liability
Type Pledged	Amount	Offsetting Liability

Legal Proceedings: (If any legal proceedings have been instituted by creditors, or any unsatisfied judgments remain on record, give full details starting with any unresolved Federal Indebtedness.)

Page 2 of 4

form **HUD-92417** (05/2003)
ref. Handbook 4470.1

Schedule A — Stocks and Bonds (Note: If more space is required use a separate sheet of paper)

Description	Number of Shares	Current Market Value (At date of this Statement)	If Listed, Name Exchange

Schedule B — Real Property (Indicate Private Residence, if any)

Location and Description of Land and Buildings Owned	Age	Original Cost	Market Value	Assessed Value	Mortgaged For	Insured For
Totals						

Title (The legal and/or equitable title to all pieces of the above-described real estate is solely in my name, except as follows).

Location of Real Property:	Name of Title Holders:

Page 3 of 4

form **HUD-92417** (05/2003)
ref. Handbook 4470.1

Bank and/or Trade References

Name & Address:	Account Numbers:

Other Information/Remarks

I/We hereby certify that the foregoing figures and the statements contained here, submitted to obtain mortgage insurance under the National Housing Act, are true and give a correct showing of my/our financial condition as of this date.

Warning: HUD will prosecute false claims and statements. Conviction may result in criminal and/or civil penalties. (18 U.S.C. 1001, 1010, 1012; 31 U.S.C. 3729, 3802)

Name(s) & Signature(s):*	Social Security Number(s) :	Date Signed:

* For married individuals, the signature and Social Security Number of the spouse is required. This signature also authorizes the acceptance of the Criminal Certification and allows consideration of the funds indicated herein for the HUD insured project.

Page 4 of 4

form **HUD-92417** (05/2003)
ref. Handbook 4470.1

Keep in mind that the assets that will most favorably influence the underwriter's decision are the liquid assets; those that can be quickly converted to cash.

8. Gift Letter

If an applicant lacks the necessary funds to close a transaction, a gift of the required amount from relatives is usually acceptable to the underwriter. The gift should be confirmed by means of a (gift) letter signed by the donor. The letter should clearly state that the money represents a gift and does not have to be repaid.

The gift usually must be from an immediate family member.

Even if the gift letter requirements are satisfied, the borrower will normally have to make some cash payment out of his or her own cash resources. FNMA requires that the borrower make at least a 5% down payment in addition to the gift, unless the gift is 20% or more of the purchase price. If the gift equals 20% or more, then the borrower is not required to make the additional 5% down payment.

C. CREDIT HISTORY

As a part of the loan evaluation, the underwriter will analyze the credit history of the borrower. This is accomplished by obtaining a credit report from a responsible credit rating bureau.

A high FICO credit score is the standard by which a borrower's creditworthiness is determined.

CREDIT SCORING *is the automated practice used by credit agencies to quantify a borrower's entire credit history into a single score or number so that an estimate of the risk of making a loan can be determined.* The most commonly used credit score is from Fair, Isaacs and Company and is called a FICO score (see **Figure 13-7**). See Chapter 8 for more on FICO. Of course, the rule applies: the more a borrower really needs a loan, the less chance credit agencies want to risk lending the money. Here are some helpful hints to increase your credit score:

1. **Pay bills on time.** Late payments, collection, and bankruptcy are negative factors.
2. **Limit outstanding debt.** Amounts owed close to your credit limit are negatives.
3. **Have a long credit history.** Insufficient credit history is a negative.
4. **Restrict your credit.** Applying for too many recent accounts is a negative.
5. **Too much credit.** Too many credit cards is a negative.

Figure 13-7 **FICO Score Chart**

760-850	EXCELLENT
700-759	VERY GOOD
723	MEDIAN FICO SCORE
660-699	GOOD
687	**AVERAGE FICO SCORE**
620-659	NOT GOOD
580-619	POOR
500-579	VERY POOR

If the borrower's credit history reflects a slow payment record or other derogatory credit information, the loan application could be declined. Derogatory credit information, over and above a slow payment record, includes suits, judgments, repossessions, collections, foreclosures, and bankruptcies.

In some instances, derogatory ratings do not prevent a borrower from obtaining a loan. If the credit problems can be satisfactorily explained so the underwriter is satisfied they do not represent the borrower's overall attitude towards credit obligations, and that the circumstances leading to the problems were temporary and no longer exist, the loan application might be approved.

Your FICO score determines the rate and terms and whether or not you get the loan.

1. Explaining Derogatory Credit

Most people try to meet their credit obligations on time; when they do not, there is usually a reason. A loss of job, hospitalization, illness, death in the family, or even divorce can create extraordinary financial pressures and adversely affect a credit report. It may be possible to successfully explain the ratings if the borrower can show that the problems occurred during a specific period of time for an understandable reason, and that prior and subsequent credit ratings have been good.

When explaining credit difficulties to a lender, it is a mistake to blame the problems on misunderstandings or on the creditors themselves. Too frequently, underwriters listen to explanations from borrowers who refuse to accept responsibility for their own acts, insisting instead that the blame lies elsewhere. The reaction to such explanations is very predictable: skepticism, disbelief, and rejection. Underwriters reason that a borrower's reluctance to take responsibility for prior credit problems is an indication of what can be expected from him or her in the future.

If a borrower's credit report is laced with derogatory ratings over a period of years, there is probably little hope for loan approval.

Perpetual credit problems more likely reflect an attitude instead of a circumstance, and it is reasonable to presume that the pattern will continue in the future.

All credit problems are resolved with time, and if a buyer indicates he or she has had some credit problems in the past, it would be a mistake to automatically presume the buyer cannot qualify for a loan. Refer him or her to a competent lender and get an expert's opinion.

2. Bill Consolidation, Refinancing

Even in the absence of derogatory ratings, there are matters that can be revealed by a credit report that might indicate the borrower is a marginal credit risk. If an individual's credit pattern is one of continually increasing liabilities and periodically "bailing out" through refinancing and debt consolidation, he or she may be classified as a marginal risk. The pattern suggests a tendency to live beyond a prudent level. This is a subjective consideration likely to influence the underwriter's decision if the borrower is weak in other critical areas, such as income or assets.

3. Illegal Discrimination

A borrower must be of legal age (usually age 18 or older) before he or she can qualify for a loan. After that, an applicant's age is not a valid reason for rejecting a loan.

In addition to age, a lender cannot use as a basis for denying a loan the race, color, creed, national origin, religion, handicap, familial status (children), marital status, or sex of the borrower (see **Figure 13-8**).

II. Summary of Qualifying the Borrower

A buyer's ability to qualify for a real estate loan depends on many factors, all of which relate to income, net worth, and credit history. While there are established guidelines for determining adequacy of income in relation to proposed housing expense, it would be wrong to apply them too rigidly. All aspects of the buyer's financial situation must be

Figure 13-8

Equal Housing Lender

We Do Business In Accordance With The Federal Fair Housing Law

(Title VIII of the Civil Rights Act of 1968, as Amended by the Housing and Community Development Act of 1974)

IT IS ILLEGAL TO DISCRIMINATE AGAINST ANY PERSON BECAUSE OF RACE, RELIGION, CREED, COLOR, NATIONAL ORIGIN, ANCESTRY, PHYSICAL HANDICAP, MEDICAL CONDITION, FAMILIA STATUS, SEX, OR AGE TO:

- Deny a loan for the purpose of purchasing, constructing, improving, repairing or maintaining a dwelling or
- Discriminate in fixing of the amount, interest rate, duration, application procedures or other terms or conditions of such a loan.

IF YOU BELIEVE YOU HAVE BEEN DISCRIMINATED AGAINST, YOU MAY SEND A COMPLAINT TO:

U.S. DEPARTMENT OF HOUSING AND URBAN DEVELOPMENT
Assistant Secretary for Fair Housing and Equal Opportunity
Washington, D.C. 20410

or call your local HUD Area or Insuring Office.

considered before deciding on his or her qualification for a loan. Considering the quality, quantity, and durability of a buyer's income and relating it to net worth is substantial enough to indicate an ability to manage financial affairs. Conversely, strong earnings and substantial assets may not be enough to offset the damage caused by poor credit paying habits. A borrower must be both able (income/assets) and willing (credit) to pay the housing expense.

Finally, keep in mind that a good property with a considerable cash equity can offset marginal credit or income because borrowers who make large investments (down payments) in their properties are far less likely to default than borrowers with little or no equity.

III. FHA Underwriting Standards

FHA's qualifying ratios are based on the borrower's gross income.

Once the borrower's gross income has been identified, it must be compared against the proposed housing expense. Included in FHA's estimated housing expense are the principal and interest payments, the monthly property taxes, the monthly homeowner's insurance premium, an estimated monthly maintenance expense, an estimated monthly utilities expense, monthly homeowner's association dues (if any), and monthly property assessments (if any).

Sample Housing Expense:

$538.42	principal and interest
40.00	property taxes
15.00	homeowner's insurance
33.00	maintenance expense
80.00	utilities expense
-0-	homeowners' association dues
-0-	assessments
$706.42	total housing expense

The FHA will allow a maximum ratio of housing expense-to-gross income of 31%.

$706.42 (housing expense) ÷ .31 = $2,278.77 minimum gross income necessary

In addition to its concern for the borrower's ratio of housing expense-to-income, FHA will want to know the borrower can support the family's fixed monthly payments as well. ***FIXED PAYMENTS*** *include automobile and personal loans, revolving credit card obligations, and child support or alimony payments.*

The maximum ratio for housing expense plus fixed payments-to-gross income is 43%.

Example:

$706.42	housing expense
	fixed monthly payments:
92.65	auto payment
20.00	revolving account
$819.07	Total

$819.07 (housing expense and fixed payments) ÷ .43 = $1,904.81 minimum gross income necessary.

IV. VA Qualifying Standards

Prior to 1986, the Department of Veterans Affairs (VA) used a cash flow qualifying method. In 1986, the VA began using both the cash flow method and an income ratio method. This means that those underwriting VA guaranteed loans will have to determine two separate figures in their analysis: the residual income of the borrower and the income ratio of the borrower.

***RESIDUAL INCOME** is the amount of income a loan applicant has left after taxes, recurring obligations, and the proposed housing expense has been deducted from his or her gross monthly income.*

The amount of the veteran's residual income must meet the VA's minimum requirements. The VA frequently publishes tables of residual income that are defined both by region and by family size.

A. MINIMUM RESIDUAL STANDARDS ARE GUIDELINES

The balance available for family support is an important factor in evaluating a loan application, but is not the only consideration. The VA standards are intended to be guidelines in judging the borrower's relative strength or weakness with regards to residual income, which is only one of the many factors to be considered in underwriting VA loan applications.

B. OTHER FACTORS

In addition to the residual income standards, other important factors considered in underwriting a loan application include:

1. The borrower's demonstrated ability to accumulate cash or other liquid assets.
2. The borrower's demonstrated ability to use credit wisely and to avoid incurring an excessive amount of debt.
3. The relationship between the shelter expense for the property being acquired and the expense that the borrower is accustomed to paying.
4. The number and ages of the borrower's dependents.
5. The locality and general economic level of the neighborhood where the property is located.
6. The likelihood that the borrower's income may increase or decrease.
7. The borrower's employment history and work experience.
8. The borrower's demonstrated ability and willingness to make payments on time.
9. The amount of any down payment made.
10. The borrower's available cash after paying closing costs and other prepaid items.

C. INCOME RATIO ANALYSIS

In addition to residual income, a ratio based on total monthly debt payments (housing expense, installment debts, child support, etc.) to gross monthly income will be considered by a VA underwriter. The ratio is determined by taking the sum of the housing expense (principal, interest, tax, and insurance payments) and monthly obligations and dividing that by gross income. If the obligations-to-income ratio is 41% or less, the underwriter may approve the loan. If the ratio is above 41%, the underwriter must present other factors (e.g., sufficient residual income, significant liquid assets, or a substantial down payment) before approving the loan. A VA underwriter may generally approve the loan if the residual income is at least 20% over the required minimum.

The VA has emphasized that these underwriting standards are only guidelines for approval and should not be automatic reasons for approving or rejecting a loan.

When the borrower actually applies for a loan with a lender, he or she will have already entered into a purchase and sale agreement for a particular home at a particular purchase price and will be asking for a certain loan amount. Because the lender knows the requested loan amount and purchase price, he or she can calculate (with fair accuracy) what insurance, taxes, mortgage insurance, and maintenance costs will be. When you are prequalifying a buyer, however, you will usually not have a particular purchase price in mind, but you will still need to know an approximate figure for these costs. In the qualifying forms, assume that 10% of the total mortgage payment will go towards taxes, insurance, and mortgage insurance. This is only an approximation, but it should be close enough for prequalifying purposes. Average figures for these costs will vary from place to place, depending on property tax rates and other factors. If you are prequalifying a borrower with a specific loan amount in mind, you should be able to determine approximate figures for these amounts by asking a local lender (see **Figures 13-9 through 13-13**).

Figure 13-9

INCOME QUALIFYING – CONVENTIONAL LOANS
FIXED-RATE, 90% OR LESS LTV

Monthly Gross Income:

Base salary	______
Overtime	______
Bonuses	______
Commissions	______
Other	______
Total	______

Long-Term Monthly Debt:

Car payment	______
Child support	______
Credit cards	______
Other loans	______
Other debts	______
Total	______

(Consider 5% payments on all revolving charges)

Housing Expense-to-Income Ratio:

______	Stable Monthly Income
x .28	Income Ratio
______	Maximum Mortgage Payment (PITI)

Total Debt Service Ratio:

______	Stable Monthly Income
x .36	Income Ratio
______	Maximum Monthly Obligations
______	Maximum Monthly Obligations
–	Monthly Obligations
______	Maximum Mortgage Payment (PITI)

MAXIMUM MORTGAGE PAYMENT (PITI)______

______	Maximum PITI
–	(less 10% of mortgage payment) (Insurance, taxes, PMI)
______	Maximum Principal and Interest Payment
______	**MAXIMUM LOAN AMOUNT** (using calculator or interest factor tables)

Figure 13-10

INCOME QUALIFYING – CONVENTIONAL LOANS
FIXED-RATE, MORE THAN 90% LTV

Monthly Gross Income:		**Long-Term Monthly Debt:**	
Base salary	________	Car payment	________
Overtime	________	Child support	________
Bonuses	________	Credit cards	________
Commissions	________	Other loans	________
Other	________	Other debts	________
Total	________	**Total**	________
			(Consider 5% payments on all revolving charges)

Housing Expense-to-Income Ratio:

________	Stable Monthly Income
x .28	Income Ratio
________	Maximum Mortgage Payment (PITI)

Total Debt Service Ratio:

________	Stable Monthly Income
x .36	Income Ratio
________	Maximum Monthly Obligations
________	Maximum Monthly Obligations
________	Monthly Obligations
________	Maximum Mortgage Payment (PITI)

MAXIMUM MORTGAGE PAYMENT (PITI)________

________	Maximum PITI (less 10% of mortgage payment)
– ________	(Insurance, taxes, PMI)
________	Maximum Principal and Interest Payment
________	**MAXIMUM LOAN AMOUNT** (using calculator or interest factor tables)

Figure 13-11

INCOME QUALIFYING – CONVENTIONAL LOANS
ADJUSTABLE-RATE, 90% OR LESS LTV

Monthly Gross Income:

Base salary	________
Overtime	________
Bonuses	________
Commissions	________
Other	________
Total	________

Long-Term Monthly Debt:

Car payment	________
Child support	________
Credit cards	________
Other loans	________
Other debts	________
Total	________

(Consider 5% payments on all revolving charges)

Housing Expense-to-Income Ratio:

________	Stable Monthly Income
x .28	Income Ratio
________	Maximum Mortgage Payment (PITI)

Total Debt Service Ratio:

________	Stable Monthly Income
x .36	Income Ratio
________	Maximum Monthly Obligations

________	Maximum Monthly Obligations
–	Monthly Obligations
________	Maximum Mortgage Payment (PITI)

MAXIMUM MORTGAGE PAYMENT (PITI)________

________	Maximum PITI (less 10% of mortgage payment)
–	(Insurance, taxes, PMI)
________	Maximum Principal and Interest Payment

________	**MAXIMUM LOAN AMOUNT** (using calculator or interest factor tables)

Figure 13-12

INCOME QUALIFYING – FHA-INSURED LOANS
Income Ratio Method

Monthly Gross Income:

Base salary	________
Overtime	________
Bonuses	________
Commissions	________
Other	________
Total	________

Long-Term Monthly Debt:

Car payment	________
Child support	________
Credit cards	________
Other loans	________
Other debts	________
Total	________

(Consider 5% payments on all revolving charges)

Housing Expense-to-Income Ratio: 29%

________	Stable Monthly Income
x .31	Income Ratio
________	Maximum Mortgage Payment (PITI)

Total Debt Service Ratio: 41%

________	Stable Monthly Income
x .43	Income Ratio
________	Maximum Monthly Obligations
________	Maximum Monthly Obligations
–	Monthly Obligations
________	Maximum Mortgage Payment (PITI)

MAXIMUM MORTGAGE PAYMENT (PITI)________

________	Maximum PITI (less 10% of mortgage payment)
–	(Insurance, taxes, MIP)
________	Maximum Principal and Interest Payment
________	**MAXIMUM LOAN AMOUNT** (not to exceed regional mortgage amount limitations)

Figure 13-13

INCOME QUALIFYING – VA GUARANTEED LOANS
Residual Income Method

Monthly Gross Income:

Base salary	______
Overtime	______
Bonuses	______
Commissions	______
Other	______
Total	______

Long-Term Monthly Debt:

Car payment	______
Child support	______
Credit cards	______
Other loans	______
Other debts	______
Total	______

(consider 5% payments on all revolving charges)

Less All Taxes:

Federal Income tax	______
Social Security (7.65%)	______
State Income tax	______
Other Tax	______
Total	______

Net Income	______
less:	
long-term debts	______
required reserves	______
Total	______

MAXIMUM HOUSING EXPENSE ______

Total Housing Expense	______
less 20% (taxes, insurance, maintenance, utilities)	– ______
	______

Maximum Principal and Interest Payment ______

______ **MAXIMUM LOAN AMOUNT** (not to exceed lender limitations)

Income Ratio Method

Total Debt Service Ratio: 41%

______	Stable Monthly Income
x .41	Income Ratio
______	Maximum Monthly Obligations
______	Maximum Monthly Obligations
–	Monthly Obligations
______	Maximum Mortgage Payment (PITI)

MAXIMUM MORTGAGE PAYMENT (PITI) ______

______	Maximum PITI (less 10% of mortgage payment)
–	(Insurance, taxes, PMI)
______	Maximum Principal and Interest Payment

______ **MAXIMUM LOAN AMOUNT** (not to exceed lender limitations)

V. CHAPTER SUMMARY

The loan underwriting process evaluates both the property and the borrower's willingness and ability to pay off the loan. An underwriter will make a determination of these factors by analyzing the borrower's current income, debt levels, overall net worth, and credit history (FICO scoring). This analysis will be made by applying the guidelines of the agency that will be involved in the loan. For conventional loans, these will be the guidelines of FNMA and FHLMC. FHA and VA programs have slightly different guidelines. Conventional and FHA loans emphasize income-to-debt ratios. VA standards emphasize residual income requirements as well as income-to-total debt ratios. As a result, the VA program is somewhat more lenient. Once the borrower has been qualified, the underwriter will call for a property appraisal to determine if the property qualifies for the particular loan program as well. This process will be covered in the next chapter.

VI. TERMINOLOGY

Balance Sheet
Comortgagor
Credit Scoring
Debt Service Ratio
Disintermediation
Durable Income
Equity
FICO Scores
Fixed Payments
Income Statement
Investment Quality Loan
Liquid Assets
Loan Underwriting
Net Worth
Quality Secondary Source
Request for Verification of Employment
Request for Verification of Deposit
Residual Income
Secondary Earnings
Stable Monthly Income
Total Debt Service Ratio

VII. CHAPTER QUIZ

1. The process of qualifying both a borrower's ability to pay and a property's worth is called:

   a. net worth.
   b. loan underwriting.
   c. stabilization of income.
   d. none of the above.

2. A loan that meets the requirements of FHLMC (Freddie Mac) is called a(n):

   a. investment quality loan.
   b. stable loan.
   c. equitable loan.
   d. debt serviced loan.

3. In a conventional loan, the housing expense to stable income ratio must not be more than:

   a. 25%.
   b. 31%.
   c. 33%.
   d. 43%.

4. The total debt service ratio for a VA loan is:

   a. 25%.
   b. 29%.
   c. 33%.
   d. 41%.

5. The value of a property minus the debts owed on it is called the:

   a. debt service ratio.
   b. investment quality.
   c. owner's equity.
   d. all the above.

6. In addition to the income-to-total debt service ratio, the VA uses which of the following to qualify a loan?

   a. Income ratio analysis
   b. Disintermediation
   c. Residual income
   d. Stable monthly income

7. For conventional loans exceeding 90% LTV, the expense ratios must not exceed:
   a. 28% and 36%.
   b. 25% and 33%.
   c. 29% and 41%.
   d. 33% and 41%.

8. In evaluating a borrower, an underwriter looks at:
   a. income.
   b. assets.
   c. credit history.
   d. all the above.

9. Which of the following is not considered stable monthly income?
   a. Overtime
   b. Self-employment income
   c. Alimony
   d. Unemployment benefits

10. As a general rule, a borrower should have how many years of continuous employment to obtain a home loan?
   a. 1 year
   b. 2 years
   c. 3 years
   d. Less than one year

ANSWERS: 1. *b*; 2. *a*; 3. *b*; 4. *d*; 5. *c*; 6. *c*; 7. *a*; 8. *d*; 9. *d*; 10. *b*

COMPS
mouse-scratch-pad
www.comps.com

Chapter 14
Qualifying the Property

Qualifying the property involves an analysis of its many features to determine whether it has sufficient value to serve as collateral for a real estate loan, and whether its value can be expected to remain stable in the months and years to come.

Lenders do not make loans in anticipation of foreclosure. They make loans in anticipation of being repaid in a timely manner. Every underwriting decision is based on this premise. Regardless of whether the borrower has sterling credit or not, the property will serve as security for the debt. A wise lender will make certain before extending a loan that there is enough value in the property to protect its investment.

I. The Lender's Perception of Value

Lenders utilize Licensed and Certified Appraisers to provide a professional opinion of market value for each residence they loan upon.

By both state and federal law, appraisers are required to provide an unbiased and independent analysis of the property. Appraisers are required to adhere to the Uniform Standards of Professional Appraisal Practice (USPAP) in carrying out each appraisal.

Chapter 14

CHAPTER OUTLINE

The USPAP applies to all Licensed and Certified Appraisers as well as the users of appraisals.

The seller, buyer, or their agents are not the appraiser's clients. **The lender is the primary client of the appraiser**. The USPAP makes it very clear that the appraiser is expected to safeguard the primary lender, the investors of the secondary market, and the federal insurance funds. The penalties for not doing so can be quite severe. The appraiser must follow the ***APPRAISAL PROCESS****, an outline contained in the USPAP of the material that the appraiser must address in carrying out the appraisal.* In addition, the appraiser is required to adhere to all state laws and federal lending regulator guidelines governing appraisals. All appraisals for federally related transactions must be in writing and must be made to market value. ***MARKET VALUE*** *is the price paid by a typical buyer; it is based on the analysis of a group of actual sales that occurred in the marketplace.* The exact definition of Market Value that an appraiser must follow is included in the Uniform Residential Appraisal Report (URAR), a portion of which is shown in **Figure 14-1**.

When the appraiser is retained by the lender to estimate the market value of a residence, he or she is being asked to make a thorough analysis of the property and its surroundings and to issue an objective analysis of its market value. As such, the appraiser's conclusions may not coincide with the price agreed upon by the seller and the buyer. It is not unusual for the purchase agreement to reflect the emotional or subjective considerations that are valuable to both buyer and seller, but are not pertinent to the actual market value of the property.

It is the "true" market value that a lender seeks, because if a foreclosure is ever necessary, the lender has some assurance that the property can be sold for an amount that can enable them to recover most, if not all, of their investment.

A. LTV AND MAXIMUM LOAN AMOUNT

As we discussed in a previous chapter, loans are generally made at a loan-to-value ratio of from 80% to 90% of the value of the property. Thus, if a property was appraised at $100,000 and a lender's maximum LTV ratio is 80%, the maximum loan would be $80,000. Lenders generally make loans based on either the sales price or the appraised value, **whichever is lower**.

Example:

$180,000.00 Sales Price
$150,000.00 Appraised Value

$150,000.00 Appraised Value
x .80 Loan-to-Value Ratio
$120,000.00 Maximum Loan

Figure 14-1

Uniform Residential Appraisal Report

File #

This report form is designed to report an appraisal of a one-unit property or a one-unit property with an accessory unit; including a unit in a planned unit development (PUD). This report form is not designed to report an appraisal of a manufactured home or a unit in a condominium or cooperative project.

This appraisal report is subject to the following scope of work, intended use, intended user, definition of market value, statement of assumptions and limiting conditions, and certifications. Modifications, additions, or deletions to the intended use, intended user, definition of market value, or assumptions and limiting conditions are not permitted. The appraiser may expand the scope of work to include any additional research or analysis necessary based on the complexity of this appraisal assignment. Modifications or deletions to the certifications are also not permitted. However, additional certifications that do not constitute material alterations to this appraisal report, such as those required by law or those related to the appraiser's continuing education or membership in an appraisal organization, are permitted.

SCOPE OF WORK: The scope of work for this appraisal is defined by the complexity of this appraisal assignment and the reporting requirements of this appraisal report form, including the following definition of market value, statement of assumptions and limiting conditions, and certifications. The appraiser must, at a minimum: (1) perform a complete visual inspection of the interior and exterior areas of the subject property, (2) inspect the neighborhood, (3) inspect each of the comparable sales from at least the street, (4) research, verify, and analyze data from reliable public and/or private sources, and (5) report his or her analysis, opinions, and conclusions in this appraisal report.

INTENDED USE: The intended use of this appraisal report is for the lender/client to evaluate the property that is the subject of this appraisal for a mortgage finance transaction.

INTENDED USER: The intended user of this appraisal report is the lender/client.

DEFINITION OF MARKET VALUE: The most probable price which a property should bring in a competitive and open market under all conditions requisite to a fair sale, the buyer and seller, each acting prudently, knowledgeably and assuming the price is not affected by undue stimulus. Implicit in this definition is the consummation of a sale as of a specified date and the passing of title from seller to buyer under conditions whereby: (1) buyer and seller are typically motivated; (2) both parties are well informed or well advised, and each acting in what he or she considers his or her own best interest; (3) a reasonable time is allowed for exposure in the open market; (4) payment is made in terms of cash in U. S. dollars or in terms of financial arrangements comparable thereto; and (5) the price represents the normal consideration for the property sold unaffected by special or creative financing or sales concessions* granted by anyone associated with the sale.

*Adjustments to the comparables must be made for special or creative financing or sales concessions. No adjustments are necessary for those costs which are normally paid by sellers as a result of tradition or law in a market area; these costs are readily identifiable since the seller pays these costs in virtually all sales transactions. Special or creative financing adjustments can be made to the comparable property by comparisons to financing terms offered by a third party institutional lender that is not already involved in the property or transaction. Any adjustment should not be calculated on a mechanical dollar for dollar cost of the financing or concession but the dollar amount of any adjustment should approximate the market's reaction to the financing or concessions based on the appraiser's judgment.

STATEMENT OF ASSUMPTIONS AND LIMITING CONDITIONS: The appraiser's certification in this report is subject to the following assumptions and limiting conditions:

1. The appraiser will not be responsible for matters of a legal nature that affect either the property being appraised or the title to it, except for information that he or she became aware of during the research involved in performing this appraisal. The appraiser assumes that the title is good and marketable and will not render any opinions about the title.

2. The appraiser has provided a sketch in this appraisal report to show the approximate dimensions of the improvements. The sketch is included only to assist the reader in visualizing the property and understanding the appraiser's determination of its size.

3. The appraiser has examined the available flood maps that are provided by the Federal Emergency Management Agency (or other data sources) and has noted in this appraisal report whether any portion of the subject site is located in an identified Special Flood Hazard Area. Because the appraiser is not a surveyor, he or she makes no guarantees, express or implied, regarding this determination.

4. The appraiser will not give testimony or appear in court because he or she made an appraisal of the property in question, unless specific arrangements to do so have been made beforehand, or as otherwise required by law.

5. The appraiser has noted in this appraisal report any adverse conditions (such as needed repairs, deterioration, the presence of hazardous wastes, toxic substances, etc.) observed during the inspection of the subject property or that he or she became aware of during the research involved in performing this appraisal. Unless otherwise stated in this appraisal report, the appraiser has no knowledge of any hidden or unapparent physical deficiencies or adverse conditions of the property (such as, but not limited to, needed repairs, deterioration, the presence of hazardous wastes, toxic substances, adverse environmental conditions, etc.) that would make the property less valuable, and has assumed that there are no such conditions and makes no guarantees or warranties, express or implied. The appraiser will not be responsible for any such conditions that do exist or for any engineering or testing that might be required to discover whether such conditions exist. Because the appraiser is not an expert in the field of environmental hazards, this appraisal report must not be considered as an environmental assessment of the property.

6. The appraiser has based his or her appraisal report and valuation conclusion for an appraisal that is subject to satisfactory completion, repairs, or alterations on the assumption that the completion, repairs, or alterations of the subject property will be performed in a professional manner.

Freddie Mac Form 70 March 2005 | Page 4 of 6 | Fannie Mae Form 1004 March 2005

Uniform Residential Appraisal Report

File #

APPRAISER'S CERTIFICATION: The Appraiser certifies and agrees that:

1. I have, at a minimum, developed and reported this appraisal in accordance with the scope of work requirements stated in this appraisal report.

2. I performed a complete visual inspection of the interior and exterior areas of the subject property. I reported the condition of the improvements in factual, specific terms. I identified and reported the physical deficiencies that could affect the livability, soundness, or structural integrity of the property.

3. I performed this appraisal in accordance with the requirements of the Uniform Standards of Professional Appraisal Practice that were adopted and promulgated by the Appraisal Standards Board of The Appraisal Foundation and that were in place at the time this appraisal report was prepared.

4. I developed my opinion of the market value of the real property that is the subject of this report based on the sales comparison approach to value. I have adequate comparable market data to develop a reliable sales comparison approach for this appraisal assignment. I further certify that I considered the cost and income approaches to value but did not develop them, unless otherwise indicated in this report.

5. I researched, verified, analyzed, and reported on any current agreement for sale for the subject property, any offering for sale of the subject property in the twelve months prior to the effective date of this appraisal, and the prior sales of the subject property for a minimum of three years prior to the effective date of this appraisal, unless otherwise indicated in this report.

6. I researched, verified, analyzed, and reported on the prior sales of the comparable sales for a minimum of one year prior to the date of sale of the comparable sale, unless otherwise indicated in this report.

7. I selected and used comparable sales that are locationally, physically, and functionally the most similar to the subject property.

8. I have not used comparable sales that were the result of combining a land sale with the contract purchase price of a home that has been built or will be built on the land.

9. I have reported adjustments to the comparable sales that reflect the market's reaction to the differences between the subject property and the comparable sales.

10. I verified, from a disinterested source, all information in this report that was provided by parties who have a financial interest in the sale or financing of the subject property.

11. I have knowledge and experience in appraising this type of property in this market area.

12. I am aware of, and have access to, the necessary and appropriate public and private data sources, such as multiple listing services, tax assessment records, public land records and other such data sources for the area in which the property is located.

13. I obtained the information, estimates, and opinions furnished by other parties and expressed in this appraisal report from reliable sources that I believe to be true and correct.

14. I have taken into consideration the factors that have an impact on value with respect to the subject neighborhood, subject property, and the proximity of the subject property to adverse influences in the development of my opinion of market value. I have noted in this appraisal report any adverse conditions (such as, but not limited to, needed repairs, deterioration, the presence of hazardous wastes, toxic substances, adverse environmental conditions, etc.) observed during the inspection of the subject property or that I became aware of during the research involved in performing this appraisal. I have considered these adverse conditions in my analysis of the property value, and have reported on the effect of the conditions on the value and marketability of the subject property.

15. I have not knowingly withheld any significant information from this appraisal report and, to the best of my knowledge, all statements and information in this appraisal report are true and correct.

16. I stated in this appraisal report my own personal, unbiased, and professional analysis, opinions, and conclusions, which are subject only to the assumptions and limiting conditions in this appraisal report.

17. I have no present or prospective interest in the property that is the subject of this report, and I have no present or prospective personal interest or bias with respect to the participants in the transaction. I did not base, either partially or completely, my analysis and/or opinion of market value in this appraisal report on the race, color, religion, sex, age, marital status, handicap, familial status, or national origin of either the prospective owners or occupants of the subject property or of the present owners or occupants of the properties in the vicinity of the subject property or on any other basis prohibited by law.

18. My employment and/or compensation for performing this appraisal or any future or anticipated appraisals was not conditioned on any agreement or understanding, written or otherwise, that I would report (or present analysis supporting) a predetermined specific value, a predetermined minimum value, a range or direction in value, a value that favors the cause of any party, or the attainment of a specific result or occurrence of a specific subsequent event (such as approval of a pending mortgage loan application).

19. I personally prepared all conclusions and opinions about the real estate that were set forth in this appraisal report. If I relied on significant real property appraisal assistance from any individual or individuals in the performance of this appraisal or the preparation of this appraisal report, I have named such individual(s) and disclosed the specific tasks performed in this appraisal report. I certify that any individual so named is qualified to perform the tasks. I have not authorized anyone to make a change to any item in this appraisal report; therefore, any change made to this appraisal is unauthorized and I will take no responsibility for it.

20. I identified the lender/client in this appraisal report who is the individual, organization, or agent for the organization that ordered and will receive this appraisal report.

Freddie Mac Form 70 March 2005 | Page 5 of 6 | Fannie Mae Form 1004 March 2005

Uniform Residential Appraisal Report

File #

21. The lender/client may disclose or distribute this appraisal report to: the borrower; another lender at the request of the borrower; the mortgagee or its successors and assigns; mortgage insurers; government sponsored enterprises; other secondary market participants; data collection or reporting services; professional appraisal organizations; any department, agency, or instrumentality of the United States; and any state, the District of Columbia, or other jurisdictions; without having to obtain the appraiser's or supervisory appraiser's (if applicable) consent. Such consent must be obtained before this appraisal report may be disclosed or distributed to any other party (including, but not limited to, the public through advertising, public relations, news, sales, or other media).

22. I am aware that any disclosure or distribution of this appraisal report by me or the lender/client may be subject to certain laws and regulations. Further, I am also subject to the provisions of the Uniform Standards of Professional Appraisal Practice that pertain to disclosure or distribution by me.

23. The borrower, another lender at the request of the borrower, the mortgagee or its successors and assigns, mortgage insurers, government sponsored enterprises, and other secondary market participants may rely on this appraisal report as part of any mortgage finance transaction that involves any one or more of these parties.

24. If this appraisal report was transmitted as an "electronic record" containing my "electronic signature," as those terms are defined in applicable federal and/or state laws (excluding audio and video recordings), or a facsimile transmission of this appraisal report containing a copy or representation of my signature, the appraisal report shall be as effective, enforceable and valid as if a paper version of this appraisal report were delivered containing my original hand written signature.

25. Any intentional or negligent misrepresentation(s) contained in this appraisal report may result in civil liability and/or criminal penalties including, but not limited to, fine or imprisonment or both under the provisions of Title 18, United States Code, Section 1001, et seq., or similar state laws.

SUPERVISORY APPRAISER'S CERTIFICATION: The Supervisory Appraiser certifies and agrees that:

1. I directly supervised the appraiser for this appraisal assignment, have read the appraisal report, and agree with the appraiser's analysis, opinions, statements, conclusions, and the appraiser's certification.

2. I accept full responsibility for the contents of this appraisal report including, but not limited to, the appraiser's analysis, opinions, statements, conclusions, and the appraiser's certification.

3. The appraiser identified in this appraisal report is either a sub-contractor or an employee of the supervisory appraiser (or the appraisal firm), is qualified to perform this appraisal, and is acceptable to perform this appraisal under the applicable state law.

4. This appraisal report complies with the Uniform Standards of Professional Appraisal Practice that were adopted and promulgated by the Appraisal Standards Board of The Appraisal Foundation and that were in place at the time this appraisal report was prepared.

5. If this appraisal report was transmitted as an "electronic record" containing my "electronic signature," as those terms are defined in applicable federal and/or state laws (excluding audio and video recordings), or a facsimile transmission of this appraisal report containing a copy or representation of my signature, the appraisal report shall be as effective, enforceable and valid as if a paper version of this appraisal report were delivered containing my original hand written signature.

APPRAISER

Signature __________
Name __________
Company Name __________
Company Address __________
____
Telephone Number __________
Email Address __________
Date of Signature and Report __________
Effective Date of Appraisal __________
State Certification # __________
or State License # __________
or Other (describe) __________ State # __________
State __________
Expiration Date of Certification or License __________

ADDRESS OF PROPERTY APPRAISED
____
____

APPRAISED VALUE OF SUBJECT PROPERTY $ __________

LENDER/CLIENT
Name __________
Company Name __________
Company Address __________
____
Email Address __________

SUPERVISORY APPRAISER (ONLY IF REQUIRED)

Signature __________
Name __________
Company Name __________
Company Address __________
____
Telephone Number __________
Email Address __________
Date of Signature __________
State Certification # __________
or State License # __________
State __________
Expiration Date of Certification or License __________

SUBJECT PROPERTY

☐ Did not inspect subject property
☐ Did inspect exterior of subject property from street
Date of Inspection __________
☐ Did inspect interior and exterior of subject property
Date of Inspection __________

COMPARABLE SALES

☐ Did not inspect exterior of comparable sales from street
☐ Did inspect exterior of comparable sales from street
Date of Inspection __________

Freddie Mac Form 70 March 2005 — Page 6 of 6 — Fannie Mae Form 1004 March 2005

In the example, the maximum loan is predicated on the lower appraised value, not the higher sales price. If the lender were to base the loan on the higher of the two figures, it would be loaning an amount that would be 96% of the appraised market value. This is obviously unacceptable.

B. ESTIMATING MARKET VALUE

It is not necessary for agents and loan officers to be able to appraise properties. However, it is helpful to understand the mechanics of the appraisal process and to know something about the reasoning and logic that underlies many of the appraiser's conclusions.

For real estate agents, an understanding of how lenders and their appraisers perceive value will enable them to write and arrange financing for sales that will hold together.

Appraisers use three approaches to determine value in residential appraisal: the **market approach**, the **cost approach**, and the **income approach**. While all three approaches are utilized, the market approach is generally given the most weight by residential appraisers.

II. Market Approach

The market approach to value is the most easily understood by the layman.

The ***MARKET APPROACH*** *involves a comparison of the property being appraised against other similar properties in the same neighborhood that have recently sold.* Appraisers know that no informed buyer who is acting free of pressure will pay more for a particular property than he or she would have to pay for an equally desirable substitute property. An informed seller is not likely to sell for less than is necessary, and if he or she is objective, the selling price will be based on the results of recent sales in the neighborhood.

The property sales that appraisers actually use are those that have closed escrow. These are considered the best indicators of actual value.

Asking or listing prices are only helpful to the appraiser to the extent that they indicate the general upward or downward trend of the market in the area. Often the asking price of a property is set at a figure that is slightly higher than the seller expects to receive. This practice leaves the seller negotiating room, and permits the buyer to claim the victory of a successful downward negotiation in the sales price of the property.

A. IDENTIFYING LEGITIMATE COMPARABLES

When utilizing the market approach, the appraiser must be certain that the sales used as a basis for comparison are, in fact, relevant in terms of the factors that have the most impact on value.

1. Metropolitan Statistical Areas

Appraisers utilize a great deal of information from the U.S. Bureau of the Census. Much of this information involves statistical analysis and information from Metropolitan Statistical areas. A ***METROPOLITAN STATISTICAL AREA*** *is an area with a core city population of 50,000 people and the area surrounding it*. The information obtained from these areas is considered to be significant to business, industry, and consumer groups. Much of this information is provided using **graphs, bar graphs**, and **pie charts** (see **Figure 14-3**). In addition, most of this information is presented utilizing measures of **central tendency** (see **Figure 14-2**).

While statistical information may be shown in lists and charts, it is often more easily understood when shown in a visual form. *Bar graphs may be combined with a frequency curve to provide what is known as a* ***HISTOGRAM*** (see **Figure 14-3**).

A Histogram connects the centers of each bar on a bar graph.

FREQUENCY CURVES *show not only the measure of central tendency but the dispersion of the units or numbers surrounding it*. This dispersion may be **left skewed, right skewed**, or **normal** (see **Figure 14-3**). *A normal frequency curve is commonly called a* ***BELL CURVE***. The peak of the curve is the central measure. A normal frequency curve would have a **mean, median**, and **modal number** that is identical.

2. Multiple Regression Analysis

Another tool consists of the use of ***MULTIPLE REGRESSION ANALYSIS***, *which is a statistical procedure that attempts to assess the relationship between a dependent variable and two or more independent variables*. A number of electronic programs have been developed to take the information obtained from statistical analysis and compute suggested line-item value adjustments. Before computers, a simple regression analysis could require hundreds, if not thousands, of rigorous hand calculations. Now these can be performed in seconds on a computer.

3. Automated Valuation Models (AVMs)

Currently, a popular tool for the selection of comparable sales, the ***AUTOMATED VALUATION MODEL (AVM)***, *which is a computer-generated valuation report*, has become the darling of the lending industry. Many residential lenders accept AVM reports in lieu of traditional appraisals for both first and second mortgages. The

Figure 14-2

Measures of Central Tendency

Appraisers often calculate averages to determine predominant values in a neighborhood, average rent prices, and gross rent multipliers. Additionally, information from the U.S. Bureau of the Census and other statistical data is often presented as an average. Calling something average has a number of different meanings, and the appraiser has to be conversant with them all. The common ways to measure central tendency (average) are the **mean**, **median**, and **mode**.

In the sample of values listed below:

1
2
3
4
4

2.8 is the mean
3 is the median
4 is the mode
1-4 is the range

MEAN is the arithmetic average, which is calculated by adding all the values in the sample to arrive at a sum and then dividing by the number of items in the sample. This method is generally used by real estate agents when referring to "average" square footage or "average" price.

MEDIAN is the middle value in a sample of values. In the sample above, "3" is the median because there are an equal number of values above and below it (two higher and two lower). Real estate publications often refer to the median price of housing in a particular state, city, or county.

MODE is the most frequently occurring value in a sample. In the sample above, "4" is the mode. Modal prices of similar housing would be of interest to an appraiser in developing comparables.

RANGE is the spread between the lowest and highest numbers in the sample. Appraisers, for instance, would be interested in the lowest and highest prices paid for housing in a neighborhood.

STANDARD DEVIATION is a mathematical formula that measures how far the prices vary from the mean (arithmetic average). For example, a small standard deviation would mean that most of the prices are approximately the same. The greater the standard deviation, the more the prices would vary.

Figure 14-3

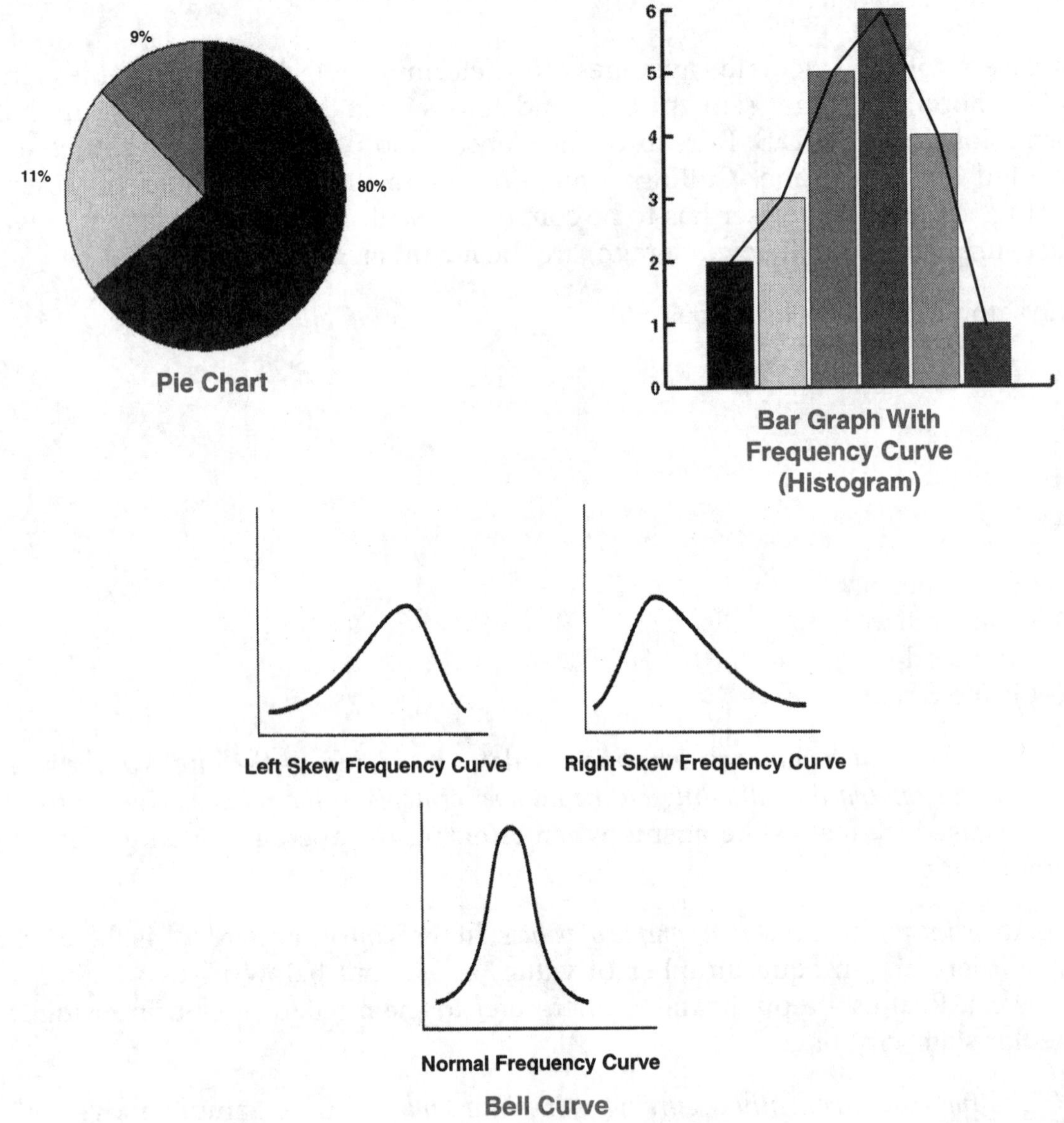

9%
11%
80%

Pie Chart

6
5
4
3
2
1
0

Bar Graph With Frequency Curve (Histogram)

Left Skew Frequency Curve

Right Skew Frequency Curve

Normal Frequency Curve

Bell Curve

concept behind the practice is that it is quick and less expensive than the traditional appraisal process. It is also assumed, by some, that because the "human element" is removed, the result is somehow less biased and more accurate.

In ancient times (twenty years ago), appraisers got information about sales from public microfiche, multiple listings sales books, and actual visits to local area brokers. The appraiser would then manually select those properties from this information that he or she considered comparable and then inspect the subject property inside and out, as well as inspect the comparable sales from outside at a minimum. This process was greatly speeded up by computers that allowed the appraisers to create incredibly rapid reports. Computers also permitted more rapid comparable selection through the development of programs to take information from **Multiple Listing Services (MLSs)** and **County Recording Offices** online.

Other analytical tools, such as multiple regression analysis (originally used by assessors) and AVM models were developed to help make comparable analysis easier. An AVM can review and select from hundreds of properties within seconds. If the AVM is combined with a regression analysis program it can provide a bottom line value in seconds. Current AVMs may use multiple regression, neural network (fuzzy logic), or appraiser-emulated programs. They may also allow manual user input or not, depending on the program. No commercially available AVM programs will allow the user to know the equations used in AVM calculations. This is considered proprietary information by the program providers. The question might be asked: "Why do we need an appraiser?"

Well, it turns out that most AVMs are only accurate about 65% of the time. This is because of the "human element" that is responsible for the design of the programs and the raw data input into the programs. All economic and appraisal modeling programs require proper calibration by the user. In addition, the raw data put into many models is often unverified and incorrect. For example, most county property data is anywhere from 10-15 years old and may not include homeowner upgrade information. New pools, spas, patios, kitchen and bath remodels, and room additions may be entirely left out or misstated by those who input the information. If a residence is waterfront property, it will most likely be compared to non-waterfront property by the AVM. The AVM program assumes that every residence in your area is of the same quality and condition. In other words, an AVM, like all so-called Artificial Intelligence Programs (AI), cannot think for itself!

This being said, many of these programs are being falsely described as "appraisals" by those who sell them to lenders and others. When they are taken at face value as such, great harm may come to those who rely on them.

Field experience has shown that AVMs can greatly undervalue and overvalue neighboring properties.

Example: Recently, two residences in the same neighborhood were valued by an AVM program for the authors. The square footage of the houses in the neighborhood range from 1,000 to 2,000 square feet. All houses were the same age and built by the same builder. The first residence was 1145 square feet, 3 bedrooms, 1.5 baths, and a patio deck. The house had new carpet. The house sold for $645,000. The AVM valued it at $645,000. The second house, which was next door, was 1560 square feet, 3 bedrooms, and 2 baths. It had a covered patio, new driveway, new garage door, new roof, recently remodeled kitchen and baths, new carpet, new vinyl windows, new interior and exterior doors, new heating and air conditioning system and new paint inside/out. This house was valued by the AVM at $638,000. All the improvements for the second house were contractor installed and had building permits. These do not show up on the tax roll however, so apparently the AVM and those who input information to it, as well as those who use this information, were not aware of them or of the value they added to this house!

The example above illustrates the dangers involved in relying on an AVM alone. Imagine the owner of the second house getting one of these online AVM reports and listing his house at the "appraised" value. Could he sue the AVM provider if he lost money as a result? What about a borrower who was allowed to borrow against an inflated AVM value? What if, after finding out that they were upside down in the loan (owe more than the house is worth), they walk away and leave the lender holding the bag?

4. Appraiser Assisted AVMs

To try to answer these problems (and they are a very real ones, indeed) the industry has developed the ***APPRAISER ASSISTED AUTOMATED VALUATION MODEL (AAAVM).*** *These programs are modified to allow an appraiser to manually input information, make some adjustments, and do minimal calibration (depending on the program).* Also, the appraiser signs off on the result which takes care of who is liable for the accuracy of the AVM. So much for leaving out the "human element"!

In their October 2006 newsletter, FNMA announced that they will allow AVM assisted appraisals in conjunction with their ***PROPERTY INSPECTION ALTERNATIVE PROGRAM,*** *which allows a lender to loan without a property inspection.* As of our publication date, they have not as yet published specific guidelines of how this system is expected to work.

AVMs have the potential in the hands of an appraiser who understands the theory and mathematical formulae behind the model and can thus calibrate it properly, to shorten the necessary research time of an appraisal. Once again, an AVM is one of the tools that may be used in an appraisal. It is a very dangerous tool in the hands of those who seek to replace an appraisal by blindly relying on the information provided by just the AVM.

5. Sale Date of the Comparable Sale

The sale should be recent—within the past six months, if possible.

The sale may not be over one year old. Recent sales are used because they most accurately reflect what is occurring in the current market and do not require adjustments for time. Older sales, up to one year in time, may have to be adjusted to reflect any inflationary or deflationary trends that have taken place since the sale. Adjustments for time are tricky and can sometimes be based on faulty or misapplied statistical analysis. An appraiser must be able to both understand and properly apply statistical information.

> **Example:** Prices for homes in Wagner City have risen by 17% within one year. A home that was worth $300,000 eleven months ago is adjusted upwards 17%. There is nothing wrong with that, right? Wrong! First of all, the percentage was for a whole year, not eleven months. The statistical percentage, if correct, would have to be prorated. But the most important detail might be that research of sales of homes in the specific neighborhood shows that prices actually declined in value by 3%. Therefore, the comparable's time adjustment would be overvalued by 20%!

6. Location of the Comparable Sale

Comparables should be selected from the neighborhood of the subject property.

In the absence of any legitimate comparable sales in the neighborhood, the appraiser can select comparables from nearby similar neighborhoods. Care must be taken that the properties and the neighborhoods have similar physical and demographic characteristics.

It is generally conceded that location contributes more to the value of real estate than any other characteristic.

7. Physical Characteristics

To qualify as a comparable, a property should have physical characteristics that are essentially similar to the subject property.

8. Terms of Sale

With the increase of seller participation in financing today, the terms of sale have become much more of a factor when estimating value. Buyers have demonstrated a readiness that often borders on foolishness to pay inflated prices for housing. Often, eager sellers have provided extended payment terms and below-market rates while adjusting the price of the house upwards to recover the difference in interest. In these cases, the inflated price paid for the home distorts the actual values in the neighborhood. Where a seller has given extremely favorable terms, there is an excellent chance that the price of the home does not represent the true value of homes in the neighborhood. The appraiser is required to research the terms of sale of comparables to determine what influence they had on the sale price.

9. Arm's Length Transaction

Before a sale can be relied upon as an indication of what the subject property is worth, it must be an *ARM'S LENGTH TRANSACTION. This means that buyer and seller are both well informed, under no pressure to either buy or sell, and that the property is offered for a reasonable time on the open market.*

"Distress sales," REO (real estate owned) bank sales, and trust sales are not considered to be arm's length transactions.

III. Cost Approach

The cost approach is based on the presumption that buyers will not pay more for an older property than the cost of purchasing a newly constructed residence at the site.

Residential appraisers keep abreast of current construction costs in their areas and refer to them when using the cost approach. Cost handbooks utilized by appraisers for each local area are published by major construction cost service firms including **Marshall and Swift** and **Boekh**.

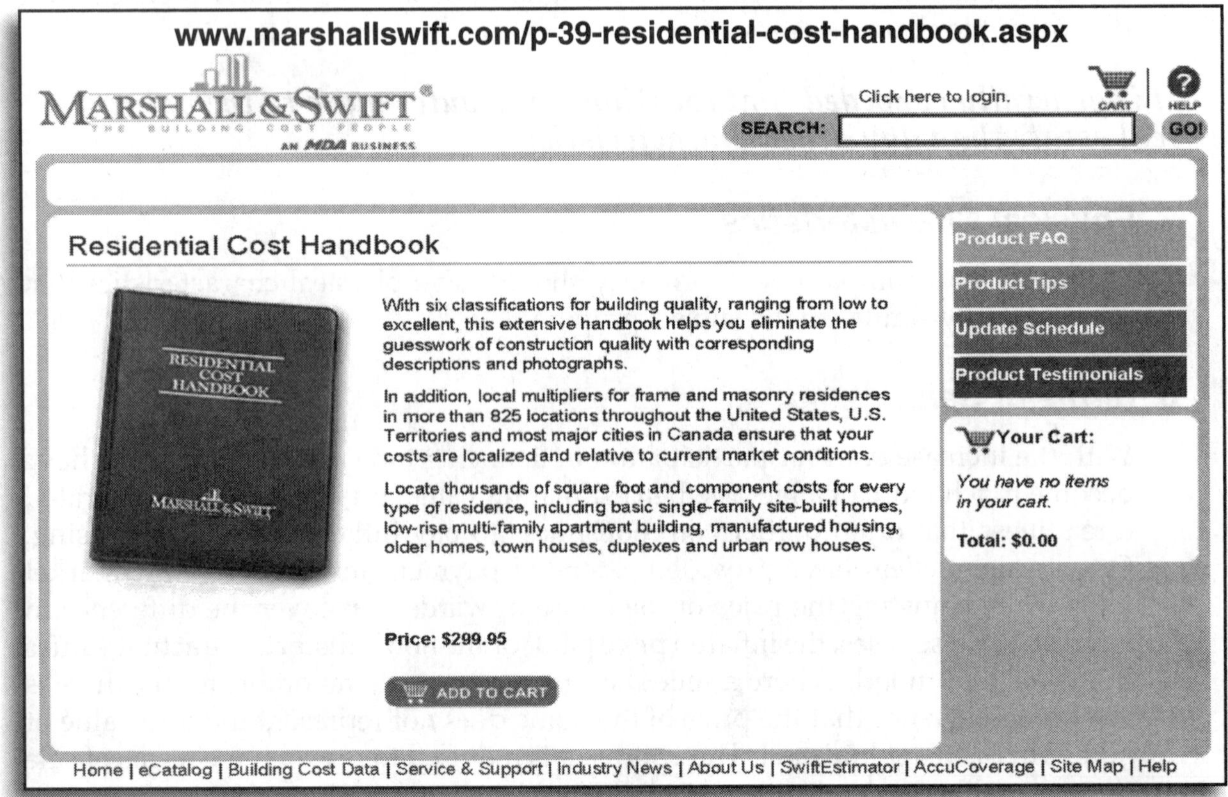

There are three steps in the cost approach:

1. Estimate the cost of replacing the house with a new home that is similar to the existing one utilizing the information from the cost handbook.
2. Estimate and deduct accrued depreciation from all sources.
3. Add the value of the lot to the depreciated value of the house.

The cost handbooks are set up to utilize the square foot method of estimating construction costs.

Once the appraiser has measured the subject property and determined the overall square footage, he or she has only to compare the square footage of the subject with the tables contained in the cost handbook to determine the cost to construct a new house. The appraiser will then deduct all sources of accrued depreciation from the new cost. This is the most difficult part of the process. It is based on the presumption that a used home is not as valuable as a new home and that it may have suffered a loss in value for one of the following three reasons:

1. *Physical deterioration or deferred maintenance (**PHYSICAL OBSOLESCENCE**).*
2. *Inadequacies caused by poor design (**FUNCTIONAL OBSOLESCENCE**).*
3. *Factors outside the property itself, such as a deteriorating neighborhood. (**ECONOMIC OBSOLESCENCE**).*

Physical obsolescence is determined from age/life charts published in the cost handbooks. Functional obsolescence is determined by comparison of the subject's floor plan, materials used, and compliance with current building codes to newly constructed housing.

In most cases, both physical and functional obsolescence are curable.

The ***COST TO CURE*** *refers to the amount of money necessary to repair or replace structural components and functional deficiencies in a structure.* If the cost to cure an item is more than the value added by it being replaced, it is said to be incurable.

Economic obsolescence is based on location and is not curable.

Economic obsolescense results in a permanent loss of value to the property in a residential use.

After depreciation is calculated, the cost of the depreciated structure is added to the land value to determine the overall value by the cost approach. Appraisers have several methods of making this calculation; however, the most desirable determination is made by comparison of actual sales prices of similar building lots.

IV. Income Approach

The majority of single-family residences are not income-producing properties (rentals), so traditional income analysis and appraisal techniques do not apply. However, some single-family residences are rented, for which lenders will request an income approach. Generally, this is provided by using a gross rent multiplier. The ***GROSS RENT MULTIPLIER (GRM)*** *is determined by dividing the sales price of a series of at least three recent sales of similar single family rental properties by their monthly rental income.*

Example: Sales price $100,000 ÷ $900 monthly rent = 111 gross rent multiplier.

The appraiser will then select a multiplier from the range that has been developed. Generally, this will be from the property that is most similar to the subject. He or she will then multiply that multiplier by the subject's rent to determine the value by the income approach. As residential properties are generally rented from month to month rather than by multiyear leases, the contract rent is generally the same as the economic or market rent. However, when there is a long-term lease, the possibility exists that the contract rent may be below market. In that case, the appraiser would have to determine what the subject's current market rent should be.

V. Understanding the Appraisal Process

Real estate agents and loan brokers need to understand the basic steps in the appraisal process because it will help them eliminate, or at least minimize, a prevalent problem that has plagued the industry—both agents and loan brokers tend to overvalue properties. This is because both are concerned with getting the maximum amount for their client, whether they are the seller or the borrower. Also, some listings are set at a higher price than the market will support. When an uninformed buyer and/or his or her agent do not negotiate that price downward, the property can sell at an unrealistic price. If the agent, broker, or loan representative has an unrealistic view of the property's value, they can be assured that an appraiser will rain on their parade. The result will be a low appraisal. There are only five possible responses to a low appraisal:

1. Reduce the sales price to the appraised value.
2. Keep the price where it is and have the buyer make up the difference.
3. Strike a compromise between buyer and seller at a new price between the appraised value and the selling price. Again, the buyer has to make up the difference.
4. Ask for a reconsideration of the appraised value in the hope that it will be increased to the selling price.
5. Terminate the sale.

While it is entirely possible to carry out options 1-3, it is entirely likely that all parties to the transaction will find that distasteful. The seller has a sale at the high price; why should he or she budge? The buyer will claim that he or she is unable to come up with the necessary additional payment. The agents and loan representatives will not want to decrease their commission. This leaves alternative number four. This is a viable response if the agent has done his or her homework, and the appraiser is unaware of data that can be used to justify the higher price or has made errors within the report. In all fairness, appraisers, being human, also make mistakes. Most appraisers are perfectly willing to look at and use information that may help all the parties achieve their goals. Unfortunately, many agents and loan officers do not know how to properly go about this and are left with alternative number five.

A. HOW TO SOLVE PROBLEMS CAUSED BY LOW APPRAISALS

Of course the best way to eliminate the problems created by low appraisals is to avoid them in the first place by pricing properties realistically. A seller should not be given an unrealistic estimate of his property's worth. Even if a buyer can be persuaded to pay the unrealistic price, the appraisal will come back low and the real problems of trying to keep the sale together will set in. If the property could not be priced correctly when listed, an attempt to do so should be made at the time of sale. No case can be made for overstating values when properties are listed and sold, because sooner or later every sale that is dependent on financing must yield to the conclusions of a professional appraiser.

1. Request for Reconsideration of Value

Regardless of how objective an appraiser may be, there are some subjective considerations and conclusions in every report.

An appraisal is an opinion of value.

If you are affected by a low appraisal and sincerely believe that the appraiser has made a mistake, you can appeal his or her decision and, with the proper documentation, get the appraisal increased, possibly to the figure originally requested. Please see the Uniform Residential Appraisal Report (URAR) in **Figure 14-4**. The market analysis is the heart of this form. It shows what informed buyers have been willing to pay in the past for similar properties. The lender can only presume that the value indicated by these comparable sales is what informed buyers will be willing to pay for the property if it is foreclosed and resold. Lenders rely heavily on this comparable sale information.

What this means is that if you disagree with the appraisal and plan to ask the lender to reconsider the appraised amount, you will have to support your request by submitting at least three comparable sales that indicate a higher value estimate

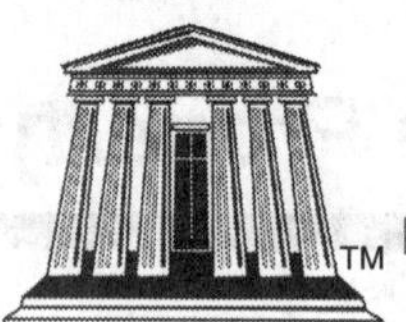

Figure 14-4

Uniform Residential Appraisal Report

File #

The purpose of this summary appraisal report is to provide the lender/client with an accurate, and adequately supported, opinion of the market value of the subject property.

SUBJECT

Property Address | City | State | Zip Code
Borrower | Owner of Public Record | County
Legal Description
Assessor's Parcel # | Tax Year | R.E. Taxes $
Neighborhood Name | Map Reference | Census Tract
Occupant ☐ Owner ☐ Tenant ☐ Vacant | Special Assessments $ | ☐ PUD | HOA $ | ☐ per year ☐ per month
Property Rights Appraised ☐ Fee Simple ☐ Leasehold ☐ Other (describe)
Assignment Type ☐ Purchase Transaction ☐ Refinance Transaction ☐ Other (describe)
Lender/Client | Address
Is the subject property currently offered for sale or has it been offered for sale in the twelve months prior to the effective date of this appraisal? ☐ Yes ☐ No
Report data source(s) used, offering price(s), and date(s).

CONTRACT

I ☐ did ☐ did not analyze the contract for sale for the subject purchase transaction. Explain the results of the analysis of the contract for sale or why the analysis was not performed.

Contract Price $ | Date of Contract | Is the property seller the owner of public record? ☐ Yes ☐ No | Data Source(s)
Is there any financial assistance (loan charges, sale concessions, gift or downpayment assistance, etc.) to be paid by any party on behalf of the borrower? ☐ Yes ☐ No
If Yes, report the total dollar amount and describe the items to be paid.

NEIGHBORHOOD

Note: Race and the racial composition of the neighborhood are not appraisal factors.

Neighborhood Characteristics	One-Unit Housing Trends	One-Unit Housing	Present Land Use %
Location ☐ Urban ☐ Suburban ☐ Rural	Property Values ☐ Increasing ☐ Stable ☐ Declining	PRICE AGE	One-Unit %
Built-Up ☐ Over 75% ☐ 25–75% ☐ Under 25%	Demand/Supply ☐ Shortage ☐ In Balance ☐ Over Supply	$ (000) (yrs)	2-4 Unit %
Growth ☐ Rapid ☐ Stable ☐ Slow	Marketing Time ☐ Under 3 mths ☐ 3–6 mths ☐ Over 6 mths	Low	Multi-Family %
Neighborhood Boundaries		High	Commercial %
		Pred.	Other %

Neighborhood Description

Market Conditions (including support for the above conclusions)

SITE

Dimensions | Area | Shape | View
Specific Zoning Classification | Zoning Description
Zoning Compliance ☐ Legal ☐ Legal Nonconforming (Grandfathered Use) ☐ No Zoning ☐ Illegal (describe)
Is the highest and best use of the subject property as improved (or as proposed per plans and specifications) the present use? ☐ Yes ☐ No If No, describe

Utilities	Public	Other (describe)		Public	Other (describe)	Off-site Improvements—Type	Public	Private
Electricity	☐	☐	Water	☐	☐	Street	☐	☐
Gas	☐	☐	Sanitary Sewer	☐	☐	Alley	☐	☐

FEMA Special Flood Hazard Area ☐ Yes ☐ No | FEMA Flood Zone | FEMA Map # | FEMA Map Date
Are the utilities and off-site improvements typical for the market area? ☐ Yes ☐ No If No, describe
Are there any adverse site conditions or external factors (easements, encroachments, environmental conditions, land uses, etc.)? ☐ Yes ☐ No If Yes, describe

IMPROVEMENTS

General Description	Foundation	Exterior Description materials/condition	Interior materials/condition
Units ☐ One ☐ One with Accessory Unit	☐ Concrete Slab ☐ Crawl Space	Foundation Walls	Floors
# of Stories	☐ Full Basement ☐ Partial Basement	Exterior Walls	Walls
Type ☐ Det. ☐ Att. ☐ S-Det./End Unit	Basement Area sq. ft.	Roof Surface	Trim/Finish
☐ Existing ☐ Proposed ☐ Under Const.	Basement Finish %	Gutters & Downspouts	Bath Floor
Design (Style)	☐ Outside Entry/Exit ☐ Sump Pump	Window Type	Bath Wainscot
Year Built	Evidence of ☐ Infestation	Storm Sash/Insulated	Car Storage ☐ None
Effective Age (Yrs)	☐ Dampness ☐ Settlement	Screens	☐ Driveway # of Cars
Attic ☐ None	Heating ☐ FWA ☐ HWBB ☐ Radiant	Amenities ☐ Woodstove(s) #	Driveway Surface
☐ Drop Stair ☐ Stairs	☐ Other Fuel	☐ Fireplace(s) # ☐ Fence	☐ Garage # of Cars
☐ Floor ☐ Scuttle	Cooling ☐ Central Air Conditioning	☐ Patio/Deck ☐ Porch	☐ Carport # of Cars
☐ Finished ☐ Heated	☐ Individual ☐ Other	☐ Pool ☐ Other	☐ Att. ☐ Det. ☐ Built-in

Appliances ☐ Refrigerator ☐ Range/Oven ☐ Dishwasher ☐ Disposal ☐ Microwave ☐ Washer/Dryer ☐ Other (describe)
Finished area **above** grade contains: | Rooms | Bedrooms | Bath(s) | Square Feet of Gross Living Area Above Grade
Additional features (special energy efficient items, etc.)
Describe the condition of the property (including needed repairs, deterioration, renovations, remodeling, etc.).

Are there any physical deficiencies or adverse conditions that affect the livability, soundness, or structural integrity of the property? ☐ Yes ☐ No If Yes, describe

Does the property generally conform to the neighborhood (functional utility, style, condition, use, construction, etc.)? ☐ Yes ☐ No If No, describe

Freddie Mac Form 70 March 2005 | Page 1 of 6 | Fannie Mae Form 1004 March 2005

Uniform Residential Appraisal Report

File #

There are comparable properties currently offered for sale in the subject neighborhood ranging in price from $ to $.

There are comparable sales in the subject neighborhood within the past twelve months ranging in sale price from $ to $.

FEATURE	SUBJECT	COMPARABLE SALE # 1		COMPARABLE SALE # 2		COMPARABLE SALE # 3	
Address							
Proximity to Subject							
Sale Price	$		$		$		$
Sale Price/Gross Liv. Area	$ sq. ft.	$ sq. ft.		$ sq. ft.		$ sq. ft.	
Data Source(s)							
Verification Source(s)							
VALUE ADJUSTMENTS	DESCRIPTION	DESCRIPTION	+(-) $ Adjustment	DESCRIPTION	+(-) $ Adjustment	DESCRIPTION	+(-) $ Adjustment
Sale or Financing Concessions							
Date of Sale/Time							
Location							
Leasehold/Fee Simple							
Site							
View							
Design (Style)							
Quality of Construction							
Actual Age							
Condition							
Above Grade Room Count	Total Bdrms. Baths	Total Bdrms. Baths		Total Bdrms. Baths		Total Bdrms. Baths	
Gross Living Area	sq. ft.	sq. ft.		sq. ft.		sq. ft.	
Basement & Finished Rooms Below Grade							
Functional Utility							
Heating/Cooling							
Energy Efficient Items							
Garage/Carport							
Porch/Patio/Deck							
Net Adjustment (Total)		☐ + ☐ -	$	☐ + ☐ -	$	☐ + ☐ -	$
Adjusted Sale Price of Comparables		Net Adj. % Gross Adj. %	$	Net Adj. % Gross Adj. %	$	Net Adj. % Gross Adj. %	$

SALES COMPARISON APPROACH

I ☐ did ☐ did not research the sale or transfer history of the subject property and comparable sales. If not, explain

My research ☐ did ☐ did not reveal any prior sales or transfers of the subject property for the three years prior to the effective date of this appraisal.

Data source(s)

My research ☐ did ☐ did not reveal any prior sales or transfers of the comparable sales for the year prior to the date of sale of the comparable sale.

Data source(s)

Report the results of the research and analysis of the prior sale or transfer history of the subject property and comparable sales (report additional prior sales on page 3).

ITEM	SUBJECT	COMPARABLE SALE # 1	COMPARABLE SALE # 2	COMPARABLE SALE # 3
Date of Prior Sale/Transfer				
Price of Prior Sale/Transfer				
Data Source(s)				
Effective Date of Data Source(s)				

Analysis of prior sale or transfer history of the subject property and comparable sales

Summary of Sales Comparison Approach

Indicated Value by Sales Comparison Approach $

RECONCILIATION

Indicated Value by: Sales Comparison Approach $ Cost Approach (if developed) $ Income Approach (if developed) $

This appraisal is made ☐ "as is", ☐ subject to completion per plans and specifications on the basis of a hypothetical condition that the improvements have been completed, ☐ subject to the following repairs or alterations on the basis of a hypothetical condition that the repairs or alterations have been completed, or ☐ subject to the following required inspection based on the extraordinary assumption that the condition or deficiency does not require alteration or repair:

Based on a complete visual inspection of the interior and exterior areas of the subject property, defined scope of work, statement of assumptions and limiting conditions, and appraiser's certification, my (our) opinion of the market value, as defined, of the real property that is the subject of this report is $, as of , which is the date of inspection and the effective date of this appraisal.

Freddie Mac Form 70 March 2005 Page 2 of 6 Fannie Mae Form 1004 March 2005

Uniform Residential Appraisal Report

File #

ADDITIONAL COMMENTS

COST APPROACH TO VALUE (not required by Fannie Mae)

Provide adequate information for the lender/client to replicate the below cost figures and calculations.

Support for the opinion of site value (summary of comparable land sales or other methods for estimating site value)

ESTIMATED ☐ REPRODUCTION OR ☐ REPLACEMENT COST NEW	OPINION OF SITE VALUE = $
Source of cost data	Dwelling Sq. Ft. @ $ =$
Quality rating from cost service Effective date of cost data	Sq. Ft. @ $ =$
Comments on Cost Approach (gross living area calculations, depreciation, etc.)	
	Garage/Carport Sq. Ft. @ $ =$
	Total Estimate of Cost-New = $
	Less Physical Functional External
	Depreciation =$( )
	Depreciated Cost of Improvements =$
	"As-is" Value of Site Improvements =$
Estimated Remaining Economic Life (HUD and VA only) Years	Indicated Value By Cost Approach =$

INCOME APPROACH TO VALUE (not required by Fannie Mae)

Estimated Monthly Market Rent $ X Gross Rent Multiplier = $ Indicated Value by Income Approach

Summary of Income Approach (including support for market rent and GRM)

PROJECT INFORMATION FOR PUDs (if applicable)

Is the developer/builder in control of the Homeowners' Association (HOA)? ☐ Yes ☐ No Unit type(s) ☐ Detached ☐ Attached

Provide the following information for PUDs ONLY if the developer/builder is in control of the HOA and the subject property is an attached dwelling unit.

Legal name of project

Total number of phases Total number of units Total number of units sold

Total number of units rented Total number of units for sale Data source(s)

Was the project created by the conversion of an existing building(s) into a PUD? ☐ Yes ☐ No If Yes, date of conversion

Does the project contain any multi-dwelling units? ☐ Yes ☐ No Data source(s)

Are the units, common elements, and recreation facilities complete? ☐ Yes ☐ No If No, describe the status of completion.

Are the common elements leased to or by the Homeowners' Association? ☐ Yes ☐ No If Yes, describe the rental terms and options.

Describe common elements and recreational facilities

Freddie Mac Form 70 March 2005 Page 3 of 6 Fannie Mae Form 1004 March 2005

is in order. If you are to convince the lender to accept your comparables over those used by the appraiser, they must be at least as similar to the subject property as the comparables utilized by the appraiser.

2. Format for Reconsideration Request

Lenders are familiar with the market data analysis format used in the URAR. It therefore makes sense to arrange your reconsideration request in much the same way. Write a cover letter making your request to the lender (see **Figure 14-5**). Do not contact the appraiser directly. Both the lender and the appraiser might consider an attempt to contact the appraiser directly as undue pressure. ***UNDUE PRESSURE*** *is an attempt to illegally coerce an appraiser's opinion.* Be aware that, generally, the appraiser has access to nationwide comparable resources, including FNC, Inc. and First American Real Estate Solutions, and in many cases, the Multiple Listing Service (MLS) for your area. ***FNC, INC.*** *provides comparable data of sales from the actual appraisals of those properties.* It is considered to be a highly reliable source of data by appraisers because it is provided by appraisers. The appraiser will have to confirm the information provided by you through at least two of these sources.

All sales that you provide must be sold and closed. Listings are not acceptable. Your best chance of success is that there are several sales that the appraiser did not consider that you feel are more similar to the subject property than those that the appraiser used. Put this information into a market data analysis similar to that shown in Figure 14-5, and provide the reasons why you believe these sales are actually more representative of the subject. Do your homework, be professional, be courteous, and you have a good chance of success. If you are sloppy, you will be facing the dreaded alternative number five.

VI. Key Considerations to a Residential Appraiser

There are many things to consider during the residential appraisal process. Some of them are very important, others are not. The principal method for appraising residential property is the market approach. Since this amounts to a series of comparisons between the subject property and similar properties that have sold recently, it stands to reason that the most critical elements of comparison are the ones that will have the greatest impact on value. If you are also aware of how these add or detract from value, than you will be less likely to be adversely impacted by a low appraisal. When you are confronted with a low appraisal, you will also be better equipped to resolve it. The following is a summary of property features that are considered important by appraisers.

Location. The subject and the comparables should be from the same neighborhood. This is a major consideration for appraisers.

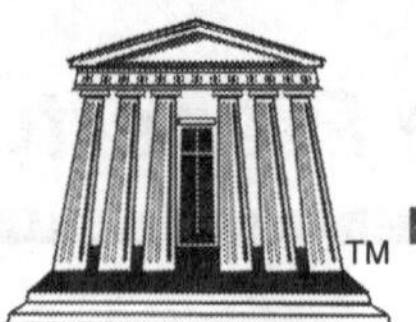

Figure 14-5

REQUEST FOR RECONSIDERATION OF VALUE

Dear Mr. Jewel:

Attached is a market data analysis that supports this request for reconsideration of your value estimate for 412 Acme Drive, dated April 17, 20xx.

I believe the market data presented indicate that an estimate of value in the amount of $138,000 is justified.

Your earliest consideration of this request will be appreciated.

Sincerely,

Thomas M. Crane

MARKET DATA ANALYSIS
412 Acme Road

Item	Subject Prop.	Comparable 1	Comparable 2	Comparable 3
Address	412 Acme Drive	131 Skip Road	221 Sutter St.	168 Bow Road
Sales Price	$135,000	$141,000	$134,500	$129,500
Data Source	sales contract	pres. owner	MLS	selling broker
Date of Sale	9/1/20xx	6/29/20xx	7/14/20xx	5/17/20xx
Location	high qual. suburb	same	same	same
Site/View	inside lot	corner lot	corner lot	inside lot
Design/Appeal	rambler/exc.	same	same	same
Constr. Quality	good	good	good	good
Age	7 yrs.	6 yrs.	8 yrs.	8 yrs.
Conditon	good	good	good	good
No. of Rooms	8	7	7	6
No. of Bedrooms	4	4	3	3
No. of Baths	2½	2½	2	2
Liv. Area (sq. ft.)	2,700	3,300	2,350	2,150
Garage/Carport	2-car attached gar.	same	same	same
Patios, Pools, etc.	15' x 21' patio	15' x 26' patio	18' x 16' patio	15' x 17' patio
Additional Data	2 fireplaces range, oven D/W, disposal central air	2 fireplaces range, oven D/ W central air	1 fireplace range, oven D/ W central air	1 fireplace range, oven D/ W
Comments	Subject has superior energy efficiency to comps 2 and 3 and is at least equal in this respect to comp 1. Principal difference between comps 1 and 2 is square footage.			

Owner Occupied. Owner-occupied neighborhoods are considered to be better maintained and less susceptible to deterioration than rental neighborhoods.

Vacancies. Vacant homes and lots are symptomatic of either declining values or low buyer interest in the area.

Rental Levels. Do rents compare favorably with other areas?

Construction Activity. New home construction indicates increased interest in an area.

Conformity. Values are protected if there is a reasonable level of social and economic homogeneity in the neighborhood. This includes styles, ages, prices, sizes, and construction quality of the housing.

Strictly enforced zoning and private restrictions do much to promote conformity. This is a major consideration for appraisers.

Changing Land Use. Is the neighborhood in transition from residential to another use? If so, the properties within the area are probably declining in value, even though the eventual change may promise higher values because of the potential for more productive use in the future. This is a major consideration for appraisers.

Size and Shape of Lots. Rectangular lots are more desirable than irregular lots. There is no premium for corner lots in residential appraisal. Corner lots have traffic on two sides and possible noise detriment from that traffic. Larger lots have additional value. However, if the lot is vastly greater in size than other lots in the neighborhood (say, a 1 acre lot in a neighborhood of 7500 sq. ft. lots), the added value might be minimal.

Contour of the Land. Mildly rolling is preferred over flat or steep lots.

Street Patterns. Cul-de-sac streets are preferable. Next, wide gently curving streets are more appealing. Streets on main traffic arteries are the least desirable.

Utilities. Are electricity, water, sewer, and telephone service readily available?

Nuisances. For example, close proximity to bad odors, industrial plants, and high noise levels from factories, aircraft, freeways, and trains. This is a major consideration for appraisers.

Proximity to Services. Is the property close to schools, employment, public transportation, and shopping? Is it closely served by police and fire departments? This is a major consideration for appraisers.

Zoning. Does the property have residential zoning and is it enforced? This is a major consideration for appraisers.

Site/View. Is the property of sufficient size for the improvements? Does it have the proper setbacks (distance of improvements from lot lines) required by zoning? Is the property under-improved (more land than is necessary to support the improvements—a 600-square-foot house on twenty acres)? These are major considerations for appraisers. While views certainly add value, the amount they add is in the eye of the beholder (subjective). Do not expect your appraiser to be unduly impressed by the view.

Design and Appeal. Is the property's appeal to the average buyer good, average, or poor? This is a subjective judgment.

Construction Quality. Is the quality of the materials and craftsmanship excellent, good, average, or fair? This is a major appraisal consideration.

Age/Condition. Are the subject and the comparable properties similar in age and condition? This is a major appraisal consideration.

Functional Utility. Is the floor plan and building orientation functional? This is a major appraisal consideration.

Energy-Efficient Items. Even though these items have assumed more importance in a high energy cost world, they can be viewed as an over-improvement of the property with little or no added value if the systems are redundant. For example, having both solar water heating and a gas fired furnace would provide two systems for heating where only one is needed.

Room Count. This includes the overall total of rooms in the house, the number of bedrooms, and the number of baths. Differences in the number of bedrooms and baths can have a notable effect on value. This is a major appraisal consideration.

Square Footage. The overall square footage can have an appreciable impact on market value. Comparables should have square footage that is not more or less than 20% different than the subject property. The closer in size to the subject, the better. This is a major appraisal consideration.

As can be seen from the above, some appraisal considerations are subjective, others are of average importance, and some are major considerations. To successfully challenge an appraisal, it is often necessary to show that a major appraisal consideration has been overlooked or that several comparables that reflect these major appraisal considerations have been overlooked. Another possibility might be that the appraiser is making large downward adjustments in areas that could be considered subjective. In any case, the authors would like to reiterate that the best defense against low appraisals is to list properties at realistic prices.

VII. Rural and Suburban Homes

Properties in outlying areas are eligible for maximum financing by both the primary and secondary market subject to the following conditions:

1. The value of the land is not more than 49% of the overall value of the property.
2. There are adequate public or private utilities in service on the property.
3. The property is accessible by a federal, state, or county highway or an all-weather secondary road.
4. The present or anticipated use of adjacent real estate does not unfavorably affect the value of the property as a residence.

VIII. Atypical Property and Loan Types

***ATYPICAL PROPERTIES**, which are also called nonconforming properties, include, but are not limited to, manufactured homes, dome homes, and log cabins.* These must be appraised by a Certified Level Appraiser only. If there is any atypical or creative financing, the services of a Certified Appraiser must be utilized. Licensed Level Appraisers are only permitted to appraise conforming properties and loans. They are also limited to appraising conforming residential properties that are less than one million dollars in value.

IX. CHAPTER SUMMARY

Lenders demand professional appraisals because they want an entirely objective opinion of the true market values of the properties they loan upon. Loan-to-value ratios are based on the sales price or the appraised value, whichever is lower. The appraisers utilized by lenders are Licensed or Certified. The appraiser's client is the lender, not anyone else associated with the transaction. All appraisers, and those who use their appraisals for federal loan transactions, must adhere to the Uniform Standards of Professional Appraisal Practice (USPAP) as well as state and federal lending and appraisal regulations. The appraiser is required to follow the appraisal process. This is a format that is laid out in the USPAP. For loans, the appraiser is asked to determine the "market value" of the property. This is a specifically defined value that may be either higher or lower than the actual selling price of a property.

Appraisers use the market approach, the cost approach, and the income approach when valuing properties.

The market approach is the most useful for residential properties, as it reflects what actually is occurring in the marketplace. Comparables used in this approach should be recent sales in the same general neighborhood or area as the subject and as similar to the subject as possible. They must be real closed sales at "arm's length."

The cost approach is carried out with the use of cost handbooks. Appraisers estimate the overall accrued depreciation of a property by taking into account any physical, functional, or economic obsolescence that it may have incurred.

The income approach is seldom used unless the property is a rental. Then a Gross Rent Multiplier (GRM) is used to determine value.

It is useful for agents, brokers, and others to understand the appraisal process in order to keep from overvaluing properties and losing sales as a result. While it is possible to successfully challenge a low appraisal, it must be done utilizing established facts that address the key considerations that lenders and appraisers consider in an appraisal. It should be presented to the lender in an understandable format. Wishful thinking and hoping on the part of agents, brokers, and others is insufficient reason for either an appraiser or the lender to change an opinion regarding value.

Atypical property and loan types must be carried out by a Certified Appraiser.

X. TERMINOLOGY

Accrued Depreciation
Appraisal Process
Appraiser Assisted Automated Valuation Model (AAAVM)
Appraiser Client - Lender
Arm's Length Transaction
Atypical Property
Automated Valuation Model (AVM)
Bell Curve
Boekh
Central Tendency
Certified Appraiser
Cost Approach
Cost to Cure
Curable
Economic Obsolescence
Frequency Curves
Functional Obsolescence
Gross Rent Multiplier (GRM)
Histogram
Income Approach
Licensed Appraiser
Market Approach
Market Value
Marshall and Swift
Mean, Median, or Mode Number
Metropolitan Statistical Area
Multiple Listing Service (MLS)
Multiple Regression Analysis
Physical Obsolescence
Property Inspection Alternative Program
Uniform Standards of Professional Appraisal Practice (USPAP)

XI. CHAPTER QUIZ

1. Appraisals of atypical properties may be carried out by:
   a. Certified Appraisers only.
   b. Licensed Appraisers only.
   c. both Licensed and Certified Appraisers.
   d. any real estate professional.

2. The most common ways to measure central tendency include:
   a. mean.
   b. median.
   c. mode.
   d. all the above.

3. The outline of the appraisal process is contained in:
   a. FNMA regulations.
   b. USPAP.
   c. state law.
   d. all the above.

4. Determining economic obsolescence (depreciation) is part of the:
   a. market approach.
   b. cost approach.
   c. income approach.
   d. all the above.

5. If a structural item can be readily repaired or replaced, it is said to be:
   a. curable.
   b. incurable.
   c. functionally obsolescent.
   d. physically obsolescent.

6. A metropolitan statistical area has a core city population of:
   a. 10,000.
   b. 15,000.
   c. 25,000.
   d. 50,000.

7. Appraisers are required to use:
   a. listings.
   b. pending sales.
   c. closed sales.
   d. all the above.

8. The appraiser's client is the:
   a. loan broker.
   b. selling and listing agents.
   c. buyer and seller.
   d. lender.

9. Market value is the:
   a. actual sale price.
   b. price to an individual buyer.
   c. price to a typical buyer.
   d. none of the above.

10. Which of the following is a major appraisal consideration?
    a. Owner-occupied
    b. Conforms to neighborhood
    c. Contour of the land
    d. Design and appeal

ANSWERS: 1. a; 2. d; 3. b; 4. b; 5. a; 6. d; 7. c; 8. d; 9. c; 10. b

LoanProspector
on the Internet

Chapter 15
Real Estate Finance Mathematics

Math is a fundamental tool used in the financing process. As you explain the various finance programs, qualify a buyer for a loan, describe discounts and buy-downs, and determine closing costs, you will be using mathematical formulas. While the prospect of mathematical computations arouses fear in the hearts of many of us, the math principles you will need to know are actually very simple. The following is a brief description of those formulas.

I. Approach to Solving Math Problems

Solving math problems is simplified by using a step-by-step approach.

The most important step is to thoroughly understand the problem.

You must know what answer you want before you can successfully work any math problem. Once you have determined what it is you are to find (for example, interest rate, loan-to-value ratio, amount, or profit), you will know what formula to use.

For example, the profit and loss formula is **value after = percent x value before (VA = % x VB)**. The formulas you will most likely be using will be explained in this chapter.

Chapter 15

CHAPTER OUTLINE

The next step is to substitute the numbers you know into the formula. In many problems you will be able to substitute the numbers into the formula without any additional steps. However, in many other problems it will be necessary to take one or more preliminary steps, for instance, converting fractions to decimals.

Once you have substituted the numbers into the formula you will have to do some computations to find the unknown. Most of the formulas have the same basic form: **A = B x C**. You will need two of the numbers (or the information that enables you to find two of the numbers) and then you will either have to divide or multiply them to find the third number—the answer you are seeking.

Whether you will need to multiply or divide is determined by which quantity (number) in the formula you are trying to discover.

For example, the formula A = B x C may be converted into three different formulas. All three formulas are equivalent, but are put into different forms, depending upon the quantity (number) to be discovered. If the quantity A is unknown, then the following formula is used:

$$A = B \times C$$

The number B is multiplied by C; the product of B times C is A.

If the quantity B is unknown, the following formula is used:

$$B = A \div C$$

The number A is divided by C; the quotient of A divided by C is B.

If the quantity C is unknown, the following formula is used:

$$C = A \div B$$

The number A is divided by B; the quotient of A divided by B is C. Notice that in all these instances, the unknown quantity is always by itself on one side of the "equal" sign.

II. Converting Fractions to Decimals

There will be many times when you will want to convert a fraction into a decimal. Most people find it much easier to work with decimals than fractions. Also, hand calculators can multiply and divide by decimals.

To convert a fraction into a decimal, you simply divide the top number of the fraction (the "numerator") by the bottom number of the fraction (the "denominator").

Example: To change 3/4 into a decimal, you must divide 3 (the top number) by 4 (the bottom number).

$$3 \div 4 = .75$$

To change 1/5 into a decimal, divide 1 by 5.

$$1 \div 5 = .20$$

If you are using a hand calculator, it will automatically give you the right answer with the decimals in the correct place.

To add or subtract by decimals, **line the decimals up by decimal point** and add or subtract.

Example:

```
   23.77
  746.1
    1.567
   82.6
+ 1134.098
  1988.135
```

To multiply by decimals, do the multiplication. **The answer should have as many decimal places as the total number of decimal places in the multiplying numbers.** Just add up the decimal places in the numbers you are multiplying and put the decimal point the same number of places to the left.

Example:

```
    57.999
    x 23.7
 1374.5763
```

To divide by decimals, move the decimal point in the outside number all the way to the right and then move the decimal point in the inside number the same number of places to the right.

Example:

44.6 ÷ 5.889
44600 ÷ 5889 = 7.57

Just as with addition and multiplication, the above steps are unnecessary if you use a hand calculator. If the numbers are punched in correctly, the calculator will automatically give you an answer with the decimal in the right place.

III. Percentage Problems

You will often be working with percentages in real estate finance problems. For example, loan-to-value ratios and interest rates are stated as percentages.

It is necessary to convert the percentages into decimals and vice versa, so that the arithmetic in a percentage problem can be done in decimals.

To convert a percentage to a decimal, remove the percentage sign and **move the decimal point two places to the left.** This may require adding zeros.

Example:

80% becomes .80
9% becomes .09
75.5% becomes .755
8.75% becomes .0875

To convert a decimal to percentage, do just the opposite. Move the decimal **two places to the right** and add a percentage sign.

Example:

.88 becomes 88%
.015 becomes 1.5%
.09 becomes 9%

Whenever something is expressed as a percent of something, it means multiply. The word "of" means to multiply.

Example: If a lender requires a loan-to-value ratio of 75% and a house is worth $89,000, what will be the maximum loan amount? (What is 75% of $89,000?)

.75 x $89,000 = $66,750 maximum loan amount

Percentage problems are usually similar to the above example. You have to find a part of something, or a percentage of the total.

A general formula is:

A percentage of the total equals the part, or part = percent x total

$$P = \% \times T$$

Example: Smith spends 24% of her monthly salary on her house payment. Her monthly salary is $2,750. What is the amount of her house payment?

1. Find amount of house payment.
2. Write down formula: P = % x T.
3. Substitute numbers into formula.

$$P = 24\% \times \$2,750$$

Before you can perform the necessary calculations, you must convert the 24% into a decimal. Move the decimal two places to the left: **24% = .24**

$$P = .24 \times \$2,750$$

4. Calculate: multiply the percentage by the total.

$$.24 \times \$2,750 = \$660$$

Smith's house payment is $660.

IV. Problems Involving Measures of Central Tendency

As was explained in Chapter 14, appraisers, finance officers, and lenders evaluate data and information by the use of averages. These average figures are known as the mean, the median, or the mode. It is useful to know how they are derived.

The average figure that is called a **Mean** is derived by taking a set of numbers and adding them up. The result is then divided by the numbers in the set.

Example:

A group of houses have the following monthly rental prices:

Rental #1 – $1,300
Rental #2 – $900

Rental #3 – $1,200
Rental #4 – $1,100
Rental #5 – $1,150
$5,650 Total

To determine the Mean, the total rentals of $5,650.00 are divided by the number of rental houses.

Thus, $\frac{\$5650}{5}$ = $1130 Mean monthly rental.

The average figure that is described as a **Median** is derived by simply selecting the middle number in a set of numbers.

Example:

Rental #1 – $1,100
Rental #2 – $1,150
Rental #3 – $1,200
Rental #4 – $1,200 = Median
Rental #5 – $1,250
Rental #6 – $1,250
Rental #7 – $1,300

There are three numbers before Rental #4 and three numbers after. Therefore, rental #4 is the median number and the median rental price is $1,200.

The example above had an odd number of rentals. The following example shows how to determine a mean with an even set of numbers.

Example:

Rental #1 – $1,100
Rental #2 – $1,150
Rental #3 – $1,200
Rental #4 – $1,200
Rental #5 – $1,250
Rental #6 – $1,250
Rental #7 – $1,275
Rental #8 – $1,275

The median is determined by adding the two middle rental numbers in the set and dividing the result by 2.

In this set the middle numbers are rentals number 4 and 5.

$1,200 +$1,250 $2,450 Therefore: $2,450 / 2 = $1,225

Thus, the median rent in this even number example is $1,225.

A **Mode** measures the most frequently occurring number in a series of numbers. Appraisers and lenders often use this benchmark to determine the predominant value of housing in a neighborhood.

Example:

Sale #1 – $325,000
Sale #2 – $328,000
Sale #4 – $332,000
Sale #6 – $335,000
Sale #7 – $335,000
Sale #8 – $340,000
Sale #9 – $345,000

There are two sales at $335,000. This would be the Mode. It would also be the predominant value of this set of sales.

The value range states from the lowest number to the highest number, in a set of numbers. Thus, the range in the example above would be expressed as from $325,000 to $345,000.

V. Interest Problems

Interest can be viewed as the "rent" paid by a borrower to a lender for the use of money (the loan amount, or principal). ***INTEREST** is the cost of borrowing money.* There are two types of interest: simple and compound.

***SIMPLE INTEREST** is interest paid only on the principal owed.* ***COMPOUND INTEREST** is interest paid on accrued interest, as well as on the principal owed.*

Simple interest problems are worked in basically the same manner as percentage problems, except that the simple interest formula has four components rather than three: interest, principal, rate, and time.

Interest = Principal x Rate x Time

$$I = P \times R \times T$$

Interest: The cost of borrowing expressed in dollars; money paid for the use of money.

Principal: The amount of the loan in dollars on which the interest is paid.

Rate: The cost of borrowing expressed as a percentage of the principal paid in interest for one year.

Time: The length of time of the loan, usually expressed in years.

One must know the number values of three of the four components in order to compute the fourth (unknown) component.

a. Interest unknown

Interest = Principal x Rate x Time

Example: Find the interest on $3,500 for six years at 11%.

$I = P \times R \times T$
$I = (\$3{,}500 \times .11) \times 6$
$I = \$385 \times 6$
$I = \$2{,}310$

b. Principal unknown

Principal = Interest ÷ Rate x Time

$P = I \div (R \times T)$

Example: How much money must be loaned to receive $2,310 interest at 11% if the money is loaned for six years?

$P = I \div (R \times T)$
$P = \$2{,}310 \div (.11 \times 6)$
$P = \$2{,}310 \div .66$
$P = \$3{,}500$

c. Rate unknown

Rate = Interest ÷ Principal x Time

$R = I \div (P \times T)$

Example: In six years $3,500 earns $2,310 interest. What is the rate of interest?

$R = I \div (P \times T)$
$R = \$2{,}310 \div (\$3{,}500 \times 6)$
$R = \$2{,}310 \div \$21{,}000$
$R = .11$ *or* 11%

d. Time unknown

Time = Interest ÷ Rate x Principal

$T = I \div (R \times P)$

Example: How long will it take $3,500 to return $2,310 at an annual rate of 11%?

$T = I \div (R \times P)$
$T = \$2{,}310 \div (\$3{,}500 \times .11)$
$T = \$2{,}310 \div \$385$
$T = 6$ *years*

A. COMPOUND INTEREST

Compound interest is more common in advanced real estate subjects, such as appraisal and annuities. Compound interest tables are readily available, but the principle is discussed here to further your understanding.

As previously stated, compound interest is interest on the total of the principal plus its accrued interest. For each time period (called the "conversion period"), interest is added to the principal to make a new principal amount. Therefore, each succeeding time period has an increased principal amount on which to compute interest. Conversion periods may be monthly, quarterly, semi-annual, or annual.

The compound interest rate is usually stated as an annual rate and must be changed to the appropriate "interest rate per conversion period" or "periodic interest rate." To do this, you must divide the annual interest rate by the number of conversion periods per year. **This periodic interest rate is called "i."** The formula used for compound interest problems is interest = principal x periodic interest rate, or

$$I = P \times i$$

Example: A $5,000 investment at 9% interest compounded annually for three years earns how much interest at maturity?

$$
\begin{aligned}
I &= P \text{ x } i \\
I &= \$5{,}000 \text{ x } (.09 \div 1) \\
\textit{First year's } I &= \$5{,}000 \text{ x } .09 \textit{ or } \$450. \\
& \textit{Add to } \$5{,}000. \\
\textit{Second year's } I &= \$5{,}450 \text{ x } .09 \textit{ or } 490.50. \\
& \textit{Add to } \$5{,}450. \\
\textit{Third year's } I &= \$5{,}940.50 \text{ x } .09 \textit{ or } \$534.65. \\
& \textit{Add to } \$5{,}940.50
\end{aligned}
$$

At maturity, the borrower will owe $6,475.15. The $5,000 loan has earned interest of $1,475.15 in three years.

Example: How much interest will a $1,000 investment earn over two years at 12% interest compounded semi-annually?

Since the conversion period is semi-annual, the interest is computed every six months. Thus, the periodic interest rate "i" is divided by two conversion periods: i = 6%.

$$I = P \text{ x } i$$

1. Original principal amount	=	*$1,000.00*
2. Interest for 1st period ($1,000 x .06)	=	*$60.00*
3. Balance beginning 2nd period	=	*$1,060.00*
4. Interest for 2nd period ($1,060 x .06)	=	*$63.60*
5. Balance beginning 3rd period	=	*$1,123.60*
6. Interest for 3rd period ($1,123.60 x .06)	=	*$67.42*
7. Balance beginning 4th period	=	*$1,191.02*
8. Interest for 4th period ($1,191.02 x .06)	=	*$71.46*
9. Compound principal balance	=	*$1,262.48*

i for 2 years = $1,262.48 - $1,000 or $262.48

The same problem, using annual simple interest, results in $22.48 less interest for the lender:

$1,000 x .12 x 2 = $240 simple interest

Obviously, no one in actual practice is going to go through the tedious process outlined above to calculate compound interest, especially if it is compounded daily over a 30-year period! Instead, standardized compound interest tables or calculators can be used to find the answer quickly.

B. EFFECTIVE INTEREST RATE

The ***NOMINAL ("NAMED") INTEREST RATE*** *is the rate of interest stated in the loan documents*. The ***EFFECTIVE INTEREST RATE*** *is the rate the borrower is actually paying (including interest, points, and loan fees)*. In other words, the loan papers may say one thing when the end result is another, depending upon how many times a year the actual earnings rate is compounded.

The effective interest rate equals the annual rate, which will produce the same interest in a year as the nominal rate converted a certain number of times.

For example, 6% converted semiannually produces $6.09 per $100; therefore, 6% is the nominal rate and 6.09% is the effective rate. A rate of 6% converted semi-annually yields the same interest as a rate of 6.09% on an annual basis.

C. DISCOUNTS

As discussed in the chapter on alternative methods of financing, often the loan proceeds disbursed by the lender are less than the face value of the note. This occurs when the borrower (or a third party) pays discount points. The lender deducts the amount of the points from the loan amount up front as compensation for making the loan on the agreed terms. The borrower thus receives less than must be repaid under the contract. When a discount is paid, the interest costs to the borrower (and the yield to the lender) are higher than the contract interest rate.

When more accurate yield and interest tables are unavailable, it is possible to approximate the effective interest cost to the borrower and the yield rate to the lender when discounted loans are involved. The formula for doing so is as follows:

$$i = (r + (d/n)) \div (P - d)$$

i: approximate effective interest rate (expressed as a decimal)

r: contract interest rate (expressed as a decimal)

d: discount rate, or points deducted (expressed as a decimal)

P: principal of loan (expressed as the whole number 1 for all dollar amounts)

n: term (years, periods, or a fraction thereof)

Example: What is the estimated effective interest rate on a $60,000 mortgage loan, with a 20-year term, contract rate, if interest being 10% per annum, discounted 3%, so that only $58,200 is disbursed to the borrower?

$$i = \frac{.10 + (.03/20)}{1 - .03} = \frac{.10 + .0015}{.97} = \frac{.10150}{.97} = .10463 \text{ or } 10.46\%$$

The effective interest rate (or yield) on the loan is 10.46%.

VI. Profit and Loss Problems

Every time a homeowner sells a house, a profit or loss is made. If the house is sold for more than was initially paid for it, the owner makes a profit. If it is sold for less, the owner suffers a loss. Many times you will want to be able to calculate the amount of that profit or loss. Profit and loss problems are solved with a formula that is a variation of the percent formula: **value after = percentage x value before.**

VA = % x VB

The ***VALUE AFTER*** *is the value of the property after the profit or loss is taken.* The ***VALUE BEFORE*** *is the value of the property before the profit or loss is taken.* The percent is 100% plus the percent of profit or minus the percent of loss. The idea is to express the value of the property after a profit or loss as a percentage of the property's value before the profit or loss. If there is no profit or loss, the value has not changed. If there is a profit, the value after will be greater than 100% of the value before, since the value has increased. If there is a loss, the value after is less than 100% of the value before, since the value has decreased.

Example: Green bought a house ten years ago for $50,000 and sold it last month for 45% more than she paid for it. What was the selling price of the house?

VA = % x VB
VA = 145% x VB (To get the percent, you must add the percent of profit to, or subtract the percent of loss from, 100%.)
VA = 1.45 x $50,000
VA = $72,500 was the selling price

Example: Now we will use the profit and loss formula to calculate another one of the components.

Green sold her house last week for $117,000. She paid $121,000 for it five years ago. What was the percent of loss?

VA = % x VB
$117,000 = % x $121,000
(Because the percent is the unknown, you must divide the value after by the value before.)

% = \$117,000 ÷ \$121,000

% = .9669 or 97% (rounded)

Now subtract 97% from 100% to find the percent of loss.

% = 100% - 97% = 3% loss

Example: Your customer just sold a house for 17% more than was paid for it. The seller's portion of the closing costs came to \$4,677. The seller received \$72,500 in cash at closing. What did the seller originally pay for the house?

VA = % x VB

\$72,500 + 4,677 = 117% x VB

VB = (\$72,500 + 4,677) ÷ 117%

(Since the value before is unknown, you must divide the value after [the total of the closing costs and the escrow proceeds] by the percent of profit.)

VB = \$77,177 ÷ 1.17

VB = \$65,963.25 was the original price

VII. Prorations

There are some expenses connected with owning real estate that are often either paid for in advance or in arrears. For example, fire insurance premiums are normally paid for in advance. Landlords usually collect rents in advance, too. On the other hand, mortgage interest accrues in arrears.

When expenses are paid in advance and the owner then sells the property, part of these expenses have already been used up by the seller and are rightfully the seller's expense. Often, however, a portion of the expenses of ownership still remain unused and when title to the property transfers to the buyer, the benefit of these advances will accrue to the buyer. It is only fair that the buyer, therefore, reimburse the seller for the unused portions of these homeownership expenses. For example, suppose the seller of a home paid \$1,400 annual property taxes for the coming year, one month before the property was sold. The seller has only benefited from one month of the tax year, but the buyer will benefit from the next 11 months of the prepaid taxes. Unless the buyer reimburses the seller for 11 months' worth of the taxes, the seller will be stuck with paying the taxes for someone else's property.

These adjustments, or reimbursements, are made by the process of ***PRORATION**, which means apportioning the expenses (or benefits) fairly to each party.*

For example, a seller sells the property six months after paying the annual property taxes for the ensuing year. One half of the tax payment will thus accrue to the benefit of the buyer. In this case, the buyer pays half of the tax amount to the seller. (This example is over-simplified, because in practice, prorations are figured down to the day.)

Prorations are usually calculated at real estate closings, where the costs of such items as taxes and insurance are allocated between the buyer and the seller. Rental income is also prorated.

The formula for proration is: **share = daily rate x number of days**:

S = *R* x *D*

To work a proration problem:

1. Find the annual or monthly amount of the expense.
2. Then find the daily rate of the expense (per diem).
3. Next, determine the number of days for which the person is responsible for the expense.
4. Finally, substitute the daily rate and number of days into the formula and calculate.

Example: The seller paid the June homeowner's insurance premium of $28 on the first of the month. The transaction closes on the 18th of the month. How much of the insurance premium does the buyer owe to the seller?

S = *R* x *D*

The premium is $28 per month. To find the daily rate of the expense, divide $28 by 30, since there are 30 days in June.

$28 ÷ 30 = $.93
The rate is $.93 per day.

Next, find out how many days the buyer is responsible for. (The buyer pays for the day of closing.) There are 13 days left in the month that the buyer is responsible for.

S = R x D
S = $.93 x 13
S = $12.09 is the amount owed to the seller.

Example: A sale closes on September 14. The annual property taxes of $1,750 have not been paid. How much will the seller owe the buyer at closing?

The property tax year runs from July 1 through June 30. The seller owes for the period from July 1 up to September 14.

The annual amount is $1,750, which must be divided by 365 days to get the daily rate.

1,750 ÷ 365 = $4.79 per day

Next, you must figure the number of days.

July - 31
August - 31
September - 13
75 days

S = R x D
S = 4.79 x 75
S = $359.25 owed to the buyer at closing.

VIII. Mathematical Tables and Their Use

The scope of this book does not permit a full discussion of the use of the various tables relating to real estate finance. Generally speaking, the following tables are most commonly used.

A. AMORTIZATION TABLES

These are commonly available in booklet form from various title companies, escrow companies, and banks. They indicate the monthly payment needed for the periodic repayment of both the principal amount of the loan and the interest due. One form of amortization table has a list of possible loan terms (expressed in years) along one axis. The other axis is the interest rate. There is a separate table for each loan amount. At the intersection of any two axes in the table is the monthly payment in dollars and cents (see **Figure 15-1**).

An alternative type of table for figuring loan payments is the **Interest Rate Factors Table** (see **Figure 15-2**). It would be helpful to take a moment to examine this table and follow the instructions set out at the beginning of the table. This table gives you interest rate factors, which, multiplied by the loan amount, give you the amount of the monthly loan payment.

B. PRORATION TABLES

This is simply a table that gives the number of days between various dates. It is used to prorate such items as interest, insurance premiums, or rents (see **Figure 15-3**).

C. REMAINING BALANCE TABLES OR LOAN PROGRESS CHARTS

Remaining balance tables show the remaining balance of a loan expressed as a percentage of the original loan amount, using the data: original loan amount, interest rate, age of loan, and original term of loan. A loan progress chart also allows you to find the remaining loan balance by giving you the amount still owing for every $1,000 borrowed (see **Figure 15-4**).

D. MORTGAGE YIELD TABLES

These are used to determine the yield on a mortgage at a specified discount. A point discount table is shown in **Figure 15-5**.

E. BALLOON PAYMENT TABLES

These are used to determine the unpaid balance due and payable on a loan. Loans, especially second trust deed loans, often have terms of four or five years, but are amortized over 12 or 15 years. This will leave a large lump sum payment of principal owing at the end of the loan term.

F. CONSTANT ANNUAL PERCENTAGE TABLES

An annual constant is the sum of 12 monthly payments expressed as a percent of a principal loan amount. When multiplied by the loan amount, the annual loan payment may be determined. The remaining term of a loan, remaining loan balance, and interest rate of a loan may also be determined by use of a constant annual percent table.

Online Mortgage Calculators
(Increasing First-Time Homebuyers' Knowledge)

Although online mortgage calculators are rapidly replacing printed amortization tables and handheld electronic amortization calculators, it is doubtful they will ever fully replace the original printed tables. We have provided several examples of printed amortization tables in this text because it is important to understand the concepts behind the shortcuts. Therefore, it is strongly recommended that you study the tables printed in the book to gain a full comprehension of how the formulas work. Then you can use the shortcuts with confidence, and will have the ability to explain the process, if necessary, to new homebuyers.

Online mortgage calculators can accomplish several things, including:

1. calculate a simple monthly payment;
2. figure the effects of prepaying a mortgage, and
3. analyze the composition of monthly payments in the future.

The latter is particularly helpful in projecting mortgage-interest tax write-offs in future years. Many online calculators offer graph and chart conversions to help illustrate how equity builds over time or how interest declines as a percentage of the monthly payment.

There are numerous mortgage calculators available at no charge on the Internet, allowing even novices in the homebuying arena the opportunity to choose a loan by calculating the monthly payments they can afford, as well as figuring how much of each payment goes towards the principal versus the interest. A better prepared customer saves time and paperwork, and can make a professional's job easier in the long run.

Although we do not endorse or guarantee any website, below is a listing of just a few of the more well-known companies that provide online mortgage calculators.

www.bloomberg.com/invest/calculators/index.html
www.quickenloans.com/mortgage-calculator
www.bankrate.com/brm/calculators/mortgages.asp
www.calculators4mortgages.com/calculators/loan/calcmonpaytable.html
www.mortgage-calc.com
www.mortgagecalculator.org

Figure 15-1 **MONTHLY AMORTIZING PAYMENTS** **4%**

AMOUNT OF LOAN	NUMBER OF YEARS IN TERM											
	1	2	3	4	5	6	7	8	9	10	11	12
$ 50	4.26	2.18	1.48	1.13	0.93	0.79	0.69	0.61	0.56	0.51	0.47	0.44
100	8.52	4.35	2.96	2.26	1.85	1.57	1.37	1.22	1.11	1.02	0.94	0.88
200	17.03	8.69	5.91	4.52	3.69	3.13	2.74	2.44	2.21	2.03	1.88	1.76
300	25.55	13.03	8.86	6.78	5.53	4.70	4.11	3.66	3.32	3.04	2.82	2.63
400	34.06	17.37	11.81	9.04	7.37	6.26	5.47	4.88	4.42	4.05	3.76	3.51
500	42.58	21.72	14.77	11.29	9.21	7.83	6.84	6.10	5.53	5.07	4.69	4.38
600	51.09	26.06	17.72	13.55	11.05	9.39	8.21	7.32	6.63	6.08	5.63	5.26
700	59.61	30.40	20.67	15.81	12.90	10.96	9.57	8.54	7.73	7.09	6.57	6.13
800	68.12	34.74	23.62	18.07	14.74	12.52	10.94	9.76	8.84	8.10	7.51	7.01
900	76.64	39.09	26.58	20.33	16.58	14.09	12.31	10.98	9.94	9.12	8.44	7.88
1,000	85.15	43.43	29.53	22.58	18.42	15.65	13.67	12.19	11.05	10.13	9.38	8.76
2,000	170.30	86.85	59.05	45.16	36.84	31.30	27.34	24.38	22.09	20.25	18.76	17.52
3,000	255.45	130.28	88.58	67.74	55.25	46.94	41.01	36.57	33.13	30.38	28.14	26.27
4,000	340.60	173.70	118.10	90.32	73.67	62.59	54.68	48.76	44.17	40.50	37.51	35.03
5,000	425.75	217.13	147.62	112.90	92.09	78.23	68.35	60.95	55.21	50.63	46.89	43.78
6,000	510.90	260.55	177.15	135.48	110.50	93.88	82.02	73.14	66.25	60.75	56.27	52.54
7,000	596.05	303.98	206.67	158.06	128.92	109.52	95.69	85.33	77.29	70.88	65.64	61.29
8,000	681.20	347.40	236.20	180.64	147.34	125.17	109.36	97.52	88.33	81.00	75.02	70.05
9,000	766.35	390.83	265.72	203.22	165.75	140.81	123.02	109.71	99.37	91.13	84.40	78.80
10,000	851.50	434.25	295.24	225.80	184.17	156.46	136.69	121.90	110.41	101.25	93.77	87.56
15,000	1277.25	651.38	442.86	338.69	276.25	234.68	205.04	182.84	165.62	151.87	140.66	131.33
20,000	1703.00	868.50	590.48	451.59	368.34	312.91	273.38	243.79	220.82	202.50	187.54	175.11
25,000	2128.75	1085.63	738.10	564.48	460.42	391.13	341.73	304.74	276.03	253.12	234.42	218.89
30,000	2554.50	1302.75	885.72	677.38	552.50	469.36	410.07	365.68	331.23	303.74	281.31	262.66
35,000	2980.25	1519.88	1033.34	790.27	644.58	547.59	478.41	426.63	386.44	354.36	328.19	306.44
40,000	3406.00	1737.00	1180.96	903.17	736.67	625.81	546.76	487.58	441.64	404.99	375.07	350.22
45,000	3831.75	1954.13	1328.58	1016.06	828.75	704.04	615.10	548.52	496.85	455.61	421.96	393.99
50,000	4257.50	2171.25	1476.20	1128.96	920.83	782.26	683.45	609.47	552.05	506.23	468.84	437.77
55,000	4683.25	2388.38	1623.82	1241.85	1012.91	860.49	751.79	670.42	607.26	556.85	515.72	481.55
60,000	5109.00	2605.50	1771.44	1354.75	1105.00	938.72	820.13	731.36	662.46	607.48	562.61	525.32
65,000	5534.75	2822.62	1919.06	1467.64	1197.08	1016.94	888.48	792.31	717.67	658.10	609.49	569.10
70,000	5960.50	3039.75	2066.68	1580.54	1289.16	1095.17	956.82	853.25	772.87	708.72	656.37	612.87
75,000	6386.25	3256.87	2214.30	1693.43	1381.24	1173.39	1025.17	914.20	828.08	759.34	703.26	656.65
80,000	6812.00	3474.00	2361.92	1806.33	1473.33	1251.62	1093.51	975.15	883.28	809.97	750.14	700.43
85,000	7237.75	3691.12	2509.54	1919.22	1565.41	1329.85	1161.85	1036.09	938.49	860.59	797.02	744.20
90,000	7663.50	3908.25	2657.16	2032.12	1657.49	1408.07	1230.20	1097.04	993.69	911.21	843.91	787.98
95,000	8089.25	4125.37	2804.78	2145.02	1749.57	1486.30	1298.54	1157.99	1048.90	961.83	890.79	831.76
100,000	8515.00	4342.50	2952.40	2257.91	1841.66	1564.52	1366.89	1218.93	1104.10	1012.46	937.67	875.53
105,000	8940.74	4559.62	3100.02	2370.81	1933.74	1642.75	1435.23	1279.88	1159.31	1063.08	984.56	919.31
110,000	9366.49	4776.75	3247.64	2483.70	2025.82	1720.98	1503.57	1340.83	1214.51	1113.70	1031.44	963.09
115,000	9792.24	4993.87	3395.26	2596.60	2117.91	1799.20	1571.92	1401.77	1269.72	1164.32	1078.32	1006.86
120,000	10217.99	5211.00	3542.88	2709.49	2209.99	1877.43	1640.26	1462.72	1324.92	1214.95	1125.21	1050.64
125,000	10643.74	5428.12	3690.50	2822.39	2302.07	1955.65	1708.61	1523.66	1380.13	1265.57	1172.09	1094.42
130,000	11069.49	5645.24	3838.12	2935.28	2394.15	2033.88	1776.95	1584.61	1435.33	1316.19	1218.97	1138.19
135,000	11495.24	5862.37	3985.74	3048.18	2486.24	2112.10	1845.29	1645.56	1490.54	1366.81	1265.86	1181.97
140,000	11920.99	6079.49	4133.36	3161.07	2578.32	2190.33	1913.64	1706.50	1545.74	1417.44	1312.74	1225.74
145,000	12346.74	6296.62	4280.98	3273.97	2670.40	2268.56	1981.98	1767.45	1600.95	1468.06	1359.62	1269.52
150,000	12772.49	6513.74	4428.60	3386.86	2762.48	2346.78	2050.33	1828.40	1656.15	1518.68	1406.51	1313.30
155,000	13198.24	6730.87	4576.22	3499.76	2854.57	2425.01	2118.67	1889.34	1711.36	1569.30	1453.39	1357.07
160,000	13623.99	6947.99	4723.84	3612.65	2946.65	2503.23	2187.01	1950.29	1766.56	1619.93	1500.27	1400.85
165,000	14049.74	7165.12	4871.46	3725.55	3038.73	2581.46	2255.36	2011.24	1821.76	1670.55	1547.16	1444.63
170,000	14475.49	7382.24	5019.08	3838.44	3130.81	2659.69	2323.70	2072.18	1876.97	1721.17	1594.04	1488.40
175,000	14901.24	7599.37	5166.70	3951.34	3222.90	2737.91	2392.05	2133.13	1932.17	1771.79	1640.92	1532.18
180,000	15326.99	7816.49	5314.32	4064.23	3314.98	2816.14	2460.39	2194.07	1987.38	1822.42	1687.81	1575.96
185,000	15752.74	8033.62	5461.94	4177.13	3407.06	2894.36	2528.73	2255.02	2042.58	1873.04	1734.69	1619.73
190,000	16178.49	8250.74	5609.56	4290.03	3499.14	2972.59	2597.08	2315.97	2097.79	1923.66	1781.57	1663.51
195,000	16604.24	8467.86	5757.18	4402.92	3591.23	3050.82	2665.42	2376.91	2152.99	1974.29	1828.46	1707.29
200,000	17029.99	8684.99	5904.80	4515.82	3683.31	3129.04	2733.77	2437.86	2208.20	2024.91	1875.34	1751.06
205,000	17455.74	8902.11	6052.42	4628.71	3775.39	3207.27	2802.11	2498.81	2263.40	2075.53	1922.22	1794.84
210,000	17881.48	9119.24	6200.04	4741.61	3867.47	3285.49	2870.45	2559.75	2318.61	2126.15	1969.11	1838.61
215,000	18307.23	9336.36	6347.66	4854.50	3959.56	3363.72	2938.80	2620.70	2373.81	2176.78	2015.99	1882.39
220,000	18732.98	9553.49	6495.28	4967.40	4051.64	3441.95	3007.14	2681.65	2429.02	2227.40	2062.87	1926.17
225,000	19158.73	9770.61	6642.90	5080.29	4143.72	3520.17	3075.49	2742.59	2484.22	2278.02	2109.76	1969.94
230,000	19584.48	9987.74	6790.52	5193.19	4235.81	3598.40	3143.83	2803.54	2539.43	2328.64	2156.64	2013.72
235,000	20010.23	10204.86	6938.14	5306.08	4327.89	3676.62	3212.17	2864.48	2594.63	2379.27	2203.52	2057.50
240,000	20435.98	10421.99	7085.76	5418.98	4419.97	3754.85	3280.52	2925.43	2649.84	2429.89	2250.41	2101.27
245,000	20861.73	10639.11	7233.38	5531.87	4512.05	3833.07	3348.86	2986.38	2705.04	2480.51	2297.29	2145.05
250,000	21287.48	10856.24	7381.00	5644.77	4604.14	3911.30	3417.21	3047.32	2760.25	2531.13	2344.17	2188.83
255,000	21713.23	11073.36	7528.62	5757.66	4696.22	3989.53	3485.55	3108.27	2815.45	2581.76	2391.06	2232.60
260,000	22138.98	11290.48	7676.24	5870.56	4788.30	4067.75	3553.89	3169.22	2870.66	2632.38	2437.94	2276.38
265,000	22564.73	11507.61	7823.86	5983.45	4880.38	4145.98	3622.24	3230.16	2925.86	2683.00	2484.82	2320.16
270,000	22990.48	11724.73	7971.48	6096.35	4972.47	4224.20	3690.58	3291.11	2981.07	2733.62	2531.71	2363.93
280,000	23841.98	12158.98	8266.72	6322.14	5156.63	4380.66	3827.27	3413.00	3091.48	2834.87	2625.47	2451.48
290,000	24693.48	12593.23	8561.96	6547.93	5340.80	4537.11	3963.96	3534.89	3201.89	2936.11	2719.24	2539.04
300,000	25544.98	13027.48	8857.20	6773.72	5524.96	4693.56	4100.65	3656.79	3312.30	3037.36	2813.01	2626.59

4% Monthly Amortizing Payments

AMOUNT OF LOAN	NUMBER OF YEARS IN TERM 13	14	15	16	17	18	19	20	25	30	35	40
$ 50	0.42	0.39	0.37	0.36	0.34	0.33	0.32	0.31	0.27	0.24	0.23	0.21
100	0.83	0.78	0.74	0.71	0.68	0.66	0.63	0.61	0.53	0.48	0.45	0.42
200	1.65	1.56	1.48	1.42	1.36	1.31	1.26	1.22	1.06	0.96	0.89	0.84
300	2.47	2.34	2.22	2.12	2.03	1.96	1.89	1.82	1.59	1.44	1.33	1.26
400	3.30	3.12	2.96	2.83	2.71	2.61	2.51	2.43	2.12	1.91	1.78	1.68
500	4.12	3.90	3.70	3.53	3.39	3.26	3.14	3.03	2.64	2.39	2.22	2.09
600	4.94	4.68	4.44	4.24	4.06	3.91	3.77	3.64	3.17	2.87	2.66	2.51
700	5.77	5.45	5.18	4.95	4.74	4.56	4.39	4.25	3.70	3.35	3.10	2.93
800	6.59	6.23	5.92	5.65	5.42	5.21	5.02	4.85	4.23	3.82	3.55	3.35
900	7.41	7.01	6.66	6.36	6.09	5.86	5.65	5.46	4.76	4.30	3.99	3.77
1,000	8.24	7.79	7.40	7.06	6.77	6.51	6.27	6.06	5.28	4.78	4.43	4.18
2,000	16.47	15.57	14.80	14.12	13.53	13.01	12.54	12.12	10.56	9.55	8.86	8.36
3,000	24.70	23.36	22.20	21.18	20.30	19.51	18.81	18.18	15.84	14.33	13.29	12.54
4,000	32.93	31.14	29.59	28.24	27.06	26.01	25.08	24.24	21.12	19.10	17.72	16.72
5,000	41.16	38.92	36.99	35.30	33.82	32.51	31.35	30.30	26.40	23.88	22.14	20.90
6,000	49.39	46.71	44.39	42.36	40.59	39.02	37.62	36.36	31.68	28.65	26.57	25.08
7,000	57.62	54.49	51.78	49.42	47.35	45.52	43.89	42.42	36.95	33.42	31.00	29.26
8,000	65.85	62.27	59.18	56.48	54.12	52.02	50.15	48.48	42.23	38.20	35.43	33.44
9,000	74.09	70.06	66.58	63.54	60.88	58.52	56.42	54.54	47.51	42.97	39.85	37.62
10,000	82.32	77.84	73.97	70.60	67.64	65.02	62.69	60.60	52.79	47.75	44.28	41.80
15,000	123.47	116.76	110.96	105.90	101.46	97.53	94.04	90.90	79.18	71.62	66.42	62.70
20,000	164.63	155.67	147.94	141.20	135.28	130.04	125.38	121.20	105.57	95.49	88.56	83.59
25,000	205.78	194.59	184.93	176.50	169.10	162.55	156.72	151.50	131.96	119.36	110.70	104.49
30,000	246.94	233.51	221.91	211.80	202.92	195.06	188.07	181.80	158.36	143.23	132.84	125.39
35,000	288.10	272.43	258.90	247.10	236.74	227.57	219.41	212.10	184.75	167.10	154.98	146.28
40,000	329.25	311.34	295.88	282.40	270.56	260.08	250.75	242.40	211.14	190.97	177.11	167.18
45,000	370.41	350.26	332.86	317.70	304.38	292.59	282.10	272.70	237.53	214.84	199.25	188.08
50,000	411.56	389.18	369.85	353.00	338.20	325.10	313.44	303.00	263.92	238.71	221.39	208.97
55,000	452.72	428.10	406.83	388.30	372.02	357.61	344.78	333.29	290.32	262.58	243.53	229.87
60,000	493.87	467.01	443.82	423.60	405.84	390.12	376.13	363.59	316.71	286.45	265.67	250.77
65,000	535.03	505.93	480.80	458.90	439.66	422.63	407.47	393.89	343.10	310.32	287.81	271.67
70,000	576.19	544.85	517.79	494.20	473.48	455.14	438.81	424.19	369.49	334.20	309.95	292.56
75,000	617.34	583.76	554.77	529.50	507.30	487.65	470.16	454.49	395.88	358.07	332.09	313.46
80,000	658.50	622.68	591.76	564.80	541.12	520.16	501.50	484.79	422.27	381.94	354.22	334.36
85,000	699.65	661.60	628.74	600.10	574.94	552.67	532.84	515.09	448.67	405.81	376.36	355.25
90,000	740.81	700.52	665.72	635.40	608.76	585.18	564.19	545.39	475.06	429.68	398.50	376.15
95,000	781.97	739.43	702.71	670.70	642.58	617.69	595.53	575.69	501.45	453.55	420.64	397.05
100,000	823.12	778.35	739.69	706.00	676.40	650.20	626.88	605.99	527.84	477.42	442.78	417.94
105,000	864.28	817.27	776.68	741.30	710.22	682.71	658.22	636.28	554.23	501.29	464.92	438.84
110,000	905.43	856.19	813.66	776.60	744.04	715.22	689.56	666.58	580.63	525.16	487.06	459.74
115,000	946.59	895.10	850.65	811.90	777.86	747.73	720.91	696.88	607.02	549.03	509.20	480.63
120,000	987.74	934.02	887.63	847.20	811.68	780.24	752.25	727.18	633.41	572.90	531.33	501.53
125,000	1028.90	972.94	924.61	882.50	845.50	812.75	783.59	757.48	659.80	596.77	553.47	522.43
130,000	1070.06	1011.85	961.60	917.80	879.32	845.26	814.94	787.78	686.19	620.64	575.61	543.33
135,000	1111.21	1050.77	998.58	953.10	913.14	877.77	846.28	818.08	712.58	644.52	597.75	564.22
140,000	1152.37	1089.69	1035.57	988.40	946.96	910.28	877.62	848.38	738.98	668.39	619.89	585.12
145,000	1193.52	1128.61	1072.55	1023.70	980.78	942.79	908.97	878.68	765.37	692.26	642.03	606.02
150,000	1234.68	1167.52	1109.54	1059.00	1014.60	975.30	940.31	908.98	791.76	716.13	664.17	626.91
155,000	1275.84	1206.44	1146.52	1094.30	1048.41	1007.81	971.65	939.27	818.15	740.00	686.31	647.81
160,000	1316.99	1245.36	1183.51	1129.60	1082.23	1040.32	1003.00	969.57	844.54	763.87	708.44	668.71
165,000	1358.15	1284.28	1220.49	1164.90	1116.05	1072.83	1034.34	999.87	870.94	787.74	730.58	689.60
170,000	1399.30	1323.19	1257.47	1200.20	1149.87	1105.34	1065.68	1030.17	897.33	811.61	752.72	710.50
175,000	1440.46	1362.11	1294.46	1235.50	1183.69	1137.85	1097.03	1060.47	923.72	835.48	774.86	731.40
180,000	1481.61	1401.03	1331.44	1270.80	1217.51	1170.36	1128.37	1090.77	950.11	859.35	797.00	752.29
185,000	1522.77	1439.94	1368.43	1306.10	1251.33	1202.87	1159.71	1121.07	976.50	883.22	819.14	773.19
190,000	1563.93	1478.86	1405.41	1341.40	1285.15	1235.38	1191.06	1151.37	1002.89	907.09	841.28	794.09
195,000	1605.08	1517.78	1442.40	1376.70	1318.97	1267.89	1222.40	1181.67	1029.29	930.96	863.42	814.99
200,000	1646.24	1556.70	1479.38	1412.00	1352.79	1300.40	1253.75	1211.97	1055.68	954.84	885.55	835.88
205,000	1687.39	1595.61	1516.37	1447.30	1386.61	1332.91	1285.09	1242.26	1082.07	978.71	907.69	856.78
210,000	1728.55	1634.53	1553.35	1482.60	1420.43	1365.42	1316.43	1272.56	1108.46	1002.58	929.83	877.68
215,000	1769.70	1673.45	1590.33	1517.90	1454.25	1397.93	1347.78	1302.86	1134.85	1026.45	951.97	898.57
220,000	1810.86	1712.37	1627.32	1553.20	1488.07	1430.44	1379.12	1333.16	1161.25	1050.32	974.11	919.47
225,000	1852.02	1751.28	1664.30	1588.50	1521.89	1462.95	1410.46	1363.46	1187.64	1074.19	996.25	940.37
230,000	1893.17	1790.20	1701.29	1623.80	1555.71	1495.46	1441.81	1393.76	1214.03	1098.06	1018.39	961.26
235,000	1934.33	1829.12	1738.27	1659.10	1589.53	1527.97	1473.15	1424.06	1240.42	1121.93	1040.53	982.16
240,000	1975.48	1868.03	1775.26	1694.40	1623.35	1560.48	1504.49	1454.36	1266.81	1145.80	1062.66	1003.06
245,000	2016.64	1906.95	1812.24	1729.70	1657.17	1592.99	1535.84	1484.66	1293.21	1169.67	1084.80	1023.95
250,000	2057.80	1945.87	1849.22	1765.00	1690.99	1625.50	1567.18	1514.96	1319.60	1193.54	1106.94	1044.85
255,000	2098.95	1984.79	1886.21	1800.30	1724.81	1658.01	1598.52	1545.25	1345.99	1217.41	1129.08	1065.75
260,000	2140.11	2023.70	1923.19	1835.60	1758.63	1690.52	1629.87	1575.55	1372.38	1241.28	1151.22	1086.65
265,000	2181.26	2062.62	1960.18	1870.89	1792.45	1723.03	1661.21	1605.85	1398.77	1265.16	1173.36	1107.54
270,000	2222.42	2101.54	1997.16	1906.19	1826.27	1755.54	1692.55	1636.15	1425.16	1289.03	1195.50	1128.44
280,000	2304.73	2179.37	2071.13	1976.79	1893.91	1820.56	1755.24	1696.75	1477.95	1336.77	1239.77	1170.23
290,000	2387.04	2257.21	2145.10	2047.39	1961.55	1885.58	1817.93	1757.35	1530.73	1384.51	1284.05	1212.03
300,000	2469.35	2335.04	2219.07	2117.99	2029.19	1950.60	1880.62	1817.95	1583.52	1432.25	1328.33	1253.82

Monthly Amortizing Payments 5%

Amount of Loan	Number of Years in Term: 1	2	3	4	5	6	7	8	9	10	11	12
$ 50	4.29	2.20	1.50	1.16	0.95	0.81	0.71	0.64	0.58	0.54	0.50	0.47
100	8.57	4.39	3.00	2.31	1.89	1.62	1.42	1.27	1.16	1.07	0.99	0.93
200	17.13	8.78	6.00	4.61	3.78	3.23	2.83	2.54	2.31	2.13	1.98	1.85
300	25.69	13.17	9.00	6.91	5.67	4.84	4.25	3.80	3.46	3.19	2.96	2.78
400	34.25	17.55	11.99	9.22	7.55	6.45	5.66	5.07	4.61	4.25	3.95	3.70
500	42.81	21.94	14.99	11.52	9.44	8.06	7.07	6.33	5.76	5.31	4.94	4.63
600	51.37	26.33	17.99	13.82	11.33	9.67	8.49	7.60	6.92	6.37	5.92	5.55
700	59.93	30.71	20.98	16.13	13.21	11.28	9.90	8.87	8.07	7.43	6.91	6.48
800	68.49	35.10	23.98	18.43	15.10	12.89	11.31	10.13	9.22	8.49	7.90	7.40
900	77.05	39.49	26.98	20.73	16.99	14.50	12.73	11.40	10.37	9.55	8.88	8.33
1,000	85.61	43.88	29.98	23.03	18.88	16.11	14.14	12.66	11.52	10.61	9.87	9.25
2,000	171.22	87.75	59.95	46.06	37.75	32.21	28.27	25.32	23.04	21.22	19.73	18.50
3,000	256.83	131.62	89.92	69.09	56.62	48.32	42.41	37.98	34.56	31.82	29.60	27.75
4,000	342.43	175.49	119.89	92.12	75.49	64.42	56.54	50.64	46.07	42.43	39.46	37.00
5,000	428.04	219.36	149.86	115.15	94.36	80.53	70.67	63.30	57.59	53.04	49.33	46.25
6,000	513.65	263.23	179.83	138.18	113.23	96.63	84.81	75.96	69.11	63.64	59.19	55.50
7,000	599.26	307.10	209.80	161.21	132.10	112.74	98.94	88.62	80.63	74.25	69.06	64.75
8,000	684.86	350.98	239.77	184.24	150.97	128.84	113.08	101.28	92.14	84.86	78.92	74.00
9,000	770.47	394.85	269.74	207.27	169.85	144.95	127.21	113.94	103.66	95.46	88.79	83.25
10,000	856.08	438.72	299.71	230.30	188.72	161.05	141.34	126.60	115.18	106.07	98.65	92.49
15,000	1284.12	658.08	449.57	345.44	283.07	241.58	212.01	189.90	172.76	159.10	147.97	138.74
20,000	1712.15	877.43	599.42	460.59	377.43	322.10	282.68	253.20	230.35	212.14	197.29	184.98
25,000	2140.19	1096.79	749.28	575.74	471.79	402.63	353.35	316.50	287.94	265.17	246.62	231.23
30,000	2568.23	1316.15	899.13	690.88	566.14	483.15	424.02	379.80	345.52	318.20	295.94	277.47
35,000	2996.27	1535.50	1048.99	806.03	660.50	563.68	494.69	443.10	403.11	371.23	345.26	323.72
40,000	3424.30	1754.86	1198.84	921.18	754.85	644.20	565.36	506.40	460.70	424.27	394.58	369.96
45,000	3852.34	1974.22	1348.70	1036.32	849.21	724.73	636.03	569.70	518.28	477.30	443.91	416.21
50,000	4280.38	2193.57	1498.55	1151.47	943.57	805.25	706.70	633.00	575.87	530.33	493.23	462.45
55,000	4708.42	2412.93	1648.40	1266.62	1037.92	885.78	777.37	696.30	633.46	583.37	542.55	508.69
60,000	5136.45	2632.29	1798.26	1381.76	1132.28	966.30	848.04	759.60	691.04	636.40	591.87	554.94
65,000	5564.49	2851.65	1948.11	1496.91	1226.64	1046.83	918.71	822.90	748.63	689.43	641.20	601.18
70,000	5992.53	3071.00	2097.97	1612.06	1320.99	1127.35	989.38	886.20	806.21	742.46	690.52	647.43
75,000	6420.57	3290.36	2247.82	1727.20	1415.35	1207.87	1060.05	949.50	863.80	795.50	739.84	693.67
80,000	6848.60	3509.72	2397.68	1842.35	1509.70	1288.40	1130.72	1012.80	921.39	848.53	789.16	739.92
85,000	7276.64	3729.07	2547.53	1957.49	1604.06	1368.92	1201.39	1076.10	978.97	901.56	838.49	786.16
90,000	7704.68	3948.43	2697.39	2072.64	1698.42	1449.45	1272.06	1139.40	1036.56	954.59	887.81	832.41
95,000	8132.72	4167.79	2847.24	2187.79	1792.77	1529.97	1342.73	1202.70	1094.15	1007.63	937.13	878.65
100,000	8560.75	4387.14	2997.09	2302.93	1887.13	1610.50	1413.40	1266.00	1151.73	1060.66	986.45	924.90
105,000	8988.79	4606.50	3146.95	2418.08	1981.48	1691.02	1484.07	1329.30	1209.32	1113.69	1035.78	971.14
110,000	9416.83	4825.86	3296.80	2533.23	2075.84	1771.55	1554.73	1392.60	1266.91	1166.73	1085.10	1017.38
115,000	9844.87	5045.21	3446.66	2648.37	2170.20	1852.07	1625.40	1455.90	1324.49	1219.76	1134.42	1063.63
120,000	10272.90	5264.57	3596.51	2763.52	2264.55	1932.60	1696.07	1519.20	1382.08	1272.79	1183.74	1109.87
125,000	10700.94	5483.93	3746.37	2878.67	2358.91	2013.12	1766.74	1582.50	1439.66	1325.82	1233.07	1156.12
130,000	11128.98	5703.29	3896.22	2993.81	2453.27	2093.65	1837.41	1645.79	1497.25	1378.86	1282.39	1202.36
135,000	11557.02	5922.64	4046.08	3108.96	2547.62	2174.17	1908.08	1709.09	1554.84	1431.89	1331.71	1248.61
140,000	11985.05	6142.00	4195.93	3224.11	2641.98	2254.70	1978.75	1772.39	1612.42	1484.92	1381.03	1294.85
145,000	12413.09	6361.36	4345.79	3339.25	2736.33	2335.22	2049.42	1835.69	1670.01	1537.95	1430.36	1341.10
150,000	12841.13	6580.71	4495.64	3454.40	2830.69	2415.74	2120.09	1898.99	1727.60	1590.99	1479.68	1387.34
155,000	13269.16	6800.07	4645.49	3569.55	2925.05	2496.27	2190.76	1962.29	1785.18	1644.02	1529.00	1433.59
160,000	13697.20	7019.43	4795.35	3684.69	3019.40	2576.79	2261.43	2025.59	1842.77	1697.05	1578.32	1479.83
165,000	14125.24	7238.78	4945.20	3799.84	3113.76	2657.32	2332.10	2088.89	1900.36	1750.09	1627.65	1526.07
170,000	14553.28	7458.14	5095.06	3914.98	3208.11	2737.84	2402.77	2152.19	1957.94	1803.12	1676.97	1572.32
175,000	14981.31	7677.50	5244.91	4030.13	3302.47	2818.37	2473.44	2215.49	2015.53	1856.15	1726.29	1618.56
180,000	15409.35	7896.86	5394.77	4145.28	3396.83	2898.89	2544.11	2278.79	2073.11	1909.18	1775.61	1664.81
185,000	15837.39	8116.21	5544.62	4260.42	3491.18	2979.42	2614.78	2342.09	2130.70	1962.22	1824.94	1711.05
190,000	16265.43	8335.57	5694.48	4375.57	3585.54	3059.94	2685.45	2405.39	2188.29	2015.25	1874.26	1757.30
195,000	16693.46	8554.93	5844.33	4490.72	3679.90	3140.47	2756.12	2468.69	2245.87	2068.28	1923.58	1803.54
200,000	17121.50	8774.28	5994.18	4605.86	3774.25	3220.99	2826.79	2531.99	2303.46	2121.32	1972.90	1849.79
205,000	17549.54	8993.64	6144.04	4721.01	3868.61	3301.52	2897.46	2595.29	2361.05	2174.35	2022.23	1896.03
210,000	17977.58	9213.00	6293.89	4836.16	3962.96	3382.04	2968.13	2658.59	2418.63	2227.38	2071.55	1942.27
215,000	18405.61	9432.35	6443.75	4951.30	4057.32	3462.57	3038.80	2721.89	2476.22	2280.41	2120.87	1988.52
220,000	18833.65	9651.71	6593.60	5066.45	4151.68	3543.09	3109.46	2785.19	2533.81	2333.45	2170.19	2034.76
225,000	19261.69	9871.07	6743.46	5181.60	4246.03	3623.61	3180.13	2848.49	2591.39	2386.48	2219.51	2081.01
230,000	19689.73	10090.42	6893.31	5296.74	4340.39	3704.14	3250.80	2911.79	2648.98	2439.51	2268.84	2127.25
235,000	20117.76	10309.78	7043.17	5411.89	4434.74	3784.66	3321.47	2975.09	2706.56	2492.54	2318.16	2173.50
240,000	20545.80	10529.14	7193.02	5527.04	4529.10	3865.19	3392.14	3038.39	2764.15	2545.58	2367.48	2219.74
245,000	20973.84	10748.50	7342.87	5642.18	4623.46	3945.71	3462.81	3101.69	2821.74	2598.61	2416.80	2265.99
250,000	21401.88	10967.85	7492.73	5757.33	4717.81	4026.24	3533.48	3164.99	2879.32	2651.64	2466.13	2312.23
255,000	21829.91	11187.21	7642.58	5872.47	4812.17	4106.76	3604.15	3228.28	2936.91	2704.68	2515.45	2358.48
260,000	22257.95	11406.57	7792.44	5987.62	4906.53	4187.29	3674.82	3291.58	2994.50	2757.71	2564.77	2404.72
265,000	22685.99	11625.92	7942.29	6102.77	5000.88	4267.81	3745.49	3354.88	3052.08	2810.74	2614.09	2450.96
270,000	23114.03	11845.28	8092.15	6217.91	5095.24	4348.34	3816.16	3418.18	3109.67	2863.77	2663.42	2497.21
280,000	23970.10	12283.99	8391.86	6448.21	5283.95	4509.39	3957.50	3544.78	3224.84	2969.84	2762.06	2589.70
290,000	24826.17	12722.71	8691.57	6678.50	5472.66	4670.44	4098.84	3671.38	3340.01	3075.90	2860.71	2682.19
300,000	25682.25	13161.42	8991.27	6908.79	5661.38	4831.48	4240.18	3797.98	3455.19	3181.97	2959.35	2774.68

5% MONTHLY AMORTIZING PAYMENTS

AMOUNT OF LOAN	NUMBER OF YEARS IN TERM											
	13	14	15	16	17	18	19	20	25	30	35	40
$ 50	0.44	0.42	0.40	0.38	0.37	0.36	0.35	0.33	0.30	0.27	0.26	0.25
100	0.88	0.83	0.80	0.76	0.73	0.71	0.69	0.66	0.59	0.54	0.51	0.49
200	1.75	1.66	1.59	1.52	1.46	1.41	1.37	1.32	1.17	1.08	1.01	0.97
300	2.62	2.49	2.38	2.28	2.19	2.11	2.05	1.98	1.76	1.62	1.52	1.45
400	3.50	3.32	3.17	3.04	2.92	2.82	2.73	2.64	2.34	2.15	2.02	1.93
500	4.37	4.15	3.96	3.79	3.65	3.52	3.41	3.30	2.93	2.69	2.53	2.42
600	5.24	4.98	4.75	4.55	4.38	4.22	4.09	3.96	3.51	3.23	3.03	2.90
700	6.12	5.81	5.54	5.31	5.11	4.93	4.77	4.62	4.10	3.76	3.54	3.38
800	6.99	6.64	6.33	6.07	5.83	5.63	5.45	5.28	4.68	4.30	4.04	3.86
900	7.86	7.46	7.12	6.82	6.56	6.33	6.13	5.94	5.27	4.84	4.55	4.34
1,000	8.74	8.29	7.91	7.58	7.29	7.04	6.81	6.60	5.85	5.37	5.05	4.83
2,000	17.47	16.58	15.82	15.16	14.58	14.07	13.61	13.20	11.70	10.74	10.10	9.65
3,000	26.20	24.87	23.73	22.74	21.86	21.10	20.41	19.80	17.54	16.11	15.15	14.47
4,000	34.93	33.16	31.64	30.31	29.15	28.13	27.22	26.40	23.39	21.48	20.19	19.29
5,000	43.66	41.45	39.54	37.89	36.44	35.16	34.02	33.00	29.23	26.85	25.24	24.11
6,000	52.39	49.74	47.45	45.47	43.72	42.19	40.82	39.60	35.08	32.21	30.29	28.94
7,000	61.12	58.03	55.36	53.04	51.01	49.22	47.62	46.20	40.93	37.58	35.33	33.76
8,000	69.85	66.31	63.27	60.62	58.30	56.25	54.43	52.80	46.77	42.95	40.38	38.58
9,000	78.58	74.60	71.18	68.20	65.58	63.28	61.23	59.40	52.62	48.32	45.43	43.40
10,000	87.31	82.89	79.08	75.77	72.87	70.31	68.03	66.00	58.46	53.69	50.47	48.22
15,000	130.96	124.34	118.62	113.66	109.30	105.46	102.05	99.00	87.69	80.53	75.71	72.33
20,000	174.62	165.78	158.16	151.54	145.74	140.61	136.06	132.00	116.92	107.37	100.94	96.44
25,000	218.27	207.22	197.70	189.43	182.17	175.76	170.07	164.99	146.15	134.21	126.18	120.55
30,000	261.92	248.67	237.24	227.31	218.60	210.92	204.09	197.99	175.38	161.05	151.41	144.66
35,000	305.58	290.11	276.78	265.19	255.03	246.07	238.10	230.99	204.61	187.89	176.65	168.77
40,000	349.23	331.55	316.32	303.08	291.47	281.22	272.12	263.99	233.84	214.73	201.88	192.88
45,000	392.88	373.00	355.86	340.96	327.90	316.37	306.13	296.99	263.07	241.57	227.11	216.99
50,000	436.53	414.44	395.40	378.85	364.33	351.52	340.14	329.98	292.30	268.42	252.35	241.10
55,000	480.19	455.88	434.94	416.73	400.77	386.67	374.16	362.98	321.53	295.26	277.58	265.21
60,000	523.84	497.33	474.48	454.61	437.20	421.83	408.17	395.98	350.76	322.10	302.82	289.32
65,000	567.49	538.77	514.02	492.50	473.63	456.98	442.19	428.98	379.99	348.94	328.05	313.43
70,000	611.15	580.21	553.56	530.38	510.06	492.13	476.20	461.97	409.22	375.78	353.29	337.54
75,000	654.80	621.66	593.10	568.27	546.50	527.28	510.21	494.97	438.45	402.62	378.52	361.65
80,000	698.45	663.10	632.64	606.15	582.93	562.43	544.23	527.97	467.68	429.46	403.76	385.76
85,000	742.11	704.55	672.18	644.03	619.36	597.58	578.24	560.97	496.91	456.30	428.99	409.87
90,000	785.76	745.99	711.72	681.92	655.79	632.74	612.25	593.97	526.14	483.14	454.22	433.98
95,000	829.41	787.43	751.26	719.80	692.23	667.89	646.27	626.96	555.37	509.99	479.46	458.09
100,000	873.06	828.88	790.80	757.69	728.66	703.04	680.28	659.96	584.60	536.83	504.69	482.20
105,000	916.72	870.32	830.34	795.57	765.09	738.19	714.30	692.96	613.82	563.67	529.93	506.31
110,000	960.37	911.76	869.88	833.45	801.53	773.34	748.31	725.96	643.05	590.51	555.16	530.42
115,000	1004.02	953.21	909.42	871.34	837.96	808.49	782.32	758.95	672.28	617.35	580.40	554.53
120,000	1047.68	994.65	948.96	909.22	874.39	843.65	816.34	791.95	701.51	644.19	605.63	578.64
125,000	1091.33	1036.09	988.50	947.11	910.82	878.80	850.35	824.95	730.74	671.03	630.86	602.75
130,000	1134.98	1077.54	1028.04	984.99	947.26	913.95	884.37	857.95	759.97	697.87	656.10	626.86
135,000	1178.64	1118.98	1067.58	1022.87	983.69	949.10	918.38	890.95	789.20	724.71	681.33	650.97
140,000	1222.29	1160.42	1107.12	1060.76	1020.12	984.25	952.39	923.94	818.43	751.56	706.57	675.08
145,000	1265.94	1201.87	1146.66	1098.64	1056.56	1019.40	986.41	956.94	847.66	778.40	731.80	699.19
150,000	1309.59	1243.31	1186.20	1136.53	1092.99	1054.56	1020.42	989.94	876.89	805.24	757.04	723.30
155,000	1353.25	1284.75	1225.74	1174.41	1129.42	1089.71	1054.44	1022.94	906.12	832.08	782.27	747.41
160,000	1396.90	1326.20	1265.27	1212.29	1165.85	1124.86	1088.45	1055.93	935.35	858.92	807.51	771.52
165,000	1440.55	1367.64	1304.81	1250.18	1202.29	1160.01	1122.46	1088.93	964.58	885.76	832.74	795.63
170,000	1484.21	1409.09	1344.35	1288.06	1238.72	1195.16	1156.48	1121.93	993.81	912.60	857.97	819.74
175,000	1527.86	1450.53	1383.89	1325.95	1275.15	1230.31	1190.49	1154.93	1023.04	939.44	883.21	843.85
180,000	1571.51	1491.97	1423.43	1363.83	1311.58	1265.47	1224.50	1187.93	1052.27	966.28	908.44	867.96
185,000	1615.17	1533.42	1462.97	1401.71	1348.02	1300.62	1258.52	1220.92	1081.50	993.13	933.68	892.07
190,000	1658.82	1574.86	1502.51	1439.60	1384.45	1335.77	1292.53	1253.92	1110.73	1019.97	958.91	916.18
195,000	1702.47	1616.30	1542.05	1477.48	1420.88	1370.92	1326.55	1286.92	1139.96	1046.81	984.15	940.29
200,000	1746.12	1657.75	1581.59	1515.37	1457.32	1406.07	1360.56	1319.92	1169.19	1073.65	1009.38	964.40
205,000	1789.78	1699.19	1621.13	1553.25	1493.75	1441.22	1394.57	1352.91	1198.41	1100.49	1034.61	988.51
210,000	1833.43	1740.63	1660.67	1591.14	1530.18	1476.38	1428.59	1385.91	1227.64	1127.33	1059.85	1012.62
215,000	1877.08	1782.08	1700.21	1629.02	1566.61	1511.53	1462.60	1418.91	1256.87	1154.17	1085.08	1036.73
220,000	1920.74	1823.52	1739.75	1666.90	1603.05	1546.68	1496.62	1451.91	1286.10	1181.01	1110.32	1060.84
225,000	1964.39	1864.96	1779.29	1704.79	1639.48	1581.83	1530.63	1484.91	1315.33	1207.85	1135.55	1084.95
230,000	2008.04	1906.41	1818.83	1742.67	1675.91	1616.98	1564.64	1517.90	1344.56	1234.69	1160.79	1109.06
235,000	2051.70	1947.85	1858.37	1780.56	1712.34	1652.13	1598.66	1550.90	1373.79	1261.54	1186.02	1133.17
240,000	2095.35	1989.29	1897.91	1818.44	1748.78	1687.29	1632.67	1583.90	1403.02	1288.38	1211.26	1157.28
245,000	2139.00	2030.74	1937.45	1856.32	1785.21	1722.44	1666.69	1616.90	1432.25	1315.22	1236.49	1181.39
250,000	2182.65	2072.18	1976.99	1894.21	1821.64	1757.59	1700.70	1649.89	1461.48	1342.06	1261.72	1205.50
255,000	2226.31	2113.63	2016.53	1932.09	1858.08	1792.74	1734.71	1682.89	1490.71	1368.90	1286.96	1229.61
260,000	2269.96	2155.07	2056.07	1969.98	1894.51	1827.89	1768.73	1715.89	1519.94	1395.74	1312.19	1253.72
265,000	2313.61	2196.51	2095.61	2007.86	1930.94	1863.04	1802.74	1748.89	1549.17	1422.58	1337.43	1277.83
270,000	2357.27	2237.96	2135.15	2045.74	1967.37	1898.20	1836.75	1781.89	1578.40	1449.42	1362.66	1301.94
280,000	2444.57	2320.84	2214.23	2121.51	2040.24	1968.50	1904.78	1847.88	1636.86	1503.11	1413.13	1350.16
290,000	2531.88	2403.73	2293.31	2197.28	2113.11	2038.80	1972.81	1913.88	1695.32	1556.79	1463.60	1398.38
300,000	2619.18	2486.62	2372.39	2273.05	2185.97	2109.11	2040.84	1979.87	1753.78	1610.47	1514.07	1446.59

MONTHLY AMORTIZING PAYMENTS 6%

AMOUNT OF LOAN	NUMBER OF YEARS IN TERM 1	2	3	4	5	6	7	8	9	10	11	12
$ 50	4.31	2.22	1.53	1.18	0.97	0.83	0.74	0.66	0.61	0.56	0.52	0.49
100	8.61	4.44	3.05	2.35	1.94	1.66	1.47	1.32	1.21	1.12	1.04	0.98
200	17.22	8.87	6.09	4.70	3.87	3.32	2.93	2.63	2.41	2.23	2.08	1.96
300	25.82	13.30	9.13	7.05	5.80	4.98	4.39	3.95	3.61	3.34	3.12	2.93
400	34.43	17.73	12.17	9.40	7.74	6.63	5.85	5.26	4.81	4.45	4.15	3.91
500	43.04	22.17	15.22	11.75	9.67	8.29	7.31	6.58	6.01	5.56	5.19	4.88
600	51.64	26.60	18.26	14.10	11.60	9.95	8.77	7.89	7.21	6.67	6.23	5.86
700	60.25	31.03	21.30	16.44	13.54	11.61	10.23	9.20	8.41	7.78	7.26	6.84
800	68.86	35.46	24.34	18.79	15.47	13.26	11.69	10.52	9.61	8.89	8.30	7.81
900	77.46	39.89	27.38	21.14	17.40	14.92	13.15	11.83	10.81	10.00	9.34	8.79
1,000	86.07	44.33	30.43	23.49	19.34	16.58	14.61	13.15	12.01	11.11	10.37	9.76
2,000	172.14	88.65	60.85	46.98	38.67	33.15	29.22	26.29	24.02	22.21	20.74	19.52
3,000	258.20	132.97	91.27	70.46	58.00	49.72	43.83	39.43	36.02	33.31	31.11	29.28
4,000	344.27	177.29	121.69	93.95	77.34	66.30	58.44	52.57	48.03	44.41	41.47	39.04
5,000	430.34	221.61	152.11	117.43	96.67	82.87	73.05	65.71	60.03	55.52	51.84	48.80
6,000	516.40	265.93	182.54	140.92	116.00	99.44	87.66	78.85	72.04	66.62	62.21	58.56
7,000	602.47	310.25	212.96	164.40	135.33	116.02	102.26	92.00	84.05	77.72	72.57	68.31
8,000	688.54	354.57	243.38	187.89	154.67	132.59	116.87	105.14	96.05	88.82	82.94	78.07
9,000	774.60	398.89	273.80	211.37	174.00	149.16	131.48	118.28	108.06	99.92	93.31	87.83
10,000	860.67	443.21	304.22	234.86	193.33	165.73	146.09	131.42	120.06	111.03	103.68	97.59
15,000	1291.00	664.81	456.33	352.28	290.00	248.60	219.13	197.13	180.09	166.54	155.51	146.38
20,000	1721.33	886.42	608.44	469.71	386.66	331.46	292.18	262.83	240.12	222.05	207.35	195.18
25,000	2151.67	1108.02	760.55	587.13	483.33	414.33	365.22	328.54	300.15	277.56	259.18	243.97
30,000	2582.00	1329.62	912.66	704.56	579.99	497.19	438.26	394.25	360.18	333.07	311.02	292.76
35,000	3012.33	1551.23	1064.77	821.98	676.65	580.06	511.30	459.96	420.21	388.58	362.85	341.55
40,000	3442.66	1772.83	1216.88	939.41	773.32	662.92	584.35	525.66	480.23	444.09	414.69	390.35
45,000	3872.99	1994.43	1368.99	1056.83	869.98	745.78	657.39	591.37	540.26	499.60	466.52	439.14
50,000	4303.33	2216.04	1521.10	1174.26	966.65	828.65	730.43	657.08	600.29	555.11	518.36	487.93
55,000	4733.66	2437.64	1673.21	1291.68	1063.31	911.51	803.48	722.78	660.32	610.62	570.19	536.72
60,000	5163.99	2659.24	1825.32	1409.11	1159.97	994.38	876.52	788.49	720.35	666.13	622.03	585.52
65,000	5594.32	2880.84	1977.43	1526.53	1256.64	1077.24	949.56	854.20	780.38	721.64	673.86	634.31
70,000	6024.66	3102.45	2129.54	1643.96	1353.30	1160.11	1022.60	919.91	840.41	777.15	725.70	683.10
75,000	6454.99	3324.05	2281.65	1761.38	1449.97	1242.97	1095.65	985.61	900.44	832.66	777.53	731.89
80,000	6885.32	3545.65	2433.76	1878.81	1546.63	1325.84	1168.69	1051.32	960.46	888.17	829.37	780.69
85,000	7315.65	3767.26	2585.87	1996.23	1643.29	1408.70	1241.73	1117.03	1020.49	943.68	881.20	829.48
90,000	7745.98	3988.86	2737.98	2113.66	1739.96	1491.56	1314.77	1182.73	1080.52	999.19	933.04	878.27
95,000	8176.32	4210.46	2890.09	2231.08	1836.62	1574.43	1387.82	1248.44	1140.55	1054.70	984.87	927.06
100,000	8606.65	4432.07	3042.20	2348.51	1933.29	1657.29	1460.86	1314.15	1200.58	1110.21	1036.71	975.86
105,000	9036.98	4653.67	3194.31	2465.93	2029.95	1740.16	1533.90	1379.86	1260.61	1165.72	1088.54	1024.65
110,000	9467.31	4875.27	3346.42	2583.36	2126.61	1823.02	1606.95	1445.56	1320.64	1221.23	1140.38	1073.44
115,000	9897.64	5096.88	3498.53	2700.78	2223.28	1905.89	1679.99	1511.27	1380.67	1276.74	1192.21	1122.23
120,000	10327.98	5318.48	3650.64	2818.21	2319.94	1988.75	1753.03	1576.98	1440.69	1332.25	1244.05	1171.03
125,000	10758.31	5540.08	3802.75	2935.63	2416.61	2071.62	1826.07	1642.68	1500.72	1387.76	1295.88	1219.82
130,000	11188.64	5761.68	3954.86	3053.06	2513.27	2154.48	1899.12	1708.39	1560.75	1443.27	1347.72	1268.61
135,000	11618.97	5983.29	4106.97	3170.48	2609.93	2237.34	1972.16	1774.10	1620.78	1498.78	1399.55	1317.40
140,000	12049.31	6204.89	4259.08	3287.91	2706.60	2320.21	2045.20	1839.81	1680.81	1554.29	1451.39	1366.20
145,000	12479.64	6426.49	4411.19	3405.33	2803.26	2403.07	2118.25	1905.51	1740.84	1609.80	1503.23	1414.99
150,000	12909.97	6648.10	4563.30	3522.76	2899.93	2485.94	2191.29	1971.22	1800.87	1665.31	1555.06	1463.78
155,000	13340.30	6869.70	4715.41	3640.18	2996.59	2568.80	2264.33	2036.93	1860.90	1720.82	1606.90	1512.57
160,000	13770.63	7091.30	4867.51	3757.61	3093.25	2651.67	2337.37	2102.63	1920.92	1776.33	1658.73	1561.37
165,000	14200.97	7312.91	5019.62	3875.03	3189.92	2734.53	2410.42	2168.34	1980.95	1831.84	1710.57	1610.16
170,000	14631.30	7534.51	5171.73	3992.46	3286.58	2817.40	2483.46	2234.05	2040.98	1887.35	1762.40	1658.95
175,000	15061.63	7756.11	5323.84	4109.89	3383.25	2900.26	2556.50	2299.76	2101.01	1942.86	1814.24	1707.74
180,000	15491.96	7977.71	5475.95	4227.31	3479.91	2983.12	2629.54	2365.46	2161.04	1998.37	1866.07	1756.54
185,000	15922.29	8199.32	5628.06	4344.74	3576.57	3065.99	2702.59	2431.17	2221.07	2053.88	1917.91	1805.33
190,000	16352.63	8420.92	5780.17	4462.16	3673.24	3148.85	2775.63	2496.88	2281.10	2109.39	1969.74	1854.12
195,000	16782.96	8642.52	5932.28	4579.59	3769.90	3231.72	2848.67	2562.58	2341.13	2164.90	2021.58	1902.91
200,000	17213.29	8864.13	6084.39	4697.01	3866.57	3314.58	2921.72	2628.29	2401.15	2220.42	2073.41	1951.71
205,000	17643.62	9085.73	6236.50	4814.44	3963.23	3397.45	2994.76	2694.00	2461.18	2275.93	2125.25	2000.50
210,000	18073.96	9307.33	6388.61	4931.86	4059.89	3480.31	3067.80	2759.71	2521.21	2331.44	2177.08	2049.29
215,000	18504.29	9528.94	6540.72	5049.29	4156.56	3563.18	3140.84	2825.41	2581.24	2386.95	2228.92	2098.08
220,000	18934.62	9750.54	6692.83	5166.71	4253.22	3646.04	3213.89	2891.12	2641.27	2442.46	2280.75	2146.88
225,000	19364.95	9972.14	6844.94	5284.14	4349.89	3728.90	3286.93	2956.83	2701.30	2497.97	2332.59	2195.67
230,000	19795.28	10193.75	6997.05	5401.56	4446.55	3811.77	3359.97	3022.53	2761.33	2553.48	2384.42	2244.46
235,000	20225.62	10415.35	7149.16	5518.99	4543.21	3894.63	3433.02	3088.24	2821.36	2608.99	2436.26	2293.25
240,000	20655.95	10636.95	7301.27	5636.41	4639.88	3977.50	3506.06	3153.95	2881.38	2664.50	2488.09	2342.05
245,000	21086.28	10858.55	7453.38	5753.84	4736.54	4060.36	3579.10	3219.66	2941.41	2720.01	2539.93	2390.84
250,000	21516.61	11080.16	7605.49	5871.26	4833.21	4143.23	3652.14	3285.36	3001.44	2775.52	2591.76	2439.63
255,000	21946.94	11301.76	7757.60	5988.69	4929.87	4226.09	3725.19	3351.07	3061.47	2831.03	2643.60	2488.42
260,000	22377.28	11523.36	7909.71	6106.11	5026.53	4308.96	3798.23	3416.78	3121.50	2886.54	2695.43	2537.22
265,000	22807.61	11744.97	8061.82	6223.54	5123.20	4391.82	3871.27	3482.48	3181.53	2942.05	2747.27	2586.01
270,000	23237.94	11966.57	8213.93	6340.96	5219.86	4474.68	3944.31	3548.19	3241.56	2997.56	2799.10	2634.80
280,000	24098.61	12409.78	8518.15	6575.81	5413.19	4640.41	4090.40	3679.61	3361.61	3108.58	2902.77	2732.39
290,000	24959.27	12852.98	8822.37	6810.66	5606.52	4806.14	4236.49	3811.02	3481.67	3219.60	3006.45	2829.97
300,000	25819.93	13296.19	9126.59	7045.51	5799.85	4971.87	4382.57	3942.43	3601.73	3330.62	3110.12	2927.56

6%

Monthly Amortizing Payments

AMOUNT OF LOAN	NUMBER OF YEARS IN TERM 13	14	15	16	17	18	19	20	25	30	35	40
$ 50	0.47	0.45	0.43	0.41	0.40	0.38	0.37	0.36	0.33	0.30	0.29	0.28
100	0.93	0.89	0.85	0.82	0.79	0.76	0.74	0.72	0.65	0.60	0.58	0.56
200	1.85	1.77	1.69	1.63	1.57	1.52	1.48	1.44	1.29	1.20	1.15	1.11
300	2.78	2.65	2.54	2.44	2.35	2.28	2.21	2.15	1.94	1.80	1.72	1.66
400	3.70	3.53	3.38	3.25	3.14	3.04	2.95	2.87	2.58	2.40	2.29	2.21
500	4.63	4.41	4.22	4.06	3.92	3.80	3.69	3.59	3.23	3.00	2.86	2.76
600	5.55	5.29	5.07	4.87	4.70	4.55	4.42	4.30	3.87	3.60	3.43	3.31
700	6.48	6.17	5.91	5.69	5.49	5.31	5.16	5.02	4.52	4.20	4.00	3.86
800	7.40	7.05	6.76	6.50	6.27	6.07	5.89	5.74	5.16	4.80	4.57	4.41
900	8.33	7.94	7.60	7.31	7.05	6.83	6.63	6.45	5.80	5.40	5.14	4.96
1,000	9.25	8.82	8.44	8.12	7.84	7.59	7.37	7.17	6.45	6.00	5.71	5.51
2,000	18.50	17.63	16.88	16.23	15.67	15.17	14.73	14.33	12.89	12.00	11.41	11.01
3,000	27.75	26.44	25.32	24.35	23.50	22.75	22.09	21.50	19.33	17.99	17.11	16.51
4,000	36.99	35.25	33.76	32.46	31.33	30.33	29.45	28.66	25.78	23.99	22.81	22.01
5,000	46.24	44.07	42.20	40.58	39.16	37.91	36.81	35.83	32.22	29.98	28.51	27.52
6,000	55.49	52.88	50.64	48.69	46.99	45.49	44.17	42.99	38.66	35.98	34.22	33.02
7,000	64.74	61.69	59.07	56.81	54.82	53.08	51.53	50.16	45.11	41.97	39.92	38.52
8,000	73.98	70.50	67.51	64.92	62.65	60.66	58.89	57.32	51.55	47.97	45.62	44.02
9,000	83.23	79.32	75.95	73.03	70.48	68.24	66.25	64.48	57.99	53.96	51.32	49.52
10,000	92.48	88.13	84.39	81.15	78.32	75.82	73.61	71.65	64.44	59.96	57.02	55.03
15,000	138.71	132.19	126.58	121.72	117.47	113.73	110.42	107.47	96.65	89.94	85.53	82.54
20,000	184.95	176.25	168.78	162.29	156.63	151.64	147.22	143.29	128.87	119.92	114.04	110.05
25,000	231.19	220.31	210.97	202.86	195.78	189.55	184.03	179.11	161.08	149.89	142.55	137.56
30,000	277.42	264.38	253.16	243.44	234.94	227.45	220.83	214.93	193.30	179.87	171.06	165.07
35,000	323.66	308.44	295.35	284.01	274.09	265.36	257.63	250.76	225.51	209.85	199.57	192.58
40,000	369.89	352.50	337.55	324.58	313.25	303.27	294.44	286.58	257.73	239.83	228.08	220.09
45,000	416.13	396.56	379.74	365.15	352.40	341.18	331.24	322.40	289.94	269.80	256.59	247.60
50,000	462.37	440.62	421.93	405.72	391.56	379.09	368.05	358.22	322.16	299.78	285.10	275.11
55,000	508.60	484.68	464.13	446.30	430.71	416.99	404.85	394.04	354.37	329.76	313.61	302.62
60,000	554.84	528.75	506.32	486.87	469.87	454.90	441.65	429.86	386.59	359.74	342.12	330.13
65,000	601.08	572.81	548.51	527.44	509.02	492.81	478.46	465.69	418.80	389.71	370.63	357.64
70,000	647.31	616.87	590.70	568.01	548.18	530.72	515.26	501.51	451.02	419.69	399.14	385.15
75,000	693.55	660.93	632.90	608.58	587.33	568.63	552.07	537.33	483.23	449.67	427.65	412.67
80,000	739.78	704.99	675.09	649.16	626.49	606.53	588.87	573.15	515.45	479.65	456.16	440.18
85,000	786.02	749.06	717.28	689.73	665.64	644.44	625.68	608.97	547.66	509.62	484.67	467.69
90,000	832.26	793.12	759.48	730.30	704.80	682.35	662.48	644.79	579.88	539.60	513.18	495.20
95,000	878.49	837.18	801.67	770.87	743.95	720.26	699.28	680.61	612.09	569.58	541.69	522.71
100,000	924.73	881.24	843.86	811.44	783.11	758.17	736.09	716.44	644.31	599.56	570.19	550.22
105,000	970.96	925.30	886.05	852.01	822.26	796.08	772.89	752.26	676.52	629.53	598.70	577.73
110,000	1017.20	969.36	928.25	892.59	861.42	833.98	809.70	788.08	708.74	659.51	627.21	605.24
115,000	1063.44	1013.43	970.44	933.16	900.57	871.89	846.50	823.90	740.95	689.49	655.72	632.75
120,000	1109.67	1057.49	1012.63	973.73	939.73	909.80	883.30	859.72	773.17	719.47	684.23	660.26
125,000	1155.91	1101.55	1054.83	1014.30	978.88	947.71	920.11	895.54	805.38	749.44	712.74	687.77
130,000	1202.15	1145.61	1097.02	1054.87	1018.04	985.62	956.91	931.37	837.60	779.42	741.25	715.28
135,000	1248.38	1189.67	1139.21	1095.45	1057.19	1023.52	993.72	967.19	869.81	809.40	769.76	742.79
140,000	1294.62	1233.74	1181.40	1136.02	1096.35	1061.43	1030.52	1003.01	902.03	839.38	798.27	770.30
145,000	1340.85	1277.80	1223.60	1176.59	1135.50	1099.34	1067.33	1038.83	934.24	869.35	826.78	797.81
150,000	1387.09	1321.86	1265.79	1217.16	1174.66	1137.25	1104.13	1074.65	966.46	899.33	855.29	825.33
155,000	1433.33	1365.92	1307.98	1257.73	1213.81	1175.16	1140.93	1110.47	998.67	929.31	883.80	852.84
160,000	1479.56	1409.98	1350.18	1298.31	1252.97	1213.06	1177.74	1146.29	1030.89	959.29	912.31	880.35
165,000	1525.80	1454.04	1392.37	1338.88	1292.12	1250.97	1214.54	1182.12	1063.10	989.26	940.82	907.86
170,000	1572.03	1498.11	1434.56	1379.45	1331.28	1288.88	1251.35	1217.94	1095.32	1019.24	969.33	935.37
175,000	1618.27	1542.17	1476.75	1420.02	1370.43	1326.79	1288.15	1253.76	1127.53	1049.22	997.84	962.88
180,000	1664.51	1586.23	1518.95	1460.59	1409.59	1364.70	1324.95	1289.58	1159.75	1079.20	1026.35	990.39
185,000	1710.74	1630.29	1561.14	1501.17	1448.74	1402.61	1361.76	1325.40	1191.96	1109.17	1054.86	1017.90
190,000	1756.98	1674.35	1603.33	1541.74	1487.90	1440.51	1398.56	1361.22	1224.18	1139.15	1083.37	1045.41
195,000	1803.22	1718.42	1645.53	1582.31	1527.05	1478.42	1435.37	1397.05	1256.39	1169.13	1111.87	1072.92
200,000	1849.45	1762.48	1687.72	1622.88	1566.21	1516.33	1472.17	1432.87	1288.61	1199.11	1140.38	1100.43
205,000	1895.69	1806.54	1729.91	1663.45	1605.36	1554.24	1508.98	1468.69	1320.82	1229.08	1168.89	1127.94
210,000	1941.92	1850.60	1772.10	1704.02	1644.52	1592.15	1545.78	1504.51	1353.04	1259.06	1197.40	1155.45
215,000	1988.16	1894.66	1814.30	1744.60	1683.67	1630.05	1582.58	1540.33	1385.25	1289.04	1225.91	1182.96
220,000	2034.40	1938.72	1856.49	1785.17	1722.83	1667.96	1619.39	1576.15	1417.47	1319.02	1254.42	1210.48
225,000	2080.63	1982.79	1898.68	1825.74	1761.98	1705.87	1656.19	1611.97	1449.68	1348.99	1282.93	1237.99
230,000	2126.87	2026.85	1940.88	1866.31	1801.14	1743.78	1693.00	1647.80	1481.90	1378.97	1311.44	1265.50
235,000	2173.11	2070.91	1983.07	1906.88	1840.29	1781.69	1729.80	1683.62	1514.11	1408.95	1339.95	1293.01
240,000	2219.34	2114.97	2025.26	1947.46	1879.45	1819.59	1766.60	1719.44	1546.33	1438.93	1368.46	1320.52
245,000	2265.58	2159.03	2067.45	1988.03	1918.60	1857.50	1803.41	1755.26	1578.54	1468.90	1396.97	1348.03
250,000	2311.81	2203.09	2109.65	2028.60	1957.76	1895.41	1840.21	1791.08	1610.76	1498.88	1425.48	1375.54
255,000	2358.05	2247.16	2151.84	2069.17	1996.91	1933.32	1877.02	1826.90	1642.97	1528.86	1453.99	1403.05
260,000	2404.29	2291.22	2194.03	2109.74	2036.07	1971.23	1913.82	1862.73	1675.19	1558.84	1482.50	1430.56
265,000	2450.52	2335.28	2236.23	2150.32	2075.22	2009.14	1950.62	1898.55	1707.40	1588.81	1511.01	1458.07
270,000	2496.76	2379.34	2278.42	2190.89	2114.38	2047.04	1987.43	1934.37	1739.62	1618.79	1539.52	1485.58
280,000	2589.23	2467.47	2362.80	2272.03	2192.69	2122.86	2061.04	2006.01	1804.05	1678.75	1596.54	1540.60
290,000	2681.70	2555.59	2447.19	2353.17	2271.00	2198.68	2134.65	2077.66	1868.48	1738.70	1653.56	1595.62
300,000	2774.18	2643.71	2531.58	2434.32	2349.31	2274.49	2208.25	2149.30	1932.91	1798.66	1710.57	1650.65

MONTHLY AMORTIZING PAYMENTS 7%

AMOUNT OF LOAN	NUMBER OF YEARS IN TERM 1	2	3	4	5	6	7	8	9	10	11	12
$ 50	4.33	2.24	1.55	1.20	1.00	0.86	0.76	0.69	0.63	0.59	0.55	0.52
100	8.66	4.48	3.09	2.40	1.99	1.71	1.51	1.37	1.26	1.17	1.09	1.03
200	17.31	8.96	6.18	4.79	3.97	3.41	3.02	2.73	2.51	2.33	2.18	2.06
300	25.96	13.44	9.27	7.19	5.95	5.12	4.53	4.10	3.76	3.49	3.27	3.09
400	34.62	17.91	12.36	9.58	7.93	6.82	6.04	5.46	5.01	4.65	4.36	4.12
500	43.27	22.39	15.44	11.98	9.91	8.53	7.55	6.82	6.26	5.81	5.45	5.15
600	51.92	26.87	18.53	14.37	11.89	10.23	9.06	8.19	7.51	6.97	6.54	6.18
700	60.57	31.35	21.62	16.77	13.87	11.94	10.57	9.55	8.76	8.13	7.62	7.20
800	69.23	35.82	24.71	19.16	15.85	13.64	12.08	10.91	10.01	9.29	8.71	8.23
900	77.88	40.30	27.79	21.56	17.83	15.35	13.59	12.28	11.26	10.45	9.80	9.26
1,000	86.53	44.78	30.88	23.95	19.81	17.05	15.10	13.64	12.51	11.62	10.89	10.29
2,000	173.06	89.55	61.76	47.90	39.61	34.10	30.19	27.27	25.02	23.23	21.77	20.57
3,000	259.59	134.32	92.64	71.84	59.41	51.15	45.28	40.91	37.52	34.84	32.66	30.86
4,000	346.11	179.10	123.51	95.79	79.21	68.20	60.38	54.54	50.03	46.45	43.54	41.14
5,000	432.64	223.87	154.39	119.74	99.01	85.25	75.47	68.17	62.54	58.06	54.43	51.42
6,000	519.17	268.64	185.27	143.68	118.81	102.30	90.56	81.81	75.04	69.67	65.31	61.71
7,000	605.69	313.41	216.14	167.63	138.61	119.35	105.65	95.44	87.55	81.28	76.19	71.99
8,000	692.22	358.19	247.02	191.57	158.41	136.40	120.75	109.07	100.06	92.89	87.08	82.28
9,000	778.75	402.96	277.90	215.52	178.22	153.45	135.84	122.71	112.56	104.50	97.96	92.56
10,000	865.27	447.73	308.78	239.47	198.02	170.50	150.93	136.34	125.07	116.11	108.85	102.84
15,000	1297.91	671.59	463.16	359.20	297.02	255.74	226.40	204.51	187.60	174.17	163.27	154.26
20,000	1730.54	895.46	617.55	478.93	396.03	340.99	301.86	272.68	250.13	232.22	217.69	205.68
25,000	2163.17	1119.32	771.93	598.66	495.03	426.23	377.32	340.85	312.66	290.28	272.11	257.10
30,000	2595.81	1343.18	926.32	718.39	594.04	511.48	452.79	409.02	375.19	348.33	326.53	308.52
35,000	3028.44	1567.05	1080.70	838.12	693.05	596.72	528.25	477.19	437.72	406.38	380.95	359.94
40,000	3461.07	1790.91	1235.09	957.85	792.05	681.97	603.71	545.35	500.26	464.44	435.37	411.36
45,000	3893.71	2014.77	1389.47	1077.59	891.06	767.21	679.18	613.52	562.79	522.49	489.79	462.78
50,000	4326.34	2238.63	1543.86	1197.32	990.06	852.46	754.64	681.69	625.32	580.55	544.21	514.20
55,000	4758.98	2462.50	1698.25	1317.05	1089.07	937.70	830.10	749.86	687.85	638.60	598.63	565.61
60,000	5191.61	2686.36	1852.63	1436.78	1188.08	1022.95	905.57	818.03	750.38	696.66	653.05	617.03
65,000	5624.24	2910.22	2007.02	1556.51	1287.08	1108.19	981.03	886.20	812.91	754.71	707.47	668.45
70,000	6056.88	3134.09	2161.40	1676.24	1386.09	1193.44	1056.49	954.37	875.44	812.76	761.89	719.87
75,000	6489.51	3357.95	2315.79	1795.97	1485.09	1278.68	1131.96	1022.53	937.98	870.82	816.31	771.29
80,000	6922.14	3581.81	2470.17	1915.70	1584.10	1363.93	1207.42	1090.70	1000.51	928.87	870.73	822.71
85,000	7354.78	3805.67	2624.56	2035.44	1683.11	1449.17	1282.88	1158.87	1063.04	986.93	925.15	874.13
90,000	7787.41	4029.54	2778.94	2155.17	1782.11	1534.42	1358.35	1227.04	1125.57	1044.98	979.57	925.55
95,000	8220.05	4253.40	2933.33	2274.90	1881.12	1619.66	1433.81	1295.21	1188.10	1103.04	1033.99	976.97
100,000	8652.68	4477.26	3087.71	2394.63	1980.12	1704.91	1509.27	1363.38	1250.63	1161.09	1088.42	1028.39
105,000	9085.31	4701.13	3242.10	2514.36	2079.13	1790.15	1584.74	1431.55	1313.16	1219.14	1142.84	1079.81
110,000	9517.95	4924.99	3396.49	2634.09	2178.14	1875.40	1660.20	1499.71	1375.70	1277.20	1197.26	1131.22
115,000	9950.58	5148.85	3550.87	2753.82	2277.14	1960.64	1735.66	1567.88	1438.23	1335.25	1251.68	1182.64
120,000	10383.21	5372.71	3705.26	2873.55	2376.15	2045.89	1811.13	1636.05	1500.76	1393.31	1306.10	1234.06
125,000	10815.85	5596.58	3859.64	2993.29	2475.15	2131.13	1886.59	1704.22	1563.29	1451.36	1360.52	1285.48
130,000	11248.48	5820.44	4014.03	3113.02	2574.16	2216.38	1962.05	1772.39	1625.82	1509.42	1414.94	1336.90
135,000	11681.12	6044.30	4168.41	3232.75	2673.17	2301.62	2037.52	1840.56	1688.35	1567.47	1469.36	1388.32
140,000	12113.75	6268.17	4322.80	3352.48	2772.17	2386.87	2112.98	1908.73	1750.88	1625.52	1523.78	1439.74
145,000	12546.38	6492.03	4477.18	3472.21	2871.18	2472.11	2188.44	1976.89	1813.42	1683.58	1578.20	1491.16
150,000	12979.02	6715.89	4631.57	3591.94	2970.18	2557.36	2263.91	2045.06	1875.95	1741.63	1632.62	1542.58
155,000	13411.65	6939.75	4785.96	3711.67	3069.19	2642.60	2339.37	2113.23	1938.48	1799.69	1687.04	1594.00
160,000	13844.28	7163.62	4940.34	3831.40	3168.20	2727.85	2414.83	2181.40	2001.01	1857.74	1741.46	1645.41
165,000	14276.92	7387.48	5094.73	3951.14	3267.20	2813.09	2490.30	2249.57	2063.54	1915.79	1795.88	1696.83
170,000	14709.55	7611.34	5249.11	4070.87	3366.21	2898.34	2565.76	2317.74	2126.07	1973.85	1850.30	1748.25
175,000	15142.19	7835.21	5403.50	4190.60	3465.21	2983.58	2641.22	2385.91	2188.60	2031.90	1904.72	1799.67
180,000	15574.82	8059.07	5557.88	4310.33	3564.22	3068.83	2716.69	2454.07	2251.13	2089.96	1959.14	1851.09
185,000	16007.45	8282.93	5712.27	4430.06	3663.23	3154.07	2792.15	2522.24	2313.67	2148.01	2013.56	1902.51
190,000	16440.09	8506.80	5866.65	4549.79	3762.23	3239.32	2867.61	2590.41	2376.20	2206.07	2067.98	1953.93
195,000	16872.72	8730.66	6021.04	4669.52	3861.24	3324.56	2943.08	2658.58	2438.73	2264.12	2122.40	2005.35
200,000	17305.35	8954.52	6175.42	4789.25	3960.24	3409.81	3018.54	2726.75	2501.26	2322.17	2176.83	2056.77
205,000	17737.99	9178.38	6329.81	4908.99	4059.25	3495.05	3094.00	2794.92	2563.79	2380.23	2231.25	2108.19
210,000	18170.62	9402.25	6484.20	5028.72	4158.26	3580.30	3169.47	2863.09	2626.32	2438.28	2285.67	2159.61
215,000	18603.26	9626.11	6638.58	5148.45	4257.26	3665.54	3244.93	2931.25	2688.85	2496.34	2340.09	2211.02
220,000	19035.89	9849.97	6792.97	5268.18	4356.27	3750.79	3320.39	2999.42	2751.39	2554.39	2394.51	2262.44
225,000	19468.52	10073.84	6947.35	5387.91	4455.27	3836.03	3395.86	3067.59	2813.92	2612.45	2448.93	2313.86
230,000	19901.16	10297.70	7101.74	5507.64	4554.28	3921.28	3471.32	3135.76	2876.45	2670.50	2503.35	2365.28
235,000	20333.79	10521.56	7256.12	5627.37	4653.29	4006.52	3546.78	3203.93	2938.98	2728.55	2557.77	2416.70
240,000	20766.42	10745.42	7410.51	5747.10	4752.29	4091.77	3622.25	3272.10	3001.51	2786.61	2612.19	2468.12
245,000	21199.06	10969.29	7564.89	5866.83	4851.30	4177.01	3697.71	3340.27	3064.04	2844.66	2666.61	2519.54
250,000	21631.69	11193.15	7719.28	5986.57	4950.30	4262.26	3773.17	3408.43	3126.57	2902.72	2721.03	2570.96
255,000	22064.33	11417.01	7873.66	6106.30	5049.31	4347.50	3848.64	3476.60	3189.11	2960.77	2775.45	2622.38
260,000	22496.96	11640.88	8028.05	6226.03	5148.32	4432.75	3924.10	3544.77	3251.64	3018.83	2829.87	2673.80
265,000	22929.59	11864.74	8182.44	6345.76	5247.32	4517.99	3999.57	3612.94	3314.17	3076.88	2884.29	2725.21
270,000	23362.23	12088.60	8336.82	6465.49	5346.33	4603.24	4075.03	3681.11	3376.70	3134.93	2938.71	2776.63
280,000	24227.49	12536.33	8645.59	6704.95	5544.34	4773.73	4225.96	3817.45	3501.76	3251.04	3047.55	2879.47
290,000	25092.76	12984.05	8954.36	6944.42	5742.35	4944.22	4376.88	3953.78	3626.83	3367.15	3156.39	2982.31
300,000	25958.03	13431.78	9263.13	7183.88	5940.36	5114.71	4527.81	4090.12	3751.89	3483.26	3265.24	3085.15

7% MONTHLY AMORTIZING PAYMENTS

AMOUNT OF LOAN	NUMBER OF YEARS IN TERM											
	13	14	15	16	17	18	19	20	25	30	35	40
$ 50	0.49	0.47	0.45	0.44	0.42	0.41	0.40	0.39	0.36	0.34	0.32	0.32
100	0.98	0.94	0.90	0.87	0.84	0.82	0.80	0.78	0.71	0.67	0.64	0.63
200	1.96	1.88	1.80	1.74	1.68	1.64	1.59	1.56	1.42	1.34	1.28	1.25
300	2.94	2.81	2.70	2.61	2.52	2.45	2.39	2.33	2.13	2.00	1.92	1.87
400	3.92	3.75	3.60	3.47	3.36	3.27	3.18	3.11	2.83	2.67	2.56	2.49
500	4.90	4.68	4.50	4.34	4.20	4.08	3.98	3.88	3.54	3.33	3.20	3.11
600	5.87	5.62	5.40	5.21	5.04	4.90	4.77	4.66	4.25	4.00	3.84	3.73
700	6.85	6.55	6.30	6.08	5.88	5.71	5.56	5.43	4.95	4.66	4.48	4.36
800	7.83	7.49	7.20	6.94	6.72	6.53	6.36	6.21	5.66	5.33	5.12	4.98
900	8.81	8.42	8.09	7.81	7.56	7.34	7.15	6.98	6.37	5.99	5.75	5.60
1,000	9.79	9.36	8.99	8.68	8.40	8.16	7.95	7.76	7.07	6.66	6.39	6.22
2,000	19.57	18.71	17.98	17.35	16.80	16.32	15.89	15.51	14.14	13.31	12.78	12.43
3,000	29.35	28.07	26.97	26.02	25.19	24.47	23.83	23.26	21.21	19.96	19.17	18.65
4,000	39.13	37.42	35.96	34.69	33.59	32.63	31.77	31.02	28.28	26.62	25.56	24.86
5,000	48.91	46.78	44.95	43.37	41.99	40.78	39.71	38.77	35.34	33.27	31.95	31.08
6,000	58.69	56.13	53.93	52.04	50.38	48.94	47.66	46.52	42.41	39.92	38.34	37.29
7,000	68.47	65.48	62.92	60.71	58.78	57.09	55.60	54.28	49.48	46.58	44.72	43.51
8,000	78.25	74.84	71.91	69.38	67.18	65.25	63.54	62.03	56.55	53.23	51.11	49.72
9,000	88.03	84.19	80.90	78.05	75.57	73.40	71.48	69.78	63.62	59.88	57.50	55.93
10,000	97.81	93.55	89.89	86.73	83.97	81.56	79.42	77.53	70.68	66.54	63.89	62.15
15,000	146.72	140.32	134.83	130.09	125.95	122.33	119.13	116.30	106.02	99.80	95.83	93.22
20,000	195.62	187.09	179.77	173.45	167.94	163.11	158.84	155.06	141.36	133.07	127.78	124.29
25,000	244.52	233.86	224.71	216.81	209.92	203.88	198.55	193.83	176.70	166.33	159.72	155.36
30,000	293.43	280.63	269.65	260.17	251.90	244.66	238.26	232.59	212.04	199.60	191.66	186.43
35,000	342.33	327.40	314.59	303.53	293.89	285.43	277.97	271.36	247.38	232.86	223.60	217.51
40,000	391.23	374.17	359.54	346.89	335.87	326.21	317.68	310.12	282.72	266.13	255.55	248.58
45,000	440.14	420.94	404.48	390.25	377.85	366.98	357.39	348.89	318.06	299.39	287.49	279.65
50,000	489.04	467.71	449.42	433.61	419.84	407.76	397.10	387.65	353.39	332.66	319.43	310.72
55,000	537.95	514.48	494.36	476.97	461.82	448.53	436.81	426.42	388.73	365.92	351.38	341.79
60,000	586.85	561.25	539.30	520.33	503.80	489.31	476.52	465.18	424.07	399.19	383.32	372.86
65,000	635.75	608.02	584.24	563.69	545.78	530.08	516.23	503.95	459.41	432.45	415.26	403.94
70,000	684.66	654.79	629.18	607.05	587.77	570.86	555.94	542.71	494.75	465.72	447.20	435.01
75,000	733.56	701.56	674.13	650.41	629.75	611.63	595.65	581.48	530.09	498.98	479.15	466.08
80,000	782.46	748.33	719.07	693.77	671.73	652.41	635.36	620.24	565.43	532.25	511.09	497.15
85,000	831.37	795.10	764.01	737.13	713.72	693.18	675.07	659.01	600.77	565.51	543.03	528.22
90,000	880.27	841.87	808.95	780.49	755.70	733.96	714.78	697.77	636.11	598.78	574.98	559.29
95,000	929.18	888.64	853.89	823.85	797.68	774.73	754.49	736.54	671.45	632.04	606.92	590.36
100,000	978.08	935.41	898.83	867.21	839.67	815.51	794.20	775.30	706.78	665.31	638.86	621.44
105,000	1026.98	982.18	943.77	910.57	881.65	856.28	833.91	814.07	742.12	698.57	670.80	652.51
110,000	1075.89	1028.95	988.72	953.93	923.63	897.06	873.62	852.83	777.46	731.84	702.75	683.58
115,000	1124.79	1075.72	1033.66	997.29	965.61	937.83	913.33	891.60	812.80	765.10	734.69	714.65
120,000	1173.69	1122.49	1078.60	1040.65	1007.60	978.61	953.04	930.36	848.14	798.37	766.63	745.72
125,000	1222.60	1169.26	1123.54	1084.02	1049.58	1019.38	992.75	969.13	883.48	831.63	798.58	776.79
130,000	1271.50	1216.03	1168.48	1127.38	1091.56	1060.16	1032.46	1007.89	918.82	864.90	830.52	807.87
135,000	1320.41	1262.80	1213.42	1170.74	1133.55	1100.93	1072.16	1046.66	954.16	898.16	862.46	838.94
140,000	1369.31	1309.57	1258.36	1214.10	1175.53	1141.71	1111.87	1085.42	989.50	931.43	894.40	870.01
145,000	1418.21	1356.34	1303.31	1257.46	1217.51	1182.48	1151.58	1124.19	1024.83	964.69	926.35	901.08
150,000	1467.12	1403.11	1348.25	1300.82	1259.50	1223.26	1191.29	1162.95	1060.17	997.96	958.29	932.15
155,000	1516.02	1449.88	1393.19	1344.18	1301.48	1264.03	1231.00	1201.72	1095.51	1031.22	990.23	963.22
160,000	1564.92	1496.65	1438.13	1387.54	1343.46	1304.81	1270.71	1240.48	1130.85	1064.49	1022.18	994.30
165,000	1613.83	1543.42	1483.07	1430.90	1385.45	1345.58	1310.42	1279.25	1166.19	1097.75	1054.12	1025.37
170,000	1662.73	1590.19	1528.01	1474.26	1427.43	1386.36	1350.13	1318.01	1201.53	1131.02	1086.06	1056.44
175,000	1711.63	1636.96	1572.95	1517.62	1469.41	1427.13	1389.84	1356.78	1236.87	1164.28	1118.00	1087.51
180,000	1760.54	1683.73	1617.90	1560.98	1511.39	1467.91	1429.55	1395.54	1272.21	1197.55	1149.95	1118.58
185,000	1809.44	1730.50	1662.84	1604.34	1553.38	1508.68	1469.26	1434.31	1307.55	1230.81	1181.89	1149.65
190,000	1858.35	1777.27	1707.78	1647.70	1595.36	1549.46	1508.97	1473.07	1342.89	1264.08	1213.83	1180.72
195,000	1907.25	1824.04	1752.72	1691.06	1637.34	1590.23	1548.68	1511.84	1378.22	1297.34	1245.77	1211.80
200,000	1956.15	1870.81	1797.66	1734.42	1679.33	1631.01	1588.39	1550.60	1413.56	1330.61	1277.72	1242.87
205,000	2005.06	1917.58	1842.60	1777.78	1721.31	1671.78	1628.10	1589.37	1448.90	1363.88	1309.66	1273.94
210,000	2053.96	1964.35	1887.54	1821.14	1763.29	1712.56	1667.81	1628.13	1484.24	1397.14	1341.60	1305.01
215,000	2102.86	2011.12	1932.49	1864.50	1805.28	1753.33	1707.52	1666.90	1519.58	1430.41	1373.55	1336.08
220,000	2151.77	2057.89	1977.43	1907.86	1847.26	1794.11	1747.23	1705.66	1554.92	1463.67	1405.49	1367.15
225,000	2200.67	2104.66	2022.37	1951.22	1889.24	1834.88	1786.94	1744.43	1590.26	1496.94	1437.43	1398.23
230,000	2249.58	2151.43	2067.31	1994.58	1931.22	1875.66	1826.65	1783.19	1625.60	1530.20	1469.37	1429.30
235,000	2298.48	2198.20	2112.25	2037.94	1973.21	1916.44	1866.36	1821.96	1660.94	1563.47	1501.32	1460.37
240,000	2347.38	2244.97	2157.19	2081.30	2015.19	1957.21	1906.07	1860.72	1696.28	1596.73	1533.26	1491.44
245,000	2396.29	2291.74	2202.13	2124.66	2057.17	1997.99	1945.78	1899.49	1731.61	1630.00	1565.20	1522.51
250,000	2445.19	2338.51	2247.08	2168.03	2099.16	2038.76	1985.49	1938.25	1766.95	1663.26	1597.15	1553.58
255,000	2494.09	2385.28	2292.02	2211.39	2141.14	2079.54	2025.20	1977.02	1802.29	1696.53	1629.09	1584.65
260,000	2543.00	2432.05	2336.96	2254.75	2183.12	2120.31	2064.91	2015.78	1837.63	1729.79	1661.03	1615.73
265,000	2591.90	2478.82	2381.90	2298.11	2225.11	2161.09	2104.61	2054.55	1872.97	1763.06	1692.97	1646.80
270,000	2640.81	2525.59	2426.84	2341.47	2267.09	2201.86	2144.32	2093.31	1908.31	1796.32	1724.92	1677.87
280,000	2738.61	2619.13	2516.72	2428.19	2351.05	2283.41	2223.74	2170.84	1978.99	1862.85	1788.80	1740.01
290,000	2836.42	2712.67	2606.61	2514.91	2435.02	2364.96	2303.16	2248.37	2049.66	1929.38	1852.69	1802.16
300,000	2934.23	2806.21	2696.49	2601.63	2518.99	2446.51	2382.58	2325.90	2120.34	1995.91	1916.57	1864.30

MONTHLY AMORTIZING PAYMENTS 8%

AMOUNT OF LOAN	NUMBER OF YEARS IN TERM											
	1	2	3	4	5	6	7	8	9	10	11	12
$ 50	4.35	2.27	1.57	1.23	1.02	0.88	0.78	0.71	0.66	0.61	0.58	0.55
100	8.70	4.53	3.14	2.45	2.03	1.76	1.56	1.42	1.31	1.22	1.15	1.09
200	17.40	9.05	6.27	4.89	4.06	3.51	3.12	2.83	2.61	2.43	2.29	2.17
300	26.10	13.57	9.41	7.33	6.09	5.26	4.68	4.25	3.91	3.64	3.43	3.25
400	34.80	18.10	12.54	9.77	8.12	7.02	6.24	5.66	5.21	4.86	4.57	4.33
500	43.50	22.62	15.67	12.21	10.14	8.77	7.80	7.07	6.51	6.07	5.71	5.42
600	52.20	27.14	18.81	14.65	12.17	10.52	9.36	8.49	7.82	7.28	6.85	6.50
700	60.90	31.66	21.94	17.09	14.20	12.28	10.92	9.90	9.12	8.50	8.00	7.58
800	69.60	36.19	25.07	19.54	16.23	14.03	12.47	11.31	10.42	9.71	9.14	8.66
900	78.29	40.71	28.21	21.98	18.25	15.78	14.03	12.73	11.72	10.92	10.28	9.75
1,000	86.99	45.23	31.34	24.42	20.28	17.54	15.59	14.14	13.02	12.14	11.42	10.83
2,000	173.98	90.46	62.68	48.83	40.56	35.07	31.18	28.28	26.04	24.27	22.84	21.65
3,000	260.97	135.69	94.01	73.24	60.83	52.60	46.76	42.42	39.06	36.40	34.25	32.48
4,000	347.96	180.91	125.35	97.66	81.11	70.14	62.35	56.55	52.08	48.54	45.67	43.30
5,000	434.95	226.14	156.69	122.07	101.39	87.67	77.94	70.69	65.10	60.67	57.08	54.13
6,000	521.94	271.37	188.02	146.48	121.66	105.20	93.52	84.83	78.12	72.80	68.50	64.95
7,000	608.92	316.60	219.36	170.90	141.94	122.74	109.11	98.96	91.14	84.93	79.91	75.78
8,000	695.91	361.82	250.70	195.31	162.22	140.27	124.69	113.10	104.15	97.07	91.33	86.60
9,000	782.90	407.05	282.03	219.72	182.49	157.80	140.28	127.24	117.17	109.20	102.74	97.43
10,000	869.89	452.28	313.37	244.13	202.77	175.34	155.87	141.37	130.19	121.33	114.16	108.25
15,000	1304.83	678.41	470.05	366.20	304.15	263.00	233.80	212.06	195.29	182.00	171.24	162.37
20,000	1739.77	904.55	626.73	488.26	405.53	350.67	311.73	282.74	260.38	242.66	228.31	216.50
25,000	2174.72	1130.69	783.41	610.33	506.91	438.34	389.66	353.42	325.47	303.32	285.39	270.62
30,000	2609.66	1356.82	940.10	732.39	608.30	526.00	467.59	424.11	390.57	363.99	342.47	324.74
35,000	3044.60	1582.96	1096.78	854.46	709.68	613.67	545.52	494.79	455.66	424.65	399.55	378.86
40,000	3479.54	1809.10	1253.46	976.52	811.06	701.33	623.45	565.47	520.75	485.32	456.62	432.99
45,000	3914.48	2035.23	1410.14	1098.59	912.44	789.00	701.38	636.16	585.85	545.98	513.70	487.11
50,000	4349.43	2261.37	1566.82	1220.65	1013.82	876.67	779.32	706.84	650.94	606.64	570.78	541.23
55,000	4784.37	2487.51	1723.51	1342.72	1115.21	964.33	857.25	777.52	716.03	667.31	627.85	595.35
60,000	5219.31	2713.64	1880.19	1464.78	1216.59	1052.00	935.18	848.21	781.13	727.97	684.93	649.48
65,000	5654.25	2939.78	2036.87	1586.84	1317.97	1139.67	1013.11	918.89	846.22	788.63	742.01	703.60
70,000	6089.20	3165.92	2193.55	1708.91	1419.35	1227.33	1091.04	989.57	911.32	849.30	799.09	757.72
75,000	6524.14	3392.05	2350.23	1830.97	1520.73	1315.00	1168.97	1060.26	976.41	909.96	856.16	811.84
80,000	6959.08	3618.19	2506.91	1953.04	1622.12	1402.66	1246.90	1130.94	1041.50	970.63	913.24	865.97
85,000	7394.02	3844.32	2663.60	2075.10	1723.50	1490.33	1324.83	1201.62	1106.60	1031.29	970.32	920.09
90,000	7828.96	4070.46	2820.28	2197.17	1824.88	1578.00	1402.76	1272.31	1171.69	1091.95	1027.40	974.21
95,000	8263.91	4296.60	2976.96	2319.23	1926.26	1665.66	1480.70	1342.99	1236.78	1152.62	1084.47	1028.33
100,000	8698.85	4522.73	3133.64	2441.30	2027.64	1753.33	1558.63	1413.67	1301.88	1213.28	1141.55	1082.46
105,000	9133.79	4748.87	3290.32	2563.36	2129.03	1841.00	1636.56	1484.36	1366.97	1273.94	1198.63	1136.58
110,000	9568.73	4975.01	3447.01	2685.43	2230.41	1928.66	1714.49	1555.04	1432.06	1334.61	1255.70	1190.70
115,000	10003.67	5201.14	3603.69	2807.49	2331.79	2016.33	1792.42	1625.72	1497.16	1395.27	1312.78	1244.83
120,000	10438.62	5427.28	3760.37	2929.56	2433.17	2103.99	1870.35	1696.41	1562.25	1455.94	1369.86	1298.95
125,000	10873.56	5653.42	3917.05	3051.62	2534.55	2191.66	1948.28	1767.09	1627.34	1516.60	1426.94	1353.07
130,000	11308.50	5879.55	4073.73	3173.68	2635.94	2279.33	2026.21	1837.77	1692.44	1577.26	1484.01	1407.19
135,000	11743.44	6105.69	4230.41	3295.75	2737.32	2366.99	2104.14	1908.46	1757.53	1637.93	1541.09	1461.32
140,000	12178.39	6331.83	4387.10	3417.81	2838.70	2454.66	2182.08	1979.14	1822.63	1698.59	1598.17	1515.44
145,000	12613.33	6557.96	4543.78	3539.88	2940.08	2542.32	2260.01	2049.82	1887.72	1759.26	1655.24	1569.56
150,000	13048.27	6784.10	4700.46	3661.94	3041.46	2629.99	2337.94	2120.51	1952.81	1819.92	1712.32	1623.68
155,000	13483.21	7010.24	4857.14	3784.01	3142.85	2717.66	2415.87	2191.19	2017.91	1880.58	1769.40	1677.81
160,000	13918.15	7236.37	5013.82	3906.07	3244.23	2805.32	2493.80	2261.87	2083.00	1941.25	1826.48	1731.93
165,000	14353.10	7462.51	5170.51	4028.14	3345.61	2892.99	2571.73	2332.56	2148.09	2001.91	1883.55	1786.05
170,000	14788.04	7688.64	5327.19	4150.20	3446.99	2980.66	2649.66	2403.24	2213.19	2062.57	1940.63	1840.17
175,000	15222.98	7914.78	5483.87	4272.27	3548.37	3068.32	2727.59	2473.92	2278.28	2123.24	1997.71	1894.30
180,000	15657.92	8140.92	5640.55	4394.33	3649.76	3155.99	2805.52	2544.61	2343.37	2183.90	2054.79	1948.42
185,000	16092.86	8367.05	5797.23	4516.40	3751.14	3243.65	2883.45	2615.29	2408.47	2244.57	2111.86	2002.54
190,000	16527.81	8593.19	5953.91	4638.46	3852.52	3331.32	2961.39	2685.97	2473.56	2305.23	2168.94	2056.66
195,000	16962.75	8819.33	6110.60	4760.52	3953.90	3418.99	3039.32	2756.66	2538.65	2365.89	2226.02	2110.79
200,000	17397.69	9045.46	6267.28	4882.59	4055.28	3506.65	3117.25	2827.34	2603.75	2426.56	2283.09	2164.91
205,000	17832.63	9271.60	6423.96	5004.65	4156.67	3594.32	3195.18	2898.02	2668.84	2487.22	2340.17	2219.03
210,000	18267.58	9497.74	6580.64	5126.72	4258.05	3681.99	3273.11	2968.71	2733.94	2547.88	2397.25	2273.16
215,000	18702.52	9723.87	6737.32	5248.78	4359.43	3769.65	3351.04	3039.39	2799.03	2608.55	2454.33	2327.28
220,000	19137.46	9950.01	6894.01	5370.85	4460.81	3857.32	3428.97	3110.07	2864.12	2669.21	2511.40	2381.40
225,000	19572.40	10176.15	7050.69	5492.91	4562.19	3944.98	3506.90	3180.76	2929.22	2729.88	2568.48	2435.52
230,000	20007.34	10402.28	7207.37	5614.98	4663.58	4032.65	3584.83	3251.44	2994.31	2790.54	2625.56	2489.65
235,000	20442.29	10628.42	7364.05	5737.04	4764.96	4120.32	3662.77	3322.12	3059.40	2851.20	2682.64	2543.77
240,000	20877.23	10854.55	7520.73	5859.11	4866.34	4207.98	3740.70	3392.81	3124.50	2911.87	2739.71	2597.89
245,000	21312.17	11080.69	7677.41	5981.17	4967.72	4295.65	3818.63	3463.49	3189.59	2972.53	2796.79	2652.01
250,000	21747.11	11306.83	7834.10	6103.24	5069.10	4383.32	3896.56	3534.17	3254.68	3033.19	2853.87	2706.14
255,000	22182.05	11532.96	7990.78	6225.30	5170.49	4470.98	3974.49	3604.86	3319.78	3093.86	2910.94	2760.26
260,000	22617.00	11759.10	8147.46	6347.36	5271.87	4558.65	4052.42	3675.54	3384.87	3154.52	2968.02	2814.38
265,000	23051.94	11985.24	8304.14	6469.43	5373.25	4646.31	4130.35	3746.23	3449.96	3215.19	3025.10	2868.50
270,000	23486.88	12211.37	8460.82	6591.49	5474.63	4733.98	4208.28	3816.91	3515.06	3275.85	3082.18	2922.63
280,000	24356.77	12663.65	8774.19	6835.62	5677.40	4909.31	4364.15	3958.28	3645.25	3397.18	3196.33	3030.87
290,000	25226.65	13115.92	9087.55	7079.75	5880.16	5084.64	4520.01	4099.64	3775.43	3518.51	3310.48	3139.12
300,000	26096.53	13568.19	9400.91	7323.88	6082.92	5259.98	4675.87	4241.01	3905.62	3639.83	3424.64	3247.36

8% — Monthly Amortizing Payments

Amount of Loan	13	14	15	16	17	18	19	20	25	30	35	40
	NUMBER OF YEARS IN TERM											
$ 50	0.52	0.50	0.48	0.47	0.45	0.44	0.43	0.42	0.39	0.37	0.36	0.35
100	1.04	1.00	0.96	0.93	0.90	0.88	0.86	0.84	0.78	0.74	0.72	0.70
200	2.07	1.99	1.92	1.85	1.80	1.75	1.71	1.68	1.55	1.47	1.43	1.40
300	3.10	2.98	2.87	2.78	2.70	2.63	2.57	2.51	2.32	2.21	2.14	2.09
400	4.14	3.97	3.83	3.70	3.60	3.50	3.42	3.35	3.09	2.94	2.85	2.79
500	5.17	4.96	4.78	4.63	4.50	4.38	4.28	4.19	3.86	3.67	3.56	3.48
600	6.20	5.95	5.74	5.55	5.39	5.25	5.13	5.02	4.64	4.41	4.27	4.18
700	7.24	6.94	6.69	6.48	6.29	6.13	5.99	5.86	5.41	5.14	4.98	4.87
800	8.27	7.94	7.65	7.40	7.19	7.00	6.84	6.70	6.18	5.88	5.69	5.57
900	9.30	8.93	8.61	8.33	8.09	7.88	7.70	7.53	6.95	6.61	6.40	6.26
1,000	10.34	9.92	9.56	9.25	8.99	8.75	8.55	8.37	7.72	7.34	7.11	6.96
2,000	20.67	19.83	19.12	18.50	17.97	17.50	17.10	16.73	15.44	14.68	14.21	13.91
3,000	31.00	29.74	28.67	27.75	26.95	26.25	25.64	25.10	23.16	22.02	21.31	20.86
4,000	41.33	39.66	38.23	37.00	35.94	35.00	34.19	33.46	30.88	29.36	28.42	27.82
5,000	51.66	49.57	47.79	46.25	44.92	43.75	42.73	41.83	38.60	36.69	35.52	34.77
6,000	61.99	59.48	57.34	55.50	53.90	52.50	51.28	50.19	46.31	44.03	42.62	41.72
7,000	72.32	69.40	66.90	64.75	62.88	61.25	59.82	58.56	54.03	51.37	49.72	48.68
8,000	82.65	79.31	76.46	74.00	71.87	70.00	68.37	66.92	61.75	58.71	56.83	55.63
9,000	92.98	89.22	86.01	83.25	80.85	78.75	76.91	75.28	69.47	66.04	63.93	62.58
10,000	103.31	99.14	95.57	92.50	89.83	87.50	85.46	83.65	77.19	73.38	71.03	69.54
15,000	154.97	148.70	143.35	138.74	134.74	131.25	128.18	125.47	115.78	110.07	106.54	104.30
20,000	206.62	198.27	191.14	184.99	179.66	175.00	170.91	167.29	154.37	146.76	142.06	139.07
25,000	258.27	247.83	238.92	231.24	224.57	218.75	213.63	209.12	192.96	183.45	177.57	173.83
30,000	309.93	297.40	286.70	277.48	269.48	262.49	256.36	250.94	231.55	220.13	213.08	208.60
35,000	361.58	346.97	334.48	323.73	314.39	306.24	299.08	292.76	270.14	256.82	248.60	243.36
40,000	413.23	396.53	382.27	369.98	359.31	349.99	341.81	334.58	308.73	293.51	284.11	278.13
45,000	464.89	446.10	430.05	416.22	404.22	393.74	384.53	376.40	347.32	330.20	319.62	312.90
50,000	516.54	495.66	477.83	462.47	449.13	437.49	427.26	418.23	385.91	366.89	355.14	347.66
55,000	568.20	545.23	525.61	508.71	494.05	481.23	469.98	460.05	424.50	403.58	390.65	382.43
60,000	619.85	594.80	573.40	554.96	538.96	524.98	512.71	501.87	463.09	440.26	426.16	417.19
65,000	671.50	644.36	621.18	601.21	583.87	568.73	555.43	543.69	501.69	476.95	461.67	451.96
70,000	723.16	693.93	668.96	647.45	628.78	612.48	598.16	585.51	540.28	513.64	497.19	486.72
75,000	774.81	743.49	716.74	693.70	673.70	656.23	640.88	627.34	578.87	550.33	532.70	521.49
80,000	826.46	793.06	764.53	739.95	718.61	699.98	683.61	669.16	617.46	587.02	568.21	556.25
85,000	878.12	842.63	812.31	786.19	763.52	743.72	726.33	710.98	656.05	623.70	603.73	591.02
90,000	929.77	892.19	860.09	832.44	808.44	787.47	769.06	752.80	694.64	660.39	639.24	625.79
95,000	981.43	941.76	907.87	878.68	853.35	831.22	811.78	794.62	733.23	697.08	674.75	660.55
100,000	1033.08	991.32	955.66	924.93	898.26	874.97	854.51	836.45	771.82	733.77	710.27	695.32
105,000	1084.73	1040.89	1003.44	971.18	943.17	918.72	897.23	878.27	810.41	770.46	745.78	730.08
110,000	1136.39	1090.46	1051.22	1017.42	988.09	962.46	939.96	920.09	849.00	807.15	781.29	764.85
115,000	1188.04	1140.02	1099.00	1063.67	1033.00	1006.21	982.68	961.91	887.59	843.83	816.81	799.61
120,000	1239.69	1189.59	1146.79	1109.92	1077.91	1049.96	1025.41	1003.73	926.18	880.52	852.32	834.38
125,000	1291.35	1239.15	1194.57	1156.16	1122.83	1093.71	1068.13	1045.56	964.78	917.21	887.83	869.14
130,000	1343.00	1288.72	1242.35	1202.41	1167.74	1137.46	1110.86	1087.38	1003.37	953.90	923.34	903.91
135,000	1394.65	1338.28	1290.14	1248.65	1212.65	1181.20	1153.58	1129.20	1041.96	990.59	958.86	938.68
140,000	1446.31	1387.85	1337.92	1294.90	1257.56	1224.95	1196.31	1171.02	1080.55	1027.28	994.37	973.44
145,000	1497.96	1437.42	1385.70	1341.15	1302.48	1268.70	1239.03	1212.84	1119.14	1063.96	1029.88	1008.21
150,000	1549.62	1486.98	1433.48	1387.39	1347.39	1312.45	1281.76	1254.67	1157.73	1100.65	1065.40	1042.97
155,000	1601.27	1536.55	1481.27	1433.64	1392.30	1356.20	1324.48	1296.49	1196.32	1137.34	1100.91	1077.74
160,000	1652.92	1586.11	1529.05	1479.89	1437.22	1399.95	1367.21	1338.31	1234.91	1174.03	1136.42	1112.50
165,000	1704.58	1635.68	1576.83	1526.13	1482.13	1443.69	1409.93	1380.13	1273.50	1210.72	1171.94	1147.27
170,000	1756.23	1685.25	1624.61	1572.38	1527.04	1487.44	1452.66	1421.95	1312.09	1247.40	1207.45	1182.03
175,000	1807.88	1734.81	1672.40	1618.62	1571.95	1531.19	1495.38	1463.78	1350.68	1284.09	1242.96	1216.80
180,000	1859.54	1784.38	1720.18	1664.87	1616.87	1574.94	1538.11	1505.60	1389.27	1320.78	1278.47	1251.57
185,000	1911.19	1833.94	1767.96	1711.12	1661.78	1618.69	1580.83	1547.42	1427.87	1357.47	1313.99	1286.33
190,000	1962.85	1883.51	1815.74	1757.36	1706.69	1662.43	1623.56	1589.24	1466.46	1394.16	1349.50	1321.10
195,000	2014.50	1933.08	1863.53	1803.61	1751.61	1706.18	1666.28	1631.06	1505.05	1430.85	1385.01	1355.86
200,000	2066.15	1982.64	1911.31	1849.86	1796.52	1749.93	1709.01	1672.89	1543.64	1467.53	1420.53	1390.63
205,000	2117.81	2032.21	1959.09	1896.10	1841.43	1793.68	1751.73	1714.71	1582.23	1504.22	1456.04	1425.39
210,000	2169.46	2081.77	2006.87	1942.35	1886.34	1837.43	1794.46	1756.53	1620.82	1540.91	1491.55	1460.16
215,000	2221.11	2131.34	2054.66	1988.59	1931.26	1881.17	1837.18	1798.35	1659.41	1577.60	1527.07	1494.93
220,000	2272.77	2180.91	2102.44	2034.84	1976.17	1924.92	1879.91	1840.17	1698.00	1614.29	1562.58	1529.69
225,000	2324.42	2230.47	2150.22	2081.09	2021.08	1968.67	1922.63	1882.00	1736.59	1650.98	1598.09	1564.46
230,000	2376.07	2280.04	2198.00	2127.33	2066.00	2012.42	1965.36	1923.82	1775.18	1687.66	1633.61	1599.22
235,000	2427.73	2329.60	2245.79	2173.58	2110.91	2056.17	2008.08	1965.64	1813.77	1724.35	1669.12	1633.99
240,000	2479.38	2379.17	2293.57	2219.83	2155.82	2099.92	2050.81	2007.46	1852.36	1761.04	1704.63	1668.75
245,000	2531.04	2428.73	2341.35	2266.07	2200.73	2143.66	2093.53	2049.28	1890.95	1797.73	1740.14	1703.52
250,000	2582.69	2478.30	2389.14	2312.32	2245.65	2187.41	2136.26	2091.11	1929.55	1834.42	1775.66	1738.28
255,000	2634.34	2527.87	2436.92	2358.56	2290.56	2231.16	2178.98	2132.93	1968.14	1871.10	1811.17	1773.05
260,000	2686.00	2577.43	2484.70	2404.81	2335.47	2274.91	2221.71	2174.75	2006.73	1907.79	1846.68	1807.82
265,000	2737.65	2627.00	2532.48	2451.06	2380.39	2318.66	2264.43	2216.57	2045.32	1944.48	1882.20	1842.58
270,000	2789.30	2676.56	2580.27	2497.30	2425.30	2362.40	2307.16	2258.39	2083.91	1981.17	1917.71	1877.35
280,000	2892.61	2775.70	2675.83	2589.80	2515.12	2449.90	2392.61	2342.04	2161.09	2054.55	1988.74	1946.88
290,000	2995.92	2874.83	2771.40	2682.29	2604.95	2537.40	2478.06	2425.68	2238.27	2127.92	2059.76	2016.41
300,000	3099.23	2973.96	2866.96	2774.78	2694.78	2624.89	2563.51	2509.33	2315.45	2201.30	2130.79	2085.94

MONTHLY AMORTIZING PAYMENTS 9%

AMOUNT OF LOAN	1	2	3	4	5	6	7	8	9	10	11	12
	NUMBER OF YEARS IN TERM											
$ 50	4.38	2.29	1.59	1.25	1.04	0.91	0.81	0.74	0.68	0.64	0.60	0.57
100	8.75	4.57	3.18	2.49	2.08	1.81	1.61	1.47	1.36	1.27	1.20	1.14
200	17.50	9.14	6.36	4.98	4.16	3.61	3.22	2.94	2.71	2.54	2.40	2.28
300	26.24	13.71	9.54	7.47	6.23	5.41	4.83	4.40	4.07	3.81	3.59	3.42
400	34.99	18.28	12.72	9.96	8.31	7.22	6.44	5.87	5.42	5.07	4.79	4.56
500	43.73	22.85	15.90	12.45	10.38	9.02	8.05	7.33	6.78	6.34	5.99	5.70
600	52.48	27.42	19.08	14.94	12.46	10.82	9.66	8.80	8.13	7.61	7.18	6.83
700	61.22	31.98	22.26	17.42	14.54	12.62	11.27	10.26	9.49	8.87	8.38	7.97
800	69.97	36.55	25.44	19.91	16.61	14.43	12.88	11.73	10.84	10.14	9.57	9.11
900	78.71	41.12	28.62	22.40	18.69	16.23	14.49	13.19	12.19	11.41	10.77	10.25
1,000	87.46	45.69	31.80	24.89	20.76	18.03	16.09	14.66	13.55	12.67	11.97	11.39
2,000	174.91	91.37	63.60	49.78	41.52	36.06	32.18	29.31	27.09	25.34	23.93	22.77
3,000	262.36	137.06	95.40	74.66	62.28	54.08	48.27	43.96	40.63	38.01	35.89	34.15
4,000	349.81	182.74	127.20	99.55	83.04	72.11	64.36	58.61	54.18	50.68	47.85	45.53
5,000	437.26	228.43	159.00	124.43	103.80	90.13	80.45	73.26	67.72	63.34	59.81	56.91
6,000	524.71	274.11	190.80	149.32	124.56	108.16	96.54	87.91	81.26	76.01	71.77	68.29
7,000	612.17	319.80	222.60	174.20	145.31	126.18	112.63	102.56	94.81	88.68	83.73	79.67
8,000	699.62	365.48	254.40	199.09	166.07	144.21	128.72	117.21	108.35	101.35	95.69	91.05
9,000	787.07	411.17	286.20	223.97	186.83	162.23	144.81	131.86	121.89	114.01	107.65	102.43
10,000	874.52	456.85	318.00	248.86	207.59	180.26	160.90	146.51	135.43	126.68	119.61	113.81
15,000	1311.78	685.28	477.00	373.28	311.38	270.39	241.34	219.76	203.15	190.02	179.42	170.71
20,000	1749.03	913.70	636.00	497.71	415.17	360.52	321.79	293.01	270.86	253.36	239.22	227.61
25,000	2186.29	1142.12	795.00	622.13	518.96	450.64	402.23	366.26	338.58	316.69	299.03	284.51
30,000	2623.55	1370.55	954.00	746.56	622.76	540.77	482.68	439.51	406.29	380.03	358.83	341.41
35,000	3060.81	1598.97	1113.00	870.98	726.55	630.90	563.12	512.76	474.01	443.37	418.63	398.32
40,000	3498.06	1827.39	1271.99	995.41	830.34	721.03	643.57	586.01	541.72	506.71	478.44	455.22
45,000	3935.32	2055.82	1430.99	1119.83	934.13	811.15	724.01	659.26	609.44	570.05	538.24	512.12
50,000	4372.58	2284.24	1589.99	1244.26	1037.92	901.28	804.46	732.52	677.15	633.38	598.05	569.02
55,000	4809.84	2512.67	1748.99	1368.68	1141.71	991.41	884.90	805.77	744.86	696.72	657.85	625.92
60,000	5247.09	2741.09	1907.99	1493.11	1245.51	1081.54	965.35	879.02	812.58	760.06	717.65	682.82
65,000	5684.35	2969.51	2066.99	1617.53	1349.30	1171.66	1045.80	952.27	880.29	823.40	777.46	739.72
70,000	6121.61	3197.94	2225.99	1741.96	1453.09	1261.79	1126.24	1025.52	948.01	886.74	837.26	796.63
75,000	6558.87	3426.36	2384.98	1866.38	1556.88	1351.92	1206.69	1098.77	1015.72	950.07	897.07	853.53
80,000	6996.12	3654.78	2543.98	1990.81	1660.67	1442.05	1287.13	1172.02	1083.44	1013.41	956.87	910.43
85,000	7433.38	3883.21	2702.98	2115.23	1764.47	1532.18	1367.58	1245.27	1151.15	1076.75	1016.67	967.33
90,000	7870.64	4111.63	2861.98	2239.66	1868.26	1622.30	1448.02	1318.52	1218.87	1140.09	1076.48	1024.23
95,000	8307.90	4340.06	3020.98	2364.08	1972.05	1712.43	1528.47	1391.77	1286.58	1203.42	1136.28	1081.13
100,000	8745.15	4568.48	3179.98	2488.51	2075.84	1802.56	1608.91	1465.03	1354.30	1266.76	1196.09	1138.04
105,000	9182.41	4796.90	3338.98	2612.93	2179.63	1892.69	1689.36	1538.28	1422.01	1330.10	1255.89	1194.94
110,000	9619.67	5025.33	3497.98	2737.36	2283.42	1982.81	1769.80	1611.53	1489.72	1393.44	1315.69	1251.84
115,000	10056.92	5253.75	3656.97	2861.78	2387.22	2072.94	1850.25	1684.78	1557.44	1456.78	1375.50	1308.74
120,000	10494.18	5482.17	3815.97	2986.21	2491.01	2163.07	1930.69	1758.03	1625.15	1520.11	1435.30	1365.64
125,000	10931.44	5710.60	3974.97	3110.64	2594.80	2253.20	2011.14	1831.28	1692.87	1583.45	1495.11	1422.54
130,000	11368.70	5939.02	4133.97	3235.06	2698.59	2343.32	2091.59	1904.53	1760.58	1646.79	1554.91	1479.44
135,000	11805.95	6167.45	4292.97	3359.49	2802.38	2433.45	2172.03	1977.78	1828.30	1710.13	1614.71	1536.35
140,000	12243.21	6395.87	4451.97	3483.91	2906.17	2523.58	2252.48	2051.03	1896.01	1773.47	1674.52	1593.25
145,000	12680.47	6624.29	4610.97	3608.34	3009.97	2613.71	2332.92	2124.28	1963.73	1836.80	1734.32	1650.15
150,000	13117.73	6852.72	4769.96	3732.76	3113.76	2703.84	2413.37	2197.54	2031.44	1900.14	1794.13	1707.05
155,000	13554.98	7081.14	4928.96	3857.19	3217.55	2793.96	2493.81	2270.79	2099.16	1963.48	1853.93	1763.95
160,000	13992.24	7309.56	5087.96	3981.61	3321.34	2884.09	2574.26	2344.04	2166.87	2026.82	1913.73	1820.85
165,000	14429.50	7537.99	5246.96	4106.04	3425.13	2974.22	2654.70	2417.29	2234.58	2090.16	1973.54	1877.76
170,000	14866.76	7766.41	5405.96	4230.46	3528.93	3064.35	2735.15	2490.54	2302.30	2153.49	2033.34	1934.66
175,000	15304.01	7994.83	5564.96	4354.89	3632.72	3154.47	2815.59	2563.79	2370.01	2216.83	2093.15	1991.56
180,000	15741.27	8223.26	5723.96	4479.31	3736.51	3244.60	2896.04	2637.04	2437.73	2280.17	2152.95	2048.46
185,000	16178.53	8451.68	5882.96	4603.74	3840.30	3334.73	2976.48	2710.29	2505.44	2343.51	2212.75	2105.36
190,000	16615.79	8680.11	6041.95	4728.16	3944.09	3424.86	3056.93	2783.54	2573.16	2406.84	2272.56	2162.26
195,000	17053.04	8908.53	6200.95	4852.59	4047.88	3514.98	3137.38	2856.79	2640.87	2470.18	2332.36	2219.16
200,000	17490.30	9136.95	6359.95	4977.01	4151.68	3605.11	3217.82	2930.05	2708.59	2533.52	2392.17	2276.07
205,000	17927.56	9365.38	6518.95	5101.44	4255.47	3695.24	3298.27	3003.30	2776.30	2596.86	2451.97	2332.97
210,000	18364.82	9593.80	6677.95	5225.86	4359.26	3785.37	3378.71	3076.55	2844.02	2660.20	2511.77	2389.87
215,000	18802.07	9822.22	6836.95	5350.29	4463.05	3875.50	3459.16	3149.80	2911.73	2723.53	2571.58	2446.77
220,000	19239.33	10050.65	6995.95	5474.71	4566.84	3965.62	3539.60	3223.05	2979.44	2786.87	2631.38	2503.67
225,000	19676.59	10279.07	7154.94	5599.14	4670.63	4055.75	3620.05	3296.30	3047.16	2850.21	2691.19	2560.57
230,000	20113.84	10507.50	7313.94	5723.56	4774.43	4145.88	3700.49	3369.55	3114.87	2913.55	2750.99	2617.48
235,000	20551.10	10735.92	7472.94	5847.99	4878.22	4236.01	3780.94	3442.80	3182.59	2976.89	2810.79	2674.38
240,000	20988.36	10964.34	7631.94	5972.42	4982.01	4326.13	3861.38	3516.05	3250.30	3040.22	2870.60	2731.28
245,000	21425.62	11192.77	7790.94	6096.84	5085.80	4416.26	3941.83	3589.30	3318.02	3103.56	2930.40	2788.18
250,000	21862.87	11421.19	7949.94	6221.27	5189.59	4506.39	4022.27	3662.56	3385.73	3166.90	2990.21	2845.08
255,000	22300.13	11649.61	8108.94	6345.69	5293.39	4596.52	4102.72	3735.81	3453.45	3230.24	3050.01	2901.98
260,000	22737.39	11878.04	8267.94	6470.12	5397.18	4686.64	4183.17	3809.06	3521.16	3293.58	3109.81	2958.88
265,000	23174.65	12106.46	8426.93	6594.54	5500.97	4776.77	4263.61	3882.31	3588.88	3356.91	3169.62	3015.79
270,000	23611.90	12334.89	8585.93	6718.97	5604.76	4866.90	4344.06	3955.56	3656.59	3420.25	3229.42	3072.69
280,000	24486.42	12791.73	8903.93	6967.82	5812.34	5047.16	4504.95	4102.06	3792.02	3546.93	3349.03	3186.49
290,000	25360.93	13248.58	9221.93	7216.67	6019.93	5227.41	4665.84	4248.56	3927.45	3673.60	3468.64	3300.29
300,000	26235.45	13705.43	9539.92	7465.52	6227.51	5407.67	4826.73	4395.07	4062.88	3800.28	3588.25	3414.10

9% MONTHLY AMORTIZING PAYMENTS

AMOUNT OF LOAN	NUMBER OF YEARS IN TERM 13	14	15	16	17	18	19	20	25	30	35	40
$ 50	0.55	0.53	0.51	0.50	0.48	0.47	0.46	0.45	0.42	0.41	0.40	0.39
100	1.09	1.05	1.02	0.99	0.96	0.94	0.92	0.90	0.84	0.81	0.79	0.78
200	2.18	2.10	2.03	1.97	1.92	1.88	1.84	1.80	1.68	1.61	1.57	1.55
300	3.27	3.15	3.05	2.96	2.88	2.81	2.76	2.70	2.52	2.42	2.36	2.32
400	4.36	4.20	4.06	3.94	3.84	3.75	3.67	3.60	3.36	3.22	3.14	3.09
500	5.45	5.25	5.08	4.93	4.80	4.69	4.59	4.50	4.20	4.03	3.92	3.86
600	6.54	6.30	6.09	5.91	5.76	5.62	5.51	5.40	5.04	4.83	4.71	4.63
700	7.63	7.35	7.10	6.90	6.72	6.56	6.42	6.30	5.88	5.64	5.49	5.40
800	8.72	8.40	8.12	7.88	7.68	7.50	7.34	7.20	6.72	6.44	6.28	6.18
900	9.81	9.45	9.13	8.87	8.63	8.43	8.26	8.10	7.56	7.25	7.06	6.95
1,000	10.90	10.49	10.15	9.85	9.59	9.37	9.17	9.00	8.40	8.05	7.84	7.72
2,000	21.80	20.98	20.29	19.70	19.18	18.73	18.34	18.00	16.79	16.10	15.68	15.43
3,000	32.70	31.47	30.43	29.54	28.77	28.10	27.51	27.00	25.18	24.14	23.52	23.15
4,000	43.59	41.96	40.58	39.39	38.36	37.46	36.68	35.99	33.57	32.19	31.36	30.86
5,000	54.49	52.45	50.72	49.23	47.95	46.83	45.85	44.99	41.96	40.24	39.20	38.57
6,000	65.39	62.94	60.86	59.08	57.53	56.19	55.02	53.99	50.36	48.28	47.04	46.29
7,000	76.28	73.43	71.00	68.92	67.12	65.56	64.19	62.99	58.75	56.33	54.88	54.00
8,000	87.18	83.92	81.15	78.77	76.71	74.92	73.36	71.98	67.14	64.37	62.72	61.71
9,000	98.08	94.41	91.29	88.61	86.30	84.29	82.53	80.98	75.53	72.42	70.56	69.43
10,000	108.97	104.90	101.43	98.46	95.89	93.65	91.69	89.98	83.92	80.47	78.40	77.14
15,000	163.46	157.35	152.14	147.68	143.83	140.47	137.54	134.96	125.88	120.70	117.60	115.71
20,000	217.94	209.79	202.86	196.91	191.77	187.29	183.38	179.95	167.84	160.93	156.80	154.28
25,000	272.43	262.24	253.57	246.13	239.71	234.12	229.23	224.94	209.80	201.16	196.00	192.85
30,000	326.91	314.69	304.28	295.36	287.65	280.94	275.07	269.92	251.76	241.39	235.20	231.41
35,000	381.39	367.13	355.00	344.59	335.59	327.76	320.92	314.91	293.72	281.62	274.40	269.98
40,000	435.88	419.58	405.71	393.81	383.53	374.58	366.76	359.90	335.68	321.85	313.60	308.55
45,000	490.36	472.03	456.42	443.04	431.47	421.41	412.61	404.88	377.64	362.09	352.80	347.12
50,000	544.85	524.47	507.14	492.26	479.41	468.23	458.45	449.87	419.60	402.32	392.00	385.69
55,000	599.33	576.92	557.85	541.49	527.35	515.05	504.30	494.85	461.56	442.55	431.20	424.25
60,000	653.81	629.37	608.56	590.71	575.29	561.87	550.14	539.84	503.52	482.78	470.40	462.82
65,000	708.30	681.81	659.28	639.94	623.23	608.69	595.99	584.83	545.48	523.01	509.60	501.39
70,000	762.78	734.26	709.99	689.17	671.17	655.52	641.83	629.81	587.44	563.24	548.80	539.96
75,000	817.27	786.71	760.70	738.39	719.11	702.34	687.68	674.80	629.40	603.47	588.00	578.53
80,000	871.75	839.16	811.42	787.62	767.05	749.16	733.52	719.79	671.36	643.70	627.20	617.09
85,000	926.23	891.60	862.13	836.84	814.99	795.98	779.37	764.77	713.32	683.93	666.40	655.66
90,000	980.72	944.05	912.84	886.07	862.93	842.81	825.21	809.76	755.28	724.17	705.60	694.23
95,000	1035.20	996.50	963.56	935.30	910.87	889.63	871.06	854.74	797.24	764.40	744.80	732.80
100,000	1089.69	1048.94	1014.27	984.52	958.81	936.45	916.90	899.73	839.20	804.63	784.00	771.37
105,000	1144.17	1101.39	1064.98	1033.75	1006.75	983.27	962.75	944.72	881.16	844.86	823.20	809.93
110,000	1198.65	1153.84	1115.70	1082.97	1054.69	1030.09	1008.59	989.70	923.12	885.09	862.40	848.50
115,000	1253.14	1206.28	1166.41	1132.20	1102.63	1076.92	1054.44	1034.69	965.08	925.32	901.60	887.07
120,000	1307.62	1258.73	1217.12	1181.42	1150.57	1123.74	1100.28	1079.68	1007.04	965.55	940.80	925.64
125,000	1362.11	1311.18	1267.84	1230.65	1198.51	1170.56	1146.13	1124.66	1049.00	1005.78	980.00	964.21
130,000	1416.59	1363.62	1318.55	1279.88	1246.45	1217.38	1191.97	1169.65	1090.96	1046.01	1019.20	1002.77
135,000	1471.07	1416.07	1369.26	1329.10	1294.39	1264.21	1237.82	1214.64	1132.92	1086.25	1058.40	1041.34
140,000	1525.56	1468.52	1419.98	1378.33	1342.33	1311.03	1283.66	1259.62	1174.88	1126.48	1097.60	1079.91
145,000	1580.04	1520.96	1470.69	1427.55	1390.27	1357.85	1329.51	1304.61	1216.84	1166.71	1136.79	1118.48
150,000	1634.53	1573.41	1521.40	1476.78	1438.21	1404.67	1375.35	1349.59	1258.80	1206.94	1175.99	1157.05
155,000	1689.01	1625.86	1572.12	1526.00	1486.15	1451.49	1421.20	1394.58	1300.76	1247.17	1215.19	1195.62
160,000	1743.49	1678.31	1622.83	1575.23	1534.09	1498.32	1467.04	1439.57	1342.72	1287.40	1254.39	1234.18
165,000	1797.98	1730.75	1673.54	1624.46	1582.03	1545.14	1512.88	1484.55	1384.68	1327.63	1293.59	1272.75
170,000	1852.46	1783.20	1724.26	1673.68	1629.97	1591.96	1558.73	1529.54	1426.64	1367.86	1332.79	1311.32
175,000	1906.95	1835.65	1774.97	1722.91	1677.91	1638.78	1604.57	1574.53	1468.60	1408.09	1371.99	1349.89
180,000	1961.43	1888.09	1825.68	1772.13	1725.85	1685.61	1650.42	1619.51	1510.56	1448.33	1411.19	1388.46
185,000	2015.91	1940.54	1876.40	1821.36	1773.79	1732.43	1696.26	1664.50	1552.52	1488.56	1450.39	1427.02
190,000	2070.40	1992.99	1927.11	1870.59	1821.73	1779.25	1742.11	1709.48	1594.48	1528.79	1489.59	1465.59
195,000	2124.88	2045.43	1977.82	1919.81	1869.67	1826.07	1787.95	1754.47	1636.44	1569.02	1528.79	1504.16
200,000	2179.37	2097.88	2028.54	1969.04	1917.61	1872.89	1833.80	1799.46	1678.40	1609.25	1567.99	1542.73
205,000	2233.85	2150.33	2079.25	2018.26	1965.55	1919.72	1879.64	1844.44	1720.36	1649.48	1607.19	1581.30
210,000	2288.33	2202.77	2129.96	2067.49	2013.49	1966.54	1925.49	1889.43	1762.32	1689.71	1646.39	1619.86
215,000	2342.82	2255.22	2180.68	2116.71	2061.43	2013.36	1971.33	1934.42	1804.28	1729.94	1685.59	1658.43
220,000	2397.30	2307.67	2231.39	2165.94	2109.37	2060.18	2017.18	1979.40	1846.24	1770.17	1724.79	1697.00
225,000	2451.79	2360.11	2282.10	2215.17	2157.31	2107.01	2063.02	2024.39	1888.20	1810.41	1763.99	1735.57
230,000	2506.27	2412.56	2332.82	2264.39	2205.25	2153.83	2108.87	2069.37	1930.16	1850.64	1803.19	1774.14
235,000	2560.75	2465.01	2383.53	2313.62	2253.19	2200.65	2154.71	2114.36	1972.12	1890.87	1842.39	1812.70
240,000	2615.24	2517.46	2434.24	2362.84	2301.13	2247.47	2200.56	2159.35	2014.08	1931.10	1881.59	1851.27
245,000	2669.72	2569.90	2484.96	2412.07	2349.07	2294.29	2246.40	2204.33	2056.04	1971.33	1920.79	1889.84
250,000	2724.21	2622.35	2535.67	2461.29	2397.01	2341.12	2292.25	2249.32	2098.00	2011.56	1959.99	1928.41
255,000	2778.69	2674.80	2586.38	2510.52	2444.95	2387.94	2338.09	2294.31	2139.96	2051.79	1999.19	1966.98
260,000	2833.17	2727.24	2637.10	2559.75	2492.90	2434.76	2383.94	2339.29	2181.92	2092.02	2038.39	2005.54
265,000	2887.66	2779.69	2687.81	2608.97	2540.84	2481.58	2429.78	2384.28	2223.88	2132.25	2077.59	2044.11
270,000	2942.14	2832.14	2738.52	2658.20	2588.78	2528.41	2475.63	2429.27	2265.84	2172.49	2116.79	2082.68
280,000	3051.11	2937.03	2839.95	2756.65	2684.66	2622.05	2567.32	2519.24	2349.75	2252.95	2195.19	2159.82
290,000	3160.08	3041.92	2941.38	2855.10	2780.54	2715.70	2659.01	2609.21	2433.67	2333.41	2273.58	2236.95
300,000	3269.05	3146.82	3042.80	2953.55	2876.42	2809.34	2750.70	2699.18	2517.59	2413.87	2351.98	2314.09

MONTHLY AMORTIZING PAYMENTS 10%

AMOUNT OF LOAN	NUMBER OF YEARS IN TERM 1	2	3	4	5	6	7	8	9	10	11	12
$ 50	4.40	2.31	1.62	1.27	1.07	0.93	0.84	0.76	0.71	0.67	0.63	0.60
100	8.80	4.62	3.23	2.54	2.13	1.86	1.67	1.52	1.41	1.33	1.26	1.20
200	17.59	9.23	6.46	5.08	4.25	3.71	3.33	3.04	2.82	2.65	2.51	2.40
300	26.38	13.85	9.69	7.61	6.38	5.56	4.99	4.56	4.23	3.97	3.76	3.59
400	35.17	18.46	12.91	10.15	8.50	7.42	6.65	6.07	5.64	5.29	5.01	4.79
500	43.96	23.08	16.14	12.69	10.63	9.27	8.31	7.59	7.04	6.61	6.26	5.98
600	52.75	27.69	19.37	15.22	12.75	11.12	9.97	9.11	8.45	7.93	7.52	7.18
700	61.55	32.31	22.59	17.76	14.88	12.97	11.63	10.63	9.86	9.26	8.77	8.37
800	70.34	36.92	25.82	20.30	17.00	14.83	13.29	12.14	11.27	10.58	10.02	9.57
900	79.13	41.54	29.05	22.83	19.13	16.68	14.95	13.66	12.68	11.90	11.27	10.76
1,000	87.92	46.15	32.27	25.37	21.25	18.53	16.61	15.18	14.08	13.22	12.52	11.96
2,000	175.84	92.29	64.54	50.73	42.50	37.06	33.21	30.35	28.16	26.44	25.04	23.91
3,000	263.75	138.44	96.81	76.09	63.75	55.58	49.81	45.53	42.24	39.65	37.56	35.86
4,000	351.67	184.58	129.07	101.46	84.99	74.11	66.41	60.70	56.32	52.87	50.08	47.81
5,000	439.58	230.73	161.34	126.82	106.24	92.63	83.01	75.88	70.40	66.08	62.60	59.76
6,000	527.50	276.87	193.61	152.18	127.49	111.16	99.61	91.05	84.48	79.30	75.12	71.71
7,000	615.42	323.02	225.88	177.54	148.73	129.69	116.21	106.22	98.56	92.51	87.64	83.66
8,000	703.33	369.16	258.14	202.91	169.98	148.21	132.81	121.40	112.63	105.73	100.16	95.61
9,000	791.25	415.31	290.41	228.27	191.23	166.74	149.42	136.57	126.71	118.94	112.68	107.56
10,000	879.16	461.45	322.68	253.63	212.48	185.26	166.02	151.75	140.79	132.16	125.20	119.51
15,000	1318.74	692.18	484.01	380.44	318.71	277.89	249.02	227.62	211.19	198.23	187.80	179.27
20,000	1758.32	922.90	645.35	507.26	424.95	370.52	332.03	303.49	281.58	264.31	250.40	239.02
25,000	2197.90	1153.63	806.68	634.07	531.18	463.15	415.03	379.36	351.97	330.38	313.00	298.77
30,000	2637.48	1384.35	968.02	760.88	637.42	555.78	498.04	455.23	422.37	396.46	375.60	358.53
35,000	3077.06	1615.08	1129.36	887.70	743.65	648.41	581.05	531.10	492.76	462.53	438.20	418.28
40,000	3516.64	1845.80	1290.69	1014.51	849.89	741.04	664.05	606.97	563.15	528.61	500.80	478.04
45,000	3956.22	2076.53	1452.03	1141.32	956.12	833.67	747.06	682.84	633.55	594.68	563.40	537.79
50,000	4395.80	2307.25	1613.36	1268.13	1062.36	926.30	830.06	758.71	703.94	660.76	626.00	597.54
55,000	4835.38	2537.98	1774.70	1394.95	1168.59	1018.93	913.07	834.58	774.33	726.83	688.60	657.30
60,000	5274.96	2768.70	1936.04	1521.76	1274.83	1111.56	996.08	910.45	844.73	792.91	751.20	717.05
65,000	5714.54	2999.43	2097.37	1648.57	1381.06	1204.18	1079.08	986.33	915.12	858.98	813.80	776.81
70,000	6154.12	3230.15	2258.71	1775.39	1487.30	1296.81	1162.09	1062.20	985.51	925.06	876.40	836.56
75,000	6593.70	3460.87	2420.04	1902.20	1593.53	1389.44	1245.09	1138.07	1055.91	991.14	939.00	896.31
80,000	7033.28	3691.60	2581.38	2029.01	1699.77	1482.07	1328.10	1213.94	1126.30	1057.21	1001.60	956.07
85,000	7472.86	3922.32	2742.72	2155.82	1806.00	1574.70	1411.11	1289.81	1196.69	1123.29	1064.19	1015.82
90,000	7912.43	4153.05	2904.05	2282.64	1912.24	1667.33	1494.11	1365.68	1267.09	1189.36	1126.79	1075.58
95,000	8352.01	4383.77	3065.39	2409.45	2018.47	1759.96	1577.12	1441.55	1337.48	1255.44	1189.39	1135.33
100,000	8791.59	4614.50	3226.72	2536.26	2124.71	1852.59	1660.12	1517.42	1407.87	1321.51	1251.99	1195.08
105,000	9231.17	4845.22	3388.06	2663.08	2230.94	1945.22	1743.13	1593.29	1478.27	1387.59	1314.59	1254.84
110,000	9670.75	5075.95	3549.40	2789.89	2337.18	2037.85	1826.14	1669.16	1548.66	1453.66	1377.19	1314.59
115,000	10110.33	5306.67	3710.73	2916.70	2443.42	2130.48	1909.14	1745.03	1619.05	1519.74	1439.79	1374.35
120,000	10549.91	5537.40	3872.07	3043.52	2549.65	2223.11	1992.15	1820.90	1689.45	1585.81	1502.39	1434.10
125,000	10989.49	5768.12	4033.40	3170.33	2655.89	2315.73	2075.15	1896.78	1759.84	1651.89	1564.99	1493.85
130,000	11429.07	5998.85	4194.74	3297.14	2762.12	2408.36	2158.16	1972.65	1830.23	1717.96	1627.59	1553.61
135,000	11868.65	6229.57	4356.08	3423.95	2868.36	2500.99	2241.16	2048.52	1900.63	1784.04	1690.19	1613.36
140,000	12308.23	6460.29	4517.41	3550.77	2974.59	2593.62	2324.17	2124.39	1971.02	1850.12	1752.79	1673.11
145,000	12747.81	6691.02	4678.75	3677.58	3080.83	2686.25	2407.18	2200.26	2041.41	1916.19	1815.39	1732.87
150,000	13187.39	6921.74	4840.08	3804.39	3187.06	2778.88	2490.18	2276.13	2111.81	1982.27	1877.99	1792.62
155,000	13626.97	7152.47	5001.42	3931.21	3293.30	2871.51	2573.19	2352.00	2182.20	2048.34	1940.59	1852.38
160,000	14066.55	7383.19	5162.75	4058.02	3399.53	2964.14	2656.19	2427.87	2252.59	2114.42	2003.19	1912.13
165,000	14506.13	7613.92	5324.09	4184.83	3505.77	3056.77	2739.20	2503.74	2322.99	2180.49	2065.78	1971.88
170,000	14945.71	7844.64	5485.43	4311.64	3612.00	3149.40	2822.21	2579.61	2393.38	2246.57	2128.38	2031.64
175,000	15385.29	8075.37	5646.76	4438.46	3718.24	3242.03	2905.21	2655.48	2463.78	2312.64	2190.98	2091.39
180,000	15824.86	8306.09	5808.10	4565.27	3824.47	3334.66	2988.22	2731.35	2534.17	2378.72	2253.58	2151.15
185,000	16264.44	8536.82	5969.43	4692.08	3930.71	3427.28	3071.22	2807.23	2604.56	2444.79	2316.18	2210.90
190,000	16704.02	8767.54	6130.77	4818.90	4036.94	3519.91	3154.23	2883.10	2674.96	2510.87	2378.78	2270.65
195,000	17143.60	8998.27	6292.11	4945.71	4143.18	3612.54	3237.24	2958.97	2745.35	2576.94	2441.38	2330.41
200,000	17583.18	9228.99	6453.44	5072.52	4249.41	3705.17	3320.24	3034.84	2815.74	2643.02	2503.98	2390.16
205,000	18022.76	9459.71	6614.78	5199.33	4355.65	3797.80	3403.25	3110.71	2886.14	2709.10	2566.58	2449.92
210,000	18462.34	9690.44	6776.11	5326.15	4461.88	3890.43	3486.25	3186.58	2956.53	2775.17	2629.18	2509.67
215,000	18901.92	9921.16	6937.45	5452.96	4568.12	3983.06	3569.26	3262.45	3026.92	2841.25	2691.78	2569.42
220,000	19341.50	10151.89	7098.79	5579.77	4674.35	4075.69	3652.27	3338.32	3097.32	2907.32	2754.38	2629.18
225,000	19781.08	10382.61	7260.12	5706.59	4780.59	4168.32	3735.27	3414.19	3167.71	2973.40	2816.98	2688.93
230,000	20220.66	10613.34	7421.46	5833.40	4886.83	4260.95	3818.28	3490.06	3238.10	3039.47	2879.58	2748.69
235,000	20660.24	10844.06	7582.79	5960.21	4993.06	4353.58	3901.28	3565.93	3308.50	3105.55	2942.18	2808.44
240,000	21099.82	11074.79	7744.13	6087.03	5099.30	4446.21	3984.29	3641.80	3378.89	3171.62	3004.78	2868.19
245,000	21539.40	11305.51	7905.47	6213.84	5205.53	4538.84	4067.30	3717.68	3449.28	3237.70	3067.37	2927.95
250,000	21978.98	11536.24	8066.80	6340.65	5311.77	4631.46	4150.30	3793.55	3519.68	3303.77	3129.97	2987.70
255,000	22418.56	11766.96	8228.14	6467.46	5418.00	4724.09	4233.31	3869.42	3590.07	3369.85	3192.57	3047.45
260,000	22858.14	11997.69	8389.47	6594.28	5524.24	4816.72	4316.31	3945.29	3660.46	3435.92	3255.17	3107.21
265,000	23297.72	12228.41	8550.81	6721.09	5630.47	4909.35	4399.32	4021.16	3730.86	3502.00	3317.77	3166.96
270,000	23737.29	12459.14	8712.15	6847.90	5736.71	5001.98	4482.32	4097.03	3801.25	3568.07	3380.37	3226.72
280,000	24616.45	12920.58	9034.82	7101.53	5949.18	5187.24	4648.34	4248.77	3942.04	3700.23	3505.57	3346.22
290,000	25495.61	13382.03	9357.49	7355.15	6161.65	5372.50	4814.35	4400.51	4082.82	3832.38	3630.77	3465.73
300,000	26374.77	13843.48	9680.16	7608.78	6374.12	5557.76	4980.36	4552.25	4223.61	3964.53	3755.97	3585.24

10% Monthly Amortizing Payments

AMOUNT OF LOAN	NUMBER OF YEARS IN TERM											
	13	14	15	16	17	18	19	20	25	30	35	40
$ 50	0.58	0.56	0.54	0.53	0.52	0.50	0.50	0.49	0.46	0.44	0.43	0.43
100	1.15	1.11	1.08	1.05	1.03	1.00	0.99	0.97	0.91	0.88	0.86	0.85
200	2.30	2.22	2.15	2.10	2.05	2.00	1.97	1.94	1.82	1.76	1.72	1.70
300	3.45	3.33	3.23	3.14	3.07	3.00	2.95	2.90	2.73	2.64	2.58	2.55
400	4.60	4.44	4.30	4.19	4.09	4.00	3.93	3.87	3.64	3.52	3.44	3.40
500	5.74	5.55	5.38	5.23	5.11	5.00	4.91	4.83	4.55	4.39	4.30	4.25
600	6.89	6.65	6.45	6.28	6.13	6.00	5.89	5.80	5.46	5.27	5.16	5.10
700	8.04	7.76	7.53	7.33	7.15	7.00	6.87	6.76	6.37	6.15	6.02	5.95
800	9.19	8.87	8.60	8.37	8.17	8.00	7.86	7.73	7.27	7.03	6.88	6.80
900	10.34	9.98	9.68	9.42	9.20	9.00	8.84	8.69	8.18	7.90	7.74	7.65
1,000	11.48	11.09	10.75	10.46	10.22	10.00	9.82	9.66	9.09	8.78	8.60	8.50
2,000	22.96	22.17	21.50	20.92	20.43	20.00	19.63	19.31	18.18	17.56	17.20	16.99
3,000	34.44	33.25	32.24	31.38	30.64	30.00	29.44	28.96	27.27	26.33	25.80	25.48
4,000	45.92	44.33	42.99	41.84	40.85	40.00	39.26	38.61	36.35	35.11	34.39	33.97
5,000	57.40	55.42	53.74	52.30	51.07	50.00	49.07	48.26	45.44	43.88	42.99	42.46
6,000	68.88	66.50	64.48	62.76	61.28	60.00	58.88	57.91	54.53	52.66	51.59	50.95
7,000	80.35	77.58	75.23	73.22	71.49	69.99	68.69	67.56	63.61	61.44	60.18	59.45
8,000	91.83	88.66	85.97	83.68	81.70	79.99	78.51	77.21	72.70	70.21	68.78	67.94
9,000	103.31	99.74	96.72	94.14	91.91	89.99	88.32	86.86	81.79	78.99	77.38	76.43
10,000	114.79	110.83	107.47	104.60	102.13	99.99	98.13	96.51	90.88	87.76	85.97	84.92
15,000	172.18	166.24	161.20	156.89	153.19	149.98	147.19	144.76	136.31	131.64	128.96	127.38
20,000	229.57	221.65	214.93	209.19	204.25	199.97	196.26	193.01	181.75	175.52	171.94	169.83
25,000	286.97	277.06	268.66	261.48	255.31	249.97	245.32	241.26	227.18	219.40	214.92	212.29
30,000	344.36	332.47	322.39	313.78	306.37	299.96	294.38	289.51	272.62	263.28	257.91	254.75
35,000	401.75	387.88	376.12	366.07	357.43	349.95	343.45	337.76	318.05	307.16	300.89	297.21
40,000	459.14	443.29	429.85	418.37	408.49	399.94	392.51	386.01	363.49	351.03	343.87	339.66
45,000	516.54	498.70	483.58	470.66	459.55	449.93	441.57	434.26	408.92	394.91	386.86	382.12
50,000	573.93	554.11	537.31	522.96	510.61	499.93	490.63	482.52	454.36	438.79	429.84	424.58
55,000	631.32	609.52	591.04	575.25	561.67	549.92	539.70	530.77	499.79	482.67	472.82	467.04
60,000	688.71	664.93	644.77	627.55	612.73	599.91	588.76	579.02	545.23	526.55	515.81	509.49
65,000	746.11	720.34	698.50	679.84	663.79	649.90	637.82	627.27	590.66	570.43	558.79	551.95
70,000	803.50	775.75	752.23	732.14	714.85	699.90	686.89	675.52	636.10	614.31	601.78	594.41
75,000	860.89	831.16	805.96	784.43	765.91	749.89	735.95	723.77	681.53	658.18	644.76	636.86
80,000	918.28	886.57	859.69	836.73	816.97	799.88	785.01	772.02	726.97	702.06	687.74	679.32
85,000	975.68	941.98	913.42	889.02	868.03	849.87	834.08	820.27	772.40	745.94	730.73	721.78
90,000	1033.07	997.39	967.15	941.32	919.09	899.86	883.14	868.52	817.84	789.82	773.71	764.24
95,000	1090.46	1052.80	1020.88	993.61	970.15	949.86	932.20	916.78	863.27	833.70	816.69	806.69
100,000	1147.85	1108.21	1074.61	1045.91	1021.22	999.85	981.26	965.03	908.71	877.58	859.68	849.15
105,000	1205.25	1163.62	1128.34	1098.20	1072.28	1049.84	1030.33	1013.28	954.14	921.46	902.66	891.61
110,000	1262.64	1219.03	1182.07	1150.50	1123.34	1099.83	1079.39	1061.53	999.58	965.33	945.64	934.07
115,000	1320.03	1274.44	1235.80	1202.79	1174.40	1149.83	1128.45	1109.78	1045.01	1009.21	988.63	976.52
120,000	1377.42	1329.85	1289.53	1255.09	1225.46	1199.82	1177.52	1158.03	1090.45	1053.09	1031.61	1018.98
125,000	1434.82	1385.26	1343.26	1307.38	1276.52	1249.81	1226.58	1206.28	1135.88	1096.97	1074.60	1061.44
130,000	1492.21	1440.67	1396.99	1359.68	1327.58	1299.80	1275.64	1254.53	1181.32	1140.85	1117.58	1103.89
135,000	1549.60	1496.08	1450.72	1411.97	1378.64	1349.79	1324.70	1302.78	1226.75	1184.73	1160.56	1146.35
140,000	1606.99	1551.49	1504.45	1464.27	1429.70	1399.79	1373.77	1351.04	1272.19	1228.61	1203.55	1188.81
145,000	1664.38	1606.90	1558.18	1516.56	1480.76	1449.78	1422.83	1399.29	1317.62	1272.48	1246.53	1231.27
150,000	1721.78	1662.31	1611.91	1568.86	1531.82	1499.77	1471.89	1447.54	1363.06	1316.36	1289.51	1273.72
155,000	1779.17	1717.72	1665.64	1621.15	1582.88	1549.76	1520.96	1495.79	1408.49	1360.24	1332.50	1316.18
160,000	1836.56	1773.13	1719.37	1673.45	1633.94	1599.75	1570.02	1544.04	1453.93	1404.12	1375.48	1358.64
165,000	1893.95	1828.54	1773.10	1725.74	1685.00	1649.75	1619.08	1592.29	1499.36	1448.00	1418.46	1401.10
170,000	1951.35	1883.95	1826.83	1778.04	1736.06	1699.74	1668.15	1640.54	1544.80	1491.88	1461.45	1443.55
175,000	2008.74	1939.36	1880.56	1830.33	1787.12	1749.73	1717.21	1688.79	1590.23	1535.76	1504.43	1486.01
180,000	2066.13	1994.77	1934.29	1882.63	1838.18	1799.72	1766.27	1737.04	1635.67	1579.63	1547.42	1528.47
185,000	2123.52	2050.18	1988.02	1934.92	1889.24	1849.72	1815.33	1785.30	1681.10	1623.51	1590.40	1570.92
190,000	2180.92	2105.59	2041.75	1987.22	1940.30	1899.71	1864.40	1833.55	1726.54	1667.39	1633.38	1613.38
195,000	2238.31	2161.00	2095.48	2039.51	1991.37	1949.70	1913.46	1881.80	1771.97	1711.27	1676.37	1655.84
200,000	2295.70	2216.41	2149.22	2091.81	2042.43	1999.69	1962.52	1930.05	1817.41	1755.15	1719.35	1698.30
205,000	2353.09	2271.82	2202.95	2144.10	2093.49	2049.68	2011.59	1978.30	1862.84	1799.03	1762.33	1740.75
210,000	2410.49	2327.23	2256.68	2196.40	2144.55	2099.68	2060.65	2026.55	1908.28	1842.91	1805.32	1783.21
215,000	2467.88	2382.64	2310.41	2248.69	2195.61	2149.67	2109.71	2074.80	1953.71	1886.78	1848.30	1825.67
220,000	2525.27	2438.05	2364.14	2300.99	2246.67	2199.66	2158.77	2123.05	1999.15	1930.66	1891.28	1868.13
225,000	2582.66	2493.46	2417.87	2353.28	2297.73	2249.65	2207.84	2171.30	2044.58	1974.54	1934.27	1910.58
230,000	2640.06	2548.87	2471.60	2405.58	2348.79	2299.65	2256.90	2219.55	2090.02	2018.42	1977.25	1953.04
235,000	2697.45	2604.28	2525.33	2457.87	2399.85	2349.64	2305.96	2267.81	2135.45	2062.30	2020.24	1995.50
240,000	2754.84	2659.69	2579.06	2510.17	2450.91	2399.63	2355.03	2316.06	2180.89	2106.18	2063.22	2037.96
245,000	2812.23	2715.10	2632.79	2562.46	2501.97	2449.62	2404.09	2364.31	2226.32	2150.06	2106.20	2080.41
250,000	2869.63	2770.51	2686.52	2614.76	2553.03	2499.61	2453.15	2412.56	2271.76	2193.93	2149.19	2122.87
255,000	2927.02	2825.92	2740.25	2667.05	2604.09	2549.61	2502.22	2460.81	2317.19	2237.81	2192.17	2165.33
260,000	2984.41	2881.33	2793.98	2719.35	2655.15	2599.60	2551.28	2509.06	2362.63	2281.69	2235.15	2207.78
265,000	3041.80	2936.74	2847.71	2771.65	2706.21	2649.59	2600.34	2557.31	2408.06	2325.57	2278.14	2250.24
270,000	3099.19	2992.15	2901.44	2823.94	2757.27	2699.58	2649.40	2605.56	2453.50	2369.45	2321.12	2292.70
280,000	3213.98	3102.97	3008.90	2928.53	2859.39	2799.57	2747.53	2702.07	2544.37	2457.21	2407.09	2377.61
290,000	3328.76	3213.79	3116.36	3033.12	2961.52	2899.55	2845.66	2798.57	2635.24	2544.96	2493.06	2462.53
300,000	3443.55	3324.61	3223.82	3137.71	3063.64	2999.54	2943.78	2895.07	2726.11	2632.72	2579.02	2547.44

MONTHLY AMORTIZING PAYMENTS 11%

AMOUNT OF LOAN	NUMBER OF YEARS IN TERM 1	2	3	4	5	6	7	8	9	10	11	12
$ 50	4.42	2.34	1.64	1.30	1.09	0.96	0.86	0.79	0.74	0.69	0.66	0.63
100	8.84	4.67	3.28	2.59	2.18	1.91	1.72	1.58	1.47	1.38	1.31	1.26
200	17.68	9.33	6.55	5.17	4.35	3.81	3.43	3.15	2.93	2.76	2.62	2.51
300	26.52	13.99	9.83	7.76	6.53	5.72	5.14	4.72	4.39	4.14	3.93	3.77
400	35.36	18.65	13.10	10.34	8.70	7.62	6.85	6.29	5.86	5.52	5.24	5.02
500	44.20	23.31	16.37	12.93	10.88	9.52	8.57	7.86	7.32	6.89	6.55	6.27
600	53.03	27.97	19.65	15.51	13.05	11.43	10.28	9.43	8.78	8.27	7.86	7.53
700	61.87	32.63	22.92	18.10	15.22	13.33	11.99	11.00	10.24	9.65	9.17	8.78
800	70.71	37.29	26.20	20.68	17.40	15.23	13.70	12.57	11.71	11.03	10.48	10.03
900	79.55	41.95	29.47	23.27	19.57	17.14	15.42	14.14	13.17	12.40	11.79	11.29
1,000	88.39	46.61	32.74	25.85	21.75	19.04	17.13	15.71	14.63	13.78	13.10	12.54
2,000	176.77	93.22	65.48	51.70	43.49	38.07	34.25	31.42	29.26	27.56	26.19	25.08
3,000	265.15	139.83	98.22	77.54	65.23	57.11	51.37	47.13	43.88	41.33	39.28	37.61
4,000	353.53	186.44	130.96	103.39	86.97	76.14	68.49	62.84	58.51	55.11	52.37	50.15
5,000	441.91	233.04	163.70	129.23	108.72	95.18	85.62	78.55	73.13	68.88	65.47	62.68
6,000	530.29	279.65	196.44	155.08	130.46	114.21	102.74	94.26	87.76	82.66	78.56	75.22
7,000	618.68	326.26	229.18	180.92	152.20	133.24	119.86	109.96	102.39	96.43	91.65	87.75
8,000	707.06	372.87	261.91	206.77	173.94	152.28	136.98	125.67	117.01	110.21	104.74	100.29
9,000	795.44	419.48	294.65	232.61	195.69	171.31	154.11	141.38	131.64	123.98	117.84	112.82
10,000	883.82	466.08	327.39	258.46	217.43	190.35	171.23	157.09	146.26	137.76	130.93	125.36
15,000	1325.73	699.12	491.09	387.69	326.14	285.52	256.84	235.63	219.39	206.63	196.39	188.04
20,000	1767.64	932.16	654.78	516.92	434.85	380.69	342.45	314.17	292.52	275.51	261.85	250.72
25,000	2209.55	1165.20	818.47	646.14	543.57	475.86	428.07	392.72	365.65	344.38	327.31	313.39
30,000	2651.45	1398.24	982.17	775.37	652.28	571.03	513.68	471.26	438.78	413.26	392.78	376.07
35,000	3093.36	1631.28	1145.86	904.60	760.99	666.20	599.29	549.80	511.91	482.13	458.24	438.75
40,000	3535.27	1864.32	1309.55	1033.83	869.70	761.37	684.90	628.34	585.04	551.01	523.70	501.43
45,000	3977.18	2097.36	1473.25	1163.05	978.41	856.54	770.51	706.88	658.17	619.88	589.16	564.10
50,000	4419.09	2330.40	1636.94	1292.28	1087.13	951.71	856.13	785.43	731.30	688.76	654.62	626.78
55,000	4861.00	2563.44	1800.63	1421.51	1195.84	1046.88	941.74	863.97	804.43	757.63	720.08	689.46
60,000	5302.90	2796.48	1964.33	1550.74	1304.55	1142.05	1027.35	942.51	877.56	826.51	785.55	752.14
65,000	5744.81	3029.51	2128.02	1679.96	1413.26	1237.22	1112.96	1021.05	950.69	895.38	851.01	814.82
70,000	6186.72	3262.55	2291.72	1809.19	1521.97	1332.39	1198.58	1099.59	1023.82	964.26	916.47	877.49
75,000	6628.63	3495.59	2455.41	1938.42	1630.69	1427.56	1284.19	1178.14	1096.94	1033.13	981.93	940.17
80,000	7070.54	3728.63	2619.10	2067.65	1739.40	1522.73	1369.80	1256.68	1170.07	1102.01	1047.39	1002.85
85,000	7512.45	3961.67	2782.80	2196.87	1848.11	1617.90	1455.41	1335.22	1243.20	1170.88	1112.85	1065.53
90,000	7954.35	4194.71	2946.49	2326.10	1956.82	1713.07	1541.02	1413.76	1316.33	1239.76	1178.32	1128.20
95,000	8396.26	4427.75	3110.18	2455.33	2065.54	1808.24	1626.64	1492.31	1389.46	1308.63	1243.78	1190.88
100,000	8838.17	4660.79	3273.88	2584.56	2174.25	1903.41	1712.25	1570.85	1462.59	1377.51	1309.24	1253.56
105,000	9280.08	4893.83	3437.57	2713.78	2282.96	1998.58	1797.86	1649.39	1535.72	1446.38	1374.70	1316.24
110,000	9721.99	5126.87	3601.26	2843.01	2391.67	2093.75	1883.47	1727.93	1608.85	1515.26	1440.16	1378.92
115,000	10163.90	5359.91	3764.96	2972.24	2500.38	2188.92	1969.09	1806.47	1681.98	1584.13	1505.63	1441.59
120,000	10605.80	5592.95	3928.65	3101.47	2609.10	2284.09	2054.70	1885.02	1755.11	1653.01	1571.09	1504.27
125,000	11047.71	5825.98	4092.34	3230.70	2717.81	2379.26	2140.31	1963.56	1828.24	1721.88	1636.55	1566.95
130,000	11489.62	6059.02	4256.04	3359.92	2826.52	2474.44	2225.92	2042.10	1901.37	1790.76	1702.01	1629.63
135,000	11931.53	6292.06	4419.73	3489.15	2935.23	2569.61	2311.53	2120.64	1974.50	1859.63	1767.47	1692.30
140,000	12373.44	6525.10	4583.43	3618.38	3043.94	2664.78	2397.15	2199.18	2047.63	1928.51	1832.93	1754.98
145,000	12815.35	6758.14	4747.12	3747.61	3152.66	2759.95	2482.76	2277.73	2120.75	1997.38	1898.40	1817.66
150,000	13257.25	6991.18	4910.81	3876.83	3261.37	2855.12	2568.37	2356.27	2193.88	2066.26	1963.86	1880.34
155,000	13699.16	7224.22	5074.51	4006.06	3370.08	2950.29	2653.98	2434.81	2267.01	2135.13	2029.32	1943.02
160,000	14141.07	7457.26	5238.20	4135.29	3478.79	3045.46	2739.59	2513.35	2340.14	2204.01	2094.78	2005.69
165,000	14582.98	7690.30	5401.89	4264.52	3587.50	3140.63	2825.21	2591.90	2413.27	2272.88	2160.24	2068.37
170,000	15024.89	7923.34	5565.59	4393.74	3696.22	3235.80	2910.82	2670.44	2486.40	2341.76	2225.70	2131.05
175,000	15466.80	8156.38	5729.28	4522.97	3804.93	3330.97	2996.43	2748.98	2559.53	2410.63	2291.17	2193.73
180,000	15908.70	8389.42	5892.97	4652.20	3913.64	3426.14	3082.04	2827.52	2632.66	2479.51	2356.63	2256.40
185,000	16350.61	8622.46	6056.67	4781.43	4022.35	3521.31	3167.66	2906.06	2705.79	2548.38	2422.09	2319.08
190,000	16792.52	8855.49	6220.36	4910.65	4131.07	3616.48	3253.27	2984.61	2778.92	2617.26	2487.55	2381.76
195,000	17234.43	9088.53	6384.05	5039.88	4239.78	3711.65	3338.88	3063.15	2852.05	2686.13	2553.01	2444.44
200,000	17676.34	9321.57	6547.75	5169.11	4348.49	3806.82	3424.49	3141.69	2925.18	2755.01	2618.47	2507.12
205,000	18118.24	9554.61	6711.44	5298.34	4457.20	3901.99	3510.10	3220.23	2998.31	2823.88	2683.94	2569.79
210,000	18560.15	9787.65	6875.14	5427.56	4565.91	3997.16	3595.72	3298.77	3071.44	2892.76	2749.40	2632.47
215,000	19002.06	10020.69	7038.83	5556.79	4674.63	4092.33	3681.33	3377.32	3144.57	2961.63	2814.86	2695.15
220,000	19443.97	10253.73	7202.52	5686.02	4783.34	4187.50	3766.94	3455.86	3217.69	3030.51	2880.32	2757.83
225,000	19885.88	10486.77	7366.22	5815.25	4892.05	4282.67	3852.55	3534.40	3290.82	3099.38	2945.78	2820.50
230,000	20327.79	10719.81	7529.91	5944.48	5000.76	4377.84	3938.17	3612.94	3363.95	3168.26	3011.25	2883.18
235,000	20769.69	10952.85	7693.60	6073.70	5109.47	4473.01	4023.78	3691.49	3437.08	3237.13	3076.71	2945.86
240,000	21211.60	11185.89	7857.30	6202.93	5218.19	4568.18	4109.39	3770.03	3510.21	3306.01	3142.17	3008.54
245,000	21653.51	11418.93	8020.99	6332.16	5326.90	4663.35	4195.00	3848.57	3583.34	3374.88	3207.63	3071.22
250,000	22095.42	11651.96	8184.68	6461.39	5435.61	4758.52	4280.61	3927.11	3656.47	3443.76	3273.09	3133.89
255,000	22537.33	11885.00	8348.38	6590.61	5544.32	4853.70	4366.23	4005.65	3729.60	3512.63	3338.55	3196.57
260,000	22979.24	12118.04	8512.07	6719.84	5653.03	4948.87	4451.84	4084.20	3802.73	3581.51	3404.02	3259.25
265,000	23421.14	12351.08	8675.77	6849.07	5761.75	5044.04	4537.45	4162.74	3875.86	3650.38	3469.48	3321.93
270,000	23863.05	12584.12	8839.46	6978.30	5870.46	5139.21	4623.06	4241.28	3948.99	3719.26	3534.94	3384.60
280,000	24746.87	13050.20	9166.85	7236.75	6087.88	5329.55	4794.29	4398.36	4095.25	3857.01	3665.86	3509.96
290,000	25630.69	13516.28	9494.23	7495.21	6305.31	5519.89	4965.51	4555.45	4241.50	3994.76	3796.79	3635.32
300,000	26514.50	13982.36	9821.62	7753.66	6522.73	5710.23	5136.74	4712.53	4387.76	4132.51	3927.71	3760.67

11% Monthly Amortizing Payments

AMOUNT OF LOAN	13	14	15	16	17	18	19	20	25	30	35	40
	NUMBER OF YEARS IN TERM											
$ 50	0.61	0.59	0.57	0.56	0.55	0.54	0.53	0.52	0.50	0.48	0.47	0.47
100	1.21	1.17	1.14	1.11	1.09	1.07	1.05	1.04	0.99	0.96	0.94	0.93
200	2.42	2.34	2.28	2.22	2.18	2.14	2.10	2.07	1.97	1.91	1.88	1.86
300	3.63	3.51	3.41	3.33	3.26	3.20	3.15	3.10	2.95	2.86	2.82	2.79
400	4.84	4.68	4.55	4.44	4.35	4.27	4.19	4.13	3.93	3.81	3.75	3.72
500	6.04	5.85	5.69	5.55	5.43	5.33	5.24	5.17	4.91	4.77	4.69	4.65
600	7.25	7.02	6.82	6.66	6.52	6.40	6.29	6.20	5.89	5.72	5.63	5.57
700	8.46	8.19	7.96	7.77	7.60	7.46	7.34	7.23	6.87	6.67	6.56	6.50
800	9.67	9.36	9.10	8.88	8.69	8.53	8.38	8.26	7.85	7.62	7.50	7.43
900	10.87	10.53	10.23	9.99	9.77	9.59	9.43	9.29	8.83	8.58	8.44	8.36
1,000	12.08	11.70	11.37	11.10	10.86	10.66	10.48	10.33	9.81	9.53	9.37	9.29
2,000	24.16	23.39	22.74	22.19	21.71	21.31	20.95	20.65	19.61	19.05	18.74	18.57
3,000	36.23	35.08	34.10	33.28	32.57	31.96	31.43	30.97	29.41	28.57	28.11	27.85
4,000	48.31	46.77	45.47	44.37	43.42	42.61	41.90	41.29	39.21	38.10	37.48	37.14
5,000	60.38	58.46	56.83	55.46	54.27	53.26	52.38	51.61	49.01	47.62	46.85	46.42
6,000	72.46	70.15	68.20	66.55	65.13	63.91	62.85	61.94	58.81	57.14	56.22	55.70
7,000	84.53	81.84	79.57	77.64	75.98	74.56	73.33	72.26	68.61	66.67	65.59	64.99
8,000	96.61	93.53	90.93	88.73	86.84	85.21	83.80	82.58	78.41	76.19	74.96	74.27
9,000	108.68	105.22	102.30	99.82	97.69	95.86	94.28	92.90	88.22	85.71	84.33	83.55
10,000	120.76	116.91	113.66	110.91	108.54	106.51	104.75	103.22	98.02	95.24	93.70	92.83
15,000	181.13	175.36	170.49	166.36	162.81	159.76	157.12	154.83	147.02	142.85	140.55	139.25
20,000	241.51	233.82	227.32	221.81	217.08	213.01	209.50	206.44	196.03	190.47	187.40	185.66
25,000	301.89	292.27	284.15	277.26	271.35	266.27	261.87	258.05	245.03	238.09	234.24	232.08
30,000	362.26	350.72	340.98	332.71	325.62	319.52	314.24	309.66	294.04	285.70	281.09	278.49
35,000	422.64	409.17	397.81	388.16	379.89	372.77	366.62	361.27	343.04	333.32	327.94	324.91
40,000	483.02	467.63	454.64	443.61	434.16	426.02	418.99	412.88	392.05	380.93	374.79	371.32
45,000	543.39	526.08	511.47	499.06	488.43	479.28	471.36	464.49	441.06	428.55	421.64	417.74
50,000	603.77	584.53	568.30	554.51	542.70	532.53	523.74	516.10	490.06	476.17	468.48	464.15
55,000	664.15	642.98	625.13	609.96	596.96	585.78	576.11	567.71	539.07	523.78	515.33	510.57
60,000	724.52	701.44	681.96	665.41	651.23	639.03	628.48	619.32	588.07	571.40	562.18	556.98
65,000	784.90	759.89	738.79	720.86	705.50	692.29	680.86	670.93	637.08	619.02	609.03	603.40
70,000	845.27	818.34	795.62	776.31	759.77	745.54	733.23	722.54	686.08	666.63	655.88	649.81
75,000	905.65	876.80	852.45	831.76	814.04	798.79	785.60	774.15	735.09	714.25	702.72	696.23
80,000	966.03	935.25	909.28	887.21	868.31	852.04	837.98	825.76	784.10	761.86	749.57	742.64
85,000	1026.40	993.70	966.11	942.66	922.58	905.30	890.35	877.37	833.10	809.48	796.42	789.06
90,000	1086.78	1052.15	1022.94	998.11	976.85	958.55	942.72	928.97	882.11	857.10	843.27	835.47
95,000	1147.16	1110.61	1079.77	1053.56	1031.12	1011.80	995.10	980.58	931.11	904.71	890.11	881.88
100,000	1207.53	1169.06	1136.60	1109.01	1085.39	1065.05	1047.47	1032.19	980.12	952.33	936.96	928.30
105,000	1267.91	1227.51	1193.43	1164.46	1139.65	1118.31	1099.84	1083.80	1029.12	999.94	983.81	974.71
110,000	1328.29	1285.96	1250.26	1219.91	1193.92	1171.56	1152.22	1135.41	1078.13	1047.56	1030.66	1021.13
115,000	1388.66	1344.42	1307.09	1275.36	1248.19	1224.81	1204.59	1187.02	1127.14	1095.18	1077.51	1067.54
120,000	1449.04	1402.87	1363.92	1330.81	1302.46	1278.06	1256.96	1238.63	1176.14	1142.79	1124.35	1113.96
125,000	1509.41	1461.32	1420.75	1386.26	1356.73	1331.32	1309.33	1290.24	1225.15	1190.41	1171.20	1160.37
130,000	1569.79	1519.78	1477.58	1441.71	1411.00	1384.57	1361.71	1341.85	1274.15	1238.03	1218.05	1206.79
135,000	1630.17	1578.23	1534.41	1497.16	1465.27	1437.82	1414.08	1393.46	1323.16	1285.64	1264.90	1253.20
140,000	1690.54	1636.68	1591.24	1552.61	1519.54	1491.07	1466.45	1445.07	1372.16	1333.26	1311.75	1299.62
145,000	1750.92	1695.13	1648.07	1608.06	1573.81	1544.33	1518.83	1496.68	1421.17	1380.87	1358.59	1346.03
150,000	1811.30	1753.59	1704.90	1663.51	1628.08	1597.58	1571.20	1548.29	1470.17	1428.49	1405.44	1392.45
155,000	1871.67	1812.04	1761.73	1718.96	1682.34	1650.83	1623.57	1599.90	1519.18	1476.11	1452.29	1438.86
160,000	1932.05	1870.49	1818.56	1774.41	1736.61	1704.08	1675.95	1651.51	1568.19	1523.72	1499.14	1485.28
165,000	1992.43	1928.94	1875.39	1829.86	1790.88	1757.34	1728.32	1703.12	1617.19	1571.34	1545.99	1531.69
170,000	2052.80	1987.40	1932.22	1885.31	1845.15	1810.59	1780.69	1754.73	1666.20	1618.95	1592.83	1578.11
175,000	2113.18	2045.85	1989.05	1940.76	1899.42	1863.84	1833.07	1806.33	1715.20	1666.57	1639.68	1624.52
180,000	2173.55	2104.30	2045.88	1996.21	1953.69	1917.09	1885.44	1857.94	1764.21	1714.19	1686.53	1670.93
185,000	2233.93	2162.76	2102.71	2051.66	2007.96	1970.35	1937.81	1909.55	1813.21	1761.80	1733.38	1717.35
190,000	2294.31	2221.21	2159.54	2107.11	2062.23	2023.60	1990.19	1961.16	1862.22	1809.42	1780.22	1763.76
195,000	2354.68	2279.66	2216.37	2162.56	2116.50	2076.85	2042.56	2012.77	1911.23	1857.04	1827.07	1810.18
200,000	2415.06	2338.11	2273.20	2218.01	2170.77	2130.10	2094.93	2064.38	1960.23	1904.65	1873.92	1856.59
205,000	2475.44	2396.57	2330.03	2273.46	2225.04	2183.36	2147.31	2115.99	2009.24	1952.27	1920.77	1903.01
210,000	2535.81	2455.02	2386.86	2328.91	2279.30	2236.61	2199.68	2167.60	2058.24	1999.88	1967.62	1949.42
215,000	2596.19	2513.47	2443.69	2384.36	2333.57	2289.86	2252.05	2219.21	2107.25	2047.50	2014.46	1995.84
220,000	2656.57	2571.92	2500.52	2439.81	2387.84	2343.11	2304.43	2270.82	2156.25	2095.12	2061.31	2042.25
225,000	2716.94	2630.38	2557.35	2495.26	2442.11	2396.37	2356.80	2322.43	2205.26	2142.73	2108.16	2088.67
230,000	2777.32	2688.83	2614.18	2550.71	2496.38	2449.62	2409.17	2374.04	2254.27	2190.35	2155.01	2135.08
235,000	2837.69	2747.28	2671.01	2606.16	2550.65	2502.87	2461.55	2425.65	2303.27	2237.96	2201.86	2181.50
240,000	2898.07	2805.74	2727.84	2661.61	2604.92	2556.12	2513.92	2477.26	2352.28	2285.58	2248.70	2227.91
245,000	2958.45	2864.19	2784.67	2717.06	2659.19	2609.38	2566.29	2528.87	2401.28	2333.20	2295.55	2274.33
250,000	3018.82	2922.64	2841.50	2772.51	2713.46	2662.63	2618.66	2580.48	2450.29	2380.81	2342.40	2320.74
255,000	3079.20	2981.09	2898.33	2827.96	2767.73	2715.88	2671.04	2632.09	2499.29	2428.43	2389.25	2367.16
260,000	3139.58	3039.55	2955.16	2883.41	2821.99	2769.13	2723.41	2683.69	2548.30	2476.05	2436.09	2413.57
265,000	3199.95	3098.00	3011.99	2938.86	2876.26	2822.39	2775.78	2735.30	2597.30	2523.66	2482.94	2459.99
270,000	3260.33	3156.45	3068.82	2994.31	2930.53	2875.64	2828.16	2786.91	2646.31	2571.28	2529.79	2506.40
280,000	3381.08	3273.36	3182.48	3105.21	3039.07	2982.14	2932.90	2890.13	2744.32	2666.51	2623.49	2599.23
290,000	3501.83	3390.26	3296.14	3216.11	3147.61	3088.65	3037.65	2993.35	2842.33	2761.74	2717.18	2692.06
300,000	3622.59	3507.17	3409.80	3327.01	3256.15	3195.15	3142.40	3096.57	2940.34	2856.98	2810.88	2784.89

MONTHLY AMORTIZING PAYMENTS — 12%

AMOUNT OF LOAN	1	2	3	4	5	6	7	8	9	10	11	12
	NUMBER OF YEARS IN TERM											
$ 50	4.45	2.36	1.67	1.32	1.12	0.98	0.89	0.82	0.76	0.72	0.69	0.66
100	8.89	4.71	3.33	2.64	2.23	1.96	1.77	1.63	1.52	1.44	1.37	1.32
200	17.77	9.42	6.65	5.27	4.45	3.92	3.54	3.26	3.04	2.87	2.74	2.63
300	26.66	14.13	9.97	7.91	6.68	5.87	5.30	4.88	4.56	4.31	4.11	3.95
400	35.54	18.83	13.29	10.54	8.90	7.83	7.07	6.51	6.08	5.74	5.48	5.26
500	44.43	23.54	16.61	13.17	11.13	9.78	8.83	8.13	7.60	7.18	6.84	6.57
600	53.31	28.25	19.93	15.81	13.35	11.74	10.60	9.76	9.12	8.61	8.21	7.89
700	62.20	32.96	23.26	18.44	15.58	13.69	12.36	11.38	10.63	10.05	9.58	9.20
800	71.08	37.66	26.58	21.07	17.80	15.65	14.13	13.01	12.15	11.48	10.95	10.51
900	79.97	42.37	29.90	23.71	20.03	17.60	15.89	14.63	13.67	12.92	12.32	11.83
1,000	88.85	47.08	33.22	26.34	22.25	19.56	17.66	16.26	15.19	14.35	13.68	13.14
2,000	177.70	94.15	66.43	52.67	44.49	39.11	35.31	32.51	30.37	28.70	27.36	26.27
3,000	266.55	141.23	99.65	79.01	66.74	58.66	52.96	48.76	45.56	43.05	41.04	39.41
4,000	355.40	188.30	132.86	105.34	88.98	78.21	70.62	65.02	60.74	57.39	54.72	52.54
5,000	444.25	235.37	166.08	131.67	111.23	97.76	88.27	81.27	75.93	71.74	68.39	65.68
6,000	533.10	282.45	199.29	158.01	133.47	117.31	105.92	97.52	91.11	86.09	82.07	78.81
7,000	621.95	329.52	232.51	184.34	155.72	136.86	123.57	113.77	106.29	100.43	95.75	91.94
8,000	710.80	376.59	265.72	210.68	177.96	156.41	141.23	130.03	121.48	114.78	109.43	105.08
9,000	799.64	423.67	298.93	237.01	200.21	175.96	158.88	146.28	136.66	129.13	123.11	118.21
10,000	888.49	470.74	332.15	263.34	222.45	195.51	176.53	162.53	151.85	143.48	136.78	131.35
15,000	1332.74	706.11	498.22	395.01	333.67	293.26	264.80	243.80	227.77	215.21	205.17	197.02
20,000	1776.98	941.47	664.29	526.68	444.89	391.01	353.06	325.06	303.69	286.95	273.56	262.69
25,000	2221.22	1176.84	830.36	658.35	556.12	488.76	441.32	406.33	379.61	358.68	341.95	328.36
30,000	2665.47	1412.21	996.43	790.02	667.34	586.51	529.59	487.59	455.53	430.42	410.34	394.03
35,000	3109.71	1647.58	1162.51	921.69	778.56	684.26	617.85	568.85	531.45	502.15	478.73	459.70
40,000	3553.96	1882.94	1328.58	1053.36	889.78	782.01	706.11	650.12	607.37	573.89	547.12	525.37
45,000	3998.20	2118.31	1494.65	1185.03	1001.01	879.76	794.38	731.38	683.30	645.62	615.51	591.04
50,000	4442.44	2353.68	1660.72	1316.70	1112.23	977.51	882.64	812.65	759.22	717.36	683.90	656.71
55,000	4886.69	2589.05	1826.79	1448.37	1223.45	1075.27	970.91	893.91	835.14	789.10	752.29	722.39
60,000	5330.93	2824.41	1992.86	1580.04	1334.67	1173.02	1059.17	975.18	911.06	860.83	820.68	788.06
65,000	5775.18	3059.78	2158.94	1711.70	1445.89	1270.77	1147.43	1056.44	986.98	932.57	889.07	853.73
70,000	6219.42	3295.15	2325.01	1843.37	1557.12	1368.52	1235.70	1137.70	1062.90	1004.30	957.46	919.40
75,000	6663.66	3530.52	2491.08	1975.04	1668.34	1466.27	1323.96	1218.97	1138.82	1076.04	1025.85	985.07
80,000	7107.91	3765.88	2657.15	2106.71	1779.56	1564.02	1412.22	1300.23	1214.74	1147.77	1094.24	1050.74
85,000	7552.15	4001.25	2823.22	2238.38	1890.78	1661.77	1500.49	1381.50	1290.66	1219.51	1162.62	1116.41
90,000	7996.40	4236.62	2989.29	2370.05	2002.01	1759.52	1588.75	1462.76	1366.59	1291.24	1231.01	1182.08
95,000	8440.64	4471.98	3155.36	2501.72	2113.23	1857.27	1677.01	1544.02	1442.51	1362.98	1299.40	1247.75
100,000	8884.88	4707.35	3321.44	2633.39	2224.45	1955.02	1765.28	1625.29	1518.43	1434.71	1367.79	1313.42
105,000	9329.13	4942.72	3487.51	2765.06	2335.67	2052.78	1853.54	1706.55	1594.35	1506.45	1436.18	1379.10
110,000	9773.37	5178.09	3653.58	2896.73	2446.89	2150.53	1941.81	1787.82	1670.27	1578.19	1504.57	1444.77
115,000	10217.62	5413.45	3819.65	3028.40	2558.12	2248.28	2030.07	1869.08	1746.19	1649.92	1572.96	1510.44
120,000	10661.86	5648.82	3985.72	3160.07	2669.34	2346.03	2118.33	1950.35	1822.11	1721.66	1641.35	1576.11
125,000	11106.10	5884.19	4151.79	3291.73	2780.56	2443.78	2206.60	2031.61	1898.03	1793.39	1709.74	1641.78
130,000	11550.35	6119.56	4317.87	3423.40	2891.78	2541.53	2294.86	2112.87	1973.96	1865.13	1778.13	1707.45
135,000	11994.59	6354.92	4483.94	3555.07	3003.01	2639.28	2383.12	2194.14	2049.88	1936.86	1846.52	1773.12
140,000	12438.84	6590.29	4650.01	3686.74	3114.23	2737.03	2471.39	2275.40	2125.80	2008.60	1914.91	1838.79
145,000	12883.08	6825.66	4816.08	3818.41	3225.45	2834.78	2559.65	2356.67	2201.72	2080.33	1983.30	1904.46
150,000	13327.32	7061.03	4982.15	3950.08	3336.67	2932.53	2647.91	2437.93	2277.64	2152.07	2051.69	1970.13
155,000	13771.57	7296.39	5148.22	4081.75	3447.89	3030.28	2736.18	2519.20	2353.56	2223.80	2120.08	2035.80
160,000	14215.81	7531.76	5314.29	4213.42	3559.12	3128.04	2824.44	2600.46	2429.48	2295.54	2188.47	2101.48
165,000	14660.06	7767.13	5480.37	4345.09	3670.34	3225.79	2912.71	2681.72	2505.40	2367.28	2256.85	2167.15
170,000	15104.30	8002.50	5646.44	4476.76	3781.56	3323.54	3000.97	2762.99	2581.32	2439.01	2325.24	2232.82
175,000	15548.54	8237.86	5812.51	4608.43	3892.78	3421.29	3089.23	2844.25	2657.25	2510.75	2393.63	2298.49
180,000	15992.79	8473.23	5978.58	4740.10	4004.01	3519.04	3177.50	2925.52	2733.17	2582.48	2462.02	2364.16
185,000	16437.03	8708.60	6144.65	4871.76	4115.23	3616.79	3265.76	3006.78	2809.09	2654.22	2530.41	2429.83
190,000	16881.27	8943.96	6310.72	5003.43	4226.45	3714.54	3354.02	3088.04	2885.01	2725.95	2598.80	2495.50
195,000	17325.52	9179.33	6476.80	5135.10	4337.67	3812.29	3442.29	3169.31	2960.93	2797.69	2667.19	2561.17
200,000	17769.76	9414.70	6642.87	5266.77	4448.89	3910.04	3530.55	3250.57	3036.85	2869.42	2735.58	2626.84
205,000	18214.01	9650.07	6808.94	5398.44	4560.12	4007.79	3618.82	3331.84	3112.77	2941.16	2803.97	2692.51
210,000	18658.25	9885.43	6975.01	5530.11	4671.34	4105.55	3707.08	3413.10	3188.69	3012.89	2872.36	2758.19
215,000	19102.49	10120.80	7141.08	5661.78	4782.56	4203.30	3795.34	3494.37	3264.62	3084.63	2940.75	2823.86
220,000	19546.74	10356.17	7307.15	5793.45	4893.78	4301.05	3883.61	3575.63	3340.54	3156.37	3009.14	2889.53
225,000	19990.98	10591.54	7473.22	5925.12	5005.01	4398.80	3971.87	3656.89	3416.46	3228.10	3077.53	2955.20
230,000	20435.23	10826.90	7639.30	6056.79	5116.23	4496.55	4060.13	3738.16	3492.38	3299.84	3145.92	3020.87
235,000	20879.47	11062.27	7805.37	6188.46	5227.45	4594.30	4148.40	3819.42	3568.30	3371.57	3214.31	3086.54
240,000	21323.71	11297.64	7971.44	6320.13	5338.67	4692.05	4236.66	3900.69	3644.22	3443.31	3282.70	3152.21
245,000	21767.96	11533.01	8137.51	6451.79	5449.89	4789.80	4324.92	3981.95	3720.14	3515.04	3351.09	3217.88
250,000	22212.20	11768.37	8303.58	6583.46	5561.12	4887.55	4413.19	4063.22	3796.06	3586.78	3419.47	3283.55
255,000	22656.45	12003.74	8469.65	6715.13	5672.34	4985.30	4501.45	4144.48	3871.98	3658.51	3487.86	3349.22
260,000	23100.69	12239.11	8635.73	6846.80	5783.56	5083.06	4589.72	4225.74	3947.91	3730.25	3556.25	3414.89
265,000	23544.93	12474.48	8801.80	6978.47	5894.78	5180.81	4677.98	4307.01	4023.83	3801.99	3624.64	3480.57
270,000	23989.18	12709.84	8967.87	7110.14	6006.01	5278.56	4766.24	4388.27	4099.75	3873.72	3693.03	3546.24
280,000	24877.67	13180.58	9300.01	7373.48	6228.45	5474.06	4942.77	4550.80	4251.59	4017.19	3829.81	3677.58
290,000	25766.15	13651.31	9632.15	7636.82	6450.89	5669.56	5119.30	4713.33	4403.43	4160.66	3966.59	3808.92
300,000	26654.64	14122.05	9964.30	7900.16	6673.34	5865.06	5295.82	4875.86	4555.27	4304.13	4103.37	3940.26

12% MONTHLY AMORTIZING PAYMENTS

AMOUNT OF LOAN	13	14	15	16	17	18	19	20	25	30	35	40
	NUMBER OF YEARS IN TERM											
$ 50	0.64	0.62	0.61	0.59	0.58	0.57	0.56	0.56	0.53	0.52	0.51	0.51
100	1.27	1.24	1.21	1.18	1.16	1.14	1.12	1.11	1.06	1.03	1.02	1.01
200	2.54	2.47	2.41	2.35	2.31	2.27	2.24	2.21	2.11	2.06	2.04	2.02
300	3.81	3.70	3.61	3.53	3.46	3.40	3.35	3.31	3.16	3.09	3.05	3.03
400	5.08	4.93	4.81	4.70	4.61	4.53	4.47	4.41	4.22	4.12	4.07	4.04
500	6.35	6.16	6.01	5.87	5.76	5.66	5.58	5.51	5.27	5.15	5.08	5.05
600	7.62	7.39	7.21	7.05	6.91	6.80	6.70	6.61	6.32	6.18	6.10	6.06
700	8.89	8.63	8.41	8.22	8.06	7.93	7.81	7.71	7.38	7.21	7.11	7.06
800	10.15	9.86	9.61	9.39	9.21	9.06	8.93	8.81	8.43	8.23	8.13	8.07
900	11.42	11.09	10.81	10.57	10.37	10.19	10.04	9.91	9.48	9.26	9.14	9.08
1,000	12.69	12.32	12.01	11.74	11.52	11.32	11.16	11.02	10.54	10.29	10.16	10.09
2,000	25.38	24.63	24.01	23.48	23.03	22.64	22.31	22.03	21.07	20.58	20.32	20.17
3,000	38.06	36.95	36.01	35.22	34.54	33.96	33.47	33.04	31.60	30.86	30.47	30.26
4,000	50.75	49.26	48.01	46.95	46.05	45.28	44.62	44.05	42.13	41.15	40.63	40.34
5,000	63.44	61.58	60.01	58.69	57.57	56.60	55.77	55.06	52.67	51.44	50.78	50.43
6,000	76.12	73.89	72.02	70.43	69.08	67.92	66.93	66.07	63.20	61.72	60.94	60.51
7,000	88.81	86.21	84.02	82.17	80.59	79.24	78.08	77.08	73.73	72.01	71.09	70.60
8,000	101.50	98.52	96.02	93.90	92.10	90.56	89.24	88.09	84.26	82.29	81.25	80.68
9,000	114.18	110.83	108.02	105.64	103.61	101.88	100.39	99.10	94.80	92.58	91.40	90.77
10,000	126.87	123.15	120.02	117.38	115.13	113.20	111.54	110.11	105.33	102.87	101.56	100.85
15,000	190.30	184.72	180.03	176.06	172.69	169.80	167.31	165.17	157.99	154.30	152.34	151.28
20,000	253.74	246.29	240.04	234.75	230.25	226.40	223.08	220.22	210.65	205.73	203.11	201.70
25,000	317.17	307.86	300.05	293.44	287.81	282.99	278.85	275.28	263.31	257.16	253.89	252.13
30,000	380.60	369.43	360.06	352.12	345.37	339.59	334.62	330.33	315.97	308.59	304.67	302.55
35,000	444.04	431.01	420.06	410.81	402.93	396.19	390.39	385.39	368.63	360.02	355.45	352.98
40,000	507.47	492.58	480.07	469.50	460.49	452.79	446.16	440.44	421.29	411.45	406.22	403.40
45,000	570.90	554.15	540.08	528.18	518.05	509.38	501.93	495.49	473.96	462.88	457.00	453.83
50,000	634.34	615.72	600.09	586.87	575.61	565.98	557.70	550.55	526.62	514.31	507.78	504.25
55,000	697.77	677.29	660.10	645.55	633.17	622.58	613.47	605.60	579.28	565.74	558.56	554.68
60,000	761.20	738.86	720.11	704.24	690.73	679.18	669.24	660.66	631.94	617.17	609.33	605.10
65,000	824.64	800.43	780.11	762.93	748.30	735.77	725.01	715.71	684.60	668.60	660.11	655.53
70,000	888.07	862.01	840.12	821.61	805.86	792.37	780.77	770.77	737.26	720.03	710.89	705.95
75,000	951.50	923.58	900.13	880.30	863.42	848.97	836.54	825.82	789.92	771.46	761.67	756.38
80,000	1014.94	985.15	960.14	938.99	920.98	905.57	892.31	880.87	842.58	822.90	812.44	806.80
85,000	1078.37	1046.72	1020.15	997.67	978.54	962.16	948.08	935.93	895.25	874.33	863.22	857.23
90,000	1141.80	1108.29	1080.16	1056.36	1036.10	1018.76	1003.85	990.98	947.91	925.76	914.00	907.65
95,000	1205.24	1169.86	1140.16	1115.04	1093.66	1075.36	1059.62	1046.04	1000.57	977.19	964.78	958.08
100,000	1268.67	1231.43	1200.17	1173.73	1151.22	1131.96	1115.39	1101.09	1053.23	1028.62	1015.55	1008.50
105,000	1332.10	1293.01	1260.18	1232.42	1208.78	1188.55	1171.16	1156.15	1105.89	1080.05	1066.33	1058.93
110,000	1395.54	1354.58	1320.19	1291.10	1266.34	1245.15	1226.93	1211.20	1158.55	1131.48	1117.11	1109.35
115,000	1458.97	1416.15	1380.20	1349.79	1323.90	1301.75	1282.70	1266.25	1211.21	1182.91	1167.89	1159.78
120,000	1522.40	1477.72	1440.21	1408.48	1381.46	1358.35	1338.47	1321.31	1263.87	1234.34	1218.66	1210.20
125,000	1585.84	1539.29	1500.22	1467.16	1439.02	1414.94	1394.24	1376.36	1316.54	1285.77	1269.44	1260.63
130,000	1649.27	1600.86	1560.22	1525.85	1496.59	1471.54	1450.01	1431.42	1369.20	1337.20	1320.22	1311.05
135,000	1712.70	1662.43	1620.23	1584.53	1554.15	1528.14	1505.78	1486.47	1421.86	1388.63	1371.00	1361.48
140,000	1776.14	1724.01	1680.24	1643.22	1611.71	1584.74	1561.54	1541.53	1474.52	1440.06	1421.77	1411.90
145,000	1839.57	1785.58	1740.25	1701.91	1669.27	1641.33	1617.31	1596.58	1527.18	1491.49	1472.55	1462.33
150,000	1903.00	1847.15	1800.26	1760.59	1726.83	1697.93	1673.08	1651.63	1579.84	1542.92	1523.33	1512.75
155,000	1966.44	1908.72	1860.27	1819.28	1784.39	1754.53	1728.85	1706.69	1632.50	1594.35	1574.11	1563.18
160,000	2029.87	1970.29	1920.27	1877.97	1841.95	1811.13	1784.62	1761.74	1685.16	1645.79	1624.88	1613.60
165,000	2093.30	2031.86	1980.28	1936.65	1899.51	1867.72	1840.39	1816.80	1737.82	1697.22	1675.66	1664.03
170,000	2156.74	2093.44	2040.29	1995.34	1957.07	1924.32	1896.16	1871.85	1790.49	1748.65	1726.44	1714.45
175,000	2220.17	2155.01	2100.30	2054.02	2014.63	1980.92	1951.93	1926.91	1843.15	1800.08	1777.22	1764.88
180,000	2283.60	2216.58	2160.31	2112.71	2072.19	2037.52	2007.70	1981.96	1895.81	1851.51	1827.99	1815.30
185,000	2347.04	2278.15	2220.32	2171.40	2129.75	2094.11	2063.47	2037.01	1948.47	1902.94	1878.77	1865.73
190,000	2410.47	2339.72	2280.32	2230.08	2187.31	2150.71	2119.24	2092.07	2001.13	1954.37	1929.55	1916.15
195,000	2473.90	2401.29	2340.33	2288.77	2244.88	2207.31	2175.01	2147.12	2053.79	2005.80	1980.33	1966.58
200,000	2537.34	2462.86	2400.34	2347.46	2302.44	2263.91	2230.78	2202.18	2106.45	2057.23	2031.10	2017.00
205,000	2600.77	2524.44	2460.35	2406.14	2360.00	2320.50	2286.55	2257.23	2159.11	2108.66	2081.88	2067.43
210,000	2664.20	2586.01	2520.36	2464.83	2417.56	2377.10	2342.31	2312.29	2211.78	2160.09	2132.66	2117.85
215,000	2727.64	2647.58	2580.37	2523.51	2475.12	2433.70	2398.08	2367.34	2264.44	2211.52	2183.44	2168.28
220,000	2791.07	2709.15	2640.37	2582.20	2532.68	2490.30	2453.85	2422.39	2317.10	2262.95	2234.21	2218.70
225,000	2854.50	2770.72	2700.38	2640.89	2590.24	2546.89	2509.62	2477.45	2369.76	2314.38	2284.99	2269.13
230,000	2917.94	2832.29	2760.39	2699.57	2647.80	2603.49	2565.39	2532.50	2422.42	2365.81	2335.77	2319.55
235,000	2981.37	2893.86	2820.40	2758.26	2705.36	2660.09	2621.16	2587.56	2475.08	2417.24	2386.55	2369.98
240,000	3044.80	2955.44	2880.41	2816.95	2762.92	2716.69	2676.93	2642.61	2527.74	2468.68	2437.32	2420.40
245,000	3108.24	3017.01	2940.42	2875.63	2820.48	2773.28	2732.70	2697.67	2580.40	2520.11	2488.10	2470.83
250,000	3171.67	3078.58	3000.43	2934.32	2878.04	2829.88	2788.47	2752.72	2633.07	2571.54	2538.88	2521.25
255,000	3235.10	3140.15	3060.43	2993.00	2935.60	2886.48	2844.24	2807.77	2685.73	2622.97	2589.66	2571.68
260,000	3298.54	3201.72	3120.44	3051.69	2993.17	2943.08	2900.01	2862.83	2738.39	2674.40	2640.43	2622.10
265,000	3361.97	3263.29	3180.45	3110.38	3050.73	2999.67	2955.78	2917.88	2791.05	2725.83	2691.21	2672.53
270,000	3425.40	3324.86	3240.46	3169.06	3108.29	3056.27	3011.55	2972.94	2843.71	2777.26	2741.99	2722.95
280,000	3552.27	3448.01	3360.48	3286.44	3223.41	3169.47	3123.08	3083.05	2949.03	2880.12	2843.54	2823.80
290,000	3679.14	3571.15	3480.49	3403.81	3338.53	3282.66	3234.62	3193.15	3054.36	2982.98	2945.10	2924.65
300,000	3806.00	3694.29	3600.51	3521.18	3453.65	3395.86	3346.16	3303.26	3159.68	3085.84	3046.65	3025.50

Monthly Amortizing Payments 13%

AMOUNT OF LOAN	NUMBER OF YEARS IN TERM 1	2	3	4	5	6	7	8	9	10	11	12
$ 50	4.47	2.38	1.69	1.35	1.14	1.01	0.91	0.85	0.79	0.75	0.72	0.69
100	8.94	4.76	3.37	2.69	2.28	2.01	1.82	1.69	1.58	1.50	1.43	1.38
200	17.87	9.51	6.74	5.37	4.56	4.02	3.64	3.37	3.16	2.99	2.86	2.75
300	26.80	14.27	10.11	8.05	6.83	6.03	5.46	5.05	4.73	4.48	4.29	4.13
400	35.73	19.02	13.48	10.74	9.11	8.03	7.28	6.73	6.31	5.98	5.72	5.50
500	44.66	23.78	16.85	13.42	11.38	10.04	9.10	8.41	7.88	7.47	7.14	6.88
600	53.60	28.53	20.22	16.10	13.66	12.05	10.92	10.09	9.46	8.96	8.57	8.25
700	62.53	33.28	23.59	18.78	15.93	14.06	12.74	11.77	11.03	10.46	10.00	9.63
800	71.46	38.04	26.96	21.47	18.21	16.06	14.56	13.45	12.61	11.95	11.43	11.00
900	80.39	42.79	30.33	24.15	20.48	18.07	16.38	15.13	14.18	13.44	12.85	12.38
1,000	89.32	47.55	33.70	26.83	22.76	20.08	18.20	16.81	15.76	14.94	14.28	13.75
2,000	178.64	95.09	67.39	53.66	45.51	40.15	36.39	33.62	31.51	29.87	28.56	27.50
3,000	267.96	142.63	101.09	80.49	68.26	60.23	54.58	50.43	47.27	44.80	42.83	41.24
4,000	357.27	190.17	134.78	107.31	91.02	80.30	72.77	67.23	63.02	59.73	57.11	54.99
5,000	446.59	237.71	168.47	134.14	113.77	100.38	90.96	84.04	78.77	74.66	71.39	68.74
6,000	535.91	285.26	202.17	160.97	136.52	120.45	109.16	100.85	94.53	89.59	85.66	82.48
7,000	625.23	332.80	235.86	187.80	159.28	140.52	127.35	117.66	110.28	104.52	99.94	96.23
8,000	714.54	380.34	269.56	214.62	182.03	160.60	145.54	134.46	126.03	119.45	114.21	109.98
9,000	803.86	427.88	303.25	241.45	204.78	180.67	163.73	151.27	141.79	134.38	128.49	123.72
10,000	893.18	475.42	336.94	268.28	227.54	200.75	181.92	168.08	157.54	149.32	142.77	137.47
15,000	1339.76	713.13	505.41	402.42	341.30	301.12	272.88	252.11	236.31	223.97	214.15	206.20
20,000	1786.35	950.84	673.88	536.55	455.07	401.49	363.84	336.15	315.08	298.63	285.53	274.93
25,000	2232.94	1188.55	842.35	670.69	568.83	501.86	454.80	420.19	393.84	373.28	356.91	343.66
30,000	2679.52	1426.26	1010.82	804.83	682.60	602.23	545.76	504.22	472.61	447.94	428.29	412.39
35,000	3126.11	1663.97	1179.29	938.97	796.36	702.60	636.72	588.26	551.38	522.59	499.67	481.12
40,000	3572.70	1901.68	1347.76	1073.10	910.13	802.97	727.68	672.30	630.15	597.25	571.05	549.86
45,000	4019.28	2139.39	1516.23	1207.24	1023.89	903.34	818.64	756.33	708.92	671.90	642.43	618.59
50,000	4465.87	2377.10	1684.70	1341.38	1137.66	1003.71	909.60	840.37	787.68	746.56	713.81	687.32
55,000	4912.46	2614.81	1853.17	1475.52	1251.42	1104.08	1000.56	924.40	866.45	821.21	785.19	756.05
60,000	5359.04	2852.51	2021.64	1609.65	1365.19	1204.45	1091.52	1008.44	945.22	895.87	856.57	824.78
65,000	5805.63	3090.22	2190.11	1743.79	1478.95	1304.82	1182.48	1092.48	1023.99	970.52	927.95	893.51
70,000	6252.21	3327.93	2358.58	1877.93	1592.72	1405.19	1273.44	1176.51	1102.76	1045.18	999.33	962.24
75,000	6698.80	3565.64	2527.05	2012.07	1706.49	1505.56	1364.40	1260.55	1181.52	1119.84	1070.71	1030.97
80,000	7145.39	3803.35	2695.52	2146.20	1820.25	1605.93	1455.36	1344.59	1260.29	1194.49	1142.09	1099.71
85,000	7591.97	4041.06	2863.99	2280.34	1934.02	1706.30	1546.32	1428.62	1339.06	1269.15	1213.47	1168.44
90,000	8038.56	4278.77	3032.46	2414.48	2047.78	1806.67	1637.28	1512.66	1417.83	1343.80	1284.85	1237.17
95,000	8485.15	4516.48	3200.93	2548.62	2161.55	1907.04	1728.24	1596.69	1496.60	1418.46	1356.24	1305.90
100,000	8931.73	4754.19	3369.40	2682.75	2275.31	2007.42	1819.20	1680.73	1575.36	1493.11	1427.62	1374.63
105,000	9378.32	4991.90	3537.87	2816.89	2389.08	2107.79	1910.16	1764.77	1654.13	1567.77	1499.00	1443.36
110,000	9824.91	5229.61	3706.34	2951.03	2502.84	2208.16	2001.12	1848.80	1732.90	1642.42	1570.38	1512.09
115,000	10271.49	5467.31	3874.81	3085.17	2616.61	2308.53	2092.08	1932.84	1811.67	1717.08	1641.76	1580.82
120,000	10718.08	5705.02	4043.28	3219.30	2730.37	2408.90	2183.04	2016.88	1890.44	1791.73	1713.14	1649.56
125,000	11164.66	5942.73	4211.75	3353.44	2844.14	2509.27	2274.00	2100.91	1969.20	1866.39	1784.52	1718.29
130,000	11611.25	6180.44	4380.22	3487.58	2957.90	2609.64	2364.96	2184.95	2047.97	1941.04	1855.90	1787.02
135,000	12057.84	6418.15	4548.69	3621.72	3071.67	2710.01	2455.92	2268.98	2126.74	2015.70	1927.28	1855.75
140,000	12504.42	6655.86	4717.16	3755.85	3185.44	2810.38	2546.88	2353.02	2205.51	2090.36	1998.66	1924.48
145,000	12951.01	6893.57	4885.63	3889.99	3299.20	2910.75	2637.84	2437.06	2284.28	2165.01	2070.04	1993.21
150,000	13397.60	7131.28	5054.10	4024.13	3412.97	3011.12	2728.80	2521.09	2363.04	2239.67	2141.42	2061.94
155,000	13844.18	7368.99	5222.57	4158.27	3526.73	3111.49	2819.76	2605.13	2441.81	2314.32	2212.80	2130.67
160,000	14290.77	7606.70	5391.04	4292.40	3640.50	3211.86	2910.72	2689.17	2520.58	2388.98	2284.18	2199.41
165,000	14737.36	7844.41	5559.51	4426.54	3754.26	3312.23	3001.68	2773.20	2599.35	2463.63	2355.56	2268.14
170,000	15183.94	8082.11	5727.98	4560.68	3868.03	3412.60	3092.64	2857.24	2678.11	2538.29	2426.94	2336.87
175,000	15630.53	8319.82	5896.45	4694.82	3981.79	3512.97	3183.60	2941.27	2756.88	2612.94	2498.32	2405.60
180,000	16077.11	8557.53	6064.92	4828.95	4095.56	3613.34	3274.56	3025.31	2835.65	2687.60	2569.70	2474.33
185,000	16523.70	8795.24	6233.39	4963.09	4209.32	3713.71	3365.52	3109.35	2914.42	2762.25	2641.08	2543.06
190,000	16970.29	9032.95	6401.86	5097.23	4323.09	3814.08	3456.48	3193.38	2993.19	2836.91	2712.47	2611.79
195,000	17416.87	9270.66	6570.33	5231.37	4436.85	3914.46	3547.44	3277.42	3071.95	2911.56	2783.85	2680.52
200,000	17863.46	9508.37	6738.80	5365.50	4550.62	4014.83	3638.40	3361.46	3150.72	2986.22	2855.23	2749.26
205,000	18310.05	9746.08	6907.27	5499.64	4664.38	4115.20	3729.36	3445.49	3229.49	3060.88	2926.61	2817.99
210,000	18756.63	9983.79	7075.73	5633.78	4778.15	4215.57	3820.32	3529.53	3308.26	3135.53	2997.99	2886.72
215,000	19203.22	10221.50	7244.20	5767.92	4891.92	4315.94	3911.28	3613.56	3387.03	3210.19	3069.37	2955.45
220,000	19649.81	10459.21	7412.67	5902.05	5005.68	4416.31	4002.24	3697.60	3465.79	3284.84	3140.75	3024.18
225,000	20096.39	10696.92	7581.14	6036.19	5119.45	4516.68	4093.20	3781.64	3544.56	3359.50	3212.13	3092.91
230,000	20542.98	10934.62	7749.61	6170.33	5233.21	4617.05	4184.16	3865.67	3623.33	3434.15	3283.51	3161.64
235,000	20989.56	11172.33	7918.08	6304.47	5346.98	4717.42	4275.12	3949.71	3702.10	3508.81	3354.89	3230.37
240,000	21436.15	11410.04	8086.55	6438.60	5460.74	4817.79	4366.08	4033.75	3780.87	3583.46	3426.27	3299.11
245,000	21882.74	11647.75	8255.02	6572.74	5574.51	4918.16	4457.04	4117.78	3859.63	3658.12	3497.65	3367.84
250,000	22329.32	11885.46	8423.49	6706.88	5688.27	5018.53	4548.00	4201.82	3938.40	3732.77	3569.03	3436.57
255,000	22775.91	12123.17	8591.96	6841.02	5802.04	5118.90	4638.96	4285.86	4017.17	3807.43	3640.41	3505.30
260,000	23222.50	12360.88	8760.43	6975.15	5915.80	5219.27	4729.92	4369.89	4095.94	3882.08	3711.79	3574.03
265,000	23669.08	12598.59	8928.90	7109.29	6029.57	5319.64	4820.88	4453.93	4174.71	3956.74	3783.17	3642.76
270,000	24115.67	12836.30	9097.37	7243.43	6143.33	5420.01	4911.84	4537.96	4253.47	4031.39	3854.55	3711.49
280,000	25008.84	13311.72	9434.31	7511.70	6370.87	5620.75	5093.75	4706.04	4411.01	4180.71	3997.32	3848.96
290,000	25902.01	13787.13	9771.25	7779.98	6598.40	5821.50	5275.67	4874.11	4568.55	4330.02	4140.08	3986.42
300,000	26795.19	14262.55	10108.19	8048.25	6825.93	6022.24	5457.59	5042.18	4726.08	4479.33	4282.84	4123.88

13% Monthly Amortizing Payments

AMOUNT OF LOAN	NUMBER OF YEARS IN TERM 13	14	15	16	17	18	19	20	25	30	35	40
$ 50	0.67	0.65	0.64	0.62	0.61	0.61	0.60	0.59	0.57	0.56	0.55	0.55
100	1.34	1.30	1.27	1.24	1.22	1.21	1.19	1.18	1.13	1.11	1.10	1.09
200	2.67	2.60	2.54	2.48	2.44	2.41	2.37	2.35	2.26	2.22	2.20	2.18
300	4.00	3.89	3.80	3.72	3.66	3.61	3.56	3.52	3.39	3.32	3.29	3.27
400	5.33	5.19	5.07	4.96	4.88	4.81	4.74	4.69	4.52	4.43	4.39	4.36
500	6.66	6.48	6.33	6.20	6.10	6.01	5.93	5.86	5.64	5.54	5.48	5.45
600	7.99	7.78	7.60	7.44	7.32	7.21	7.11	7.03	6.77	6.64	6.58	6.54
700	9.32	9.07	8.86	8.68	8.54	8.41	8.30	8.21	7.90	7.75	7.67	7.63
800	10.65	10.37	10.13	9.92	9.75	9.61	9.48	9.38	9.03	8.85	8.77	8.72
900	11.99	11.66	11.39	11.16	10.97	10.81	10.67	10.55	10.16	9.96	9.86	9.81
1,000	13.32	12.96	12.66	12.40	12.19	12.01	11.85	11.72	11.28	11.07	10.96	10.90
2,000	26.63	25.91	25.31	24.80	24.38	24.01	23.70	23.44	22.56	22.13	21.91	21.80
3,000	39.94	38.86	37.96	37.20	36.56	36.02	35.55	35.15	33.84	33.19	32.86	32.69
4,000	53.25	51.82	50.61	49.60	48.75	48.02	47.40	46.87	45.12	44.25	43.81	43.59
5,000	66.57	64.77	63.27	62.00	60.94	60.03	59.25	58.58	56.40	55.31	54.76	54.48
6,000	79.88	77.72	75.92	74.40	73.12	72.03	71.10	70.30	67.68	66.38	65.72	65.38
7,000	93.19	90.67	88.57	86.80	85.31	84.04	82.95	82.02	78.95	77.44	76.67	76.27
8,000	106.50	103.63	101.22	99.20	97.49	96.04	94.80	93.73	90.23	88.50	87.62	87.17
9,000	119.81	116.58	113.88	111.60	109.68	108.04	106.65	105.45	101.51	99.56	98.57	98.06
10,000	133.13	129.53	126.53	124.00	121.87	120.05	118.49	117.16	112.79	110.62	109.52	108.96
15,000	199.69	194.29	189.79	186.00	182.80	180.07	177.74	175.74	169.18	165.93	164.28	163.43
20,000	266.25	259.06	253.05	248.00	243.73	240.09	236.98	234.32	225.57	221.24	219.04	217.91
25,000	332.81	323.82	316.32	310.00	304.66	300.11	296.23	292.90	281.96	276.55	273.80	272.38
30,000	399.37	388.58	379.58	372.00	365.59	360.13	355.47	351.48	338.36	331.86	328.56	326.86
35,000	465.93	453.35	442.84	434.00	426.52	420.16	414.72	410.06	394.75	387.17	383.32	381.33
40,000	532.49	518.11	506.10	496.00	487.45	480.18	473.96	468.64	451.14	442.48	438.08	435.81
45,000	599.05	582.87	569.36	558.00	548.38	540.20	533.21	527.21	507.53	497.79	492.84	490.29
50,000	665.61	647.64	632.63	620.00	609.31	600.22	592.45	585.79	563.92	553.10	547.60	544.76
55,000	732.17	712.40	695.89	682.00	670.24	660.24	651.70	644.37	620.31	608.41	602.36	599.24
60,000	798.73	777.16	759.15	744.00	731.17	720.26	710.94	702.95	676.71	663.72	657.12	653.71
65,000	865.29	841.93	822.41	806.00	792.10	780.29	770.19	761.53	733.10	719.03	711.88	708.19
70,000	931.85	906.69	885.67	868.00	853.04	840.31	829.43	820.11	789.49	774.34	766.64	762.66
75,000	998.41	971.45	948.94	930.00	913.97	900.33	888.68	878.69	845.88	829.65	821.40	817.14
80,000	1064.97	1036.22	1012.20	992.00	974.90	960.35	947.92	937.27	902.27	884.96	876.16	871.62
85,000	1131.53	1100.98	1075.46	1053.99	1035.83	1020.37	1007.17	995.84	958.67	940.27	930.92	926.09
90,000	1198.09	1165.74	1138.72	1115.99	1096.76	1080.39	1066.41	1054.42	1015.06	995.58	985.68	980.57
95,000	1264.65	1230.51	1201.99	1177.99	1157.69	1140.42	1125.66	1113.00	1071.45	1050.89	1040.44	1035.04
100,000	1331.22	1295.27	1265.25	1239.99	1218.62	1200.44	1184.90	1171.58	1127.84	1106.20	1095.20	1089.52
105,000	1397.78	1360.03	1328.51	1301.99	1279.55	1260.46	1244.15	1230.16	1184.23	1161.51	1149.96	1143.99
110,000	1464.34	1424.79	1391.77	1363.99	1340.48	1320.48	1303.39	1288.74	1240.62	1216.82	1204.72	1198.47
115,000	1530.90	1489.56	1455.03	1425.99	1401.41	1380.50	1362.64	1347.32	1297.02	1272.13	1259.48	1252.95
120,000	1597.46	1554.32	1518.30	1487.99	1462.34	1440.52	1421.88	1405.90	1353.41	1327.44	1314.24	1307.42
125,000	1664.02	1619.08	1581.56	1549.99	1523.27	1500.55	1481.13	1464.47	1409.80	1382.75	1369.00	1361.90
130,000	1730.58	1683.85	1644.82	1611.99	1584.20	1560.57	1540.37	1523.05	1466.19	1438.06	1423.76	1416.37
135,000	1797.14	1748.61	1708.08	1673.99	1645.13	1620.59	1599.62	1581.63	1522.58	1493.37	1478.52	1470.85
140,000	1863.70	1813.37	1771.34	1735.99	1706.07	1680.61	1658.86	1640.21	1578.97	1548.68	1533.28	1525.32
145,000	1930.26	1878.14	1834.61	1797.99	1767.00	1740.63	1718.11	1698.79	1635.37	1603.99	1588.04	1579.80
150,000	1996.82	1942.90	1897.87	1859.99	1827.93	1800.65	1777.35	1757.37	1691.76	1659.30	1642.79	1634.28
155,000	2063.38	2007.66	1961.13	1921.99	1888.86	1860.68	1836.60	1815.95	1748.15	1714.61	1697.55	1688.75
160,000	2129.94	2072.43	2024.39	1983.99	1949.79	1920.70	1895.84	1874.53	1804.54	1769.92	1752.31	1743.23
165,000	2196.50	2137.19	2087.65	2045.98	2010.72	1980.72	1955.09	1933.10	1860.93	1825.23	1807.07	1797.70
170,000	2263.06	2201.95	2150.92	2107.98	2071.65	2040.74	2014.33	1991.68	1917.33	1880.54	1861.83	1852.18
175,000	2329.62	2266.72	2214.18	2169.98	2132.58	2100.76	2073.58	2050.26	1973.72	1935.85	1916.59	1906.65
180,000	2396.18	2331.48	2277.44	2231.98	2193.51	2160.78	2132.82	2108.84	2030.11	1991.16	1971.35	1961.13
185,000	2462.74	2396.24	2340.70	2293.98	2254.44	2220.81	2192.07	2167.42	2086.50	2046.47	2026.11	2015.61
190,000	2529.30	2461.01	2403.97	2355.98	2315.37	2280.83	2251.31	2226.00	2142.89	2101.78	2080.87	2070.08
195,000	2595.87	2525.77	2467.23	2417.98	2376.30	2340.85	2310.56	2284.58	2199.28	2157.09	2135.63	2124.56
200,000	2662.43	2590.53	2530.49	2479.98	2437.23	2400.87	2369.80	2343.16	2255.68	2212.40	2190.39	2179.03
205,000	2728.99	2655.30	2593.75	2541.98	2498.16	2460.89	2429.05	2401.74	2312.07	2267.71	2245.15	2233.51
210,000	2795.55	2720.06	2657.01	2603.98	2559.10	2520.91	2488.29	2460.31	2368.46	2323.02	2299.91	2287.98
215,000	2862.11	2784.82	2720.28	2665.98	2620.03	2580.93	2547.54	2518.89	2424.85	2378.33	2354.67	2342.46
220,000	2928.67	2849.58	2783.54	2727.98	2680.96	2640.96	2606.78	2577.47	2481.24	2433.64	2409.43	2396.94
225,000	2995.23	2914.35	2846.80	2789.98	2741.89	2700.98	2666.03	2636.05	2537.63	2488.95	2464.19	2451.41
230,000	3061.79	2979.11	2910.06	2851.98	2802.82	2761.00	2725.27	2694.63	2594.03	2544.26	2518.95	2505.89
235,000	3128.35	3043.87	2973.32	2913.98	2863.75	2821.02	2784.52	2753.21	2650.42	2599.57	2573.71	2560.36
240,000	3194.91	3108.64	3036.59	2975.98	2924.68	2881.04	2843.76	2811.79	2706.81	2654.88	2628.47	2614.84
245,000	3261.47	3173.40	3099.85	3037.98	2985.61	2941.06	2903.00	2870.37	2763.20	2710.19	2683.23	2669.31
250,000	3328.03	3238.16	3163.11	3099.97	3046.54	3001.09	2962.25	2928.94	2819.59	2765.50	2737.99	2723.79
255,000	3394.59	3302.93	3226.37	3161.97	3107.47	3061.11	3021.49	2987.52	2875.99	2820.81	2792.75	2778.27
260,000	3461.15	3367.69	3289.63	3223.97	3168.40	3121.13	3080.74	3046.10	2932.38	2876.12	2847.51	2832.74
265,000	3527.71	3432.45	3352.90	3285.97	3229.33	3181.15	3139.98	3104.68	2988.77	2931.43	2902.27	2887.22
270,000	3594.27	3497.22	3416.16	3347.97	3290.26	3241.17	3199.23	3163.26	3045.16	2986.74	2957.03	2941.69
280,000	3727.39	3626.74	3542.68	3471.97	3412.13	3361.22	3317.72	3280.42	3157.94	3097.36	3066.55	3050.64
290,000	3860.51	3756.27	3669.21	3595.97	3533.99	3481.26	3436.21	3397.57	3270.73	3207.98	3176.07	3159.60
300,000	3993.64	3885.80	3795.73	3719.97	3655.85	3601.30	3554.70	3514.73	3383.51	3318.60	3285.58	3268.55

Figure 15-2

Interest Rate Factors Tables

Example: $50,000 loan @ 12¼% for 30 years

Problem: find monthly payment

Step 1: Find the **column** that corresponds to the interest rate of the proposed loan.

Step 2: Find the **row** that corresponds to the term of the proposed loan. For example, calculations for a loan of 30 years would use the last (bottom) row of the charts.

Step 3: Take the number found at the intersection of the appropriate column and row, and **add a decimal point and a zero at the front** of the number. In our example, the chart shows a figure of 104789, which should be converted to **.0**104789.

Step 4: **Multiply** the proposed **loan amount** by the answer from step 3 to get the monthly loan payment. In our example, multiply $50,000 times .0104789.

$50,000
×.0104789
$523.95

Thus, the monthly payment on a $50,000, 30-year loan at 12¼% is $523.95 per month.

YEARS	12%	12¼%
1	888487	889657
1½	609820	610982
2	470734	471903
2½	387481	388661
3	332143	333338
3½	292756	293968
4	263338	264567
4½	240565	241812
5	222444	223709
6	195501	196804
7	176527	177867
8	162528	163905
9	151842	153255
10	143470	144919
12	131341	132859
15	120016	121629
20	110108	111856
21	108869	110641
22	107793	109586
23	106856	108670
24	106038	107871
25	105322	107174
26	104695	106564
27	104144	106030
28	103661	105562
29	103235	105150
30	102861	104789

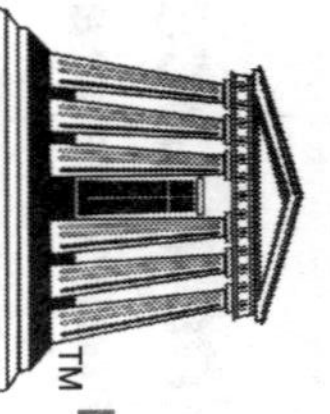

YEARS	8%	8¼%	8½%	8¾%	9%	9¼%	9½%	9¾%	10%	10¼%	10½%	YEARS
1	869884	871041	872198	873356	874515	875675	876835	877996	879158	880322	881486	1
1½	591403	592544	593687	594831	595977	597123	598271	599420	600570	601722	602875	1½
2	452273	453414	454557	455701	456847	457995	459144	460296	461449	462603	463760	2
2½	368883	370030	371178	372329	373482	374637	375793	376952	378114	379277	380443	2½
3	313364	314518	315675	316835	317997	319162	320329	321499	322671	323846	325024	3
3½	273770	274934	276102	277272	278445	279621	280800	281982	283168	284356	285547	3½
4	244129	245304	246483	247665	248850	250039	251231	252426	253625	254828	256033	4
4½	221124	222311	223501	224696	225894	227096	228301	229510	230724	231941	233161	4½
5	202764	203963	205165	206372	207584	208779	210018	211242	212470	213702	214939	5
6	175332	176556	177784	179017	180255	181499	182746	184000	185258	186521	187789	6
7	155862	157111	158365	159625	160891	162162	163439	164722	166011	167306	168606	7
8	141367	142641	143921	145208	146502	147802	149108	150422	151741	153067	154400	8
9	130187	131487	132794	134108	135429	136758	138093	139436	140786	142144	143508	9
10	121328	122653	123986	125327	126676	128033	129397	130770	132150	133539	134934	10
12	108245	109621	111006	112400	113803	115216	116637	118068	119507	120956	122414	12
15	095565	097014	098474	099945	101427	102919	104422	105936	107460	108995	110539	15
20	083644	085207	086782	088371	089973	091587	093213	948516	096502	098164	099837	20
21	082043	083627	085224	086835	088458	090094	091743	093404	095078	096763	098459	21
22	080618	082222	083841	085472	087117	088775	090446	092129	093824	095531	097250	22
23	079345	080970	082609	084261	085927	087606	089297	091001	092718	094446	096186	23
24	078205	079850	081508	083181	084866	086566	088277	090002	091738	093487	095248	24
25	077182	078845	080523	082214	083920	085638	087369	089113	090870	092638	094418	25
26	076260	077942	079638	081348	083072	084810	086559	088322	090097	091884	093682	26
27	075428	077128	078842	080570	082313	084068	085836	087616	089409	091214	093030	27
28	074676	076393	078125	079871	081630	083403	085188	086986	088796	090617	092450	28
29	073995	075729	077477	079240	081016	082805	084607	086421	088247	090085	091934	29
30	073376	075127	076891	078670	080462	082268	084085	085915	087757	089610	091473	30

YEARS	10¾%	11%	11¼%	11½%	11¾%	12%	12¼%	12½%	12¾%	13%	13¼%	YEARS
1	882650	883816	884983	886150	887318	888487	889657	890828	892001	893173	894347	1
1½	604029	605185	606342	607500	608659	609820	610982	612145	613311	614476	615643	1½
2	464918	466078	467239	468403	469568	470734	471903	473073	474245	475419	476594	2
2½	381610	382780	383952	385126	386302	387481	388661	389844	391029	392216	393405	2½
3	326045	327387	328572	329760	330950	332143	333338	334536	335737	336940	338145	3
3½	286741	287938	289138	290341	291547	292756	293968	295182	296401	297621	298845	3½
4	257242	258455	259670	260890	262112	263338	264567	265799	267036	268275	269518	4
4½	234386	235614	236846	238082	239322	240565	241812	243063	244319	245577	246839	4½
5	216179	217424	218673	219926	221183	222444	223709	224979	226254	227531	228813	5
6	189062	190340	191623	192911	194204	195501	196804	198111	199425	200742	202063	6
7	169912	171224	172541	173864	175193	176527	177867	179212	180564	181920	183282	7
8	155739	157084	158435	159793	161157	162528	163905	165288	166678	168073	169475	8
9	144880	146258	147644	149036	150436	151842	153255	154675	156103	157536	158977	9
10	136338	137750	139168	140595	142029	143470	144919	146376	147840	149311	150789	10
12	123880	125355	126839	128331	129832	131341	132859	134385	135912	137463	139014	12
15	112094	113659	115234	116818	118413	120016	121629	123252	124884	126525	128174	15
20	101522	103218	104925	106642	108370	110108	111856	113614	115382	117158	118944	20
21	100167	101887	103617	105357	107108	108869	110641	112421	114213	116012	117820	21
22	098980	100722	102474	104237	106010	107793	109586	111389	113202	115023	116853	22
23	097382	099700	101474	103258	105052	106856	108670	110493	112327	114168	116018	23
24	097019	098802	100596	102400	104214	106038	107871	109714	111567	113427	115296	24
25	096209	098011	099823	101646	103479	105322	107174	109035	110906	112784	114671	25
26	095492	097312	099143	100984	102835	104695	106564	108442	110330	112225	114128	26
27	094857	096695	098542	100400	102268	104144	106030	107924	109828	111738	113656	27
28	094293	096147	098012	099885	101769	103661	105562	107471	109389	111314	113246	28
29	093793	095662	097542	099431	101329	103235	105150	107074	109005	110944	112889	29
30	093348	095232	097126	099029	100940	102861	104789	106725	108670	110620	112578	30

YEARS	13½%	13¾%	14%	14¼%	14½%	14¾%	15%	15¼%	15½%	15¾%	16%	YEARS
1	895521	896696	897872	899048	900226	901404	902584	903764	904945	906126	907309	1
1½	616812	617981	619152	620324	621498	622672	623848	625026	626204	627384	628565	1½
2	477771	478949	480129	481311	482495	483680	484867	486056	487246	488438	489632	2
2½	394596	395789	396984	398181	399381	400582	407186	402992	404199	405209	406621	2½
3	339353	340564	341777	342992	344210	345431	346654	347879	349107	350338	351571	3
3½	300071	301301	302533	303768	305006	306247	307491	308738	309988	311240	312496	3½
4	270764	272013	273265	274521	275780	277042	278308	279577	280849	282125	283403	4
4½	248105	249374	250647	251924	253205	254489	255777	257068	258363	259662	260964	4½
5	230099	231389	232683	233981	235283	236590	237900	239214	240532	241855	243181	5
5½	215476	216787	218102	219422	220746	222074	223407	224744	226086	227432	228782	5½
6	203390	204722	206058	207399	208745	210095	211451	212811	214175	215545	216919	6
6½	193254	194606	195964	197326	198694	200066	201444	202827	204215	205607	207005	6½
7	184649	186022	187401	188784	190174	191568	192968	194373	195784	197200	198621	7
8	170882	172296	173716	175141	176573	178011	179455	180904	182360	183821	185288	8
9	160424	161877	163338	164804	166278	167758	169244	170737	172236	173741	175253	9
10	152275	153767	155267	156774	158287	159808	161335	162870	164411	165959	167514	10
12	140572	142139	143713	145295	146885	148483	150088	151701	153321	154948	156583	12
15	129832	131499	133175	134858	136551	138251	139959	141675	143400	145131	146871	15
20	120738	122541	124353	126172	128000	129836	131679	133530	135389	137254	139126	20
21	119637	121463	123297	125139	126989	128847	130712	132585	134464	136351	138244	21
22	118692	120538	122393	124256	126127	128005	129890	131783	133682	135587	137500	22
23	117877	119743	121618	123500	125390	127287	129190	131101	133018	134942	136871	23
24	117173	119058	120951	122851	124758	126673	128593	130521	132454	134394	136340	24
25	116565	118467	120377	122293	124217	126147	128084	130026	131975	133929	135889	25
26	116038	117956	119881	121813	123752	125697	127648	129604	131567	133535	135508	26
27	115582	117514	119454	121400	123352	125310	127274	129244	131219	133199	135184	27
28	115185	117132	119084	121043	123008	124978	126954	128936	130922	132913	134909	28
29	114841	116800	118764	120735	122712	124693	126680	128672	130669	132670	134675	29
29½	114686	116651	118621	120597	122579	124566	126558	128555	130556	132562	134572	29½
30	114542	116512	118488	120469	122456	124448	126445	128446	130452	132462	134476	30

YEARS	16¼%	16½%	16¾%	17%	17¼%	17½%	17¾%	18%	18¼%	18½%	18¾%	YEARS
1	908493	909677	910862	912048	913235	914423	915611	916800	917991	919182	920374	1
1½	629747	639031	632115	633301	634489	635677	636867	638058	639251	640444	641639	1½
2	490827	492024	493223	494423	495625	496829	498034	499242	500450	501661	502873	2
2½	407835	409052	410270	411490	412713	413937	415164	416392	417623	418856	420091	2½
3	352806	354044	355285	356528	357773	359021	360272	361524	362780	364038	365298	3
3½	313754	315015	316279	317546	318816	320089	321365	322643	323924	325209	326496	3½
4	284685	285971	287259	288551	289846	291144	292446	293750	295058	296370	297684	4
4½	262270	263580	264894	266210	267531	268855	270183	271514	272849	274188	275530	4½
5	244511	245846	247184	248526	249872	251223	252577	253935	255297	256663	258032	5
5½	230136	231495	232859	234226	235598	236974	238354	239739	241128	242521	243918	5½
6	218298	219681	221069	222462	223859	225261	226667	228078	229494	230914	232339	6
6½	208408	209816	211228	212646	214068	215496	216928	218365	219807	221254	222705	6½
7	200048	201479	202916	204359	205806	207258	208716	210179	211647	213120	214598	7
8	186761	188240	189725	191215	192711	194213	195720	197233	198751	200275	201804	8
9	176771	178295	179826	181362	182905	184454	186009	187569	189136	190709	192287	9
10	169075	170643	172217	173798	175386	176979	178579	180186	181798	183417	185042	10
12	158225	159874	161530	163193	164863	166539	168223	169912	171609	173312	175021	12
15	148617	150371	152133	153901	155676	157458	159247	161043	162845	164653	166467	15
20	141005	142891	144782	146681	148585	150495	152410	154332	156258	158190	160127	20
21	140143	142049	143961	145879	147802	149732	151666	153606	155551	157501	159455	21
22	139418	141342	143272	145208	147149	149096	151048	153004	154966	156932	158902	22
23	138807	140748	142695	144647	146604	148566	150533	152505	154481	156461	158446	23
24	138291	140247	142209	144176	146147	148123	150104	152089	154078	156072	158069	24
25	137855	139825	141800	143780	145765	147753	149746	151743	153744	155749	157757	25
26	134786	139469	141456	143448	145444	147444	149448	151456	153467	155481	157499	26
27	137173	139167	141166	143167	145175	147185	149198	151216	153236	155259	157286	27
28	136909	138913	140921	142933	144949	146968	148990	151015	153044	155075	157109	28
29	136684	138698	140715	142735	144759	146786	148816	150848	152884	154922	156963	29
29½	136585	138603	140624	142648	144675	146706	148739	150776	152814	154856	156899	29½
30	136494	138515	140540	142568	144599	146633	148670	150709	152751	154795	156841	30

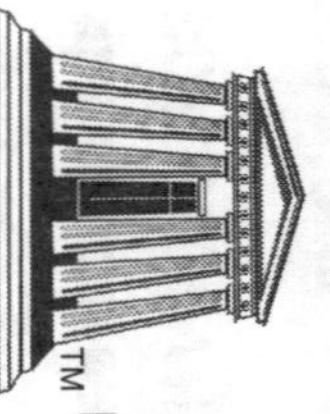

YEARS	19%	19½%	20%	20½	21	YEARS
1	921566	923954	926346	928740	931138	1
1½	642835	645231	647633	650039	652450	1½
2	504087	506519	508959	511404	513857	2
2½	421328	423808	426296	428793	431298	2½
3	366561	369094	371636	374189	376751	3
3½	327785	330374	332973	335584	338206	3½
4	299002	301647	304304	306974	309657	4
4½	276875	279577	282293	285024	287768	4½
5	259406	262165	264939	267729	270534	5
5½	245320	248135	250968	253817	256682	5½
6	233768	236639	239529	242436	245360	6
6½	224161	227088	230034	232998	235981	6½
7	216081	219062	222062	225083	228123	7
8	203339	206425	209533	212661	215811	8
9	193871	197057	200266	203496	206749	9
10	186673	189953	193256	196583	199932	10
12	176737	180187	183661	187159	190681	12
15	168288	171948	175630	179335	183062	15
20	162069	165967	169883	173816	177765	20
21	161415	165347	169295	173260	177239	21
22	160877	164839	168816	172808	176814	22
23	160434	164423	168426	172442	176470	23
24	160069	164081	168106	172144	176192	24
25	159769	163801	167846	171901	175967	25
26	159520	163571	167632	171704	175784	26
27	159315	163382	167458	171543	175637	27
28	159146	163226	167315	171412	175517	28
29	159006	163098	167198	171306	175419	29
29½	158945	163043	167148	171260	175378	29½
30	158890	162993	167102	171219	175314	30

Figure 15-3

Proration Table

Counting Days of the Year*
Numbering from January 1

Day of the month	Jan.	Feb.	March	April	May	June	July	Aug.	Sept.	Oct.	Nov.	Dec.
1	1	32	60	91	121	152	182	213	244	274	305	335
2	2	33	61	92	122	153	183	214	245	275	306	336
3	3	34	62	93	123	154	184	215	246	276	307	337
4	4	35	63	94	124	155	185	216	247	277	308	338
5	5	36	64	95	125	156	186	217	248	278	309	339
6	6	37	65	96	126	157	187	218	249	279	310	340
7	7	38	66	97	127	158	188	219	250	280	311	341
8	8	39	67	98	128	159	189	220	251	281	312	342
9	9	40	68	99	129	160	190	221	252	282	313	343
10	10	41	69	100	130	161	191	222	253	283	314	344
11	11	42	70	101	131	162	192	223	254	284	315	345
12	12	43	71	102	132	163	193	224	255	285	316	346
13	13	44	72	103	133	164	194	225	256	286	317	347
14	14	45	73	104	134	165	195	226	257	287	318	348
15	15	46	74	105	135	166	196	227	258	288	319	349
16	16	47	75	106	136	167	197	228	259	289	320	350
17	17	48	76	107	137	168	198	229	260	290	321	351
18	18	49	77	108	138	169	199	230	261	291	322	352
19	19	50	78	109	139	170	200	231	262	292	323	353
20	20	51	79	110	140	171	201	232	263	293	324	354
21	21	52	80	111	141	172	202	233	264	294	325	355
22	22	53	81	112	142	173	203	234	265	295	326	356
23	23	54	82	113	143	174	204	235	266	296	327	357
24	24	55	83	114	144	175	205	236	267	297	328	358
25	25	56	84	115	145	176	206	237	268	298	329	359
26	26	57	85	116	146	177	207	238	269	299	330	360
27	27	58	86	117	147	178	208	239	270	300	331	361
28	28	59	87	118	148	179	209	240	271	301	332	362
29	29	—	88	119	149	180	210	241	272	302	333	363
30	30	—	89	120	150	181	211	242	273	303	334	364
31	31	—	90	—	151	—	212	243	—	304	—	365

* In a leap year, add one to each number after 59 (February 28)

Figure 15-4

Loan Progress Charts

Example: $50,000 loan @ 12¼% for 30 years

Problem: find balance after three years

Step 1

Choose the **chart** that corresponds to the interest rate of the loan in question.

Step 2

Choose the **column** that corresponds to the original term of the loan. For example, 30-year loans are found in the farthest right hand column of the chart.

12¼%

ORIGINAL LOAN TERM

AGE OF LOAN	22	23	24	25	26	27	28	29	[30]	
1	990	992	993	994	994	995	996	996	997	1
2	980	982	984	986	988	989	991	992	993	2
[3]	968	972	975	978	981	983	985	987	988	3
4	954	959	964	969	972	976	979	981	983	4
5	938	946	952	958	963	968	971	975	978	5

DOLLARS STILL OWED FOR EVERY $1000 BORROWED

Step 3

Choose the **row** that corresponds to the age of the loan. For example, a three-year-old loan would utilize row three of the chart.

Step 4

Multiply the number at the intersection by the number of **$1,000 increments** in the original loan.

$988
× 50 ($50,000)
$49,400 present balance

If the original loan amount had been **$50,600**, you would multiply 988 times 50.6.

4.00%

AGE OF LOAN	ORIGINAL TERM IN YEARS													
	2	3	4	5	6	7	8	10	15	20	25	30	35	40
1	.5100	.6799	.7648	.8156	.8495	.8737	.8918	.9170	.9503	.9667	.9762	.9824	.9866	.9897
2	.0000	.3467	.5200	.6238	.6929	.7422	.7791	.8306	.8986	.9320	.9515	.9641	.9727	.9789
3		.0000	.2652	.4241	.5299	.6054	.6619	.7407	.8448	.8959	.9257	.9450	.9582	.9677
4			.0000	.2163	.3603	.4630	.5398	.6471	.7889	.8583	.8989	.9251	.9431	.9560
5				.0000	.1837	.3148	.4129	.5498	.7306	.8192	.8710	.9045	.9274	.9439
6					.0000	.1605	.2807	.4484	.6699	.7785	.8420	.8830	.9111	.9313
7						.0000	.1432	.3429	.6068	.7362	.8118	.8606	.8941	.9181
8							.0000	.2331	.5412	.6921	.7804	.8373	.8764	.9045
9								.1189	.4728	.6463	.7476	.8131	.8580	.8902
10								.0000	.4016	.5985	.7136	.7878	.8388	.8754
11									.3276	.5488	.6782	.7616	.8189	.8600
12									.2505	.4971	.6413	.7343	.7982	.8440
13									.1703	.4433	.6029	.7058	.7766	.8273
14									.0869	.3873	.5629	.6762	.7541	.8099
15									.0000	.3290	.5213	.6454	.7307	.7918
16										.2684	.4781	.6134	.7063	.7730
17										.2053	.4330	.5800	.6810	.7534
18										.1395	.3862	.5453	.6546	.7330
19										.0712	.3374	.5092	.6272	.7118
20										.0000	.2866	.4715	.5986	.6897
21											.2338	.4324	.5689	.6667
22											.1788	.3917	.5379	.6428
23											.1216	.3493	.5057	.6179
24											.0620	.3052	.4722	.5920
25											.0000	.2592	.4373	.5650
26												.2114	.4010	.5370
27												.1617	.3632	.5078
28												.1099	.3239	.4774
29												.0561	.2830	.4457
30												.0000	.2404	.4128
35													.0000	.2269
40														.0000

4.25%

AGE OF LOAN	ORIGINAL TERM IN YEARS													
	2	3	4	5	6	7	8	10	15	20	25	30	35	40
1	.5106	.6807	.7657	.8166	.8505	.8747	.8928	.9180	.9513	.9676	.9770	.9831	.9873	.9903
2	.0000	.3476	.5212	.6253	.6945	.7439	.7809	.8324	.9005	.9337	.9531	.9656	.9741	.9801
3		.0000	.2661	.4256	.5318	.6075	.6641	.7432	.8474	.8984	.9281	.9472	.9602	.9696
4			.0000	.2173	.3620	.4651	.5423	.6500	.7921	.8616	.9020	.9281	.9458	.9585
5				.0000	.1848	.3166	.4152	.5528	.7344	.8231	.8749	.9081	.9308	.9470
6					.0000	.1617	.2827	.4514	.6742	.7830	.8465	.8872	.9151	.9350
7						.0000	.1443	.3457	.6113	.7412	.8169	.8655	.8987	.9224
8							.0000	.2353	.5458	.6976	.7860	.8428	.8816	.9093
9								.1201	.4774	.6520	.7538	.8191	.8638	.8957
10								.0000	.4060	.6045	.7201	.7944	.8452	.8814
11									.3315	.5549	.6850	.7687	.8258	.8666
12									.2538	.5032	.6484	.7418	.8056	.8511
13									.1728	.4492	.6103	.7137	.7845	.8349
14									.0882	.3929	.5704	.6845	.7624	.8180
15									.0000	.3342	.5288	.6539	.7395	.8004
16										.2729	.4855	.6221	.7155	.7821
17										.2090	.4402	.5888	.6904	.7629
18										.1422	.3930	.5542	.6643	.7429
19										.0726	.3438	.5180	.6371	.7220
20										.0000	.2924	.4802	.6087	.7003
21											.2387	.4408	.5790	.6775
22											.1828	.3998	.5481	.6538
23											.1244	.3569	.5158	.6291
24											.0635	.3122	.4821	.6033
25											.0000	.2655	.4470	.5764
26												.2168	.4103	.5483
27												.1660	.3721	.5190
28												.1130	.3322	.4885
29												.0577	.2906	.4566
30												.0000	.2471	.4233
35													.0000	.2340
40														.0000

4.50%

AGE OF LOAN	ORIGINAL TERM IN YEARS 2	3	4	5	6	7	8	10	15	20	25	30	35	40
1	.5112	.6815	.7666	.8176	.8515	.8757	.8937	.9190	.9522	.9684	.9778	.9839	.9880	.9909
2	.0000	.3484	.5224	.6267	.6961	.7456	.7826	.8342	.9023	.9354	.9547	.9670	.9754	.9813
3		.0000	.2671	.4271	.5336	.6096	.6664	.7456	.8500	.9009	.9304	.9493	.9622	.9713
4			.0000	.2184	.3637	.4673	.5448	.6529	.7953	.8648	.9051	.9309	.9484	.9609
5				.0000	.1859	.3185	.4176	.5559	.7381	.8270	.8786	.9116	.9340	.9499
6					.0000	.1628	.2846	.4545	.6783	.7875	.8508	.8914	.9190	.9385
7						.0000	.1455	.3484	.6158	.7462	.8218	.8703	.9032	.9265
8							.0000	.2374	.5503	.7029	.7915	.8482	.8867	.9140
9								.1214	.4819	.6577	.7598	.8251	.8695	.9009
10								.0000	.4103	.6104	.7266	.8009	.8514	.8873
11									.3355	.5610	.6919	.7756	.8326	.8729
12									.2572	.5092	.6556	.7492	.8128	.8580
13									.1753	.4551	.6176	.7215	.7922	.8423
14									.0896	.3985	.5779	.6926	.7706	.8259
15									.0000	.3393	.5363	.6623	.7481	.8088
16										.2774	.4929	.6307	.7244	.7909
17										.2127	.4474	.5976	.6997	.7722
18										.1449	.3999	.5630	.6739	.7525
19										.0741	.3502	.5268	.6469	.7320
20										.0000	.2981	.4889	.6186	.7106
21											.2437	.4493	.5891	.6882
22											.1869	.4079	.5582	.6647
23											.1273	.3645	.5258	.6402
24											.0651	.3192	.4920	.6145
25											.0000	.2718	.4566	.5877
26												.2222	.4196	.5596
27												.1703	.3809	.5302
28												.1161	.3405	.4995
29												.0593	.2981	.4674
30												.0000	.2539	.4338
35													.0000	.2411
40														.0000

4.75%

AGE OF LOAN	ORIGINAL TERM IN YEARS 2	3	4	5	6	7	8	10	15	20	25	30	35	40
1	.5118	.6823	.7675	.8185	.8524	.8766	.8947	.9200	.9531	.9693	.9786	.9846	.9886	.9914
2	.0000	.3493	.5237	.6282	.6977	.7473	.7844	.8360	.9040	.9371	.9562	.9684	.9766	.9824
3		.0000	.2680	.4286	.5355	.6117	.6686	.7480	.8525	.9033	.9327	.9514	.9641	.9730
4			.0000	.2194	.3654	.4694	.5473	.6557	.7985	.8679	.9081	.9336	.9509	.9631
5				.0000	.1870	.3203	.4200	.5590	.7419	.8308	.8822	.9150	.9371	.9527
6					.0000	.1640	.2866	.4575	.6825	.7919	.8551	.8954	.9227	.9419
7						.0000	.1467	.3511	.6202	.7511	.8267	.8749	.9075	.9305
8							.0000	.2396	.5549	.7083	.7969	.8534	.8916	.9185
9								.1226	.4865	.6634	.7657	.8309	.8749	.9060
10								.0000	.4147	.6163	.7330	.8072	.8575	.8929
11									.3394	.5670	.6986	.7824	.8391	.8791
12									.2605	.5153	.6626	.7564	.8199	.8646
13									.1778	.4610	.6249	.7292	.7998	.8495
14									.0910	.4042	.5853	.7006	.7786	.8336
15									.0000	.3445	.5438	.6706	.7565	.8170
16										.2820	.5002	.6392	.7333	.7995
17										.2164	.4546	.6063	.7089	.7812
18										.1477	.4067	.5717	.6834	.7620
19										.0756	.3566	.5355	.6566	.7418
20										.0000	.3040	.4975	.6285	.7207
21											.2488	.4577	.5990	.6986
22											.1909	.4159	.5682	.6754
23											.1303	.3722	.5358	.6511
24											.0667	.3262	.5018	.6255
25											.0000	.2781	.4663	.5988
26												.2276	.4289	.5707
27												.1747	.3898	.5413
28												.1192	.3488	.5105
29												.0610	.3057	.4781
30												.0000	.2606	.4442
35													.0000	.2483
40														.0000

5.00%

AGE OF LOAN	ORIGINAL TERM IN YEARS													
	2	3	4	5	6	7	8	10	15	20	25	30	35	40
1	.5125	.6832	.7684	.8194	.8534	.8776	.8957	.9209	.9541	.9701	.9794	.9852	.9892	.9920
2	.0000	.3501	.5249	.6297	.6993	.7490	.7861	.8378	.9058	.9387	.9577	.9697	.9778	.9835
3		.0000	.2690	.4301	.5374	.6137	.6709	.7504	.8550	.9057	.9349	.9534	.9659	.9746
4			.0000	.2204	.3671	.4716	.5497	.6586	.8017	.8710	.9110	.9363	.9533	.9653
5				.0000	.1881	.3222	.4224	.5620	.7456	.8345	.8858	.9183	.9401	.9554
6					.0000	.1651	.2886	.4606	.6866	.7962	.8593	.8994	.9263	.9451
7						.0000	.1479	.3539	.6246	.7559	.8315	.8795	.9117	.9343
8							.0000	.2418	.5595	.7136	.8023	.8585	.8964	.9228
9								.1239	.4910	.6690	.7716	.8365	.8803	.9109
10								.0000	.4190	.6222	.7392	.8134	.8633	.8982
11									.3434	.5730	.7053	.7891	.8455	.8850
12									.2639	.5213	.6696	.7636	.8268	.8711
13									.1803	.4669	.6321	.7367	.8071	.8564
14									.0924	.4098	.5926	.7085	.7865	.8410
15									.0000	.3497	.5512	.6788	.7647	.8248
16										.2866	.5076	.6477	.7419	.8078
17										.2202	.4618	.6149	.7179	.7900
18										.1504	.4136	.5804	.6926	.7712
19										.0771	.3630	.5442	.6661	.7514
20										.0000	.3098	.5061	.6382	.7306
21											.2538	.4661	.6089	.7088
22											.1951	.4240	.5781	.6859
23											.1333	.3798	.5457	.6618
24											.0683	.3333	.5116	.6364
25											.0000	.2845	.4758	.6098
26												.2331	.4382	.5818
27												.1791	.3986	.5523
28												.1224	.3571	.5214
29												.0627	.3134	.4888
30												.0000	.2674	.4546
35													.0000	.2555
40														.0000

5.25%

AGE OF LOAN	ORIGINAL TERM IN YEARS													
	2	3	4	5	6	7	8	10	15	20	25	30	35	40
1	.5131	.6840	.7693	.8204	.8544	.8786	.8967	.9219	.9550	.9709	.9801	.9859	.9898	.9925
2	.0000	.3509	.5262	.6311	.7009	.7506	.7878	.8396	.9075	.9403	.9592	.9710	.9790	.9845
3		.0000	.2700	.4317	.5392	.6158	.6731	.7528	.8575	.9081	.9371	.9554	.9676	.9761
4			.0000	.2215	.3688	.4737	.5522	.6614	.8048	.8741	.9138	.9389	.9556	.9673
5				.0000	.1892	.3240	.4248	.5651	.7492	.8382	.8893	.9215	.9430	.9580
6					.0000	.1663	.2905	.4636	.6907	.8005	.8635	.9032	.9297	.9482
7						.0000	.1491	.3566	.6290	.7607	.8362	.8839	.9157	.9379
8							.0000	.2439	.5641	.7188	.8075	.8635	.9010	.9270
9								.1252	.4956	.6746	.7773	.8421	.8854	.9155
10								.0000	.4234	.6280	.7454	.8195	.8690	.9034
11									.3474	.5790	.7119	.7957	.8517	.8907
12									.2672	.5273	.6765	.7706	.8335	.8773
13									.1828	.4728	.6392	.7441	.8143	.8631
14									.0938	.4154	.5999	.7163	.7941	.8482
15									.0000	.3549	.5585	.6869	.7728	.8325
16										.2912	.5149	.6560	.7503	.8159
17										.2240	.4689	.6234	.7267	.7985
18										.1532	.4205	.5890	.7017	.7801
19										.0786	.3694	.5528	.6755	.7607
20										.0000	.3156	.5147	.6478	.7403
21											.2589	.4745	.6186	.7188
22											.1992	.4321	.5879	.6962
23											.1362	.3875	.5555	.6723
24											.0699	.3404	.5213	.6471
25											.0000	.2908	.4854	.6206
26												.2386	.4474	.5926
27												.1836	.4075	.5632
28												.1255	.3654	.5321
29												.0644	.3210	.4994
30												.0000	.2743	.4650
35													.0000	.2628
40														.0000

5.50%

AGE OF LOAN	ORIGINAL TERM IN YEARS													
	2	3	4	5	6	7	8	10	15	20	25	30	35	40
1	.5137	.6848	.7702	.8213	.8553	.8796	.8977	.9228	.9558	.9717	.9808	.9865	.9903	.9929
2	.0000	.3518	.5274	.6326	.7025	.7523	.7895	.8413	.9092	.9419	.9606	.9723	.9801	.9855
3		.0000	.2709	.4332	.5411	.6179	.6753	.7552	.8599	.9104	.9392	.9573	.9693	.9776
4			.0000	.2225	.3705	.4759	.5547	.6643	.8079	.8771	.9166	.9414	.9579	.9692
5				.0000	.1903	.3259	.4272	.5682	.7529	.8419	.8927	.9246	.9458	.9604
6					.0000	.1674	.2925	.4666	.6948	.8047	.8675	.9069	.9331	.9511
7						.0000	.1503	.3594	.6334	.7654	.8409	.8882	.9196	.9413
8							.0000	.2461	.5686	.7240	.8127	.8684	.9054	.9309
9								.1264	.5001	.6801	.7830	.8475	.8904	.9200
10								.0000	.4278	.6338	.7516	.8254	.8745	.9084
11									.3513	.5849	.7184	.8021	.8577	.8961
12									.2706	.5333	.6833	.7775	.8400	.8832
13									.1853	.4787	.6463	.7514	.8213	.8696
14									.0952	.4210	.6072	.7239	.8016	.8551
15									.0000	.3601	.5658	.6949	.7807	.8399
16										.2958	.5222	.6642	.7586	.8238
17										.2278	.4761	.6318	.7353	.8068
18										.1560	.4273	.5976	.7107	.7888
19										.0801	.3759	.5614	.6847	.7698
20										.0000	.3215	.5232	.6572	.7498
21											.2641	.4828	.6282	.7286
22											.2034	.4402	.5976	.7062
23											.1393	.3951	.5652	.6826
24											.0715	.3475	.5310	.6576
25											.0000	.2973	.4948	.6312
26												.2441	.4566	.6034
27												.1880	.4163	.5739
28												.1288	.3737	.5428
29												.0661	.3287	.5100
30												.0000	.2811	.4752
35													.0000	.2700
40														.0000

5.75%

AGE OF LOAN	ORIGINAL TERM IN YEARS													
	2	3	4	5	6	7	8	10	15	20	25	30	35	40
1	.5143	.6856	.7711	.8223	.8563	.8805	.8986	.9238	.9567	.9725	.9815	.9871	.9908	.9934
2	.0000	.3526	.5286	.6340	.7041	.7540	.7912	.8431	.9109	.9434	.9620	.9735	.9811	.9864
3		.0000	.2719	.4347	.5429	.6200	.6775	.7576	.8623	.9126	.9412	.9591	.9709	.9789
4			.0000	.2236	.3722	.4780	.5571	.6671	.8109	.8800	.9193	.9438	.9600	.9711
5				.0000	.1914	.3277	.4296	.5712	.7565	.8455	.8961	.9276	.9485	.9628
6					.0000	.1686	.2945	.4697	.6989	.8089	.8714	.9105	.9363	.9539
7						.0000	.1515	.3622	.6378	.7701	.8454	.8923	.9233	.9446
8							.0000	.2483	.5731	.7291	.8178	.8731	.9097	.9347
9								.1277	.5047	.6856	.7885	.8528	.8952	.9242
10								.0000	.4321	.6396	.7576	.8312	.8798	.9131
11									.3553	.5909	.7248	.8084	.8636	.9014
12									.2740	.5392	.6901	.7842	.8464	.8890
13									.1878	.4846	.6533	.7586	.8281	.8758
14									.0966	.4267	.6144	.7315	.8088	.8618
15									.0000	.3653	.5731	.7028	.7884	.8471
16										.3004	.5294	.6723	.7667	.8314
17										.2316	.4832	.6401	.7438	.8148
18										.1588	.4342	.6060	.7195	.7973
19										.0817	.3823	.5699	.6938	.7787
20										.0000	.3274	.5316	.6665	.7590
21											.2692	.4911	.6377	.7382
22											.2076	.4482	.6071	.7161
23											.1423	.4028	.5748	.6927
24											.0732	.3546	.5405	.6679
25											.0000	.3037	.5042	.6417
26												.2497	.4658	.6139
27												.1925	.4251	.5845
28												.1320	.3820	.5534
29												.0679	.3364	.5204
30												.0000	.2880	.4855
35													.0000	.2773
40														.0000

6.00%

AGE OF LOAN	ORIGINAL TERM IN YEARS 2	3	4	5	6	7	8	10	15	20	25	30	35	40
1	.5150	.6864	.7720	.8232	.8572	.8815	.8996	.9247	.9576	.9733	.9822	.9877	.9913	.9938
2	.0000	.3535	.5299	.6355	.7057	.7556	.7929	.8448	.9126	.9450	.9633	.9747	.9821	.9872
3		.0000	.2729	.4362	.5448	.6220	.6797	.7600	.8647	.9149	.9432	.9608	.9724	.9802
4			.0000	.2246	.3739	.4802	.5596	.6699	.8140	.8829	.9219	.9461	.9620	.9728
5				.0000	.1926	.3296	.4320	.5743	.7601	.8490	.8993	.9305	.9510	.9650
6					.0000	.1697	.2965	.4727	.7029	.8130	.8753	.9140	.9393	.9566
7						.0000	.1527	.3649	.6421	.7748	.8498	.8964	.9270	.9477
8							.0000	.2505	.5776	.7342	.8228	.8777	.9138	.9383
9								.1290	.5092	.6911	.7940	.8579	.8998	.9283
10								.0000	.4365	.6453	.7635	.8369	.8850	.9177
11									.3593	.5967	.7311	.8145	.8692	.9064
12									.2774	.5452	.6968	.7908	.8525	.8945
13									.1904	.4904	.6602	.7656	.8347	.8818
14									.0980	.4323	.6215	.7389	.8159	.8683
15									.0000	.3706	.5803	.7105	.7959	.8540
16										.3051	.5367	.6804	.7746	.8388
17										.2355	.4903	.6484	.7521	.8226
18										.1616	.4410	.6144	.7281	.8055
19										.0832	.3888	.5783	.7027	.7873
20										.0000	.3333	.5400	.6757	.7680
21											.2743	.4994	.6470	.7475
22											.2118	.4562	.6166	.7257
23											.1454	.4104	.5843	.7026
24											.0749	.3618	.5500	.6781
25											.0000	.3101	.5136	.6520
26												.2553	.4749	.6244
27												.1971	.4339	.5950
28												.1353	.3903	.5638
29												.0697	.3440	.5307
30												.0000	.2949	.4956
35													.0000	.2846
40														.0000

6.25%

AGE OF LOAN	ORIGINAL TERM IN YEARS 2	3	4	5	6	7	8	10	15	20	25	30	35	40
1	.5156	.6872	.7729	.8241	.8582	.8824	.9005	.9257	.9584	.9741	.9829	.9883	.9918	.9942
2	.0000	.3543	.5311	.6369	.7073	.7573	.7946	.8465	.9142	.9464	.9646	.9758	.9831	.9880
3		.0000	.2738	.4377	.5466	.6241	.6820	.7623	.8671	.9170	.9452	.9625	.9738	.9815
4			.0000	.2257	.3756	.4823	.5620	.6727	.8170	.8858	.9245	.9484	.9640	.9745
5				.0000	.1937	.3315	.4344	.5773	.7636	.8525	.9025	.9334	.9535	.9671
6					.0000	.1709	.2985	.4758	.7069	.8170	.8791	.9174	.9423	.9592
7						.0000	.1539	.3677	.6465	.7793	.8542	.9003	.9304	.9507
8							.0000	.2527	.5821	.7392	.8276	.8822	.9178	.9418
9								.1303	.5137	.6965	.7994	.8629	.9043	.9322
10								.0000	.4409	.6510	.7694	.8424	.8900	.9221
11									.3633	.6026	.7374	.8205	.8747	.9113
12									.2808	.5511	.7033	.7973	.8585	.8998
13									.1930	.4963	.6671	.7725	.8412	.8875
14									.0995	.4379	.6286	.7461	.8228	.8745
15									.0000	.3758	.5875	.7181	.8032	.8606
16										.3097	.5438	.6883	.7824	.8459
17										.2394	.4974	.6565	.7602	.8302
18										.1645	.4479	.6227	.7366	.8135
19										.0848	.3952	.5867	.7114	.7957
20										.0000	.3392	.5484	.6847	.7767
21											.2795	.5076	.6562	.7566
22											.2160	.4642	.6259	.7351
23											.1485	.4180	.5937	.7123
24											.0765	.3689	.5594	.6880
25											.0000	.3166	.5229	.6621
26												.2609	.4840	.6346
27												.2016	.4426	.6053
28												.1386	.3986	.5741
29												.0714	.3517	.5410
30												.0000	.3019	.5056
35													.0000	.2919
40														.0000

6.50%

AGE OF LOAN	ORIGINAL TERM IN YEARS 2	3	4	5	6	7	8	10	15	20	25	30	35	40
1	.5162	.6880	.7738	.8251	.8591	.8834	.9015	.9266	.9593	.9748	.9835	.9888	.9923	.9946
2	.0000	.3552	.5324	.6384	.7088	.7589	.7963	.8482	.9158	.9479	.9659	.9769	.9840	.9888
3		.0000	.2748	.4392	.5485	.6262	.6842	.7647	.8694	.9192	.9471	.9642	.9752	.9826
4			.0000	.2267	.3774	.4845	.5645	.6755	.8200	.8886	.9270	.9506	.9659	.9761
5				.0000	.1948	.3333	.4368	.5803	.7672	.8559	.9056	.9361	.9558	.9691
6					.0000	.1721	.3005	.4788	.7108	.8210	.8828	.9207	.9452	.9616
7						.0000	.1551	.3705	.6507	.7838	.8584	.9042	.9338	.9536
8							.0000	.2549	.5866	.7441	.8324	.8866	.9216	.9451
9								.1316	.5182	.7018	.8047	.8678	.9086	.9360
10								.0000	.4452	.6566	.7751	.8478	.8948	.9263
11									.3673	.6084	.7435	.8264	.8800	.9159
12									.2842	.5570	.7099	.8036	.8642	.9049
13									.1956	.5021	.6739	.7793	.8474	.8931
14									.1009	.4435	.6356	.7533	.8295	.8805
15									.0000	.3811	.5946	.7256	.8103	.8671
16										.3144	.5510	.6960	.7899	.8528
17										.2433	.5044	.6645	.7681	.8375
18										.1674	.4547	.6309	.7448	.8212
19										.0864	.4017	.5950	.7200	.8038
20										.0000	.3451	.5567	.6935	.7852
21											.2847	.5158	.6653	.7654
22											.2203	.4722	.6352	.7443
23											.1516	.4257	.6030	.7218
24											.0782	.3760	.5687	.6977
25											.0000	.3230	.5321	.6721
26												.2665	.4930	.6447
27												.2062	.4513	.6155
28												.1419	.4069	.5843
29												.0732	.3594	.5511
30												.0000	.3088	.5156
35													.0000	.2992
40														.0000

6.75%

AGE OF LOAN	ORIGINAL TERM IN YEARS 2	3	4	5	6	7	8	10	15	20	25	30	35	40
1	.5168	.6888	.7746	.8260	.8601	.8843	.9024	.9275	.9601	.9755	.9841	.9893	.9927	.9949
2	.0000	.3560	.5336	.6398	.7104	.7606	.7980	.8499	.9174	.9493	.9671	.9779	.9849	.9895
3		.0000	.2758	.4407	.5503	.6282	.6863	.7670	.8717	.9213	.9489	.9657	.9766	.9837
4			.0000	.2278	.3791	.4866	.5669	.6783	.8229	.8913	.9295	.9527	.9676	.9776
5				.0000	.1959	.3352	.4392	.5834	.7707	.8593	.9087	.9388	.9581	.9709
6					.0000	.1732	.3025	.4818	.7148	.8250	.8864	.9238	.9479	.9639
7						.0000	.1563	.3733	.6550	.7883	.8626	.9079	.9370	.9563
8							.0000	.2571	.5911	.7491	.8371	.8908	.9253	.9482
9								.1329	.5227	.7071	.8099	.8725	.9128	.9395
10								.0000	.4496	.6622	.7808	.8530	.8994	.9302
11									.3713	.6142	.7496	.8321	.8851	.9203
12									.2877	.5628	.7163	.8098	.8698	.9097
13									.1981	.5079	.6806	.7859	.8535	.8984
14									.1024	.4491	.6425	.7603	.8360	.8863
15									.0000	.3863	.6017	.7330	.8173	.8733
16										.3191	.5581	.7037	.7972	.8594
17										.2472	.5114	.6724	.7758	.8445
18										.1703	.4615	.6389	.7529	.8287
19										.0880	.4081	.6032	.7284	.8117
20										.0000	.3510	.5649	.7022	.7935
21											.2899	.5239	.6742	.7741
22											.2246	.4801	.6442	.7533
23											.1547	.4332	.6122	.7311
24											.0800	.3831	.5779	.7073
25											.0000	.3295	.5412	.6818
26												.2722	.5020	.6546
27												.2108	.4600	.6255
28												.1452	.4151	.5944
29												.0751	.3671	.5611
30												.0000	.3157	.5255
35													.0000	.3065
40														.0000

7.00%

AGE OF LOAN	ORIGINAL TERM IN YEARS													
	2	3	4	5	6	7	8	10	15	20	25	30	35	40
1	.5174	.6896	.7755	.8269	.8610	.8853	.9033	.9284	.9609	.9762	.9847	.9898	.9931	.9953
2	.0000	.3569	.5348	.6413	.7120	.7622	.7997	.8516	.9190	.9507	.9683	.9789	.9857	.9902
3		.0000	.2767	.4423	.5522	.6303	.6885	.7693	.8740	.9233	.9507	.9673	.9778	.9848
4			.0000	.2288	.3808	.4888	.5693	.6810	.8258	.8940	.9318	.9547	.9693	.9790
5				.0000	.1970	.3371	.4415	.5864	.7741	.8626	.9116	.9413	.9602	.9727
6					.0000	.1744	.3045	.4849	.7187	.8288	.8899	.9269	.9505	.9660
7						.0000	.1576	.3760	.6593	.7927	.8667	.9115	.9400	.9589
8							.0000	.2593	.5955	.7539	.8417	.8949	.9288	.9512
9								.1342	.5272	.7123	.8150	.8772	.9168	.9429
10								.0000	.4539	.6677	.7863	.8581	.9039	.9341
11									.3754	.6199	.7556	.8377	.8901	.9246
12									.2911	.5687	.7226	.8158	.8752	.9144
13									.2008	.5137	.6873	.7923	.8593	.9035
14									.1039	.4547	.6494	.7672	.8423	.8918
15									.0000	.3915	.6087	.7402	.8240	.8792
16										.3238	.5651	.7112	.8044	.8658
17										.2511	.5184	.6802	.7834	.8514
18										.1732	.4683	.6469	.7609	.8359
19										.0896	.4146	.6113	.7367	.8193
20										.0000	.3569	.5730	.7108	.8015
21											.2952	.5320	.6830	.7825
22											.2289	.4880	.6532	.7620
23											.1579	.4408	.6212	.7401
24											.0817	.3902	.5870	.7166
25											.0000	.3360	.5502	.6914
26												.2778	.5108	.6643
27												.2155	.4686	.6354
28												.1486	.4233	.6043
29												.0769	.3747	.5710
30												.0000	.3226	.5352
35													.0000	.3138
40														.0000

7.25%

AGE OF LOAN	ORIGINAL TERM IN YEARS													
	2	3	4	5	6	7	8	10	15	20	25	30	35	40
1	.5181	.6904	.7764	.8278	.8619	.8862	.9043	.9293	.9617	.9769	.9853	.9903	.9935	.9956
2	.0000	.3577	.5361	.6427	.7135	.7638	.8013	.8533	.9205	.9521	.9695	.9799	.9865	.9909
3		.0000	.2777	.4438	.5540	.6323	.6907	.7716	.8763	.9254	.9524	.9687	.9790	.9858
4			.0000	.2299	.3825	.4909	.5718	.6838	.8287	.8967	.9342	.9567	.9710	.9803
5				.0000	.1982	.3390	.4439	.5894	.7776	.8658	.9145	.9438	.9623	.9744
6					.0000	.1756	.3065	.4879	.7226	.8327	.8934	.9299	.9530	.9681
7						.0000	.1588	.3788	.6635	.7970	.8707	.9150	.9430	.9613
8							.0000	.2616	.6000	.7587	.8463	.8989	.9322	.9540
9								.1355	.5317	.7175	.8200	.8817	.9207	.9461
10								.0000	.4583	.6732	.7918	.8631	.9082	.9377
11									.3794	.6256	.7615	.8432	.8949	.9286
12									.2946	.5745	.7289	.8217	.8805	.9189
13									.2034	.5195	.6938	.7987	.8650	.9084
14									.1054	.4603	.6562	.7739	.8484	.8971
15									.0000	.3968	.6157	.7473	.8306	.8850
16										.3285	.5721	.7187	.8114	.8720
17										.2550	.5254	.6879	.7908	.8580
18										.1761	.4751	.6548	.7686	.8429
19										.0912	.4210	.6193	.7448	.8267
20										.0000	.3629	.5811	.7191	.8093
21											.3004	.5400	.6916	.7906
22											.2332	.4958	.6620	.7705
23											.1610	.4484	.6302	.7489
24											.0834	.3973	.5959	.7257
25											.0000	.3425	.5592	.7007
26												.2835	.5196	.6739
27												.2201	.4771	.6450
28												.1520	.4315	.6140
29												.0787	.3823	.5807
30												.0000	.3296	.5449
35													.0000	.3211
40														.0000

7.50%

AGE OF LOAN	ORIGINAL TERM IN YEARS													
	2	3	4	5	6	7	8	10	15	20	25	30	35	40
1	.5187	.6913	.7773	.8287	.8629	.8871	.9052	.9302	.9625	.9776	.9858	.9908	.9939	.9959
2	.0000	.3585	.5373	.6442	.7151	.7655	.8030	.8550	.9221	.9534	.9706	.9808	.9873	.9915
3		.0000	.2787	.4453	.5558	.6344	.6929	.7739	.8785	.9273	.9541	.9701	.9802	.9867
4			.0000	.2310	.3842	.4931	.5742	.6865	.8315	.8993	.9364	.9586	.9725	.9816
5				.0000	.1993	.3409	.4463	.5924	.7810	.8690	.9173	.9462	.9643	.9760
6					.0000	.1768	.3085	.4909	.7264	.8364	.8967	.9328	.9554	.9700
7						.0000	.1600	.3816	.6677	.8013	.8746	.9183	.9458	.9636
8							.0000	.2638	.6044	.7634	.8507	.9028	.9355	.9567
9								.1368	.5362	.7226	.8249	.8860	.9244	.9492
10								.0000	.4626	.6787	.7972	.8679	.9124	.9412
11									.3834	.6313	.7673	.8485	.8995	.9325
12									.2980	.5802	.7350	.8275	.8855	.9231
13									.2060	.5252	.7003	.8049	.8705	.9131
14									.1069	.4659	.6629	.7805	.8544	.9022
15									.0000	.4020	.6226	.7543	.8370	.8905
16										.3332	.5791	.7260	.8182	.8779
17										.2590	.5323	.6955	.7979	.8643
18										.1790	.4818	.6626	.7761	.8497
19										.0929	.4274	.6272	.7526	.8339
20										.0000	.3688	.5891	.7273	.8169
21											.3056	.5479	.7000	.7986
22											.2376	.5036	.6706	.7788
23											.1642	.4559	.6390	.7575
24											.0852	.4044	.6048	.7346
25											.0000	.3489	.5680	.7099
26												.2892	.5284	.6833
27												.2248	.4856	.6546
28												.1554	.4396	.6236
29												.0806	.3900	.5903
30												.0000	.3365	.5544
35													.0000	.3284
40														.0000

7.75%

AGE OF LOAN	ORIGINAL TERM IN YEARS													
	2	3	4	5	6	7	8	10	15	20	25	30	35	40
1	.5193	.6921	.7782	.8296	.8638	.8880	.9061	.9311	.9633	.9782	.9864	.9912	.9942	.9962
2	.0000	.3594	.5385	.6456	.7166	.7671	.8046	.8566	.9236	.9547	.9717	.9817	.9880	.9920
3		.0000	.2797	.4468	.5577	.6364	.6950	.7762	.8807	.9293	.9558	.9715	.9813	.9876
4			.0000	.2320	.3859	.4952	.5766	.6893	.8344	.9018	.9386	.9604	.9740	.9827
5				.0000	.2004	.3427	.4487	.5954	.7843	.8722	.9201	.9485	.9662	.9775
6					.0000	.1780	.3105	.4940	.7303	.8401	.9000	.9356	.9577	.9719
7						.0000	.1613	.3844	.6719	.8055	.8784	.9216	.9485	.9658
8							.0000	.2660	.6088	.7681	.8550	.9065	.9386	.9592
9								.1381	.5406	.7277	.8297	.8903	.9279	.9521
10								.0000	.4670	.6841	.8025	.8727	.9164	.9445
11									.3874	.6369	.7730	.8537	.9039	.9362
12									.3015	.5860	.7411	.8331	.8904	.9272
13									.2086	.5309	.7067	.8110	.8759	.9175
14									.1084	.4715	.6695	.7870	.8601	.9071
15									.0000	.4073	.6294	.7611	.8431	.8958
16										.3379	.5860	.7331	.8248	.8836
17										.2629	.5391	.7029	.8049	.8704
18										.1820	.4885	.6703	.7835	.8562
19										.0945	.4338	.6350	.7604	.8408
20										.0000	.3747	.5970	.7354	.8242
21											.3109	.5558	.7083	.8062
22											.2419	.5114	.6792	.7869
23											.1674	.4633	.6476	.7659
24											.0869	.4115	.6136	.7433
25											.0000	.3554	.5768	.7188
26												.2949	.5370	.6924
27												.2295	.4941	.6639
28												.1588	.4477	.6331
29												.0825	.3975	.5998
30												.0000	.3434	.5638
35													.0000	.3357
40														.0000

8.00%

AGE OF LOAN	ORIGINAL TERM IN YEARS													
	2	3	4	5	6	7	8	10	15	20	25	30	35	40
1	.5199	.6929	.7791	.8306	.8647	.8890	.9070	.9319	.9640	.9789	.9869	.9916	.9946	.9964
2	.0000	.3602	.5398	.6471	.7182	.7687	.8063	.8582	.9251	.9560	.9727	.9826	.9887	.9926
3		.0000	.2806	.4483	.5595	.6384	.6972	.7784	.8829	.9312	.9574	.9728	.9823	.9884
4			.0000	.2331	.3877	.4974	.5791	.6920	.8372	.9043	.9407	.9622	.9754	.9839
5				.0000	.2016	.3446	.4511	.5984	.7877	.8753	.9227	.9507	.9680	.9790
6					.0000	.1792	.3126	.4970	.7341	.8438	.9032	.9383	.9599	.9736
7						.0000	.1625	.3872	.6760	.8097	.8821	.9248	.9511	.9679
8							.0000	.2683	.6131	.7727	.8592	.9102	.9416	.9617
9								.1395	.5451	.7327	.8345	.8944	.9314	.9549
10								.0000	.4713	.6894	.8076	.8772	.9202	.9476
11									.3915	.6425	.7786	.8587	.9082	.9397
12									.3050	.5917	.7471	.8386	.8952	.9311
13									.2113	.5367	.7130	.8169	.8810	.9218
14									.1099	.4771	.6761	.7933	.8657	.9118
15									.0000	.4125	.6361	.7678	.8491	.9009
16										.3426	.5929	.7402	.8312	.8891
17										.2669	.5460	.7103	.8118	.8763
18										.1849	.4952	.6779	.7907	.8625
19										.0962	.4402	.6428	.7679	.8475
20										.0000	.3806	.6048	.7432	.8313
21											.3162	.5636	.7165	.8137
22											.2463	.5191	.6875	.7947
23											.1707	.4708	.6562	.7741
24											.0887	.4185	.6222	.7517
25											.0000	.3619	.5854	.7276
26												.3006	.5456	.7014
27												.2342	.5024	.6731
28												.1622	.4557	.6423
29												.0844	.4051	.6091
30												.0000	.3503	.5731
35													.0000	.3429
40														.0000

8.25%

AGE OF LOAN	ORIGINAL TERM IN YEARS													
	2	3	4	5	6	7	8	10	15	20	25	30	35	40
1	.5205	.6937	.7799	.8315	.8656	.8899	.9079	.9328	.9648	.9795	.9874	.9921	.9949	.9967
2	.0000	.3611	.5410	.6485	.7197	.7703	.8079	.8599	.9265	.9572	.9738	.9834	.9893	.9931
3		.0000	.2816	.4498	.5614	.6405	.6993	.7807	.8850	.9330	.9589	.9741	.9833	.9892
4			.0000	.2342	.3894	.4995	.5815	.6947	.8399	.9068	.9428	.9639	.9768	.9849
5				.0000	.2027	.3465	.4535	.6013	.7910	.8783	.9253	.9528	.9697	.9803
6					.0000	.1804	.3146	.5000	.7378	.8473	.9064	.9409	.9620	.9753
7						.0000	.1638	.3900	.6801	.8138	.8858	.9278	.9536	.9699
8							.0000	.2705	.6175	.7773	.8634	.9137	.9445	.9639
9								.1408	.5495	.7377	.8391	.8984	.9347	.9575
10								.0000	.4756	.6947	.8127	.8817	.9240	.9506
11									.3955	.6480	.7841	.8636	.9123	.9430
12									.3085	.5974	.7530	.8440	.8997	.9348
13									.2140	.5423	.7193	.8227	.8860	.9259
14									.1114	.4826	.6826	.7995	.8711	.9162
15									.0000	.4178	.6428	.7744	.8550	.9058
16										.3474	.5996	.7471	.8374	.8944
17										.2709	.5528	.7175	.8184	.8820
18										.1879	.5018	.6853	.7977	.8685
19										.0978	.4466	.6504	.7753	.8540
20										.0000	.3866	.6125	.7509	.8381
21											.3214	.5714	.7245	.8209
22											.2507	.5267	.6957	.8023
23											.1739	.4782	.6646	.7820
24											.0905	.4255	.6307	.7600
25											.0000	.3683	.5939	.7361
26												.3063	.5540	.7102
27												.2389	.5107	.6820
28												.1657	.4637	.6515
29												.0862	.4126	.6183
30												.0000	.3572	.5822
35													.0000	.3501
40														.0000

8.50%

AGE OF LOAN	ORIGINAL TERM IN YEARS													
	2	3	4	5	6	7	8	10	15	20	25	30	35	40
1	.5212	.6945	.7808	.8324	.8665	.8908	.9088	.9337	.9655	.9801	.9879	.9924	.9952	.9969
2	.0000	.3619	.5422	.6499	.7213	.7719	.8095	.8615	.9280	.9584	.9747	.9842	.9900	.9935
3		.0000	.2826	.4514	.5632	.6425	.7015	.7829	.8871	.9349	.9604	.9753	.9843	.9899
4			.0000	.2352	.3911	.5017	.5839	.6974	.8426	.9092	.9448	.9655	.9781	.9859
5				.0000	.2038	.3484	.4559	.6043	.7942	.8813	.9279	.9549	.9713	.9816
6					.0000	.1816	.3166	.5030	.7416	.8509	.9094	.9434	.9640	.9768
7						.0000	.1650	.3928	.6842	.8178	.8893	.9308	.9560	.9717
8							.0000	.2728	.6218	.7818	.8674	.9171	.9473	.9661
9								.1422	.5539	.7426	.8436	.9022	.9378	.9600
10								.0000	.4800	.6999	.8177	.8860	.9275	.9534
11									.3995	.6535	.7895	.8684	.9163	.9462
12									.3119	.6030	.7588	.8492	.9041	.9384
13									.2166	.5480	.7254	.8283	.8908	.9298
14									.1129	.4881	.6890	.8056	.8764	.9205
15									.0000	.4230	.6495	.7808	.8606	.9104
16										.3521	.6064	.7539	.8435	.8994
17										.2749	.5595	.7246	.8248	.8874
18										.1909	.5085	.6927	.8046	.8744
19										.0995	.4529	.6580	.7825	.8602
20										.0000	.3925	.6202	.7584	.8448
21											.3267	.5790	.7323	.8279
22											.2551	.5343	.7038	.8096
23											.1771	.4855	.6728	.7897
24											.0923	.4325	.6391	.7680
25											.0000	.3748	.6024	.7445
26												.3120	.5624	.7188
27												.2436	.5189	.6908
28												.1692	.4716	.6604
29												.0882	.4201	.6273
30												.0000	.3640	.5913
35													.0000	.3573
40														.0000

8.75%

AGE OF LOAN	ORIGINAL TERM IN YEARS													
	2	3	4	5	6	7	8	10	15	20	25	30	35	40
1	.5218	.6953	.7817	.8333	.8674	.8917	.9097	.9345	.9662	.9807	.9884	.9928	.9955	.9971
2	.0000	.3628	.5435	.6514	.7228	.7735	.8111	.8631	.9294	.9596	.9757	.9850	.9905	.9940
3		.0000	.2836	.4529	.5650	.6445	.7036	.7851	.8892	.9366	.9619	.9764	.9852	.9906
4			.0000	.2363	.3928	.5038	.5863	.7001	.8453	.9116	.9468	.9671	.9793	.9868
5				.0000	.2050	.3503	.4583	.6073	.7975	.8842	.9303	.9569	.9729	.9828
6					.0000	.1828	.3186	.5060	.7453	.8543	.9124	.9458	.9659	.9783
7						.0000	.1663	.3956	.6883	.8218	.8928	.9336	.9583	.9735
8							.0000	.2750	.6261	.7862	.8714	.9204	.9499	.9682
9								.1435	.5583	.7474	.8481	.9060	.9408	.9624
10								.0000	.4843	.7051	.8226	.8902	.9309	.9561
11									.4035	.6590	.7948	.8730	.9201	.9492
12									.3154	.6086	.7645	.8543	.9083	.9417
13									.2193	.5536	.7314	.8338	.8955	.9336
14									.1144	.4936	.6954	.8115	.8814	.9246
15									.0000	.4282	.6560	.7871	.8661	.9149
16										.3568	.6130	.7606	.8494	.9043
17										.2789	.5662	.7316	.8311	.8927
18										.1939	.5150	.6999	.8112	.8800
19										.1012	.4593	.6654	.7895	.8662
20										.0000	.3984	.6277	.7658	.8512
21											.3320	.5866	.7399	.8347
22											.2595	.5418	.7117	.8168
23											.1804	.4928	.6809	.7972
24											.0941	.4395	.6473	.7759
25											.0000	.3812	.6107	.7526
26												.3176	.5707	.7272
27												.2483	.5271	.6994
28												.1726	.4795	.6692
29												.0901	.4275	.6362
30												.0000	.3709	.6002
35													.0000	.3645
40														.0000

9.00%

AGE OF LOAN	ORIGINAL TERM IN YEARS													
	2	3	4	5	6	7	8	10	15	20	25	30	35	40
1	.5224	.6961	.7826	.8342	.8684	.8926	.9106	.9354	.9669	.9813	.9888	.9932	.9957	.9973
2	.0000	.3636	.5447	.6528	.7244	.7751	.8127	.8647	.9308	.9608	.9766	.9857	.9911	.9944
3		.0000	.2846	.4544	.5668	.6465	.7057	.7873	.8912	.9384	.9633	.9775	.9860	.9912
4			.0000	.2374	.3946	.5060	.5887	.7028	.8480	.9139	.9487	.9686	.9804	.9877
5				.0000	.2061	.3522	.4607	.6102	.8007	.8871	.9327	.9588	.9744	.9839
6					.0000	.1840	.3207	.5090	.7489	.8577	.9153	.9481	.9677	.9797
7						.0000	.1675	.3984	.6923	.8257	.8962	.9364	.9604	.9751
8							.0000	.2773	.6304	.7906	.8753	.9236	.9525	.9701
9								.1449	.5627	.7522	.8524	.9096	.9437	.9647
10								.0000	.4886	.7103	.8274	.8943	.9342	.9587
11									.4076	.6644	.8000	.8775	.9238	.9521
12									.3190	.6141	.7701	.8592	.9124	.9449
13									.2220	.5592	.7374	.8392	.8999	.9371
14									.1160	.4991	.7016	.8173	.8863	.9285
15									.0000	.4334	.6625	.7933	.8714	.9192
16										.3616	.6197	.7671	.8551	.9089
17										.2829	.5728	.7384	.8372	.8977
18										.1969	.5216	.7070	.8177	.8854
19										.1029	.4656	.6727	.7963	.8720
20										.0000	.4043	.6352	.7730	.8573
21											.3372	.5941	.7474	.8413
22											.2639	.5492	.7195	.8237
23											.1837	.5001	.6889	.8045
24											.0960	.4464	.6555	.7835
25											.0000	.3876	.6189	.7605
26												.3233	.5789	.7354
27												.2530	.5351	.7079
28												.1761	.4873	.6778
29												.0920	.4349	.6449
30												.0000	.3777	.6089
35													.0000	.3716
40														.0000

9.25%

AGE OF LOAN	ORIGINAL TERM IN YEARS													
	2	3	4	5	6	7	8	10	15	20	25	30	35	40
1	.5230	.6969	.7834	.8351	.8693	.8935	.9114	.9362	.9676	.9818	.9893	.9935	.9960	.9975
2	.0000	.3645	.5459	.6542	.7259	.7766	.8143	.8662	.9322	.9619	.9775	.9864	.9916	.9948
3		.0000	.2855	.4559	.5687	.6485	.7079	.7895	.8933	.9401	.9647	.9786	.9868	.9918
4			.0000	.2384	.3963	.5081	.5911	.7054	.8506	.9161	.9505	.9700	.9815	.9885
5				.0000	.2073	.3541	.4631	.6132	.8039	.8899	.9351	.9606	.9758	.9849
6					.0000	.1852	.3227	.5121	.7526	.8611	.9181	.9504	.9694	.9810
7						.0000	.1688	.4012	.6963	.8295	.8994	.9391	.9625	.9767
8							.0000	.2796	.6347	.7949	.8790	.9267	.9549	.9720
9								.1462	.5671	.7570	.8566	.9131	.9465	.9668
10								.0000	.4929	.7153	.8321	.8982	.9374	.9611
11									.4116	.6697	.8052	.8819	.9273	.9548
12									.3225	.6197	.7757	.8640	.9163	.9480
13									.2247	.5648	.7433	.8444	.9042	.9405
14									.1175	.5046	.7078	.8229	.8910	.9323
15									.0000	.4386	.6689	.7993	.8765	.9233
16										.3663	.6262	.7735	.8606	.9134
17										.2870	.5794	.7451	.8431	.9025
18										.2000	.5281	.7140	.8240	.8906
19										.1046	.4718	.6799	.8030	.8776
20										.0000	.4101	.6426	.7800	.8633
21											.3425	.6016	.7547	.8476
22											.2683	.5566	.7271	.8304
23											.1870	.5073	.6967	.8116
24											.0978	.4533	.6635	.7909
25											.0000	.3940	.6270	.7682
26												.3290	.5870	.7434
27												.2578	.5431	.7161
28												.1796	.4950	.6862
29												.0939	.4423	.6535
30												.0000	.3845	.6175
35													.0000	.3787
40														.0000

9.50%

AGE OF LOAN	ORIGINAL TERM IN YEARS													
	2	3	4	5	6	7	8	10	15	20	25	30	35	40
1	.5236	.6977	.7843	.8360	.8701	.8944	.9123	.9370	.9683	.9824	.9897	.9938	.9962	.9977
2	.0000	.3653	.5472	.6556	.7274	.7782	.8159	.8678	.9335	.9630	.9784	.9871	.9921	.9952
3		.0000	.2865	.4574	.5705	.6506	.7100	.7917	.8953	.9418	.9660	.9796	.9876	.9924
4			.0000	.2395	.3980	.5102	.5935	.7081	.8532	.9184	.9523	.9714	.9826	.9893
5				.0000	.2084	.3560	.4655	.6161	.8070	.8927	.9373	.9624	.9771	.9859
6					.0000	.1864	.3248	.5151	.7562	.8644	.9208	.9525	.9711	.9822
7						.0000	.1701	.4040	.7003	.8333	.9027	.9416	.9645	.9782
8							.0000	.2818	.6389	.7992	.8827	.9297	.9572	.9737
9								.1476	.5714	.7616	.8608	.9165	.9492	.9688
10								.0000	.4972	.7204	.8367	.9021	.9404	.9634
11									.4156	.6750	.8102	.8862	.9307	.9574
12									.3260	.6251	.7811	.8687	.9201	.9509
13									.2274	.5703	.7491	.8495	.9084	.9437
14									.1191	.5101	.7139	.8284	.8956	.9358
15									.0000	.4438	.6752	.8052	.8814	.9272
16										.3710	.6327	.7797	.8659	.9176
17										.2910	.5859	.7517	.8488	.9071
18										.2030	.5346	.7209	.8301	.8956
19										.1063	.4781	.6870	.8095	.8830
20										.0000	.4160	.6498	.7868	.8690
21											.3478	.6089	.7619	.8537
22											.2727	.5639	.7345	.8369
23											.1903	.5145	.7044	.8184
24											.0996	.4601	.6713	.7981
25											.0000	.4004	.6350	.7758
26												.3347	.5950	.7512
27												.2625	.5510	.7242
28												.1831	.5027	.6945
29												.0959	.4496	.6619
30												.0000	.3912	.6260
35													.0000	.3857
40														.0000

9.75%

AGE OF LOAN	ORIGINAL TERM IN YEARS													
	2	3	4	5	6	7	8	10	15	20	25	30	35	40
1	.5243	.6985	.7852	.8368	.8710	.8952	.9132	.9378	.9690	.9829	.9901	.9941	.9965	.9979
2	.0000	.3662	.5484	.6571	.7289	.7798	.8175	.8694	.9349	.9641	.9793	.9877	.9926	.9955
3		.0000	.2875	.4589	.5723	.6526	.7121	.7939	.8972	.9434	.9673	.9806	.9883	.9929
4			.0000	.2406	.3997	.5124	.5959	.7107	.8558	.9205	.9541	.9727	.9836	.9900
5				.0000	.2096	.3579	.4679	.6191	.8101	.8954	.9395	.9641	.9784	.9869
6					.0000	.1876	.3268	.5181	.7597	.8676	.9235	.9546	.9727	.9834
7						.0000	.1713	.4068	.7043	.8371	.9058	.9441	.9663	.9796
8							.0000	.2841	.6431	.8034	.8863	.9326	.9594	.9753
9								.1489	.5757	.7662	.8649	.9198	.9517	.9707
10								.0000	.5015	.7253	.8412	.9058	.9433	.9656
11									.4197	.6802	.8151	.8903	.9340	.9599
12									.3295	.6306	.7864	.8733	.9237	.9537
13									.2301	.5758	.7548	.8545	.9124	.9468
14									.1207	.5155	.7199	.8338	.8999	.9392
15									.0000	.4490	.6815	.8110	.8862	.9309
16										.3758	.6391	.7859	.8711	.9217
17										.2950	.5924	.7582	.8544	.9116
18										.2061	.5410	.7277	.8360	.9004
19										.1080	.4843	.6941	.8158	.8881
20										.0000	.4219	.6570	.7935	.8746
21											.3530	.6162	.7689	.8597
22											.2772	.5712	.7418	.8432
23											.1936	.5216	.7120	.8251
24											.1015	.4669	.6791	.8051
25											.0000	.4067	.6428	.7831
26												.3404	.6028	.7588
27												.2672	.5588	.7321
28												.1867	.5103	.7026
29												.0979	.4568	.6701
30												.0000	.3979	.6344
35													.0000	.3927
40														.0000

10.00%

AGE OF LOAN	ORIGINAL TERM IN YEARS													
	2	3	4	5	6	7	8	10	15	20	25	30	35	40
1	.5249	.6993	.7860	.8377	.8719	.8961	.9140	.9387	.9697	.9835	.9905	.9944	.9967	.9980
2	.0000	.3670	.5496	.6585	.7304	.7813	.8191	.8709	.9362	.9652	.9801	.9883	.9930	.9958
3		.0000	.2885	.4604	.5741	.6546	.7142	.7960	.8992	.9450	.9685	.9815	.9890	.9934
4			.0000	.2417	.4015	.5145	.5983	.7133	.8583	.9227	.9557	.9740	.9845	.9907
5				.0000	.2107	.3598	.4703	.6220	.8132	.8980	.9416	.9657	.9796	.9878
6					.0000	.1888	.3288	.5210	.7633	.8708	.9261	.9566	.9742	.9845
7						.0000	.1726	.4096	.7082	.8407	.9088	.9465	.9681	.9809
8							.0000	.2864	.6473	.8075	.8898	.9353	.9615	.9769
9								.1503	.5801	.7708	.8688	.9230	.9542	.9725
10								.0000	.5058	.7302	.8456	.9094	.9460	.9676
11									.4237	.6854	.8200	.8943	.9371	.9622
12									.3330	.6360	.7917	.8777	.9272	.9563
13									.2329	.5813	.7604	.8593	.9163	.9497
14									.1222	.5209	.7258	.8391	.9042	.9425
15									.0000	.4542	.6876	.8166	.8908	.9345
16										.3805	.6454	.7919	.8761	.9256
17										.2991	.5988	.7645	.8598	.9158
18										.2091	.5474	.7343	.8418	.9050
19										.1098	.4905	.7009	.8219	.8931
20										.0000	.4277	.6641	.8000	.8799
21											.3583	.6233	.7757	.8654
22											.2816	.5783	.7489	.8493
23											.1969	.5286	.7193	.8315
24											.1034	.4737	.6866	.8119
25											.0000	.4130	.6505	.7902
26												.3460	.6106	.7662
27												.2720	.5665	.7398
28												.1902	.5178	.7105
29												.0998	.4640	.6782
30												.0000	.4046	.6426
35													.0000	.3997
40														.0000

10.25%

AGE OF LOAN	ORIGINAL TERM IN YEARS													
	2	3	4	5	6	7	8	10	15	20	25	30	35	40
1	.5255	.7001	.7869	.8386	.8728	.8970	.9149	.9395	.9703	.9840	.9909	.9947	.9969	.9982
2	.0000	.3679	.5509	.6599	.7320	.7829	.8206	.8724	.9375	.9662	.9809	.9889	.9935	.9961
3		.0000	.2895	.4620	.5760	.6565	.7163	.7982	.9011	.9465	.9697	.9824	.9896	.9939
4			.0000	.2428	.4032	.5166	.6007	.7159	.8608	.9248	.9574	.9752	.9854	.9914
5				.0000	.2119	.3617	.4727	.6249	.8162	.9006	.9437	.9673	.9808	.9886
6					.0000	.1901	.3309	.5240	.7668	.8739	.9286	.9585	.9756	.9855
7						.0000	.1739	.4124	.7121	.8443	.9118	.9488	.9699	.9821
8							.0000	.2887	.6515	.8116	.8933	.9380	.9635	.9783
9								.1517	.5844	.7753	.8727	.9261	.9565	.9742
10								.0000	.5100	.7351	.8499	.9129	.9487	.9696
11									.4277	.6906	.8247	.8982	.9401	.9644
12									.3366	.6413	.7968	.8820	.9305	.9588
13									.2356	.5867	.7659	.8641	.9200	.9525
14									.1238	.5263	.7316	.8442	.9083	.9456
15									.0000	.4594	.6937	.8221	.8953	.9379
16										.3852	.6517	.7978	.8809	.9293
17										.3031	.6052	.7708	.8650	.9199
18										.2122	.5537	.7408	.8474	.9095
19										.1115	.4967	.7077	.8279	.8979
20										.0000	.4335	.6710	.8063	.8851
21											.3635	.6304	.7824	.8709
22											.2861	.5854	.7559	.8552
23											.2003	.5356	.7266	.8377
24											.1052	.4804	.6941	.8185
25											.0000	.4193	.6581	.7971
26												.3516	.6183	.7735
27												.2767	.5742	.7473
28												.1937	.5253	.7183
29												.1018	.4712	.6862
30												.0000	.4113	.6506
35													.0000	.4066
40														.0000

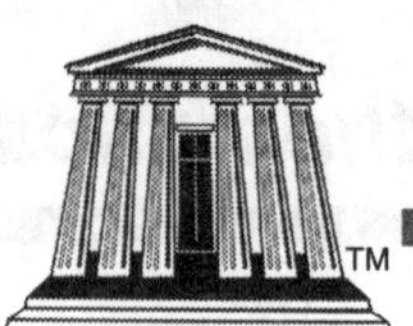

10.50%

AGE OF LOAN	ORIGINAL TERM IN YEARS 2	3	4	5	6	7	8	10	15	20	25	30	35	40
1	.5261	.7008	.7877	.8395	.8737	.8978	.9157	.9403	.9710	.9845	.9913	.9950	.9971	.9983
2	.0000	.3687	.5521	.6613	.7335	.7844	.8222	.8739	.9388	.9672	.9816	.9894	.9939	.9964
3		.0000	.2905	.4635	.5778	.6585	.7183	.8003	.9030	.9481	.9709	.9833	.9903	.9943
4			.0000	.2438	.4049	.5188	.6030	.7185	.8633	.9268	.9590	.9764	.9863	.9919
5				.0000	.2130	.3636	.4750	.6278	.8192	.9032	.9457	.9688	.9818	.9894
6					.0000	.1913	.3329	.5270	.7703	.8770	.9310	.9604	.9769	.9865
7						.0000	.1752	.4152	.7159	.8479	.9147	.9510	.9715	.9833
8							.0000	.2910	.6556	.8156	.8966	.9406	.9654	.9797
9								.1531	.5886	.7797	.8765	.9290	.9587	.9758
10								.0000	.5143	.7399	.8542	.9162	.9512	.9714
11									.4317	.6957	.8294	.9020	.9429	.9665
12									.3401	.6466	.8019	.8862	.9337	.9611
13									.2384	.5921	.7713	.8686	.9235	.9551
14									.1254	.5316	.7374	.8491	.9122	.9485
15									.0000	.4645	.6997	.8275	.8996	.9411
16										.3899	.6579	.8035	.8856	.9329
17										.3072	.6115	.7768	.8701	.9238
18										.2153	.5600	.7473	.8529	.9137
19										.1133	.5028	.7144	.8337	.9025
20										.0000	.4393	.6779	.8125	.8900
21											.3688	.6374	.7889	.8762
22											.2905	.5924	.7627	.8608
23											.2036	.5425	.7337	.8438
24											.1071	.4871	.7014	.8249
25											.0000	.4256	.6656	.8038
26												.3573	.6258	.7805
27												.2814	.5817	.7546
28												.1972	.5327	.7259
29												.1038	.4783	.6940
30												.0000	.4179	.6585
35													.0000	.4134
40														.0000

10.75%

AGE OF LOAN	ORIGINAL TERM IN YEARS 2	3	4	5	6	7	8	10	15	20	25	30	35	40
1	.5267	.7016	.7886	.8404	.8746	.8987	.9166	.9410	.9716	.9849	.9916	.9953	.9973	.9984
2	.0000	.3696	.5533	.6627	.7350	.7860	.8237	.8754	.9400	.9682	.9823	.9900	.9942	.9967
3		.0000	.2914	.4650	.5796	.6605	.7204	.8024	.9049	.9495	.9720	.9841	.9908	.9947
4			.0000	.2449	.4067	.5209	.6054	.7211	.8657	.9288	.9605	.9775	.9871	.9925
5				.0000	.2142	.3655	.4774	.6307	.8222	.9057	.9477	.9703	.9829	.9901
6					.0000	.1925	.3350	.5300	.7737	.8800	.9334	.9622	.9782	.9874
7						.0000	.1764	.4180	.7198	.8514	.9175	.9531	.9730	.9844
8							.0000	.2933	.6597	.8195	.8998	.9431	.9672	.9810
9								.1545	.5929	.7841	.8802	.9319	.9608	.9773
10								.0000	.5185	.7446	.8583	.9195	.9537	.9731
11									.4358	.7007	.8339	.9056	.9457	.9685
12									.3436	.6519	.8068	.8902	.9368	.9634
13									.2411	.5975	.7766	.8731	.9269	.9576
14									.1270	.5370	.7430	.8540	.9160	.9513
15									.0000	.4696	.7057	.8328	.9037	.9442
16										.3947	.6641	.8091	.8901	.9363
17										.3112	.6178	.7828	.8750	.9275
18										.2184	.5662	.7535	.8581	.9177
19										.1150	.5089	.7209	.8394	.9069
20										.0000	.4450	.6847	.8185	.8948
21											.3740	.6443	.7953	.8813
22											.2949	.5994	.7694	.8663
23											.2069	.5494	.7406	.8496
24											.1090	.4937	.7086	.8311
25											.0000	.4318	.6730	.8104
26												.3629	.6333	.7874
27												.2862	.5891	.7618
28												.2008	.5400	.7333
29												.1058	.4853	.7016
30												.0000	.4244	.6663
35													.0000	.4202
40														.0000

11.00%

AGE OF LOAN	ORIGINAL TERM IN YEARS													
	2	3	4	5	6	7	8	10	15	20	25	30	35	40
1	.5273	.7024	.7894	.8412	.8754	.8996	.9174	.9418	.9722	.9854	.9920	.9955	.9974	.9985
2	.0000	.3704	.5545	.6641	.7365	.7875	.8253	.8769	.9413	.9691	.9831	.9905	.9946	.9969
3		.0000	.2924	.4665	.5814	.6625	.7225	.8045	.9067	.9510	.9731	.9849	.9914	.9951
4			.0000	.2460	.4084	.5230	.6078	.7237	.8681	.9307	.9620	.9786	.9878	.9930
5				.0000	.2154	.3674	.4798	.6336	.8251	.9081	.9495	.9716	.9839	.9908
6					.0000	.1937	.3370	.5330	.7771	.8829	.9357	.9639	.9794	.9882
7						.0000	.1777	.4208	.7236	.8548	.9203	.9552	.9745	.9854
8							.0000	.2956	.6638	.8234	.9030	.9455	.9690	.9822
9								.1559	.5971	.7884	.8838	.9347	.9628	.9787
10								.0000	.5228	.7493	.8623	.9226	.9560	.9748
11									.4398	.7057	.8384	.9092	.9483	.9704
12									.3472	.6571	.8117	.8942	.9398	.9655
13									.2439	.6028	.7819	.8774	.9302	.9600
14									.1286	.5423	.7486	.8587	.9196	.9539
15									.0000	.4747	.7115	.8379	.9077	.9471
16										.3994	.6701	.8146	.8945	.9395
17										.3153	.6239	.7887	.8797	.9311
18										.2215	.5724	.7597	.8633	.9216
19										.1168	.5149	.7274	.8449	.9111
20										.0000	.4508	.6913	.8244	.8993
21											.3792	.6511	.8015	.8862
22											.2994	.6063	.7759	.8716
23											.2103	.5562	.7474	.8553
24											.1109	.5003	.7157	.8371
25											.0000	.4380	.6802	.8167
26												.3685	.6406	.7941
27												.2909	.5965	.7688
28												.2043	.5472	.7405
29												.1078	.4923	.7090
30												.0000	.4309	.6739
35													.0000	.4270
40														.0000

11.25%

AGE OF LOAN	ORIGINAL TERM IN YEARS													
	2	3	4	5	6	7	8	10	15	20	25	30	35	40
1	.5280	.7032	.7903	.8421	.8763	.9004	.9182	.9426	.9728	.9859	.9923	.9957	.9976	.9986
2	.0000	.3713	.5558	.6655	.7379	.7890	.8268	.8784	.9425	.9701	.9837	.9910	.9949	.9971
3		.0000	.2934	.4680	.5832	.6645	.7245	.8066	.9085	.9524	.9741	.9856	.9919	.9954
4			.0000	.2471	.4101	.5251	.6101	.7263	.8705	.9326	.9634	.9797	.9886	.9935
5				.0000	.2165	.3693	.4822	.6364	.8280	.9105	.9514	.9730	.9848	.9914
6					.0000	.1950	.3391	.5359	.7805	.8858	.9379	.9655	.9806	.9890
7						.0000	.1790	.4236	.7273	.8582	.9229	.9572	.9759	.9863
8							.0000	.2979	.6679	.8272	.9061	.9478	.9706	.9834
9								.1573	.6014	.7926	.8873	.9374	.9648	.9800
10								.0000	.5270	.7539	.8663	.9257	.9582	.9763
11									.4438	.7107	.8427	.9126	.9508	.9721
12									.3507	.6623	.8164	.8980	.9426	.9675
13									.2466	.6081	.7870	.8816	.9334	.9623
14									.1302	.5476	.7541	.8633	.9231	.9564
15									.0000	.4798	.7173	.8429	.9116	.9499
16										.4041	.6761	.8200	.8987	.9426
17										.3193	.6301	.7944	.8843	.9345
18										.2246	.5785	.7657	.8682	.9254
19										.1186	.5209	.7337	.8502	.9152
20										.0000	.4565	.6979	.8300	.9037
21											.3844	.6578	.8075	.8910
22											.3038	.6130	.7823	.8767
23											.2136	.5629	.7541	.8607
24											.1128	.5069	.7226	.8429
25											.0000	.4442	.6873	.8229
26												.3740	.6478	.8005
27												.2956	.6037	.7756
28												.2079	.5544	.7476
29												.1097	.4992	.7163
30												.0000	.4374	.6814
35													.0000	.4336
40														.0000

11.50%

AGE OF LOAN	ORIGINAL TERM IN YEARS													
	2	3	4	5	6	7	8	10	15	20	25	30	35	40
1	.5286	.7040	.7912	.8430	.8772	.9013	.9191	.9434	.9734	.9863	.9926	.9960	.9978	.9987
2	.0000	.3721	.5570	.6669	.7394	.7906	.8283	.8799	.9437	.9710	.9844	.9914	.9952	.9973
3		.0000	.2944	.4695	.5850	.6664	.7266	.8086	.9103	.9538	.9751	.9863	.9924	.9957
4			.0000	.2482	.4118	.5272	.6125	.7288	.8729	.9345	.9648	.9806	.9892	.9940
5				.0000	.2177	.3712	.4846	.6393	.8309	.9129	.9532	.9742	.9857	.9920
6					.0000	.1962	.3411	.5389	.7838	.8887	.9401	.9671	.9817	.9898
7						.0000	.1803	.4264	.7311	.8615	.9255	.9590	.9772	.9873
8							.0000	.3002	.6719	.8310	.9091	.9500	.9722	.9844
9								.1587	.6056	.7968	.8907	.9399	.9666	.9813
10								.0000	.5312	.7585	.8701	.9286	.9603	.9778
11									.4478	.7155	.8470	.9159	.9532	.9738
12									.3543	.6674	.8211	.9017	.9453	.9694
13									.2494	.6134	.7921	.8857	.9364	.9644
14									.1318	.5528	.7595	.8678	.9265	.9588
15									.0000	.4849	.7230	.8477	.9153	.9526
16										.4088	.6820	.8252	.9028	.9456
17										.3234	.6361	.8000	.8887	.9377
18										.2277	.5846	.7717	.8730	.9289
19										.1203	.5269	.7399	.8554	.9190
20										.0000	.4622	.7044	.8356	.9080
21											.3896	.6645	.8134	.8955
22											.3082	.6197	.7885	.8816
23											.2170	.5696	.7606	.8660
24											.1147	.5133	.7293	.8485
25											.0000	.4503	.6943	.8289
26												.3796	.6549	.8069
27												.3003	.6109	.7822
28												.2114	.5614	.7545
29												.1118	.5060	.7235
30												.0000	.4438	.6887
35													.0000	.4403
40														.0000

11.75%

AGE OF LOAN	ORIGINAL TERM IN YEARS													
	2	3	4	5	6	7	8	10	15	20	25	30	35	40
1	.5292	.7048	.7920	.8438	.8780	.9021	.9199	.9441	.9740	.9868	.9930	.9962	.9979	.9988
2	.0000	.3730	.5582	.6683	.7409	.7921	.8298	.8813	.9449	.9719	.9850	.9919	.9955	.9975
3		.0000	.2954	.4710	.5868	.6684	.7286	.8107	.9120	.9551	.9761	.9870	.9929	.9961
4			.0000	.2493	.4136	.5294	.6148	.7313	.8752	.9363	.9661	.9816	.9899	.9944
5				.0000	.2189	.3731	.4870	.6421	.8337	.9152	.9549	.9755	.9865	.9925
6					.0000	.1974	.3432	.5419	.7871	.8914	.9422	.9686	.9827	.9904
7						.0000	.1816	.4292	.7348	.8647	.9280	.9609	.9785	.9881
8							.0000	.3025	.6759	.8347	.9120	.9522	.9737	.9855
9								.1601	.6097	.8009	.8941	.9424	.9683	.9825
10								.0000	.5354	.7630	.8739	.9314	.9623	.9792
11									.4518	.7204	.8512	.9191	.9555	.9754
12									.3578	.6725	.8257	.9052	.9479	.9712
13									.2522	.6186	.7970	.8897	.9393	.9664
14									.1335	.5580	.7648	.8721	.9297	.9611
15									.0000	.4900	.7286	.8524	.9189	.9551
16										.4135	.6879	.8303	.9067	.9484
17										.3275	.6421	.8054	.8930	.9408
18										.2308	.5907	.7775	.8777	.9323
19										.1221	.5328	.7460	.8604	.9228
20										.0000	.4678	.7107	.8409	.9120
21											.3948	.6710	.8191	.8999
22											.3127	.6263	.7946	.8864
23											.2204	.5762	.7670	.8711
24											.1166	.5198	.7360	.8540
25											.0000	.4564	.7011	.8347
26												.3851	.6619	.8130
27												.3050	.6179	.7886
28												.2150	.5684	.7613
29												.1138	.5128	.7305
30												.0000	.4502	.6959
35													.0000	.4469
40														.0000

12.00%

AGE OF LOAN	ORIGINAL TERM IN YEARS 2	3	4	5	6	7	8	10	15	20	25	30	35	40
1	.5298	.7056	.7928	.8447	.8789	.9029	.9207	.9449	.9746	.9872	.9932	.9964	.9980	.9989
2	.0000	.3738	.5594	.6697	.7424	.7936	.8313	.8827	.9460	.9727	.9856	.9923	.9958	.9977
3		.0000	.2964	.4725	.5886	.6703	.7306	.8127	.9138	.9565	.9771	.9877	.9933	.9963
4			.0000	.2504	.4153	.5315	.6172	.7339	.8775	.9381	.9674	.9825	.9905	.9948
5				.0000	.2200	.3750	.4893	.6450	.8365	.9174	.9565	.9766	.9873	.9931
6					.0000	.1987	.3453	.5448	.7904	.8942	.9443	.9700	.9837	.9911
7						.0000	.1829	.4320	.7384	.8679	.9305	.9626	.9797	.9889
8							.0000	.3048	.6799	.8383	.9149	.9542	.9751	.9864
9								.1615	.6139	.8050	.8973	.9448	.9700	.9836
10								.0000	.5395	.7675	.8776	.9342	.9642	.9804
11									.4558	.7252	.8553	.9222	.9577	.9769
12									.3613	.6775	.8302	.9087	.9504	.9729
13									.2550	.6237	.8019	.8935	.9421	.9684
14									.1351	.5632	.7700	.8764	.9328	.9633
15									.0000	.4950	.7341	.8571	.9223	.9575
16										.4181	.6936	.8353	.9105	.9511
17										.3315	.6480	.8108	.8972	.9438
18										.2339	.5966	.7832	.8822	.9356
19										.1239	.5387	.7520	.8652	.9263
20										.0000	.4735	.7169	.8462	.9159
21											.4000	.6774	.8247	.9042
22											.3171	.6329	.8005	.8909
23											.2237	.5827	.7732	.8760
24											.1185	.5261	.7425	.8592
25											.0000	.4624	.7078	.8403
26												.3906	.6688	.8190
27												.3097	.6248	.7949
28												.2185	.5753	.7678
29												.1158	.5195	.7373
30												.0000	.4565	.7029
35													.0000	.4534
40														.0000

12.25%

AGE OF LOAN	ORIGINAL TERM IN YEARS 2	3	4	5	6	7	8	10	15	20	25	30	35	40
1	.5304	.7064	.7937	.8456	.8797	.9038	.9215	.9456	.9752	.9876	.9935	.9966	.9982	.9990
2	.0000	.3747	.5606	.6711	.7439	.7951	.8328	.8842	.9471	.9736	.9862	.9927	.9961	.9979
3		.0000	.2974	.4741	.5904	.6723	.7327	.8148	.9155	.9577	.9780	.9883	.9937	.9966
4			.0000	.2515	.4170	.5336	.6195	.7364	.8797	.9399	.9687	.9833	.9911	.9952
5				.0000	.2212	.3769	.4917	.6478	.8393	.9196	.9581	.9777	.9880	.9935
6					.0000	.1999	.3473	.5478	.7936	.8968	.9463	.9714	.9847	.9917
7						.0000	.1842	.4348	.7421	.8710	.9328	.9643	.9808	.9896
8							.0000	.3071	.6838	.8419	.9176	.9562	.9765	.9873
9								.1629	.6180	.8090	.9005	.9471	.9716	.9847
10								.0000	.5437	.7719	.8812	.9368	.9661	.9817
11									.4597	.7299	.8593	.9252	.9598	.9783
12									.3649	.6824	.8346	.9121	.9528	.9745
13									.2577	.6289	.8067	.8972	.9448	.9702
14									.1367	.5684	.7752	.8805	.9358	.9653
15									.0000	.5000	.7395	.8615	.9256	.9598
16										.4228	.6993	.8402	.9141	.9536
17										.3356	.6539	.8160	.9012	.9466
18										.2370	.6026	.7887	.8865	.9387
19										.1257	.5446	.7579	.8700	.9298
20										.0000	.4791	.7231	.8512	.9196
21											.4051	.6838	.8301	.9082
22											.3215	.6393	.8063	.8953
23											.2271	.5891	.7793	.8808
24											.1205	.5325	.7488	.8643
25											.0000	.4684	.7144	.8458
26												.3961	.6756	.8248
27												.3144	.6317	.8010
28												.2221	.5821	.7743
29												.1178	.5261	.7440
30												.0000	.4628	.7098
35													.0000	.4598
40														.0000

12.50%

AGE OF LOAN	ORIGINAL TERM IN YEARS													
	2	3	4	5	6	7	8	10	15	20	25	30	35	40
1	.5310	.7072	.7945	.8464	.8806	.9046	.9223	.9463	.9757	.9880	.9938	.9967	.9983	.9991
2	.0000	.3755	.5619	.6725	.7453	.7966	.8343	.8856	.9483	.9744	.9868	.9931	.9963	.9980
3		.0000	.2984	.4756	.5922	.6742	.7347	.8168	.9172	.9590	.9789	.9889	.9941	.9969
4			.0000	.2526	.4188	.5357	.6219	.7389	.8819	.9416	.9699	.9842	.9916	.9955
5				.0000	.2224	.3788	.4941	.6506	.8420	.9218	.9597	.9788	.9888	.9940
6					.0000	.2012	.3494	.5507	.7968	.8994	.9482	.9728	.9855	.9923
7						.0000	.1855	.4375	.7457	.8741	.9351	.9659	.9819	.9903
8							.0000	.3094	.6877	.8454	.9203	.9581	.9778	.9881
9								.1643	.6221	.8130	.9036	.9493	.9731	.9856
10								.0000	.5478	.7762	.8847	.9394	.9678	.9828
11									.4637	.7345	.8632	.9281	.9618	.9796
12									.3684	.6874	.8389	.9153	.9550	.9760
13									.2605	.6340	.8114	.9008	.9474	.9719
14									.1384	.5735	.7802	.8845	.9387	.9673
15									.0000	.5050	.7449	.8659	.9288	.9620
16										.4274	.7049	.8449	.9177	.9560
17										.3396	.6597	.8211	.9050	.9493
18										.2402	.6084	.7942	.8907	.9417
19										.1275	.5504	.7637	.8745	.9330
20										.0000	.4846	.7291	.8562	.9232
21											.4102	.6900	.8354	.9121
22											.3259	.6457	.8119	.8996
23											.2305	.5955	.7852	.8854
24											.1224	.5387	.7551	.8693
25											.0000	.4744	.7209	.8510
26												.4015	.6822	.8304
27												.3190	.6384	.8070
28												.2256	.5888	.7805
29												.1198	.5327	.7505
30												.0000	.4690	.7166
35													.0000	.4662
40														.0000

12.75%

AGE OF LOAN	ORIGINAL TERM IN YEARS													
	2	3	4	5	6	7	8	10	15	20	25	30	35	40
1	.5317	.7079	.7954	.8473	.8814	.9054	.9231	.9471	.9763	.9884	.9941	.9969	.9984	.9991
2	.0000	.3764	.5631	.6739	.7468	.7981	.8358	.8870	.9494	.9752	.9873	.9934	.9965	.9982
3		.0000	.2994	.4771	.5940	.6762	.7367	.8188	.9188	.9602	.9797	.9895	.9945	.9971
4			.0000	.2536	.4205	.5378	.6242	.7413	.8841	.9432	.9710	.9850	.9921	.9958
5				.0000	.2236	.3807	.4965	.6534	.8447	.9239	.9612	.9798	.9894	.9944
6					.0000	.2024	.3515	.5536	.8000	.9020	.9500	.9740	.9864	.9928
7						.0000	.1869	.4403	.7493	.8771	.9374	.9674	.9829	.9910
8							.0000	.3117	.6916	.8489	.9230	.9600	.9790	.9889
9								.1657	.6262	.8168	.9066	.9515	.9745	.9866
10								.0000	.5520	.7804	.8881	.9418	.9695	.9839
11									.4677	.7391	.8670	.9309	.9637	.9809
12									.3720	.6922	.8431	.9185	.9572	.9774
13									.2633	.6390	.8160	.9044	.9498	.9735
14									.1400	.5786	.7851	.8883	.9414	.9691
15									.0000	.5100	.7502	.8702	.9319	.9641
16										.4321	.7105	.8495	.9210	.9584
17										.3437	.6654	.8261	.9087	.9519
18										.2433	.6142	.7995	.8948	.9445
19										.1294	.5561	.7693	.8789	.9362
20										.0000	.4902	.7350	.8610	.9267
21											.4153	.6961	.8405	.9159
22											.3303	.6520	.8174	.9037
23											.2339	.6018	.7911	.8898
24											.1243	.5449	.7612	.8740
25											.0000	.4803	.7273	.8562
26												.4069	.6888	.8359
27												.3237	.6451	.8128
28												.2291	.5955	.7866
29												.1218	.5392	.7569
30												.0000	.4752	.7232
35													.0000	.4726
40														.0000

13.00%

AGE OF LOAN	ORIGINAL TERM IN YEARS													
	2	3	4	5	6	7	8	10	15	20	25	30	35	40
1	.5323	.7087	.7962	.8481	.8823	.9062	.9239	.9478	.9768	.9888	.9943	.9971	.9985	.9992
2	.0000	.3772	.5643	.6753	.7483	.7995	.8373	.8884	.9504	.9760	.9879	.9938	.9968	.9983
3		.0000	.3004	.4786	.5958	.6781	.7387	.8208	.9204	.9614	.9805	.9900	.9948	.9973
4			.0000	.2547	.4222	.5399	.6265	.7438	.8863	.9448	.9722	.9857	.9926	.9961
5				.0000	.2248	.3827	.4988	.6562	.8474	.9260	.9627	.9808	.9901	.9948
6					.0000	.2037	.3535	.5566	.8031	.9045	.9518	.9753	.9872	.9933
7						.0000	.1882	.4431	.7528	.8801	.9395	.9689	.9839	.9916
8							.0000	.3141	.6955	.8523	.9255	.9617	.9801	.9897
9								.1672	.6303	.8207	.9096	.9535	.9759	.9874
10								.0000	.5561	.7847	.8914	.9442	.9711	.9849
11									.4716	.7437	.8707	.9336	.9656	.9820
12									.3755	.6971	.8472	.9215	.9593	.9788
13									.2661	.6440	.8205	.9078	.9522	.9751
14									.1417	.5836	.7900	.8921	.9440	.9708
15									.0000	.5149	.7554	.8743	.9348	.9660
16										.4367	.7159	.8540	.9243	.9605
17										.3477	.6710	.8310	.9123	.9543
18										.2464	.6200	.8047	.8987	.9472
19										.1312	.5618	.7749	.8832	.9391
20										.0000	.4957	.7409	.8656	.9300
21											.4204	.7022	.8455	.9195
22											.3347	.6582	.8227	.9076
23											.2372	.6081	.7967	.8941
24											.1263	.5511	.7672	.8786
25											.0000	.4862	.7335	.8611
26												.4123	.6952	.8412
27												.3283	.6516	.8184
28												.2327	.6020	.7926
29												.1239	.5456	.7632
30												.0000	.4813	.7297
35													.0000	.4788
40														.0000

13.25%

AGE OF LOAN	ORIGINAL TERM IN YEARS													
	2	3	4	5	6	7	8	10	15	20	25	30	35	40
1	.5329	.7095	.7970	.8490	.8831	.9071	.9247	.9485	.9773	.9891	.9946	.9972	.9986	.9993
2	.0000	.3781	.5655	.6767	.7497	.8010	.8387	.8897	.9515	.9767	.9884	.9941	.9970	.9984
3		.0000	.3014	.4801	.5976	.6800	.7407	.8227	.9220	.9626	.9813	.9905	.9951	.9975
4			.0000	.2558	.4240	.5420	.6288	.7462	.8884	.9464	.9733	.9864	.9930	.9964
5				.0000	.2259	.3846	.5012	.6590	.8500	.9280	.9641	.9818	.9906	.9952
6					.0000	.2049	.3556	.5595	.8062	.9070	.9536	.9764	.9879	.9938
7						.0000	.1895	.4459	.7563	.8830	.9416	.9703	.9848	.9922
8							.0000	.3164	.6993	.8556	.9280	.9634	.9812	.9903
9								.1686	.6343	.8244	.9124	.9555	.9772	.9883
10								.0000	.5602	.7888	.8946	.9465	.9726	.9859
11									.4756	.7482	.8744	.9362	.9673	.9832
12									.3790	.7018	.8513	.9244	.9613	.9801
13									.2689	.6490	.8249	.9110	.9544	.9765
14									.1433	.5886	.7948	.8958	.9466	.9725
15									.0000	.5198	.7605	.8783	.9376	.9679
16										.4413	.7213	.8584	.9274	.9626
17										.3518	.6766	.8357	.9158	.9566
18										.2496	.6256	.8098	.9025	.9498
19										.1330	.5675	.7803	.8874	.9420
20										.0000	.5012	.7466	.8701	.9331
21											.4255	.7081	.8504	.9230
22											.3391	.6643	.8279	.9114
23											.2406	.6142	.8023	.8982
24											.1282	.5571	.7730	.8831
25											.0000	.4920	.7396	.8659
26												.4177	.7015	.8463
27												.3329	.6581	.8239
28												.2362	.6085	.7984
29												.1259	.5519	.7693
30												.0000	.4874	.7360
35													.0000	.4851
40														.0000

13.50%

AGE OF LOAN	ORIGINAL TERM IN YEARS													
	2	3	4	5	6	7	8	10	15	20	25	30	35	40
1	.5335	.7103	.7979	.8498	.8839	.9079	.9254	.9492	.9779	.9895	.9948	.9974	.9987	.9993
2	.0000	.3789	.5667	.6781	.7512	.8025	.8402	.8911	.9526	.9774	.9889	.9944	.9972	.9986
3		.0000	.3024	.4816	.5993	.6820	.7426	.8247	.9236	.9637	.9821	.9910	.9954	.9977
4			.0000	.2569	.4257	.5441	.6311	.7487	.8905	.9480	.9743	.9871	.9935	.9967
5				.0000	.2271	.3865	.5036	.6618	.8526	.9300	.9654	.9826	.9912	.9955
6					.0000	.2062	.3577	.5624	.8093	.9094	.9553	.9775	.9886	.9942
7						.0000	.1908	.4487	.7598	.8858	.9437	.9717	.9857	.9927
8							.0000	.3187	.7031	.8589	.9304	.9650	.9823	.9910
9								.1700	.6383	.8281	.9152	.9574	.9784	.9890
10								.0000	.5642	.7929	.8978	.9487	.9740	.9868
11									.4795	.7526	.8779	.9387	.9689	.9842
12									.3826	.7066	.8552	.9273	.9632	.9813
13									.2717	.6539	.8292	.9142	.9566	.9779
14									.1450	.5936	.7995	.8993	.9490	.9740
15									.0000	.5247	.7655	.8822	.9403	.9696
16										.4459	.7266	.8627	.9304	.9646
17										.3558	.6821	.8404	.9191	.9589
18										.2527	.6313	.8148	.9062	.9523
19										.1348	.5731	.7856	.8914	.9447
20										.0000	.5066	.7522	.8745	.9361
21											.4305	.7140	.8551	.9263
22											.3435	.6703	.8330	.9150
23											.2440	.6203	.8077	.9021
24											.1302	.5632	.7787	.8874
25											.0000	.4978	.7456	.8706
26												.4230	.7077	.8513
27												.3375	.6644	.8293
28												.2397	.6149	.8040
29												.1279	.5582	.7752
30												.0000	.4934	.7423
35													.0000	.4912
40														.0000

13.75%

AGE OF LOAN	ORIGINAL TERM IN YEARS													
	2	3	4	5	6	7	8	10	15	20	25	30	35	40
1	.5341	.7111	.7987	.8507	.8848	.9087	.9262	.9499	.9784	.9898	.9950	.9975	.9988	.9994
2	.0000	.3798	.5679	.6794	.7526	.8039	.8416	.8925	.9536	.9782	.9893	.9947	.9974	.9987
3		.0000	.3033	.4831	.6011	.6839	.7446	.8266	.9251	.9648	.9828	.9915	.9957	.9979
4			.0000	.2580	.4274	.5462	.6334	.7511	.8926	.9495	.9753	.9878	.9939	.9969
5				.0000	.2283	.3884	.5059	.6645	.8552	.9319	.9668	.9835	.9917	.9958
6					.0000	.2075	.3597	.5653	.8123	.9117	.9569	.9786	.9893	.9946
7						.0000	.1921	.4515	.7632	.8886	.9456	.9730	.9865	.9932
8							.0000	.3211	.7069	.8621	.9327	.9666	.9833	.9916
9								.1715	.6423	.8317	.9179	.9592	.9796	.9897
10								.0000	.5683	.7969	.9009	.9508	.9754	.9876
11									.4834	.7570	.8814	.9411	.9705	.9852
12									.3861	.7112	.8591	.9300	.9650	.9824
13									.2746	.6587	.8335	.9173	.9586	.9792
14									.1466	.5986	.8041	.9027	.9513	.9755
15									.0000	.5296	.7704	.8860	.9429	.9713
16										.4505	.7318	.8669	.9333	.9665
17										.3598	.6876	.8449	.9223	.9610
18										.2559	.6368	.8197	.9097	.9546
19										.1367	.5787	.7908	.8953	.9474
20										.0000	.5120	.7577	.8787	.9390
21											.4355	.7198	.8597	.9295
22											.3479	.6762	.8379	.9185
23											.2473	.6263	.8129	.9060
24											.1321	.5691	.7843	.8916
25											.0000	.5035	.7515	.8751
26												.4283	.7138	.8561
27												.3421	.6706	.8344
28												.2433	.6212	.8096
29												.1299	.5644	.7810
30												.0000	.4994	.7483
35													.0000	.4973
40														.0000

14.00%

AGE OF LOAN	ORIGINAL TERM IN YEARS													
	2	3	4	5	6	7	8	10	15	20	25	30	35	40
1	.5347	.7118	.7995	.8515	.8856	.9095	.9270	.9506	.9789	.9902	.9953	.9977	.9988	.9994
2	.0000	.3807	.5691	.6808	.7541	.8054	.8430	.8938	.9546	.9789	.9898	.9950	.9975	.9988
3		.0000	.3043	.4846	.6029	.6858	.7466	.8285	.9267	.9659	.9835	.9919	.9960	.9980
4			.0000	.2591	.4292	.5483	.6357	.7535	.8946	.9509	.9763	.9884	.9942	.9971
5				.0000	.2295	.3903	.5083	.6673	.8577	.9338	.9680	.9843	.9922	.9961
6					.0000	.2087	.3618	.5682	.8153	.9140	.9585	.9796	.9899	.9950
7						.0000	.1935	.4543	.7666	.8913	.9476	.9743	.9873	.9937
8							.0000	.3234	.7106	.8653	.9350	.9681	.9842	.9922
9								.1729	.6463	.8353	.9205	.9610	.9807	.9904
10								.0000	.5723	.8009	.9039	.9528	.9767	.9884
11									.4873	.7613	.8848	.9435	.9720	.9861
12									.3897	.7158	.8628	.9327	.9667	.9835
13									.2774	.6636	.8376	.9203	.9606	.9804
14									.1483	.6035	.8086	.9061	.9535	.9769
15									.0000	.5344	.7753	.8897	.9454	.9729
16										.4551	.7370	.8709	.9361	.9683
17										.3638	.6930	.8493	.9254	.9630
18										.2590	.6423	.8245	.9132	.9569
19										.1385	.5842	.7959	.8990	.9499
20										.0000	.5173	.7631	.8828	.9418
21											.4405	.7254	.8642	.9325
22											.3522	.6821	.8427	.9219
23											.2507	.6323	.8181	.9096
24											.1341	.5750	.7897	.8956
25											.0000	.5092	.7572	.8794
26												.4336	.7198	.8608
27												.3467	.6768	.8395
28												.2468	.6274	.8149
29												.1320	.5706	.7867
30												.0000	.5053	.7543
35													.0000	.5033
40														.0000

14.25%

AGE OF LOAN	ORIGINAL TERM IN YEARS													
	2	3	4	5	6	7	8	10	15	20	25	30	35	40
1	.5354	.7126	.8004	.8523	.8864	.9102	.9277	.9513	.9794	.9905	.9955	.9978	.9989	.9995
2	.0000	.3815	.5704	.6822	.7555	.8068	.8445	.8951	.9556	.9795	.9902	.9953	.9977	.9989
3		.0000	.3053	.4861	.6047	.6877	.7485	.8304	.9282	.9669	.9842	.9923	.9963	.9982
4			.0000	.2603	.4309	.5504	.6380	.7559	.8966	.9524	.9773	.9890	.9946	.9974
5				.0000	.2307	.3922	.5106	.6700	.8602	.9356	.9693	.9851	.9927	.9964
6					.0000	.2100	.3639	.5711	.8183	.9163	.9600	.9806	.9905	.9953
7						.0000	.1948	.4571	.7700	.8940	.9494	.9755	.9880	.9941
8							.0000	.3257	.7144	.8684	.9372	.9695	.9851	.9927
9								.1744	.6502	.8388	.9231	.9627	.9818	.9910
10								.0000	.5764	.8048	.9068	.9548	.9779	.9892
11									.4912	.7656	.8881	.9457	.9735	.9870
12									.3932	.7204	.8665	.9353	.9683	.9845
13									.2802	.6683	.8417	.9232	.9625	.9816
14									.1500	.6084	.8131	.9093	.9557	.9782
15									.0000	.5392	.7801	.8933	.9478	.9744
16										.4596	.7421	.8749	.9388	.9700
17										.3679	.6983	.8536	.9284	.9649
18										.2621	.6478	.8291	.9165	.9590
19										.1403	.5897	.8009	.9027	.9522
20										.0000	.5227	.7684	.8868	.9444
21											.4455	.7310	.8685	.9355
22											.3565	.6878	.8474	.9251
23											.2541	.6381	.8231	.9132
24											.1360	.5809	.7951	.8994
25											.0000	.5149	.7628	.8836
26												.4388	.7257	.8654
27												.3512	.6828	.8444
28												.2503	.6335	.8201
29												.1340	.5766	.7922
30												.0000	.5111	.7601
35													.0000	.5093
40														.0000

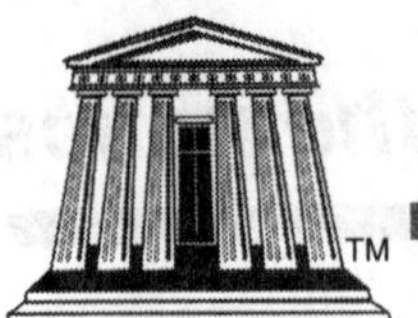

14.50%

AGE OF LOAN	ORIGINAL TERM IN YEARS													
	2	3	4	5	6	7	8	10	15	20	25	30	35	40
1	.5360	.7134	.8012	.8532	.8872	.9110	.9285	.9519	.9798	.9908	.9957	.9979	.9990	.9995
2	.0000	.3824	.5716	.6835	.7569	.8083	.8459	.8964	.9565	.9802	.9906	.9955	.9978	.9989
3		.0000	.3063	.4876	.6064	.6896	.7505	.8323	.9296	.9679	.9849	.9927	.9965	.9983
4			.0000	.2614	.4326	.5525	.6403	.7583	.8986	.9537	.9782	.9895	.9949	.9975
5				.0000	.2319	.3941	.5130	.6728	.8627	.9374	.9704	.9858	.9932	.9967
6					.0000	.2113	.3660	.5740	.8212	.9185	.9615	.9815	.9911	.9957
7						.0000	.1961	.4599	.7733	.8966	.9512	.9766	.9887	.9945
8							.0000	.3281	.7180	.8714	.9393	.9709	.9859	.9932
9								.1758	.6542	.8423	.9256	.9643	.9828	.9916
10								.0000	.5804	.8087	.9097	.9567	.9791	.9899
11									.4951	.7698	.8913	.9479	.9748	.9878
12									.3967	.7249	.8701	.9377	.9699	.9854
13									.2830	.6731	.8457	.9260	.9642	.9827
14									.1517	.6132	.8174	.9124	.9577	.9795
15									.0000	.5440	.7848	.8968	.9501	.9758
16										.4641	.7470	.8787	.9414	.9716
17										.3719	.7035	.8578	.9313	.9667
18										.2653	.6532	.8337	.9197	.9610
19										.1422	.5951	.8058	.9062	.9545
20										.0000	.5279	.7736	.8906	.9470
21											.4504	.7365	.8727	.9383
22											.3609	.6935	.8519	.9282
23											.2574	.6439	.8280	.9166
24											.1380	.5866	.8003	.9032
25											.0000	.5205	.7683	.8877
26												.4440	.7314	.8698
27												.3558	.6888	.8491
28												.2538	.6395	.8252
29												.1360	.5826	.7976
30												.0000	.5169	.7658
35													.0000	.5152
40														.0000

14.75%

AGE OF LOAN	ORIGINAL TERM IN YEARS													
	2	3	4	5	6	7	8	10	15	20	25	30	35	40
1	.5366	.7142	.8020	.8540	.8880	.9118	.9292	.9526	.9803	.9911	.9959	.9980	.9991	.9996
2	.0000	.3832	.5728	.6849	.7584	.8097	.8473	.8977	.9575	.9808	.9910	.9958	.9980	.9990
3		.0000	.3073	.4891	.6082	.6915	.7524	.8342	.9311	.9689	.9855	.9931	.9967	.9984
4			.0000	.2625	.4344	.5546	.6425	.7606	.9005	.9551	.9790	.9901	.9953	.9977
5				.0000	.2331	.3961	.5153	.6755	.8651	.9391	.9716	.9865	.9936	.9969
6					.0000	.2125	.3680	.5768	.8241	.9206	.9630	.9824	.9916	.9960
7						.0000	.1975	.4626	.7766	.8992	.9530	.9777	.9894	.9949
8							.0000	.3304	.7217	.8744	.9414	.9722	.9867	.9936
9								.1773	.6580	.8457	.9280	.9659	.9837	.9922
10								.0000	.5843	.8124	.9124	.9585	.9802	.9905
11									.4990	.7739	.8945	.9500	.9761	.9886
12									.4002	.7294	.8737	.9401	.9714	.9863
13									.2858	.6778	.8496	.9287	.9660	.9837
14									.1534	.6180	.8217	.9155	.9596	.9807
15									.0000	.5488	.7894	.9002	.9523	.9772
16										.4686	.7520	.8824	.9439	.9731
17										.3759	.7086	.8619	.9341	.9684
18										.2684	.6585	.8381	.9227	.9630
19										.1440	.6004	.8106	.9096	.9567
20										.0000	.5332	.7787	.8944	.9494
21											.4553	.7418	.8768	.9410
22											.3652	.6991	.8564	.9312
23											.2608	.6496	.8327	.9199
24											.1399	.5923	.8054	.9068
25											.0000	.5260	.7737	.8916
26												.4492	.7371	.8741
27												.3603	.6946	.8537
28												.2573	.6455	.8302
29												.1381	.5885	.8029
30												.0000	.5226	.7713
35													.0000	.5210
40														.0000

15.00%

AGE OF LOAN	2	3	4	5	6	7	8	10	15	20	25	30	35	40
1	.5372	.7149	.8028	.8548	.8888	.9126	.9300	.9533	.9808	.9914	.9960	.9981	.9991	.9996
2	.0000	.3841	.5740	.6863	.7598	.8111	.8487	.8990	.9584	.9814	.9914	.9960	.9981	.9991
3		.0000	.3083	.4906	.6100	.6934	.7543	.8361	.9325	.9699	.9861	.9935	.9969	.9985
4			.0000	.2636	.4361	.5567	.6448	.7630	.9024	.9564	.9799	.9906	.9956	.9979
5				.0000	.2343	.3980	.5177	.6782	.8675	.9408	.9727	.9872	.9940	.9971
6					.0000	.2138	.3701	.5797	.8270	.9227	.9643	.9833	.9921	.9963
7						.0000	.1988	.4654	.7799	.9017	.9546	.9787	.9900	.9953
8							.0000	.3327	.7253	.8773	.9434	.9735	.9875	.9941
9								.1787	.6619	.8490	.9303	.9674	.9846	.9927
10								.0000	.5883	.8162	.9151	.9602	.9812	.9911
11									.5029	.7780	.8975	.9520	.9774	.9893
12									.4037	.7338	.8771	.9424	.9728	.9871
13									.2887	.6824	.8534	.9313	.9676	.9847
14									.1551	.6227	.8259	.9184	.9615	.9818
15									.0000	.5535	.7939	.9034	.9545	.9784
16										.4731	.7568	.8861	.9463	.9746
17										.3799	.7137	.8659	.9367	.9701
18										.2716	.6638	.8425	.9257	.9648
19										.1459	.6057	.8153	.9129	.9588
20										.0000	.5384	.7837	.8980	.9517
21											.4602	.7471	.8807	.9436
22											.3695	.7046	.8607	.9341
23											.2642	.6553	.8374	.9230
24											.1419	.5980	.8104	.9103
25											.0000	.5315	.7790	.8954
26												.4543	.7426	.8782
27												.3648	.7004	.8582
28												.2608	.6513	.8350
29												.1401	.5944	.8081
30												.0000	.5283	.7768
35													.0000	.5268
40														.0000

15.25%

AGE OF LOAN	2	3	4	5	6	7	8	10	15	20	25	30	35	40
1	.5378	.7157	.8037	.8556	.8896	.9134	.9307	.9539	.9812	.9917	.9962	.9982	.9992	.9996
2	.0000	.3849	.5752	.6876	.7612	.8125	.8501	.9003	.9594	.9820	.9918	.9962	.9982	.9992
3		.0000	.3093	.4922	.6117	.6952	.7562	.8379	.9339	.9708	.9867	.9938	.9971	.9987
4			.0000	.2647	.4378	.5587	.6471	.7653	.9043	.9577	.9807	.9911	.9958	.9981
5				.0000	.2355	.3999	.5200	.6809	.8699	.9425	.9738	.9878	.9943	.9974
6					.0000	.2151	.3722	.5826	.8298	.9248	.9657	.9841	.9926	.9965
7						.0000	.2002	.4682	.7832	.9042	.9563	.9798	.9906	.9956
8							.0000	.3351	.7289	.8802	.9453	.9747	.9882	.9945
9								.1802	.6657	.8523	.9326	.9688	.9855	.9932
10								.0000	.5923	.8199	.9178	.9619	.9823	.9917
11									.5067	.7821	.9005	.9539	.9785	.9900
12									.4073	.7381	.8805	.9447	.9742	.9879
13									.2915	.6870	.8571	.9338	.9692	.9856
14									.1568	.6275	.8300	.9213	.9633	.9828
15									.0000	.5582	.7983	.9066	.9565	.9797
16										.4776	.7616	.8896	.9485	.9759
17										.3838	.7188	.8698	.9393	.9716
18										.2747	.6690	.8467	.9286	.9666
19										.1477	.6110	.8199	.9160	.9608
20										.0000	.5436	.7886	.9015	.9539
21											.4651	.7523	.8846	.9460
22											.3738	.7100	.8648	.9368
23											.2675	.6608	.8419	.9261
24											.1439	.6036	.8152	.9136
25											.0000	.5370	.7842	.8991
26												.4594	.7480	.8822
27												.3692	.7060	.8626
28												.2643	.6571	.8397
29												.1421	.6002	.8131
30												.0000	.5339	.7821
35													.0000	.5325
40														.0000

15.50%

AGE OF LOAN	ORIGINAL TERM IN YEARS													
	2	3	4	5	6	7	8	10	15	20	25	30	35	40
1	.5384	.7165	.8045	.8564	.8904	.9141	.9314	.9546	.9817	.9920	.9964	.9983	.9992	.9996
2	.0000	.3858	.5764	.6890	.7626	.8140	.8515	.9016	.9603	.9826	.9922	.9964	.9983	.9992
3		.0000	.3103	.4937	.6135	.6971	.7581	.8398	.9353	.9717	.9872	.9942	.9973	.9988
4			.0000	.2658	.4396	.5608	.6493	.7676	.9062	.9590	.9815	.9915	.9961	.9982
5				.0000	.2367	.4018	.5224	.6835	.8722	.9441	.9748	.9885	.9947	.9975
6					.0000	.2163	.3743	.5854	.8326	.9268	.9670	.9849	.9930	.9968
7						.0000	.2015	.4709	.7864	.9066	.9579	.9807	.9911	.9959
8							.0000	.3374	.7324	.8830	.9472	.9758	.9889	.9949
9								.1817	.6695	.8555	.9348	.9702	.9863	.9937
10								.0000	.5962	.8235	.9203	.9635	.9832	.9922
11									.5106	.7861	.9034	.9558	.9796	.9906
12									.4108	.7424	.8838	.9468	.9755	.9887
13									.2943	.6915	.8608	.9363	.9707	.9864
14									.1585	.6321	.8340	.9240	.9650	.9838
15									.0000	.5629	.8027	.9097	.9584	.9808
16										.4821	.7662	.8930	.9507	.9772
17										.3878	.7237	.8736	.9418	.9731
18										.2779	.6741	.8508	.9313	.9683
19										.1496	.6162	.8244	.9191	.9626
20										.0000	.5487	.7935	.9049	.9561
21											.4699	.7574	.8883	.9484
22											.3780	.7154	.8689	.9395
23											.2709	.6663	.8463	.9290
24											.1458	.6091	.8200	.9169
25											.0000	.5423	.7892	.9027
26												.4645	.7534	.8861
27												.3737	.7116	.8668
28												.2677	.6628	.8442
29												.1442	.6059	.8180
30												.0000	.5395	.7873
35													.0000	.5381
40														.0000

15.75%

AGE OF LOAN	ORIGINAL TERM IN YEARS													
	2	3	4	5	6	7	8	10	15	20	25	30	35	40
1	.5390	.7173	.8053	.8573	.8912	.9149	.9322	.9552	.9821	.9923	.9965	.9984	.9993	.9997
2	.0000	.3866	.5776	.6903	.7640	.8154	.8528	.9028	.9611	.9832	.9925	.9966	.9985	.9993
3		.0000	.3114	.4952	.6152	.6990	.7600	.8416	.9366	.9726	.9878	.9945	.9975	.9989
4			.0000	.2669	.4413	.5629	.6516	.7700	.9080	.9602	.9822	.9920	.9963	.9983
5				.0000	.2379	.4037	.5247	.6862	.8745	.9457	.9758	.9890	.9950	.9977
6					.0000	.2176	.3763	.5882	.8353	.9288	.9682	.9856	.9935	.9970
7						.0000	.2029	.4737	.7895	.9090	.9594	.9816	.9916	.9962
8							.0000	.3398	.7360	.8858	.9490	.9770	.9895	.9952
9								.1832	.6733	.8587	.9370	.9715	.9870	.9941
10								.0000	.6001	.8270	.9228	.9651	.9841	.9928
11									.5144	.7900	.9063	.9576	.9807	.9912
12									.4143	.7467	.8870	.9489	.9767	.9894
13									.2971	.6960	.8643	.9386	.9721	.9873
14									.1602	.6368	.8379	.9267	.9666	.9848
15									.0000	.5675	.8070	.9127	.9603	.9819
16										.4865	.7709	.8964	.9528	.9785
17										.3918	.7286	.8772	.9441	.9745
18										.2810	.6792	.8549	.9340	.9699
19										.1515	.6214	.8287	.9221	.9644
20										.0000	.5538	.7982	.9082	.9581
21											.4747	.7624	.8919	.9507
22											.3823	.7206	.8729	.9420
23											.2742	.6717	.8506	.9318
24											.1478	.6145	.8246	.9200
25											.0000	.5477	.7942	.9061
26												.4695	.7586	.8899
27												.3781	.7170	.8709
28												.2712	.6684	.8487
29												.1462	.6115	.8227
30												.0000	.5450	.7924
35													.0000	.5437
40														.0000

16.00%

AGE OF LOAN	ORIGINAL TERM IN YEARS													
	2	3	4	5	6	7	8	10	15	20	25	30	35	40
1	.5397	.7180	.8061	.8581	.8920	.9156	.9329	.9558	.9825	.9925	.9967	.9985	.9993	.9997
2	.0000	.3875	.5788	.6917	.7654	.8168	.8542	.9041	.9620	.9837	.9928	.9968	.9986	.9994
3		.0000	.3124	.4967	.6170	.7008	.7619	.8434	.9380	.9735	.9883	.9948	.9976	.9989
4			.0000	.2680	.4430	.5650	.6538	.7722	.9098	.9614	.9830	.9924	.9966	.9985
5				.0000	.2391	.4057	.5270	.6888	.8768	.9473	.9767	.9896	.9953	.9979
6					.0000	.2189	.3784	.5911	.8380	.9307	.9694	.9863	.9939	.9972
7						.0000	.2042	.4765	.7927	.9113	.9609	.9825	.9921	.9965
8							.0000	.3421	.7395	.8885	.9508	.9780	.9901	.9955
9								.1846	.6771	.8618	.9390	.9727	.9877	.9945
10								.0000	.6040	.8305	.9252	.9666	.9850	.9932
11									.5182	.7939	.9090	.9593	.9817	.9918
12									.4178	.7509	.8901	.9509	.9779	.9900
13									.3000	.7005	.8678	.9409	.9734	.9880
14									.1619	.6414	.8418	.9293	.9682	.9857
15									.0000	.5721	.8112	.9156	.9621	.9829
16										.4909	.7754	.8996	.9549	.9797
17										.3957	.7334	.8808	.9464	.9758
18										.2841	.6842	.8588	.9365	.9714
19										.1533	.6265	.8330	.9249	.9662
20										.0000	.5588	.8028	.9113	.9600
21											.4795	.7673	.8954	.9528
22											.3865	.7258	.8767	.9444
23											.2775	.6770	.8548	.9346
24											.1498	.6199	.8291	.9230
25											.0000	.5530	.7990	.9094
26												.4745	.7637	.8935
27												.3825	.7224	.8749
28												.2746	.6739	.8530
29												.1482	.6170	.8274
30												.0000	.5504	.7973
35													.0000	.5492
40														.0000

16.25%

AGE OF LOAN	ORIGINAL TERM IN YEARS													
	2	3	4	5	6	7	8	10	15	20	25	30	35	40
1	.5403	.7188	.8069	.8589	.8928	.9164	.9336	.9565	.9829	.9928	.9968	.9986	.9994	.9997
2	.0000	.3883	.5800	.6930	.7668	.8182	.8555	.9053	.9629	.9843	.9931	.9970	.9987	.9994
3		.0000	.3134	.4982	.6187	.7027	.7638	.8452	.9393	.9743	.9888	.9950	.9978	.9990
4			.0000	.2691	.4448	.5670	.6560	.7745	.9116	.9626	.9837	.9928	.9968	.9986
5				.0000	.2403	.4076	.5294	.6915	.8790	.9488	.9777	.9901	.9956	.9980
6					.0000	.2202	.3805	.5939	.8407	.9326	.9706	.9870	.9942	.9974
7						.0000	.2056	.4792	.7958	.9135	.9623	.9833	.9926	.9967
8							.0000	.3445	.7429	.8912	.9525	.9790	.9907	.9959
9								.1861	.6808	.8649	.9411	.9740	.9884	.9948
10								.0000	.6078	.8340	.9276	.9680	.9858	.9937
11									.5220	.7977	.9117	.9610	.9827	.9923
12									.4212	.7550	.8931	.9528	.9790	.9907
13									.3028	.7049	.8713	.9431	.9747	.9887
14									.1636	.6459	.8456	.9318	.9697	.9865
15									.0000	.5767	.8153	.9184	.9638	.9839
16										.4953	.7798	.9027	.9568	.9808
17										.3997	.7381	.8843	.9486	.9771
18										.2873	.6891	.8627	.9390	.9728
19										.1552	.6315	.8372	.9277	.9678
20										.0000	.5638	.8073	.9144	.9619
21											.4842	.7722	.8988	.9549
22											.3907	.7308	.8804	.9468
23											.2809	.6823	.8589	.9372
24											.1517	.6253	.8335	.9259
25											.0000	.5582	.8038	.9126
26												.4795	.7688	.8970
27												.3869	.7276	.8787
28												.2781	.6793	.8572
29												.1502	.6225	.8319
30												.0000	.5558	.8022
35													.0000	.5547
40														.0000

16.50%

AGE OF LOAN	ORIGINAL TERM IN YEARS													
	2	3	4	5	6	7	8	10	15	20	25	30	35	40
1	.5409	.7196	.8077	.8597	.8936	.9171	.9343	.9571	.9833	.9930	.9970	.9987	.9994	.9997
2	.0000	.3892	.5812	.6944	.7682	.8195	.8569	.9065	.9637	.9848	.9934	.9971	.9987	.9994
3		.0000	.3144	.4997	.6205	.7045	.7657	.8469	.9406	.9751	.9893	.9953	.9979	.9991
4			.0000	.2703	.4465	.5691	.6582	.7768	.9133	.9637	.9843	.9932	.9970	.9987
5				.0000	.2415	.4095	.5317	.6941	.8812	.9503	.9785	.9906	.9959	.9982
6					.0000	.2215	.3826	.5967	.8434	.9344	.9717	.9877	.9946	.9976
7						.0000	.2069	.4820	.7988	.9158	.9637	.9841	.9930	.9969
8							.0000	.3468	.7463	.8938	.9542	.9800	.9912	.9961
9								.1876	.6845	.8679	.9430	.9751	.9891	.9952
10								.0000	.6116	.8374	.9299	.9694	.9866	.9941
11									.5258	.8014	.9144	.9626	.9836	.9928
12									.4247	.7591	.8961	.9546	.9801	.9912
13									.3056	.7092	.8746	.9453	.9760	.9894
14									.1653	.6504	.8493	.9342	.9711	.9873
15									.0000	.5812	.8194	.9212	.9654	.9848
16										.4997	.7842	.9058	.9587	.9818
17										.4036	.7428	.8877	.9507	.9783
18										.2904	.6940	.8664	.9414	.9742
19										.1571	.6365	.8413	.9303	.9694
20										.0000	.5688	.8117	.9174	.9636
21											.4889	.7769	.9021	.9569
22											.3949	.7358	.8841	.9490
23											.2842	.6875	.8628	.9397
24											.1537	.6305	.8378	.9287
25											.0000	.5634	.8084	.9157
26												.4844	.7737	.9004
27												.3912	.7328	.8825
28												.2815	.6847	.8613
29												.1523	.6279	.8363
30												.0000	.5611	.8069
35													.0000	.5601
40														.0000

16.75%

AGE OF LOAN	ORIGINAL TERM IN YEARS													
	2	3	4	5	6	7	8	10	15	20	25	30	35	40
1	.5415	.7203	.8085	.8605	.8944	.9179	.9350	.9577	.9837	.9933	.9971	.9988	.9995	.9998
2	.0000	.3901	.5824	.6957	.7696	.8209	.8582	.9077	.9645	.9853	.9937	.9973	.9988	.9995
3		.0000	.3154	.5012	.6222	.7064	.7675	.8487	.9418	.9759	.9897	.9956	.9981	.9992
4			.0000	.2714	.4482	.5711	.6605	.7790	.9150	.9648	.9850	.9935	.9972	.9988
5				.0000	.2427	.4114	.5340	.6967	.8834	.9517	.9794	.9911	.9961	.9983
6					.0000	.2228	.3847	.5995	.8460	.9362	.9728	.9883	.9949	.9978
7						.0000	.2083	.4847	.8019	.9179	.9650	.9849	.9935	.9972
8							.0000	.3492	.7497	.8963	.9558	.9809	.9917	.9964
9								.1891	.6882	.8708	.9449	.9762	.9897	.9955
10								.0000	.6155	.8407	.9321	.9707	.9873	.9945
11									.5296	.8051	.9169	.9642	.9845	.9932
12									.4282	.7631	.8990	.9564	.9811	.9918
13									.3084	.7135	.8779	.9473	.9771	.9901
14									.1670	.6549	.8529	.9365	.9725	.9880
15									.0000	.5857	.8234	.9238	.9670	.9856
16										.5040	.7885	.9088	.9604	.9828
17										.4075	.7474	.8910	.9527	.9795
18										.2935	.6988	.8701	.9437	.9755
19										.1590	.6414	.8453	.9329	.9708
20										.0000	.5737	.8161	.9202	.9653
21											.4936	.7815	.9053	.9588
22											.3991	.7408	.8876	.9511
23											.2875	.6926	.8667	.9421
24											.1557	.6357	.8420	.9314
25											.0000	.5686	.8129	.9187
26												.4892	.7785	.9038
27												.3956	.7379	.8861
28												.2849	.6899	.8653
29												.1543	.6333	.8406
30												.0000	.5664	.8116
35													.0000	.5654
40														.0000

Figure 15-5

Points Discount Tables

Example: $50,000 loan@12.25% for 30 years
Problem: Find lender's yield if two points are charged

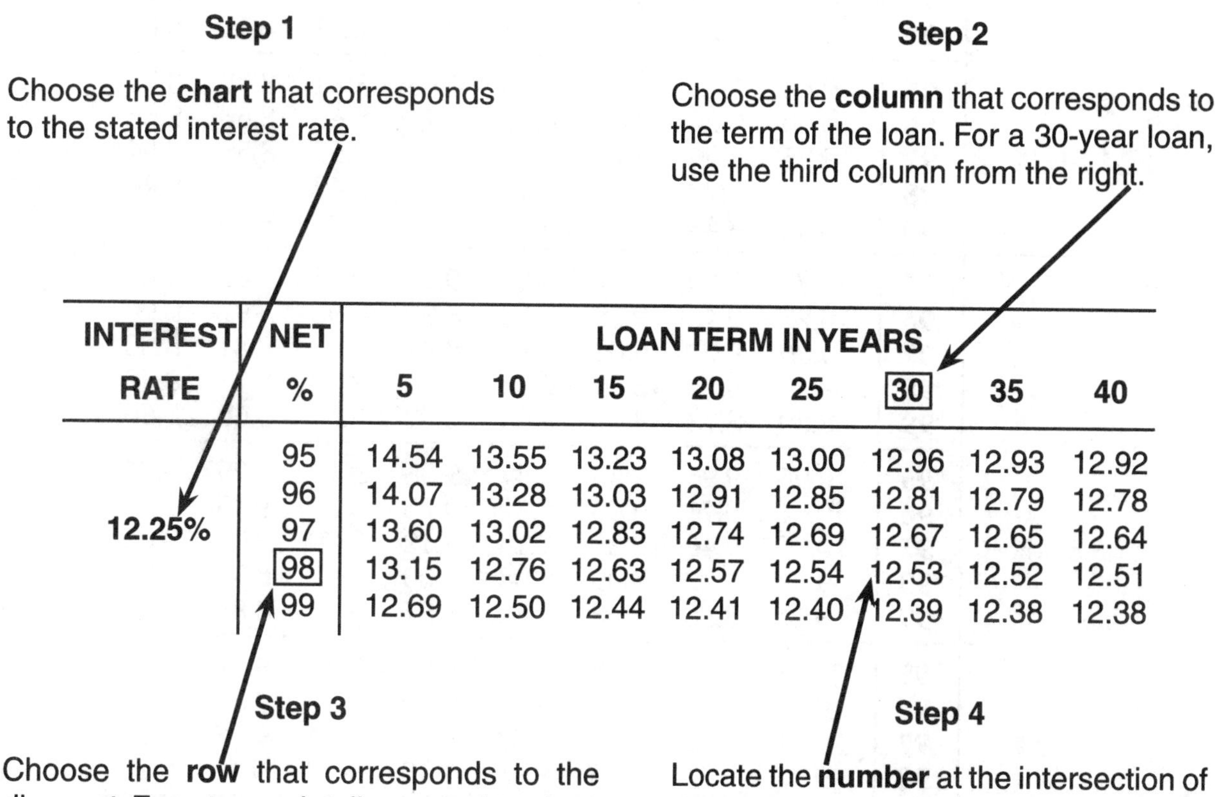

Step 1

Choose the **chart** that corresponds to the stated interest rate.

Step 2

Choose the **column** that corresponds to the term of the loan. For a 30-year loan, use the third column from the right.

INTEREST RATE	NET %	5	10	15	20	25	30	35	40
	95	14.54	13.55	13.23	13.08	13.00	12.96	12.93	12.92
	96	14.07	13.28	13.03	12.91	12.85	12.81	12.79	12.78
12.25%	97	13.60	13.02	12.83	12.74	12.69	12.67	12.65	12.64
	98	13.15	12.76	12.63	12.57	12.54	12.53	12.52	12.51
	99	12.69	12.50	12.44	12.41	12.40	12.39	12.38	12.38

(Columns 5–40: LOAN TERM IN YEARS)

Step 3

Choose the **row** that corresponds to the discount. For a two-point discount, the net % of the loan (the amount the borrower actually receives) is 98 (100% - 2% = 98%).

Step 4

Locate the **number** at the intersection of the appropriate column and row. This is the lender's yield. For a 30-year, 12.25% loan with two points charged, the yield is **12.53%.**

If the discount had been **four** points, the net % would be **96** (100 - 4 = 96) and the lender's yield would be **12.81%.**

INTEREST RATE	NET %	LOAN TERM IN YEARS 5	10	15	20	25	30	35	40
8%	95	10.20	9.19	8.86	8.70	8.61	8.55	8.51	8.48
	96	9.74	8.95	8.68	8.55	8.48	8.44	8.40	8.38
	97	9.30	8.70	8.51	8.41	8.36	8.32	8.30	8.29
	98	8.86	8.47	8.34	8.27	8.24	8.21	8.20	8.19
	99	8.43	8.23	8.17	8.14	8.12	8.11	8.10	8.09
8¼%	95	10.45	9.45	9.12	8.96	8.86	8.81	8.77	8.74
	96	10.00	9.20	8.94	8.81	8.74	8.69	8.66	8.64
	97	9.55	8.96	8.76	8.67	8.61	8.58	8.56	8.54
	98	9.11	8.72	8.59	8.53	8.49	8.47	8.45	8.44
	99	8.68	8.48	8.42	8.39	8.37	8.36	8.35	8.35
8½	95	10.71	9.70	9.37	9.21	9.12	9.07	9.03	9.00
	96	10.25	9.46	9.19	9.07	8.99	8.95	8.92	8.90
	97	9.80	9.21	9.02	8.92	8.87	8.83	8.81	8.80
	98	9.36	8.97	8.84	8.78	8.74	8.72	8.71	8.70
	99	8.39	8.73	8.67	8.64	8.62	8.61	8.60	8.60
8¾%	95	10.96	9.96	9.63	9.47	9.38	9.32	9.29	9.26
	96	10.51	9.71	9.45	9.32	9.25	9.21	9.18	9.16
	97	10.06	9.46	9.27	9.18	9.12	9.09	9.07	9.05
	98	9.62	9.22	9.09	9.03	9.00	8.97	8.96	8.95
	99	9.18	8.98	8.92	8.89	8.87	8.86	8.85	8.85
9%	95	11.12	10.11	9.78	9.63	9.54	9.48	9.44	9.42
	96	10.66	9.86	9.60	9.48	9.40	9.36	9.33	9.31
	97	10.21	9.62	9.42	9.33	9.27	9.24	9.22	9.21
	98	9.77	9.37	9.25	9.18	9.15	9.13	9.11	9.10
	99	9.33	9.14	9.07	9.04	9.02	9.01	9.01	9.00
9¼%	95	11.47	10.47	10.14	9.99	9.90	9.84	9.81	9.78
	96	11.01	10.22	9.96	9.83	9.76	9.72	9.69	9.67
	97	10.56	9.97	9.78	9.68	9.63	9.60	9.58	9.56
	98	10.12	9.73	9.60	9.54	9.50	9.48	9.47	9.46
	99	9.68	9.49	9.42	9.39	9.38	9.36	9.36	9.35

INTEREST RATE	NET %	LOAN TERM IN YEARS 5	10	15	20	25	30	35	40
9½%	95	11.73	10.73	10.40	10.24	10.16	10.10	10.07	10.05
	96	11.27	10.47	10.21	10.09	10.02	9.98	9.95	9.93
	97	10.82	10.22	10.03	9.94	9.89	9.85	9.83	9.82
	98	10.37	9.98	9.85	9.79	9.76	9.73	9.72	9.71
	99	9.93	9.74	9.67	9.64	9.63	9.62	9.61	9.61
9¾%	95	11.98	10.98	10.66	10.50	10.41	10.36	10.33	10.31
	96	11.52	10.73	10.47	10.35	10.28	10.23	10.21	10.19
	97	11.07	10.48	10.29	10.19	10.14	10.11	10.09	10.08
	98	10.62	10.23	10.10	10.04	10.01	9.99	9.97	9.97
	99	10.18	9.99	9.93	9.90	9.88	9.87	9.86	9.86
10%	95	12.24	11.34	10.91	10.76	10.67	10.62	10.59	10.57
	96	11.78	10.98	10.72	10.60	10.53	10.49	10.47	10.45
	97	11.32	10.73	10.54	10.45	10.40	10.37	10.35	10.33
	98	10.88	10.48	10.36	10.30	10.26	10.24	10.23	10.22
	99	10.43	10.24	10.18	10.15	10.13	10.12	10.11	10.11
10¼%	95	12.49	11.50	11.17	11.02	10.93	10.88	10.85	10.83
	96	12.03	11.24	10.98	10.86	10.79	10.75	10.72	10.71
	97	11.58	10.99	10.79	10.70	10.65	10.62	10.60	10.59
	98	11.13	10.74	10.61	10.55	10.52	10.50	10.48	10.47
	99	10.69	10.49	10.43	10.40	10.38	10.37	10.37	10.36
10½%	95	12.75	11.75	11.43	11.27	11.19	11.14	11.11	11.09
	96	12.29	11.49	11.24	11.11	11.05	11.01	10.98	10.97
	97	11.83	11.24	11.05	10.96	10.91	10.88	10.86	10.85
	98	11.38	10.99	10.86	10.80	10.77	10.75	10.74	10.73
	99	10.94	10.74	10.68	10.65	10.63	10.62	10.62	10.61
10¾%	95	13.01	12.01	11.68	11.53	11.45	11.40	11.37	11.35
	96	12.54	11.75	11.49	11.37	11.30	11.26	11.24	11.22
	97	12.08	11.49	11.30	11.21	11.16	11.13	11.11	11.10
	98	11.63	11.24	11.11	11.06	11.02	11.00	10.99	10.98
	99	11.19	10.99	10.93	10.90	10.89	10.88	10.87	10.87
11%	95	13.26	12.26	11.94	11.79	11.71	11.66	11.63	11.61
	96	12.80	12.00	11.75	11.63	11.56	11.52	11.50	11.48
	97	12.34	11.75	11.56	11.47	11.42	11.39	11.37	11.36
	98	11.88	11.49	11.37	11.31	11.28	11.26	11.24	11.24
	99	11.44	11.25	11.18	11.15	11.14	11.13	11.12	11.12

INTEREST RATE	NET %	LOAN TERM IN YEARS 5	10	15	20	25	30	35	40
11¼%	95	13.52	12.52	12.20	12.05	11.97	11.92	11.89	11.87
	96	13.05	12.26	12.00	11.88	11.82	11.78	11.76	11.74
	97	12.59	12.00	11.81	11.72	11.67	11.64	11.63	11.62
	98	12.14	11.75	11.62	11.56	11.53	11.51	11.50	11.49
	99	11.69	11.50	11.43	11.40	11.39	11.38	11.37	11.37
11½%	95	13.77	12.78	12.46	12.31	12.23	12.18	12.15	12.13
	96	13.30	12.51	12.26	12.14	12.08	12.04	12.02	12.00
	97	12.84	12.25	12.06	11.98	11.93	11.90	11.88	11.87
	98	12.39	12.00	11.87	11.81	11.78	11.76	11.75	11.75
	99	11.94	11.75	11.69	11.66	11.64	11.63	11.63	11.62
11¾%	95	14.03	13.03	12.71	12.57	12.49	12.44	12.41	12.39
	96	13.56	12.77	12.51	12.40	12.33	12.30	12.27	12.26
	97	13.10	12.51	12.32	12.23	12.18	12.16	12.14	12.13
	98	12.64	12.25	12.13	12.07	12.04	12.02	12.01	12.00
	99	12.19	12.00	11.94	11.91	11.89	11.88	11.88	11.87
12%	95	14.28	13.29	12.97	12.82	12.74	12.70	12.67	12.66
	96	13.81	13.02	12.77	12.65	12.59	12.55	12.53	12.52
	97	13.35	12.76	12.57	12.49	12.44	12.41	12.40	12.39
	98	12.89	12.50	12.38	12.32	12.29	12.27	12.26	12.25
	99	12.44	12.25	12.19	12.16	12.14	12.13	12.13	12.13
12¼%	95	14.54	13.55	13.23	13.08	13.00	12.96	12.93	12.92
	96	14.07	13.28	13.03	12.91	12.85	12.81	12.79	12.78
	97	13.60	13.02	12.83	12.74	12.69	12.67	12.65	12.64
	98	13.15	12.76	12.63	12.57	12.54	12.53	12.52	12.51
	99	12.69	12.50	12.44	12.41	12.40	12.39	12.38	12.38
12½%	95	14.79	13.80	13.49	13.34	13.26	13.22	13.19	13.18
	96	14.32	13.53	13.28	13.17	13.11	13.07	13.05	13.04
	97	13.86	13.27	13.08	13.00	12.95	12.92	12.91	12.90
	98	13.40	13.01	12.88	12.83	12.80	12.78	12.77	12.76
	99	12.95	12.75	12.69	12.66	12.65	12.64	12.63	12.63
12¾%	95	15.05	14.06	13.74	13.60	13.52	13.48	13.46	13.44
	96	14.58	13.79	13.54	13.42	13.36	13.33	13.31	13.30
	97	14.11	13.52	13.34	13.25	13.21	13.18	13.17	13.16
	98	13.65	13.26	13.14	13.08	13.05	13.03	13.02	13.02
	99	13.20	13.00	12.94	12.91	12.90	12.89	12.89	12.88

INTEREST RATE	NET %	LOAN TERM IN YEARS 5	10	15	20	25	30	35	40
	95	15.31	14.32	14.00	13.86	13.78	13.74	13.72	13.70
	96	14.83	14.04	13.79	13.68	13.62	13.59	13.57	13.56
13%	97	14.36	13.78	13.59	13.51	13.46	13.44	13.42	13.41
	98	13.90	13.51	13.39	13.33	13.30	13.29	13.28	13.27
	99	13.45	13.26	13.19	13.17	13.15	13.14	13.14	13.14
	95	15.56	14.57	14.26	14.12	14.04	14.00	13.98	13.97
	96	15.09	14.30	14.05	13.94	13.88	13.85	13.83	13.82
13¼%	97	14.62	14.03	13.85	13.76	13.72	13.69	13.68	13.67
	98	14.15	13.77	13.64	13.59	13.56	13.54	13.53	13.53
	99	13.70	13.51	13.45	13.42	13.40	13.39	13.39	13.39
	95	15.82	14.83	14.52	14.38	14.30	14.26	14.24	14.23
	96	15.34	14.55	14.31	14.19	14.14	14.10	14.09	14.08
13½	97	14.87	14.28	14.10	14.02	13.97	13.95	13.94	13.93
	98	14.41	14.02	13.90	13.84	13.81	13.80	13.79	13.78
	99	13.95	13.76	13.70	13.67	13.65	13.65	13.64	13.64
	95	16.07	15.09	14.77	14.63	14.56	14.52	14.50	14.49
	96	15.59	14.81	14.56	14.45	14.39	14.36	14.35	14.34
13¾%	97	15.12	14.54	14.35	14.27	14.23	14.21	14.19	14.18
	98	14.66	14.27	14.15	14.09	14.07	14.05	14.04	14.04
	99	14.20	14.01	13.95	13.92	13.91	13.90	13.89	13.89
	95	16.33	15.34	15.03	14.89	14.82	14.78	14.76	14.75
	96	15.85	15.07	14.82	14.71	14.65	14.62	14.60	14.60
14%	97	15.38	14.79	14.61	14.53	14.48	14.46	14.45	14.44
	98	14.91	14.52	14.40	14.35	14.32	14.30	14.30	14.29
	99	14.45	14.26	14.20	14.17	14.16	14.15	14.15	14.14
	95	16.58	15.60	15.29	15.15	15.08	15.05	15.02	15.01
	96	16.10	15.32	15.08	14.97	14.91	14.88	14.86	14.85
14¼%	97	15.63	15.05	14.86	14.78	14.74	14.72	14.71	14.70
	98	15.16	14.78	14.66	14.60	14.57	14.56	14.55	14.55
	99	14.70	14.51	14.45	14.42	14.41	14.40	14.40	14.40
	95	16.84	15.86	15.55	15.41	15.34	15.31	15.29	15.28
	96	16.36	15.58	15.33	15.22	15.17	15.14	15.12	15.11
14½%	97	15.88	15.30	15.12	15.04	15.00	14.97	14.96	14.96
	98	15.42	15.03	14.91	14.86	14.83	14.81	14.81	14.80
	99	14.95	14.76	14.70	14.68	14.66	14.66	14.65	14.65

INTEREST RATE	NET %	5	10	15	20	25	30	35	40
		LOAN TERM IN YEARS							
14¾%	95	17.10	16.11	15.81	15.67	15.60	15.57	15.55	15.54
	96	16.61	15.83	15.59	15.48	15.43	15.40	15.38	15.37
	97	16.14	15.55	15.37	15.29	15.25	15.23	15.22	15.21
	98	15.67	15.28	15.16	15.11	15.08	15.07	15.06	15.06
	99	15.21	15.01	14.95	14.93	14.91	14.91	14.90	14.90
15%	95	17.35	16.37	16.07	15.93	15.86	15.83	15.81	15.80
	96	16.87	16.09	15.84	15.74	15.68	15.66	15.64	15.63
	97	16.39	15.81	15.63	15.55	15.51	15.49	15.48	15.47
	98	15.92	15.54	15.42	15.36	15.34	15.32	15.31	15.31
	99	15.46	15.27	15.21	15.18	15.17	15.16	15.16	15.15
15¼%	95	17.61	16.63	16.32	16.19	16.12	16.09	16.07	16.06
	96	17.12	16.34	16.10	16.00	15.94	15.92	15.90	15.89
	97	16.64	16.06	15.88	15.80	15.77	15.74	15.73	15.73
	98	16.17	15.79	15.67	15.62	15.59	15.58	15.57	15.57
	99	15.71	15.52	15.46	15.43	15.42	15.41	15.41	15.41
15½%	95	17.86	16.88	16.58	16.45	16.39	16.35	16.33	16.33
	96	17.38	16.60	16.36	16.25	16.20	16.17	16.16	16.15
	97	16.90	16.32	16.14	16.06	16.02	16.00	15.99	15.99
	98	16.42	16.04	15.92	15.87	15.84	15.83	15.82	15.82
	99	15.96	15.77	15.71	15.68	15.67	15.66	15.66	15.66
15¾%	95	18.12	17.14	16.84	16.71	16.65	16.61	16.60	16.59
	96	17.63	16.85	16.61	16.51	16.46	16.43	16.42	16.41
	97	17.15	16.57	16.39	16.32	16.28	16.26	16.25	16.24
	98	16.68	16.29	16.18	16.12	16.10	16.09	16.08	16.08
	99	16.21	16.20	15.96	15.94	15.92	15.92	15.91	15.91
16%	95	18.38	17.40	17.10	16.97	16.91	16.88	16.86	16.85
	96	17.89	17.11	16.87	16.77	16.72	16.69	16.68	16.67
	97	17.40	16.83	16.65	16.57	16.53	16.51	16.51	16.50
	98	16.93	16.55	16.43	16.38	16.35	16.34	16.33	16.33
	99	16.46	16.27	16.21	16.19	16.17	16.17	16.17	16.16
16¼%	95	18.63	17.66	17.36	17.23	17.17	17.14	17.12	17.11
	96	18.14	17.37	17.13	17.03	16.98	16.95	16.94	16.93
	97	17.66	17.08	16.90	16.83	16.79	16.77	16.76	16.76
	98	17.18	16.80	16.68	16.63	16.61	16.59	16.59	16.58
	99	16.71	16.52	16.46	16.44	16.43	16.42	16.42	16.42

INTEREST RATE	NET %	LOAN TERM IN YEARS 5	10	15	20	25	30	35	40
16½%	95	18.89	17.91	17.62	17.49	17.43	17.40	17.38	17.38
	96	18.40	17.62	17.38	17.28	17.24	17.21	17.20	17.19
	97	17.91	17.33	17.16	17.08	17.05	17.03	17.02	17.01
	98	17.43	17.05	16.93	16.89	16.86	16.85	16.84	16.84
	99	16.96	16.77	16.72	16.69	16.68	16.67	16.67	16.67
16¾%	95	19.14	18.17	17.87	17.75	17.69	17.66	17.65	17.64
	96	18.65	17.88	17.64	17.54	17.49	17.47	17.46	17.45
	97	18.16	17.59	17.41	17.34	17.30	17.29	17.28	17.27
	98	17.69	17.30	17.19	17.14	17.12	17.10	17.10	17.09
	99	17.21	17.03	16.97	16.94	16.93	16.93	16.92	16.92
17%	95	19.40	18.43	18.13	18.01	17.95	17.92	17.91	17.90
	96	18.90	18.13	17.90	17.80	17.75	17.73	17.72	17.71
	97	18.42	17.84	17.67	17.59	17.56	17.54	17.53	17.53
	98	17.94	17.56	17.44	17.39	17.37	17.36	17.35	17.35
	99	17.47	17.28	17.22	17.19	17.18	17.18	17.17	17.17
17¼%	95	19.66	18.68	18.39	18.27	18.21	18.18	18.17	18.16
	96	19.16	18.39	18.16	18.06	18.01	17.99	17.98	17.97
	97	18.67	18.10	17.92	17.85	17.82	17.80	17.79	17.79
	98	18.19	17.81	17.70	17.65	17.62	17.61	17.61	17.60
	99	17.72	17.53	17.47	17.45	17.44	17.43	17.43	17.43
17½%	95	19.91	18.94	18.65	18.53	18.47	18.45	18.43	18.43
	96	19.41	18.64	18.41	18.32	18.27	18.25	18.24	18.23
	97	18.92	18.35	18.18	18.11	18.07	18.06	18.05	18.04
	98	18.44	18.06	17.95	17.90	17.88	17.87	17.86	17.86
	99	17.97	17.78	17.72	17.70	17.69	17.68	17.68	17.68
17¾%	95	20.17	19.20	18.91	18.79	18.73	18.71	18.70	18.69
	96	19.67	18.90	18.67	18.57	18.53	18.51	18.50	18.49
	97	19.18	18.61	18.43	18.36	18.33	18.31	18.31	18.30
	98	18.70	18.32	18.20	18.15	18.13	18.12	18.12	18.11
	99	18.22	18.03	17.97	17.95	17.94	17.93	17.93	17.93
18%	95	20.42	19.46	19.17	19.05	19.00	18.97	18.96	18.95
	96	19.92	19.16	18.96	18.83	18.79	18.77	18.76	18.75
	97	19.43	18.86	18.69	18.62	18.59	18.57	18.56	18.56
	98	18.95	18.57	18.46	18.41	18.39	18.38	18.37	18.37
	99	18.47	18.28	18.23	18.20	18.19	18.19	18.18	18.18

IX. CHAPTER SUMMARY

Agents, brokers, and loan officers need to be able to solve basic real estate math problems in order to provide professional service to their clients. It is of particular importance to be able to answer a client's questions regarding interest rates, appreciation in value, and proration of closing costs. The development of financial tables, and particularly of financial calculators, not only has made the process easier but has resulted in time savings for the real estate professional as well.

X. TERMINOLOGY

Compound Interest
Denominator
Effective Interest Rate
Interest
Interest Rate Factors Table
Mean
Nominal ("Named") Interest Rate
Numerator
Proration
Simple Interest
Value After
Value Before

XI. CHAPTER QUIZ

1. A stated interest rate of 6% on a promissory note is an example of:

 a. simple interest.
 b. compound interest.
 c. an effective rate.
 d. a nominal rate.

2. If a borrower is actually paying more than the stated rate due to a quarterly conversion, the rate is an example of:

 a. simple interest.
 b. an effective rate.
 c. a nominal rate.
 d. proration.

3. The bottom number of a fraction is the:

 a. denominator.
 b. numerator.
 c. decimal.
 d. formulator.

4. 56.337 x 21.77 =

 a. 122.645
 b. 1,226.456
 c. 12.264
 d. 1,226.000

5. 12.24 + (3.36 -2.08) x 1.23 =

 a. 18.93
 b. 13.81
 c. 16.63
 d. none of the above

6. The profit and loss formula is:

 a. P = % x T
 b. I = P x R x T
 c. VA = % x VB
 d. none of the above

7. If the interest is unknown the formula should be:
   a. R = I ÷ P x T
   b. I = P x R x T
   c. I = P ÷ R x T
   d. none of the above

8. If the principal is unknown the formula should be:
   a. P = I ÷ (R x T)
   b. P = I x R x T
   c. P = T ÷ (I x R)
   d. none of the above.

9. Dividing prepaid property expenses fairly between buyer and seller is known as:
   a. discounting.
   b. proration.
   c. conversion.
   d. compounding.

10. Interest paid on accrued interest as well as principal is known as:
    a. compound.
    b. simple.
    c. prorated.
    d. all the above.

ANSWERS: *1. d; 2. b; 3. a; 4. b; 5. b; 6. c; 7. b; 8. a; 9. b; 10. a*

– Part VI –

Chapters 16, 17, and 18
Appendix (State-Specific Concepts)

Chapter 16 – State-Sponsored Home Loan Programs

Many states offer low interest home loan programs for veterans, first-time homeowners, and low-to-middle-income borrowers. Several are listed here, with suggestions as to how to look up a particular state's program on the Internet.

Chapter 17 – CalVet Loans (California Example)

Since 1921, an additional type of government-sponsored financing is available to California veterans and veterans who move to California. Funding for the program has been provided since the program's inception through the sale of General Obligation Bonds and Revenue Bonds. The bonds have always been repaid by the veterans who participated in the program and thus, there has never been any direct cost to California taxpayers.

Chapter 18 – Escrow Procedures

The typical escrow involves many more participants than just the buyer and seller. It includes the broker, lender, and escrow agent. Important functions are also performed by title companies, notaries public, local county officials (recording office and inspectors), and structural pest inspectors.

Chapter 16
State-Sponsored Home Loan Programs

Many state and local governments provide low and moderate mortgage loan programs, as well as other benefits, to qualified borrowers. Many of these programs train participating banks, mortgage companies, credit unions, and real estate professionals in the use of their particular programs, enabling them to match the right loan with the right borrower. Programs include financing, down payment assistance, closing cost assistance, and other programs for first-time homebuyers.

In New York, for example, the State of New York Mortgage Agency (SONYMA) has a low interest rate mortgage program which provides qualified low- and moderate-income first-time homebuyers with low down payment mortgage financing on one-to-four-unit dwellings, including condominiums and cooperative apartments, as well as manufactured homes permanently attached to real property. These loans are at fixed interest rates, which are below prevailing conventional rates. The program is financed by SONYMA through the sale of tax-exempt bonds.

The various state programs are too numerous and too diversified to list here, but a simple search of the Internet will provide each state's home loan opportunities. For a list of state housing agencies, go to:

www.trackproservices.com/links/statelnk.html

The Department of Veterans Affairs (VA) also sponsors state-run programs, such as that offered by the Texas Veterans Housing Assistance Program (VHAP), which provides financing up to $200,000 toward the purchase of a home to qualified Texas veterans. Any amount in excess of the maximum must be provided by the veteran, or through a commercial lending institution. As Texas veterans' loan programs are not directly associated with the federal VA loan programs, veterans who have used their VA benefits may still be eligible for state loan programs. (See Chapter 17 for details on California's CalVet program.)

For information on federal home loan programs, call 1-800-827-1000 or visit their web page at:

www.homeloans.va.gov

You can also look up county and city governments for information at:

www.statelocalgov.net

The following is just a partial list of state programs available to first-time homeowners, low- to moderate-income borrowers, and/or qualified veterans.

California

California Housing Finance Agency (Cal HFA)

Sacramento Headquarters
1415 L Street, Ste. 500
Sacramento, CA 95814
(877) 922-5432

Los Angeles Office
100 Corporate Pointe, Ste. 250
Culver City, CA 90230
www.calhfa.ca.gov

Delaware

Delaware State Housing Authority (DSHA) (Numerous loan programs available)
820 N. French Street
Wilmington, DE 19801
(302) 739-4263 or (302) 577-5001
www.destatehousing.com

Florida

Florida Housing Finance Corporation (FHFC)
227 North Bronough Street
Suite 5000
Tallahassee, FL 32301-1329
(850) 488-4197 or Fax: (850) 488-9809
www.floridahousing.org/home

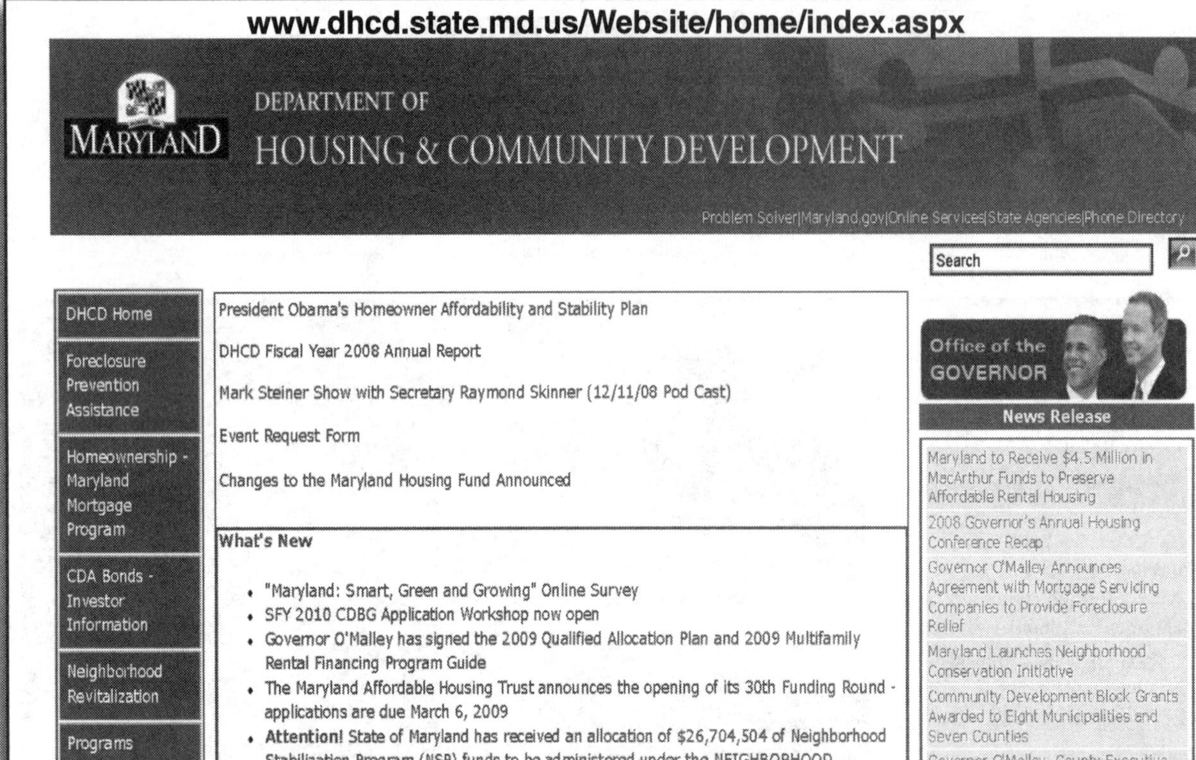

Maryland

Department of Housing and Community Development (DHCD)
Maryland Mortgage Program (MMP) also known as CDA Mortgage Loans
100 Community Place
Crownsville, MD 21032-2023
(800) 756-0119 or (410) 514-7000
www.dhcd.state.md.us/Website/home/index.aspx

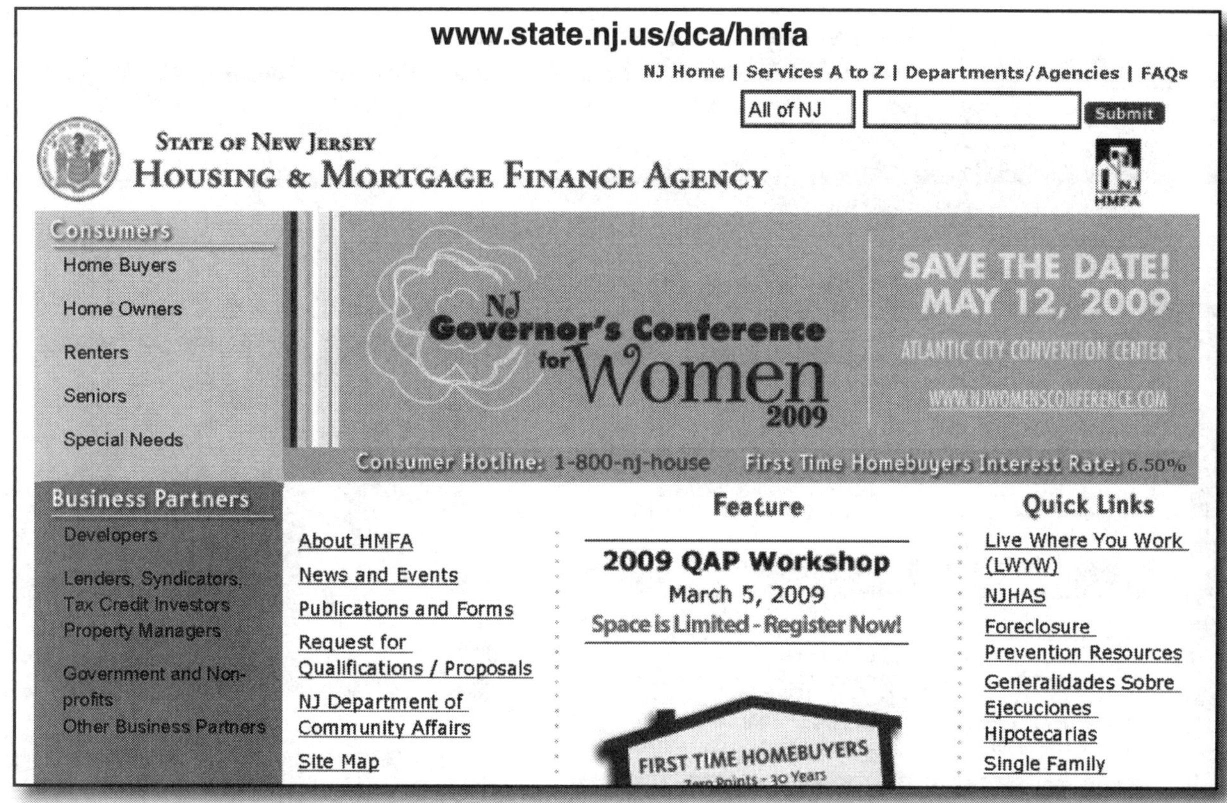

New Jersey

New Jersey Housing and Mortgage Finance Agency
Mortgage Opportunity Program (MOP)
637 South Clinton Avenue
PO Box 18550
Trenton, NJ 08650-2085
(800) NJ-HOUSE or (609) 278-7400
www.state.nj.us/dca/hmfa

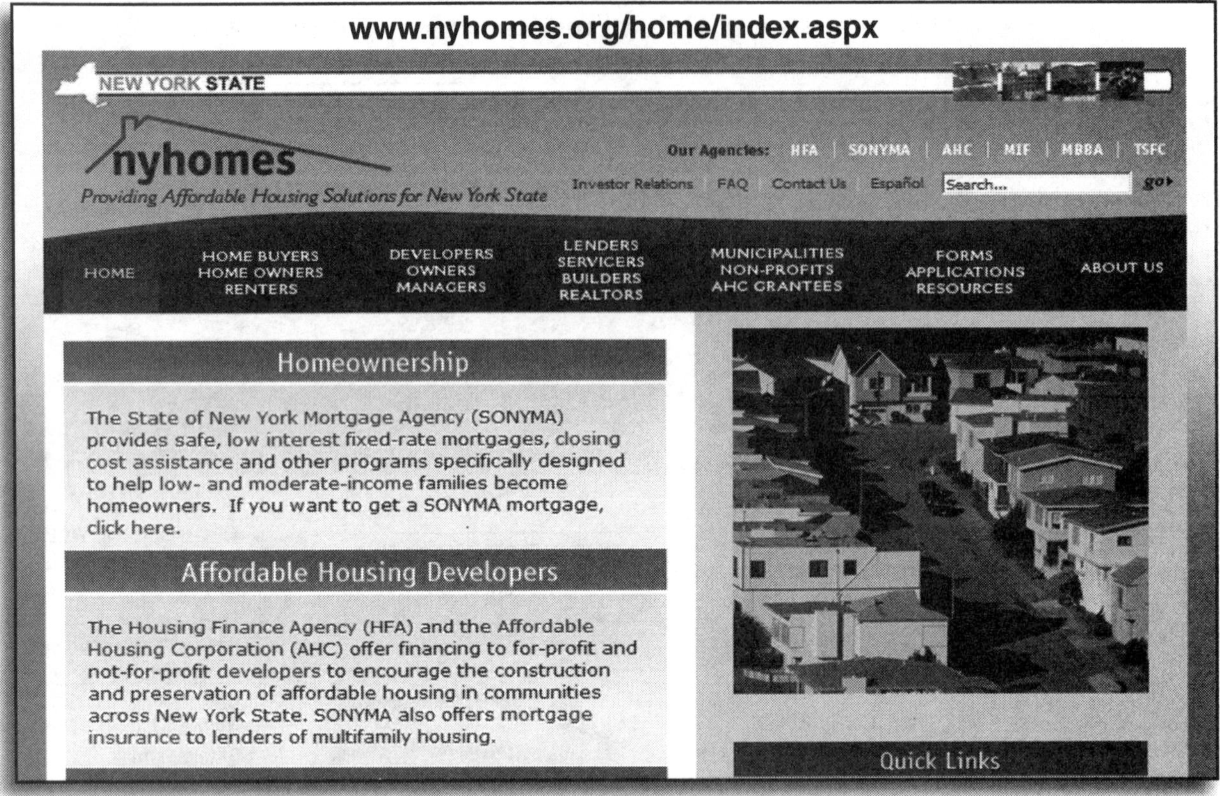

New York

State of New York Mortgage Agency (SONYMA)
641 Lexington Avenue - 4th Floor
New York, NY 10022
(800) 382-HOME (4663) or (212) 688-4000
www.nyhomes.org/home/index.asp

www.oregon.gov/OHCS/SFF_OregonBondHome.shtml

OREGON.gov

Enter search term(s)

Oregon Housing and Community Services

- Department
  - Housing/Community Services Department
  - Boards
    - Oregon State Housing Council

Welcome to www.OregonBond.us!

OHCS Homepage / OregonBond.us

- Search
- About Us
- Contact Us
- Housing Council
- Homelessness Council
- News and Events
- Community Resources
- Energy / Weatherization
- Home Buying
- Grants / Tax Credits
- CFC Overview
- Multifamily Loans
- Manufactured Home

Homeownership Starts here ...

Learn how to qualify ...

English Brochure

En Español

Homebuyer Services

Current Interest Rate
(effective 01/05/09)
Rate*Advantage*
Home Loan
4.50%
BEST RATE
1-877-ST8-BOND
(1-877-788-2663)

Contact Us Today - Click Here!

Oregon

Oregon Housing and Community Services
725 Summer Street NE, Suite B
Salem, OR 97301-1266
(503) 986-2000
www.oregon.gov/OHCS/SFF_OregonBondHome.shtml

www.glo.state.tx.us/vlb/vhap/index.html

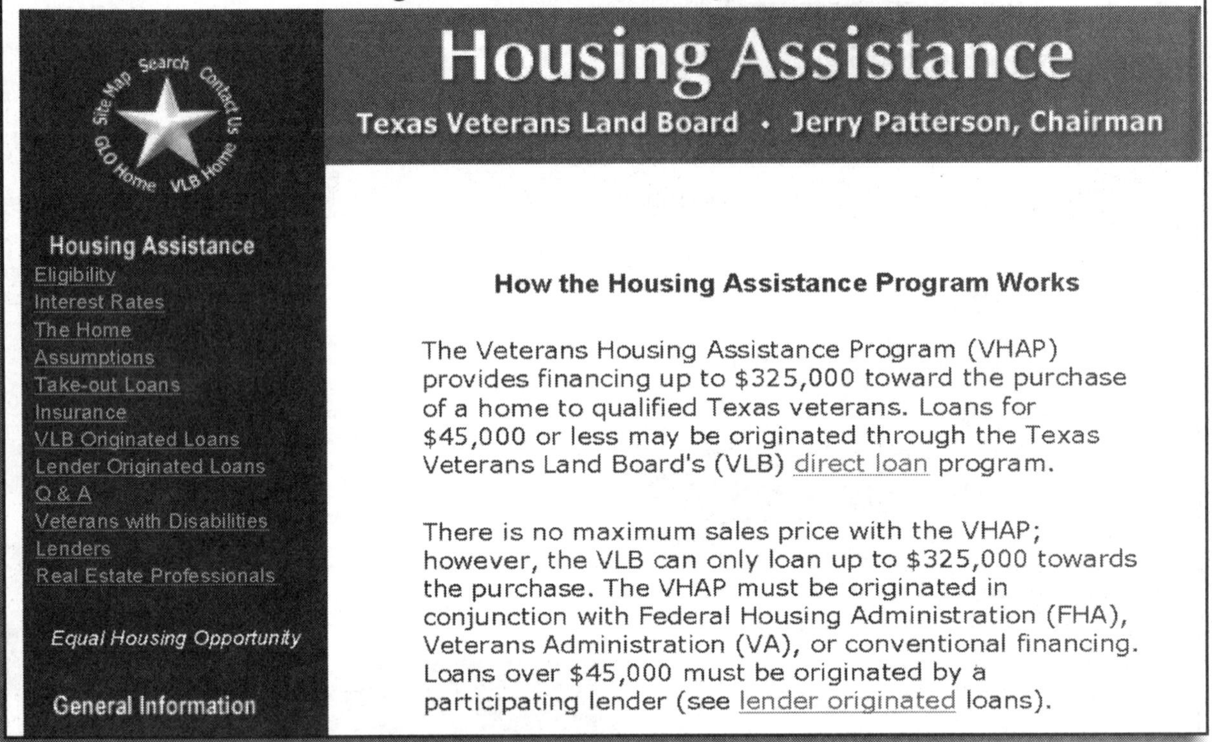

Housing Assistance

Texas Veterans Land Board • Jerry Patterson, Chairman

Site Map · Search · Contact Us · GLO Home · VLB Home

Housing Assistance

- Eligibility
- Interest Rates
- The Home
- Assumptions
- Take-out Loans
- Insurance
- VLB Originated Loans
- Lender Originated Loans
- Q & A
- Veterans with Disabilities
- Lenders
- Real Estate Professionals

Equal Housing Opportunity

General Information

How the Housing Assistance Program Works

The Veterans Housing Assistance Program (VHAP) provides financing up to $325,000 toward the purchase of a home to qualified Texas veterans. Loans for $45,000 or less may be originated through the Texas Veterans Land Board's (VLB) direct loan program.

There is no maximum sales price with the VHAP; however, the VLB can only loan up to $325,000 towards the purchase. The VHAP must be originated in conjunction with Federal Housing Administration (FHA), Veterans Administration (VA), or conventional financing. Loans over $45,000 must be originated by a participating lender (see lender originated loans).

Texas

Texas Veterans Land Board (VLB) - Veterans' Housing Assistance Program (VHAP)
P.O. Box 12873
Austin, TX 78711-2873
(800) 252-VETS (8387) or (512) 463-9592
www.glo.state.tx.us/vlb/vhap/index.html
E-mail: vlbinfo@glo.state.tx.us

http://dva.state.wi.us/

Wisconsin Department of Veterans Affairs

"Making a difference in the lives of Wisconsin Veterans"

> Home

- **Home**
- About WDVA
- Current Events
- Forms & Brochures
- News & Publications
- Federal Veterans Benefits
- State Veterans Benefits
- Veterans Cemeteries
- Veterans Homes
- Veterans Memorials
- Veterans Museum
- Veterans Service Offices
- Women Veterans
- Veterans Links

John A. Scocos
Secretary

Welcome to the web site of the Wisconsin Department of Veterans Affairs (WDVA).

I often speak about my four-point vision for WDVA. First and foremost, I believe that we must fully honor our commitment to Wisconsin's veterans. As long as I am Secretary, that commitment to Wisconsin's veterans will never waiver.

Second, I firmly believe that WDVA must always ensure stakeholder involvement, working hard to extend and expand the department's critically important relationships with all the veterans' service organizations, county veterans service officers, key leaders, VA officials, and many others.

Wisconsin

Wisconsin Department of Veteran Affairs (WDVA)
Veterans' Home Mortgage Loan Program
30 W. Mifflin St.
Madison, WI 53703
PO Box 7843
(800) 947-8387 or (608) 266-1311
http://dva.state.wi.us/

Chapter 17
CalVet Loans (California Example)

An additional type of government sponsored financing is available to California veterans. In 1921, the California legislature enacted the California Veteran Farm and Home Purchase Program, which enabled the California Department of Veterans Affairs to provide eligible veterans with affordable financing to purchase home or farm property.

Funding for the program has been provided since the program's inception through the sale of General Obligation Bonds and Revenue Bonds. The bonds have always been repaid by the veterans who participated in the program and thus there has never been any direct cost to California taxpayers. Originally the program was restricted to veterans who were born in California. Due to recent changes the program has been vastly broadened.

I. Eligibility for CalVet Program

The most important change to the new CalVet program is that all veterans who either live in California or who plan to live in California are eligible.

1. No prior residency requirement. Any veteran who moves to California may qualify for a CalVet Loan.
2. Both wartime and peacetime veterans are eligible.

CHAPTER OUTLINE

3. Veterans who previously used a CalVet loan may obtain another subject to current eligibility and funding requirements.
4. Loans may be obtained for outright purchase, rehabilitation, or construction.

II. Qualifying and Fees

CalVet now uses the VA underwriting and packaging requirements. Qualifying now follows the VA requirements. Mortgage Insurance is required for loans in which the down payment is less than 20%. The fee for the mortgage insurance is charged in escrow and may be paid either by the buyer or the seller. There is no fee for monthly mortgage insurance. There is no mortgage insurance fee if the down payment is 20% or more or if the veteran has a 10% or more VA Disability rating. The veteran will also have to provide a VA Certificate of Eligibility.

Currently, the maximum loan amount is $521,250 and loans are for a term of thirty years.

CalVet interest rates tend to be stable with infrequent upward or downward changes. The interest rate is subject to a .5% one-time upward increase at any time during the length of the loan. This feature allows CalVet to enhance the desirability of their bonds to investors. Veterans who served before 1977 and who apply before thirty years from release from the service qualify for the same rate. All other veterans will be charged 5.5%. Down payments are as low as 2%, if VA mortgage insurance is utilized. If VA mortgage insurance is utilized, the maximum loan amount is $521,250. Private mortgage insurance (PMI) is available with only 3% down. Currently the cost of the insurance is from .63% to 1.38% of the loan amount.

Down payment funds may come from any source other than the seller.

If the veteran needs help in raising down payment funds, CalVet participates with community housing loan agencies to provide loans for this purpose.

III. Broker Origination

Effective March 1, 2001, veterans were allowed to originate their loans through a Certified CalVet Brokerage Firm. CalVet allows certified mortgage brokers to receive a 1% loan origination fee. Brokers who wish to participate in the program must comply with the following requirements:

1. Brokers and loan officers must attend a CalVet lending seminar conducted by CalVet personnel.
2. CalVet will only certify mortgage brokerage companies, not individual loan officers.
3. The company must sign a CalVet Mortgage Broker Agreement and send all their loan officer personnel to CalVet training.
4. Certification is "conditional" until the company has originated at least three CalVet loans within 24 months. At that time certification becomes finalized.
5. Only loan officers who work for a certified mortgage brokerage and have attended CalVet training are eligible to receive the 1% origination fee for a CalVet loan.
6. Previous individual certification obtained before March 1, 2001 is now invalid.

CalVet instituted this new program to insure that participants better understand the program and to insure optimum performance and accountability standards from their brokers.

Further information regarding the CalVet Loan program may be obtained at their website (**www.cdva.ca.gov**).

www.cdva.ca.gov
CA.GOV
CALIFORNIA DEPARTMENT OF
VETERANS AFFAIRS
Skip to: Content | Footer | Accessibility
This Site All CA.gov
Search
GO
Home About Us Home Loans Vets Homes Vet Services CalVet Board Resources News Jobs Education
CALIFORNIA DEPARTMENT OF VETERANS AFFAIRS
DVA
GOVERNOR SCHWARZENEGGER
Visit His Website
Home
Honoring California's Veterans
Announcements
HOME
About Us
Home Loans
Vets Homes
Vet Services
CalVet Board
Veterans Now Eligible to Take State Promotional Exams
As a result of legislation signed by Governor Schwarzenegger (AB 3065, Chapter 590, Statutes of 2008) that went into effect 1 January 2009 Veterans are now eligible to take promotional civil service exams, even though they are currently not a civil service employee. This new law allows veterans who meet the minimum qualifications for promotional job openings to be admitted to state interviews and exams. For further information please

Figure 17-1

CALVET HOME LOAN APPLICATION PACKAGE

This package contains forms and instructions for obtaining a CalVet Home Loan. If you are planning to build a new home on property that you currently own or intend to purchase, you will also need to download the Construction Loan Supplemental Package of forms and instructions.

Before you begin:

You must have a property selected before applying for your loan. We suggest that you carefully review the material on the CalVet Home Loan Program on our web site. If you have questions feel free to e-mail us at loanserv@cdva.ca.gov or contact the nearest CalVet District Office. A list of CalVet District Offices and the areas they cover with complete contact information including direct e-mail address for each office is available on our website at http://www.cdva.ca.gov/CalVetLoans/Offices2.aspx.

Optional, but highly recommended: Prequalify for your loan using the **Apply Online** feature on our website. Answering a few questions about your military service, current income, and monthly obligations will confirm your eligibility and give you an estimate of the amount of loan you can qualify for. You can also prequalify by downloading and completing the Prequalification Form available at http://www.cdva.ca.gov/CalVetLoans/prequal.pdf. Send the completed form to the CalVet District Office for the area where you plan to buy your home. Keep in mind that prequalification is not the same as loan approval, which generally requires verification of your income and a review of your credit history. If you have concerns about either of these issues please contact us to discuss them.

CalVet uses the Universal Residential Loan Application (URLA), which is also known as FannieMae Form 1003 or FreddieMac Form 65. You can complete and submit this form on our website by clicking on the **Apply Online** button. First complete the Eligibility and Prequalification screens and then proceed to the Loan Application. After you complete and submit the application form, complete the remaining forms in this package and mail them to the CalVet office nearest your property. If you prefer you may obtain an application form from one of our district offices and fill it out by hand.

The first group of forms listed below contain information about CalVet Home Loans and the application process. Please review the information and contact us if you have any questions.

- Form C-13: Thank You for Choosing CalVet - These pages summarize the features and eligibility requirements of the CalVet Home Loan Program.
- Loan Terms - This document contains the current loan terms, fees and interest rates.
- Form A-1T: CalVet Home Loan Application Instruction Sheet - These instructions explain how to submit the application forms in this package and what additional information you will need to send to CalVet.
- Form A-2: CalVet Home Loan Processing Cycle - This chart explains how CalVet processes a home loan application.
- Form C-4: Important Notice - This document provides information about recent changes in the CalVet Home Loan program concerning Loan Guarantees and Loan Processing.
- Form L-8: Special Notice Regarding your CalVet Home Loan Application - This notice explains Internal Revenue Service limitations placed on funds used for CalVet Home Loans for refinancing a home loan. It also contains the notice required by the California Information Practices Act of 1977 concerning how CalVet may use the information that you submit to us.

A-1C (1/2007) Page 1of 2

CALVET HOME LOAN APPLICATION PACKAGE

- Address List - This document contains a list of CalVet offices throughout the state along with addresses and telephone numbers.

....

The forms listed below must be completed and submitted with your application. If you apply online please mail these forms to the CalVet District Office responsible for your application.

- ❑ Fannie Mae Form 1003 7/05 – This is the Uniform Residential Loan Application used by most lenders to collect the information necessary for loan processing.
- ❑ Form C-14: CalVet Home Loan Origination Fee/Funding Fee - This form allows the applicant to notify CalVet concerning their choices for payment of the Loan Origination Fee and CDVA/USDVA Funding Fee.
- ❑ Form C-11-3 / V-11: Borrower's Authorization / Verification of Borrower(s) Name(s) - This form is used to authorize CalVet to obtain verifications of your income, employment, assets, and other credit matters and to verify the exact legal name(s) of the loan applicant or applicants.
- ❑ Form L-9: Fair Lending Notice - This notice explains your rights under the Housing Financial Discrimination Act of 1977. Sign this form to show that you have read and understood it and return it with your loan application.
- ❑ Buyer's Information - This form provides us with basic information about you and the property you are purchasing that is not included on the application form.

....

The following forms are optional:

- ❑ Form A-3: Designation of Agent and General Release - You may designate another person to act as your agent in connection with the processing of your CalVet Home Loan application. The use of this form is completely optional.
- ❑ Real Estate Agent Internet Access Registration - Complete this form with the assistance of your Real Estate Agent if you want your agent to be able to monitor loan processing status on line and receive email notifications when the status changes.

....

Also available on our website:

- ❑ Minimum Property Standards – This document summarizes the standards that properties purchased with a CalVet Home Loan must meet. If you have questions about these requirements or about whether or not the property you are considering will qualify please contact one of our CalVet District Offices. The document is on our website at http://www.cdva.ca.gov/CalVetLoans/MPS.aspx and is also available in our District Offices.

A-1C (1/2007) Page 2 of 2

THANK YOU FOR CHOOSING CAL-VET

You will be pleased with your selection of CalVet financing for the purchase of your home. CalVet has many features and benefits that will save you money and provide protections for you and your investment. We want to make it as convenient as possible for you to apply for a CalVet Home Loan.

- You can apply directly to CalVet at any one of the field offices listed on the following page. If you are not certain which office to contact use the District Office locator on our website at http://www.cdva.ca.gov/calvet/offices.asp. You will need to download the second part the application package, CalVet Home Loans Application Forms.
- You can apply online at https://calvethomeloans.cdva.ca.gov/welcome.html. First complete the Eligibility screen, and then you can proceed to the Loan Application when you are ready. The additional forms that you need can be downloaded at CalVet Home Loans Application Forms. One of our field offices will contact you to confirm your application, answer any questions you may have, and advise you how to proceed.
- CalVet has trained mortgage brokers statewide that have been certified to originate CalVet Hoem Loans. A list of brokers is on our website at http://www.cdva.ca.gov/calvet/brindex.asp.

If you have a real estate agent, we encourage you to have them be active in the processing of your loan. A form to designate them to act on your behalf is included in our application package, however this is optional. If you have any questions, please discuss them with your real estate agent or mortgage broker. Of course, you may always call us at the district office.

The CalVet Loan

You must have a property selected before applying for your CalVet Home Loan. If you have not yet selected a property you can still start processing by completing the Eligibility & Prequalification page on our website (https://calvethomeloans.cdva.ca.gov/welcome.html), or obtain a prequalification form at http://www.cdva.ca.gov/calvet/prequal.asp , or at one of our District Offices.

CalVet is an authorized VA lender and can provide a VA guaranteed loan to eligible veterans. You must be eligible for the full VA loan guarantee entitlement. For applicants or properties that are not eligible for VA loans, the Department obtains private mortgage protection at a cost equivalent to the VA loan guarantee funding fee. All loans are retained for servicing by CalVet. Other features of your CalVet Home Loan include the following:

☞ **A competitive, below market interest rate.**

☞ Maximum loans up to **$521,250** for houses, condominiums and manufactured homes on land, and up to **$175,000** for manufactured homes in rental parks.

☞ A **1%** loan origination fee (collected in escrow)

☞ A **one-time** loan guarantee fee for all loans with down payments of less than 20% which may be paid by the seller or buyer. If the loan is a VA guaranteed loan the funding fee may be financed with the loan. If the loan is guaranteed by the Department's private mortgage protection, the guarantee fee can be financed if you make a minimum down payment of 5%of the purchase price.

☞ No down payment for VA guaranteed loans (CalVet/VA), and **3%** for loans using the private mortgage protection program (CalVet97). The loan term is 30 years with shorter terms available upon request.

C-13 (1/2006) Page 1 of 2

- All CalVet properties are covered by the Department's Disaster Indemnity program which provides **low cost** protection against loss due to floods and earthquakes.
- All applicants under age 62 are required to apply for mandatory life insurance, which provides 1 to 5 years (as determined by the insurance carrier) of principal and interest installments in the event of the death of the insured. Supplemental life insurance, disability coverage, and spousal life insurance are available if desired.
- Veterans may assign their interest in the CalVet property into joint tenancy with a legally married spouse or a registered domestic partner

Eligibility

Recent changes in the Military & Veterans Code have made most veterans eligible under state law, including those whose entire active service was during peacetime. Federal law restricts Qualified Veterans Mortgage Bond funds to veterans with wartime service who served prior to 1/1/1977 and apply within 30 years from their release from active duty. We currently have a limited amount of funds which are not subject to federal restrictions and are available to all veterans who meet the basic eligibility requirements of the California Military & Veterans Code.

- Applicants who were released or discharged from active duty under honorable conditions are eligible, as are applicants currently serving on active duty. (Active duty solely for training does not qualify). Applicants must have served at least 90 days on active duty, unless:
  - discharged sooner due to service-connected disability, **or**
  - eligible to receive a U.S. campaign or expeditionary medal, **or**
  - called to active duty from the Reserve or National Guard due to Presidential Order.

Current members of the California National Guard or the US Military Reserves who have served a minimum of one year of a six year obligation are also eligible provided they qualify for Qualified Mortgage Bond (QMB) funding which means they must be first time home buyers or purchase in a Targeted area, and comply with income and purchase price limits (please request a copy of Form L-10).

If your loan will be guaranteed by the USDVA you will be required to submit your VA Certificate of Eligibility (Form 26-8320). If you do not have the Certificate our District Offices can assist you in obtaining one.

For all eligibility questions, please call your local district office:

Bakersfield:	866.653.2507	**San Diego:**	866.653.2504
Fresno:	866.653.2511	**Redding:**	866.653.2508
Riverside:	800.700.2127	**Sacramento:**	866-653.2510

You may also reach the California Department of Veterans Affairs at:

Toll Free Automated Information Number: 800.952.5626

Internet Web Site: http://www.cdva.ca.gov

C-13 (1/2006) Page 2 of 2

CALVET LOAN APPLICATION INSTRUCTION SHEET

Thank you for your interest in the CalVet Loan Program. These instructions will assist you in completing your application. Staff in the local district office will be pleased to assist you further. Verification and documentation requirements vary for the different CalVet Home Loan programs. Please feel free to contact us if you have questions. ***Please note that whenever original documents are requested we will make certified copies and return your originals.***

Check when submitted ↓

1. **Fees**
   a) **Submit your non-refundable $50 APPLICATION FEE** in the form of a guaranteed or personal check made payable to the "Department of Veterans Affairs." ☐
   b) **Appraisal Fee** For existing properties, $400; for existing condominiums, $425; for proposed construction, $450. Please be prepared to pay appraiser directly with certified funds when contacted. If your loan will be VA Guaranteed, we will advise you when to remit payment directly to Cal-Vet.
   c) **A Loan Origination Fee of 1% of the basic loan, and a funding fee based on your down payment amount will be charged and collected at close of escrow. (See enclosed "C-14" form)**
   d) **A Loan Guarantee or Funding Fee** is charged on all loans with down payments of less than 20%. See the enclosed C-14 Form.

2. **Submit your completed UNIFORM RESIDENTIAL LOAN APPLICATION (Form 1003).** Note: PLEASE TYPE OR COMPLETE IN INK. Answer all questions completely. Mark questions that are not applicable "N/A." If you are married or have a registered domestic partner, they must also sign the loan application. This form may be completed and submitted on our website at www.cdva.ca.gov and then printed out for your signature. ☐

3. **Submit verification of all income sources listed on your application.** ☐
   a) Submit your most recent pay stub(s) covering at least one full month **(originals)**, plus your W-2s for the past two years, **OR**, if self employed, submit current year-to-date financial statements including a profit and loss statement and balance sheet, and copies of your federal income tax returns (1040 and Schedule C) for the past two years.
   b) Submit verification of other types of income; for example: a *current* copy of your Award Letter for retirement, VA compensation or Social Security, or *current* verification of alimony, child support, interest, or dividends.

4. **Submit original statements for the past two consecutive months** for all accounts holding funds for the down payment or closing costs. (Not required if your down payment is 20 % or more.) ☐

5. **Submit a legible copy of your NOTICE OF SEPARATION FROM ARMED FORCES (form "DD214").** If this form does not verify your Cal-Vet eligibility, we will request additional military documentation. Original documents will be returned to you after copies have been made. If you are still on active duty and have never received a "DD214," submit a Statement of Service signed by your commanding officer. ☐

6. **If you are applying for a VA Guaranteed loan with Cal-Vet submit your original VA Certificate of Eligibility (Form 26-8320).** If you do not have a Certificate of Eligibility issued by the United States Department of Veterans Affairs please complete the REQUEST FOR DETERMINATION OF ELIGIBILITY (VA Form 26-1880) included in this application package and submit it with your application. Note: Some veterans are not eligible for both Cal-Vet Loans and VA Loan Guaranties. In order to obtain a Cal-Vet Loan you must meet California veteran eligibility requirements. If you are eligible for Cal-Vet and not for a VA Loan Guaranty, Cal-Vet can still fund your loan. ☐

7. **Property Requirements**
   a) **Submit copies of the signed ESCROW INSTRUCTIONS AND SALES AGREEMENT,** and all **AMENDMENTS,** together with the **REAL ESTATE TRANSFER DISCLOSURE STATEMENT** covering the proposed transaction, executed by all parties. Include any addendums or counter offers. ☐
   b) **Submit two legible copies of a PRELIMINARY REPORT OF TITLE** *not more than three months old,* with a plat map covering the property.

8. **DESIGNATION OF AGENT AND GENERAL RELEASE (Form A-3).** This form is OPTIONAL. Submit it if you wish to have an agent act on your behalf and receive all loan correspondence during the processing of your loan. ☐

9. **Sign and return one copy of the FAIR LENDING NOTICE and WORD OF CAUTION (L-9), the BORROWER'S AUTHORIZATION (C-11-3) and VERIFICATION OF BORROWER'S NAME (V-11) Forms.** ☐

10. **Life & Disability Insurance -** All veteran applicants under the age of 62 must participate in the mandatory life insurance program and must complete and submit a medical history statement directly to The Standard Insurance Company. You may apply for optional supplemental life insurance and/or disability insurance, and your spouse or domestic partner may apply for life insurance. The application package will be provided to you at the time you submit your loan application. Additional information and the Medical History Statement are also available on our website. ☐

Page 1 of 2

☞ **THE FOLLOWING ITEMS MAY BE REQUESTED AFTER LOAN APPROVAL:**

11. **TERMITE REPORT**. If the dwelling you are purchasing is more than *one year old or has been previously occupied*, the department will require a termite report and clearance. The report must not be over *four months old.*

12. **ROOF INSPECTION REPORT**. A roof inspection completed by a licensed roofer may be required if *recommended by either the appraisal or the termite inspection report.*

13. **WELL/SEPTIC SYSTEM**. If the dwelling you are purchasing has private water and/or sewage disposal, you may be required to obtain an inspection verifying the adequacy of the systems.

14. **PERMITS/BUILDING CODE COMPLIANCE INSPECTION**. If the dwelling you are purchasing has had additions or substantial remodeling, the department may require copies of building permits or, in some cases, a code compliance inspection and clearance.

15. **SECONDARY FINANCING DOCUMENTS**. If the maximum CalVet loan is not adequate to purchase the property submitted, secondary financing may be permitted to assist in the purchase. The combined Cal-Vet loan and secondary financing must not exceed the appraised value of the property (as determined by the department). If secondary financing is used, you will be required to submit a copy of the Note and Deed of Trust, and CalVet's Subordination Agreement signed by the secondary lender.
NOTE: Cal-Vet will participate with most Community Housing down payment assistance programs.

16. **CONDOMINIUM/PLANNED UNIT DEVELOPMENT**. If you are purchasing this type of property and the Homeowners' Association of the condominium or planned unit development has not been previously approved by CalVet, you will be required to submit documents governing the development.

17. **MOBILE HOME OR MANUFACTURED HOME ON YOUR LAND**. If you are purchasing this type of property, you may be required to place the mobile home on a permanent foundation and furnish a copy of the recorded HCD Form 433a as evidence that this requirement has been completed. You must also obtain your own fire insurance coverage. Manufactured housing cannot be covered under CalVet's master policy. The home will be covered under the disaster program for flood and earthquake damage. You will be advised of the required amount of coverage after completion of the appraisal.

18. **MOBILE HOME IN A RENTAL PARK**. ***Maximum Loan Amount is $125,000.00. The interest rate will be 1% above the current CalVet rate.*** If you are purchasing this type of property, you will also be asked to:

    a) Submit, in writing, the name of the rental park, and the name and phone number of park manager.
    b) Submit a copy of the proposed rental agreement, space number and address, amount of monthly space rental, and map of the park.
    c) Advise whether the mobile home is used or new, and whether the mobile home is already in place on the space. If the mobile home is new, advise when it will be installed on the space.
    d) Submit a copy of the Sales Agreement (if a used mobile home), or a copy of the Purchase Order (if new).
    e) If a used mobile home, submit a Formal Title Search from the Department of Housing and Community Development (HCD).
    f) When the appraisal has been completed, submit a Certificate of Coverage verifying that the mobile home will be insured for the required amount. Also submit verification that a Loss Payable Endorsement, which names the Department of Veterans Affairs as the insured, will be provided in escrow when the loan is funded.
    g) If the mobile home you wish to purchase has had structural modifications, you may be required to provide evidence that the modifications were completed in accordance with appropriate building codes.
    h) Provide the name, address, and escrow number of the company handling your escrow. If the escrow company you have chosen is not approved to handle Cal-Vet transactions, your local Cal-Vet district office will advise you.

MINIMUM PROPERTY STANDARDS: All properties submitted for CalVet financing must comply with the Department's minimum property standards which are published on the CalVet Home Loans website at www.cdva.ca.gov. A copy is included in this loan application package. These standards are to protect you and the CalVet Home Loan program from conditions that may impact the utility and marketability of the property. Our goal is to assist you in purchasing a property that will be a home for you and your family and an investment in your future.

CalVet Home Loans and the Department of Veterans Affairs of the State of California do not warrant the condition, desirability, suitability, or actual value of the property you are purchasing, such determinations being entirely the responsibility of the purchaser. You are encouraged to inspect the property thoroughly, review the seller's/agent's disclosure statements, and obtain any inspection reports that you deem necessary.

APPEALS

Persons who disagree or are dissatisfied with actions taken or decisions made regarding their application may appeal to the Division Chief, Farm and Home Purchases Division, P. O. Box 942895, Sacramento, 94295-0001. If the problem is not resolved satisfactorily at that level, it may qualify for an appeal to the California Veterans Board. Further information regarding the appeal procedure is available upon request.

Page 2 of 2

A-1T (8/2005)

Loan Processing Cycle

Step 1 Loan application (URLA Form 1003 including those submitted on the CalVet Home Loans website) is received in CalVet office and is reviewed for completeness. At a minimum, applications must specify a property to be purchased and a loan amount requested, and must include sufficient information to confirm military eligibility to be considered valid. Please review the *CalVet Loan Application Instruction Sheet* for required documents. Processing may be delayed if necessary information is not provided.

Step 2 After an initial review of your eligibility, credit, and income qualification you will be advised of any additional items or documentation needed. In most cases processing of your loan will continue, however you should act promptly to submit requested items. Note: Loan processing is performed both in our field offices and Sacramento Headquarters. We will advise you of where your loan is being processed and who to contact if you have questions.

Step 3 When your CalVet eligibility, credit worthiness, and financial qualification have been established the appraisal will be ordered. You will receive a commitment letter advising you that the loan has been approved subject to receipt and review of the appraisal and any other outstanding requirements.

Step 4 Upon receipt of the appraisal you will receive a loan approval letter listing any property requirements that must be completed before the loan can be funded. In some cases items will be required prior to issuing loan documents to your escrow.

Step 5 Your application package will be forwarded to the CalVet Escrow Unit who will prepare loan documents and instructions for the private escrow holder you have chosen.

Step 6 You will be contacted by your escrow holder to sign the CalVet Contract and complete any final purchase requirements.

Step 7 The escrow holder will return the completed loan documents to CalVet and funds will be issued to close the loan.

Step 8 Your first CalVet Loan payment will be due on the first of the month occurring 30 days after closing (for example, if you loan closes on May 15, your first payment would be due on July 1).

How do I find out the status of my loan? We will try to keep you advised of your status throughout the processing, however, you can call the CalVet District Office or the Headquarters Loan Processing Unit any time if you have questions. If you provide us with your email address at the time you apply, you will receive automated notices any time the status of your application changes. If you applied on line, you can log in to check loan status at any time, day or night. If you did not apply on line, we can still set you up with access. Just contact the field office where you submitted your application. Your Real Estate Agent or Mortgage Broker can obtain this access and the automated email notification as well.

A-2 (6/2004)

IMPORTANT NOTICE

Loan Guaranty: In order to protect the program from losses should any loan go into default, and to insure that the CalVet Home Loan continues to offer the best possible value to the veterans of our state, the California Department of Veterans Affairs obtains mortgage protection coverage on all loans when the down payment is less than 20% of the purchase price. When the applicant and property are eligible and have their full entitlement remaining, the loan guaranty provided by the United States Department of Veterans Affairs (USDVA) is obtained. In all other cases the Department obtains private mortgage protection. Adding this protection to the CalVet Loan made it possible for us to reduce the cost of the funds that we use, and thereby reduce the interest rate that we charge.

The cost of the VA Guaranty is 1.25 to 3.35% of the amount of the loan and may be paid by the seller or the veteran applicant at close of escrow, or it may be financed as part of the loan. The cost of the private mortgage insurance is 0.63 to 1.38% of the loan amount, and may also be paid by either the buyer or seller, but must be paid at close of escrow and cannot be added to the loan. Both the VA Guaranty and the private mortgage insurance are one-time fees. They do not increase your monthly installment. Form C-14 in this package has additional information and must be completed to indicate how the fee will be paid.

Interest Rate: It is important for applicants to realize that the CalVet loan is not technically a fixed interest rate loan. You will be advised of the rate on your loan shortly after your application is received. **The CalVet Contract you sign will indicate that the rate may be increased during the loan term by a maximum of one-half of one percent (0.5%).** This feature of the loan has been retained in order to enhance the rating received on the bonds sold to fund CalVet loans and thereby make lower interest rates possible. Please inquire further if you are not clear on this important point.

C-4 (1/2007)

SPECIAL NOTICE REGARDING YOUR CALVET LOAN APPLICATION

CalVet loans are funded at no cost to California taxpayers with proceeds from the sale of bonds which are exempt from both state and federal taxes. Because of this method of financing, the program is subject to both state and federal laws.

Except in certain limited circumstances, CalVet is prohibited from refinancing existing loans on real property. Federal regulations prohibit refinancing except for "construction period loans, bridge loans, or similar temporary initial financing." The regulations define temporary initial financing as "any financing which has a term of twenty-four months or less." The 24 months commences with the date stated on the note and deed of trust and ends with the date the loan is due and payable in full. There must be no provisions for extension or renewal. A construction period loan should have as short a term as possible which is reasonably consistent with the anticipated construction period, and should not be converted to an interim loan with a term in excess of 24 months.

- **You must file your CalVet loan application before acquiring an interest of record in the property you wish to purchase with CalVet funds.**
- **If you intend to obtain temporary financing, show this notice to your lender to assure that your loan complies with all state and federal regulations. If you are uncertain about whether or not your interim or construction financing complies with these restrictions contact CalVet before proceeding.**

CalVet cannot and will not refinance an existing loan which does not comply with these regulations.

INFORMATION PRIVACY

The California Information Practices Act of 1977 requires that all applicants be informed of the purposes and uses to be made of information solicited. The following is furnished to explain the reasons why information is requested and the general uses to which that information may be put.

AUTHORITY: The California Department of Veterans Affairs is authorized to request information under the authority of the Military and Veterans Code of the State of California, particularly Section 987.56.

PURPOSE: The information requested is considered relevant and necessary to determine entitlement to and qualification for the benefit for which you are applying.

USES: The information will be used in your best interest in determining eligibility for the maximum benefits allowable by law. There is presently no known or foreseeable interagency or intergovernmental transfer which may be made of the information. However, the information may be transferred to a governmental entity when required by state or federal law, and certain other disclosures or transfers may be made as permitted by Section 1798.24 of the California Civil Code.

EFFECTS OF NOT PROVIDING INFORMATION: Disclosure of the information is voluntary. No penalty will be imposed for failure to respond. However, your qualifications for the benefit requested must be made on the basis of the available evidence of record. This may result in a delay in the processing of the application, receipt of less than the maximum benefit, or deferral or complete disallowance of your loan request. Failure to provide information in connection with the benefit currently being sought will have no detrimental effect on any other benefit to which you are entitled.

RIGHT OF REVIEW: Individuals have the right of access to records containing personal information on them at all times during regular office hours of the department.

DEPARTMENT OFFICIAL RESPONSIBLE FOR INFORMATION MAINTENANCE: CalVet Headquarters Operations Manager

L-8 (6/2004)

To learn more about the Life and Disability coverages offered with your home loan, please contact the Cal-Vet Home Loans call center at 800.952.5626 or Standard Insurance Company's information line at 866.825.5796 or talk to your Cal-Vet Home Loans Field Office Representative.

Is Your Investment Protected?

Life and Disability Mortgage Protection Insurance

While the need for homeowners insurance is widely recognized, it's equally important to plan how to cover mortgage payments in the event of death or disability. Consider the following:

- Four out of 10 Americans report their household does not have enough life insurance.[1]
- At age 35, there's a 50 percent chance of becoming unable to work for more than three months due to a disability before age 65.[2]

To best meet your needs for mortgage protection, Cal-Vet Home Loans offers a wide range of Life and Disability insurance coverage through Standard Insurance Company. Depending upon your age and loan origination date, Regular Life and Disability insurance coverages may be mandatory, with a number of other coverage options also available to you.

Features and Advantages

- Disability insurance provides financial protection to help cover monthly mortgage payments in the event of disability, while Life insurance provides coverage to pay off all or a portion of your mortgage.
- The Standard's plan offers a wide range of coverage options, including Spouse Life coverage to pay off the mortgage in the event of the death of the spouse.
- With coverage from The Standard, you have the peace of mind knowing you're insured with a financially sound and nationally recognized industry leader.
- The Standard offers an easy application process, generally requiring the completion of only one form.
- From the application process through the payment of any claims, both Cal-Vet Home Loans and The Standard are committed to providing you with superior customer service.

Once you complete and submit your application to the Loan Processing Unit at Cal-Vet Home Loans, you will receive a booklet containing additional information about the plans, eligibility, coverage options and rates. We will also provide an enrollment form for you to designate which plans best meet your financial needs. Cal-Vet Home Loans and Standard Insurance Company representatives are available to answer any questions you may have about the plans.

[1] Trends in Life Insurance ownership, LIMRA International, 1999
[2] Society of Actuaries, as referenced in *Money*, April 2000

Cal-Vet Home Loans

www.cdva.ca.gov

SIC **11222** (1/03)

The California Department of Veterans Affairs currently has offices in the locations listed below. It is suggested that you call the nearest office to confirm office hours before visiting. Any of our offices will be pleased to answer your questions and provide loan application materials. All numbers listed are toll free.

Fresno: **866.653.2511**
1752 E. Bullard Ave., Suite 101
93710 **Fresno@cdva.ca.gov**

Bakersfield: **866-653-2507**
5500 Ming Avenue, Suite 155
93309 **Bakersfield@cdva.ca.gov**

Redding: **866-653-2508**
1900 Churn Creek Rd., Suite 221
96002 **Redding@cdva.ca.gov**

Sacramento: **866-653-2510**
1227 O Street
95814 **Sacramento@cdva.ca.gov**

San Diego: **866.653.2504**
1350 Front Street, Room 2023
92101 **SanDiego@cdva.ca.gov**

Riverside: **800.700.2127**
1770 Iowa Avenue, Suite 260
92507 **Riverside@cdva.ca.gov**

You may also reach the California Department of Veterans Affairs at:

California Department of Veterans Affairs
P.O. Box 942895
Sacramento, CA 94295-0001

Toll Free Information Number: 800.952.5626

Internet Web Site: www.cdva.ca.gov
General Information Email address: loanserv@.cdva.ca.gov

ADDRESS LIST (3/2007)

Figure 17-2

CALVET HOME LOAN APPLICATION PACKAGE

This package contains forms and instructions for obtaining a CalVet Home Loan. If you are planning to build a new home on property that you currently own or intend to purchase, you will also need to download the Construction Loan Supplemental Package of forms and instructions.

Before you begin:

You must have a property selected before applying for your loan. We suggest that you carefully review the material on the CalVet Home Loan Program on our web site. If you have questions feel free to e-mail us at loanserv@cdva.ca.gov or contact the nearest CalVet District Office. A list of CalVet District Offices and the areas they cover with complete contact information including direct e-mail address for each office is available on our website at http://www.cdva.ca.gov/CalVetLoans/Offices2.aspx.

Optional, but highly recommended: Prequalify for your loan using the **Apply Online** feature on our website. Answering a few questions about your military service, current income, and monthly obligations will confirm your eligibility and give you an estimate of the amount of loan you can qualify for. You can also prequalify by downloading and completing the Prequalification Form available at http://www.cdva.ca.gov/CalVetLoans/prequal.pdf. Send the completed form to the CalVet District Office for the area where you plan to buy your home. Keep in mind that prequalification is not the same as loan approval, which generally requires verification of your income and a review of your credit history. If you have concerns about either of these issues please contact us to discuss them.

Apply online CALVET HOME LOANS

CalVet uses the Universal Residential Loan Application (URLA), which is also known as FannieMae Form 1003 or FreddieMac Form 65. You can complete and submit this form on our website by clicking on the **Apply Online** button. First complete the Eligibility and Prequalification screens and then proceed to the Loan Application. After you complete and submit the application form, complete the remaining forms in this package and mail them to the CalVet office nearest your property. If you prefer you may obtain an application form from one of our district offices and fill it out by hand.

The first group of forms listed below contain information about CalVet Home Loans and the application process. Please review the information and contact us if you have any questions.

- Form C-13: Thank You for Choosing CalVet - These pages summarize the features and eligibility requirements of the CalVet Home Loan Program.
- Loan Terms - This document contains the current loan terms, fees and interest rates.
- Form A-1T: CalVet Home Loan Application Instruction Sheet - These instructions explain how to submit the application forms in this package and what additional information you will need to send to CalVet.
- Form A-2: CalVet Home Loan Processing Cycle - This chart explains how CalVet processes a home loan application.
- Form C-4: Important Notice - This document provides information about recent changes in the CalVet Home Loan program concerning Loan Guarantees and Loan Processing.
- Form L-8: Special Notice Regarding your CalVet Home Loan Application - This notice explains Internal Revenue Service limitations placed on funds used for CalVet Home Loans for refinancing a home loan. It also contains the notice required by the California Information Practices Act of 1977 concerning how CalVet may use the information that you submit to us.

A-1C (1/2007) Page 1of 2

CALVET HOME LOAN APPLICATION PACKAGE

- Address List - This document contains a list of CalVet offices throughout the state along with addresses and telephone numbers.

The forms listed below must be completed and submitted with your application. If you apply online please mail these forms to the CalVet District Office responsible for your application.

- ❑ Fannie Mae Form 1003 7/05 – This is the Uniform Residential Loan Application used by most lenders to collect the information necessary for loan processing.
- ❑ Form C-14: CalVet Home Loan Origination Fee/Funding Fee - This form allows the applicant to notify CalVet concerning their choices for payment of the Loan Origination Fee and CDVA/USDVA Funding Fee.
- ❑ Form C-11-3 / V-11: Borrower's Authorization / Verification of Borrower(s) Name(s) - This form is used to authorize CalVet to obtain verifications of your income, employment, assets, and other credit matters and to verify the exact legal name(s) of the loan applicant or applicants.
- ❑ Form L-9: Fair Lending Notice - This notice explains your rights under the Housing Financial Discrimination Act of 1977. Sign this form to show that you have read and understood it and return it with your loan application.
- ❑ Buyer's Information - This form provides us with basic information about you and the property you are purchasing that is not included on the application form.

The following forms are optional:

- ❑ Form A-3: Designation of Agent and General Release - You may designate another person to act as your agent in connection with the processing of your CalVet Home Loan application. The use of this form is completely optional.
- ❑ Real Estate Agent Internet Access Registration - Complete this form with the assistance of your Real Estate Agent if you want your agent to be able to monitor loan processing status on line and receive email notifications when the status changes.

Also available on our website:

- ❑ Minimum Property Standards – This document summarizes the standards that properties purchased with a CalVet Home Loan must meet. If you have questions about these requirements or about whether or not the property you are considering will qualify please contact one of our CalVet District Offices. The document is on our website at http://www.cdva.ca.gov/CalVetLoans/MPS.aspx and is also available in our District Offices.

A-1C (1/2007) Page 2 of 2

Uniform Residential Loan Application

This application is designed to be completed by the applicant(s) with the Lender's assistance. Applicants should complete this form as "Borrower" or "Co-Borrower," as applicable. Co-Borrower information must also be provided (and the appropriate box checked) when ☐ the income or assets of a person other than the Borrower (including the Borrower's spouse) will be used as a basis for loan qualification or ☐ the income or assets of the Borrower's spouse or other person who has community property rights pursuant to state law will not be used as a basis for loan qualification, but his or her liabilities must be considered because the spouse or other person has community property rights pursuant to applicable law and Borrower resides in a community property state, the security property is located in a community property state, or the Borrower is relying on other property located in a community property state as a basis for repayment of the loan.

If this is an application for joint credit, Borrower and Co-Borrower each agree that we intend to apply for joint credit (sign below):

Borrower ____________________ Co-Borrower ____________________

I. TYPE OF MORTGAGE AND TERMS OF LOAN

Mortgage Applied for:	☐ VA ☐ FHA	☐ Conventional ☐ USDA/Rural Housing Service	☐ Other (explain):	Agency Case Number	Lender Case Number
Amount $	Interest Rate %	No. of Months	**Amortization Type:**	☐ Fixed Rate ☐ GPM	☐ Other (explain): ☐ ARM (type):

II. PROPERTY INFORMATION AND PURPOSE OF LOAN

Subject Property Address (street, city, state & ZIP)	No. of Units
Legal Description of Subject Property (attach description if necessary)	Year Built

Purpose of Loan	☐ Purchase ☐ Refinance	☐ Construction ☐ Construction-Permanent	☐ Other (explain):	Property will be: ☐ Primary Residence	☐ Secondary Residence	☐ Investment

Complete this line if construction or construction-permanent loan.

Year Lot Acquired	Original Cost	Amount Existing Liens	(a) Present Value of Lot	(b) Cost of Improvements	Total (a + b)
	$	$	$	$	$

Complete this line if this is a refinance loan.

Year Acquired	Original Cost	Amount Existing Liens	Purpose of Refinance	Describe Improvements ☐ made ☐ to be made
	$	$		Cost: $

Title will be held in what Name(s)	Manner in which Title will be held	Estate will be held in: ☐ Fee Simple ☐ Leasehold (show expiration date)
Source of Down Payment, Settlement Charges, and/or Subordinate Financing (explain)		

III. BORROWER INFORMATION

Borrower				Co-Borrower			
Borrower's Name (include Jr. or Sr. if applicable)				Co-Borrower's Name (include Jr. or Sr. if applicable)			
Social Security Number	Home Phone (incl. area code)	DOB (mm/dd/yyyy)	Yrs. School	Social Security Number	Home Phone (incl. area code)	DOB (mm/dd/yyyy)	Yrs. School
☐ Married ☐ Unmarried (include single, divorced, widowed) ☐ Separated	Dependents (not listed by Co-Borrower) no.	ages		☐ Married ☐ Unmarried (include single, divorced, widowed) ☐ Separated	Dependents (not listed by Borrower) no.	ages	
Present Address (street, city, state, ZIP)	☐ Own	☐ Rent ____No. Yrs.		Present Address (street, city, state, ZIP)	☐ Own	☐ Rent ____No. Yrs.	
Mailing Address, if different from Present Address				Mailing Address, if different from Present Address			

If residing at present address for less than two years, complete the following:

Former Address (street, city, state, ZIP)	☐ Own	☐ Rent ____No. Yrs.	Former Address (street, city, state, ZIP)	☐ Own	☐ Rent ____No. Yrs.

IV. EMPLOYMENT INFORMATION

Borrower			Co-Borrower		
Name & Address of Employer	☐ Self Employed	Yrs. on this job Yrs. employed in this line of work/profession	Name & Address of Employer	☐ Self Employed	Yrs. on this job Yrs. employed in this line of work/profession
Position/Title/Type of Business	Business Phone (incl. area code)		Position/Title/Type of Business	Business Phone (incl. area code)	

If employed in current position for less than two years or if currently employed in more than one position, complete the following:

Uniform Residential Loan Application
Freddie Mac Form 65 7/05 (rev.6/09) **Page 1 of 5** **Fannie Mae Form 1003 7/05 (rev.6/09)**

Borrower		IV. EMPLOYMENT INFORMATION (cont'd)		Co-Borrower	
Name & Address of Employer	☐ Self Employed	Dates (from – to) Monthly Income $	Name & Address of Employer	☐ Self Employed	Dates (from – to) Monthly Income $
Position/Title/Type of Business	Business Phone (incl. area code)		Position/Title/Type of Business	Business Phone (incl. area code)	
Name & Address of Employer	☐ Self Employed	Dates (from – to) Monthly Income $	Name & Address of Employer	☐ Self Employed	Dates (from – to) Monthly Income $
Position/Title/Type of Business	Business Phone (incl. area code)		Position/Title/Type of Business	Business Phone (incl. area code)	

V. MONTHLY INCOME AND COMBINED HOUSING EXPENSE INFORMATION

Gross Monthly Income	Borrower	Co-Borrower	Total	Combined Monthly Housing Expense	Present	Proposed
Base Empl. Income*	$	$	$	Rent	$	
Overtime				First Mortgage (P&I)		$
Bonuses				Other Financing (P&I)		
Commissions				Hazard Insurance		
Dividends/Interest				Real Estate Taxes		
Net Rental Income				Mortgage Insurance		
Other (before completing, see the notice in "describe other income," below)				Homeowner Assn. Dues		
				Other:		
Total	$	$	$	**Total**	$	$

* **Self Employed Borrower(s) may be required to provide additional documentation such as tax returns and financial statements.**

Describe Other Income *Notice:* **Alimony, child support, or separate maintenance income need not be revealed if the Borrower (B) or Co-Borrower (C) does not choose to have it considered for repaying this loan.**

B/C		Monthly Amount
		$

VI. ASSETS AND LIABILITIES

This Statement and any applicable supporting schedules may be completed jointly by both married and unmarried Co-Borrowers if their assets and liabilities are sufficiently joined so that the Statement can be meaningfully and fairly presented on a combined basis; otherwise, separate Statements and Schedules are required. If the Co-Borrower section was completed about a non-applicant spouse or other person, this Statement and supporting schedules must be completed about that spouse or other person also.

Completed ☐ Jointly ☐ Not Jointly

ASSETS Description	Cash or Market Value
Cash deposit toward purchase held by:	$
List checking and savings accounts below	
Name and address of Bank, S&L, or Credit Union	
Acct. no.	$
Name and address of Bank, S&L, or Credit Union	
Acct. no.	$
Name and address of Bank, S&L, or Credit Union	
Acct. no.	$

Liabilities and Pledged Assets. List the creditor's name, address, and account number for all outstanding debts, including automobile loans, revolving charge accounts, real estate loans, alimony, child support, stock pledges, etc. Use continuation sheet, if necessary. Indicate by (*) those liabilities, which will be satisfied upon sale of real estate owned or upon refinancing of the subject property.

LIABILITIES	Monthly Payment & Months Left to Pay	Unpaid Balance
Name and address of Company Acct. no.	$ Payment/Months	$
Name and address of Company Acct. no.	$ Payment/Months	$
Name and address of Company Acct. no.	$ Payment/Months	$

VI. ASSETS AND LIABILITIES (cont'd)

Assets		Liabilities		
Name and address of Bank, S&L, or Credit Union		Name and address of Company	$ Payment/Months	$
Acct. no.	$	Acct. no.		
Stocks & Bonds (Company name/ number & description)	$	Name and address of Company	$ Payment/Months	$
		Acct. no.		
Life insurance net cash value Face amount: $	$	Name and address of Company	$ Payment/Months	$
Subtotal Liquid Assets	$			
Real estate owned (enter market value from schedule of real estate owned)	$			
Vested interest in retirement fund	$			
Net worth of business(es) owned (attach financial statement)	$	Acct. no.		
Automobiles owned (make and year)	$	Alimony/Child Support/Separate Maintenance Payments Owed to:	$	
Other Assets (itemize)	$	Job-Related Expense (child care, union dues, etc.)	$	
		Total Monthly Payments	$	
Total Assets a.	$	Net Worth (a minus b) ▶ $	**Total Liabilities b.**	$

Schedule of Real Estate Owned (If additional properties are owned, use continuation sheet.)

Property Address (enter S if sold, PS if pending sale or R if rental being held for income) ▼		Type of Property	Present Market Value	Amount of Mortgages & Liens	Gross Rental Income	Mortgage Payments	Insurance, Maintenance, Taxes & Misc.	Net Rental Income
			$	$	$	$	$	$
		Totals	$	$	$	$	$	$

List any additional names under which credit has previously been received and indicate appropriate creditor name(s) and account number(s):

Alternate Name	Creditor Name	Account Number

VII. DETAILS OF TRANSACTION

a.	Purchase price	$
b.	Alterations, improvements, repairs	
c.	Land (if acquired separately)	
d.	Refinance (incl. debts to be paid off)	
e.	Estimated prepaid items	
f.	Estimated closing costs	
g.	PMI, MIP, Funding Fee	
h.	Discount (if Borrower will pay)	
i.	Total costs (add items a through h)	

VIII. DECLARATIONS

If you answer "Yes" to any questions a through i, please use continuation sheet for explanation.	Borrower Yes	Borrower No	Co-Borrower Yes	Co-Borrower No
a. Are there any outstanding judgments against you?	☐	☐	☐	☐
b. Have you been declared bankrupt within the past 7 years?	☐	☐	☐	☐
c. Have you had property foreclosed upon or given title or deed in lieu thereof in the last 7 years?	☐	☐	☐	☐
d. Are you a party to a lawsuit?	☐	☐	☐	☐
e. Have you directly or indirectly been obligated on any loan which resulted in foreclosure, transfer of title in lieu of foreclosure, or judgment? (This would include such loans as home mortgage loans, SBA loans, home improvement loans, educational loans, manufactured (mobile) home loans, any mortgage, financial obligation, bond, or loan guarantee. If "Yes," provide details, including date, name, and address of Lender, FHA or VA case number, if any, and reasons for the action.)	☐	☐	☐	☐

Uniform Residential Loan Application
Freddie Mac Form 65 7/05 (rev.6/09) **Page 3 of 5** **Fannie Mae Form 1003 7/05 (rev.6/09)**

VII. DETAILS OF TRANSACTION		
j.	Subordinate financing	
k.	Borrower's closing costs paid by Seller	
l.	Other Credits (explain)	
m.	Loan amount (exclude PMI, MIP, Funding Fee financed)	
n.	PMI, MIP, Funding Fee financed	
o.	Loan amount (add m & n)	
p.	Cash from/to Borrower (subtract j, k, l & o from i)	

VIII. DECLARATIONS	Borrower Yes	Borrower No	Co-Borrower Yes	Co-Borrower No
If you answer "Yes" to any questions a through i, please use continuation sheet for explanation.				
f. Are you presently delinquent or in default on any Federal debt or any other loan, mortgage, financial obligation, bond, or loan guarantee?	☐	☐	☐	☐
g. Are you obligated to pay alimony, child support, or separate maintenance?	☐	☐	☐	☐
h. Is any part of the down payment borrowed?	☐	☐	☐	☐
i. Are you a co-maker or endorser on a note?	☐	☐	☐	☐
j. Are you a U.S. citizen?	☐	☐	☐	☐
k. Are you a permanent resident alien?	☐	☐	☐	☐
l. **Do you intend to occupy the property as your primary residence?** If Yes," complete question m below.	☐	☐	☐	☐
m. Have you had an ownership interest in a property in the last three years?	☐	☐	☐	☐
(1) What type of property did you own—principal residence (PR), second home (SH), or investment property (IP)?	______		______	
(2) How did you hold title to the home— by yourself (S), jointly with your spouse (SP), or jointly with another person (O)?	______		______	

IX. ACKNOWLEDGEMENT AND AGREEMENT

Each of the undersigned specifically represents to Lender and to Lender's actual or potential agents, brokers, processors, attorneys, insurers, servicers, successors and assigns and agrees and acknowledges that: (1) the information provided in this application is true and correct as of the date set forth opposite my signature and that any intentional or negligent misrepresentation of this information contained in this application may result in civil liability, including monetary damages, to any person who may suffer any loss due to reliance upon any misrepresentation that I have made on this application, and/or in criminal penalties including, but not limited to, fine or imprisonment or both under the provisions of Title 18, United States Code, Sec. 1001, et seq.; (2) the loan requested pursuant to this application (the "Loan") will be secured by a mortgage or deed of trust on the property described in this application; (3) the property will not be used for any illegal or prohibited purpose or use; (4) all statements made in this application are made for the purpose of obtaining a residential mortgage loan; (5) the property will be occupied as indicated in this application; (6) the Lender, its servicers, successors or assigns may retain the original and/or an electronic record of this application, whether or not the Loan is approved; (7) the Lender and its agents, brokers, insurers, servicers, successors, and assigns may continuously rely on the information contained in the application, and I am obligated to amend and/or supplement the information provided in this application if any of the material facts that I have represented herein should change prior to closing of the Loan; (8) in the event that my payments on the Loan become delinquent, the Lender, its servicers, successors or assigns may, in addition to any other rights and remedies that it may have relating to such delinquency, report my name and account information to one or more consumer reporting agencies; (9) ownership of the Loan and/or administration of the Loan account may be transferred with such notice as may be required by law; (10) neither Lender nor its agents, brokers, insurers, servicers, successors or assigns has made any representation or warranty, express or implied, to me regarding the property or the condition or value of the property; and (11) my transmission of this application as an "electronic record" containing my "electronic signature," as those terms are defined in applicable federal and/or state laws (excluding audio and video recordings), or my facsimile transmission of this application containing a facsimile of my signature, shall be as effective, enforceable and valid as if a paper version of this application were delivered containing my original written signature.

Acknowledgement. Each of the undersigned hereby acknowledges that any owner of the Loan, its servicers, successors and assigns, may verify or reverify any information contained in this application or obtain any information or data relating to the Loan, for any legitimate business purpose through any source, including a source named in this application or a consumer reporting agency.

Borrower's Signature X	Date	Co-Borrower's Signature X	Date

X. INFORMATION FOR GOVERNMENT MONITORING PURPOSES

The following information is requested by the Federal Government for certain types of loans related to a dwelling in order to monitor the lender's compliance with equal credit opportunity, fair housing and home mortgage disclosure laws. You are not required to furnish this information, but are encouraged to do so. The law provides that a lender may not discriminate either on the basis of this information, or on whether you choose to furnish it. If you furnish the information, please provide both ethnicity and race. For race, you may check more than one designation. If you do not furnish ethnicity, race, or sex, under Federal regulations, this lender is required to note the information on the basis of visual observation and surname if you have made this application in person. If you do not wish to furnish the information, please check the box below. (Lender must review the above material to assure that the disclosures satisfy all requirements to which the lender is subject under applicable state law for the particular type of loan applied for.)

BORROWER ☐ I do not wish to furnish this information	CO-BORROWER ☐ I do not wish to furnish this information
Ethnicity: ☐ Hispanic or Latino ☐ Not Hispanic or Latino	**Ethnicity:** ☐ Hispanic or Latino ☐ Not Hispanic or Latino
Race: ☐ American Indian or Alaska Native ☐ Asian ☐ Black or African American ☐ Native Hawaiian or Other Pacific Islander ☐ White	**Race:** ☐ American Indian or Alaska Native ☐ Asian ☐ Black or African American ☐ Native Hawaiian or Other Pacific Islander ☐ White
Sex: ☐ Female ☐ Male	**Sex:** ☐ Female ☐ Male

To be Completed by Loan Originator:
This information was provided:
- ☐ In a face-to-face interview
- ☐ In a telephone interview
- ☐ By the applicant and submitted by fax or mail
- ☐ By the applicant and submitted via e-mail or the Internet

Loan Originator's Signature X		Date
Loan Originator's Name (print or type)	Loan Originator Identifier	Loan Originator's Phone Number (including area code)
Loan Origination Company's Name	Loan Origination Company Identifier	Loan Origination Company's Address

Uniform Residential Loan Application
Freddie Mac Form 65 7/05 (rev.6/09) Page 4 of 5 Fannie Mae Form 1003 7/05 (rev.6/09)

CONTINUATION SHEET/RESIDENTIAL LOAN APPLICATION		
Use this continuation sheet if you need more space to complete the Residential Loan Application. Mark B f or Borrower or C for Co-Borrower.	Borrower:	Agency Case Number:
	Co-Borrower:	Lender Case Number:

I/We fully understand that it is a Federal crime punishable by fine or imprisonment, or both, to knowingly make any false statements concerning any of the above facts as applicable under the provisions of Title 18, United States Code, Section 1001, et seq.

Borrower's Signature	Date	Co-Borrower's Signature	Date
X		X	

Uniform Residential Loan Application
Freddie Mac Form 65 7/05 (rev.6/09) Page 5 of 5 Fannie Mae Form 1003 7/05 (rev.6/09)

HOME LOANS

Interest Rate / Loan Origination Fee / Funding Fee

All CALVET Applicants – Please complete and sign the following statement:

I understand that CALVET has multiple interest rates, and that the rate on my loan will be "locked in" at the interest rate in effect for the funding source that I qualify for as of the date my application is received. If the interest rate is reduced during loan processing prior to funding of my loan, I will receive the benefit of the reduced rate. **I also understand that the CALVET interest rate is a variable rate that can be increased by no more than one half of one percent (0.5%) over the term of the loan.** I further understand that a 1% Loan Origination Fee will be charged and I will be charged a funding fee. **I intend to pay these fees as follows:**

Application Fee - $50 Must be submitted with application. This fee will be credited to the Loan Origination Fee at close of escrow. (Exception: not required for loans submitted through a CALVET certified mortgage broker)

Loan Origination Fee of 1% (of base loan amount) to be:
(If the application is submitted through a Mortgage Broker certified by CALVET this fee will be paid to the broker.)

☐ Paid in escrow by me
☐ Paid in escrow by seller*

Funding Fee (see table) to be:

☐ Paid in escrow by me
☐ Paid in escrow by seller*
☐ Added to my loan (**CalVet/VA only**)

Down payment	Funding Fee ▶	
	CALVET/VA	CalVet
20% or more	1.25%	1.25%
15 – 19%	1.25%	1.25%
11 – 14%	1.25%	1.25%
5 – 10%	1.50%	1.50%
3 – 4%	2.15%**	2.15%
0%	2.15%**	2.15%

The funding fee for VA loans is waived for veterans who have a service connected disability of 10% or greater and for un-remarried spouses of veterans whose **death, either while on active duty or after release from active duty, is determined to be service connected.** **For veterans who have previously used their VA or CalVet guarantee entitlement, the funding fee is increased to 3.30% for subsequent guarantees.

This fee is a percentage of the loan amount and will be used by CDVA to purchase a loan guarantee from VA. **This is a one time charge and does not affect your interest rate or monthly payment (unless you choose to finance the fee with your loan.)**

Veteran Applicant: ______________________ **Date:** ____________

Seller: ______________________ **Date:** ____________

*Seller must sign if you are indicating above that fees will be paid by the seller.

C-14 (2/19/2009)

OMB Control No. 2900-0086
Respondent Burden: 15 minutes

Department of Veterans Affairs

REQUEST FOR A CERTIFICATE OF ELIGIBILITY

FOR VA USE ONLY
COE REF. NO.

MAIL COMPLETED APPLICATION TO:
Atlanta Regional Loan Center
Attn: COE (262)
P. O. Box 100034
Decatur, GA 30031

NOTE: Please read information on reverse before completing this form. If additional space is required, attach a separate sheet.

1. NAME OF VETERAN *(First, Middle, Last)*
2. DATE OF BIRTH
3. SOCIAL SECURITY NUMBER

4A. DID YOU SERVE UNDER ANOTHER NAME? ☐ YES ☐ NO *(If "Yes," complete Item 4B)*
4B. NAME(S) USED DURING MILITARY SERVICE *(If different from name in Item 1)*

5. DAYTIME TELEPHONE NUMBER
6. E-MAIL ADDRESS *(If applicable)*

7A. ADDRESS *(Number and street or rural route, city or P.O., State and ZIP Code)*
7B. MAIL CERTIFICATE OF ELIGIBILITY TO: *(Complete ONLY if the Certificate is to be mailed to an address different from the one listed in Item 7A.)*

8A. WERE YOU DISCHARGED, RETIRED, OR SEPARATED FROM SERVICE BECAUSE OF DISABILITY? ☐ YES ☐ NO
8B. VA CLAIM NUMBER *(If known)*

MILITARY SERVICE (SEE INSTRUCTIONS FOR PROOF OF SERVICE ON THE NEXT PAGE)

9A. ARE YOU CURRENTLY ON ACTIVE DUTY? *(If you currently serving on active duty, leave the "Date Separated" field blank.)* ☐ YES ☐ NO

IMPORTANT: Please provide your dates of service. In many cases eligibility can be established based on data in VA systems. However, it is recommended that proof of service be provided, if readily available. Proof of service is required for persons who entered service after September 7, 1980 and were discharged after serving less than 2 years.	BRANCH OF SERVICE	DATE ENTERED	DATE SEPARATED	OFFICER OR ENLISTED	SERVICE NUMBER *(if different from Social Security Number)*
9B. ACTIVE SERVICE - ***Do not** include any periods of Active Duty for Training or Active Guard Reserve service. **Do** include any activation for duty under Title 10 U.S.C. (e.g. Reserve or Guard unit mobilized.)*					
9C. RESERVE OR NATIONAL GUARD SERVICE *Include any periods of Active Duty for Training (ADT) or Active Guard Reserve service. **Do not** include any activation for duty under Title 10 U.S.C. (e.g. Reserve or Guard unit mobilized.)*					

PREVIOUS VA LOANS (SEE INSTRUCTIONS ON THE NEXT PAGE - Attach a separate sheet if information for all homes will not fit in Item 10)

10A. DO YOU NOW OWN ANY HOME(S) PURCHASED OR REFINANCED WITH A VA-GUARANTEED LOAN? ☐ YES *(If "Yes," complete Items 10B through 10D)* ☐ NO *(If "No," skip to Item 14)* ☐ NOT APPLICABLE (NA) - I HAVE NEVER OBTAINED A VA-GUARANTEED HOME LOAN *(If "NA," skip to Item 14)*	10B. DATE OF LOAN *(Month and Year)*	10C. STREET ADDRESS	10D. CITY AND STATE
11A. ARE YOU APPLYING FOR THE **ONE-TIME ONLY RESTORATION** OF ENTITLEMENT TO PURCHASE ANOTHER HOME? ☐ YES ☐ NO *(If "Yes," complete Items 11B through 11D)*	11B. DATE OF LOAN *(Month and Year)*	11C. STREET ADDRESS	11D. CITY AND STATE
12A. ARE YOU APPLYING FOR A RESTORATION OF ENTITLEMENT TO OBTAIN A **REGULAR (CASH-OUT) REFINANCE** ON YOUR CURRENT HOME? ☐ YES ☐ NO *(If "Yes," complete Items 12B through 12D)*	12B. DATE OF LOAN *(Month and Year)*	12C. STREET ADDRESS	12D. CITY AND STATE
13A. ARE YOU REFINANCING AN EXISTING VA LOAN TO OBTAIN A LOWER INTEREST RATE **WITHOUT RECEIVING** ANY CASH PROCEEDS (IRRRL)? ☐ YES ☐ NO *(If "Yes," complete Items 13B through 13D)*	13B. DATE OF LOAN *(Month and Year)*	13C. STREET ADDRESS	13D. CITY AND STATE

I CERTIFY THAT the statements in this document are true and complete to the best of my knowledge.

14A. SIGNATURE OF VETERAN *(Do NOT print)*
14B. DATE SIGNED

FEDERAL STATUTES PROVIDE SEVERE PENALTIES FOR FRAUD, INTENTIONAL MISREPRESENTATION, CRIMINAL CONNIVANCE OR CONSPIRACY PURPOSED TO INFLUENCE THE ISSUANCE OF ANY GUARANTY OR INSURANCE BY THE SECRETARY OF VETERANS AFFAIRS

FOR VA USE ONLY *(Please do not write below this line)*
DATE RETURNED

REASON(S) FOR RETURN

VA FORM SEP 2011 **26-1880**
SUPERSEDES VA FORM 26-1880, MAR 2011, WHICH WILL NOT BE USED.

INSTRUCTIONS FOR VA FORM 26-1880

PRIVACY ACT NOTICE - VA will not disclose information collected on this form to any source other than what has been authorized under the Privacy Act of 1974 or Title 38, Code of Federal Regulations 1.576 for routine uses (for example: the authorized release of information to Congress when requested for statistical purposes) identified in the VA system of records, 55VA26, Loan Guaranty Home, Condominium and Manufactured Home Loan Applicant Records, Specially Adapted Housing Applicant Records, and Vendee Loan Applicant Records - VA, and published in the Federal Register. Your obligation to respond is required in order to determine the qualifications for a loan.

RESPONDENT BURDEN - This information is needed to help determine a veteran's qualifications for a VA guaranteed home loan. Title 38, U.S.C., section 3702, authorizes collection of this information. We estimate that you will need an average of 15 minutes to review the instructions, find the information, and complete this form. VA cannot conduct or sponsor a collection of information unless a valid OMB control number is displayed. You are not required to respond to a collection of information if this number is not displayed. Valid OMB control numbers can be located on the OMB Internet Page at www.reginfo.gov/public/do/PRAMain. If desired, you can call 1-800-827-1000 to get information on where to send comments or suggestions about this form.

A. YOUR IDENTIFYING INFORMATION

Item 1 - Tell us your complete name, *as you would like it to appear on your Certificate of Eligibility (COE).*
Item 4B - If you served under another name, provide the name as it appears on your discharge certificate (DD Form 214).
Item 7 - You can have your Certiticate of Eligibility sent to you at your current mailing address, or directly to your lender, or to any mailing address you provide in Item 7B.
Item 8B - In most cases, your VA claim number is the same as your Social Security Number. If you are not sure of your VA claim number, leave this field blank.

B. MILITARY SERVICE

Item 9 - **NOTE** - Cases involving other than honorable discharges will usually require further development by VA. This is necessary to determine if the service was under other than dishonorable conditions.

Item 9A - If you are currently serving on regular active duty, eligibility can usually be established based on data in VA systems. However, in some situations you may be asked to provide a statement of service signed by, or by direction of, the adjutant, personnel officer, or commander of your unit or higher headquarters. The statement may be in any format; usually a standard or bulleted memo is sufficient. It should identify you by name and social security number, and provide: (1) your date of entry on your current active duty period and (2) the duration of any time lost (or a statement noting there has been no lost time). Generally this should be on military letterhead.

Item 9B - **Active Service** *(not including Active Duty Training or Active Guard Reserve service)* - the best evidence to show your service is your discharge certificate (DD Form 214) showing active duty dates and type of discharge. If you were separated after October 1, 1979, the DD214 was issued in several parts (copies). We are required to have a copy showing the character of service (Item 24) and the narrative reason for separation (Item 28). We prefer the MEMBER-4 copy, however, we can accept any copy that contains these items. The copy number is shown on the bottom right of the form. We don't need the original; a photocopy is acceptable. Any Veterans Services Representative in the nearest Department of Veterans Affairs office or center will assist you in securing necessary proof of military service.

NOTE - A reservist or member of the National Guard can be called to active duty under either of two legal authorities. Title 10 U.S. Code covers those who are ordered to regular active duty under federal call up. Reservists may also be called to active service under the authority of Title 32 U.S. Code. Service covered under Title 32 U.S. Code includes basic training (Initial Active Duty for Training or IADT) annual training, as well as certain types of full-time duty may be called Active Guard Reserve, Active Duty for Special Work. Full-time National Guard Duty or Active Duty Support. Service under Title 10 U.S. Code is qualifying active duty for the VA Home Loan Benefit. Active service under Title 32 U.S. Code, however, does NOT qualify under the active duty requirements. Service under Title 32 U.S. Code can be used to meet the 6-year requirement to qualify as a member of the Selected Reserve or National Guard.

Item 9C - **National Guard Service:** You may submit NGB Form 22, Report of Separation and Record of Service, or NGB Form 23, Retirement Points Accounting, or their equivalent. We are required to have a copy showing character of service.

Selected Reserve Service (Including Active Duty Training and Active Guard Reserve) - You may submit (Including Active Duty Training and Active Guard Reserve) a copy of your latest annual retirement points statement and evidence of honorable service. There is no single form used by the Reserves similar to the DD Form 214 or NGB Form 22. The following forms are commonly used, but others may be acceptable:

Army Reserve	DARP FM 249-2E
Naval Reserve	NRPC 1070-124
Air Force Reserve	AF 526
Marine Corps Reserve	NA VMC 798
Coast Guard Reserve	CG 4174 or 4175

If you are still serving in the Selected Reserves or the National Guard, you must include an original statement of service signed by, or by the direction of, the adjutant, personnel officer, or commander of your unit or higher headquarters showing your date of entry and the length of time that you have been a member of the Selected Reserves. At least 6 years of honorable service must be documented.

C. PREVIOUS VA LOANS

Items 10 through 14. Your eligibility is reusable depending on the circumstances. Normally, if you have paid off your prior VA loan and no longer own the home, you can have your used eligibility restored for additional use. Also, on a one-time only basis, you may have your eligibility restored if your prior VA loan has been paid in full but you still own the home. Normally VA receives notification that a loan has been paid. In some instances, it may be necessary to include evidence that a previous VA loan has been paid in full. Evidence can be in the form of a paid-in-full statement from the former lender, a satisfaction of mortgage from the clerk of court in the county where the home is located, or a copy of the HUD-1 settlement statement completed in connection with a sale of the home or refinance of the prior loan. Many counties post public documents (like the satisfaction of mortgage) online.

Item 11A. **One-Time Restoration.** If you have paid off your VA loan, but still own the home purchased with that loan, you may apply for a one-time only restoration of your entitlement in order to purchase another home that will be your primary residence. Once you have used your one-time restoration, you must sell all homes before any other entitlement can be restored.

Item 12A. **Regular (cash-out) Refinance.** You may refinance your current VA or non-VA loan in order to pay off the mortgage and/or other liens of record on the home. This type of refinance requires an appraisal and credit qualifying.

Item 13A. **Interest Rate Reduction Refinancing Loan (IRRRL).** You may refinance the balance of your current VA loan in order to obtain a lower interest rate, or convert a VA adjustable rate mortgage to a fixed rate. The new loan may not exceed the sum of the outstanding balance on the existing VA loan, plus allowable fees and closing costs, including VA funding fee and up to 2 discount points. You may also add up to $6,000 of energy efficiency improvements into the loan. **A certificate of eligibility is not required for IRRRL.** Instead, a Prior Loan Validation, obtained through our online system WebLGY can be used in lieu of a COE. Presently, this application is only available to lenders. In WebLGY, a lender can select Eligibility from the toolbar and then Prior Loan Validation. Enter the veteran's Social Security Number and Last Name. The system will then, in most cases, pull up the veteran's active loan information. Print the prior Loan Validation screen and use it in lieu of the COE.

VA FORM 26-1880, SEP 2011

BORROWER'S AUTHORIZATION

We hereby give our consent to have CalVet Home Loans, or any credit reporting bureau which it may designate, obtain any and all credit information concerning our employment, checking and/or savings accounts, obligations, and all other credit matters which they may require in connection with our application for a loan and any quality control review of such loan. This form may be reproduced and photocopied and a copy shall be effective as the original which we have signed.

Signature of Veteran Applicant   Date   Signature of Spouse or Registered Domestic Partner   Date

I hereby certify this to be a true and correct copy of the original.

CalVet Home Loans   Date

Privacy Act Notice: This information is to be used by the agency collecting it or it's assignees in determining whether you qualify as a prospective mortgagor under its program. It will not be disclosed outside the agency except as required and permitted by law. You do not have to provide this information, but if you do not, your application for approval as a prospective borrower may be delayed or rejected. The information requested in this form is authorized by Title 38, USC, Chapter 37.

Verification of Borrower(s) Name(s)

I understand and agree that I will take title as my name is shown below, regardless of the way my name is shown or signed on my loan application. I am aware that all legal documents will carry my name exactly as shown below and understand that I will be required to sign exactly as it is shown below.

Print Name (Veteran)   Signature

Print Name (Spouse or Registered Domestic Partner)   Signature

C-11-3 / V-11 (1/2005)

HOME LOANS

THE HOUSING FINANCIAL DISCRIMINATION ACT OF 1977

(Pursuant to Title 21, California Code of Regulations, Section 7114)

FAIR LENDING NOTICE

It is illegal to discriminate in the provision of or in the availability of financial assistance because of the consideration of:

1. Trends, characteristics or conditions in the neighborhood or geographic area surrounding a housing accommodation, unless the financial institution can demonstrate in the particular case that such consideration is required to avoid an unsafe and unsound business practice; or
2. Race, color, religion, sex, marital status, national origin or ancestry.

It is illegal to consider the racial, ethnic, religious or national origin composition of a neighborhood or geographic area surrounding a housing accommodation or whether or not such composition is undergoing change, or is expected to undergo change, in appraising a housing accommodation or in determining whether or not, or under what terms and conditions, to provide financial assistance.

These provisions govern financial assistance for the purpose of the purchase, construction, rehabilitation or refinancing of one-to four-unit family residences occupied by the owner and for the purpose of the home improvement of any one-to four-unit family residence.

If you have questions about your rights, or if you wish to file a complaint, contact the management of this financial institution or the Office of the Secretary, Business, Transportation and Housing Agency, 1120 N Street, Sacramento, CA 95814

Acknowledgment of receipt

I (we) received a copy of this notice.

Signature of Veteran Applicant Date Signature of Spouse or Registered Domestic Partner Date

WORD OF CAUTION

The processing of your home loan is a detailed process and requires accurate information. Please keep in mind that this process may take longer than expected and requires final updating prior to the funding of your loan. Because of these last minute updates, it is imperative that the information you give us, and subsequently verified by our office, does not change appreciably. Therefore, please continue to make your mortgage payments and all other financial obligations as usual until the close of escrow.

Please notify us before you do any of the following, or please delay doing the following if at all possible:

1) Change employment or department.
2) Move any funds from one bank account to another or close an existing account.
3) Make any large purchases such as an automobile, furniture, or high cost items.

All of the above situations might be dealt with appropriately if we know about the changes prior to their occurrence. Failure to notify us about any significant changes to your original loan file, or any material fact regarding your financial condition could seriously affect the outcome of your loan transaction. **YOUR LOAN FILE MAY BE UPDATED PRIOR TO THE CLOSE OF ESCROW!**

CalVet Home Loans and the Department of Veterans Affairs of the State of California **do not warrant** the condition, desirability, suitability, or actual value of the property you are purchasing, such determinations being entirely the responsibility of the purchaser. You are encouraged to inspect the property thoroughly, review the seller's/agent's disclosure statements, and obtain any inspection reports that you deem necessary.

Signature of Veteran Applicant Date Signature of Spouse or Registered Domestic Partner Date

L-9 (6/2006)

BUYERS INFORMATION FORM

The following information will assist us in making certain your application is set up correctly from the beginning.

1. Have you had a CalVet loan before? Yes ☐ No ☐

   If yes; Loan number ______________________

   Date (mo/yr) loan was paid off ______________________

   Location of property ______________________

   Have you had a VA loan before? Yes ☐ No ☐

   If yes; Loan number ______________________

   Date (mo/yr) loan was paid off ______________________

   Location of property ______________________

2. Are you buying a new home that has never been previously occupied? Yes ☐ No ☐

   If not already completed, when is the estimated completion date? ______________________

3. Is the property either a Condominium, or located in a Planned Unit Development (PUD)?

   Condominium ☐ Planned Unit Development ☐ If yes to either;

   - What is the name of the Association and how much are the monthly dues?

     Association Name______________________ $ __________per mo.

   - Is the hazard insurance on the unit a master policy carried through the Association?

     Yes ☐ No ☐

4. Is this loan to purchase a mobile home in a rental park? Yes ☐ No ☐

   If yes, what is the monthly space rental? $______________

6. Are you currently in receipt of or eligible to receive VA Compensation? Yes ☐ No ☐

   If yes, VA Case # ______________ Disability Rating ______________%

7. In order to gain access to the home you are buying the appraiser should contact:

   Name: ______________________________ at phone # (   ) ______________

BUYER'S INFORMATION (6/2004)

Designation of Agent and General Release

I hereby appoint and designate ____________________________ as my agent for all purposes in connection with the processing of my application for a CalVet Home Loan to include, but not be limited to, working with CDVA staff in the field offices and in Department Headquarters to provide and obtain any and all information necessary to complete the processing of my loan and the purchase of the farm or home I have selected.

I understand that if the person or firm designated by me is licensed as a real estate agent or broker, they may also be the agent or broker for the seller of the property. I also understand that the Department assumes no responsibility for and makes no recommendations as to the acts, conduct, duties, qualifications, or status of the person or firm I have designated. Nevertheless, I so designate said person or firm freely and voluntarily, on my own accord, with full knowledge of all necessary facts.

I authorize the department to obtain from and disclose or release to my designated agent any and all information, whether confidential, personal, or otherwise, which may be desirable or necessary in the processing and completion of my CalVet Home Loan, and this authorization and consent will be effective from the date hereof to the date my loan is completed or otherwise terminated. I understand that all communications and contacts concerning my CalVet Home Loan will be made through or with my designated agent, and that it is the agent's responsibility to keep me informed and to provide me with copies of all correspondence and documents.

This authorization and designation may be revoked only by me in writing, and such revocation shall be effective only when received by the department.

In consideration of the department's acceptance of this designation and the terms thereof, the undersigned hereby releases the State of California, the Department of Veterans Affairs of the State of California, and their assignees, employees, officers, and successors, from any and all actions, claims, demands, liability, or suits of any kind, arising out of or by reason of this designation, the department's working with the designated agent pursuant hereto, and the obtaining, disclosure or release of any and all information pursuant to this designation.

The undersigned agree, in further consideration hereof, that this Release shall apply to all unknown and unanticipated claims arising out of said matters, as well as to those now known, if any, and expressly waive the provisions of Section 1542 of the California Civil Code which reads as follows: "A general release does not extend to claims which the creditor does not know or suspect to exist in his favor at the time of executing the release, which if known by him must have materially affected his settlement with the debtor."

The undersigned declares that the terms of this designation and release have been read completely by them, and that the terms are fully understood and freely and voluntarily accepted by them.

IN WITNESS WHEREOF, the undersigned have executed this Designation of Agent and General Release

this ____________ day of ________________, ____________

____________________________	____________________________
Veteran Applicant	Spouse or Registered Domestic Partner

ACCEPTANCE BY AGENT

I hereby accept the above designation as agent, and assume all responsibilities incident thereto.

Dated: ________________, ____________

Signature of Agent

Print Name of Agent

Business Name

( ) Business Telephone

( ) Fax Number

Business Address

( ) Mobile #

E-mail address

City State Zip

A-3 (1/2005)

REAL ESTATE AGENT
INTERNET ACCESS REGISTRATION

As a licensed real estate agent CalVet can now provide you with up-to-the-minute status of your clients loan application. You can also use our *Apply online* system to confirm eligibility or pre-qualify a new client. If you wish to become registered to access this information please complete this form and either mail, E-mail, or fax it to your local CalVet office. Upon receipt of the required information you will be assigned a Real Estate Agent ID number along with a user ID and Password by E-mail within one business day. Once you have registered with us just check the "Authorization for subsequent application box" and enter the

Please note that you must also obtain authorization from your client in order for you to be able to access their account. Your veteran client's signature on this form is his/her authorization to enable you to access their loan information. They should understand that they are not required to provide access to anyone.

For information on office locations please select
http://www.cdva.ca.gov/calvet/offices.asp

California Department of Veterans Affairs

REAL ESTATE AGENT
INTERNET ACCESS

☐ **REGISTRATION**
☐ **AUTHORIZATION - Agent ID # __________**

(Instructions: All fields are required. Please print or type)

First Name MI:	Last Name:		
Bus. Address:	City – State – Zip code		
E-Mail	Phone	Fax	Pager or Mobile
DRE License #	Client's Name	Subj. Property Address	

Approved: ______________________________
Veterans Signature Date

REA Internet Access (10/2004)

Figure 17-3

Standard Insurance Company
Cal-Vet Team, 920 SW Sixth Avenue Portland OR 97204

Medical History Statement for Life and Disability Coverage

DIRECTIONS FOR APPLYING FOR COVERAGE

This form must be completed when Evidence Of Insurability is required. To apply for coverage (as a Contractholder or Spouse), read the Information Practices Notice(s). Then complete all items, date, and sign as instructed. Send the original to Standard Insurance Company, at the address above. Please keep a copy for your records.

CONTRACTHOLDER INFORMATION

Name of Group **Department of Veterans Affairs, State of California**	Group Number **642177**	Loan Number	Loan Amount	Are You a Veteran? ☐ Yes ☐ No
Contractholder		Birthdate (Mo/Day/Year)		Date Hired (Mo/Day/Year)
No. of Hours Scheduled to Work per Week	Salary	Social Security Number		Check who is Applying (One per form) ☐ Contractholder ☐ Spouse

APPLICANT INFORMATION

Applicant's Name (Person to be insured)				
Current Address:			Future Address:	
Sex ☐M ☐F	Birthdate (Mo/Day/Year)	Birthplace	Social Security Number	Work Phone ( ) Home Phone ( )

APPLICATION INFORMATION

Type of Application *(check one)* ☐ Initial application ☐ Change in coverage

Check the insurance coverage you are requesting.

☐ Regular Life ☐ Optional Regular Life ☐ Spouse Life Disability – ☐ Option 1 ☐ Option 1a ☐ Option 2

Are you now receiving or eligible for Veterans Compensation for a military service-connected disability? ☐ Yes ☐ No

If yes, what percent? ________ Specify disability/condition: ________________

If yes, please provide the USDVA document which verifies the service-connected disability. You may contact USDVA at 1-800-827-1000 to obtain a copy of this information.

Veterans Compensation Claim No. ________________ and/or Military Services No. ________________

MEDICAL HISTORY STATEMENT QUESTIONS

Check yes or no for each of these questions, and give details for any "yes" answers. Attach a separate sheet if necessary.

1. Have you had any physical, mental or emotional condition, injury, sickness, or surgery in the past 5 years? ...... ☐Yes ☐ No
2. Have you consulted or been attended by a physician or practitioner for any cause in the past 5 years? .... ☐Yes ☐ No
3. Are you now unable to work full time because of any physical, mental or emotional condition, injury, or sickness? . ☐Yes ☐ No
4. Has a medical professional ever treated you for, diagnosed you as having, or prescribed medication for you for any of the following:
   A. High blood pressure, cardiovascular disease, heart ailment, arteriosclerosis, or stroke? .... ☐Yes ☐ No
   B. Mental condition, depression, epilepsy, or nervous system disorder? .... ☐Yes ☐ No
   C. Cancer, diabetes, or nephritis? .... ☐Yes ☐ No
   D. Arthritis, strained or injured back, slipped disc, or any bone, joint, or muscle disorder? .... ☐Yes ☐ No
   E. Lung, kidney, stomach, genital, urinary, liver, pancreas, or intestinal ailment? .... ☐Yes ☐ No
   F. Blindness or deafness? .... ☐Yes ☐ No
   G. An immune system disorder not related to Human Immunodeficiency Virus (HIV)? .... ☐Yes ☐ No
5. Has a medical professional ever diagnosed you as having or prescribed medication to you for Acquired Immune Deficiency Syndrome (AIDS), AIDS-Related Complex (ARC), or HIV infection? .... ☐Yes ☐ No
6. Have you sought or received advice or treatment for the use of alcohol or drugs in the past 10 years? .... ☐Yes ☐ No
7. In the past 10 years have you had a persistent cough, unintentional weight loss of 10 pounds or more, persistent fatigue, persistent lymph node enlargement, prolonged night sweats, pneumonia, lesions, or growths? .... ☐Yes ☐ No
8. Do you take medication for any physical, mental or emotional condition, injury, or sickness? .... ☐Yes ☐ No
9. Do you plan any operation or visit to a doctor or practitioner for an existing physical, mental or emotional condition, injury, or sickness? .... ☐Yes ☐ No
10. Are you now pregnant? .... ☐Yes ☐ No

Height	Weight	Physician or Medical Facility with Applicant's Complete Medical Records
		Name and Full Mailing Address

SI 9340-642177 1 of 3 (12/05)

Applicant Name	Social Security Number

Describe below any "yes" answers. (Please provide the entire question number.)

Question Number	*Description of Injuries, Disorders and Operations*	*Month/Year*	*Duration*	*Final Result*	*Physicians Consulted, City & State*

ACKNOWLEDGMENT AND AUTHORIZATION FOR RELEASE OF INFORMATION *(Please read carefully)*

- I represent that the statements contained herein, including those made in response to the Medical History Statement questions and any attachments, are true and complete, to the best of my knowledge and belief, and I understand that they form the basis of any coverage under the Group Policy(ies). I understand that any misstatements or failure to report information which is material to the issuance of coverage may be used as a basis for rescission of my insurance and/or denial of payment of a claim. I agree to notify Standard Insurance Company of any change in my medical condition while my enrollment application is pending. I agree that if my application is approved by Standard Insurance Company, the effective date of any coverage will be determined in accordance with the terms of the Group Policy(ies), including any applicable Active Work requirement. I agree that if my application is declined, Standard Insurance Company's liability is limited to the return of any premium which may have been paid.
- To any physician, health care provider, hospital, insurance or reinsurance company, the Medical Information Bureau, Inc. (MIB), or any employer: I authorize you to release to Standard Insurance Company or its reinsurers all medical information you have about me including medical history, diagnosis, prognosis and treatment of any physical, mental or emotional condition. I understand that Standard Insurance Company will use the information obtained by this authorization to determine my eligibility for group insurance coverage. I further authorize Standard Insurance Company to release this information to its reinsurers, MIB, and to other insurance companies to which I have applied for insurance coverage or benefits.
- I understand that if my application is approved, premiums shall be paid in accordance with the provisions of the Group Policy(ies), and my coverage will be subject to all terms and conditions of the Group Policy(ies) and state limitations.
- For the Contractholder: Regular Life Insurance, Optional Regular Life Insurance, and Disability Insurance benefits will be paid to the Policyholder.
- Benefits paid to the Policyholder will be applied against the loan contract which is subject to insurance under the Group Policy.
- I understand that Spouse Life Insurance if any, is payable to the Policyholder.
- I acknowledge that I have read and received the Information Practices Notice and I have kept a copy of this Medical History Statement.
- I understand a copy of this authorization will be provided to me, or my authorized representative, upon request. This authorization will remain valid one year from the date below. A photocopy of this authorization shall be as valid as the original.
- I understand that I have the right to revoke this authorization at any time by sending a written statement to Standard Insurance Company. I further understand that the revocation of the authorization, or the failure to sign the authorization, may impair Standard Insurance Company's ability to evaluate or process my application and may be a basis for denying my application for insurance coverage.
- I understand that I will not be rated uninsurable for life insurance coverages other than Spouse Life solely on the basis of a military service-connected disability, and that I must be actively working at least 30 hours per week in order to be eligible for disability coverage.

Signature of Applicant	**Dated**

Note: Declinations do not affect either Guarantee Issue Amounts not subject to Evidence Of Insurability or other coverages already inforce with Standard Insurance Company.

SI 9340-642177 2 of 3 (12/05)

Applicant Name	Social Security Number

INFORMATION PRACTICES NOTICE

- To help us determine your eligibility for group insurance we may request information about you from other persons and organizations. For example, we may request information from your doctor or hospital, other insurance companies, or MIB, Inc. (Medical Information Bureau). We will use the authorization you signed on this form when we seek this information.
- MIB (MEDICAL INFORMATION BUREAU) – Information regarding your insurability will be treated as confidential. Standard Insurance Company or its reinsurers may, however, make a brief report thereon to MIB, a not-for-profit membership organization of insurance companies, which operates an information exchange on behalf of its Members. If you apply to another MIB Member company for life or health insurance coverage, or a claim for benefits is submitted to such a company, MIB, upon request, will supply such company with the information in its file.

  Upon receipt of a request from you MIB will arrange disclosure of any information it may have in your file. Please contact MIB at 866-692-6901 (TTY 866-346-3642). If you question the accuracy of information in MIB's file, you may contact MIB and seek a correction in accordance with the procedures set forth in the federal Fair Credit Reporting Act. The address of MIB's information office is: Post Office Box 105, Essex Station, Boston, Massachusetts 02112.

  Standard Insurance Company may release information in its file to its reinsurers, and Standard Insurance Company, or its reinsurers, may release information in its file to other insurance companies to whom you may apply for life or health insurance, or to whom a claim for benefits may be submitted.
- DISCLOSURE TO OTHERS – The information collected about you is confidential. We will not release any information about you without your authorization, except to the extent necessary to conduct our business or as required or permitted by law.
- YOUR RIGHTS – You have a right to know what information we have about you in our underwriting file. You also have a right to ask us to correct any information you think is incorrect. We will carefully review your request and make changes when justified. If you would like more information about this right or our information practices please write to us, at Medical Underwriting, Standard Insurance Company, 900 SW Fifth Avenue, Portland, Oregon 97204-1282 or call 1-800-843-7979.

SI 9340-642177 3 of 3 (12/05)

CalVet Office Locations

Sacramento Office

1227 O Street, 4th floor
Sacramento, CA 95814
Robert Washington, Manager
(866) 653-2510 - Toll Free
(916) 503-8359 - PHONE
(916) 651-9085 - FAX
E-Mail: Sacramento@cdva.ca.gov
Office Hours: 8:00 AM to 5:00 PM Monday through Friday

Counties

Alameda
Alpine
Amador
Calaveras
Colusa
Contra Costa
El Dorado
Marin
Napa
Nevada
Placer
Sacramento
San Francisco
San Joaquin
San Mateo
Santa Clara
Santa Cruz
Solano
Sonoma
Sutter
Yolo
Yuba

Redding Office

930 Executive Way, Suite 125
Redding, CA 96002
(866) 653-2508 - Toll Free
(530) 224-4955 - PHONE
(530) 224-4959 - FAX
E-Mail: Redding@cdva.ca.gov
Office Hours: 8:00 AM to 5:00 PM Monday through Friday

Counties

Butte
Del Norte
Glenn
Humboldt
Lake
Lassen
Mendocino
Modoc
Plumas
Shasta
Sierra
Siskiyou
Tehama
Trinity

Fresno Office

1752 East Bullard Avenue, Suite 101
Fresno, CA 93710
(866) 653-2511 - Toll Free
(559) 440-5132 - PHONE
(559) 440-5172 - FAX
E-Mail: Fresno@cdva.ca.gov
Office Hours: 8:00 AM to 5:00 PM Monday through Friday

Counties

Fresno
Kings
Madera
Mariposa
Merced
Monterey
San Benito
San Luis Obispo
Stanislaus
Tuolumne

San Diego Office

3160 Camino Del Rio South, Room 112
San Diego, CA 92108
(866) 653-2504 - Toll Free
(619) 641-5840 - PHONE
(619) 641-5851 - FAX
E-Mail: SanDiego@cdva.ca.gov
Office Hours: 8:00 AM to 5:00 PM Monday through Friday

Counties

Imperial
Orange
San Diego

Bakersfield Office

5500 Ming Avenue, Suite 155
Bakersfield, CA 93309
(866) 653-2507 - Toll Free
(661) 833-4720 - PHONE
(661) 833-4732 - FAX
E-Mail: Bakersfield@cdva.ca.gov
Office Hours: 8:00 AM to 5:00 PM Monday through Friday

Counties

Inyo
Kern
Mono
North and West Los Angeles County
Santa Barbara
Tulare
Ventura

Riverside Office

1770 Iowa Ave., Suite 260
Riverside, CA 92507
(800) 700-2127 - Toll Free
(951) 774-0102 - PHONE
(951) 774-0111 - FAX
E-Mail: Riverside@cdva.ca.gov
Office Hours: 8:00 AM to 5:00 PM Monday through Friday

Counties

Riverside
San Bernardino
South and East Los Angeles County

Chapter 18
Escrow Procedures

The last step in the loan process is ***CLOSING****, when the loan proceeds are distributed and a deed to the property is transferred and recorded*. These steps are usually carried out by an escrow agent. The escrow agent makes sure that all necessary documents are prepared and properly signed, calculates any necessary prorations, makes sure that all necessary funds have been deposited, and provides a settlement statement. Once everything is in order, the loan funds are disbursed, the deed and other documents are recorded, and the transaction is completed.

An ***ESCROW*** *is where a neutral third party holds the items deposited by the parties to a transaction and disburses them after the conditions of the transaction have been met*. Attorneys, title companies, and independent escrow companies all perform this function. Many lending institutions have their own escrow departments for the transactions that they finance.

Every state has laws governing the operation of escrow agents.

The typical escrow involves many people. In addition to the buyer/borrower, seller, broker, lender, and escrow agent, important functions are performed by title companies, notaries public, local county officials (recording office and inspectors), and structural pest inspectors.

Chapter 18

CHAPTER OUTLINE

One of the key functions of the escrow process is the recordation of documents.

Any document relating to real estate ownership should be recorded.

While agents and loan officers do not act as escrow agents, they need to be very aware of the steps in the process. All real estate escrows involve the following essential steps:

1. Gathering information necessary to prepare escrow instructions
2. Obtaining a preliminary title report from the title company
3. Satisfying existing loans secured by the property
4. Preparing documents such as escrow instructions, loan documents, deeds, etc.
5. Depositing funds from a buyer or a seller
6. Prorating expenses and allocating closing costs
7. Preparing a Uniform Settlement Statement
8. Issuing policies of title insurance for the buyer and the lender
9. Disbursing funds and delivering documents

I. Opening Escrow

It is a good idea for agents and loan brokers to use an escrow progress chart (see **Figure 18-1**). By utilizing such a chart, the progress of the escrow can be monitored and the parties can be reminded of items that still need to be completed to close the transaction.

The first step in the process is to open the escrow. This is done by providing the escrow agent with the preliminary escrow instructions. Once the instructions are prepared and signed, the escrow agent will order a preliminary title report. This preliminary report will then be forwarded to the buyer/borrower's lender along with the escrow instructions.

Figure 18-1

Escrow Progress Chart

	Sch. Date	Actual Date	Escrow Operations
1			Notice of Sale to multiple listing service
2			Buyer's deposit increased to $
3			Escrow opened with
4			Preliminary title searched
5			Clouds on title eliminated
6			Credit report ordered from
7			Credit report received
8			Report of residential record ordered
9			Report of residential record received
10			Pest control inspection ordered
11			Pest control report received; work —
12			Pest control report accepted by seller
13			Pest control work ordered
14			Pest control work completed
15			Other inspections ordered
16			Report received; work —
17			Report accepted by
18			Special contingencies eliminated
19			Payoff or beneficiary statement ordered
20			Payoff or beneficiary statement received
21			Payoff or beneficiary statement ordered
22			Payoff or beneficiary statement received
23			1st loan commitment ordered from
24			Received: @ % Fee Pts.
25			2nd loan commitment ordered from
26			Received: @ % Fee Pts.
27			Loan application submitted to
28			Loan application approved
29			Loan/assumption papers received by escrow
30			Hazard insurance placed with
31			Escrow closing instructions requested
32			Client called for closing appointment
33			Closing papers signed
34			Closing papers to escrow holder
35			Funds ordered
36			Deed recorded

After Close of Escrow

Received	Delivered	
		Final adjusted closing statement
		Check of seller's proceeds
		Check of buyer's refund
		Commission check
		Seller's "Loss Payee" insurance policy
		Recorded deed
		Title insurance policy

Notations

Note that the escrow instructions must correspond to the lender's terms. Any discrepancy will require amended escrow instructions since the lender will not disburse funds into the escrow account until the instructions correspond to their loan terms.

Early in the process, the escrow agent will send a "demand for payoff" to the previous lender, if necessary. A structural pest inspection will also be immediately ordered so as to complete any needed repairs and not unduly delay the close of escrow. The results of the pest control inspection will then be forwarded to the borrower's lender.

Once the lender has carried out its underwriting functions and obtained an appraisal (if necessary), it will then issue loan approval and forward the loan documents (note, deed of trust, and Truth in Lending Statement) to the escrow agent.

Once all contingent conditions have been met (such as purchase of a new hazard insurance policy), the escrow agent will have the borrower sign the loan documents and record them. Copies of the documents will be provided to the lender. The borrower will then have a statutory rescission period before final closing. At the end of the rescission period, the lender will disburse funds into the account.

At final closing, the prior lender will be paid off, the final closing statements will be prepared, and all other parties to the escrow will receive their funds. The policy of title insurance will be issued at this time and the borrower will receive his or her copies of all the loan documents and inspection reports.

II. Settlement Statement and Closing Costs

A ***SETTLEMENT STATEMENT*** *is a listing of all the amounts involved in a transaction.* In sales of residential property financed by institutional investors, the Uniform Settlement Statement is used (see **Figure 18-2**).

Items on the statement are listed as either debits or credits. A ***DEBIT*** *is any charge payable by any party.* For instance, the purchase price is a debit to the buyer and the sales commission is a debit to the seller. A ***CREDIT*** *is any item that's payable to any party.* The buyer would be credited with the new loan and the seller would be credited with the sales price. The easy way to think of the statement is to compare it to a check register. Debits are checks written against the account or payouts. Credits are similar to deposits to the account or pay-ins. When the transaction closes, the balances for both the buyer and the seller should equal zero. Loan officers and agents are often asked to calculate an estimate of the buyer's cash requirements for closing and the seller's net proceeds. This can be done by utilizing a worksheet similar to that shown in **Figure 18-3**.

Figure 18-2

A. **Settlement Statement**

U.S. Department of Housing and Urban Development

B. Type of Loan

1. ☐ FHA 2. ☐ FmHA 3. ☐ Conv. Unins. 4. ☐ VA 5. ☐ Conv. Ins.	6. File Number:	7. Loan Number:	8. Mortgage Insurance Case Number:

C. Note: This form is furnished to give you a statement of actual settlement costs. Amounts paid to and by the settlement agent are shown. Items marked "(p.o.c.)" were paid outside the closing; they are shown here for informational purposes and are not included in the totals.

D. Name & Address of Borrower:	E. Name & Address of Seller:	F. Name & Address of Lender:

G. Property Location:	H. Settlement Agent:	
	Place of Settlement:	I. Settlement Date:

J. Summary of Borrower's Transaction		K. Summary of Seller's Transaction	
100. Gross Amount Due From Borrower		**400. Gross Amount Due To Seller**	
101. Contract sales price		401. Contract sales price	
102. Personal property		402. Personal property	
103. Settlement charges to borrower (line 1400)		403.	
104.		404.	
105.		405.	
Adjustments for items paid by seller in advance		**Adjustments for items paid by seller in advance**	
106. City/town taxes to		406. City/town taxes to	
107. County taxes to		407. County taxes to	
108. Assessments to		408. Assessments to	
109.		409.	
110.		410.	
111.		411.	
112.		412.	
120. Gross Amount Due From Borrower		**420. Gross Amount Due To Seller**	
200. Amounts Paid By Or In Behalf Of Borrower		**500. Reductions In Amount Due To Seller**	
201. Deposit or earnest money		501. Excess deposit (see instructions)	
202. Principal amount of new loan(s)		502. Settlement charges to seller (line 1400)	
203. Existing loan(s) taken subject to		503. Existing loan(s) taken subject to	
204.		504. Payoff of first mortgage loan	
205.		505. Payoff of second mortgage loan	
206.		506.	
207.		507.	
208.		508.	
209.		509.	
Adjustments for items unpaid by seller		**Adjustments for items unpaid by seller**	
210. City/town taxes to		510. City/town taxes to	
211. County taxes to		511. County taxes to	
212. Assessments to		512. Assessments to	
213.		513.	
214.		514.	
215.		515.	
216.		516.	
217.		517.	
218.		518.	
219.		519.	
220. Total Paid By/For Borrower		**520. Total Reduction Amount Due Seller**	
300. Cash At Settlement From/To Borrower		**600. Cash At Settlement To/From Seller**	
301. Gross Amount due from borrower (line 120)		601. Gross amount due to seller (line 420)	
302. Less amounts paid by/for borrower (line 220)	( )	602. Less reductions in amt. due seller (line 520)	( )
303. Cash ☐ From ☐ To Borrower		**603. Cash ☐ To ☐ From Seller**	

Section 5 of the Real Estate Settlement Procedures Act (RESPA) requires the following: • HUD must develop a Special Information Booklet to help persons borrowing money to finance the purchase of residential real estate to better understand the nature and costs of real estate settlement services; • Each lender must provide the booklet to all applicants from whom it receives or for whom it prepares a written application to borrow money to finance the purchase of residential real estate; • Lenders must prepare and distribute with the Booklet a Good Faith Estimate of the settlement costs that the borrower is likely to incur in connection with the settlement. These disclosures are manadatory.

Section 4(a) of RESPA mandates that HUD develop and prescribe this standard form to be used at the time of loan settlement to provide full disclosure of all charges imposed upon the borrower and seller. These are third party disclosures that are designed to provide the borrower with pertinent information during the settlement process in order to be a better shopper.

The Public Reporting Burden for this collection of information is estimated to average one hour per response, including the time for reviewing instructions, searching existing data sources, gathering and maintaining the data needed, and completing and reviewing the collection of information.

This agency may not collect this information, and you are not required to

L. Settlement Charges	Paid From Borrowers Funds at Settlement	Paid From Seller's Funds at Settlement
700. Total Sales/Broker's Commission based on price $ @ % =		
Division of Commission (line 700) as follows:		
701. $ to		
702. $ to		
703. Commission paid at Settlement		
704.		
800. Items Payable In Connection With Loan		
801. Loan Origination Fee %		
802. Loan Discount %		
803. Appraisal Fee to		
804. Credit Report to		
805. Lender's Inspection Fee		
806. Mortgage Insurance Application Fee to		
807. Assumption Fee		
808.		
809.		
810.		
811.		
900. Items Required By Lender To Be Paid In Advance		
901. Interest from to @$ /day		
902. Mortgage Insurance Premium for months to		
903. Hazard Insurance Premium for years to		
904. years to		
905.		
1000. Reserves Deposited With Lender		
1001. Hazard insurance months @ $ per month		
1002. Mortgage insurance months @ $ per month		
1003. City property taxes months @ $ per month		
1004. County property taxes months @ $ per month		
1005. Annual assessments months @ $ per month		
1006. months @ $ per month		
1007. months @ $ per month		
1008. months @ $ per month		
1100. Title Charges		
1101. Settlement or closing fee to		
1102. Abstract or title search to		
1103. Title examination to		
1104. Title insurance binder to		
1105. Document preparation to		
1106. Notary fees to		
1107. Attorney's fees to		
(includes above items numbers:)		
1108. Title insurance to		
(includes above items numbers:)		
1109. Lender's coverage $		
1110. Owner's coverage $		
1111.		
1112.		
1113.		
1200. Government Recording and Transfer Charges		
1201. Recording fees: Deed $; Mortgage $; Releases $		
1202. City/county tax/stamps: Deed $; Mortgage $		
1203. State tax/stamps: Deed $; Mortgage $		
1204.		
1205.		
1300. Additional Settlement Charges		
1301. Survey to		
1302. Pest inspection to		
1303.		
1304.		
1305.		
1400. Total Settlement Charges (enter on lines 103, Section J and 502, Section K)		

Figure 18-3

SETTLEMENT STATEMENT

	BUYER'S STATEMENT		SELLER'S STATEMENT	
	Debit	**Credit**	**Debit**	**Credit**
Sales Price	52,000.00			52,000.00
Deposit		1,500.00		
Commission – 7%			3,640.00	
Mortgage Balance			35,822.24	
Prepaid Interest	261.00		156.70	
New Loan		45,000.00		
Taxes – Prorated		327.10	327.10	
Loan Origination Fee - 1%	450.00			
Fire Insurance	192.00			
Title Insurance – standard			238.10	
Title Insurance - extended	135.00			
Tax Reserve – 2 months	183.00			
Appraisal Fee	75.00			
Credit Report	50.00			
Survey Fee	255.00			
Discount Points			2,850.00	
Documentary Stamps			57.20	
Balance Due From Buyer		6,773.90		
Balance Due To Seller			8,908.66	
TOTALS	$53,601.00	$53,601.00	$52,000.00	$52,000.00

Settlement statements are written interpretations of the financial elements of the contract.

A. BUYER'S COSTS

The main cost to the buyer is the purchase price.

In most transactions, the purchase price cost is offset by some form of financing. The difference between the sales price and the loan amount is partially accounted for by a down payment. However, this is only one of the many costs the borrower will incur. There is generally a loan origination fee to cover the lender's administrative costs. The lender may also charge points to make the loan. There is an appraisal fee, a credit report fee, attorney fees, notary fees, a fee for the lenders title insurance policy, and possibly impound fees for taxes and insurance. Depending on the escrow agreement, the borrower may share costs with the seller for escrow and recording fees and possibly the title insurance policy, as well as any inspections and repairs. In addition, the borrower/buyer is responsible for any special costs that he or she incurs.

B. SELLER'S FEES

The seller will have to pay off any existing loans, including any prepayment penalties, at the close of escrow. The seller will also pay the sales commission and his or her

portion of the attorney fees, escrow fees, notary fees, and recording fees. Depending on local custom, the seller may also pay none, all, or a portion of the title insurance premium, the structural pest control inspection/repairs, the buyer/borrower's loan discount, and a home warranty contract.

C. BUYER'S CREDITS

The buyer will normally be credited with any payments initially made out of pocket for an earnest money deposit, appraisal fee, credit report, and prorated taxes or rents due.

D. SELLER'S CREDITS

In addition to receiving funds from the purchase price, the seller may be due credits for items such as prorated taxes, insurance premiums, and the balance in any existing impound account that was required for the seller's prior loan. If the property is income property, there might be a credit for prorated rents.

III. Real Estate Settlement Procedures Act (RESPA)

The ***REAL ESTATE SETTLEMENT PROCEDURES ACT (RESPA)*** *applies to the sale of one-to-four unit properties that involve financing from institutional lenders where the purchase loan is secured by a first trust mortgage.*

RESPA does not apply to purchases of vacant land, properties of 25 or more acres, or transactions where the borrower assumes an existing first mortgage loan.

In transactions subject to RESPA, the lender must give the borrower a **good faith estimate** of the closing costs at the time of the loan application (see **Figure 18-4**). The lender is also required to give the borrower a booklet published by HUD which describes closing costs, settlement procedures, and the borrower's rights. The entity handling the closing must prepare the settlement statement on the Uniform Settlement Statement.

RESPA prohibits all kickbacks and unearned fees.

If the lender requires a particular closing agent, any business relationship between the escrow agent and the lender must be disclosed, and an estimate of the agent's charges for the services to be provided must be given. Also, a sale may not be conditioned upon the use of a particular title insurer or escrow company chosen by the seller.

Figure 18-4

GOOD FAITH ESTIMATE

Applicants: Prepared By:

Property Address:

App No/Loan Prog: Date Prepared:

The information provided below reflects estimates of the charges which you are likely to incur at the settlement of your loan. The fees listed are estimates - actual charges may be more or less. Your transaction may not involve a fee for every item listed.

The numbers listed beside the estimates generally correspond to the numbered lines contained in the HUD-1 settlement statement which you will be receiving at settlement. The HUD-1 settlement statement will show you the actual cost for items paid at settlement.

Total Loan Amount $ Interest Rate: % Term: mths MIP/FF Financed $

800	**ITEMS PAYABLE IN CONNECTION WITH LOAN:**	
801	Loan Origination Fee	$
802	Loan Discount	
803	Appraisal Fee	
804	Credit Report	
805	Lender's Inspection Fee	
808	Mortgage Broker Fee	
809	Tax Related Service Fee	
810	Processing Fee	
811	Underwriting Fee	
812	Wire Transfer Fee	
900	**ITEMS REQUIRED BY LENDER TO BE PAID IN ADVANCE:**	
901	Interest for days @ $ per day	$
902	Mortgage Insurance Premium	
903	Hazard Insurance Premium	
904	Tax and Assessment	
905	VA Funding Fee	
1000	**RESERVES DEPOSITED WITH LENDER:**	
1001	Hazard Insurance Premiums months @ $ per month	$
1002	Mortgage Ins. Premium Reserves months @ $ per month	
1004	Taxes and Assessment Reserves months @ $ per month	
1100	**TITLE CHARGES:**	
1101	Closing or Escrow Fee:	$
1105	Document Preparation Fee	
1106	Notary Fees	
1107	Attorney Fees	
1108	Title Insurance:	
1200	**GOVERNMENT RECORDING & TRANSFER CHARGES:**	
1201	Recording Fees:	$
1202	City/County Tax/Stamps:	
1203	State Tax/Stamps:	
1300	**ADDITIONAL SETTLEMENT CHARGES:**	
1302	Pest Inspection	$

TOTAL ESTIMATED SETTLEMENT CHARGES

COMPENSATION TO BROKER (Not Paid Out of Loan Proceeds): $

TOTAL ESTIMATED FUNDS NEEDED TO CLOSE:		**TOTAL ESTIMATED MONTHLY PAYMENT:**	
Purchase Price/Payoff	$	Principal & Interest	$
Loan Amount	0.00	Other Financing (P & I)	
Est. Closing Costs		Hazard Insurance	
Est. Prepaid Items/Reserv		Real Estate Taxes	
Amount Paid by Seller		Mortgage Insurance	
		Homeowner Assn. Dues	
Total Est. Funds **needed to close**	0.00	Total Monthly Payment	

☐ This Good Faith Estimate is being provided by , a mortgage broker, and no lender has been obtained. A lender will provide you with an additional Good Faith Estimate within three business days of the receipt of your loan application.

These estimates are provided pursuant to the Real Estate Settlement Procedures Act of 1974, as amended (RESPA). Additional information can be found in the HUD Special Information Booklet, which is to be provided to you by your mortgage broker or lender. The undersigned acknowledges receipt of the booklet "Settlement Costs," and if applicable the Consumer Handbook on ARM Mortgages.

Applicant Date Applicant Date

IV. Additional Disclosures

Many states require additional documentation to transfer property or to obtain a loan. In many cases, this consists of disclosures to the prospective borrower or purchaser. The following are a list of the disclosures required by the state of California.

1. **Real Estate Transfer Disclosure.** This disclosure divulges the material facts about a property that could affect its value. It lists the age, structural components, the presence or absence of easements, fences, and driveways. The disclosure statement also lists alterations or additions without building permits, zoning violations, deed restrictions, lawsuits involving the property, environmental contamination, adverse soil conditions, and flooding hazards.
2. **Pest Control Inspection Report.** While the law does not require a pest control report, virtually all lenders do.
3. **Disclosure of Geologic Hazards.** By law, disclosure of possible landslide activity, erosion, expansive soil, and proximity to a fault line is required.
4. **Disclosure of Hazardous Waste Deposits.** The owner of any property that was utilized for the disposal of hazardous waste, or within 2,000 feet of such a property, must disclose this information to a buyer.
5. **Thermal Insulation Disclosure.** Sellers of new homes must disclose the type of material used, and the thickness or R-value to prospective buyers.
6. **Special Flood Area Disclosure.** The seller must disclose to a potential buyer if the property is included in a special flood hazard area, as shown on a flood hazard map.
7. **City and County Ordinances.** Sellers must inform buyers of any special ordinances that affect the property being sold, including occupancy standards, zoning and use, building code compliance, and fire, health, and safety requirements.
8. **Condominium Documents Disclosure.** The seller must provide the buyer a copy of the governing documents of the project (CCRs), a copy of the subdivision restrictions, including any limitation on occupancy due to age, a copy of the most recent financial statement of the homeowner's association, and a written statement from the association as to the amount of any unpaid assessments.
9. **Disclosure for Real Property Loans.** This is a written statement on a form approved by the Commissioner of the California Department of Real Estate. It details the expected maximum overall costs to be paid by a borrower for a loan. It includes all taxes, fees, commissions, points, bonuses, and charges. If the loan is an ARM, the *Consumer Handbook on Adjustable-Rate Mortgages*, published by the Federal Reserve Board, must be provided to the borrower. All information required by Regulation Z, RESPA, and ECOA must be provided. Finally, the lender must comply with the Housing Financial Discrimination Act (Holden Act). This is a state act that forbids discrimination based on race, religion, color, sex, marital status, national origin or ancestry. The act also prohibits the practice of redlining.

In effect, these state disclosures and laws extend protection to purchasers and borrowers who might be outside of the federal umbrella. In many cases, they extend additional protections that are somewhat localized in nature and might not apply to other areas or be a necessary part of federal legislation.

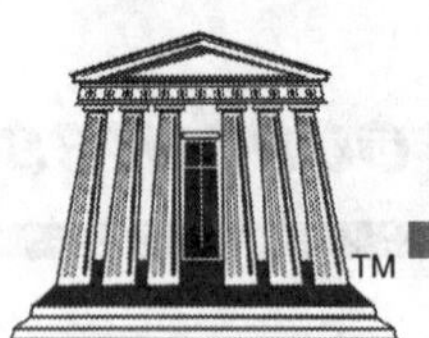

Chapter 18

A

Acceleration: The process of calling an entire loan balance immediately due and payable, usually because of default or sale of the secured property.

Accrued Depreciation: The loss in value to a property due to physical, functional, and economic detrimental conditions.

Appraisal: An opinion of value stated by a professional appraiser.

APR: The annual percentage rate. The rate of interest on a loan on an annual basis.

Alienation: The transfer of title to real estate by any means.

All-Inclusive Trust Deed: A trust deed that is the equivalent of a wraparound mortgage.

Amortize: To structure loan payments so that a series of level payments, including principal and interest, will retire the debt in full at the end of the loan term.

ARM: Adjustable rate mortgage; a loan in which the interest rate is tied to an index and periodically changed to reflect market trends as indicated by the index.

Arm's Length Transaction: A sale where neither the buyer nor the seller is acting under unusual pressure; the property is offered in the marketplace for a reasonable time, and both buyer and seller are aware of the property's merits and defects.

Assumption: The substitution of a buyer for the seller as the person primarily responsible for the continued repayment of an existing loan.

Automated Valuation Model (AVM): A computer-generated residential property appraisal report.

B

Bailout (Government): The act of loaning or giving capital to a failing business in order to save it from bankruptcy, insolvency, or total liquidation and ruin.

Balance: Economic principle stating that maximum value is achieved when the four agents of production (land, labor, capital, and coordination) are in balance.

Balloon Payment: The payment due at the end of the term of a partially amortized loan.

Bank Insurance Fund (BIF): A fund under the control of the Deposit Insurance Corporation, which insures commercial bank and savings bank deposits.

Beneficiary: The person entitled to payment on a loan secured by a deed of trust.

Bearer Note: A banknote that is payable to the bearer on demand, rather than a specific individual.

Block Busting: The illegal practice of persuading people to sell their property by creating and spreading fear that people of other races and religions moving into a neighborhood will lower property values.

Bonds: Instruments of debt issued by a corporation or government agency.

Bond Type Securities: Debt instruments issued by the secondary market that are backed by mortgages.

Buydown: When points are paid to a lender to buy down the interest rate on a loan so the borrower will be able to afford the payments.

Buyer's Market: A market in which there are more sellers than buyers. Prices tend to decrease at these times.

C

Cash Flow Analysis: A method of qualifying borrowers by analyzing the amount of income left over after all monthly obligations have been met.

CAP: The maximum amount of interest for an adjustable rate mortgage.

Call Provision: The right of a lender to accelerate payment of a loan if a property is sold or transferred.

Census Tracts: Demographic areas that have similar economic characteristics as determined by the Bureau of the Census.

Central Bank: A bank of last resort. In the United States, this is the Federal Reserve System.

Certified Appraiser: An appraiser that holds a license at the state certification level. Certified Appraisers may appraise any property without limitation.

Certificate of Eligibility: A VA document that certifies that a veteran is eligible for a VA loan.

Chattel: Personal property as opposed to real property (real estate and the bundle of rights).

Civil Rights Act of 1866: A federal law that makes it illegal to discriminate by race in the sale of real estate.

Civil Rights Act of 1968: An extension of the 1866 act that outlaws discrimination on the basis of sex, religion, or ethnicity, as well as race.

Commercial Bank: A financial institution whose main function is to facilitate commercial transactions. Commercial banks hold most of their assets in the form of demand deposits (checking accounts).

Commercial Paper: Unsecured promissory notes sold by large banks to meet short-term debt obligations.

Community Reinvestment Act: A federal law that prohibits "redlining."

Community Support Statement: Federally required documentation from lenders that shows the amount of loans and to whom they are made in the local area.

Co-Mortgager: A cosigner on a loan.

Compound Interest: Interest calculated as a percentage of both principal and accumulated unpaid interest.

Conforming Loans: Loans that may be readily sold into the secondary market.

Contingent Interest: A lender's share of the appreciation on a SAM loan.

Conventional Loan: Any loan that is not directly guaranteed by the federal government.

Convertible ARM: An ARM that gives the borrower the option of converting to a fixed rate loan within the first few years of the loan term.

Cost Approach: An appraisal methodology that determines value by finding the cost to build a new residence, subtracting accrued depreciation, and adding the result to the value of the land.

Cost of Funds Index (COFI): An average of the rates paid by savings institutions on deposits. The index is often used as a basis for mortgage interest rates.

Credit Report: A listing of a borrower's credit history, including amount of debt and record of repayment.

CRV: A certificate of reasonable value; an appraisal form used by the VA.

D

Deed: A written legal document that conveys title to a property.

Deed of Reconveyance: A document to release and convey title to a property to the borrower when the mortgage debt on it is paid in full.

Deed of Trust: An instrument that makes real property the security for a loan; unlike a mortgage, it may be foreclosed nonjudicially.

Default: The failure to fulfill a legal obligation. The nonrepayment of a legal debt.

Deferred Interest: Interest that is accumulated over the course of one or more payment periods, but not payable until some future time. This is a common element of adjustable rate and graduated payment plans.

Deficiency Judgment: A court judgment ordering a debtor to pay the difference between the amount of a debt and the proceeds raised by foreclosure and sale of the secured property.

Demand: The economic principle that states that the quantity desired for a good or service is dependent on the price level.

Demand Deposit: A deposit that may be withdrawn at any time, such as a checking account.

Demographics: The study of economic trends in a geographic area.

Deposit Insurance Fund: The federal fund that controls the Bank Insurance Fund (BIF) and the Savings Association Insurance Fund (SAIF), which insure customer deposits in banks and savings banks.

Direct Endorsement Lender: A lender that has been approved to make loans that are insured/guaranteed directly by the federal government.

Disclosure: A written statement that details for a buyer/borrower all the information involved in the transaction. Real estate agents, lenders, and appraisers are all required to provide disclosure statements.

Discount: The charging of points on a loan for the purpose of increasing the yield of the loan.

Discount Rate: The interest rate charged by the Federal Reserve to member banks who borrow funds on a short-term basis.

Disintermediation: The process by which savings institutions lose deposits to higher-paying investments.

Due-on-Sale Clause: A clause in a mortgage allowing the lender to accelerate the loan if the property is sold; also called an alienation clause.

E

Economic Obsolescence: A loss in property value due to outside forces over which the owner has no control.

Effective Interest Rate: The actual rate of interest after all discounting, fees, and points have been paid.

Entitlement: The loan amount that the VA will provide for a veteran based on their military service.

Equal Credit Opportunity Act: A 1974 Act of Congress to further eliminate discrimination (Chapter 5).

Equitable Interest: The real property interest of the vendee in a land contract; it includes the right to possession of the property and the right to acquire title by paying the contract according to its terms.

Equitable Right of Redemption: A borrower's right to redeem a property during the foreclosure process.

Equity: The difference between the value of a property and the outstanding indebtedness secured by the property.

Escrow: The use of a disinterested third party to hold documents and funds when a property is being transferred.

Estate: An interest in a property or in the property rights.

Estoppel: A legal doctrine that requires lenders and others to abide by prior agreements.

F

Federal Reserve System: The government body that regulates the activities of the nation's commercial banks.

FDIC: The Federal Deposit Insurance Corporation provides insurance for depositors. This program provides stability to the banking system, as well as security for depositors.

Federal Funds Rate: The rate of interest the Federal Reserve charges its member banks for unsecured loans.

Federal Housing Finance Board (FHFB): A board created by FIRREA to take over the duties of the Federal Home Loan Bank board.

Federal Open Market Committee: The committee in charge of selling government securities. Open Market Operations control the nation's money supply.

Federally Related Transaction: Any transaction that involves an institution that is federally regulated.

Fee Simple Absolute: The highest form of property ownership. It includes all property rights.

FHA: A government agency that provides federal insurance for mortgage loans.

FHLMC: The Federal Home Loan Mortgage Corporation (Freddie Mac).

Fiat Money: Literally, money by decree. Money that has no backing other than a government's decree that it is money.

Fiduciary: A person in a position of financial trust.

Financial Statement: A statement that summarizes an individual's financial condition. It lists assets and liabilities and is used to determine net worth.

FIRREA: The Financial Institutions Reform, Recovery and Enforcement Act was enacted in 1989 in response to a crisis in the S&L industry. The legislation governs lending activity for all federally related transactions.

Fixed-Rate Mortgage: A mortgage wherein the interest rate remains constant throughout the life of the loan.

FNMA: The Federal National Mortgage Association (Fannie Mae). A government sponsored enterprise (GSE) overseen by the Federal Housing Finance Agency (FHFA). FNMA is a major secondary market entity.

Functional Obsolescence: An appraisal term to describe a property that has faulty or outmoded design features.

G

GEM: A growth equity mortgage is characterized by gradually increasing payments over the term of the loan. The interest rate is constant.

General Warranty Deed: A type of deed used to convey the highest form of ownership in a property. Used in the eastern states.

G.I. Bill: The federal legislation that provided for VA loan insurance.

Good Faith Estimate: A document required by RESPA. In it, the lender must state all of the costs of the loan to the borrower before closing the loan.

GNMA: The Government National Mortgage Association or "Ginnie Mae" is a government agency supervised by HUD. It promotes investment by guaranteeing payment on FHA, FMHA, and VA loans.

GPM: A graduated payment mortgage is a loan in which the payments are increased periodically during the early years of the loan.

Graduated Payment Term: The number of years during which payments may be adjusted in a GPM.

Grant Deed: A bare or "naked" transfer of real property. Used in the western states.

Grantee: A person who receives a transfer of real property.

Grantor: A person who transfers real property to the grantee.

Gross Income: Income from all sources before deductions for expenditures and taxes.

Gross Rent Multiplier: A GRM is developed by dividing the monthly rental payment into the sales price of an income property. This method is often used by brokers and appraisers to help develop an estimate of an income property's value.

H-J

Homebuyer's Summary: An FHA document that must be presented to the borrower by the lender. It lists all property defects found by the FHA appraiser.

Income Approach: An appraisal methodology used to value properties based on their income.

Indemnity Obligation: An obligation by a VA borrower to pay back the loan, even in the case of a default by a subsequent purchaser.

Index: A measure of the cost of money used as the basis of rate adjustments for an ARM.

Interest: The charge for renting or borrowing money. Usually expressed as a percentage of the outstanding loan amount.

Interest Rate Cap: The maximum rate of interest that may be charged on an ARM.

Interest Shortfall: The failure to collect accumulated interest due to the graduated payment or adjustable-rate feature of a loan.

Intermediary: A person or institution who originates loans on behalf of another.

Investment Quality Loan: A loan that meets the guidelines of the secondary market.

Judicial Foreclosure: A court supervised foreclosure proceeding.

Jumbo Loan: A nonconforming loan. A loan that exceeds the maximum limits of the secondary market.

L

Law of Supply and Demand: The basic law of economics stating that prices rise when supply decreases or demand increases, and that prices fall when supply increases or demand decreases.

Legal Tender: Lawful money. U.S. banknotes are legal tender for payment of any debt.

Lease/Option: A combination of a lease on real property and an option to purchase the real property during the term of the lease.

Leased Fee Estate: A landlord's property interest.

Leasehold Estate: A tenant's property interest.

Level Payment Loan: A loan that is repaid in equal periodic payments over its entire term.

Licensed Appraiser: An appraiser whose practice is limited to conforming loans and SFRs valued at under $1,000,000.00.

Life Estate: An estate that is held by an individual for their own lifetime and that will revert to the original owner(s) upon their death.

Line of Credit: An amount of money held by the lender against which a borrower may draw funds. The account is secured by the borrower's equity in his/her real estate.

Liquidity: A term that describes the relative ability to convert property quickly to cash. A liquid investment is easily convertible to cash.

Loan Application: A document filled out by a borrower that details the amount to be borrowed and information regarding the borrower's credit and employment history.

Loan Fee: A one-time fee charged by the lender for origination of a loan; often a percentage of the loan amount; also called a loan service fee or loan origination fee.

Loan Underwriting: The process of determining if a loan may be made that will provide minimum risk for the investor.

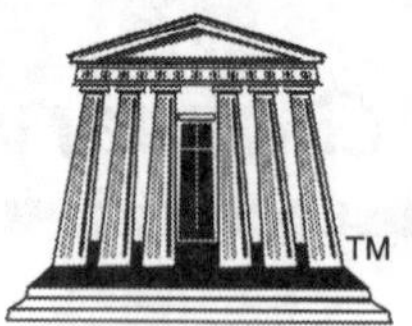

LTV: The loan-to-value ratio is the percentage of a property's market value that a lender is willing to loan, with the property offered as collateral.

M

Maker: A person who signs a promissory note.

Margin: The difference between the index rate and the interest charged on an ARM.

Market Approach: An appraisal technique that utilizes sales of comparable properties to determine value.

Market Value: The highest price a property would bring if sold in a competitive market, where all conditions for a fair sale are met. The conditions for a fair sale are: reasonable exposure to the market, arms-length transaction, knowledgeable buyer and seller, no coercion to either buy or sell, and terms in cash or the equivalent.

Measures of Central Tendency (or Central Location): Numerical values that are indicative of the central point or the greatest frequency concerning a set of data. The most common measures of central location are the mean, median, and mode.

MIP: Mortgage insurance premium; especially the one time premium charged by FHA.

Mixed-Use Property: A property that has two or more uses, such as a combination of residential and commercial use.

Money: From the Latin word *moneta*. Money is a medium of exchange. It is portable, in the form of currency or coins; and is accepted by the public due to its legal tender status. The U.S. dollar is the world's most acceptable form of money.

Money Market Funds: Noninsured, private market investment funds.

Mortgage: An instrument wherein property is pledged as a security for a debt, creating a lien on the secured property. A mortgage must be foreclosed judicially.

Mortgage-Backed Securities: Instruments issued by various agencies such as GNMA FHLMC to raise investment funds.

Mortgage Banker: An individual or company that makes mortgage loans.

Mortgage Broker: An individual who acts as a go-between for lending institutions and borrowers. The mortgage broker handles the paperwork involved in a transaction. The mortgage broker does not make loans.

Mortgage Company: An institution designed to originate and service real estate loans on behalf of large institutional investors.

Mortgagee: The one who receives a mortgage (the lender).

Mortgagor: The person who gives a mortgage (the borrower).

Multiple Regression Analysis: A statistical procedure that attempts to assess the relationship between a dependent variable and two or more independent variables.

Mutual Savings Bank: A type of financial institution designed for small savers; often found in the Northeast.

N

Negative Amortization: An increase in an outstanding loan balance brought about by deferred interest.

Negative Amortization Cap: A limit on the amount of negative amortization allowable in an ARM or GPM.

Negotiable Instrument: An instrument, such as a promissory note, that is freely transferable.

Net Income: A person's after-tax income.

Net Worth: The worth of an individual after personal liabilities are subtracted from personal assets.

Nominal Rate: The interest rate specified in a promissory note.

Nonjudicial Foreclosure: Foreclosure of a trust deed without judicial proceedings by means of a trustee's sale.

O-P

Open Market Operations: The purchase or sale of treasury bonds by the Federal Reserve. This process helps control the money supply.

Optionee: A person who receives an option.

Optionor: A person who gives an option.

Option Money: An amount paid by the optionee to have the optionor grant an option.

Origination: The process of making a new loan.

Participation Loan: A loan made in exchange for a portion of a borrower's equity in the secured property. Also known as a shared appreciation mortgage.

Pass-Through Securities: A GNMA program wherein the principal and interest payments on mortgages purchased by investors are passed through to them as they are collected.

Payee: The party to whom a mortgage is made payable.

Payment Adjustment Period: The minimum interval between successive adjustments of payments on an ARM or GPM.

Payment Cap: A limit on the size of payments on an ARM.

Physical Obsolescence: An appraisal term that describes the ordinary aging process of a building.

PMI: Private mortgage insurance; protects against loss from default on conventional loans.

Points: A point is 1% of a loan. Points are charged by lenders in order to increase yields on below-market interest rate loans.

Portfolio: The collection of mortgages held by a primary lending institution and not sold into the secondary market.

Power of Issue: The legal right to issue or create money.

Predatory Lending: The usage of unethical and often criminal lending practices.

Primary Market: Local lending institutions.

Prime Rate: The lowest rate that a bank charges its best customers.

Principal: The amount of a loan balance representing the original funds advanced.

Private Mortgage Insurance: See PMI.

Promissory Note: Written evidence of debt.

Proration: The apportionment between buyer and seller of previously paid expenses, such as the refund of the unused portion of a seller's prepaid property tax for the year.

Purchase Agreement: A simple real estate contract that lists the price of the property and acknowledges any down payment made by the buyer.

Purchase Money Loan: A loan made by a lender or a seller of a property that is used to finance the purchase of the property.

Q-R

Qualifying: The process of checking to make sure that the borrower is not likely to default, and that the property has sufficient value to satisfy the loan in the event of a default.

Quiet Title: A court action to settle any dispute to a title, such as liens or other encumbrances. The court will issue a new title to the property.

Rate Adjustment Period: The minimum interval between successive adjustments of the interest rate on an ARM.

Real Estate: The physical land and buildings of a property.

Real Estate Contract: An installment sales contract for the purchase of real estate.

Real Estate Cycle: The upward and downward movements of real estate prices created by the forces of supply and demand.

Real Property: The rights enjoyed by an owner of real estate.

Re-Amortization: The recalculation of level payments for a loan, necessitated by either a change in the loan term or an increase in the loan balance due to negative amortization.

Recast: To re-amortize.

Recording Acts: State laws requiring that information regarding property transfers become part of the public record by being recorded by public authorities.

Redemption: The process of recovering foreclosed property after a sheriff's sale.

Redlining: The illegal practice of not making loans in certain neighborhoods due to religious, racial, ethnic, or other social reasons.

Reduction-Option Mortgage: A fixed rate mortgage with an option to reduce the interest rate once during the life of the loan.

Regulation Z: The Truth in Lending Law overseen by the Federal Reserve.

REIT: A Real Estate Investment Trust is an association that invests in real estate mortgages. If the trust is properly constituted, there are tax advantages.

REMIC: A Real Estate Mortgage Investment Trust is an entity that can avoid double taxation when issuing collateralized mortgage obligations.

Reserve Requirement: The percentage of a bank's deposits that may not be loaned out.

RESPA: The Real Estate Settlement Procedures Act of 1974 seeks to prevent fraud by requiring full disclosures to consumers before loan closings.

Reversion: The return of real estate and real property rights to an owner at the end of a lease term.

Right of Rescission: The right of a borrower to refuse a loan.

RTC: The Resolution Trust Corporation was an agency formed to manage the disposition of the assets of failed S&Ls.

S

SAFE Act: The Secure and Fair Enforcement for Mortgage Licensing Act of 2008. Sets minimum standards for federal and state Mortgage Loan Originators (MLOs) licensing, testing, and registration.

SAM: A shared appreciation mortgage. See participation mortgage.

Savings Banks (formerly called S&Ls): Savings banks hold long-term deposits and invest them in long-term loans such as real estate markets. Savings banks are primary lenders.

Secondary Financing: Money borrowed from any source to pay a portion of the required down payment or settlement costs of a loan.

Secondary Liability: Liability that arises only in the event that the person primarily liable cannot satisfy the debt.

Secondary Market: Institutions such as FNMA, FHLMC, and others who purchase mortgages from the primary market.

Securities: Instruments, such as mortgages and trust deeds, that pledge assets as security for debt.

Seller's Market: A time period of high demand for real estate and a low supply being offered for sale.

Senior Pass-Through: The principal amount of a pass-through.

Servicing: The process of collecting loan payments, keeping records, and handling defaults.

Shared Equity Loan: See participation loan.

Simple Interest: Interest calculated as a percentage of the principle only.

Special Warranty Deed: While similar to a Warranty Deed, defects in title are only covered as far back as the time when the grantor acquired title.

Spread: The difference between the note rate and the payment rate on a GPM.

Stable Monthly Income: A borrower's base income plus earnings from reliable secondary sources.

Steering: The illegal practice of directing clients only into neighborhoods that are similar in racial or ethnic background to the client.

Step-Rate Loan: A loan using a temporary buydown that decreases over the buydown period. See buydown.

Stock: An ownership interest in a corporation.

Subordinate Pass-Through: The overcollateralized portion of a pass-through.

Subprime Borrowers: Borrowers with lesser ability to repay the loan based on various criteria like credit score and credit history.

Subprime Mortgage Crisis: A financial crisis triggered by a dramatic rise in mortgage delinquencies and foreclosures in America, negatively affecting banks and financial markets around the world.

Supply: The available amount of a good or service that is in demand.

T

Teaser Rate: A below-market rate of interest. It often applies only under very specific conditions.

Title: A legal document that shows evidence of property ownership.

Total Debt Service Ratio: The ratio between the total of housing expense plus long-term obligations and the borrower's stable monthly income.

Trigger Words: Language in advertisement that triggers the federal disclosure laws.

Troubled Asset Relief Program (TARP): A U.S. government program to purchase assets and equity from financial institutions in order to strengthen the financial sector.

Trustee: A person or entity that holds property in trust for another. This is a fiduciary relationship.

Trustor: The person or entity that creates the trust.

Truth in Lending Law: See Regulation Z.

U-Z

Underwriting: The process of evaluating a borrower's willingness and ability to pay, along with the collateral offered as security. The person who does this is called an underwriter.

USPAP: The Uniform Standards of Professional Appraisal Practice require appraisers to follow certain ethical and professional requirements for all appraisal assignments involving federally related loan transactions.

U.S. Treasury: An executive department of the U.S. government that serves as the nation's fiscal manager.

Usury: Charging more interest than is legally allowed.

VA Entitlement: See Entitlement.

VA Guaranty: The dollar amount of a loan that the VA will pay in the event of a default.

Valuation Conditions Form: An FHA document that requires the appraiser to report all property deficiencies.

Vendee: The purchaser/borrower under a real estate sales contract.

Vendor: The seller/lender under a real estate contract.

Verification of Deposit: A form sent by a lender to a borrower's bank requesting verification of a borrower's funds.

VRM: A variable rate mortgage. Any loan in which the interest rate may change, whether the rate is tied to an index or not. Such loans have been replaced by ARMs and AMLs.

Warranty Deed: A deed used to convey real property which contains warranties of title and quiet possession, and the grantor thus agrees to defend the premises against the lawful claims of third persons. It is commonly used in many states, but in others, the grant deed has supplanted it due to the practice of securing title insurance policies which have reduced the importance of express and implied warranty in deeds.

Wraparound Mortgage: A type of mortgage where part of the payments are used to retire an existing loan.

Yield: The lender's overall rate of return on a loan, taking into account interest, points, and fees.

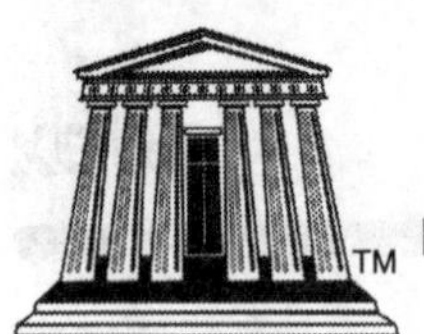

G

P

Q-R